CHILDREN'S WRITER'S & ILLUSTRATOR'S MARKET

2016

includes a one-year online subscription to **Children's Writer's & Illustrator's Market** on

WritersMarket.com

Where & How to Sell What You Write

THE ULTIMATE MARKET RESEARCH TOOL FOR WRITERS

To register your *Children's Writer's & Illustrator's Market 2016* book and **start your one-year online genre-only subscription**, scratch off the block below to reveal your activation code, then go to www.WritersMarket.com. Find the box that says "Purchased a Deluxe Edition?" then click on "Activate Your Account" and enter the activation code. It's that easy!

UPDATED MARKET LISTINGS FOR YOUR INTEREST AREA
EASY-TO-USE SEARCHABLE DATABASE • RECORD-KEEPING TOOLS
PROFESSIONAL TIPS & ADVICE • INDUSTRY NEWS

Your purchase of *Children's Writer's & Illustrator's Market* gives you access to updated listings related to this genre of writing (valid through 12/31/16). For just $9.99, you can upgrade your subscription and get access to listings from all of our best-selling Market Books. Visit **www.WritersMarket.com** for more information.

WritersMarket.com
Where & How to Sell What You Write

Activate your WritersMarket.com subscription to get instant access to:

- **UPDATED LISTINGS IN YOUR WRITING GENRE:** Find additional listings that didn't make it into the book, updated contact information, and more. WritersMarket.com provides the most comprehensive database of verified markets available anywhere.

- **EASY-TO-USE SEARCHABLE DATABASE:** Looking for a specific magazine or book publisher? Just type in its name. Or widen your prospects with the Advanced Search. You can also search for listings that have been recently updated!

- **PERSONALIZED TOOLS:** Store your best-bet markets, and use our popular recording-keeping tools to track your submissions. Plus, get new and updated market listings, query reminders, and more—every time you log in!

- **PROFESSIONAL TIPS & ADVICE:** From pay-rate charts to sample query letters, and from how-to articles to Q&As with literary agents, we have the resources writers need.

YOU'LL GET ALL OF THIS WITH YOUR INCLUDED SUBSCRIPTION TO

WritersMarket.com
Where & How to Sell What You Write

CWIM16

CHILDREN'S WRITER'S & ILLUSTRATOR'S MARKET

2016

Chuck Sambuchino, *Editor*

Nancy Parish, *Contributing Editor*

WD

WRITER'S DIGEST
BOOKS

WritersDigest.com
Cincinnati, Ohio

Children's Writer's & Illustrator's Market 2016. Copyright © 2015 F+W: A Content & E-Commerce Company. Published by Writer's Digest Books, an imprint of F+W, 10151 Carver Road, Suite 200, Blue Ash, Ohio 45242. Printed and bound in the United States of America. All rights reserved. No part of this book may be reproduced in any form or by any electronic or mechanical means including information storage and retrieval systems without permission in writing from the publisher, except by a reviewer, who may quote brief passages in a review.

Publisher: Phil Sexton

Writer's Market website: www.writersmarket.com
Writer's Digest website: www.writersdigest.com

Distributed in Canada by Fraser Direct
100 Armstrong Avenue
Georgetown, Ontario, Canada L7G 5S4
Tel: (905) 877-4411

Distributed in the U.K. and Europe by F&W Media International
Brunel House, Newton Abbot, Devon, TQ12 4PU, England
Tel: (+44) 1626-323200, Fax: (+44) 1626-323319
E-mail: postmaster@davidandcharles.co.uk

Distributed in Australia by Capricorn Link
P.O. Box 704, Windsor, NSW 2756 Australia
Tel: (02) 4577-3555

Library of Congress Catalog Number 31-20772
ISSN: 0897-9790
ISBN-13: 978-1-59963-943-7
ISBN-10: 1-59963-943-2

Attention Booksellers: This is an annual directory of F+W: A Content & E-Commerce Company. Return deadline for this edition is December 31, 2016.

Edited by: Chuck Sambuchino
Designed by: Alexis Brown
Production coordinated by: Debbie Thomas

CONTENTS

FROM THE EDITOR

Flip through the pages of this *Children's Writer's & Illustrator's Market* edition and you'll immediately see some cool changes. First of all, we've tried as much as ever to provide plenty of upfront instructional content to burgeoning illustrators—by talking to artists who just finished drawing their first published books, and interviewing professionals who've been working in the field for years. Secondly, we've scoured around for new publishers and found plenty to add. These are book publishers that accept direct submissions for picture books, middle grade, young adult, and more. This way, whether you want to try for a literary agent first, or whether you opt to send your work directly to a traditional publishing house editor, you'll have plenty of choices for either pathway.

It's a return to basics. Even 28 years after its first publication, the goal of *CWIM* remains simple: Give writers lots of markets for their original writing and illustration. In this guide, you'll find listings for US publishers, Canadian publishers, literary agents, magazines, conferences, contests, international publishers, and more. If your goal is to create books for children, you've come to the right place—so read on.

Please stay in touch with me at guidetoliteraryagents.com/blog and on Twitter (@chucksambuchino). I love hearing feedback and success stories. (And don't forget to download your free supplemental webinar at www.writersmarket.com/cwim16-webinar.)

Chuck Sambuchino
literaryagent@fwmedia.com; chucksambuchino.com
Editor, *Guide to Literary Agents / Children's Writer's & Illustrator's Market*
Author, *How to Survive a Garden Gnome Attack* (2010); *Get a Literary Agent* (2014); *Create Your Writer Platform* (2012); *When Clowns Attack* (2015)

HOW TO USE CWIM

Maximize your education.

As a writer, illustrator, or photographer first picking up *Children's Writer's & Illustrator's Market*, you may not know quite how to start using the book. Your impulse may be to flip through the book and quickly make a mailing list, then submit to everyone in hopes that someone will take interest in your work. Well, there's more to it. Finding the right market takes time and research. The more you know about a market that interests you, the better chance you have of getting work accepted. We've made your job a little easier by putting a wealth of information at your fingertips. Besides providing listings, this directory includes a number of tools to help you determine which markets are the best ones for your work. By using these tools, as well as researching on your own, you raise your odds of being published.

USING THE INDEXES

This book lists hundreds of potential buyers of freelance material. To learn which companies want the type of material you're interested in submitting, start with the indexes.

Editor and Agent Names Index

This index lists book editors, magazine editors, art directors, agents and art reps—indicating the companies they work for. Use this specific index to find company and contact information for individual publishing professionals.

Age-Level Index

Age groups are broken down into these categories in the Age-Level Index:

- **PICTURE BOOKS OR PICTURE-ORIENTED MATERIAL** are written and illustrated for preschoolers to 8-year-olds.
- **YOUNG READERS** are for 5- to 8-year-olds.
- **MIDDLE READERS** are for 9- to 11-year-olds.
- **YOUNG ADULT** is for ages 12 and up.

Age breakdowns may vary slightly from publisher to publisher, but using them as general guidelines will help you target appropriate markets. For example, if you've written an article about trends in teen fashion, check the Magazines Age-Level

Index under the Young Adult subheading. Using this list, you'll quickly find the listings for young adult magazines.

Subject Index

But let's narrow the search further. Take your list of young adult magazines, turn to the Subject Index, and find the Fashion subheading. Then highlight the names that appear on both lists (Young Adult and Fashion). Now you have a smaller list of all the magazines that would be interested in your teen fashion article. Read through those listings and decide which ones sound best for your work.

Illustrators and photographers can use the Subject Index as well. If you specialize in painting animals, for instance, consider sending samples to book and magazine publishers listed under Animals and, perhaps, Nature/Environment. Because illustrators can simply send general examples of their style to art directors to keep on file, the indexes may be more helpful to artists sending manuscript/illustration packages who need to search for a specific subject. Always read the listings for the potential markets to see the type of work art directors prefer and what type of samples they'll keep on file, and obtain art or photo guidelines if they're available online.

Photography Index

In this index, you'll find lists of book and magazine publishers that buy photos from freelancers. Refer to the list and read the listings for companies' specific photography needs. Obtain photo guidelines if they're offered online.

USING THE LISTINGS

Many listings begin with symbols. Refer to the pull-out bookmark (shown later in this article).

⊕ market new to this edition

Ⓐ market accepts agented submissions only

☻ award-winning market

♻ Canadian market

↪ market located outside of the U.S. and Canada

⬉ online opportunity

💬 comment from the editor of *Children's Writer's & Illustrator's Market*

○ publisher producing educational material

▢ book packager/producer

ms, mss manuscript(s)

SCBWI Society of Children's Book Writers and Illustrators

SASE self-addressed, stamped envelope

IRC International Reply Coupon, for use in countries other than your own

b&w black & white (photo)

(For definitions of unfamiliar words and expressions relating to writing, illustration and publishing, see the Glossary.)

Many listings indicate whether submission guidelines are indeed available. If a publisher you're interested in offers guidelines, get them and read them. The same is true with catalogs. Sending for and reading catalogs or browsing them online gives you a better idea of whether your work would fit in with the books a publisher produces. (You should also look at a few of the books in the catalog at a library or bookstore to get a feel for the publisher's material.)

Especially for artists & photographers

Along with information for writers, listings provide information for illustrators and photographers. Illustrators will find numerous markets that maintain files of samples for possible future assignments. If you're both a writer and an illustrator, look for markets that accept manuscript/illustration packages and read the information offered under the **Illustration** subhead within the listings.

If you're a photographer, after consulting the Photography Index, read the information under the **Photography** subhead within listings to see what format buyers prefer. For example, some want the highest resolution .jpg available of an image. Note the type of photos a buyer wants to purchase and the procedures for submitting. It's not uncommon for a market to want a résumé and promotional literature, as well as sample URLS linking to previous work. Listings also note whether model releases and/or captions are required.

ADDRESSES AND WEBSITES

SPECIFIC CONTACT NAMES

INFO ON WHAT A PUBLISHER HANDLES

SUBMISSION TIPS

⊕ MERIT PRESS

A DIVISION OF ADAMS MEDIA (PART OF F+W MEDIA), 57 LITTLEFIELD ST, AVON, MA 02322. (508)427-7100. **E-MAIL:** MERITPRESS@FWMEDIA.COM. **WEBSITE:** WWW.ADAMSMEDIA.COM/MERIT-PRESS-BOOKS. **CONTACT:** JACQUELYN MITCHARD, EDITOR-IN-CHIEF.

Focuses on contemporary YA, usually based in reality.

FICTION "Natural is good; a little bit of supernatural (as in, perhaps foreseeing the future) is okay, too. Normal is great (at least until something happens) but not paranormal. What we are not seeking right now is tryphids, blood drinkers, flesh eaters and even yetis (much though we love them)."

HOW TO CONTACT "We do accept direct submissions as well as submissions from literary agents. We don't accept submissions in hard copy. Send full or partial manuscripts and queries to meritpress@fwmedia.com."

TIPS "I want to publish the next *Carrie, The Book Thief, National Velvet, Tuck Everlasting, Mr. and Mrs. Bo Jo Jones,* and *The Outsiders.* These will be the classics for a new generation, and they're being written right now. Since suspense (noir or pastel, comic or macabre) is my love, I hope I have a sense for finding those stories. As it turns out, a big part of my vocation, at this point in my career, is the desire to discover and nurture great new writers, and to put great books in the hands of great readers."

QUICK TIPS FOR WRITERS & ILLUSTRATORS

If you're new to the world of children's publishing, buying *Children's Writer's & Illustrator's Market* may have been one of the first steps in your journey to publication. What follows is a list of suggestions and resources that can help make that journey a smooth and swift one:

1. MAKE THE MOST OF *CHILDREN'S WRITER'S & ILLUSTRATOR'S MARKET*. Be sure to take advantage of the articles and interviews in the book. The insights of the authors, illustrators, editors, and agents we've interviewed will inform and inspire you.

2. JOIN THE SOCIETY OF CHILDREN'S BOOK WRITERS AND ILLUSTRATORS. SCBWI, more than 22,000 members strong, is an organization for both beginners and professionals interested in writing and illustrating for children, with more than 70 active regional chapters worldwide. It offers members a slew of information and support through publications, a website, and a host of Regional Advisors overseeing chapters in almost every state in the U.S. and a growing number of locations around the globe. SCBWI puts on a number of conferences, workshops, and events on the regional and national levels (many listed in the Conferences & Workshops section of this book). For more information, visit scbwi.org.

3. READ NEWSLETTERS. Newsletters, such as *Children's Book Insider*, *Children's Writer* and the *SCBWI Bulletin*, offer updates and new information about publishers on a timely basis and are relatively inexpensive. Many local chapters of SCBWI offer regional newsletters as well.

4. READ TRADE AND REVIEW PUBLICATIONS. Magazines like *Publishers Weekly* (which offers two special issues each year devoted to children's publishing and is available on newsstands as well as through a digital subscription) offer news, articles, reviews of newly published titles, and ads featuring upcoming and current releases. Referring to them will help you get a feel for what's happening in children's publishing.

5. READ GUIDELINES. Most publishers and magazines offer writers' and artists' guidelines that provide detailed information on needs and submission requirements, and some magazines offer theme lists for upcoming issues. Many publishers and magazines state the availability of guidelines within their listings. You'll often find submission information on publishers' and magazines' websites.

6. LOOK AT PUBLISHERS' CATALOGS. Perusing publishers' catalogs can give you a feel for their line of books and help you decide where your work might fit in. If catalogs are available (often stated within listings), visit publishers' websites, which often contain their full catalogs. You can also ask librarians to look at catalogs they have on hand. You can even search Amazon.com by publisher and year. (Click on "book search" then "publisher, date" and plug in, for example, "Lee & Low" under *publisher* and "2015" under *year*. You'll get a list of Lee & Low titles published in 2015, which you can peruse.)

7. VISIT BOOKSTORES. It's not only informative to spend time in bookstores—it's fun, too! Frequently visit the children's section of your local bookstore (whether a chain or an independent) to see the latest from a variety of publishers and the most current issues of children's magazines. Look for books in the genre you're writing or with illustrations similar in style to yours, and spend some time studying them. It's also wise to get to know your local booksellers; they can tell you what's new in the store and provide insight into what kids and adults are buying.

8. READ, READ, READ! While you're at that bookstore, pick up a few things, or keep a list of the books that interest you and check them out of your library. Read and study the latest releases, the award winners and the classics. You'll learn from other writers, get ideas, and get a feel for what's being published. Think about what works and doesn't work in a story. Pay attention to how plots are constructed and how characters are developed, or the rhythm and pacing of picture book text. It's certainly enjoyable research!

9. TAKE ADVANTAGE OF INTERNET RESOURCES. There are innumerable sources of information available online about writing for children (and anything else you could possibly think of). It's also a great resource for getting (and staying) in touch with other writers and illustrators through listservs, blogs, social networking sites, and e-mail, and it can serve as a vehicle for self-promotion.

10. CONSIDER ATTENDING A CONFERENCE. If time and finances allow, attending a conference is a great way to meet peers and network with professionals in the field of children's publishing. As mentioned earlier, SCBWI offers conferences in various locations year round. (See scbwi.org and click on "Events" for a full conference calendar.) General writers' conferences often offer specialized sessions just for those interested in children's writing. Many conferences offer optional manuscript and portfolio critiques as well, giving you feedback from seasoned professionals. See the Conferences section of this book for information on conferences.

11. NETWORK, NETWORK, NETWORK! Don't work in a vacuum. You can meet other writers and illustrators through a number of the things listed earlier—SCBWI, conferences, online. Attend local meetings for writers and illustrators whenever you can. Befriend other writers in your area (SCBWI offers members a roster broken down by state)—share guidelines, share subscriptions, be conference buddies and roommates, join a critique group or writing group, exchange information, and offer support. Get online—sign on to listservs, post on message boards and blogs, visit social networking sites and chatrooms. Exchange addresses, phone numbers, and e-mail addresses with writers or illustrators you meet at events. And at conferences, don't be afraid to talk to people, ask strangers to join you for lunch, approach speakers and introduce yourself, or chat in elevators and hallways.

12. PERFECT YOUR CRAFT AND DON'T SUB-MIT UNTIL YOUR WORK IS ITS BEST. It's often been said that a writer should try to write every day. Great manuscripts don't happen overnight; there's time, research and revision involved. As you visit bookstores and study what others have written and illustrated, really step back and look at your own work and ask yourself—honestly—*How does my work measure up? Is it ready for editors or art directors to see?* If it's not, keep working. Join a critique group or get a professional manuscript or portfolio critique.

13. BE PATIENT, LEARN FROM REJECTION, AND DON'T GIVE UP! Thousands of manuscripts land on editors' desks; thousands of illustration samples line art directors' file drawers. There are so many factors that come into play when evaluating submissions. Keep in mind that you might not hear back from publishers promptly. Persistence and patience are important qualities in writers and illustrators working toward publication. Keep at it—it will come. It can take a while, but when you get that first book contract or first assignment, you'll know it was worth the wait. (For proof, read the "First Books" article later in this book!)

BEFORE YOUR FIRST SALE

If you're just beginning to pursue your career as a children's book writer or illustrator, it's important to learn the proper procedures, formats and protocol for the publishing industry. This article outlines the basics you need to know before you submit your work to a market.

FINDING THE BEST MARKETS FOR YOUR WORK

Researching markets thoroughly is a basic element of submitting your work successfully. Editors and art directors hate to receive inappropriate submissions; handling them wastes a lot of their time, not to mention your time and money, and they are the main reason some publishers have chosen not to accept material over the transom. By randomly sending out material without knowing a company's needs, you're sure to meet with rejection.

If you're interested in submitting to a particular magazine, see if it's available in your local library or bookstore, or read past articles online. For a book publisher, obtain a book catalog and check a library or bookstore for titles produced by that publisher. Most publishers and magazines have websites that include catalogs or sample articles (websites are given within the listings). Studying such materials carefully will better acquaint you with a publisher's or magazine's writing, illustration and photography styles and formats.

Many of the book publishers and magazines listed in this book offer some sort of writers', artists' or photographers' guidelines on their websites. It's important to read and study guidelines before submitting work. You'll get a better understanding of what a particular publisher wants. You may even decide, after reading the submission guidelines, that your work isn't right for a company you considered.

SUBMITTING YOUR WORK

Throughout the listings, you'll read requests for particular elements to include when contacting markets. Here are explanations of some of these important submission components.

Queries, cover letters & proposals

A query is a no-more-than-one-page, well-written letter meant to arouse an editor's interest in your work. Query letters briefly outline the work you're proposing and include facts, anecdotes, interviews or other pertinent information that give the editor a feel for the manuscript's premise—enticing her to want to know more. End your letter with a straightforward request to submit the work, and include information on its approximate length, date it could be completed, and whether accompanying photos or artwork are available.

In a query letter, think about presenting your book as a publisher's catalog would present it. Read through a good catalog and examine how the publishers give enticing summaries of their books in a spare amount of words. It's also important that query letters give editors a taste of your writing style. For good advice and samples of queries, cover letters and other correspondence, consult the article "Crafting a Query" in this book, as well as *Formatting & Submitting Your Manuscript, 3rd Ed.* and *The Writer's Digest Guide to Query Letters* (both Writer's Digest Books).

• **QUERY LETTERS FOR NONFICTION.** Queries are usually required when submitting nonfiction material to a publisher. The goal of a nonfiction query is to convince the editor your idea is perfect for her readership and that you're qualified to do the job. Note any previous writing experience and include published samples to prove your credentials, especially samples related to the subject matter you're querying about.

• **QUERY LETTERS FOR FICTION.** For a fiction query, explain the story's plot, main characters, conflict and resolution. Just as in nonfiction queries, make the editor eager to see more.

• **COVER LETTERS FOR WRITERS.** Some editors prefer to review complete manuscripts, especially for picture books or fiction. In such cases, the cover letter (which should be no longer than one page) serves as your introduction, establishes your credentials as a writer, and gives the editor an overview of the manuscript. If the editor asked for the manuscript because of a query, note this in your cover letter.

• **COVER LETTERS FOR ILLUSTRATORS AND PHOTOGRAPHERS.** For an illustrator or photographer, the cover letter serves as an introduction to the art director and establishes professional credentials when submitting samples. Explain what services you can provide as well as what type of follow-up contact you plan to make, if any. Be sure to include the URL of your online portfolio if you have one.

• **RÉSUMÉS.** Often writers, illustrators and photographers are asked to submit résumés with cover letters and samples. They can be created in a variety of formats, from a single-page listing information to color brochures featuring your work. Keep your résumé brief, and focus on your achievements, including your clients and the work you've done for them, as well as your educational background and any awards you've received. Do not use the same résumé you'd use for a typical job application.

• **BOOK PROPOSALS.** Throughout the listings in the Book Publishers section, publishers refer to submitting a synopsis, outline and sample chapters. Depending on an editor's preference, some or all of these components, along with a cover letter, make up a book proposal.

A *synopsis* summarizes the book, covering the basic plot (including the ending). It should be easy to read and flow well. The gold standard for synopsis length is one page, single-spaced.

An *outline* covers your book chapter by chapter and provides highlights of each. If you're developing an outline for fiction, include major characters, plots and subplots, and book length. Requesting an outline is uncommon, and the word is somewhat interchangeable with "synopsis."

Sample chapters give a more comprehensive idea of your writing skill. Some editors may request the first two or three chapters to determine if they're interested in seeing the whole book. Some may request a set number of pages.

Manuscript formats

When submitting a complete manuscript, follow some basic guidelines. In the upper-left corner of your title page, type your legal name (not pseudonym), address and phone number. In the upper-right corner, type the approximate word count. All material in the upper corners should be single-spaced. Then type the title (centered) almost halfway down that page, the word "by" two spaces under that, and your name or pseudonym two spaces under "by."

The first page should also include the title (centered) one-third of the way down. Two spaces under that, type "by" and your name or pseudonym. To begin the body of your manuscript, drop down two double spaces and indent five spaces for each new paragraph. There should be one-inch margins around all sides of a full typewritten page. (Manuscripts with wide margins are more readable and easier to edit.)

Set your computer to double-space the manuscript body. From page two to the end of the manuscript, include your last name followed by a comma and the title (or key words of the title) in the upper-left corner. The page number should go in the top right corner. Drop down two double spaces to begin the body of each page. If you're submitting a novel, type each chapter title one-third of the way down the page. For more information on manuscript formats, read *Formatting & Submitting Your Manuscript, 3rd Ed.* (Writer's Digest Books).

Picture book formats

The majority of editors prefer to see complete manuscripts for picture books. When typing the text of a picture book, don't indicate page breaks and don't type each page of text on a new sheet of paper. And unless you are an illustrator, don't worry about supplying art. Editors will find their own illustrators for picture books. Most of the time, a writer and an illustrator who work on the same book never meet or interact. The editor acts as a go-between and works with the writer and illustrator throughout the publishing process. *How to Write and Sell Children's Picture Books*, by Jean E. Karl (Writer's Digest Books), offers advice on preparing text and marketing your work.

If you're an illustrator who has written your own book, consider creating a dummy or storyboard containing both art and text, and then submit it along with your complete manuscript and sample pieces of final art (hi-res PDFs or .jpgs—never originals). Publishers interested in picture books specify in their listings what should be submitted. For tips on creating a dummy, refer to *How to Write and Illustrate Children's Books and Get Them Published*, edited by Treld Pelkey Bicknell and Felicity Trotman (North Light Books), or Frieda Gates' book, *How to Write, Illustrate, and Design Children's Books* (Lloyd-Simone Publishing Company).

Writers may also want to learn the art of dummy-making to help them through their writing process with things like pacing, rhythm and length. For a great explanation and helpful hints, see *You Can Write Children's Books*, by Tracey E. Dils (Writer's Digest Books).

Mailing submissions

Your main concern when packaging material is to be sure it arrives undamaged. If your manuscript is fewer than six pages, simply fold it in thirds and send it in a #10 (business-size) envelope. For a SASE, either fold another #10 envelope in thirds or insert a #9 (reply) envelope, which fits in a #10 neatly without folding.

Another option is folding your manuscript in half in a 6x9 envelope, with a #9 or #10 SASE enclosed. For larger manuscripts, use a 9x12 envelope both for mailing the submission and as a SASE (which can be folded in half). Book manuscripts require sturdy packaging for mailing. Include a self-addressed mailing label and return postage. If asked to send artwork and photographs, remember they require a bit more care in packaging to guarantee they arrive in good condition. Sandwich illustrations and photos between heavy cardboard that is slightly larger than the work. The cardboard can be secured by rubber bands or with tape. If you tape the cardboard together, check that the artwork doesn't stick to the tape. Be sure your name and address appear on the back of each piece of art or each photo in case the material becomes separated. For the packaging, use either a manila envelope, a foam-padded envelope, or a mailer lined with plastic air bubbles. Bind nonjoined edges with reinforced mailing tape and affix a typed mailing label or clearly write your address.

Mailing material first class ensures quick delivery. Also, first-class mail is forwarded for one year if the addressee has moved, and it can be returned if undeliverable. If you're concerned about your original material safely reaching its destination, consider other mailing options such as UPS. No matter which way you send material, never send it where it requires a signature. Agents and editors are too busy to sign for packages.

Remember, companies outside your own country can't use your country's postage when returning a manuscript to you. When mailing a submission to another country, include a self-addressed envelope and International Reply Coupons, or IRCs. (You'll see this term in many listings in the Canadian & International Book Publishers section.) Your postmaster can tell you, based on a package's weight, the correct number of IRCs to include to ensure its return. If it's not necessary for an editor to return your work (such as with photocopies), don't include return postage.

Unless requested, it's never a good idea to use a company's fax number to send manuscript submissions. This can disrupt a company's internal business. Study the listings for specifics and visit publishers' and market websites for more information.

E-Mailing submissions

Most correspondence with editors today is handled over e-mail. This type of communication is usually preferred by publishing professionals because it is easier to deal with as well as free. When sending an e-mailed submission, make sure to follow submission guidelines. Double-check the recipient's e-mail address. Make sure your subject line has the proper wording, if specific wording was asked for. Keep your introduction letter short and sweet. Also, editors and agents usually do not like opening unsolicited attachments, which makes for an awkward situation for illustrators who want to attach .jpgs. One easy way around this is to post some sample illustrations on your web-

site. That way, you can simply paste URL hyperlinks to your work. Editors can click through to look over your illustration samples, and there is no way your submission will get accidentally deleted because of attachments. That said, if editors are asking for illustration samples, they are most likely used to receiving unsolicited attachments.

Keeping submission records

It's important to keep track of the material you submit. When recording each submission, include the date it was sent, the business and contact name, and any enclosures (such as samples of writing, artwork or photography). You can create a record-keeping system of your own or look for record-keeping software in your area computer store.

Keep copies of articles or manuscripts you send together with related correspondence to make follow-up easier. When you sell rights to a manuscript, artwork or photos, you can "close" your file on a particular submission by noting the date the material was accepted, what rights were purchased, the publication date and payment.

Often writers, illustrators and photographers fail to follow up on overdue responses. If you don't hear from a publisher within their stated response time, wait another month or so and follow up with an e-mail asking about the status of your submission. Include the title or description, date sent and a SASE (if applicable) for response. Ask the contact person when she anticipates making a decision. You may refresh the memory of a buyer who temporarily forgot about your submission. At the very least, you'll receive a definite "no" and free yourself to send the material to another publisher.

Simultaneous submissions

Writers and illustrators are encouraged to simultaneously submit—sending the same material to several markets at the same time. Almost all markets are open to this type of communication; those that do not take simultaneous submissions will directly say so in their submission guidelines.

It's especially important to keep track of simultaneous submissions, so if you get an offer on a manuscript sent to more than one publisher, you can instruct other publishers to withdraw your work from consideration. (Or, you can always use the initial offer as a way to ignite interest from other agents and editors. It's very possible to procure multiple offers on your book using this technique.)

AGENTS & ART REPS

Most children's writers, illustrators and photographers, especially those just beginning, are confused about whether to enlist the services of an agent or representative. The decision is strictly one that each writer, illustrator or photographer must make for herself. Some are confident with their own negotiation skills and believe acquiring an agent or rep is not in their best interest. Others feel uncomfortable in the business arena or are not willing to sacrifice valuable creative time for marketing.

About half of children's publishers accept unagented work, so it's possible to break into children's publishing without an agent. Writers targeting magazine markets don't need the services of an agent. In fact, it's practically impossible to find an agent interested in marketing articles and short stories—there simply isn't enough financial incentive.

One benefit of having an agent, though, is it may speed up the process of getting your work reviewed, especially by publishers who don't accept unagented submissions. If an agent has a good reputation and submits your manuscript to an editor, that manuscript will likely bypass the first-read stage (which is generally done by editorial assistants and junior editors) and end up on the editor's desk sooner.

When agreeing to have a reputable agent represent you, remember that she should be familiar with the needs of the current market and evaluate your manuscript/artwork/photos accordingly. She should also determine the quality of your piece and whether it is saleable. When your manuscript sells, your agent should negotiate a favorable contract and clear up any questions you have about payments.

Keep in mind that however reputable the agent or rep is, she has limitations. Representation does not guarantee sale of your work. It just means an agent or rep sees potential in your writing, art or photos. Though an agent or rep may offer criticism or advice on how to improve your work, she cannot make you a better writer, artist or photographer.

Literary agents typically charge a 15 percent commission from the sale of writing; art and photo representatives usually charge a 25–30 percent commission. Such fees are taken from advances and royalty earnings. If your agent sells foreign rights or film rights to your work, she will deduct a higher percentage because she will most likely be dealing with an overseas agent with whom she must split the fee.

Be advised that not every agent is open to representing a writer, artist or photographer who lacks an established track record. Just as when approaching a publisher, the manuscript, artwork or photos, and que-

ry or cover letter you submit to a potential agent must be attractive and professional looking. Your first impression must be as an organized, articulate person. For listings of agents and reps, turn to the Agents & Art Reps section.

For additional listings of art reps, consult *Artist's & Graphic Designer's Market*; for photo reps, see *Photographer's Market*; for more information and additional listings of literary agents, see *Guide to Literary Agents* (all Writer's Digest Books).

MIDDLE GRADE VS. YOUNG ADULT

Different audiences, different styles.

by Marie Lamba

OK, class. What sets a middle-grade novel apart from a young adult novel? If you said MG is for readers ages 8–12, and YA is for readers ages 13–18, then give yourself a check plus. But if you're writing for the juvenile market and that's *all* you know about these two categories, then I'm afraid you still need to stick around for the rest of this class. A book that doesn't fit within the parameters of either age category is a book you won't be able to sell.

In my work with The Jennifer De Chiara Literary Agency, I see my inbox flooded every day with queries for manuscripts that suffer from an MG/YA identity crisis. Like when a query says, "I've written a 100,000-word MG novel about a seventh-grader who falls in love and has sex for the first time." Or when one states, "In my 20,000-word YA novel, a 14-year-old holds her first sleepover and learns the meaning of true friendship." Both queries would earn a swift rejection, based on both inappropriate manuscript lengths and on content that's either too mature or too young for the audience they're targeting. Sadly, by not understanding what makes a book a true MG

or a solid YA, these writers have hamstrung their chances for success, regardless of how well written their stories may be. It's like they showed up to a final exam without ever cracking a book.

On the bright side, writers who study up on the many key differences between MG and YA will be able to craft the kind of well-targeted manuscript that will make both agents and editors take notice. Pay attention, because someday your manuscript *will* be tested.

MG at a Glance

AGE OF READERS: 8–12. **LENGTH:** Generally 30,000–50,000 words (although fantasy can run longer to allow for more complex world-building). **CONTENT RESTRICTIONS:** No profanity, graphic violence or sexuality (romance, if any, is limited to a crush or a first kiss). **AGE OF PROTAGONIST:** Typically age 10 for a younger MG novel, and up to age 13 for older, more complex books. **MIND-SET:** Focus on friends, family and the character's immediate world and relationship to it; characters react to what happens to them, with minimal self-reflection.

VOICE: Often third person.

YA at a Glance

AGE OF READERS: 13–18. **LENGTH:** Generally 50,000–75,000 words (although there's also a length allowance for fantasy). **CONTENT RE-STRICTIONS:** Profanity, graphic violence, romance and sexuality (except for eroticism) are all allowable (though not required). **AGE OF PROTAGONIST:** Ages 14–15 for a younger YA with cleaner content aimed at the middle-school crowd; for older and more edgy YA, characters can be up to 18 (but not in college). **MIND-SET:** YA heroes discover how they fit in the world beyond their friends and family; they spend more time reflecting on what happens and analyzing the meaning of things. **VOICE:** Often first person.

MG vs. YA Characters

When picking your hero's age, remember that kids "read up," which means they want to read about characters who are older than they are. So an 8-year-old protagonist won't fly for the MG category, though it'd be OK for a younger chapter book or easy reader. For the widest audience, you'll generally want your protagonist to be on the oldest side of your readership that your plot will allow. That means a 12- or even 13-year-old hero for MG, and a 17- or 18-year-old for YA (just remember your hero can't be in college yet—that would push it into the "new adult" category).

MG vs. YA Readers

Middle-grade is *not* synonymous with middle school. Books for the middle-school au-dience tend to be divided between the MG and YA shelves. So which shelf do those readers go to? While there is no such thing as a 'tween category in bookstores, there are degrees of maturity in both MG and YA novels that'll appeal to the younger and older sides of the middle-school crowd. A longer, more complex MG novel with characters who are 13 could take place in middle school and be considered an "upper-MG novel." But the material can't be too mature. It's still an MG novel, after all, and most readers will be younger. Writing a sweeter, more innocent YA? Then it's pretty likely that your readers will be 'tweens, that your characters should be around 15 years old, and that your book will be marketed as a "young YA." But

While it's useful for you to understand these nuances as you craft your story and relate to your true audience, when it comes time to submit, don't go so far as to define your novel as upper MG or younger YA in your query. That's already pointing to a more limited readership. Instead, just stick to calling it either MG or YA when you submit, and let an interested agent draw conclusions about nuances from there.

MG vs. YA Content and Voice

What's cool to a fourth-grader differs from what a 10th-grader will idolize. Same goes for the way they speak and the way they view the world. Which is why if romance appears in an MG novel, it's limited to a crush and maybe an innocent kiss, as it is in *Shug* by Jenny Han. A YA could involve deep, true love as well as sexuality, as in *The Fault in Our Stars* by John Green. Another key difference? Overall, MG novels end on a hopeful note, while YA novels could have less optimistic endings, as in Green's tearful story. You could say that that's youth vs. experience coming into play.

When it comes to content, here's another important thing to keep in mind: There are gatekeepers between your book and your targeted audience. MG readers typically don't have direct access to their novels. To get a book, kids first go through a parent, a teacher or a librarian. While you might want to have that gritty character in your upper-MG novel drop a few four-letter words, doing so *will* hurt book sales, so choose your language wisely.

Also, think *carefully* about your content. MG is not the place for graphic or persistent violence, but can it be scary and dark? Sure—look at *Holes* by Louis Sachar, where boys are threatened by a crazy warden and nearly killed by poisonous lizards. (Note, however, that book *does* have a happy ending.)

If you're writing a YA, you don't have to worry about those gatekeepers as much. But while YA authors cover just about anything in their novels, keep in mind that *gratuitous* sex, foul language or violence won't fly in *any* great literature. And do remember that school and library support can really catapult a YA title to success. While dropping a ton of F-bombs is OK if it fits with your characters and setting, be prepared for your book to be perhaps on fewer school shelves as a result, and make sure it's worth that risk.

Exceptions to Every Rule

Like any rebellious teen can tell you, rules are made to be broken. Word counts often vary from the suggested norms. Just don't deviate too low or too high, especially for a debut. I know what you're thinking: J.K. Rowling. True, *Harry Potter and the Deathly Hallows* came close to a whopping 200,000 words, but her debut novel, *Harry Potter and the Sorcerer's Stone*, was roughly 77,000 words—which is still long for the genre, but not outrageously so for an MG fantasy. Hey, once you get as popular as Rowling, you can write doorstopper-sized tomes, too.

Content can also stray from the stated guidelines, *with good reason*. You might, say, choose to have an MG with a swear word, or with a more edgy storyline. Whatever norm you do stray from, just make sure you do so for a specific and valid purpose, that your book still fits your audience's point of view, and that you understand what deviating from the norm might mean for your book's marketability.

Whether you aim to write a YA or an MG novel, there is one thing you absolutely *must* do: Tell a story that is meaningful to your intended reader. And to do that, you must first know *who* that reader is.

So which shelf does your book belong on? Know *that* and your book will surely graduate with full honors, moving on to a long and happy future in your readers' appreciative hands.

MARIE LAMBA (marielamba.com) is author of the YA novels *What I Meant...*, *Over My Head* and *Drawn*. She's also an associate literary agent at The Jennifer De Chiara Literary Agency (jdlit.com).

WRITER FOR HIRE

Opportunities in children's educational publishing.

by Jenna Glatzer

My first published book was the result of an online job listing: a book packager asked for writers who could contribute to a series of nonfiction books for fourth graders. Despite that I had no book experience, I thought, *Couldn't hurt to try.* I sent over my résumé and clips from magazine articles, and within a few days, I had my first-ever book assignment: a 64-page picture book about the exploration of the moon.

The pay was a modest flat fee and it was a work-for-hire, meaning that the publisher would own all rights and I would never see royalties, even if the book sold millions of copies in multiple languages. But that wasn't very important to me; what mattered at the time was getting experience and my first book credit.

The publisher liked my work and hired me again, and I began looking around for similar opportunities. I soon realized that there were many opportunities for intrepid writers who were willing to search for them: Numerous book publishers and packagers in the children's educational markets develop new series ideas in-house every year and then hire writers, consultants, and sometimes illustrators to work on the books.

Although not in every case, most deals are very similar:

• The publisher will have a theme for the series—for instance, inventors, seasons, endangered animals, or presidents—and will assign one (or more) titles in the series to you.

• These are not textbooks, but supplemental nonfiction books that go along with themes and lessons kids learn in class, or are subjects of high interest to particular age groups.

• You're given a specific format to follow. It will tell you the grade level, reading level, page count, and word count, plus details of specific things to include and where to include them (for instance, guided reading questions, related websites, recommended books, sidebars, and your "About the Author" bio).

• They are work-for-hire deals, with payments split into two or three installments (often half up front and half on acceptance of the final draft). Typical pay for an elementary-level text is a flat fee of $500-8,000 depending on length, research required, deadline, and projected sales. Some publishers offer an advance against royalties.

• They're fairly fast turnarounds: You won't get a year to write your book. One to four months is common.

THE GOOD

Less Competition

This type of work is attractive to new writers because it provides a less-competitive way to break into the publishing world than trying to pitch your own original manuscripts. The work is out there, but many writers don't know about it.

You Don't Need an Agent

In fact, few agents bother representing this type of work because the commissions are too low. You can submit directly and skip that step.

Loyalty

Many publishers in this field use the same writers over and over for years. If you turn in good work on time, you can expect that you'll be hired again. "If we're happy with a particular writer, she or he could stay busy working with us," says Ashley Kuehl, associate editorial director of Lerner Publications.

Fast Credits

If you're looking to boost your résumé, this is a way to do it quickly (or at least less slowly—book publishing is rarely speedy). After author Linda Tagliaferro submitted her first children's manuscript, an editor hired her to write *ten more* books in a series! In addition to just adding to your list of credits, it can also give you much-needed experience and confidence when working with editors and understanding the publication process.

Local Prestige

If you've always wanted to speak at children's schools or libraries, this can give you the clout you need. Libraries and schools are often hungry for children's authors to come read their work and speak to kids about the book topic or about writing—and you can make some extra money this way.

A Change of Pace

Tagliaferro spends most of her time writing for adults, but likes taking a break to write for kids. "It's a nice way to use another part of my brain," she says. These are fairly short-term projects and are on an array of topics that you may enjoy learning about. There is often flexibility in the topics, too—an editor may give you a list of titles in the series and ask which one (or ones) you want to take on.

No Pressure to Come Up With Ideas

If you don't have dozens of ideas for books of your own, that's fine—you can let the publishing team do the brainstorming for you. No worries about whether or not your idea is good enough to be published, no crafting a perfect query letter, no submission waiting game or rejections ... they've already "bought" the topic. If, on the other hand, you want to be involved with the idea-generating part, some publishers and packagers are interested in hearing that, too. (Publishers Enslow Press and Nomad Press welcome your ideas, for instance.)

THE LESS GOOD

You Don't Always Get Credit

The author's name doesn't always appear on the cover when you do series work. When it doesn't appear on the cover, sometimes it does appear inside the book on the title or copyright page, but sometimes it's nowhere to be seen.

Low Pay

Considering the time you may put into research, writing, editing, rewriting, and proofreading, the hourly fees to write series books are typically low.

Lack of Control

You won't have much creative control. You're being hired to do a job and match the tone and "voice" of the series. Straying from the topic or format is not OK. You likely won't have any say in the title, cover, or artwork, though there are exceptions.

Not in Bookstores

These series books are usually not stocked on bookstore shelves (though they can be ordered through bookstores) or in other brick-and-mortar stores. They're sold to schools and libraries and available online. Many are available as e-books as well.

Non-Negotiable Terms

Contract terms in this market are typically less negotiable than in trade publishing. It's always worth trying for better terms, but there is often not much wiggle room, and even experienced writers won't shake out much more fruit from the tree. You may be able to negotiate for more free books—writers typically get 10-25 authors' copies and discounted rates on additional copies.

SKILLS YOU NEED

A background in education is necessary for some subjects and some publishers, but not the majority. What's more important are your research skills, and ability to write clearly and concisely.

Research should consist of primary sources whenever possible: Direct interviews with experts or people involved with the story, studies printed in peer-reviewed journals, oral histories, autobiographies, and so on. When these are not available, reliable secondary sources are the next pick: newspaper articles, reference books, magazine articles, interviews with sources who are connected with the original source. What's never acceptable are sources like Wikipedia, personal blogs, or other children's books. You will normally need to footnote your manuscript so that a fact-checker can ... well, check your facts!

Despite that it's not a very hard market to get into, that doesn't mean it's easy to do a good job. Most of these books have tight word counts and limited vocabulary. "You have to know how to write tight," says Tagliaferro. "You also have to know how to communicate sophisticated concepts in short, meaningful words that even young children can understand. On several books about animals and their babies, I had to mention how the parent animal keeps its babies safe from predators. Well, 'predator' is a word they won't use in books for four- and five-year-olds. I finally came up with the idea of mentioning where the parent animal hides its young, and then added, 'Hungry animals can't find them.' It's fun for me to think of ways to get these concepts across in short, simple words."

And unless you have a child in the target age group or teach that age group, you're probably not all that familiar with what's expected. Author Tish Davidson, who's done several work-for-hires for Scholastic, Mason Crest, and Scribner, cautions that writing nonfiction for kids is different from writing fiction for kids. "Go to the library and ask the children's librarian for nonfiction books at the appropriate grade level. The topic is unimportant. Pay attention to the vocabulary level, sentence lengths, sentence complexity, and paragraph length. After you've read a dozen or so, you will have a good sense of the elements appropriate for a specific age group."

You also need to understand how to follow guidelines very precisely, how to keep yourself on track without a boss looming over your shoulder, and you need a willingness to revise and rewrite when an editor asks. Kuehl says that they also value writers who have an awareness of their own capabilities—those who are realistic about how much they can handle in a given time frame, and who ask questions up front when they're at all unclear about what an assignment entails.

Deadlines in book publishing are critical—you can't hold up publication because you didn't budget your time correctly. Delia Greve, senior editor at becker&mayer! Books, says that if you want to impress her once you have an assignment, it's pretty simple: "Hit the dates set out in a schedule. And if an author can't hit them, I really like him or her to be realistic and honest. Let me know if a date will be missed ahead of time. I can then make a plan and work with an author, but if I don't know something will be late until after the due date has past, planning gets much trickier."

If you miss deadlines, plagiarize, or submit unacceptable work and don't get it fixed on the first revision, it's unlikely for you to get a second chance—and more likely that your book will get reassigned to another writer. Davidson has picked up several assignments when another writer dropped the ball.

Finally, you need the ability to not be boring. All of us can remember "required reading" in school that nearly put us to sleep. Don't be that writer. Even though this type of work is not a creative smorgasbord where you can stretch your literary prowess to the max, you still have to tell stories in ways that are engaging to kids. Your book should not just be a collection of facts, but a cohesive story that may contain dialogue, funny or gripping anecdotes, and rich imagery.

FINDING OPPORTUNITIES

You know what a book publisher is. A book packager (or producer) is an entity that puts together the various elements for a publisher—they hire writers and designers, take care of editing and layout, and often even print the books for a publisher. Your manuscript will have to be approved by both the packager and the publisher. Not all publishers use packagers, but many do.

You can search for educational book publishers and packagers online (and I've listed many here), but another effective way to get assignments is through in-person meetings at writers' conferences and book fairs. That's how Barbara Radcliffe Rogers began writing kids' social studies books. She liked a publisher's line at a book fair, so she asked them what countries they had not yet covered in a particular series. Not only did she end up writing for them, but the publisher sent her and her photographer husband to Africa on assignment.

Rogers found her opportunity by asking what was available; you can also find opportunities by looking for the gaps in a series. My third published book was part of a series about disabilities; I noticed that they hadn't yet covered Down syndrome, and considering my brother has Down syndrome, I knew plenty about it. I asked if they were interested in adding that topic to their series, and they did—it's still in print more than a decade later.

WHY SERIES?

These types of books are almost always parts of series because that's how the educational market prefers to buy. Publishers pay attention to trends, state and national educational standards, and feedback from educators and librarians in determining new titles.

"Our series are delineated by age, so someone looking for science books for eight-year-olds can check our Explore series and find dozens of books that fit that description," says Susan Hale Kahan of Nomad Press. "If teachers use one of our books and discover they can rely on Nomad for compelling content and rigorous learning, they have a whole series to choose from."

WHAT PUBLISHERS WANT TO SEE

Well, let's start out with what they don't want: traditional query letters.

They don't want your ideas for original books, for the most part, unless it fits in with a series they're publishing. And they don't want to see your already-written manuscript. They just want to know about you and your expertise.

So what you actually need are three things: a letter of introduction, a couple of writing samples, and a résumé. And while book credits are a plus, not every publisher insists that you have any. This is a great avenue for people who have *some* sort of publishing credentials (like magazine or newspaper articles), but who don't necessarily have books to their name yet.

You need to convey a few things in your letter:

• That you can write
• That you are careful about proofreading (double-check your grammar and spelling)

• Any areas of expertise you might have (history, travel, science, technology, fitness, crafting, etc.)
• Anything that qualifies you to write for them: past writing experience, teaching experience, educational experience, or relevant degrees.

"Most often it's the quality of writing that gets our attention before we even focus on the content," says Susan Hale Kahan of Nomad Press. If you can demonstrate in your cover letter that you can write, they're willing to work with you even if you've never had a book published before (though they will need to see writing samples that show you can handle the kind of topics they assign).

You'll probably get an acknowledgment from someone on the editorial staff— "Thanks for sending your stuff—we'll let you know if we have anything that fits," but then it could be a long time before you hear again. Don't get too discouraged: This is one field where publishers really do hold onto résumés for a very long time. Both Tagliaferro and I have had assignments show up a year or more after we submitted résumés to a publisher. If a long time passes and your résumé improves, feel free to send out updated ones. (No need to send updates for every new credit, but every six months or so is fine if you have substantial additions.)

My career has come a long way since those first few educational books—I'm Celine Dion's authorized biographer, my latest health book sold out in three days, and my resume includes 24 other books from publishers like Simon & Schuster and Penguin Random House. They're in lots of languages and one even got made into a movie. I certainly don't need to write work-for-hire educational books anymore ... and yet I still do it from time to time because I enjoy it. It's enabled me to learn more about some interesting topics (my latest release is about the inventor of the Ferris wheel) and to stretch my writing muscles.

You may find the same satisfaction. And best of all, you'll contribute to educating today's children while you're building your career.

JENNA GLATZER (jennaglatzer.com) is the award-winning author of 26 books for grown-ups and kids, including the authorized biography *Celine Dion: For Keeps*, *The Marilyn Monroe Treasures*, *Never Ever Give Up: The Inspiring Story of Jessie and Her JoyJars* with Erik Rees, and *Bullyproof Your Child for Life* with Dr. Joel Haber. Her most recent children's book is *George Ferris' Grand Idea: The Ferris Wheel*.

CHILDREN'S EDUCATIONAL PUBLISHERS AND PACKAGERS THAT HIRE WRITERS

ABDO: www.abdopublishing.com

Amicus: www.amicuspublishing.us

Bearport Publishing: www.bearportpublishing.com

Bow Publications: www.bowpublications.com

Capstone: www.capstonepub.com

Carson-Dellosa: www.carsondellosa.com

Continental: www.continentalpress.com

Delta Publishing Company: www.deltapublishing.com

Enslow Publishing: www.enslow.com

JayJo Books: www.jayjo.com

Jump Start Press: www.jumpstartpress.com

Infobase: www.infobasepublishing.com

Innovative Kids: www.innovativekids.com

Lerner: www.lernerbooks.com

Nomad Press: www.nomadpress.net

Oomf, Inc.: www.oomf.com

OTTN Publishing: www.ottnpublishing.com

Perfection Learning: www.perfectionlearning.com

Red Line Editorial: www.reditorial.com

MAKING YOUNG READERS LAUGH

The power of humor in a manuscript.

by Kerrie Flanagan

Humor is a tool all writers should have in their toolbox, but especially when writing for children. Making kids laugh while they are reading creates an emotional connection to the work and makes it a memorable experience. That connection with the reader is what all writers crave. And thanks to pioneers in children's literature like Dr. Seuss, writing fun and entertaining books for kids is a valued pursuit for writers.

Humor is all about the unexpected; pushing boundaries, going against the norm, irony, and exaggeration. Sometimes it shows up as physical humor, sometimes in the situation (plot), with the language (puns, misunderstandings), and/or with the characters (exaggerated personalities, flaws, etc.).

Some very talented authors have figured out how to make kids laugh. Jeff Kinney, the mastermind behind the wildly successful Diary of a Wimpy Kid series, did not set out to write for children. His dream was to be a syndicated newspaper cartoonist. He tried for three years to make that happen.

"Eventually I had to come to terms with the fact that I didn't have what it took to illustrate a professional comic strip ... my style wasn't refined enough. So I had the idea to create comics as a middle school kid, and that's when Diary of a Wimpy Kid was born."

John Erickson, creator of Hank the Cowdog, a popular series for grades 3–5 told from the dog's point of view, had a similar experience. A rancher in Texas, Erickson originally wrote a story about Hank the Cowdog for *The Cattleman Magazine* whose target audience was ranchers like himself. His wife told him he should write for children and after some coaxing, that's what he decided to do.

Even with their success in the children's market, both Kinney and Erickson, still don't feel they are writing for a younger audience. Though he's written 75 published books, Erickson said, "I don't know a thing about writing for children. I'm just trying to make people laugh."

Kinney originally submitted the first *Diary of a Wimpy Kid* book to the publisher as a book for adults. "I didn't change a thing after I was told it would be market-ed for kids. I realized that if I had been thinking of a kids' audience as I was writing, I would've written down to kids. Even now, when I write, I think of adult readers, not kids."

Sometimes an idea for a book can come from something very simple. Gordon McAlpine, author of *The Misadventures of Edgar & Allan Poe*, shared, "Initially, it was the sound of the names Edgar *and* Allan Poe, which I thought was funny." Going with this idea he introduces Em and Milly Dickinson in the second book of the trilogy. But he said he managed to fend off the temptation toward overkill by not bringing in more twins like Arthur and Conan Doyle, or Robert and Louis Stevenson.

Creating storylines and characters to keep kids engaged and laughing takes a special kind of writer. Ursula Vernon, author and illustrator of the Dragonbreath series for grades 3–5, isn't always sure what will make kids laugh, but she has a few staples in her repertoire. "Sometimes the kids think parts of a book are hysterically funny that I hadn't expected. Generally, though, I find that kids like pizza, farts, weird diseases, and made-up animals. If I get stuck, I go for one of those."

Lisa Doan, author of The Berenson Schemes series, also writes for grades 3–5, and she has a little different take on what kids find funny. "Middle graders have been flooded with society's rules and expectations; they know what the norms are. In humor, the unexpected rides in on the back of the skewed world view character—that guy who either doesn't understand the norms or doesn't care what they are—creating a space between what is assumed will happen and what actually happens. Tone dictates whether that space is humor or tragedy."

McAlpine says that young readers love to see holes poked in cynical individuals or institutions. "Merely deflating the overblown is not enough. Young readers appreciate characters who can also create, inspire, and connect, standing up at times for those who do not enjoy the compensations/liabilities of being, say, the uniquely conjoined great-great-great-great grandnephews of Edgar Allan Poe."

Debbie Dadey, author of more than 160 books including The Adventures of the Bailey School Kids series, has found that if it's not funny to her, it won't be funny to kids. "I think unusual or unexpected situations can be funny. And underwear is always funny. Also, taking something normal and going wild can be funny. For instance, in *Treasure in Trident City* (Mermaid Tales series) a simple book report is funny because of the unexpected and silly way the character dresses. A visit to the ice cream store gets silly in *Ghouls Don't Scoop Ice Cream* when Eddie accidently squirts whipped cream everywhere (while in his underwear, of course)!"

A variety of experiences and activities provide inspiration and ideas for these authors. Erickson watches his dog do things like snap at snowflakes and imitate the howling coyotes on the ranch. He then imagines what is going on in his dog's mind.

Vernon found you can't always rely on your own experiences from growing up, be-cause some things have changed. "I thought school lunches being awful would be funny forever ... and then I started doing book tours in California, and students would all tell me how wonderful the lunches were and I lost some of my 'A' material!"

Kinney finds some of his best material from real life, things that would be too difficult to make up. "The more outlandish or unrealistic my jokes are, the less the reader can relate to them. The problem is, funny things don't happen around me fast enough. So I have to pad the real-life stuff with things from my imagination."

The best humor lurks in the darkest corner of the mind, Doan says. It's a corner she says where we store everything we would like to forget. "There are two departments in that corner: the true tragedies department, which is usually small and best left undisturbed, and the next door down—the department of cringe-inducing incidents. That door can be flung wide open to reveal a vast landscape of hilarity. I have a feeling that people who claim to have no sense of humor are just too scaredy-cat to open that door."

McAlpine finds inspiration from others stories. "Infiltrate a good book and you'll find a dozen untold stories hovering like fireflies in the shadows. Capture them, enchant them with your own voice and perspective, and then allow them to illuminate a story that is all your own."

So what is it agents and editors are looking for? Kelly Sonnack, literary agent with the Andrea Brown Literary Agency, has seen many manuscripts come across her desk. For her, the authors that miss the mark are the ones trying too hard. "It's a difficult thing to try to explain because when you're funny you're *just funny* and it's really hard to force the issue. I think it's important to remember that children have a different sense of humor than adults and that doesn't just mean gross humor. Kids are really smart and you have to give them credit for that. My favorite humor for kids is the clever kind."

Her advice is to go read your manuscript to a group of kids with no personal connection to you, or better yet, let them read it themselves and see what they think.

One of the biggest pieces of advice that these authors have for writers trying to break into the children's market is not to talk down to kids. "It's important to write what you think is funny," Kinney says. "Kids are pretty sophisticated when it comes to humor. If what you're writing is good, they'll get it."

Vernon feels if kids get a whiff that you're patronizing them, you're done. "I have to write jokes that I think are funny as an adult, too. If it comes across like I'm writing jokes because The Dear Children Will Find This Amusing, the readers will not be amused."

McAlpine adds: "Young readers are smart and imaginative. They delight at the prospect of *those* characteristics being used against bullies or condescending, arrogant, overblown grown-ups."

Finally, Doan says: "I write what makes me laugh. Which apparently falls on the juvenile side. (I'll never be mature enough to write YA)."

So, get out your old yearbooks, dig up all those embarrassing moments from childhood, think about all the adventures you had with your friends growing up, reminisce about family trips and write them all down. Then pull out all the stories, spice them up with some humor and who knows, maybe you will have a bestseller on your hands.

KERRIE FLANAGAN (KerrieFlanagan.com) is a freelance writer, Director of Northern Colorado Writers (NorthernColoradoWriters.com), a writing organization going strong since 2007, and author of *Write Away; A Year of Musings & Motivations for Writers*.

LAUGHTER BY THE AGES

Dr. Paul McGhee researched humor and laughter for 20 years, and found that young children experience the following different stages as they develop.

STAGE 1: LAUGHTER AT THE ATTACHMENT FIGURE (6–12 MONTHS)

During this stage children are reacting to other people, not creating their own humor. They respond when something is unusual. You can find infants laughing at a parent waddling like a penguin, making silly faces, and making exaggerated animal sounds.

STAGE 2: TREATING AN OBJECT AS A DIFFERENT OBJECT (12 MONTHS TO 5 YEARS)

This is when children begin pretend play and it paves the way for some of the earliest humor created by children. They start to understand their world and begin playing around with it. They may put socks on their hands or bowls on their head. They know this is not the norm, so they find it funny.

STAGE 3: MISNAMING OBJECTS OR ACTIONS (2–4 YEARS)

Two- and three-year-olds find it funny to simply give the wrong name for things. Calling a cat a dog or a squirrel an elephant or calling mommy, daddy. It's all very funny to them.

STAGE 4A: PLAYING WITH WORD SOUNDS, NOT MEANINGS (3–5 YEARS)

Several new forms of humor emerge by the end of the third year. One is when children begin experimenting with the sounds of words. They may repeat words over and over like "silly, frilly, pilly." Sound play may also show up by altering the sound of a single word in an otherwise normal sentence, such as "I want tato-wato-chatos" for potatoes.

STAGE 4B: NONSENSE REAL-WORD COMBINATIONS (3–5 YEARS)

In addition to playing with the sounds of words, most (but not all) three-year-olds also start putting real words together in nonsensical combinations known to be wrong. For instance: "Can I have more flower milk please?" or "Look at that lollipop tree."

STAGE 4C: DISTORTION OF FEATURES OF OBJECTS, PEOPLE OR ANIMALS (3–5 YEARS)

By age three, children have a good grasp of their world, generating many new kinds of humor. These include:
- Adding or removing features that don't belong: a dog's head on a man's body, a tree with cakes growing on it, or a car with no wheels.

- Changing the shape, size, location, color, length, etc., of familiar things: a boy with a square head or a dog with polka dots.
- Exaggerating features: a long neck, big ears, enormous or very pointy nose.
- Using impossible behavior: a duck on roller skates, a dog walking a human, or a fish playing the piano

PRE-RIDDLE STAGE: TRANSITION PERIOD (5-7 YEARS)

This is the point at which children have been exposed to riddles but don't really understand them. What they do understand is that you ask a question, then give an answer and laugh. As far as they're concerned, their answer is just as funny as yours. This is when absolutely ridiculous knock-knock jokes become big for a child, such as: "Knock-knock." "Who's there?" "My hat!"

HOW TO SELL YOUR PICTURE BOOK

An agent shares insider tips.

by Lara Perkins

Pitching a picture book? Things are looking up. Although the Association of American Publishers reports that book sales in the children's/young adult segment declined from January to October 2013, many agents observed an uptick in picture book acquisitions throughout 2013 and into 2014. By no means a perfect measure, it's nonetheless telling that approximately 400 picture book deals were announced in Publishers Marketplace in 2013 compared to approximately 300 in 2012. Still, the market is very competitive, and going head-to-head with the classics as well as new work by high-profile authors can be daunting. It needn't be. As a literary agent specializing in children's fiction and nonfiction, I'd like to share some observations about the current picture book market and tips for crafting picture books that sell.

KNOW THE MARKET.

Picture books typically hit the shelves two to five years after acquisition, so predicting current acquisition trends from new releases is difficult—as is trying to capitalize on a perceived hot trend. Yet successful new releases can suggest the larger strengths and reader appeal that publishers are seeking. For example, the success of *Goodnight, Goodnight, Construction Site* by Sherri Duskey Rinker and Tom Lichtenheld suggests stories that infuse a lulling, dreamy bedtime sweetness into active (building, traveling) daytime play are finding an audience.

The current market also reveals strong interest in character-driven stories that have series potential (*Clark the Shark* by Bruce Hale and Guy Francis, new classics like Ian Falconer's *Olivia*) and capture a universally relatable "kid experience" in a funny, larger-than-life way (*Crankenstein* by Samantha Berger and Dan Santat, *The Dark* by Lemony Snicket and Jon Klassen, *No Fits, Nilson!* by Zachariah OHora). We're also seeing interest in off-the-wall, kid-friendly humor (*Dragons Love Tacos* by Adam Rubin and Daniel Salmieri, *The Day the Crayons Quit* by Drew Daywalt and Oliver Jeffers); stories that cleverly turn familiar relationships upside down (*Nugget and Fang* by Tammi Sauer and Michael Slack, *Children Make Terrible Pets* by Peter Brown, *How to Babysit a Grandpa* by Jean Reagan and Lee Wildish); and books that are seasonal but work year-round (*Creepy Carrots!* by Aaron Reynolds and Peter Brown, *Bear Has a Story to Tell* by Philip C. Stead and Erin Stead).

There's significant interest in beautiful nonfiction picture books, biographies and others (*On a Beam of Light: A Story of Albert Einstein* by Jennifer Berne and Vladimir Radunsky and *Nelson Mandela* by Kadir Nelson).

Lovely, lyrical picture books with a hook for parents as well as kids are sought after (*Once Upon a Memory* by Nina Laden and Renata Liwska)—particularly for the younger set—as are innovative storytelling formats that take witty, fun narrative risks (*Battle Bunny* by Jon Scieszka, Mac Barnett and Matthew Myers). Many of these titles could fit more than one description as well.

Ideally, a new manuscript should share some proven strengths with recent successful picture books, while giving readers something new and fresh.

BEGIN WITH A STRONG IDEA.

Every picture book needs a plot and story structure. Even young picture books like Hervé Tullet's *Press Here*, concept books, and picture books with cumulative structures like Oliver Jeffers' *Stuck* or unusual formats like *Battle Bunny* must have tension, rising and falling action, and a satisfying final resolution.

Any story for young readers must tap into a universal childhood experience, no matter how wacky the premise. With *Dragons Love Tacos*, for example, hosting taco parties for dragons may not be a universal experience of childhood, but avoiding certain foods and attending parties where shenanigans ensue are. Similarly, John Rocco's *Blackout* transforms a commonplace neighborhood blackout into something magical and resonant. This universality is key to winning the hearts of parents, librarians and teachers—the gatekeepers who will share your book with kids.

Childhood experiences like bedtime rituals or the first day of school are evergreen, but a fresh angle with strong kid appeal is a must. For example, many picture books deal with fear of the dark, but *The Dark* takes an inventive approach, personifying the dark and following the relationship arc between housemates Laszlo and the dark.

To give your story that all-important kid appeal, tell it from a child's-eye point of view, even if your main character is a shark or President Obama. This is true even for the youngest picture books and nonfiction picture books. For example, Susan B. Katz's and Alicia Padrón's board book *ABC Baby Me!* brings readers directly into the perspective of a baby, and *On a Beam of Light* focuses on imagination, wonder and curiosity to bring Albert Einstein and his work to life for kids. Your main character or characters must be relatable and approach the world in a way that is recognizable to your audience.

If you're tackling a more serious subject such as loss or grief, be honest in your treatment of the subject but keep the mood positive and reassuring for this age group. For example, the final phrase in *Once Upon a Memory*, "Will you remember you once were a child?" is a beautiful nod to the passage of time and inevitable end of childhood, but framed in a gentle and child-friendly way.

Keep in mind that beloved picture books are read again and again by parents and kids. For that reason, successful picture books are filled with pitch-perfect character details that readers can continue to enjoy on the 10th or 20th or 100th reading. For example, every time I read Oliver Jeffers' *This Moose Belongs to Me*, I'm newly charmed by another hilarious character detail.

CRAFT STORIES THAT SELL.

How you choose to tell your story is as important as the story you tell. Picture book texts must be lean and mean, with exceptionally tight pacing. Although word counts can soar up to 1,200–1,300 words, most picture book texts for ages 3–8 are around 250–600 words. Infant/toddler board books will be even shorter, often with just a few words per page. With no words to spare, picture books must begin in media res, with the central tension and stakes of the story or the central concept clearly evident from the opening page. For example, the first line of *This Moose Belongs to Me* is "Wilfred owned a moose," which immediately establishes the central conflict and misunderstanding that drives the story.

Rhyme is understandably a hot-button issue in the picture book world, as it's no secret that rhyming texts can be a more difficult sell in today's market. However, skilled, creative rhyme can still sell very well (see Rinker and Lichtenheld's *Goodnight, Goodnight, Construction Site* or *Steam Train, Dream Train*), and even editors and agents who are hesitant about rhyme may often be swayed by terrific, well-executed stanzas coupled with a strong story and characters.

Unfortunately, rhyme all too often masks larger issues with story, character or voice. If you write in rhyme, I recommend also composing in prose to make sure the story and characters are compelling and fully drawn independent of the rhyming structure.

Whether you write in prose or rhyme, be thoughtful about rhythm and cadence, the musicality of language and the resulting effect on mood and tone. Picture books are meant to be read aloud, and *Once Upon a Memory* is just one example of how rhythm and cadence can enhance the mood of a story.

Similarly, because kids have an experimental, whole-hearted way of interacting with the world, having a child's-eye-view approach to storytelling means employing a creative and playful use of language. For example, in *Mostly Monsterly* by Tammi Sauer and Scott Magoon, Sauer has fun using the most "monsterly" words possible: *lurched*, *growled* and especially the neologism *monsterly*!

Nothing is more fun for kids than getting the joke and being part of the story, so repeating jokes and phrases makes young readers feel like "insiders" in the best way. The key however is repetition with a difference, so the story remains surprising and forward moving. For example, in *The Day the Crayons Quit*, each crayon's letter of complaint follows a similar format but has a different voice and delightfully surprising variations that keep readers hooked and the joke fresh.

Finally, picture books are like jazz collaborations. If the author does her best work and invites the illustrator to do the same, then the whole will be stronger, more surprising and more satisfying than the sum of its parts. For example, in *The Dark*, the dark gives Laszlo a gift that is never specified in the text, but the glowing illustration says it all. Making a dummy of your work can help you judge the illustration potential and visual rhythm of your story as a whole.

KNOW THE COMPETITION— THEN SUBMIT.

If you've followed the advice above and done your best to craft a story that sells, look once again at successful new releases. Make sure you (and your beta readers) can articulate both why your picture book is likely to find an audience based on successful recent picture books and how you're doing something new and different that still has major kid appeal. If you can, then chances are you've written a picture book that can sell in today's upward-moving market.

LARA PERKINS is an associate agent and digital manager at Andrea Brown Literary Agency. She represents all categories of children's literature, from picture books through young adult.

CRAFTING A QUERY

How to write a great letter.

by Kara Gebhart Uhl

So you've written a book. And now you want an agent. If you're new to publishing, you probably assume that the next step is to send your finished, fabulous book out to agents, right? Wrong. Agents don't want your finished, fabulous book. In fact, they probably don't even want *part* of your finished, fabulous book—at least, not yet. First, they want your query.

A query is a short, professional way of introducing yourself to an agent. If you're frustrated by the idea of this step, imagine yourself at a cocktail party. Upon meeting someone new, you don't greet them with a boisterous hug and kiss and, in three minutes, reveal your entire life story including the fact that you were late to the party because of some gastrointestinal problems. Rather, you extend your hand. You state your name. You comment on the hors d'oeuvres, the weather, the lovely shade of someone's dress. Perhaps, after this introduction, the person you're talking to politely excuses himself. Or, perhaps, you begin to forge a friendship. It's

basic etiquette, formality, professionalism—it's simply how it's done.

Agents receive hundreds of submissions every month. Often they read these submissions on their own time—evenings, weekends, on their lunch break. Given the number of writers submitting, and the number of agents reading, it would simply be impossible for agents to ask for and read entire book manuscripts off the bat. Instead, a query is a quick way for you to, first and foremost, pitch your book. But it's also a way to pitch yourself. If an agent is intrigued by your query, she may ask for a partial (say, the first three chapters of your book). Or she may ask for your entire manuscript. And only then may you be signed.

As troublesome as it may first seem, try not to be frustrated by this process. Because, honestly, a query is a really great way to help speed up what is already a monumentally slow-paced industry. Have you ever seen pictures of slush piles—those piles of unread queries on many well-known agents' desk? Imagine the size of those slush piles if they held full manuscripts instead of one-page query letters. Thinking of it this way, query letters begin to make more sense.

Here we share with you the basics of a query, including its three parts and a detailed list of dos and don'ts.

PART I: THE INTRODUCTION

Whether you're submitting a 100-word picture book or a 90,000-word novel, you must be able to sum up the most basic aspects of it in one sentence. Agents are busy. And they constantly receive submissions for types of work they don't represent. So upfront they need to know that, after reading your first paragraph, the rest of your query is going to be worth their time.

An opening sentence designed to "hook" an agent is fine—if it's good and if it works. But this is the time to tune your right brain down and your left brain up—agents desire professionalism and queries that are short and to the point. Remember the cocktail party. Always err on the side of formality. Tell the agent, in as few words as possible, what you've written, including the title, genre and length.

Within the intro you also must try to connect with the agent. Simply sending 100 identical query letters out to "Dear Agent" won't get you published. Instead, your letter should be addressed not only to a specific agency but a specific agent within that agency. (And double, triple, quadruple check that the agent's name is spelled correctly.) In addition, you need to let the agent know why you chose her specifically. A good author-agent relationship is like a good marriage. It's

important that both sides invest the time to find a good fit that meets their needs. So how do you connect with an agent you don't know personally? Research.

1. Make a connection based on an author or book the agent already represents.

Most agencies have websites that list who and what they represent. Research those sites. Find a book similar to yours and explain that, because such-and-such book has a similar theme or tone or whatever, you think your book would be a great fit. In addition, many agents will list specific topics they're looking for, either on their websites or in interviews. If your book is a match, state that.

2. Make a connection based on an interview you read.

Search by agents' names online and read any and all interviews they've participated in. Perhaps they mentioned a love for X and your book is all about X. Or, perhaps they mentioned that they're looking for Y and your book is all about Y. Mention the specific interview. Prove that you've invested as much time researching them as they're about to spend researching you.

3. Make a connection based on a conference you both attended.

Was the agent you're querying the keynote speaker at a writing conference you were recently at? Mention it, specifically commenting on an aspect of his speech you liked. Even better, did you meet the agent in person? Mention it, and if there's something you can say to jog her memory about the meeting, say it. And better yet, did the agent specifically ask you to send your manuscript? Mention it.

Finally, if you're being referred to a particular agent by an author who that agent already represents—that's your opening sentence. That referral is guaranteed to get your query placed on the top of the stack.

PART II: THE PITCH

Here's where you really get to sell your book—but in only three to 10 sentences. Consider the jacket flap and its role in convincing readers to plunk down $24.95 to buy what's in between those flaps. Like a jacket flap, you need to hook an agent in the confines of very limited space. What makes your story interesting and unique? Is your story about a woman going through a midlife crisis? Fine, but there are hundreds of stories about women going through midlife crises. Is your story about a woman who, because of a midlife crisis, leaves her life and family behind to spend three months in India? Again, fine, but this story, too, already exists—in many forms. Is your story about a woman who, because of a midlife crisis, leaves her life and family behind to spend three months in India, falls in love with someone new while there and starts a new life—and family?—and then has to deal with everything she left behind upon her return? *Now* you have a hook.

Practice your pitch. Read it out loud, not only to family and friends, but to people willing to give you honest, intelligent criticism. If you belong to a writing group, workshop your pitch. Share it with members of an online writing forum. Know anyone in the publishing industry? Share it with them. Many writers spend years writing their books. We're not talking about querying magazines here, we're talking about querying an agent who could become a lifelong partner. Spend time on your pitch. Perfect it. Turn it into jacket-flap material so detailed, exciting and clear that it would be near impossible to read your pitch and not want to read more. Use active verbs. Write your pitch, put it aside for a week, then look at it again. Don't send a query simply because you finished a book. Send a query because you finished your pitch and are ready to take the next steps.

PART III: THE BIO

If you write fiction, unless you're a household name, an agent is much more interested in your pitch than in who you are. If you write nonfiction, who you are—more specifically, your platform and publicity—is much more important. Regardless, these are key elements that must be present in every bio:

1. Publishing credits

If you're submitting fiction, focus on your fiction credits—previously published works and short stories. That said, if you're submitting fiction and all your previously published work is nonfiction—magazine articles, essays, etc.—that's still fine and good to mention. Just don't be overly long about it. Mention your publications in bigger magazines or well-known literary journals. If you've never had anything published, don't say you lack official credits. Simply skip this altogether and thank the agent for his time.

2. Contests and awards

If you've won many, focus on the most impressive ones and the ones that most directly relate to your work. Don't mention contests you entered and weren't named in. Also, feel free to leave titles and years out of it. If you took first place at the Delaware Writers Conference for your fiction manuscript, that's good enough. Mentioning details isn't necessary.

3. MFAs

If you've earned or are working toward a Master of Fine Arts in writing, say so and state the program. Don't mention English degrees or online writing courses.

4. Large, recognized writing organizations

Agents don't want to hear about your book club and the fact that there's always great food, or the small critique group you meet with once a week. And they really don't want to hear about the online writing forum you belong to. But if you're a member of something like the Romance Writers of America (RWA), the Mystery Writers of America (MWA), the Society of Children's Book Writers and Illustrators (SCBWI), the Society of Professional Journalists (SPJ), etc., say so. This shows you're serious about what you do and you're involved in groups that can aid with publicity and networking.

5. Platform and publicity

If you write nonfiction, who you are and how you're going to help sell the book once it's published becomes very important. Why are you the best person to write it and what do you have now—public speaking engagements, an active website or blog, substantial cred in your industry—that will help you sell this book?

Finally, be cordial. Thank the agent for taking the time to read your query and consider your manuscript. Ask if you may send more, in the format she desires (partial, full, etc.).

Think of the time you spent writing your book. Unfortunately, you can't send your book to an agent for a first impression. Your query *is* that first impression. Give it the time it deserves. Keep it professional. Keep it formal. Let it be a firm handshake—not a sloppy kiss. Let it be a first meeting that evolves into a lifetime relationship—not a rejection slip. But expect those slips. Just like you don't become lifelong friends with everyone you meet at a cocktail party, you can't expect every agent you pitch to sign you. Be patient. Keep pitching. And in the meantime, start writing that next book.

KARA GEBHART UHL, formerly a managing editor at *Writer's Digest* magazine, now freelance writes and edits in Fort Thomas, KY. She also blogs about parenting at pleiadesbee.com. Her essays have appeared on *The Huffington Post*, *The New York Times'* Motherlode and *TIME: Healthland*. Her parenting essay, "Apologies to the Parents I Judged Four Years Ago" was named one of *TIME's* "Top 10 Opinions of 2012."

DOS AND DON'TS FOR QUERYING AGENTS

DO:

- Keep the tone professional.
- Query a specific agent at a specific agency.
- Proofread. Double-check the spelling of the agency and the agent's name.
- Keep the query concise, limiting the overall length to one page (single space, 12-point type in a commonly used font).
- Focus on the plot, not your bio, when pitching fiction.
- Pitch agents who represent the type of material you write.
- Check an agency's submission guidelines to see how it would like to be queried—for example, via e-mail or mail—and whether or not to include a SASE.
- Keep pitching, despite rejections.

DON'T:

- Include personal info not directly related to the book. For example, stating that you're a parent to three children doesn't make you more qualified than someone else to write a children's book.
- Say how long it took you to write your manuscript. Some bestselling books took 10 years to write—others, six weeks. An agent doesn't care how long it took—an agent only cares if it's good. Same thing goes with drafts—an agent doesn't care how many drafts it took you to reach the final product.
- Mention that this is your first novel or, worse, the first thing you've ever written aside from grocery lists. If you have no other publishing credits, don't advertise that fact. Don't mention it at all.
- State that your book has been edited by peers or professionals. Agents expect manuscripts to be edited, no matter how the editing was done.
- Bring up screenplays or film adaptations; you're querying an agent about publishing a book, not making a movie.
- Mention any previous rejections.
- State that the story is copyrighted with the U.S. Copyright Office or that you own all rights. Of course you own all rights. You wrote it.
- Rave about how much your family and friends loved it. What matters is that the agent loves it.
- Send flowers, baked goods or anything else except a self-addressed stamped envelope (and only if the SASE is required).
- Follow up with a phone call. After the appropriate time has passed (many agencies say how long it will take to receive a response) follow up in the manner you queried—via e-mail or mail.

SAMPLE QUERY NO. 1: YOUNG ADULT
AGENT'S COMMENTS: LAUREN MACLEOD (STROTHMAN AGENCY)

Dear Ms. MacLeod,

I am seeking literary representation and hope you will consider my tween novel, REAL MERMAIDS DON'T WEAR TOE RINGS.

First zit. First crush. First … mermaid's tail?

1 Jade feels like enough of a freak-of-nature when she gets her first period at almost fifteen. She doesn't need to have it happen at the mall while trying on that XL tankini she never wanted to buy in the first place. And she really doesn't need to run into Luke Martin in the Feminine Hygiene Products **2** aisle while her dad Googles "menstruation" on his Blackberry **4** .

3 But "freak-of-nature" takes on a whole new meaning when raging hormones and bath salts bring on another metamorphosis—complete with scales and a tail. And when Jade learns she's inherited her mermaid tendencies from her late mother's side of the family, it raises the question: if Mom was once a mermaid, did she really drown that day last summer?

Jade is determined to find out. Though, how does a plus-sized, aquaphobic mer-girl go about doing that, exactly … especially when Luke from aisle six seems to be the only person who might be able to help?

5 REAL MERMAIDS DON'T WEAR TOE RINGS is a light-hearted fantasy novel for tweens (10-14). It is complete at 44,500 words and available at your request. The first ten pages and a synopsis are included below my signature. I also have a completed chapter book for boys (MASON AND THE MEGANAUTS), should that be of interest to you.

My middle grade novel, ACADIAN STAR, was released last fall by Nimbus Publishing and has been nominated for the 2009/2010 Hackmatack Children's Choice Book Award. I have three nonfiction children's books with Crabtree Publishing to my credit (one forthcoming) as well as an upcoming early chapter book series. Thank you for taking the time to consider this project.

Kind regards,
Hélène Boudreau
www.heleneboudreau.com

1 One of the things that can really make a query letter stand out is a strong voice, and it seems that is one of the things writers struggle with the most. Hélène, however, knocked it out of the park with her query letter. I find young readers are very sensitive to inauthentic voices, but you can tell by just the first few paragraphs that she is going to absolutely nail the tween voice in the manuscript—you can see this even by the way she capitalized Feminine Hygiene Products **2** .

3 The first time I read this query, I actually did laugh out loud. Instead of merely promising me RMDWTR was funny (which it absolutely is), Hélène showed me how funny she can be, which made me want to request the manuscript even before I got to her sample pages.

I also loved how clearly and with just a few words she could invoke an entire scene. Hélène doesn't tell us Jade gets embarrassed in front of a local hunk, she plops us right down in the middle of the pink aisle with the well-intentioned but hopelessly nerdy Dad **4** . I felt this really spoke to her talents—if she could bring bits of a query to life, I couldn't wait to see what she could do with a whole manuscript. **5** And on top of all of this, she had a phenomenal title, a bio that made it very clear she was ready to break out, and a hook so strong it even made it onto the cover!

SAMPLE QUERY NO. 2: YOUNG ADULT
AGENT'S COMMENTS: MICHELLE HUMPHREY (MARTHA KAPLAN LITERARY)

Dear Ms. Humphrey,

I'm contacting you because I've read on various writing websites that you are expanding your young adult client list.

In LOSING FAITH, fifteen-year-old Brie Jenkins discovers her sister's death may not have been an accident ❶. At the funeral, an uncorroborated story surfaces about Faith's whereabouts the night of her tragic fall from a cliff. When Brie encounters a strange, evasive boy ❸ at Faith's gravesite, she tries to confront him, but he disappears into a nearby forest.

Brie searches out and questions the mysterious boy, finding more information than she bargained for: Faith belonged to a secret ritualistic group, which regularly held meetings at the cliff where she died. Brie suspects foul play, but the only way to find out for sure is to risk her own life and join the secret cult. ❷

LOSING FAITH (76k/YA) will appeal to readers of ❹ John Green's LOOKING FOR ALASKA and Laurie Halse Anderson's CATALYST. My published stories have won an editor's choice award in *The Greensilk Journal* and appeared in *Mississippi Crow* magazine. I'm a member of Romance Writers of America, where my manuscript is a finalist in the Florida chapter's Launching a Star Contest. For your convenience, I've pasted the first chapter at the bottom of this e-mail. Thank you for your time and consideration.

Sincerely,
Denise Jaden
www.denisejaden.com ❺

Everything about Denise's query appealed to me. She gave me a quick sentence about why she chose to query me, and then went right into the gist of her novel. ❶ Her "gist" is very much a teaser, or like the back blurb of a book. She gives plot clues without revealing too much of the plot. She keeps the plot points brief and keeps the teaser moving; most important is where she ends—on a note that makes the agent curious to know more. ❷ Denise also gives us vivid characters ❸ in this teaser: the smart, investigative protagonist, Brie; the mysterious boy at the gravesite; the sister, Faith, who's not what she seems. By creating hints of vivid characters and quick engaging plot points in a paragraph, Denise demonstrates her storytelling ability in the query—and I suspected it would carry through to her novel. ❹ Denise includes some other elements that I like to see in queries: comparisons to other well-known books (two or three is enough) and credentials that show her ability to write fiction. ❺ I like, too, that she included her website—I often visit websites when considering queries.

SAMPLE QUERY NO. 3: MIDDLE GRADE
AGENT'S COMMENTS: ELANA ROTH (RED TREE LITERARY)

Dear Ms. Roth,

A boy with a hidden power and the girl who was sent to stop him have 24 hours to win a pickle contest.

1 12-year-old Pierre La Bouche is a *cornichon*. That's French for "pickle," but it also means "good-for-nothing." A middle child who gets straight C's, he's never been No. 1 at anything. When the family farm goes broke, grandfather Henri gives Pierre a mission: to save the farm by winning an international pickle contest.

2 En route to the contest, Pierre meets Aurore, the charming but less-than-truthful granddaughter of a rival farmer. She's been sent to ensnare Pierre, but after a wake up call from her conscience, she rescues him. Together, they navigate the ghostly Paris catacombs, figure out how to crash-land a plane, and duel with a black-hearted villain who will stop at nothing to capture their pickles. In their most desperate hour, it is Pierre's incredible simplicity that saves the day. Always bickering but becoming friends, Pierre and Aurore discover that anything is possible, no matter how hard it may seem.

3 *Pickle Impossible* is complete at 32,500 words. I'm a technical writer by day, optimistic novelist by night. Recently, I've interviewed a host of pickle makers and French natives. My own pickles are fermenting in the kitchen. I grew up in Toronto and live with my wife and children in Israel.

Thank you for your consideration. I hope to hear from you.

Kind Regards,

Eli Stutz

1 The first paragraph introduces the main character and the set-up. He uses concrete things to describe Pierre. He throws in the French flair of the book right away. And he doesn't beat around the bush to tell me what Pierre has to accomplish. **2** The second delves a little deeper into the plot. It gives me the complication that will drive the story forward—someone is out to stop Pierre. And then Eli accomplishes the most important trick here: He gives me some fun examples of what will happen in the book without summarizing the entire plot. That is key because I don't want to read the whole book in the query letter. But he gives me flavor. **3** The bio paragraph is straight to the point, not overcrowded with his whole life history, and also ties light-heartedly right back to the subject of the book. I loved that he tried fermenting his own pickles. (He later told me they weren't very good.) Here's the kicker. The total word count on this letter is 242 words. 242! Look how much he fits into 242 words. There's plot, character, personality and quirk. From this tightly written letter I know I'm going to get a fun, zany story. Those of you who wanted 250 words just to pitch your book, take heed! Shorter is better.

MAKE A LIVING AS A WRITER

by Carmela Martino

For traditionally published children's authors, the economic facts of life can be disheartening. Unless your books are bestsellers, advances and royalties are generally modest. This is especially true for beginning writers. First-time picture book authors can expect to split an advance of about $8,000-$12,000 with the illustrator, each receiving royalties of 4–6 percent (usually of the list price). Advances for debut novels are generally around $5,000–$20,000 (though they can go significantly higher). The royalties for novels aren't split with an illustrator, and typically run around 10 percent. But you won't receive *any* royalties until the advance is earned back, and many books go out of print without ever earning out. And, according to literary agent Jennifer Laughran of the Andrea Brown Literary Agency, even large advances don't guarantee a steady income stream.

It's no surprise, then, that published authors often have "day jobs" to pay the bills while they build up their readership and sales. However, some authors prefer to support themselves by taking on freelance assignments. These assignments can cover a wide variety of activities, such as magazine writing, work-for-hire projects, editing, teaching, and presenting at schools and conferences. We've invited four traditionally published trade book authors who are also successful freelancers to share their experiences finding creative ways to make a living writing.

Vijaya Bodach is a scientist-turned-children's author. Her first trade book, *Ten Easter Eggs*, was published by Cartwheel/Scholastic in 2015. She has written more than 40 books for educational publishers, including *How Do Toys Work?* (Macmillan), and the Compass Media books *India, My Pocket Hamster,* and *Caring for Your Turtle.* She has also published 60 stories, articles, and poems in *Highlights for Children, Cricket, Odyssey,* and other magazines. You can learn more about her at vijayabodach.blogspot.com.

Lisa Bullard's trade books for children include picture books and the middle-grade mystery *Turn Left at the Cow* (Harcourt). She has also written 80 titles for educational publishers, most recently the We Are Alike and Different series (Lerner). Her how-to book for adults, *Get Started in Writing for Children* (McGraw-Hill), draws on her longtime background as a writer, writing teacher, and publishing professional. She co-founded the coaching and critique service Mentors for Rent (MentorsForRent.com) with author Laura Purdie Salas. Together they publish the Children's Writer Insider Guides, a series of books about how to succeed in children's publishing. Bullard regularly teaches writing at venues such as The Loft Literary Center in Minneapolis. For more information, visit lisabullard.com.

JoAnn Early Macken is the author of five trade books for children, including *Baby Says "Moo!"* (Disney-Hyperion), *Waiting Out the Storm* (Candlewick Press), and *Flip, Float, Fly: Seeds on the Move* (Holiday House). She also wrote the poetry instruction guide *Write a Poem Step by Step* and more than 130 nonfiction books for young readers. Her poems appear often in children's magazines and anthologies. She earned her MFA in Writing for Children and Young Adults from Vermont College of Fine Arts and has taught writing at four Wisconsin colleges. She contributes regularly to the TeachingAuthors.com blog and speaks at schools, libraries, and conferences. Visit her website at www.joannmacken.com.

Laura Purdie Salas has written more than 120 books for children and teens, including the award-winning trade picture books from Millbrook Press: *A Rock Can Be ..., Water Can Be ...,* and *A Leaf Can Be ...,* as well as numerous titles from educational publishers, such as the Capstone Press books *Colors of Fall* and *P Is for Pom Pom! A Cheerleading Alphabet.* Her adult credits include *Writing for the Educational Market: Informational Books for Kids,* a do-it-yourself guidebook based on a six-week course she has taught. She is also a visiting author, assessment writer, copyeditor, and co-founder (with Lisa Bullard) of the coaching and critiquing service Mentors for Rent (MentorsForRent.com). Visit her online at laurasalas.com

Like many published authors, all of you supplement your income by writing work-for-hire (WFH) books for educational publishers and/or packagers who pay a set fee instead of royalties. How did you get started writing for these publishers/packagers? What types of WFH books have you written?

BODACH: I'd been writing for children's magazines for a few years and trying to break into the picture book market when one of my critique group partners wailed about having to write some books on the physical sciences. "I would love to write them," I told her. So she put me in touch with her editor. I wrote a sample and the rest is history.

I sent samples to other educational companies and found out that my ability to write simply and clearly about difficult topics was in high demand. Most of my WFH books are on the sciences and mathematics since this material is part of my cellular makeup—I have a

BS in microbiology and a PhD in Bio-chemistry/biophysics, and worked as a scientist for fifteen years before staying home to raise my children.

BULLARD: My first work-for-hire assignment came about when an editor I knew moved to a new job for an educational publisher. She contacted me and asked if I was interested in writing books for that market. Although I knew I'd have to figure it out as I went, I said "yes."

I've written about a wide variety of subjects—ranging from lowrider cars to monster mythology to money management—but I really enjoy writing for new readers in grades 1–3.

MACKEN: After my first trade book was published, I enrolled in the MFA in Writing for Children and Young Adults program at Vermont College of Fine Arts. Then a writer friend introduced me to an editor of educational books for children. I started working with her as a freelance editor, proofreader, and fact checker, and then wrote several series of nonfiction beginning readers. Most of those books describe animal life cycles. Since then, I've written about poetry, people, pets, and many other fascinating subjects.

SALAS: In October 1999, I went to a local SCBWI conference. Editors from two educational publishers, Capstone Press and Lerner, spoke there. Because I was a conference volunteer (always a great idea), I got to be one editor's helper, and I had a manuscript critique with

the other. I ended up writing books for both companies. I didn't go to the conference thinking, *Educational publishing—that's for me!* But I was one of those kids who liked writing reports in school. So as the editors described how they worked, I thought, "I could do this!"

As of 2015, I've written about 120 nonfiction books for the educational market. I write mostly for the K-6 market. In addition to nonfiction, I've done themed poetry collections, and nonfiction and fiction leveled readers.

What do you see as the advantages and disadvantages of taking on WFH projects? Do you have any personal guidelines for what types of projects you'll accept?

BODACH: The advantages are many: I get to write about topics I am passionate about, share my love of science with kids, get published and paid quickly, and build credibility and a good reputation. I've learned how to become a professional writer. I've also expanded my repertoire. I am not content just to write about science. I've written about the history of India, pets and pet care, and religion, too. Best of all, I have beautiful books to share with children.

The disadvantages are few: The tight deadlines mean I often have to drop everything to focus on the project at hand. Often I'm only working on WFH projects instead of my own projects, so the works of my heart take second place. Once in a while there is a dispute about wording or phrasing and the editorial team has the last say. And if one of my books becomes a bestseller, I don't earn a penny more than my contract. However, all of this I know going into the project.

If I am not agreeable with the timeframe or the pay, or I do not have enthusiasm for the project, I do not take it on. I always try to estimate how long a book will take to write and how much research will be involved. I shoot for $50/hour. Sometimes, the research takes much longer than estimated and my hourly rate will drop to $25. But I cannot in good faith take anything less than $20/hr.

BULLARD: For me, the advantages of work-for-hire projects are that they allow me to pursue my love of writing for kids with a guarantee of help to pay the bills—there is no doubt about whether these projects will ultimately sell to a publisher (unfortunately, some of my trade book attempts have ended up unsold in a drawer). One "disadvantage" is that initially, I am not always as inherently interested in some of the topics I take on. However, I have found that there is something intriguing to be discovered about almost any topic! Another disadvantage is that some people rank these books as having a lesser stature than trade titles; teachers and students, however, have sent me fan letters for my work-for-hire titles.

My personal guidelines regarding what I'll accept almost always hinge on the payment offered and whether I can meet the deadlines.

MACKEN: Work-for-hire projects taught me how to write within strict requirements and tight deadlines. They give me the freedom to set my own hours and good reasons to research an amazing variety of topics. They can be a reliable source of income. I especially like to write about writing, science, and nature. I've learned to turn down projects that sound too vague, require too much work, or need to be completed too quickly.

SALAS: WFH books made me feel like a working writer, and they gave me the confidence to call myself a writer. They have provided a small but steady income, with the amount earned known up-front and almost always paid promptly. They've provided me with credits for my cover letter. They've given me the opportunity to learn about a lot of different topics!

The disadvantages: I am not always passionate about the topics. But being passionate about a topic can actually make it harder to write about to someone *else's* specifications, so that might be a good thing. The deadlines are sometimes ridiculously short, but, again, that usually ends up being a plus for me. Who has time to get bored with a topic when you only have eight weeks to write a book about it?

Regarding my personal guidelines: I no longer accept any project that requires me to include excerpts from many sources *and* to secure the reprint rights. Even if a publisher is willing to pay reprint fees, it's unbelievably time-consuming to track down copyright holders and get fees, etc. I will never attempt that again!

Besides work-for-hire books, what other kinds of freelance assignments have you taken on to supplement your income? What was your most unusual or fun assignment? How did you get these assignments? Did they require any special skills, such as a degree or hands-on experience?

BODACH: I have written for testing companies. My kids now know that the standardized tests they take are written by regular folks like me who take great pains to make their passages fun to read! I've also written manuals for teachers. Most of these assignments were posted on a listserv I belong to: NFforKids. (See groups.yahoo.com/neo/groups/NFforKids/info.) Some were requests that came directly to me since people know my background. I don't think one even needs a science degree unless you are writing at the high school or college level. But you need to have interest!

My most fun assignment was writing *How Do Toys Work?* (Macmillan). We already had a lot of mechanical toys and I bought a few more, like Newton's Cradle, Drinking Bird, and Magic Tops. My kids and I had a great time playing with all the toys!

BULLARD: Outside of writing work-for-hire, many of my freelance assignments involve teaching in some way—which is a great way for me to build some "people" time into the more introverted task of sitting in front of a computer and writing. I have taught classes to adult writers who want to write children's books, in a variety of settings, including online.

I've taught children, too, in schools and libraries, at writing "camp," and for a homeschool co-op. Perhaps the most unusual teaching arrangement has been acting as a creative writing tutor, where I work with small groups of children who are friends (similar perhaps to group piano lessons).

In some cases I went through a formal application process or submitted a proposal to get these gigs. But many of my teaching jobs have come through connections I've built through writing assignments or other teaching jobs.

MACKEN: I love working with writers of all ages! I started by volunteering in our kids' classrooms. Now I present poetry and writing workshops to students, adult writers, and teachers at schools, libraries, and conferences. I also do picture book critiques, both privately and through SCBWI, and I've written test passages for several testing companies. The first one contacted me after a poem I wrote appeared in a children's magazine.

Earning my MFA enabled me to teach at the university level. For eight years as an adjunct instructor, I taught graduate and undergraduate credit writing courses. At first, I taught assigned courses; later, I was able to propose my own ideas. I also proposed and taught noncredit courses through Continuing Education Departments at other universities. For each course, I created a syllabus, developed writing exercises and assignments, organized peer critiques, and critiqued student work. All four of my teaching jobs resulted from referrals from other authors.

SALAS: I do a lot of assessment writing for testing companies. Sometimes I get fun assignments like "write a poem comparing a tiger to a housecat." Random things like that generally come from packagers I've written for. They tend to mostly be poetry-related, since word has gotten around that I'm very good at writing poetry on assignment.

Besides freelance writing assignments, I do school visits; teach/present at conferences for educators, children's writers, and young authors; copyedit (usually education-related materials); and critique and coach children's writers through Mentors for Rent (MentorsForRent.com) with Lisa Bullard.

Regarding skill requirements: Some assessment companies only use writers with teaching experience, which I do have. Or master's degrees, which I do not have. Professional copyediting experience is probably necessary to get copyediting gigs. (I was a part-time copyeditor for the Minneapolis *Star Tribune* for ten years.)

What kind of income can writers expect from work-for-hire projects and the other types of freelance assignments you've taken on? What types of assignments have you found most lucrative? Least lucrative?

BODACH: Income varies widely for WFH. I've been paid $100 for a short book (500 words) to $1,000. For a longer book, I've been paid $1,000 (5,000 words) to $4,000. Note that sometimes a longer book is easier to write.

Books have been the most rewarding, both financially and emotionally. You have a book baby to hold after all that work. Writing for testing companies has also paid well. But you can't talk about it. Teaching is a labor of love. It doesn't pay well, but it's in my bones. Last, I like being able to defray the cost of a writing conference by giving a workshop. It's great being with your tribe.

BULLARD: My work-for-hire payments probably average out to around $1,000 per book. Keep in mind that most of the books I write are for younger readers, and some publishers pay based on word count. I've definitely been offered much less—in the neighborhood of only $400 per book. I usually can't accept those lower offers because the hourly rate, between researching and writing, is simply not enough.

The rate for teaching really varies, and sometimes I have to propose the rate I'll accept. In those cases, I usually base my fee on $50 per hour for student contact time, as well as some additional money to cover my prep time; I also need to consider travel time and mileage if those are significant factors.

My most lucrative assignments have been large editing projects that were funded through the local university. Conference presentations are also sometimes well-paid gigs.

MACKEN: Work-for-hire projects have a wide range of pay scales because length, reading level, and other requirements vary a lot. I've written poems for test publishers for as little as $25 and as much as $400. Most of my beginning reader books paid from $250–$500 each, but that range might be higher now. Longer books can pay $1,200–$1,600 or more.

SALAS: These fees vary a lot. For my nonfiction WFH picture books: $600–$1,200. Leveled readers: $1,500–3,000. Passage or poem for assessment companies: $200–300. Copyediting: $30/hour. School visits: $700–800 per day. Library programs, teacher in-services, writing conferences, etc., are often $300 per session. Young author conferences: $300/day.

My most lucrative assignments have been short books on topics I love for clients who have a very clear idea about what they want me to do. The least lucrative: writing fiction for hire—for me, because that's not *my* sweet spot. What is lucrative varies with each individual writer. What you can write *fast* and revise easily is going to be most lucrative for you.

How do you balance your freelance work with your trade book writing? Has your freelance work helped or hindered your overall career?

BODACH: I'm doing a better job now of balancing mostly because I don't actively pursue WFH. If it comes knocking at my door, I'll consider it. Do I love the project? If yes, then, is the pay good? If yes, I'll take it on. My freelance work has inspired many of my pet projects and vice versa. There is cross-pollination. In the same way, other arts like singing, piano-playing, and cooking also feed the various types of writing I do (WFH, blogging, novels, picture books, etc.).

BULLARD: My freelance work, for the most part, has been a very positive thing for my overall writing career. It funds my trade book writing and allows me to forego returning to a "day job." I also find having outside deadlines to be very motivating, so even during the past couple of years, when I've been very distracted by a family health crisis, I've managed to write many work-for-hire titles while getting very little done on potential trade titles. And I often get ideas that I incorporate into my trade writing through the research I'm doing for work-for-hire projects, or because I've been inspired by young readers at a school visit or writing class.

MACKEN: I enjoy both trade book and freelance writing. I used to switch back and forth, but I had trouble getting back into my own projects if I spent too much time away from them. Now I try to keep doing some of each most days. If I don't have another project lined up, I try to look for more work before I finish a freelance project so I don't have long gaps between projects.

SALAS: I try to make time for thirty minutes of writing daily on my trade book projects. It doesn't always happen, though. It's not all freelance work that keeps me from my own writing. A lot of it is correspondence and marketing related to my existing or forthcoming trade books. Still, I try to dive into my trade writing projects for a little bit daily to stay connected to them and remember *why* I'm doing all the other stuff.

What advice do you have for writers trying to find ways to supplement their income? Can you recommend any specific resources?

BODACH: Network. By this I mean participate in the communities you join. Don't just peddle your services. Develop relationships. I am a part of the SCBWI Blueboards (www.scbwi.org/boards/index.php), which includes a board specifically for "Work-for-hire & Calls for Submissions."

Evelyn B. Christensen, puzzle creator extraordinaire, maintains a directory of educational publishers on her website (www.evelynchristensen.com/markets.html). Study Laura Purdie Salas's book, *Writing for the Educational Market: Informational Books for Kids*, and then send out packets to these publishers.

Also, you'll be surprised how many editors read magazines, so do not discount developing stories for the magazine market. It's a great place to hone your writing skills. Perhaps the next call will come because an editor read your well-written article on porcupines or navigation or the stars. You never know.

BULLARD: My key advice is to work really hard to build positive relationships. That includes personal relationships as well as work relationships. I've gotten freelance jobs through writing students, editor referrals, a friend at church, and through other writers and freelancers. My most recent possibility came about just last week, when I was contacted by a former co-worker whom I haven't seen in years—he wants to talk about a potentially large editorial/management project. Sometimes things like this don't work out, but my approach is to stay as open as possible to new possibilities! I kid with my dad that rather than getting new work through cold calling, my best tactic for finding new income streams is to take people I've met out for coffee.

MACKEN: Most educational publishers develop their own series ideas and assign books to writers. If you want to be considered for this kind of work, see which publishers publish the kinds of books you'd like to write. Explore the publishers' websites and look for submission information. Check this book you're reading right now [*Children's Writer's and Illustrator's Market*], the SCBWI Market Surveys, and Evelyn B. Christensen's online list of Educational Markets for Children's Writers. Then prepare a submission packet. Include a cover letter, résumé, and writing sample. If you have published work, send a photocopy. Include enough pages to give an editor a sense of your skills.

You can also take classes, especially if you're trying to develop a specific skill. Join or start a writing group; you can learn as much from critiquing other people's work as you do from their comments on yours. Learn how to check readability statistics and practice writing for different reading levels. Understand end matter requirements.

SALAS: One way to jump-start your thinking is to visit freelance writing job boards (such as educationwriting. blogspot.com) and read through them for a couple of weeks. See what, exactly, companies are hiring writers to *do*. Then brainstorm to find your own unique angle.

At Mentors for Rent, we talk with clients about career-building often. It's a very personal process, and it can be confusing and scary. But most of us do have skills we can parlay into income that is somehow related to kidlit. Sometimes you just have to talk to other writers who have a little bit broader range of experience than you do.

CARMELA MARTINO has an MFA in Writing for Children and Young Adults from Vermont College. Her most recent trade book credits include a humorous short story in the middle-grade anthology *I Fooled You: Ten Stories of Tricks, Jokes, and Switcheroos* edited by Johanna Hurwitz (Candlewick Press), and poems in several anthologies. In addition to writing stories and poems for children and teens, Carmela works as a freelance writer and writing teacher. She founded TeachingAuthors.com, a blog by six children's authors who are also writing teachers. For more information, see carmelamartino.com.

DEBUT AUTHORS TELL ALL (FIRST BOOKS)

Learn how first-time kidlit writers got published.

compiled by Chuck Sambuchino

There's something fresh and amazing about debut novels that's inspiring to other writers. It's with that in mind that we collected 14 successful debuts from the past year and sat down to ask the authors questions about how they broke in, what they did right, and what advice they have for scribes who are trying to follow in their footsteps. These are writers of picture books, middle grade stories, and young adult novels—same as you—who saw their work come to life through hard work and determination. Read on to learn more about their individual journeys.

PICTURE BOOKS

❶ DEV PETTY

DEVPETTY.COM

I Don't Want to Be a Frog **(FEBRUARY 2015, DOUBLEDAY BOOK S FOR YOUNG READERS, MIKE BOLDT ILLUSTRATIONS)**

QUICK TAKE: A story about about a frog who doesn't want to be a frog, but discovers the bright side of his frog-ness and learns to accept himself as he is."

WRITES FROM: Albany, California

PRE-BOOK: *Frog* is my debut book and was among the first I ever wrote. I was exploring writing in only dialogue and was finding a lot of joy in writing funny picture books, which pretty much sums up *I Don't Want to be a Frog*: dialogue and funny.

TIME FRAME: I wrote the rough draft pretty quickly—in an afternoon I think—but at first it was sort of a thin story. It wasn't about a whole lot—just a frog who wanted to be a different animal. But I found a lot of material in a frog who, at his core, didn't want to be what he was. It was funny to me, since he's a frog and there's sort of no changing that.

ENTER THE AGENT: My agent at the time was Sara Sciuto who I queried when she was at Full Circle Literary [and she is now at Fuse Literary]. She liked the humor I used in my writing and got the deal with Doubleday. I switched agents along the way and my current agent is Danielle Smith at Red Fox Literary.

WHAT I DID RIGHT: I just trusted my gut and my voice, and was willing to come at picture books from a weird angle knowing some people just wouldn't go for my style, but hoping enough would. I also read a lot about keeping picture books short and punchy and fresh.

I WISH I WOULD HAVE DONE DIFFERENT: I would have taken a bit more time to consider what type of writer I wanted to be. I'm lucky that *Frog* is a book I really love, because early on, I was just so eager for a book deal, I would have been delighted to have sold anything, even if it was a book I didn't like so much. I'm much more reflective now about what I'm putting out there, and I write and throw a way a lot that just doesn't feel like it's what I want it to be or who I want to be as a writer.

BEST ADVICE FOR WRITERS: I would say to do more thinking than writing. It's really easy to get mired in language and sentence structure and sort of lose the forest for the trees. It's important to really think about your idea inside and out and up and down and all around before penning a word so that you really know what you're getting at and how you want to get at it.

NEXT UP: I have a book coming out in 2017 with Little Brown called *Claymates*.

② KATHERYN RUSSELL-BROWN
KRBROWN.NET

Little Melba and Her Big Trombone (SEPTEMBER 2014, LEE & LOW, FRANK MORRISON ILLUSTRATIONS)

QUICK TAKE: A lively biography of little-known jazz arranger Melba Liston—a little girl with a big heart who fell in love with the trombone.

WRITES FROM: Gainesville, Florida.

PRE-BOOK: I had a sabbatical from my day job. As part of a larger research project, I looked at how children learn about race, when they learn about it and what they learn. It was during this period that I decided to try my hand at writing books for young people. Prior to *Little Melba*, I had published four academic nonfiction books that address issues of race and the criminal justice system.

TIME FRAME: I heard an NPR broadcast in February 2010, "Melba Liston: Bones of An Arranger." Before it was over, I had decided to write a children's story about Melba. It took about two months to get a solid first draft of the story.

ENTER THE AGENT: In the spring of 2010, I saw a discussion about agent Adriana Dominguez on a blog post. It stated that she worked with Full Circle Literary Agency and was looking for new children's book authors. So, I sent her a query.

BIGGEST SURPRISE: The amount of editing required was a surprise. I was already used to edits, but the level of detailed rewriting required for a picture book was new to me. Because picture books have so few words, each one must earn its keep on the page. This means lots of editing.

WHAT I DID RIGHT: Three things. First, I joined my local SCBWI chapter. It is wonderful to have a weekly space to meet and talk with other children's book writers—a mix of will-be and already published authors. Second, I sent out my work for critique as much as possible. I'm a fan of constructive criticism. Even some harsh criticism can be valuable. Third, I tried not to take the massive number of rejections personally. In some ways it was pretty easy since they were usually form letters. However, they still sting. I just kept moving forward hoping that someone would hear the song I was singing.

I WISH I WOULD HAVE DONE DIFFERENT: I should have had more patience with the process. The world of children's book publishing works very differently than the world of academic publishing.

NEXT UP: Another picture book.

③ MARCIA BERNEGER
MARCIABERNEGER.COM

Buster the Little Garbage Truck (**APRIL 2015, SLEEPING BEAR PRESS, KEVIN ZIMMER ILLUSTRATIONS**)

QUICK TAKE: Buster the little garbage truck works to overcome his fear of the loud noises all around him.

WRITES FROM: San Diego, California.

PRE-BOOK: Although I have written many stories for children, my publishing credits before *Buster* were limited to stories in magazines. *Buster* is my first book.

WHAT I LEARNED: The biggest two things the writing/publishing process teaches you are flexibility and patience. Patience, because the publishing process takes a minimum of two years from the time the editor says yes, to holding your book in your hands. Flexibility in that what you start out with may wind up being quite different from your final product.

WHAT I DID RIGHT: I think one of the most important things you can do to ensure success is to join an organization such as SCBWI and learn as much as you can about all aspects of the journey you are undertaking. Then join a critique group. Getting honest feedback about your story is vital to its success. I read, and then dismiss many of the ideas suggested by my critique group members, but some of the changes I have made based on those amazing writer-friends have made all the difference in the world.

PLATFORM: I have a website I am particularly pleased with, and my SCBWI friend created the perfect banner for it. I also am on Facebook and Twitter. I'm researching ecological-themed organizations to tie in with Buster being a garbage truck and have created the first of several kid-friendly art projects using recycled materials commonly found around the house.

ADVICE FOR WRITERS: Don't give up and don't try to change your story every time someone reads it and offers "helpful" suggestions. Think about what they say, try out some of the better ideas, and remember that, in the end, it is *your* story.

NEXT UP: I'm going to be quite busy for the next few months with *Buster*-related activities (book signings, school visits, etc.), but I'm also working on a sequel: *Buster and the Bullies*.

④ BARBARA LOWELL
George Ferris, What a Wheel (Penguin Core Concepts) **(JUNE 2014, GROSSET & DUNLAP, JERRY HOARE ILLUSTRATIONS)**

QUICK TAKE: A nonfiction picture book biography about George Ferris, who designed and built a 250-foot wheel that could hold 2,160 people—something never done before.

WRITES FROM: Tulsa, Oklahoma

PRE-BOOK: I had written a few fiction picture book manuscripts based on true stories, but writing about George Ferris was my first attempt at a nonfiction picture book.

ENTER THE AGENT: My agent is Abigail Samoun of Red Fox Literary. I sent a manuscript to her as an SCBWI Oklahoma conference submission. At that time, she was an editor at Tricycle Press. She asked me to send her more, and she bought the second manuscript I sent. About six months later, Tricycle Press shuttered and the manuscript was not published. I kept in touch and when I won the Katherine Patterson Prize at Hunger Mountain for a picture book manuscript, she read it on their website. She liked that manuscript and offered to represent it, and she negotiated the *George Ferris, What a Wheel* contract.

WHAT I LEARNED: My big surprise was when I learned that the illustrator, Jerry Hoare, lived in Wales. When I sent him an e-mail letting him know how much I loved his illustrations, he wrote back, "Splendid working with you." I liked how very British his response was.

WHAT I DID RIGHT: The best thing I did was to join SCBWI, Soon after, I helped form a critique group, attended conferences, and sent submissions to the speakers. From the start, I studied the craft of writing and I still look for opportunities to learn.

I WISH I WOULD HAVE DONE DIFFERENT: I would have built a platform sooner.

PLATFORM: I have an Activity Guide and a Reader's Theater written for teachers which is on my website.

BEST ADVICE FOR WRITERS: Think positive, be polite, learn your craft, don't take rejection personally; instead, learn from it, look for opportunities, and never give up.

NEXT UP: I am working on a nonfiction picture book biography and researching another.

⑤ MIRANDA PAUL
MIRANDAPAUL.COM
One Plastic Bag: Isatou Ceesay And The Recycling Women of the Gambia (**FEBRUARY 2015, MILLBROOK PRESS, ELIZABETH ZUNON ILLUSTRATIONS**)

QUICK TAKE: A nonfiction picture book that tells the true story of how five Gambian women used creativity and determination to clean up their village and become financially empowered.

WRITES FROM: Green Bay, Wisconsin

PRE-BOOK: I was working as a teacher and as a freelance writer. I'd also previously been a teacher in the Gambia and had traveled there on five different occasions. I'd previously published articles in magazines, newspapers, and done other for-hire work.

TIME FRAME: From the first time I picked up one of Isatou's recycled creations until the day the book was published was about 12 years. The idea for a book stewed around in my head for a year before I could pinpoint the way I could best tell it. It was only about six months from final draft of the manuscript until I submitted to the publishing house that would eventually express interest in publishing it.

BIGGEST SURPRISE: How selling your second book (and third, and fourth) can be just as difficult. I think there's this notion that once you land an agent, or editor, somehow there's less work. Maybe there is when it comes to paperwork or submitting manuscripts, but not the actual writing!

WHAT I DID RIGHT: I grew a thick skin, always queried in a professional manner, and wrote and polished a lot of manuscripts before I even began querying. Rejection is a lot less painful if you have another story or idea you can move on to.

I WISH I WOULD HAVE DONE DIFFERENT: I'd spend less time reading all the advice on the Internet. There's a lot out there, and while there are so many helpful sites, reading too much advice about the market, or trends, or "what not to do" stifled me a few times.

NEXT UP: Several picture books. In 2015, my book *Water is Water* will be published by Neal Porter Books/Macmillan.

MIDDLE GRADE

⑥ JEFF ANDERSON
WRITEGUY.NET

Zack Delacruz: Me and My Big Mouth (**AUGUST 2015, STERLING**)

QUICK TAKE: Happily invisible sixth grader Zack Delacruz forgets who he is for a moment and stands up to a bully, which throws him into a whirlwind of dances, difficult people, and chocolate bars.

WRITES FROM: San Antonio, Texas

PRE-BOOK: I've been writing middle grade fiction and other genres [for myself] for the last 22 years. After several years of being fairly successful at publishing books on teaching writing and grammar for teachers, I realized my writing career would be incomplete without reaching the audience I originally wanted: kids. I doubled down, searched out retreats, feedback, and writing conferences.

TIME FRAME: I attended an SCBWI conference in Indiana and opted for an editor critique. By that point, I had given up on *Zack Delacruz* and moved on to something else. The new piece wasn't ready to submit by the conference deadline, so I handed in the first ten pages of *Zack Delacruz*—the book I'd given up on, the one a handful of editors and agents had rejected. Once the editor, Brett Duquette from Sterling, read my pages, he asked to see more. He even gave some pointers for a revision he asked me to submit to him. Excited, of course, I made those changes. It took another year of work after that.

ENTER THE AGENT: When I told her a publisher was interested in *Zack Delacruz*, a friend of mine referred me to a "sharp cookie" literary agent she'd met at another conference—Roseanne Wells from The Jennifer De Chiara Literary Agency.

BIGGEST SURPRISE: The most surprising thing happened before the book was signed. I was instructed to double the length with no feedback or suggestions on how to do that—they'd only give the feedback after I'd signed, and they'd only sign me if I doubled the length. So, without guidance from my editor, I doubled the length. This was a place where Roseanne stepped in and offered feedback.

WHAT I DID RIGHT: [After early rejection], I felt the pain and kept writing. I know that's how writers get better. They write. I often reminded myself: Until I've sent it 80 times, I am not finished with a piece. I think it was helpful that I was willing to hear feedback, willing to rewrite, and willing to work hard at it over long periods of time with little reward beyond the joy of doing it.

I WISH I WOULD HAVE DONE DIFFERENT: I'd go to more writing conferences earlier. Until you are around the people who make books, you'll make choices that may not support your career unfolding.

PLATFORM: I had a platform as a staff developer and writer of professional books on teaching writing and grammar for teachers, many of whom teach the age group to which my middle grade fiction novel appeals. Because of this interaction, I am approaching 10,000 Twitter followers. I present at conferences. I am willing to do my own publicity and footwork and support the team at my publisher. In fact, per their request, I gave them a month of my work life to tour.

BEST ADVICE FOR WRITERS: "Ass in Chair." Fingers above keyboard. Don't talk about what you're going to write—write it.

NEXT UP: Since Zack Delacruz is a new series for Sterling, I am currently working on revisions for book two.

❼ CONSTANCE LOMBARDO
CONSTANCELOMBARDO.COM
Mr. Puffball: Stunt Cat to the Stars **(SEPTEMBER 2015, KATHERINE TEGEN BOOKS)**

QUICK TAKE: The illustrated story of how a young cat follows his movie star dreams all the way from New Jersey to Hollywood, where he catapults himself into the role of stunt cat to his celebrity hero, El Gato.

WRITES FROM: Asheville, North Carolina

PRE-BOOK: I joined SCBWI about nine years ago and then started a critique group here in Asheville. I attended several SCBWI conferences and workshops. After writing many picture books without finding a publisher, I wrote two YA novels and one middle grade novel.

Then somebody in my critique group said, "I want to do a graphic novel," and I thought, *So do I!* Through working on drawings of cats, the character of Mr. Puffball emerged, told me his story and … the rest is history.

TIME FRAME: In December 2011, I started work on a novelty book of cats with funny captions. By spring of 2012, that had morphed into a series of comic strips I thought I'd submit to magazines. That led to the development of Mr. Puffball as a standout character, and he demanded an entire novel to himself. I enrolled in the SCBWI Carolinas sponsored Graphic Novel Workshop with Mark Siegel in May 2012, pulled together a completed (written and illustrated) manuscript for the workshop and started subbing soon after.

ENTER THE AGENT: I'd been subbing projects to agents for a few years with many nibbles and no bites. I found Lori Nowicki (Painted Words) online and was super impressed with her client list. I submitted two picture book manuscripts. She was not taken with those, but liked my writing and asked to see more. I submitted *Mr. Puffball*. She loved the concept and wanted to work with me.

BIGGEST SURPRISE: My agent totally gets me and is so supportive. Her encouragement and feedback has taken Mr. Puffball to a whole new level of fabulous. Also, I'm constantly amazed at the kindness and generosity of children's book writers and illustrators. I totally rely on my local SCBWI chapter listserv and author friends to help me negotiate all the intricacies of writing, publishing, marketing, etc.

I WISH I WOULD HAVE DONE DIFFERENT: I started subbing books before I was ready. It's so easy to become attached to your writing and so hard to know whether something is truly submission quality.

PLATFORM: I post drawings of Mr. Puffball (and other cats!) on Facebook and Twitter (@ MisterPuffball) and connect with other book people on those sites.

BEST ADVICE FOR WRITERS: To paraphrase Jay Asher: "Don't give up because that *NY Times* bestseller could be right around the corner!"

NEXT UP: I am currently working on the second Mr. Puffball book, then on to book #3 … and hopefully that series will continue.

YOUNG ADULT

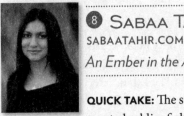

⑧ SABAA TAHIR
SABAATAHIR.COM

An Ember in the Ashes (**APRIL 2015, RAZORBILL**)

QUICK TAKE: The story of an orphan girl fighting for her family, and a tormented soldier fighting for his freedom.

WRITES FROM: San Francisco, California

PRE-BOOK: Before I began writing, I was an editor at *The Washington Post*. I wrote very rarely for the newspaper, and *Ember* is actually my first novel.

TIME FRAME: It took me about six years to write. During that time, I did a great deal of research to enrich the world I was creating. One of my characters is a warrior, so part of my research included interviews with modern-day warriors. What I learned in the interviews helped me write characters who (I hope) are more authentic and three-dimensional.

ENTER THE AGENT: A friend of mine in publishing told me about Alexandra Machinist [of ICM Partners], and said that she might be a good fit for me and for the book. I queried her and she offered.

WHAT I LEARNED: You don't have to write alone. I was really isolated while writing *Ember*. It wasn't until after I got my book deal that I realized there's a huge, wonderful YA writing community online. It's supportive, fun, and a great place to find a sympathetic ear or advice when you're struggling.

WHAT I DID RIGHT: I revised the heck out of my book so that by the time I sent it in, it was in good shape. I also did a ton of agent research before I began querying. I figured out what my comps were and which agents were looking for what. I read the "Successful Queries" series on the Guide to Literary Agents Blog, as well as the Query Shark's entire archive of letters.

BEST ADVICE FOR WRITERS: Never give up. Keep writing through the rejections, the revisions, the never-ending explanations to your friends about why you aren't published yet. Keep writing when you hear that other people have gotten agents and book deals. Keep writing, even if it takes you years to finally accomplish your goal.

⑨ LISA FREEMAN
LISA-FREEMAN.COM

Honey Girl (**MARCH 2015, SKY PONY PRESS**)

QUICK TAKE: When fifteen-year-old Haunani "Nani" Grace Nuuhiwa's father dies of a sudden heart attack in 1972, she is forced to move to Santa Monica with her alcoholic mother, and fit in at the hottest surf spot in California.

WRITES FROM: Santa Monica, California

PRE-BOOK: *Honey Girl* originated from a thesis I began and never finished about young women rejecting feminism. I was still working as an illustrator and publishing poetry at the time.

TIME FRAME: Well, I actually was very unorganized in my early drafts of *Honey Girl*. Once I got organized, it was about five years until I finished a draft that could go to market.

ENTER THE AGENT: I had just gotten word that my first agent was retiring when I had a final first draft of *Honey Girl*. It was devastating, especially after working so hard with one person. Having said that, I am a big *Writer's Digest* reader, and knew that Thao Le [of Sandra Dijkstra Literary Agency] was going to be at a Writer's Digest Conference pitch slam in Los Angeles. I got to the slam two hours early so I would be one of the first people in the room. I made a beeline to Thao Le and was the first person she heard pitch. At the end of the pitch when the bell rang, I asked her, "Ms. Le, may I please send you three pages of *Honey Girl*?" That began a long correspondence and our eventual signing.

WHAT I DID RIGHT: I never gave up. I knew this was a good story and I didn't send out a draft until it was the best I could make it.

I WISH I WOULD HAVE DONE DIFFERENT: I would have drunk more water, exercised more, and worn my glasses to take better care of myself. I didn't realize what the long haul would demand of me. Writing is a sport that takes great physical strength. This I did not know.

BEST ADVICE FOR WRITERS: Don't send out your novel before it's ready. Take your time. If it's as good as you think it is, everything will work out.

NEXT UP: Currently I am finishing the first draft of a YA paranormal romance.

10 J.E. ANCKORN
TWITTER.COM/ULTRA_LILAC

Untaken **(MARCH 2015, CURIOSITY QUILLS PRESS)**

QUICK TAKE: Three kids survive an alien invasion, but one of them has a secret that puts them all in danger.

WRITES FROM: Boston, Massachusetts

PRE-BOOK: I started out as an illustrator and toy designer. After eight years of illustrating other people's work, I decided to write the books that went with the pictures I *really* wanted to be drawing.

TIME FRAME: For months I had one random scene lodged in my brain: three kids are lost in an abandoned, pitch dark shopping mall—and something else is in there with them. I wrote that one scene, and then said, "I guess I need the rest of a book to go with this." It took me about six months to write the rest, which is quick for me.

ENTER THE AGENT: I'm represented by the awesome Rebecca Podos of the Rees Literary Agency. I found her the way most authors do these days: via online resources and databases.

WHAT I LEARNED: How helpful it is to have a fresh perspective on your work. I had the input of some great editors during the revision of *Untaken*. I think every writer can benefit from feedback beyond their circle of friends and family. Even when you don't agree with edits, it can be helpful to examine *why* you don't.

WHAT I DID RIGHT: I did my research. It pays to research the industry, to find out what common practice is, and what potential routes to publication exist well before you are ready to submit.

I WISH I WOULD HAVE DONE DIFFERENT: I'd have tried to enjoy the ride more. Publishing for me has been a mix of white-knuckle speed and long, long stretches of "wait and see." I had the almost superhuman stamina and resolve to worry throughout all of it. It was impressive.

BEST ADVICE FOR WRITERS: Write every day, but don't set your word count so high you get afflicted with the dreaded "don't wannas." I aim for five hundred words a day and usually write two thousand. When I aimed for two thousand I'd sulk and spin in my chair, and on a *really* good day, erase half a sentence.

NEXT UP: I'm currently working on a YA contemporary.

⑪ HEATHER W. PETTY
HEATHERWPETTY.COM

Lock & Mori **(SEPTEMBER 2015, SIMON & SCHUSTER BOOKS FOR YOUNG READERS)**

QUICK TAKE: A modern day Sherlock Holmes origin story told from the perspective of a 16-year-old, female Moriarty.

WRITES FROM: Reno, Nevada

PRE-BOOK: I normally write YA urban fantasy or paranormal, and had a paranormal mystery on submission that wasn't selling because the market was dead for that genre in YA. When I told my agent about this book idea, she pretty much told me to drop everything and write it.

ENTER THE AGENT: Within the year I was drafting *Lock & Mori*, I had two successive agents who ended up retiring before the book was ready to submit. So I was left with a freshly drafted novel and looking for an agent. I queried a few, and a friend of mine who was working with Laurie McLean (of what is now Fuse Literary) told her about the book over lunch one day. My friend asked me if she could pass along the manuscript to Laurie, because she was a huge fan of Sherlock Holmes and really wanted to read it. I agreed. Laurie called me the next day to offer representation. I ended up with a couple other offers, but Laurie was definitely the best fit for me and my work.

WHAT I LEARNED: *Lock & Mori* was my third book on submission, which means I'd gone through the process twice without selling a book. It was rough, but I think it's also important to know that publishing is never a sure thing. Just because an agent loves your work doesn't mean your manuscript will meet the market needs or find the right editor right away. It also taught me a lot about patience and persistence.

WHAT I DID RIGHT: I kept going. Honestly, if I weren't so stubborn, I might have given up at some point. But I was determined to break into the industry and decided I wasn't going to give up.

I WISH I WOULD HAVE DONE DIFFERENT: I was probably a little too stubborn when it came to writing in the genres that I preferred and was more comfortable writing, even though I knew the market was dead in those areas. I don't believe in chasing the market, necessarily, but when you know there has been a shift away from a certain kind of book, it's fruitless to keep writing in that genre. That was especially true for me, because there are so many genres that I love.

BEST ADVICE FOR WRITERS: The one way you'll ensure that you never sell a book is if you give up. Be persistent and be willing to do the hard work it takes to grow.

NEXT UP: There are two more books in the Lock & Mori series, so I'm busy working on that!

⑫ MICHAELA DEPRINCE WITH ELAINE DE- PRINCE (ANSWERS FROM ELAINE)
MICHAELADEPRINCE.COM

Taking Flight: From War Orphan to Star Ballerina (OCTOBER 2014, KNOPF BOOKS FOR YOUNG READERS)

QUICK TAKE: The [nonfiction true story] of a small child, orphaned during the civil war in Sierra Leone, who dreamt of becoming a ballerina, and made her dream come true after being adopted by an American family.

PRE-BOOK: Michaela and I submitted a 700-word children's picture book manuscript to Full Circle Literary. It was based on an anecdote about a homemade tutu that I had sewn for Michaela. Literary agent Adriana Dominguez asked if we would be willing to turn it into a 200-page young adult memoir because Michaela had gained a certain degree of celebrity as a professional ballerina with the Dance Theatre of Harlem by that time, and our agent believed that her story would be inspiring to other young people who experienced adversity.

TIME FRAME: We had to work quickly on this manuscript because a few months after signing a contract with Knopf, Michaela was invited to join the Dutch National Ballet. She flew off to Amsterdam at age eighteen. Michaela would call me almost daily on Viber and confer on the writing.

BIGGEST SURPRISE: How long it took for a book to go from submission to release, and how much of her time would be demanded for interviews. Perhaps because I'm so much older, and consequently more patient than Michaela, nothing seemed to surprise me, except for the difficulty we had in deciding on a title.

WHAT WE DID RIGHT: Many decades ago when I was in school, my teachers always advised, "Write what you know." This is what Michaela and I did, and it got the attention of an excellent agent and amazing publisher.

BEST ADVICE FOR WRITERS: Follow submission guidelines, and work on your query. Find a hook that will grab an agent/publisher. After acceptance be willing to accept constructive criticism and make recommended changes.

13 AISHA SAEED
AISHASAEED.COM

Written in the Stars (MARCH 2015, NANCY PAULSEN BOOKS)

QUICK TAKE: When Naila's parents find out she broke their one rule—to never fall in love— the consequences are greater than she could ever have imagined.

WRITES FROM: Atlanta, Georgia

PRE-BOOK: I wrote freelance articles for various publications and also had an essay published in an anthology *Love Insh'Allah: The Secret Love Lives of American Muslim Women.*

TIME FRAME: My story covers the issue of forced marriage. I had childhood friends who got pressured into marriages they didn't want, so the threads of this story lingered in my heart since I was a teenager myself. It took a lot longer to overcome the self-doubt and actually begin putting pen to paper to actually write the story. Thanks to NaNoWriMo, I pushed through and finished my first draft November 2008. It then took quite a few revisions to get it ready to show an agent.

ENTER THE AGENT: I found my amazing agent Taylor Martindale [of Full Circle Literary] through the old-fashioned slush pile. I was careful with who I submitted to and made sure to only query agents who had an interest in the type of story I wrote. I feel inordinately lucky because Taylor has been an incredible champion for this story.

BIGGEST SURPRISE: I always knew there was a team behind each book, but I never knew how vast that team was. An author might write the book but from the agent to the editor, copyeditors, publicists, etc., it truly takes a village to produce a book. Another huge surprise was how social media will connect you to writers from all over the globe and give you kindred spirits who completely understand what you're going through every step of the way.

WHAT I DID RIGHT: I was very specific on who I queried to get as my agent. It's quality over quantity and I only queried agents who I thought would truly get my story. I also think being open to critique and feedback is vital. Most authors who go on submission will get rejections. Being open to hearing the *why*, and working on it, is vital.

PLATFORM: My passion for seeing a more diverse literary world organically led to me being a founding member of We Need Diverse Books. WNDB began as a hashtag that went viral and sparked conversations around the world, and is now also an organization committed to promoting diverse narratives and amplifying the voices of diverse authors. While the organization is not about promoting my own book, highlighting the importance of diverse books does help all diverse books, including my own.

BEST ADVICE FOR WRITERS: Find a trusted critique partner to give you honest feedback, and be sure to return the favor in critiquing their work. There is a lot to be learned about the art of writing from editing other people's work.

NEXT UP: I'm working on a few different young adult and middle grade projects. It's exciting to venture into writing new and different things!

⑭ KATIE M. STOUT
KATIEMSTOUT.COM

Hello, I Love You **(JUNE 2015, ST. MARTIN'S GRIFFITH)**

QUICK TAKE: After a tough year at home, the daughter of country music royalty attends boarding school in Korea, where she falls for a KPOP idol.

WRITES FROM: Atlanta, Georgia

PRE-BOOK: I was a college kid when I wrote *Hello, I Love You*, so mostly, I was just writing essays and research papers. I'd been published in my university's literary journal twice I'd also written two books before this, but they were terrible, and I did nothing with them.

TIME FRAME: I wrote the book in the span of two months during my last semester of college, but it took me a year to edit it.

ENTER THE AGENT: I found my awesome literary agent, Emily S. Keyes of Fuse Literary, on querytracker.com.

BIGGEST SURPRISE: Just how supportive a team your publisher can be. I was expecting to get lost in the shuffle of a major publishing house that has so many authors, but I've genuinely felt supported. My editor especially has been so encouraging and helpful throughout the process.

WHAT I DID RIGHT: I didn't give up. I queried widely. *Widely.* Like more than 100 queries. I was getting a good number of requests, but the partials and fulls would keep getting rejected, for different reasons. I felt like I should quit—shelve the project and start on something new—but this was the book I loved and wanted to debut with, so I kept researching and kept querying. In the end, I got two offers of representation, and it was worth all those horrible months in the querying trenches.

WHAT I LEARNED: Everyone's road to publication is different; your story won't be like anyone else's, so don't be disappointed if your journey differs from another writer's.

PLATFORM: I was a YA book blogger before I started querying, so I had a lot of contacts in that sphere. I've found it really helpful with word-of-mouth, because bloggers support each other.

BEST ADVICE FOR WRITERS: Write what *you* want to write. Before I received the offer from St. Martin's, I heard (quite a lot, actually) that the market wasn't ready for a YA book about Korean pop music. One agent actually gave me a very nice rejection on the full manuscript, saying she loved the book but had no idea how she would pitch it to editors. Don't follow trends. Write the stories from your heart.

NEXT UP: Next on my plate is a YA fantasy, but I feel sure I'll return to my contemporary roots.

CHUCK SAMBUCHINO (chucksambuchino.com, @chucksambuchino) edits the *Guide to Literary Agents* (guidetoliteraryagents.com/blog) as well as the *Children's Writer's & Illustrator's Market*. His pop humor books include *How to Survive a Garden Gnome Attack* (film rights optioned by Sony) and *When Clowns Attack: A Survival Guide* (Sept. 2015, Ten Speed Press). Chuck's other writing guides include *Formatting & Submitting Your Manuscript (3rd. Ed.)*, *Create Your Writer Platform*, and *Get a Literary Agent*. Besides that, he is a husband, guitarist, father, dog owner, and cookie addict.

DEBUT ILLUSTRATORS TELL ALL

Learn from these 6 success stories.

....

by Kerrie Flanagan

Getting that first book deal as an illustrator is a defining moment that imprints itself into your memory. It affirms your decision to be an artist. Here are six debut illustrators who we asked to share their insights about their journeys and how they successfully crossed over into the world of professional children's illustrators. They were asked how they got started illustrating. Where do they find their inspiration? How did they end up getting this illustration job? How did they find representation? What surprised them most about the whole book publishing process? What did they learn along the way? How do they incorporate social media into building their platform? What advice do they have for others trying to become children's book illustrators? Read on to find out more about these talented illustrators and their unique experiences.

❶ KAREN ROMAGNA (KARENROMAGNA.COM)
Voyage (BUNKER HILL PUBLISHING, OCTOBER 2014, WORDS BY BILLY COLLINS)

THE BOOK: A boy climbs into a boat and begins reading a book that carries him to faraway places and adventures.

HOW I GOT STARTED: In the early 1990s, I studied illustration with Milton Charles, a retired art director from Pocket Books. For years I used the tools and techniques I had learned from him to paint children's portraits and landscapes. In recent years I have gotten very involved with SCBWI. I have been actively working to illustrate and develop my own manuscripts for publication.

SOURCE OF INSPIRATION: My inspiration comes from life: funny moments, beautiful skies, baby ducks in spring, and from other illustrators. I love the work of classic illustrators like Beatrix Potter, Howard Pyle, Molly Brett and E.H. Shepard. However, I also find it incredibly helpful to study other picture book illustrators that I admire and try to discover what works for them.

HOW I GOT THIS ILLUSTRATING JOB: Former U.S. Poet Laureate Billy Collins found me. "Voyage" is a poem he had written to celebrate the 25 years that John Cole had been director of the Center for the Book in the Library of Congress. The publishers at Bunker Hill Publishing had discovered the poem hanging on the wall in John Cole's office and thought it would make a wonderful picture book. When he was approached by Bunker Hill Publishing about turning his poem into a picture book, Billy told them that he usually chooses the illustrator for his books. He searched the web and came up with me! I was asked to submit thumbnail sketches of the layout for the book and one finished illustration. Bunker Hill Publishing also had an illustrator that they wanted to use for this project. Before I began the illustration, I asked the publisher, "Exactly which illustration did Billy Collins find online that made him choose me for this book?" They replied, "It's the one of the boy and the boat." Billy Collins had found a portrait I had painted of my younger son, Tim, 20 years earlier!

BIGGEST SURPRISE: I thought that painting the illustrations was all I needed to do. I had no idea how much effort goes into marketing once the book is published. I have been attending book fairs, scheduling book signings at local book stores, and running workshops. I have hired a professional to write a teacher guide to accompany *Voyage*. I know that I need to be able to tie *Voyage* into the Core Curriculum so that I can participate in school visits.

WHAT I LEARNED: One must stay focused and on track, and develop a process for the illustrations. Keep in contact with the editors and art directors. Don't be afraid to ask questions. It is important to show up every morning and begin to work. I worked hard to develop my computer skills—not because I work digitally, but because it is necessary for sending images, cleaning up sketches, etc. Good quality tools make the work so much easier.

PLATFORM: I made a trailer for *Voyage* with images from the book with music that my son wrote to go along with it. I created a Facebook page for my illustration work. On my website I have two other videos that were made for *Voyage*. Lastly, I find that bloggers are generally very happy to review your book and blog about you.

ADVICE FOR ILLUSTRATORS: Put yourself out there. It can be intimidating to show your work. Join organizations such as SCBWI. You will find that you are not alone. *Everyone* is a beginner at some time. Look for an illustrator critique group in your area. Work to put together a great portfolio. Put only your best work in that portfolio. When you do finally get out there, make sure that you have promotional postcards so people know how to reach you.

FINAL THOUGHTS: Just keep at it! It can really happen.

② Dana Simpson (danasimpson.com) *Phoebe and Her Unicorn* **(Andrews McMeel Publishing, September 2014)**

THE BOOK: The comic strip story of the friendship between an unusual little girl and a magical unicorn.

AWARDS: Powell's Books and the New York Public Library both named it one of the best children's books of 2014. And today, BookRiot.com named it one of the best feminist children's books.

HOW I GOT STARTED: Career-wise, I started out as a webcomic artist. I drew one of the earliest web-based comic strips, *Ozy and Millie,* for a decade. It was how I learned the art form.

SOURCE OF INSPIRATION: Honestly, my two protagonists are two sides of my personality talking to each other. I just think of situations to put them in and see what they do.

THE DEAL: I won the development contract and book contract that ended up producing *Phoebe and Her Unicorn* in the Comic Strip Superstar contest. It would be a difficult career path to emulate.

REPRESENTATION: I don't have an agent. I do have a lawyer, who negotiated my contract. His name is Stu, and he's basically every syndicated cartoonist's lawyer.

BIGGEST SURPRISE: That they actually let me make the cover bright pink. Everybody seems to assume that was imposed on me by my publisher, but it was my idea. I half expected them to tell me I couldn't do it. Also that Peter S. Beagle offered to write the introduction. That kind of came out of nowhere, from my perspective—and it was amazing.

WHAT I LEARNED: I learned that I'm my publisher's favorite author because I'm "always so positive." My surly teenage self would be appalled. I also learned that while my work is for children; I write for myself and I wasn't going out of my way to write a children's comic strip necessarily. I have no complaints about it because kids are the best fans to have anyway.

PLATFORM: Like I said, I was a webcomic artist for ten years (and really, for a couple more when the current strip launched online before it launched in print). It's hard to get noticed doing that now, but in 1998 when I started, there wasn't so much competition.

ADVICE FOR ILLUSTRATORS: Draw what you love, love what you draw, and if possible, marry someone with an actual job.

FINAL THOUGHTS: Unicorn!

 ③ JULIE-ANNE GRAHAM (JULIEANNEGRAHAM. COM) *The Perfect Percival Priggs* (**RUNNING PRESS KIDS, MAY 2015**)

THE BOOK: A boy believes he has to be perfect to be loved by his high-achieving parents, but he soon realizes that's not the case, and they're not as perfect as they seem.

AWARDS: The original dummy book was Highly Commended for The Macmillan Prize for Children's Picture Book Illustration in 2013.

HOW I GOT STARTED: I've always been creative and loved drawing. My first degree was in fashion design, and I loved the fashion illustration aspect of it. Then I spent years doing freelance graphic design and got a large commission to illustrate an Irish-language course. I always loved writing and telling stories and decided I wanted to develop my work in that direction, so I joined the MA in Children's Book Illustration at Cambridge School of Art (Anglia Ruskin University).

SOURCE OF INSPIRATION: I find textiles and fashion very inspiring, and I usually include some kind of repeat patterns or fabrics in my work. For some of the work I did on the MA, I actually was sewing the characters faces! Going to the Children's Book Fair in Bologna every year is a huge source of inspiration; you get to see the beautiful illustrations that are being produced globally. The variation is amazing, and it's so interesting to see the differences between countries and what they produce. I love looking at the French, Italian, and Spanish publishers in particular. I have discovered some real gems there. One of my favorite books ever is by Charlotte Gastaut. It's called *Le Grand Voyage De Mademoiselle Prudence* and it has the most amazing cut-outs and transparencies that layer up on top of each other.

THE DEAL: I was studying on the MA and as part of the course we had to create a variety of projects and dummy books, which the college then took with them to display at a stand at the Bologna Book Fair. An agent saw my work and loved it, so I signed with her. She helped me tweak the dummy book and we submitted it to publishers about six months later. There were a few publishers interested, then Running Press made me an offer and I accepted it.

REPRESENTATION: Having the stand at the Bologna Book Fair was incredible exposure. So many publishers and agents came to view the work and my agent was one of them. She e-mailed me ASAP after seeing the dummy book and then we talked on the phone (she's based in the U.S. and I am in the U.K.) and I ended up signing with her. She's been brilliant.

BIGGEST SURPRISE: The story changed quite a lot from the original dummy book and most of the illustrations I had done originally ended up being reworked. It was a long process and took nearly a year to complete. It was definitely worthwhile as the book has improved as a result. One surprising thing is that you don't need to be in the same country as your publisher. Because the publisher and I are based in different parts of the world, we did everything by phone calls and e-mail.

WHAT I LEARNED: I learned about consistency. It's important that the characters look the same on each page (proportions) and that there is a consistent color palette across the whole book. I kept a note of the digital colors I used along with opacities and when I was using paints, the name of the colors, etc. I had a color profile for each character. It sounds geeky but it was very helpful. I also learned that it was important to label and group the layers in my Photoshop files so that I could send them to the publisher and they would be able to make sense of them.

PLATFORM: I have a website and blog, and I am on Facebook and Twitter. I created an activity pack to go with the book, which is downloadable from my website and allows teachers or parents to do activities based on the book.

ADVICE FOR ILLUSTRATORS: Educate yourself either by reading books or doing a course. Picture books in particular have a very defined format and it's important that you understand it so that you can approach publishers or agents in a professional manner. Read *Children's Picture Books: The Art of Visual Storytelling* and *Illustrating Children's Books: Creating Pictures for Publication*, both by Martin Salisbury. Develop your work as much as possible, drawing from life wherever possible. Have a selection of color and black-and-white work in your portfolio; make sure you feature children, adults, and animals in your illustrations. Make a website. Contact publishers or agents through the *Children's Writer's & Illustrator's Market*. Don't be scared of approaching them; they are looking for new talent and you could be it! Enter competitions. If you are feeling adventurous, go to the Bologna Book Fair with your portfolio. You can e-mail publishers a couple of months in advance to book appointments or just ask at the desks when you arrive. Each publisher has a different policy—some may not see illustrators at all, others may schedule in time to do that, others may see you in between other appointments. If you submit your work into the Bologna Illustrators Exhibition you'll also get a free ticket into the fair, but check the deadline, it's always *very* early!

FINAL THOUGHTS: Tools! These are some of the essential tools that help me create my work. In addition to all the usual paints, pencils, computers, etc., these are must-haves.

• Lightbox! It's essential for revising your own illustrations and improving them. Spend the money and get a good one.

• Wacom Tablet for drawing directly into the computer. It's great for editing and cleaning up images.

• Adobe Photoshop. Illustrator is good too, but you can get away without it, whereas I think Photoshop is essential.

• A good quality scanner.

• Lynda.com. You can teach yourself *any* graphics program at your own speed. It's an invaluable resource. Don't be intimidated if you're not techy; you can learn anything on here.

④ SHAWN SHEEHY (SHAWNSHEEHY.COM) *Welcome to the Neighborwood* (CANDLEWICK, MARCH 2015)

THE BOOK: *Welcome to the Neighborwood* showcases seven animal builders, along with the structures they make and the interrelationships they share.

HOW I GOT STARTED: I don't call myself an illustrator. Primarily, I'm a book artist that focuses on pop-up engineering. I made my first pop-up book in 1997 while studying graphic design. I got pretty excited about that project, and decided to follow my design studies with an MFA in Book and Paper Arts. Soon I was making books regularly, involving myself in the writing, image development, paper making, printing, binding and design, as well as engineering.

SOURCE OF INSPIRATION: Nearly all of my artist books—and *Welcome to the Neighborwood* would be included—focus on ecological concerns. Many of my projects result from having read or heard stories in the news about environmental issues. Also, I enjoy highlighting unusual traits or habits of wild creatures.

THE DEAL: *Welcome to the Neighborwood* was originally created as a limited-edition artist book. A partner in a Chicago book design company expressed willingness to share my book with publishers at a New York book fair. A representative of Candlewick showed interest, and after several years of conversation and negotiation, Candlewick decided to publish *Neighborwood*, maintaining nearly all of the original concept and execution.

REPRESENTATION: We—partners in the design firm and I—decided that, if a publisher showed interest, it would be mutually beneficial if we entered into a contracted agent/client relationship. Serving as agent isn't their primary function, but it worked out well for all of us.

WHAT SURPRISED ME MOST ABOUT THE PROCESS: Since this is my first trade book, the process was packed with new experiences. Near the top of the surprise list would be Candlewick's utter devotion to maintaining the integrity of the original book. They were really terrific.

WHAT I LEARNED: Many, many things. Certainly, I learned a lot in the development of the text. This was the first time I had worked closely with a copy editor. We labored to be thorough with the biology while keeping tight reins on the word count.

PLATFORM: I regularly and faithfully maintain a website that features all of my book projects and public engagements. I'm somewhat active on Facebook. I frequently teach pop-up engineering workshops and provide public presentations of my work. I make announcements on a listserv. I attend the conference of The Movable Book Society, which provides the opportunity to network with many other pop-up professionals, academics, and aficionados.

ADVICE FOR ILLUSTRATORS: When I was young, I didn't have the ambition of becoming a children's book creator. I was in my thirties when I made my first book. I spent a good deal of time in my twenties feeling frustrated about career direction. I don't remember the source, but sometime in that period of my life I read/heard something along these lines: "Find the people who are doing the things you like to do or want to be doing, and go be with them." For me, searching out that intersection of passions and networking has often led to opportunity.

FINAL THOUGHTS: I can't wait to work on the next project!

⑤ JEAN JULLIEN (JEANJULLIEN.COM) *Hoot Owl, Master of Disguise* (CANDLEWICK, FEBRUARY 2015, AUTHOR SEAN TAYLOR)

THE BOOK: It's the story of a young owl who is as hungry as he is ambitious!

HOW I GOT STARTED: I've always drawn. I grew up reading American comic books, watching Japanese and American cartoons, and being fed modernist art by my mother. I then studied graphic design for eight years, going from a very practical course in France to Central Saint Martins to the Royal College of Art. This taught me a lot about the history and rules of image making. I never studied illustration and am grateful that I got into it naturally, strengthened by a rigorous learning in composition, typography, colors, and everything that makes an image not beautiful but efficient. I felt like I learned how to use the tools so that I could go and play with them, which is what I'm doing every day.

SOURCE OF INSPIRATION: All the aforementioned: cartoon, comics, and masters of design and image making.

THE DEAL: I do a lot of commercial jobs; it's half of my practice really. I enjoy the "realness" of it. So I did this series of table cards for Byron Hamburgers in London, and Deirdre Mc-Dermott (the art director at Walker Books) liked it and gave me a call to come in and have a chat. We got on really well—I loved what they do and had never done a children's book before. Matter of fact, I was quite wary of doing one, due to my already deceitfully naive aesthetic. But their intelligence when it comes to making picture books convinced me to give it a go and I am stoked by the experience.

REPRESENTATION: I have an agent for commercial projects like advertising, editorial, etc. I do not have an agent for picture books.

WHAT SURPRISED ME MOST ABOUT THE PROCESS: How passionate the people I worked with were. I was expecting the world of picture books to be driven by over-the-top rules of what is acceptable for children, etc.—a sort of nightmare of political correctness (which would have put me off). But all that mattered to Deirdre was for the result to be the best possible. Every meeting felt focused on the process and the development of something fluid and enjoyable, not the commercial end. From what I've heard so far, it seems like they got it right and that people are really enjoying it.

WHAT I LEARNED: To trust people's experience and knowledge. So ... a bit of humility, I guess! I enjoyed getting feedback and seeing the pacing and fluidity grow as we were exchanging [ideas]. I never use narrative nor repetition in my work, which is often a one-liner. So that storytelling was really new to me, and I've learned a lot.

PLATFORM: I just produce a lot. I take more work on than I should and still try to do as many solo shows as I can and to post daily on social media. I work best when I'm really busy. It allows me to develop a dialogue with people who don't judge me on a piece that is meant to sum my work up and that would have taken ages to produce, but more on a constant stream of work: a visual language that allows me to speak out with honesty. It feels like people take well to that, this sharing of intimacy and of the process that is heralded by social medias.

ADVICE FOR ILLUSTRATORS: Go for it and trust your collaborators!

6 ADAM F. WATKINS (ADAMFWATKINS.COM) *R is For Robot: A Noisy Alphabet* (**PRICE STERN SLOAN, JUNE 2014**)

THE BOOK: A loud, fun book for youngsters learning the alphabet.

HOW I GOT STARTED: I started drawing when I was very young. I think most kids do. But drawing was something I really enjoyed and was pretty good at. I didn't really know what an illustrator was until I went to art college. My four years at the Columbus College of Art & Design was where I not only honed my skills as an illustrator, but also where I learned what illustration was, the different types of careers illustrators have, and of course, the many talented professionals, past and present.

SOURCE OF INSPIRATION: One source of inspiration, for me, is good work. Guys like: AG Ford, Loren Long, Adam Rex ... the list goes on and on. I am also inspired by different careers of fellow author/illustrators. Once you start to achieve some early career goals, it's important to always have at least one person whose career is (or was) where you hope to be in ten years.

THE DEAL: There was an editor at Penguin Random House who saw some examples of my work and thought I'd be a good fit for an alphabet book concept they'd been kicking around. After some more samples, I got the job!

REPRESENTATION: Yes, I have an agent. I am a proud client of the wonderful team at New Leaf Literary & Media, Inc. My agent and good friend is the one and only Joanna Volpe. She found me at the 2010 SCBWI Winter Conference. I signed with her a few weeks after and haven't looked back since.

WHAT SURPRISED ME MOST ABOUT THE PROCESS: I'd say it's the ups and downs of the marathon that is the book-making process. It was basically like this: very excited about the opportunity. Stoked about the finished concept and idea of the book. Work very hard and tirelessly on the illustrations. Hate all the work you've done and feel it's totally inadequate by the time you send it in to the publisher. Then, fall in love with the whole project again once you get your first copies of the finished book in the mail. It sounds kind of weird, but I have found this to be a pretty common turn of events for authors and/or illustrators.

WHAT I LEARNED: I learned that people in the publishing business are extremely genuine and good. That personal relationships are very important and valued. And that I will never do anything else for a living.

PORTFOLIO AND PLATFORM: I'm horrible at this! I'm not very big on social media. I only use Facebook and Twitter and only have about 200 or so followers on each site. I have a website (www.adamfwatkins.com) with my portfolio, but I don't really "work" on a portfolio these days.

ADVICE FOR ILLUSTRATORS: Outside of the "never give up on your dreams" speech, it would have to be get an agent. They make all the difference in the world, as far as I'm concerned.

KERRIE FLANAGAN (KerrieFlanagan.com) is a freelance writer, director of Northern Colorado Writers (NorthernColoradoWriters.com), a writing organization going strong since 2007, and author of *Write Away: A Year of Musings & Motivations for Writers.*

HENRY WINKLER AND LIN OLIVER

Meet the star duo behind Hank Zipzer.

by Kerrie Flanagan

Individually, Henry Winkler and Lin Oliver both have impressive resumes. Winkler as an actor, director, and producer, and Oliver as the co-founder of Society of Children's Book Writers & Illustrators (SCBWI), a producer, television writer, and author. When they combined their talents to co-author the *New York Times* bestselling series, Hank Zipzer, The World's Greatest Underachiever, the results were amazing.

Winkler received his MFA from the Yale School of Drama in 1970 and is best known for his role as Fonzie on the sitcom "Happy Days." In addition, he acted in other television shows and movies including "Arrested Development," *The Waterboy* and *The Practice*. He also directed and produced "MacGyver" in the 1980's and "Sabrina, the Teenage Witch" in the late 1990s. Winkler has a passion for children and in 1990

helped form the Children's Action Network, which uses the power of the entertainment community to increase awareness about children's issues and to make them a top priority in everyday life.

Oliver graduated from UCLA and UC Berkeley with a degree in English. After an unsuccessful semester as a high school teacher, she got a job writing educational books for children. She and her writing partner, Steve Mooser, wanted to learn more about writing for children, but had a hard time finding resources and conferences. So together they formed SCBWI, which now has over 22,000 members. Oliver eventually went on to work for television as a vice president of Universal Studios for eleven years, where she wrote and produced shows such as "Harry and the Hendersons." She now has her own production company where she writes and produces television shows for families. Plus, she is a children's author of the Almost Identical series and the book, *Little Poems for Tiny Ears*.

In early 2000, Winkler's agent suggested he write children's books. Winkler didn't feel he had enough experience to do that so his agent introduced Oliver. The two hit it off and began collaborating on a book series based on Winkler's childhood and his challenges with dyslexia. The Hank Zipzer books were born and are now a bestselling series.

Once you two knew you wanted to work together, what were the steps you took to getting a publisher?

Henry: The first thing we did was Lin, as always, sat at the computer and I walked around her office. We figured out a book proposal together, which I never heard of before, but Lin was very familiar with. We hammered out who Hank was, what his life was like, where he lived (which was easy because it was the apartment I grew up in) and we created friends for Hank. We put together the book proposal and when Lin was satisfied we had done it the way it should be done, we sent it to the agent at ICM, Esther Newberg. She handles clients like Thomas Friedman, Bill Clinton, and everyone else you can imagine.

Lin: She was the head of the literary department at ICM [now ICM Partners].

Henry: She said, "I don't do children's books." And I said to her, "There's always a first time. I think you

should look at this." She sent it out to five publishers. Three said no, one said maybe and Penguin Putnam said yes. And they came back with a contract for four books.

Lin: That was 11 years ago and since then, there are now 18 Hank Zipzer, the World's Great Underachiever books.

Henry: They are for third-, fourth-, and fifth-graders.

Lin: Those Hank Zipzer books have sold about four million copies. We got a lot of letters from kids wanting to know what Hank was like before he got diagnosed. Because early on in the series he gets diagnosed with dyslexia. So we created Here's Hank, who is the younger Hank. They are true chapter books with illustrations and about 10,000 words.

Henry: We are working on chapter eight of the seventh novel of that series right now. The fourth one that came out was on the *New York Times* bestseller list for series.

Lin: It's called *Fake Snakes and Weird Wizards*. It's a story about Hank's annoying little sister who loves reptiles. She wants to have a birthday party with a reptile show and the family can't afford it. Hank volunteers to step forward as the West Side Magician and produce a reptile. Things go very much wrong at the birthday party. By the way, making the bestseller list as a series is a big deal because it's exclusively big movie titles like *Harry Potter, Divergent, Maze Runner*, so

Bookmarks Are People Too!

Fake Snakes and Weird Wizards

it was great for a chapter book to in-filtrate that series list. So, in the ensu-ing 10 years since we started, we have written 18 of the Hank Zipzer novels, we've completed 6.5 Here's Hank books and there are four more in our contract. Then we also did another four-book series called Ghost Buddy that we did with Scholastic.

Henry: I'm going to brag again. We were on the bestseller list [a few months ago] and that was the second time. The first time was a few years ago with Hank Zipzer, the older novels. We were on the list at No. 8.

Henry, was there anything that sur-prised you about the process of writ-ing a book?

Henry: How many rules I didn't know. And how many rules Lin did know. I learned everything from Lin. All the rules about going in the same door and leaving the same door you came in on every little rule that is part of the liter-ary process I learned from Lin.

Are there one or two rules that stand out?

Lin: I think the thing that Henry strug-gles with most is narrative point of view. We are writing in the first person. You can only write about things that Hank is seeing or experiencing. Henry will say, "Let's go in the next room and see what the mom is doing." Well, we can't be there unless Hank is there. I think this is tricky for all writers. That's why so much is written in third person or omniscient third person, because you want to be able to move around. But what we traded off for that was the in-timacy of the first person voice.

Henry: The personality of Hank gets to come out.

Lin: Henry and I debate these is-sues day in and day out. We very much collaborate. There is a lot of give and take in the conversation about what we agree on. The other thing that comes up often is the pacing of the story. Hen-ry loves the tale, and I love to move on. I am always saying that this is getting a little slow, this is getting a little boring. He keeps saying, "Oh, but this is so funny and so interesting." We do a lot of negotiation on how long a scene should go, what to dramatize, and what to skip over.

Henry: Sometimes my actor self starts to feel like, *Oh my gosh, the jeopardy*; and *Oh my gosh the emotion*. We can't move until we know how he feels about the women yelling at him. I need to know how he is feeling. I need to know that he can't use the blender until he figures out how to plug it in because he doesn't know where the plug is. He's worried. And actually, that was a real conversation. This kind of thing comes up almost every day.

Lin: It's one of the hardest things about writing; deciding what to leave in and what to take out. Especially when you are writing for young kids. We are writing for second graders. You have to be aware of their attention span and providing enough action to move the story along. But enough depth to understand how your characters feel. That's a balance. We are collaborating, so we need two people to agree on it. It's hard enough to agree with yourself on it.

Can you explain your writing process?
Lin: Because we know we are writing a series, we don't have to go through a lot of character development. We now know our cast of characters. The first thing we do is come up with a premise that is meaningful. Not just a good

story premise, but one that resonates in terms of saying something to kids. Whether it is about friendship or honesty or not judging people. We go through many premises until we land on one that we feel is rich enough to carry the theme we want express.

Henry: We know right away when it is rich enough because as soon as we say what the premise could be, we say, oh my god, then this could happen ... oh yeah, and that could happen and she could come over here and meet this person and he could lose his homework. I'm telling you without fail, when we come up with story, we either sit there like bumps on a log and nothing spurs up or it's so dynamic that it is electric.

Lin: I think that's true.

Henry: It is true; it happens every time.

Lin: Then after the premise we do an outline where we do the beats for the story. The outline is subject to change. We start to feel where it begins and where it ends and where the turning point is. Then we allow ourselves enough leeway to go back in and change that if the pacing requires it.

Henry: This is really important. We have an airtight outline. We know exactly where this is going to go and as we start writing the book, honest to God, the book has a life of its own. All of a sudden at chapter five it takes a left turn and there goes the outline and here comes the story. We end up in a place we did not consider. It's shocking how organic the process is.

Lin: We do the outline so we have a road map. If the road map changes and we decide to go to Wisconsin instead of Washington, then we'll go there. But we don't start out with just winging it. Particularly with the younger books; they are short. You can't wander through the story. They have to be very targeted. Then we send the outline to the publisher and get their feedback. After that, the next thing we do is decide on a title. We are really big believers in titles. Especially for children's books. They are not reading a review in the *New York Times*. They are making a decision because the book is at a book fair or they are at a store with their parents looking at books. They make a decision based on something that appeals to them in the title. We try to have titles that are distinctive, maybe funny, and maybe enticing.

Henry: Lin is stickler for titles. She told me we have three seconds. The kid picks a book up off the shelf looks at it, reads the title and either it goes in the basket or it goes back on the shelf. So we work on those titles, sometimes for days.

Lin: We love it because when we go and speak at schools, and we say a title of a book, it gets a laugh. We did a Hank Zipzer book called *The Curtain Went Up, My Pants Fell Down*. Kids are going to want to read that. One of our new Here's Hank books is called

A Short Tale About a Long Dog. It really matters to us that the title intrigues kids and makes them laugh.

Then once we have the title, the premise, and what we want to say to kids and the outline, then we write. We write in my office. I am at the computer because Henry is kind of allergic to them. Given that we both came out of television writing and television production, this process is very familiar to us. Television sitcom writing happens when you do a draft on your own, but then you really refine the script in a room together with other writers. We write for about 2–2.5 hours. But we are very focused on it for that time. On the little books we try to do a chapter in that time. For the longer books it might take 3–4 days to do a chapter. We have draft usually in about three months.

Then we each take it home separately and read it over for rhythm and style, and punch up the jokes and words that don't resonate. Then that first draft goes to our editor. We get back their reactions, revisions, and notes, which we discuss ad nauseam. One of us is more resilient to the notes than the other one. I look forward to the editorial notes, especially since they can point out where we are not clear on something. Then we do the revisions, which takes a couple of weeks. Usually we work well enough with our editors now that only one revision is required and sometimes there is a third take, which is a polish. Then we are done with the official writing part. Sometimes we talk with the illustrator.

Henry: That I found really, really important. The illustrator for the young books, for Here's Hank, is really terrific. I think the covers are just edible. They are colorful and fun and just really wonderful. Something I could never do in a million years. We called him up in England and talked him through the character. [How Hank was drawn] changed from his first concept to what it is now because we took the time to tell him anecdotes about my real life, about Hank, how we see him and how hard things are for him. I think every author should do that.

You take serious topics like learning challenges and bullying, and approach them with humor. Why do you take this approach?

Henry: We believe the way to a kid's heart is through humor. We did not set out, in any such way or form, to write a self-help book. *Oh isn't that sad, the poor kid has a learning problem.* He just happens to be a really inventive child who's working on all cylinders, except he can't spell and his math is beyond him. But his thinking process, his imagination is on fire.

When we go into schools and all of the kids are sitting there, 300–400 kids at a time, we ask, "Does anybody know what they are great at?" There is not a hand that does not shoot up in the air. Every child knows what they are great at. We believe that is where

the focus should be. Not everybody is going to be great at algebra or geometry. But they might be good at art, at running, at being a friend, at English, at writing. One kid said, "I am great at being me." There is more than one way to solve a problem. There is not really one way to figure it out. You can do it your way and if you get to where you want to be, then your way is brilliant. Children are not defined by school. It has nothing to do with their brilliance if they don't do well in academic subjects. We encourage the parents to come. It is just a fact; the parents come because I was the Fonz. They come because they know me from TV. But when they leave, they go, "Oh my God, I am going to look at my child differently. Oh my God I never considered that. My kid came home and said, 'I just found the first book I'm going to read.'" When a child reads one, they say, "Hey, that's just like me." Libraries tell us that all time. Reluctant readers who won't read just have to read one and then they read five as fast as they can.

Lin, what changes have you seen in the publishing industry and how does that affect writers today?

Lin: The publishing industry is in a huge state of flux. That has to do with the creation and popularity of self-publishing. When I first started, vanity publishing was really an ugly stepsister. You only published yourself if you were desperate or narcissistic or needed something to show your grandchildren. Now, it is a viable option for a lot of people in a lot of categories. All of that makes a huge difference in democratizing the publishing industry. Publishing is available to many more people. They don't have to get through gatekeepers. They can go directly out there. Whether it's creating a blog or publishing your own novel or your own works of nonfiction, you can do it in electronic form; you can do it in book form. Suddenly, the industry is available to everyone. In many senses it's a great thing and in many senses it is problematic. It puts everyone on an equal footing. Whether or not you're a trained writer or whether or not your ideas have been vetted, there is no one between you and your reader with self-publishing. Part of the problem is that in traditional publishing there is a tremendous bottleneck. People who have things to say more often than not, can't get through. On the other hand, maybe some of that is valid. Maybe they shouldn't be getting through. I am not opposed to it, but I think caution needs to be considered. I think publishing companies provide a very significant vetting role in our society. That is the biggest change in publishing overall.

In children's publishing that has had less of an effect. From what I have read and been told, electronic publishing in the children's field is actually down and not up. Parents find it and then discover what they really want is a book in their kids' hands. Sitting with an iPad at bedtime or having their child read from their iPad when they are putting themselves to sleep when they are older, is not necessarily the experience people are looking for. So, electronic publishing has not had as much an effect in the children's field. But what has had a tremendous impact is the enormous success of children and young adult genres. It used to be that people who published children's books, it was a nice little business. And now what you will find is that the major publishing companies use their children's book divisions to help support the adult publishing division. That's come about by the huge growth in the YA market and in YA popularity, and in the genre that people refer to as new adult. The line between a young adult book and an adult book is blurred a bit. As many people read *The Fault in Our Stars* in their twenties, as kids in their teens.

This, plus the giant series successes like Harry Potter and the Rick Riordan books and the Wimpy Kids and Divergents and Maze Runners. These big series books have become a source for hit feature films and that helps drive the book industry, too. One of the huge changes I've seen in children's books is that they are not just part of the market, they often drive the market, which is a very good thing.

What advice do you have for writers wanting to write children's books?

Henry: Here's what I've learned: I did not know I could write a book. I did not know I could be part of a team that would write so many books. So, you sit in front of your computer or in front of your pad of paper and you spend five minutes a day and you write down whatever is in your mind. The biggest thing is to not edit until you are finished. Do not write and think, *Oh no, I shouldn't write that because someone's going to read it and think this or my mother's going to be angry or my aunt is going to see herself.* Write everything that is in your head, in your heart and then see what you've got at the end. I believe you will be pleasantly surprised.

KERRIE FLANAGAN (KerrieFlanagan.com) is a freelance writer, Director of Northern Colorado Writers (NorthernColoradoWriters.com), a writing organization going strong since 2007, and author of *Write Away: A Year of Musings & Motivations for Writers.*

CINDY CALLAGHAN

On writing well, and what it's like to see your
work adapted into a TV series.

....

by Ramona Long

Cindy Callaghan's
debut middle grade
novel, *Just Add
Magic*, is—in Cal-
laghan's words—
"a super cute story
about Kelly Quinn
and her secret cook-
ing club."

Just Add Magic was published in 2010
by Simon & Schuster / Aladdin M!X, and
has been followed by four other middle
grade novels: *Lost in London*; (2013); *Lucky
Me* (2014); *Lost in Paris* (2015); and *Lost in
Rome* (2015).

Each story centers around a contemporary middle grade girl navigating family,
friendship, and school—plus adventures in
magic, fashion, scavenger hunts, chain letters, international travel, and a little *amore*.
The stories are told with lots of humor and
laughs, and celebrates girls and what they
can gain from unlikely friendships.

Some of the books are set in the countryside near Callaghan's current home in
Delaware. The Lost in series takes her characters to big European cities.

In 2015, Amazon Studios adapted *Just
Add Magic* for a live-action TV series pilot aimed at young viewers ages 6-11. Callaghan worked with Amazon to develop the
novel to screen. After the pilot was viewed
and reviewed, Amazon made the decision
to expand to a full season of 13 episodes
featuring Kelly and her secret cooking club.
Callaghan will continue to act as consultant for the series while she works on new
projects.

Callaghan grew up in New Jersey and
attended college at the University of Southern California before earning a BA in English and French, and an MBA from the University of Delaware. She recently exited corporate America after nearly 20 years, and is
now fully entrenched in writing and family.
Callaghan lives and writes in Wilmington,
Delaware with her family and numerous
rescued pets.

ABOUT THE "JUST ADD MAGIC" TV SERIES:

Your first middle grade novel, *Just Add Magic*, was adapted by Amazon Studios and is in development for a TV series. What chain of events happened from book to television pilot to series?

Just Add Magic landed me a literary agent and my first publishing contract. Shortly after the book's 2010 release, my agent and I went our separate ways, leaving the book unrepresented. I continued to believe that *Just Add Magic* had more in its future—the screen.

Enter: college roommate. Like everyone, I friended my freshman college roommate on Facebook. We'd gone to the University of Southern California to be film writers, but ... yadda yadda ... I got an MBA and have worked for twenty years in pharmaceuticals. Anyway, she wasn't living far from me, so we lunched and I learned that she was transitioning from an animation writing career. She said, "Talk to my agent and see if she has some advice for *Just Add Magic*." I sent her agent a copy of the book.

Months passed.

One day I got a call from California: "I'd love to represent it."

My film agent submitted *Just Add Magic* to studios.

Weeks passed.

I was at the International Thriller Writers meeting in New York City. In the evening, I attended a session called "Book to TV," (hello, irony) when my cell phone rang again from California. (FYI: *Always* take a call from California.)

My film agent said, "Amazon wants to option it!"

So, I totally freaked out. Totally.

Months passed.

Drafts were written and sent up the Amazon ladder waiting for the green light. One night I was at the local coffee joint debating semi-colons with my writing group when a call came in from you-know-where. They said, "Can you come to Los Angeles? We're moving ahead."

Everyone at the coffee joint got to see my happy dance. (Poor folks).

Fast forward more months.

The pilot was tested for a month and got the green light to move ahead to a series—that's a full season of 13 episodes. Pretty cool.

What kind of input did you have as the novel was adapted for screen?

I was a consultant on the project. In that role I helped with script writer selection. Amazon had narrowed it down to two writers whose bios I reviewed carefully in advance. With credentials like Disney, Nickelodeon or ABC Family hits to their names, I was instantly wow-ed.

After listening to their ideas, I knew which visions resonated for me, but I wasn't confident in my own judgment since this was all so new. I mean, what if I said the wrong thing? So mostly I listened, but then I was asked my opinion ... *Yikes!* I very carefully crafted my

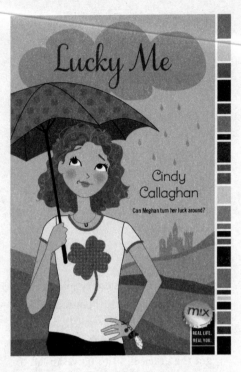

there for something that was in my head, an idea of freckle-faced Kelly Quinn and her secret cooking club. Does that thought give you chills? It does to me. Every time.

The casting is phenomenal. The girls did an amazing job representing the characters I'd created in my head. The thought of working with them all again on 12 more episodes is awesome.

Has the possibility of a future adaptation for the screen changed your approach to writing new works?

I've always thought of my work visually, but this underscores the importance of getting to the action quickly. Movies don't have fluff and usually no interior thought. We see so much in terms of action. It's also helped sharpen my dialogue.

Do you plan to write an original screenplay yourself, or adapt one of your published novels for TV?

I hope that *all* of my books will be adapted for screen—either movie or TV. As far as writing the screenplay myself, I could definitely see that in my future, although I don't have any immediate plans.

ABOUT WRITING FOR MIDDLE GRADE READERS:

What drew you to write for the middle grade audience? What challenges did you discover once you began?

I had middle-graders in my home, so that inspiration was always around

response and was pleasantly surprised that the Amazon team was on the same page. *Yay!*

I also reviewed drafts of the scripts and provided comments. Lastly, I was on the set and offered my opinion during the filming.

How did viewing your story being adapted to the screen make you feel? Did the pilot match the images in your head of the characters you'd created, or were you surprised?

This is difficult to put into words, but I'll try. The school where we filmed was filled with people—actors, extras, cinematographers, directors, security, food service people, set and costume designers, make-up artists, etc. *They were all*

do have one project for boys that I toy with from time to time, but it's still in a very sloppy preliminary stage.

You have daughters and you've shared how a kitchen full of girls sparked *Just Add Magic*. Do you use your daughters and their friends as inspiration, to bounce off ideas, for reality checks on how girls think in 2015?

Actually, my daughter and two of her kooky friends cooking in my kitchen one day was the inspiration for a "cooking club." Then, my wheels got spinning and I thought about a "secret cooking club." Why is it secret? And then I became obsessed with the notion of "Kelly Quinn's Secret Cooking Club," which was the book's original title. I wrote furiously for weeks until a very rough draft was done. Then, of course, I edited for years.

What factors influence where you set each story? Once the location (London, Ireland, Rome, Paris) is determined, how do you decide where to set particular scenes?

My "lost in" books all have a city/country mouse theme. The country side is in Wilmington, Delaware, where I live, or locales nearby. For the city side, I select locations that I think will make middle grade girls "spark." They're interested in big, glam, European cities! When I begin my research into specific sites within each city, I investigate many more than I actually use. I map them out geographically and see how

me. I also write adult and YA, but I have a voice that lends itself nicely to middle grade.

I found dialogue challenging and would often ask my kids, "How would you say this?" or "Do you know what this word means?" or "How would you describe an XYZ?" And they helped me out. I'm better at it now, but the "in" lingo changes quickly. I eavesdrop a lot.

Your main characters are all girls. Why is this, and have you considered writing a male main character?

Being a girl, I feel I can connect with girl situations easily. I'm often asked to write boy books because many teachers and parents feel there is a gap in the middle-grade boy market. I've tried, but I haven't nailed the voice. I

first or beta readers before sending them to your agent or editor?

I belong to two writing groups, both of which are fab. One I have been meeting with for eleven years! As you can imagine, it's become more than a writing critique group. I share everything from initial ideas to chapters to entire manuscripts with them. Their feedback is invaluable and an important part of my writing process. I can't imagine writing without constant feedback.

What would you call your greatest skill as a writer? For emerging writers, what would you say to them about finding and sharpening a recognized skill?

My biggest skill is my drive, if you can call that a skill. It's the will to persevere. I want this and I'm willing to work very very hard to make it happen. I wasn't a great writer when I started and I'm still not, but like muscles, the skill gets stronger with practice. I think I'm a better writer than I was ten years ago and I get better with every project. So, that's the skill I would tell beginning writers they need—fire in your belly. Everything else will follow.

What other types of writing do you do? Do you have a dream project?

I also write YA and adult thriller. I dream to write the next really big thriller that creates a swell of hype, like *The Firm* when it came out. Remember that? And then I dream that it would be made into a big screen movie, which I'm asked not only to produce,

they might play a role into the story. It's a very fun selection process, which unfortunately leaves a lot of material on the cutting room floor.

ABOUT YOU AS A WRITER:

Do you have a set writing schedule or writing habit?

Not really, except that I almost always write very early on Saturday and Sunday mornings when the world is very quiet. My mind is sharp and there is no place else that I need to or should be. Stores aren't even open! And my kids are asleep. There are no e-mails or texts coming in, and very little distraction.

Do you belong to any critique or writing groups? Do you run stories through

but act in. I don't necessarily need to be the star, but I would likely play opposite Christopher Meloni. I imagine I would be a cop, detective, secret agent of something of that ilk. And scenes would be filmed in my hometown and all my friends could be extras. We would have a huge party with the whole town and the movie stars. Then, I'd be asked to host "SNL" when Justin Timberlake is the musical guest and Mark Wahlberg does one of those surprise pop-in visits.

What? It could happen.

ABOUT YOUR BOOKS:

You will have five novels in print and more planned, but your books are not a series. What can a reader expect to find in each of your books?

For this set of five books—*Just Add Magic, Lucky Me, Lost in London, Lost in Paris* and *Lost in Rome*—readers and their parents can expect good clean fun. If I told you my positioning in the marketplace, that's what it would be: Good Clean Fun. There is adventure, humor (lots of laughs), maybe a smidgen of romance, and no bad words or risque scenes. And even though my books are not a series per se and each has a new gang of characters, I have begun infusing "crossovers." This means that you may see a character from one book pay a little visit to another. This is super fun for me and I hope readers will think so, too.

What kind of takeaway about being a girl in our world do you hope readers gain from your body of work?

One of the things I like to show in each of my books in unlikely friendships. I want girls to know that while it's OK for like to attract like, it's also really fun, cool, great, and interesting to befriend different types of people—not your age, not your gender, not interested in the same things you are, not from your country. I love that the characters in my books build seemingly unlikely friendships.

What do you like best about the books you write? This applies to as you are writing them, and after they are written.

They make me laugh. I love it when I'm writing a scene and I make myself laugh. I love it when I do a reading, and I have to take a pause to compose myself. I love it when someone who has read a book says, "OMG, Meghan McGlinchey at the magic show ... I couldn't stop laughing."

You are an active presence on social media, on the Web, at book talks and conferences, and you make many public appearances. Which of these do you enjoy best?

I really like school visits. I feel like I leave the students feeling inspired to write and with permission to write whatever they want without the thought or fear that it will be graded.

I also really want them to understand that they should *enjoy* reading. That is, that reading shouldn't feel like homework. If they aren't a big reader, or they currently don't enjoy reading, I ask them to consume stories differently—try comic books, audio books, biographies, mysteries, whatever. They don't have to finish it if they don't like it, but I ask them to try lots of different stuff until they find something that they enjoy.

RAMONA LONG (ramonadef.wordpress.com) works as an author, editor, and online writing instructor. Her short stories and creative nonfiction have appeared in literary, regional, and juvenile publications. She has been awarded artist grants and fellowships from a number of state and regional arts councils in the Mid-Atlantic area, and from national writing organizations, including the SCBWI. She lives in Delaware and is active in the Delmarva literary and arts scene.

BARNEY SALTZBERG

On how to have a career that lasts decades.

....

by Carmela Martino

In his bestselling interactive board book *Beautiful Oops!* (Workman Publishing) author/ illustrator Barney Saltzberg celebrates imagination and creative risk-taking, themes that permeate many of his books as well as his own career. He sold his first published book, *Utter Nonsense* (McGraw-Hill, 1981), by personally pitching it during a visit to New York. Saltzberg went on to find his niche in children's books, writing and illustrating over 50, including *Beautiful Oops!* and its companion, *A Little Bit of Oomph!*; the perennial favorite Touch and Feel Kisses series published by Houghton Mifflin Harcourt; and his latest, *Inside This Book (are three books)*, from Abrams Appleseed.

Illustration was *not* Saltzberg's first ambition, however. As a child, he dreamed of being a musician in a rock band, like John Lennon of the Beatles. Even after his guitar teacher told him to take up a different instrument because he'd "never be a guitar player," Saltzberg persisted. He eventually mastered the instrument, becoming a singer and songwriter, too. He has recorded four albums for children, including *Crazy Hair Day* and *The Soccer Mom from Outer Space!* (based on books of the same title published by Candlewick Press and Crown Books, respectively). He has also written and produced songs for the PBS show *Arthur*.

Saltzberg studied art at Sonoma State College. His naive style was very different from that of his classmates, who had all been trained to draw realistically. When an instructor told him that he drew "like a child," Saltzberg wanted to "crawl under the table." It wasn't until later that he realized "being different is a good thing." He eventually took a class in children's book writing and illustration taught by author/illustrator Barbara Bottner at Otis-Parsons. While in Bottner's class, Saltzberg worked on *It Must Have Been the Wind*, published by HarperCollins in 1982. Since then, he has received numerous awards for his work, including the Parents' Choice Gold Award, Teachers' Choice Award for the Family, International Reading Association Children's Choice Award, iParenting Media Award, Virginia Young Readers Medal, and an Oppenheim Award. Saltzberg is now a teacher himself, offering a course in "Writing and Illustrating Picture Books for Children" at UCLA Extension in Los Angeles. He travels frequently to speak on creativity in universities, public libraries, and schools. Those travels have included trips to Russia and China as part of the United States State Department's cultural exchange program.

Saltzberg embarked on a 15-city tour to promote the release of *Redbird: Colors, Colors Everywhere* and *Redbird: Friends Come in Different Sizes*, the first two board books in a new series from Workman Publishing. Meanwhile, sales of *Beautiful Oops!*, originally published in 2010, continue to grow. In January 2015, Workman Publishing launched a "Celebrate Oops!" initiative via the website BeautifulOops.com, inviting teachers and librarians to commit to the initiative's resolution: "We celebrate mistakes in this classroom. Every oops is an opportunity to make something beautiful." Those who accept the invitation receive an Educators Guide and other materials to help them "Celebrate Oops!" with their students. Within weeks of the site's launch, teachers from around the world had posted images of their students' Beautiful Oops!-inspired projects on the website and on other social media—using the hashtags #BeautifulOops and #CelebrateOops.

For more information about *Beautiful Oops!* and Satlzberg's other books, visit BeautifulOops.com and barneysaltzberg. com. You can also find Saltzberg on Facebook and Twitter.

The central theme of *Beautiful Oops!*—that instead of being discouraged by our mistakes, we can embrace them as opportunities—is such an empowering idea, not only for children, but for adults, too. Has it always been your personal philosophy? Can you tell us how (and why) you came to turn the idea into a book?

I think I have always been inventive. My mother never bought coloring books. She bought pads of paper for me to fill with my own drawings. She always said, "Why would you want to color in other people's artwork?" I think that philosophy helped me to be creative from an early age.

Traveling around the world and showing images of my creative process, two pictures sparked requests from teachers, with the same request. "Can you teach how you fix your mistakes?" The first picture is a photo of an illustration I made that a dog stepped on. I thought I was going to have to throw the artwork out until I realized I could cover all the paw prints with clouds. The second image is of a sketchbook I had spilled coffee on. I turned the stain into the face of a coffee blob monster. After being asked to write a book dealing with fixing mistakes, I finally de-

cided to see what I could do. I didn't want a "story" about someone who did this. I really wanted a hands-on book which would be interactive. Let's "see" the oops and then with a page turn or lifted flap, we will see how the mistake becomes something beautiful. I tore a piece of paper halfway across and realized it looked like the mouth of an alligator. *Beautiful Oops!* was born!

Was the "Celebrate Oops!" initiative your idea, or did that come from your publisher? Are you surprised by the response it has received?

Peter H. Reynolds' book *The Dot* (Candlewick Press)—a book I love!—has an International Dot Day. I loved the idea and asked Peter if he would mind my making Oops! a movement. We decided one day wasn't enough! Peter gave me his blessings and I presented the idea to my publisher. I brought my daughter with me and they had a team

ready to brainstorm and fly. It's pretty spectacular to find a publisher who has the flexibility and resources to jump in like that. Especially with a book that was four years old when I pitched the idea. They have been amazing!

I have been completely floored by the mail I have received, the artwork I have seen, and the continual stories I hear from people who have read and shared *Beautiful Oops!*—countless tales about perfectionists and how my book helped them loosen up and to embrace the beauty in an oops. The book really models creative problem solving, but the concept of turning a perceived mistake into something beautiful goes beyond just making art.

You've said that, as a boy, you wanted to be a musician and play in a band. Did you try to make a go as a musician before becoming an author/illustrator? When and why did you decide to try writing/illustrating?

I was in my first band at the age of eight. I played music through college and came back to Los Angeles, where I grew up, just in time for Disco to hit. I recorded a lot of songs but never broke into the singer/songwriter market. I was working as a shoe leather salesman (taking over my father's business), when I decided to take an art class at night. The admissions person mentioned Barbara Bottner's picture book writing and illustration class. I don't know what possessed me to sign up, but I did. Somehow, the years of writing songs and my love of drawing fit in very well with creating picture books.

Has your songwriting experience influenced your book writing, or vice versa? How do you go about writing songs for the albums that are based on your books?

As I mentioned, I do think songwriting has helped me with book writing. That said, I can make a song rhyme, but it's a different art to write poetry. You can fudge a lot of the rhythm when you sing something, but it is a different animal when it comes to writing a book that rhymes. After years of attempting that, I have published a few rhyming books over the past few years.

I have written some songs to go along with books I have written. Unless the book rhymes and I "sing" the book, I use the book as a roadmap to give me direction in the lyrics. I view music to lyrics the same way I approach artwork to text. Music enhances the lyrics. Artwork illuminates the text. It's fun to demonstrate this with children. I can sing something with power chords and make a heavy metal sounding tune or I can switch to a slower, minor key ballad and make the same lyrics sound sad. It gets the point across and encourages taking chances and experimenting.

Reviewers have called your illustrations "sweetly childlike," "simple but expressive," "cheerful," and "whimsical." In *Andrew Drew and Drew* **(Abrams), the title character is**

a "doodle boy" who loves to draw. **Were you like Andrew as a child? Is that when you first began developing your illustration style, or is it something you've actively worked to acquire? Have you been inspired by any particular authors or illustrators?**

Andrew Drew and Drew is an open love letter to Crockett Johnson. His *Harold and the Purple Crayon* (HarperCollins) is one of picture book's holy grails to me. He was and continues to be a constant inspiration. Maurice Sendak, too. How can you not look to him for inspiration (and intimidation!) I was like Andrew as a child. I covered the brown paper bags my lunch came in with pencil drawings. I only wish I had a photo of one of those bags to see what they looked like. I filled countless blank books with drawings. (Those, I still have!)

Would you tell us how you sold your first book? How many books did you sell on your own? When did you get an agent? Is an agent a necessity in today's market? If so, any tips on how to find the right one?

Actually, my first picture book was taken to a New York editor by my teacher, Barbara Bottner, after she helped me make a book dummy. While I was in New York I had another dummy for a book of cartoons. I went to McGraw-Hill, which publishes educational books (but I didn't know that at the time). I saw that they were a publisher and asked a security guard where to go to get a book published. He said, "You don't do that." I said, "Well, if you did, what floor would you go to?" He told me the 36th floor and I got in the elevator. Ten minutes later, they bought my book. (That doesn't happen very often, if *ever*!) The book was called *Utter Nonsense*. After I had sold two books on my own, I asked around and met a few agents. I have had one ever since. I think an agent is incredibly necessary. To find one, you can do lots of homework online and by joining SCBWI.

How do you approach working on a new book? Do you start with the story first, or the pictures? How do you create characters that are both unique and that appeal to young children?

Every book starts differently. I don't have a formula. Sometimes I draw a character and I think it needs a story. Just an expression on a face and body language might suggest a direction I wasn't consciously thinking about until I looked at the drawing. Other times, I will write an entire story without drawing any characters. Once I add illustration to the equation, lots of editing takes place.

My goal is for my drawings to illuminate the text. I might add subplots in the visuals that don't ever get mentioned in the story. I did that for my Roaring Brook Press book with Neal Porter, *Tea with Grandpa*. I saw my father having a Skype conversation with his great-granddaughter and they were having a cup of tea together. It was the cutest thing ever. I wrote a rhyming poem to tell the story, but it became very clear to me from the start that I didn't want to give away the surprise ending that reveals these two are speaking via Skype. So, how do you make interesting spot drawings with someone speaking to another person, but without ever seeing them together? I couldn't sell the book at first. I realized the illustrations were void of the granddaughter and the grandfather having eye contact with another person, or interacting at all besides what I was describing. I decided the granddaughter should have a cat and the grandfather would have a dog. The entire feeling of the story changed with those two never-mentioned characters. And, for fun, anyone paying attention will notice the dog and cat are interested in the tea. Ultimately, at the end, we can see they are enjoying a cup as well.

Many of your books are interactive, with flaps, folds, cutouts, etc. Do these features involve special challenges for you as the creator, and/or for the publisher? Are interactive books harder to get published? Do libraries hesitate to purchase them, since the flaps and folds may make the books more fragile?

I never intentionally planned on creating interactive books. The one that really changed my feeling about interactive books is *Beautiful Oops!* I really wanted to create something that allowed the reader the opportunity to experience an element of surprise. We see a torn piece of paper (literally) and by turning the page, we see the tear has been turned into the mouth of an alligator. I wanted to show a few ways to play with a spill. I spilled juice and photographed it. Then, I made multiple copies and drew different things over each version of the same spill. This nicely unfolds with each spill solution revealing yet another flap, showing an entirely different approach to the same spill. I'm sure there are special shelves in libraries to make sure these books aren't torn apart.

You asked if making these books creates special challenges for me. I found that I "think with my hands." I can't always conceptualize a book like this without tearing paper and folding paper and seeing how things might work. I built my book, *Andrew Drew and Drew* while I was creating it. I love the challenge of seeing how I can surprise myself and ultimately, the reader, when the page reveal happens. Being a musician, the rhythm of the page turn is really important to me. I find having extra gatefold flaps allows for a different pacing of a story. I love having that flexibility. Publishers are much better about being open to creating the best book possible, so a flap here or there isn't too hard to get support for. This of course assumes that the flap adds something more than just a gimmick to a story.

How have you managed to be so prolific? Can you share any tips on how to generate ideas? How do you decide which ideas are worth pursuing?

I get asked these questions a lot. I realized recently that some people lift weights and get stronger muscles. I use my imagination every day and as corny as it sounds, I believe my imagination is getting stronger as I get older. I am in the zone a lot. Things I hear. Things I feel. Things I see. I drive my wife crazy when I say, "That would make a great book title!" I say that a lot. I'm always looking.

Wondering what ideas are worth pursing is a loaded question. I try not to think about that in the beginning. If I do that, I am already thinking about the commercial appeal of a book. That alters the way I proceed. I get a spark of an idea and if it tickles my fancy, I dive in. When it's done, I have a better sense if there's going to be a market for my work. There are no guarantees even a published story will find its audience. I vote for pursuing story lines that feel compelling to you as a writer and see where it takes you.

What is your workspace like? What is a typical workday for you? What are your favorite writing/illustrating tools?

I would love to tell you that I have a converted barn in Northern California and I look out my window at vineyards and cows. We live in Los Angeles and I work in a converted garage behind my house. It's a lovely space, but it's not a

INSIDE THIS BOOK (are three books).
by Barney Saltzberg

barn in the countryside. I have a wall of guitars, a wall where I hang illustrations I'm working on, my computer center, and my drawing table. I also have a table in the middle of the room where I sit with students that I mentor. It's a wonderful space.

Things have changed now that my children are grown. I used to drive them to school and get to work after I dropped them off. I would pick them up and take them to soccer or dance or wherever, and I would bring my work with me. I have been known to paint in the back of my old minivan when my kids were little. Now that it's just my wife and me, along with our three dogs, I walk the dogs in the morning and try to get to my studio by 8:30 or 9:00 a.m. I work most of the day, eating lunch while I work. Sometimes I take a fifteen minute nap, but the dogs want to eat by 4:30 and they are very vocal about it. I walk them after dinner and

either go back to work for a bit while I wait for my wife, or I call it a day. Sometimes I have deadlines or just inspiration which pulls me outside to the studio and I might work until midnight.

Whenever I stop working, I always think about whatever project I'm working on as I close my eyes and fall asleep. Sometimes that requires that I get up again and write something down, or record a little song, if I am working on music.

I find that the space between being awake and asleep is a delicious time to let my mind wander, in hopes of figuring out the next move for whatever I'm working on. The trick is, not to fall asleep before I write down what I'm thinking, or I won't remember what my idea was in the morning.

You travel a great deal promoting your books. How do you balance your visits and appearances with creative time?

Well, I am answering these questions as I type on my iPad, flying somewhere between Denver and Nashville after having given three short assemblies in the San Francisco bay area today. I will be in a different state each day of this week, promoting new books. It's a difficult balance. I only go out for short book tours a couple of times a year. Otherwise, it's a school visit or a keynote address, once in a while. I try not to travel that much because it takes days to prepare and days to unwind. I prefer to stay home and create. That said, I *love* interacting with students and teachers.

How did you become involved in the State Department's cultural exchange program? When you visit schools in foreign countries, do you notice any differences compared to schools in the United States?

I was invited by the State Department to travel to China and Russia. They found me. I thought they were kidding when they first called. Those were trips of a lifetime.

I definitely find that children are children, wherever I travel. In China, it was a little different because I found that using brainstorming techniques and playing with ideas was a really foreign concept to them. They aren't being taught to think outside of the box. The educational system there is much more formal than here. Now that I think of it, Russia was pretty formal as well.

The backflap for *Chengdu Could Not, Would Not Fall Asleep* (Disney-Hyperion) says the art was inspired by photographs your wife took while you were in China. The book also contains a note about the illustrations, which were created in pencil and watercolors and then composed using Photoshop. Can you explain that process? Why did you choose that approach?

My wife took a 48-hour trip to Chengdu to see the pandas while I was working. She told me the panda she photographed couldn't fall asleep and eventually climbed up and slept on top of another panda. I needed to give it a voice and a look. My amazing editor and art director, Kevin Lewis and Joann Hill, really were the catalysts for the look of this book. They really had a vision for this book. I had made pencil sketches and they wanted an even "toothier" look. It was suggested I work much smaller than the final size of the book. That way, when they blew up my artwork, it really created a line I never would have come up with on my own. Once we scanned the pencil sketches, the art department added a glow in Photoshop and I used Photoshop to add scratchy pencils lines to tie everything together. I love the way this book turned out.

How did you go about creating your first app, Nibbly's Nose, and your first digital picture book, *Would You Rather Be a Princess or a Dragon?* Are you planning to work on more apps and e-books? What do you think the future holds for printed books? Do you think publishing will shift more and more toward electronic formats?

I was very scared and intrigued when the iPad came out. I went to the first two digital book conferences in New York. I felt like a blacksmith putting horseshoes on a horse and seeing a car drive by. For now, things haven't changed as radically as I thought they would.

I thought it would be important for me to have a presence in the digital book world and had some friends create Nibbly's Nose and *Princess*. The problem I have had, I share with the large publishers. It's very hard to find these products in the iBookstore or on Amazon or the app store. Great ideas are buried in those places. A lovely company called Auryn made my book *Crazy Hair Day* (Candlewick Press) into a fantastic app. I don't think a lot of people know about it. That's been the experience for a lot of developers. There needs to be a way for people to find out about these products more easily before they will ever really grow to the level they are capable of. The good news is, I think picture books are here to stay for a very long time!

Can you tell us about your involvement with the PBS show *Arthur*? How did that come about? What did it entail?

I had sold a TV show to Disney with Laura Numeroff many years ago. Unfortunately, it was never made. We met a writer, Joe Fallon, who wrote for "Arthur," after our show fell apart. He needed an a cappella song about homework for Mr. Ratburn to sing. He asked if I would like to try it. I jumped at the chance. The song was used and then I wrote an episode, which I made about music, and then Joe asked me to write songs for an album. We wrote and produced ten songs and the last thing I did for them was to write a song for their Christmas special. I wrote a song called

"Baxter Day." I loved working on that show. I would *love* another one to come my way.

Two of your most recent books, *Redbird: Friends Come in Different Sizes* and *Redbird: Colors, Colors Everywhere*, are part of a series, as are many of your other books. Did you plan all your series books to be published that way at the outset, or did they evolve into series?

This series was created at the request of Workman Publishing. They asked me to create a character and write two concept books. My then editor, Raquel Jaramillo (of *Wonder* fame), picked a little red bird from *Beautiful Oops!* She suggested that be my character. She asked for a book about different sizes and I was completely frozen. There are so many concept books out there I honestly didn't know why we needed another one. One day, Raquel suggested I add friendship to my story. The book practically wrote itself from that point. "I have a tall friend. A taller friend, and an even taller friend than that. Hey, which one of you tall friends squished my favorite hat?"

For the color book, I thought about my mother. She was a bit indecisive. I was extolling the virtues of a color when I realized, well, yes, blue is lovely, but have you seen green? This is funny to me and ultimately Redbird has to pick a rainbow to cover all the bases. I was given a very short timeframe to illustrate these books. I wanted to keep

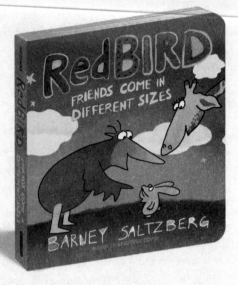

got exactly what I wanted, which is bright and bold and not too computer-generated looking.

You've been teaching writing and illustrating for a number of years. How has teaching influenced your own approach to creating? Do you have any general advice for beginning writer/illustrators?

I've taken a break from teaching formally. I do have my students that come to my studio on a regular basis. Either way, I need to be on my game to work with anyone else. The hard part about all of this is, stories are subjective. What you might love, I might not and vice-versa. My role is to help people find their voices. To make sure whatever story they are working on works.

Being able to tell me what a book idea is about in two sentences is very important. I call it the TV guide description. I should know what your book is about in two sentences. I follow that advice now when I write as well. It helps me and the people I work with zero in on what they are writing about.

the look my last few Workman books have had, with sloshed on acrylic paint, but I knew I wanted bold outlines since this was a book for little ones. I ended up painting sheet after sheet of sloshed colors and scanning them into the computer. I use a Wacom Cintiq monitor which allows me to draw on screen. I never made pencil sketches for this book. I created the drawings in Photoshop, and on other layers I dropped in my acrylic, hand painted colors. I

CARMELA MARTINO (carmelamartino.com) is a recovering perfectionist trying to embrace her own *Beautiful Oops!* moments. She has an MFA in Writing for Children and Young Adults from Vermont College. Her most recent credits include a humorous short story in the middle-grade anthology *I Fooled You: Ten Stories of Tricks, Jokes, and Switcheroos* edited by Johanna Hurwitz (Candlewick Press), and poems in several anthologies. In addition to writing stories and poems for children and teens, Carmela works as a freelance writer and writing teacher. She founded TeachingAuthors.com, a blog by six children's authors who are also writing teachers.

WILL HILLENBRAND

On his process, his inspiration, and how he writes a wordless picture book.

....

by Gloria G. Adams

If you ask award-winning illustrator/author Will Hillenbrand what the best compliment he ever received was, he'll tell you it was a hug from a child. Hillenbrand's love for children shines through his artwork and is the reason he connects so well with his young audience of loyal fans.

He grew up in Cincinnati, Ohio, where, as a boy, he began drawing pictures of the stories he overheard at his father's barbershop. He has contributed many wonderful illustrations and endearing stories to the world of picture books; his body of work, so far, contains more than 60 books. Hillenbrand not only illustrates his own books, but also illustrates the books of many well-known authors.

He travels extensively to elementary schools to read his books to children and show them how he creates his illustrations.

Children are quickly put at ease by his quiet manner. His enthusiasm for picture books, art, and reading is contagious.

Hillenbrand currently lives in Terrace Park, Ohio, with his wife, Jane, and their son, Ian.

What, for you, is the best part about being a children's picture book author/illustrator?

My audience of young people is the very, very, very best part of creating books. When I see the faces of young children who are engaged with books—my books—it delights my heart. To think that I might play a part with their becoming readers/thinkers is an additional benefit.

How (and when) did you break into the field?

Shortly after graduating from the Art Academy of Cincinnati in 1982, I began thinking about becoming a children's picture book illustrator. I began to devour as many picture books at the public library as I could. Other books were also available that instructed and guided my path regarding how to become a published children's book illustrator.

In all, it took me about five years to prepare my work to a level that I was happy with. I was working full-time, and all of my preparation time took place after I left work. Once my art portfolio was ready, I contacted publishers ... not just any publishers but those whom I had handpicked and that I felt published the very best work. I sent letters of introduction to them, following up with phone calls and scheduling trips to New York and Boston to meet with both editors and art directors. I was able to get a book contract from that very first visit.

For the first 20 years of my children's book publishing career I did not have a literary agent, although I do now. She helps with obtaining literary projects on my behalf and negotiates contract language and details with my publishers.

You use mixed media. Do you have a favorite medium?

I think my favorite medium is whatever allows me to show my audience the ideas I wish to convey in the most direct way. If I could only have one tool in my toolbox, it would be my pencil. Graphite pencil is a beautifully designed tool; it can convey so much with its directness, softness and subtleness. I love the way the pencil feels in my hand when I draw. I also love watch-ing a drawing appear right in front of my eyes. I often think of my pencil drawing as being a kind of promise. When I add color to the art and it is done successfully, I feel it has been a promise that has been kept. Currently, I am drawing on my iPad with Adobe Photoshop Sketch and my pencil is called Ink, also made by Adobe. I love the way my pencil line works using this application.

How long does it take you to finish illustrating a picture book for which you have written the text?

It is a difficult question because the books that I do are not formulaic. I hope that each is a new invention. Thus, whenever I am doing something new, I feel a bit like Thomas Edison may have when he invented the lightbulb. So many things are tried and tried again all in an effort to define the seemingly simple.

I have completed books in three months, five months, eight months, as well as a year or more. When setting up a schedule with the publisher, I try to predict when I'll be finished with the final art. I always try to meet that deadline.

Illustrating a book that I have written is a little different from doing one written by another author. When illustrating a book that I have written I can change things more fluently as I get further into making the book ... tightening it up as needed without asking my editor for permission.

Do you ever get to collaborate with authors whose manuscripts you've been assigned to illustrate?

No, never directly. I always work with my editor when I have any suggestion that may change the way the book was originally presented to me. It is the editor's/publisher's role to decide first of all if what I'd like to contribute has merit.

Tell me about your process, from the start of an idea until it is there on the page.

I start by reading and rereading and re-rereading the manuscript. I look into my mind's eye for the feel of the book-what is unique about the story, the setting, the characters and the pacing. I get to know the story intimately, personally. Then, I pick up my pencil and sketchpad and I play and play and play some more. Playing allows me to find the joy of the story.

Then, I make the book look like a duck, walk like a duck, swim like a duck, fly like a duck and quack like a duck, so to speak. That means creating the structure of the book—the book dummy. Words and pictures need to be placed on the page, pages need to be turned and read, and the drama of the page turned needs to be deployed. The sketches done for this are scanned into the computer and I figure out the shape of the book, whether it be horizontal or vertical.

The text also needs to be laid out in coordination with the illustrations-what is called the grid of the book. And I determine whether the pictures should be full bleed or spot.

Creating character sketches is very helpful. Other considerations include making decisions about how close up or far away and what angles best showcase the illustrations- bird's-eye views (viewing objects from above) or worm's eye views (viewing objects from below). Thinking about how close figures are to the picture plane is something I mull over as well as whether or not I have enough variety in and consistency with my pictures.

When the book dummy is completed, I submit it to my publisher. Once he or she has had enough time to review it, we schedule time to talk about it. This is an exciting time of a project.

After the conversation about the book dummy, I put my ducks in a row and if I'm lucky, my publisher gives me the okay to create the final art for the book. I never overlook this step, as it is an essential plateau, a kind of base camp that allows me to move to the final part of the project. If a good base

camp is not created, the summit will be unsuccessful.

At that point, it is time for me to fulfill the promise I made when I created the sketches. I need to create a colorful visual life in making the final artwork.

Your wordless picture book, *Snowman's Story*, is very popular. What are the challenges/joys of illustrating a wordless book?

I had a written story in the first several book dummies but with each revision more words were tossed out because the pictures were telling the story. Suddenly, I realized all the words were gone! Making a wordless book was different and challenging because of the obvious reasons. This kind of storytelling needs to be told in the most pure language, the international language of pictures.

What kind of editing goes into picture book illustrations after a manuscript is purchased by a publishing house?

In my experience, it is always a little different for each book. Editing is the most natural way to improve a book. I love the editors whom I work with; they are brilliant, kind and very knowledgeable about our work. They would never introduce making a visual change just for the sake of it. The level of respect I have for my editors is enormous. I'm fortunate to call them my friends.

Have you done other paintings and drawings besides illustrations for children's picture books? If not, would you like to and if so, what kind of work would you like to do?

Yes, I do drawings and paintings in addition to those for children's books. Those works are mostly gifts to family and friends. I also show new works every year at the gallery shows for the Greenacres Artists Guild in Cincinnati.

Please know that creating books for children has been, and will continue to be for me, the most satisfying of endeavors.

Do you have a favorite book that you have created?

Yes, I do. My favorite is always the book I'm currently making. To me it is the only one that exists. It demands and receives my full attention. After I am finished with that book, the next book becomes my new favorite! It is up to my audience to choose one of my books to be their favorite.

What was your inspiration for the Bear and Mole series?

That's easy—my inspiration was my relationship with my son, Ian. When he was little, my wife, Jane, and I read a book to him that he fell in love with, *The Mole Family Christmas* by Russell Hoban and Lillian Hoban. Ian loved that book so much that he role-played the boy character and the book. He started digging everywhere like a little mole.

A month or two later, Ian tried to wake me up early in the morning to play. He went to the foot of the bed, unfolded the tucked sheets, climbed underneath and tunneled, like a little mole, until he found my big fat toe which he then gave a gigantic tweak. That is what I call a mole alarm clock with no snooze button.

After making him breakfast that day we drove to his favorite playground where he played and played. Then he asked me to tell him a story. So, I thought about the main character being a little mole. I then said that the Mole had a best friend ... and Ian suggested a bear. I remembered what had happened between us that morning and with a little embellishment retold the morning's events, adding sound effects, including an enormous snore for the bear. Ian loved the story. Arriving home, I sketched out the story in my journal, just so I could remember

it. Many years later, I made it into the book *Spring Is Here!*

Has the world of digital illustration changed the way you create your books?

Yes, it has! I love using this new media although I love using the old media, too.

It has been more than a little bit challenging to learn how to use the new media but then that's true for all media. I have always been interested in presenting the best, most fresh and original art for my audience. Since I have mastered the digital tools, the benefit for my audience is that the book they hold and the art that they see is the first impression it has made on the page. That in fact, they are holding in their hands the original art the way I have intended it to be. That is so cool!

As an illustrator, how has your work evolved over the years?

My work as an illustrator and author continues to evolve. I always create images with all of the integrity that I have; as a creative person I allow myself to be open ... open and vulnerable and sensitive and strong but wanting to put my face to the wind and discover. Every creative person already knows this ... I have seen this in the art of children.

Something that has not changed but has become stronger is my devotion and love for my readers.

Why do you think children are drawn to your work?

Children may be drawn to my work because of my characters. I try to reflect to them what is both real and magical and kind.

Is there a particular book from your own childhood that still resonates with you?

Many books do but today I'll pick just one—*The Tale of Peter Rabbit* by Beatrix Potter. I love that story because my grandmother read it aloud to me ... and I love that she did.

What projects have you been working on and what's forthcoming?

I most recently completed *All for a Dime!*, the fourth book in the Bear and Mole series, as well as *Bear and Bunny* written by Daniel Pinkwater. It's the companion book to *Bear in Love*, which was published in 2012. Both books are due to be published in fall 2015. Currently I'm working on the artwork for *Me and Annie McPhee,* a fun story, which was written by Olivier Dunrea.

What advice can you offer aspiring children's book illustrators?

Learn all you can about this art form, read a ton of books for children, and pursue this calling with a burning passion. Nothing less will do.

Also, become a member of SCBWI. For a full list of things to consider, visit my website at willhillenbrand.com/aboutme.html and click on the yellow HELP! box.

GLORIA G. ADAMS spent most of her career as a children's librarian and is now a freelance writer living in Stow, Ohio. She has been published in several magazines, including *Turtle* and *Girlworks*, and has won prizes in children's and adult literary contests. Her picture book, *Ah-Choo!* (Sterling Publishing), written with co-author Lana Koehler, is due out March 1, 2016. Another book, *My Underpants Are Made From Plants* (co-author, Vera J. Hurst) is part of the Schoolwide, Inc. digital library. Gloria is a member of the Society of Children's Book Writers and Illustrators.

DEBUT DOS AND DON'TS

Advice from those who succeeded the first time.

....

by Lee Wind

As an author, illustrator, or author/illustrator, going from *aspiring* to *published* is a game-changer. So who better to help us hit that home-run when it's our turn at bat than four former Rookies of the Year who are well on their way to being inducted into the Kid Lit Hall of Fame?

Four different coaches, each with their own perspective. Get ready for training, because it's debut book season, and you've been drafted!

Your coaches:

Sara Zarr is the author of five novels for young adults, plus a sixth that she co-authored with Tara Altebrando. Zarr's 2008 debut, *Story of a Girl*, was a National Book Award Finalist, and she has twice won the Utah Book Award. Her latest book is *The Lucy Variations*. Check out her books and podcast series at sarazarr.com.

Don Tate is an illustrator, author, and author/illustrator. In all, he's worked on more than 30 published picture books. His debut as a picture book author, *It Jes' Happened: When Bill Traylor Started to Draw*, won a 2013 Ezra Jack Keats New Writer Award Honor and a Lee & Low Books New Voices Award Honor. His first authored and illustrated picture book is also his newest, *Poet: The Remarkable Story of George Moses Horton*. Find out more about Don and his work at dontate.com.

Grace Lin is an author and an illustrator of children's picture books, early readers, and middle grade novels. Her MG novel, *Where the Moun-*

tain Meets the Moon, was a 2010 Newbery Honor Book *and* a *New York Times* Bestseller. *Ling and Ting,* Grace's first early reader, received the Theodore Seuss Geisel Honor in 2011. Her latest title is *Starry River of the Sky.* Lin's website, with more info about her books (like how to make a bubblewrap Chinese firecracker), is at gracelin.com

Clare Vanderpool started to write her debut novel when her kids were one, three, five, and seven. Nine years later, *Moon Over Manifest* was published, and then it won the 2011 Newbery Medal. Her next novel, *Navigating Early*, was named a 2014 Printz Honor Book. Vanderpool's website is clarevanderpool.com.

Let's say your best friend's debut picture book/early reader/middle grade/young adult novel just sold. Yay! After joining them in a happy dance, they sit you down for some advice. To maximize the chances of their debut book being successful, what should they do right away?

ZARR: Celebrate! There can be so much anxiety in this business that sometimes we can forget to be happy. Through a combination of hard work and luck, you've reached a huge goal that you set for yourself. Take a moment to bask. Then, get back to writing something else. This is not quite the time to pour all your energy into building a "plat-

form" or "brand"—publication is probably at least a year away at this point—maybe two, maybe more. Do whatever kind of social networking you enjoy, but mostly get back to writing because this is going to be your last calm spell for a while.

TATE: Celebrate! The road to publication can be quite bumpy. But now is the time to pause and relish in this milestone. Break bread with friends and family at a special restaurant. Clink glasses of wine in a toast with your critique group. Or do a happy dance all alone in your favorite writing and/or illustrating space. Enjoy! But don't linger for too long. An offer for publication is not the end of this ride. It's only the beginning. You have a long way to go.

LIN: Debut books are wonderful because you will never have another first book again. That said, because it is a first book, almost inevitably, the release of it never meets the hoped expectations. For me, when my novel *Year of the Dog* released, I had already published many picture books and had already been jaded by the lack of fanfare concerning their release. So the first thing would be to readjust your expectations. It's unlikely your book will be a bestseller, get a movie deal, or a theme park. I'm not saying it doesn't happen, but if it does—let it be a surprise rather than something you anticipate.

The publication of a debut book is the first step in what we all hope is a long and storied career. Everything you do in terms of marketing and promotion is not really for your book, it's for the "long tail," for your next book and the book after that. I think many debut authors jump into promoting their book, thinking about the single title. It's definitely something to concentrate on, but, really, the more important thing is thinking about promoting your entire body of work, especially the books that are to come.

So, in my opinion, the first thing you need to do is make sure that you have your basic online author identity established. This consists of two important things:

1. A website, all about you as an author and your books, and hopefully more.

2. A mailing list/newsletter. Gather together all your contacts that you think would be interested and ask them if they would like to be on your mailing list. Sign up for a mailing list service like mailchimp or constant contact and put the sign-in on your website so readers can opt in. That way when your book comes out, you can contact them all to let them know!

For bonus points, I'd suggest getting familiar with the other social media platforms like Facebook, Twitter, Instagram, etc., and figure out which ones you like best. Choose one, maybe two of those platforms and start to participate in it as feels appropriate. I don't recommend doing all of them, no matter how tempting it seems. Social media can be a big time suck.

VANDERPOOL: Yes, that phone call is so exciting. Take time to enjoy the moment. Then take a deep breath because the ride is just beginning. Marketing is important but there is still

work to be done on the manuscript. Establish a good working relationship with your editor by listening carefully and collaborating from the initial editorial letter through copy-editing to make the best book possible.

In the months leading up to the release?

ZARR: Have some sort of website with your name on it, even if it's just a simple tumblr or the like. Use your real name as it will be on your book, not "catlady99" or whatever you've been using. Communicate with your publisher and agent. In a non-entitled way, ask what's going on as far as marketing and publicity and how you can help. Be pro-

active but don't go rogue. This is an important balance and it can take some fumbling to get right. You want to do what you can without stepping on toes or inadvertently working against your publisher's plans. Care (it's a book!), but have a sense of humor and some perspective (it's just a book).

You may start freaking out a tiny bit at this point. This is actually a good time to stay away from Goodreads and Amazon because you will always, always find another book in your season that is getting more buzz, better positioning, has what you think is a better cover, a higher rating or ranking, foreign sales, movie rights, etc. If this is only going to stress and distract you, turn it off. Your agent and/or editor will let you know when there's something important to share.

Some authors put a lot of energy into urging folks to pre-order, and that can

work well for them. Think about booksellers and where you'll be most happy to funnel your readers' money and go from there with a pre-order strategy.

This can also be a busy time of saying yes to any and every little invite that comes along, whether it's for a blog interview or a local conference or a school visit. Go for it. This is a season of "yes." You'll learn from it what you enjoy doing and what you hate, and then have some experience from which to work when a season of "no" comes along. Support your peers who are going through the same stresses as you. Be a champion of books you love so that you don't become completely obsessed with your own book.

If you find yourself going off the deep end, remember it's just a book. It won't be the worst book ever published, and it won't be the best. It will be somewhere in between. Remain calm. Take good care of yourself. Keep writing.

TATE: If you haven't already, establish a web presence. This might seem obvious, but I've known some well-established authors and illustrators who have not taken this important step, for whatever reason. Nowadays, children's book authors and illustrators are expected to connect with their readers through social networking. In addition, teachers, librarians, booksellers—and potentially an editor or art director in your future—will want to look you up online. Don't disappoint, invest in a

website. Create a Facebook page, Twitter, Instagram, other.

When my first authored book, *It Jes' Happened* debuted from Lee & Low in 2012, everyone within my social networking circles and beyond already knew about the book because social networking had become my megaphone. I blasted the news of my book and its positive reviews to the world.

Also, months ahead of your book's publication date, start planning a book launch celebration. Set a date, pick a venue (indie book store, maybe), establish a budget. Enlist author and illustrator friends to help you plan and carry out the big event. *It Jes' Happened* is the story of an outsider artist who created pictures with colored pencils and paint. At the launch celebration, we had drawing and painting stations set up for children to create art like Bill Traylor. In addition, be sure that your local bookstores, especially the independents, have advance reader copies (ARCs) of your book.

LIN: Write your next book! Make it your goal to have a rough draft before your book's publication, before reviews of your first book come in, before you get sales figures. Not only is this better for you as a writer, this is better for you as an author. *Your absolute best promotion is publishing another book.*

That said, I know you probably want more concrete suggestions about your upcoming book. So while you are taking a break from writing your second book, consider doing the following:

1. Play around on the one or two social platforms you've decided on and try to make friends and a community. Don't get down on yourself if you don't, though. I'm the first one to admit that I find it all kinds of difficult. Just do the best you can.

2. Here's the open secret about children's book authors. Most of them make more of their living from visiting schools and talking about their books than actually the books themselves. Have you heard about how musicians make all their money touring, not by selling songs? It's the same with children's authors.

So, if you are looking for a long-term career, school visits will probably be an important part of it. During these months, start looking around and see if there are any authors presenting at your local schools. Ask the school if you can sit in on the author's presentation and see how he/she presents. Observe more than one author's presentation and think about how you can create your own.

3. Decide if you want to have a book birthday celebration (I recommend it but not for reasons you probably think—see below) and, if you do, start planning.

VANDERPOOL: In the months leading up to the release, you can work on creating a website that will give readers a window into the book as well as your life as a writer. It's fun perusing other websites to get ideas and then to really create something that reflects your personality and interests.

On their book birthday?

ZARR: Celebrate! Once again, it's time to be happy and proud. Think ahead of time what you want to do to make it a good day. You may enjoy hanging out on Twitter all day and watching the love multiply. Or you may rather unplug everything and go on a hike. This is your day, do what makes you happy. One of my favorite things to do on publication day is go out to breakfast with a good friend and eat bacon. You've probably been beating the drum about your book for the week or two leading up to publication and you can take the day off if you want. Or, if you prefer, you can talk about it all day with impunity!

TATE: There's no such thing as a Book Birthday Fairy, though the thought of one seems kind of cool. You know, someone who'd deliver flowers and cake on the day your book is born, and then nurse the newborn to good health. But that's your job,

newbie author or illustrator. Make the day special for you and your book—again, celebrate!

Getting a book published had been a longtime dream of mine. So when my first illustrated book published in 2000, *Say Hey: A Song of Willie Mays* (Hyperion), I rounded up my wife and daughter and dragged them to the bookstore. Thankfully the book was stocked there on publication day. My teenage daughter was so proud that she waved the book in the air, announcing to everyone within earshot that her dad was the illustrator. That was a dream come true, but again, that was back in 2000. Nowadays, believe it or not, many books won't show up in bookstores—not on their book birthday or ever. That can be a huge shocker if your expectations were otherwise.

On your book birthday, plan to make a lot of noise! Do a blog tour where you discuss your book on blogs over the course of a few days or a week. Chat up your book on social networks, and invite your friends to help you to spread the word.

LIN: Celebrate!

I am a big believer in book birthday parties. If you can, throw a big one, but don't do the math. Don't think that for all the time or money you put in, you're going to get x amount of sales back. Think of it as a party for your mom's 80th or a wedding—you're doing it out of love. Have a party for the love of your book, for the love of your readers. Invite everyone you know; have book-themed treats and prizes. You wrote and published a book. That is deserving of a celebration!

And if your guests have a great time, every person will tell two or three people about it—an added bonus that will have a ripple effect on your book.

VANDERPOOL: Have a book launch at a local bookstore!

For the first three months of the book being out in the world?

ZARR: Once the initial hype of the ARC [advanced review copy] season and publication is over, it can be easy to neglect your book. By now you're probably sick of yourself. Nonetheless, this is no time to lose energy. Keep your website up to date with the latest review quotes, and post them on social media. You will be surprised to find that after six months of this, there will still be people you know who say, "I didn't know your book was out!" And you'll be like: "*It's literally all I've talked about.*" When you have news, don't be shy about sharing it. You'll continue to pick up readers and momentum. (If you use social media a lot, just make sure your book isn't literally all you talk about. Sometimes people would rather know what you had for lunch or what you thought of the latest episode of "Scandal.")

Meanwhile, you are still writing, still championing books and causes and people you care about, still taking care of yourself.

TATE: Getting the word out about your book is critical, especially in the first few months. Young readers, librarians, booksellers, love getting their hands on new books. Some will even promote your book on their social networks and blogs. It's your job along with your publisher to let these folks know about your book.

Some publishers will support your book with well-funded marketing campaigns. They'll also get your books in the hands of influential librarians, book reviewers, trade journals ... They'll put you on the road to promote your book to librarians and booksellers at conferences. Other publishers will not. In that instance, you will be mostly on your own to spread the news. Know early on where you fall in that marketing conversation so that you can plan accordingly. Who are the marketing contacts at your publishing house? Be sure to give them a list of potential media outlets where review copies can be sent. When *It Jes' Happened* first published, I contacted a very influential librarian at a review journal and asked if she'd consider writing a blog post about my book. I began to worry about my request, thinking it was out of protocol or unethical. The reviewer reassured me that asking was indeed a good thing, even if a review could not be promised. She did write a very nice review, however, which published well in advance of any other industry review. It helped set a positive tone for future buzz.

LIN: Revise your second book. If it's ready, send it to your agent/publisher. Be happy whenever someone tells you they read and loved your already published book. Try not to obsessively check your Amazon rankings. Craft a school visit program.

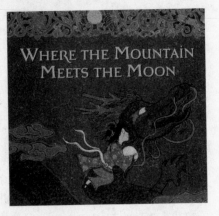

VANDERPOOL: Getting the word out is important. Send out information to schools around your area to generate interest in author visits. It's really fun when those first milestones begin to happen—getting invited to speak at a school, signing books, doing interviews, answering your first fan letter.

In the first year of the book's publication life?

ZARR: As above, share news when you have it. Find fresh ways to talk about the book every now and again, but really the book belongs to the world now and you're probably ready to move on.

TATE: Your book is your creative offspring. No one will care about your baby like you do. So as the year moves on and other books come out, you must continue to champion your book in more creative ways. Seek out opportunities to promote it at book festivals, which will mean working with your publisher to see that copies get into the hands of festival organizers. Don't take it for granted that your publisher will do this automatically. Seek out paid school and public library visits, where you can get your book in front of more students. Write an article for a professional organization where you can talk up your books. Pitch a proposal to present at a conference. Since the focus of my career has been on diverse books, I've participated at festivals on diversity panels or discussions about diversity. This has allowed me to cheer the works of other authors and illustrators of color but, no doubt, also talk about my own books. Find your niche.

LIN: Keep working on that second book. If you're ready, start the third. Try out your school visit program. Ask a local school, a scout troop, a mother-daughter reading club—any group that you think would be appropriate—if you can come in and present. Think about how to make it better, improve. When you think it's finally good enough, start offering school visits on your website. Say yes to as many offers as you can. After the first few freebies, start charging for your visits. Make sure you value yourself for what you are worth.

VANDERPOOL: Promotion can be challenging and even uncomfortable. It can feel like you're tooting your own horn. I think it's helpful to look at it more as promoting *the book*. Your characters need help for their voices to be heard.

How about reviews? Should your friend read them? Respond to them? Ask all their other friends, their mother, and their child's kindergarten teacher to post five-star reviews online?

ZARR: No. No to all of those questions! Except: Yes, read trade reviews. Most of those will come right around the book's release and provide you with snappy quotes around which you can strategically place ellipses and put on your website. Do not read reviews on sites like Amazon and Goodreads. That's my advice, anyway, though some disagree with me. I just think, well, the book is out and there's nothing you can do about it anyway. Some people won't like your book. Let it go.

TATE: I should probably suggest that authors and illustrators never read reviews of their own books. But that won't happen. You won't be able to resist reading reviews—you'll be drawn to them like a paperclip to a magnet. In fact you may even resort to creating Google Alerts of your book titles so you'll never miss a review. So I suggest that authors and illustrators do read their reviews—or at least some of them. Just remember that your book is a work of art and everyone will not

like what you've created in its entirety, or at all. And some reviewers will just plain be mean depending upon what kind of mood they are in that day, or if their breakfast agreed with them or not. What I try to remember is that my editor and I carefully considered what to include in our book. We considered the story arc. We weighed the weight of every single word, every single illustration, everything—over and over again over the course of many years. So just because someone thinks we should have done something differently does not make them right.

Given that, I would advise against responding to negative reviews. I did that once online and I felt awful afterwards—it could not be erased. Occasionally I'll see an author on Goodreads, for instance, arguing with a reviewer about negative comments or one-starred reviews. Don't go there, it's just not becoming of a book creator. Learn what you can from negative reviews, and be thankful for the positive comments. The worse thing is when no one is talking about your book at all.

LIN: It's pretty impossible not to read your reviews, but try to remember that once the book is published it is not yours anymore. The book, the story now belongs to the reader and they are allowed to think whatever they want about it (even if they are wrong). *Never* respond to a bad review. Possibly respond to a good one, but tread lightly—it's OK if, say, the reviewer tweets you and says "I loved your book, this is my review!" but I'd hesitate about a review you just stumble upon. Anything you do can be construed as you trying to take back ownership of the story. By publishing your book, it is a gift to the reader. They may love it. They may hate it. But it is now theirs and you can't take it back.

Me, personally, I don't ask anyone, friends or family, to post five starred-reviews online because I want an honest gauge of what people think of my book, no matter how painful. I try to read the negative reviews with an open heart and mind (which is hard to do, I admit) and see if what it says can help me improve my next book. Remember, everything is about making your next book better.

Whenever I get demoralized, I try to remember that the worst thing to happen to a book is not to be disliked, but to be ignored.

P.S.: Best free advice: Stay away from Goodreads! You will get such conflicting reviews—from adoration to detestation—that it's not particularly helpful but almost always depressing.

VANDERPOOL: It's a personal choice whether to read reviews or not. I would say go ahead. But it's OK to filter them a bit. And remember, by the time the reviews are coming out, you're hopefully already well into your next project. So again, the focus is all about the story you're working on. Take a peek and then get back to work!

Let's talk book tours. If your friend's publisher isn't going to send them on one, should they crowd-fund or figure out another creative way to send themselves on their own book tour? Does it make a real difference, or is it more about author ego in wanting to have those one-on-one connections with readers?

ZARR: I've been lucky enough to be sent on a few book tours and I will say this: Yes, it is good for the ego on the surface (nothing sounds cooler than telling your friends you're going on a book tour), but it can also be very rough on the ego in reality. Even for some of my most popular writer friends, it can look like awkward evenings with three people occupying the thirty chairs that have been set up at stores, or talking to a classroom full of students who neither know nor care who you are. That said, the times when you do make a connection with a reader or potential reader or bookseller or teacher or librarian can be extremely special and keep you going when you're feeling discouraged. For most writers, there's not a ton of evidence that tours have a big impact on sales so I would not freak out if you don't get a tour. They are expensive for publishers and you might rather they spend that money on ads, more ARCs, or sending you to conferences down the line. I did not go on a tour for my first book. I would not crowd-fund a tour. I think every writer has a certain amount of capital with her readers and that should be valued. I don't think crowd-funding a tour is the best use of the capital.

TATE: In all honesty, I don't have much experience with book tours, at least not an official publisher-sponsored book tour. I could offer many reasons as to why not, but hey, why screw with my own ego, right? I would love it if one of my publishers sent me on a book tour, flying me from city to city, bookstore to bookstore, signing books and taking selfies with my readers. That would be so much fun! But what would it accomplish in terms of sales and raising awareness of my book? And could we reach the same goals in other less expensive ways? Maybe.

That said, I've done several minitours myself. It usually involves reaching out to independent bookstores to arrange sales and signings while speaking at schools. Sometimes these minitours are connected to a conference where I will speak.

As a winner of the 2014 SCBWI Launch Grant, I was given $2,000 to use for marketing my first authored and illustrated book, *Poet: The Remarkable Story of George Moses Horton* (Peachtree Publishers, 2015). I've discussed ideas for launching the book with my marketing department, which will include a book tour. I will pay for the tour myself (my publisher is supporting me in many other ways), but my publisher is fully on board, arranging tour venues and dates. The money

will cover my travel and hotel accommodations, in addition to any publicity needed.

LIN: Well, I don't think it's egotistical to want to have those one-on-one connections. Creating in a vacuum is hard. Knowing versus believing that your work is actually in the living, breathing world is important soul food.

That said, I think the time needed for a debut book tour is time better spent on writing your next book. Unless you have a specific niche that you know can be counted on to come out for you (for example, you wrote a book about basset hounds and you target each basset hound-lover group in the U.S. and tour where the groups are the largest and most rabid); it's probably unlikely to be worth the time and effort. And it could possibly be demoralizing. When I did bookstore events early on, I was mainly just asked where the bathroom was.

VANDERPOOL: Book tours are great ways to create excitement and awareness of the book. Any way that an author can make connections with readers is important. Ideally, this can be done on a local level without a great deal of expense. Bookstores and schools would be a great way to connect with young readers. Authors can also team up to do a group event, which adds to the energy and excitement.

Marketing and promotion are becoming more and more DIY. What's the thing you did with your debut (or for subsequent books) that had the biggest return on your investment of time and money and effort? What's something you tried that didn't work out? What's the one thing your friend should ask their publisher for?

ZARR: I can't take any credit for this because it wasn't strategic so much as happenstance, but I think what helped me a lot was that I'd been blogging since 2000 or so. My book sold in 2005, and came out in 2007. So by the time it came out I had seven years worth of relationships with writers and readers of YA. I realize this sounds like a contradiction to what I said earlier about not spending too much time on building a platform or brand. But I never thought of it as "building a brand;" I was just doing something I enjoyed and being myself. I guess my brand is "being me" and that is probably everyone's most powerful tool. (Being you, not being me. One of me is plenty.)

One thing I tried with my fourth book was going on a group tour with some women who wrote in different genres than me. That was something I did on my own dime. I had a ton of fun, but it didn't have the desired result of connecting with a new audience. I realized that the audience on this tour was more about various fandoms than anything, and were probably never going to be my readers. I may have picked up a few but not enough to make the financial investment payoff. And that

was a moment I went "off-brand" as far as "being me."

TATE: With my debut as an author, my publisher did a fantastic job of getting review copies of *It Jes' Happened* into all of the right hands. The book was widely reviewed. It made many end-of-year lists. To top it off, it received the Ezra Jack Keats New Writer Honor award. So hats off to my publisher, they did many things right. But there was no budget for promoting the book beyond any of that. As far as conferences and other public events, yes, it was DIY for me. I did a few things on my own that I am really happy about and proud of.

R. Gregory Christie, the illustrator for *It Jes' Happened*, and I conducted a book talk and signing together at the High Museum of Art in Atlanta, Georgia, where Bill Traylor's artwork was on display. We worked with the museum to publicize the event. On that day, we offered a guided tour of the museum and discussed Traylor's artwork. Afterwards we signed books. The museum covered our overnight stay and handled all of the publicity. It was nicely attended—on Mother's Day even! In addition to being a publicity trip, I did some research for another book in progress, at the Martin Luther King Jr. National Historic Site. (Try to lump trips together, promotion and research.)

Later the next year, I hired Kirsten Cappy of Curious City, a book marketing and projects firm. She planned and coordinated an arts event at the American Folk Art Museum in New York City. Families were invited out to hear Greg and I give a brief reading and talk, and then children created pictograph journals. It was not a hugely attended event, but it was a memorable experience. I would do it again in a heartbeat.

While your publisher may not be able to support events like this, communicate with your publisher's marketing department. They can support your efforts through their blogs and social networks. And be sure to take lots of photographs and do a writeup about the event. Our event in NYC was written up in *Publishers Weekly*!

LIN: Look at your book and figure out how the marketing department is going to label it. I'm the first person to say that the labels are ridiculous, that there's no such thing as a "boy" book, etc., but the reality is the book is going to get a label no matter what. So think about what label that is going to be.

My best investment on promotion was probably for *Where the Mountain Meets the Moon* and *Starry River of the Sky*. For those books, I hired a consultant (Kirsten Cappy, Curious City) to create fun educational activities that schools and book clubs could use with my books. They've been a great resource for schools that want to prepare for a visit with me or for groups planning to read my books. While I don't know if it sells more books in terms

of hard numbers, it definitely gets the kids more excited about reading my books and that only makes them more dedicated fans.

Things that didn't work out? When you ask too much of your readers. Right now, I actually have a "write your own story and share it" promotion going on with my *Ling & Ting: Twice as Silly* book—where I ask kids to write a story and share it with me via a video. It was a fun idea and it's still ongoing but the response has been tepid. I kind of suspected it wouldn't be that successful as it is a lot to ask people to do, but I wanted to try it as an experiment. So learn from me—if you do a promotion, keep it simple and easy.

What would I tell my friend to ask the publisher for? It depends on what kind of book he/she wrote but, in general, I would suggest asking them to make some sort of teacher's guide or reading supplement that people can download. If the publisher can't do it, consider hiring someone to do it for you.

VANDERPOOL: Probably the most helpful thing I've been able to do is be accessible. I rarely turn down an invitation to talk to students or teachers about writing and stories. And I answer all my fan mail. That personal contact is rewarding in ways that go beyond book sales.

Speed round: Worth it or not worth it? Swag (buttons, erasers, stickers, temporary tattoos, bookmarks, postcards, other)?

ZARR: Meh on swag generally, except I think postcards can be great *if* you actually mail them to people in a thoughtful and targeted way.

TATE: Sure. Swag is always nice. They serve as fun mementoes as well as publicity. At a launch party for *It Jes' Happened*, I handed out art supplies to the children, which included a tiny box of colored pencils. I covered the pencil box with an image of the book cover. One event organizer created pencils with my book's name printed on the side. Made for great swag to hand out at future events.

LIN: If you can afford it, yes. Make sure you give a bunch to your publisher to give out at conferences. But if it makes your finances tight, don't sweat it.

Book plates you can mail?

ZARR: You should always have some on hand.

TATE: *Meh*. This can get tedious and time consuming. If you have time and really want to then, yes, I say go for it. Certainly can't hurt. But remember that somewhere between the launch events and swag and book plates, you need to make time for writing or illustrating your next book.

LIN: Sure. They are pretty inexpensive, easy to do, and everyone loves a signed book.

Teacher's guide?

ZARR: I hate teacher's guides! But they may be worth it.

TATE: Totally. Teacher Activity Guides increase the value of your books and offer teachers and librarians more of a justification to use your book in the classroom. Guides are not overly expensive; I offer them as free downloads for most of the books on my website. Be sure to hire a professional educator, though. Some people think they can create their own guide, and if you are a writer and a graphic artist you probably can. But guides that are in alignment with the needs of teachers—Common Core and State Standards—are more valuable in the classroom. If my publisher does not have a guide made, I hire educators to write and create them for me. My guides are Common Core aligned for English and Language Arts, which are now required by many teachers. For my next book, *Poet*, my debut as both an author and illustrator, I've hired a Texas poetry teacher to write a guide for me. He is familiar with the Texas Educational Agency's Texas Essential Knowledge and Skills requirements.

LIN: Yes. This might be where you part with a bit of money.

Blog tour?

ZARR: Can be worth it, as long as there's not so much overlap in the blogs' readerships that you're just shouting into an echo chamber.

TATE: Yes, make as much noise as possible! Although, I have not done a blog tour myself.

LIN: Doesn't hurt, but not a big deal if you don't. They take up a lot of time that might be better spent writing.

Book trailer?

ZARR: I've never done one. I like watching the ones readers do.

TATE: I love them, but they're not for everyone or every book. For *It Jes' Happened*, I created my own book trailer and 30-second teaser. I used Greg's art and downloaded royalty-free music. I put it all together in iMovie. Many students now create book trailers, so maybe you can have a student make one for you.

LIN: Doesn't hurt, but they have to be really good (no ten-minute pan and scans of each spread of your book) to stand out. A bad book trailer is not worth it. However, spending a huge amount of money on a good book trailer isn't worth it either. If you can't do it yourself well or coerce a talented family member, don't sweat it.

VANDERPOOL: All of the above can be helpful, but there is the old saying – All Things in Moderation. For me, it's important to remember that my time is best spent actually writing. So do any and all of the above as long as it doesn't become a full-time job and leave little time for writing.

Book Two is famously challenging, maybe more so when a debut—like yours—is widely acclaimed. If everything goes right and your friend's debut is a hit, what are you going to tell them about writing and/or illustrating their sophomore effort?

ZARR: Get it done. Just get it done. The sooner, the better. Best-case scenario is you get it done in that first year after you sell book one, before ARCs for it even go out. Sometimes that's not possible, in which case you really need to find a way to turn off the noise about book one. Stay away from Amazon and Goodreads, turn off your alerts and notifications, and for the love of God, don't Google yourself.

You may find yourself curled in a ball on the kitchen floor, crying in the shower, or calling your agent every other day to gently suggest they kill your contract. This is normal. Keep writing.

TATE: True, with book number two I had a mental hurdle to deal with. But you have two choices: 1) Allow success to boost your confidence; 2) Allow success to tear down your confidence. You choose.

LIN: Start writing it before book one comes out and remember, you can only do your best.

VANDERPOOL: I had a wonderful editor give me some great advice. She said it doesn't matter what accomplishments you've had in previous books. When writing a new book, it's all about falling in love with those new characters, listening to their voices, and telling their story. As tempting as it may be to ride the wave of success, it's important to get back to that quiet space to listen, to ponder, to write.

Any final do/don't advice for that debut author/illustrator friend—who's really a stand-in for our readers?

ZARR: Do find a way to keep loving books and reading. Being in the publishing industry can sometimes douse the flames of your original passion. Find something that you enjoy doing for you, that isn't about marketing or anything else. I started hosting a podcast where I get to talk to other writers, not as a way to keep my brand going but because I enjoy it.

Don't get bitter. Like I said, there will always, *always*—no matter how amazing your books do—be authors who seem to be doing better, getting more. If you get caught up in the parts that feel like a popularity contest, you'll spend a lot of time being unhappy. Just because we're writing about high school doesn't mean we have to relive it in our careers.

TATE: Try not to listen to the hype. *It Jes' Happened* published to three wonderful starred reviews, and the accolades marched on throughout the year. I didn't pay much attention to the hype at first, but by the end of the year, the book started to receive awards buzz. That's when I started to pay attention. Seemed like everyone was talking about my book winning one of the big awards. On the weekend before the big

awards were announced, someone offered advice to me about what I should do if I received the infamous call. After that, I totally swallowed the hype, every last nugget of it. So did my publisher, I learned later. I was (we were) crushed when that didn't happen. But I also learned some very important lessons: Stay humble; stay focused; don't worry about awards.

LIN: Well, my debut picturebook, *The Ugly Vegetables* was published in 1999 and my debut novel, *The Year of the Dog* was published in 2006. So needless to say, quite a bit has changed since then! However, even though a lot has changed (the advent of social media marketing) a lot has stayed the same (the importance of school and library markets). I suspect that many debut authors will be inundated with "building your platform" advice telling them to tweet, make book trailers, etc. and I am not discounting any of those things. What I am discounting (which you don't have to listen to, it's just my opinion) is the importance of all of those things. The blog tours, the book videos, the tweets—none of those things hurt your book, and can very well help it and you should do them if you want to and you have the time and resources to. But they are not the most important thing.

As you can see from my above answers, what I think is the most important thing to do (after you've established the basics like an author website) is to *write your next book*. People forget. They can forget why they loved your book so much and why they want your next one. Don't let them.

VANDERPOOL: My best advice would be to enjoy each stage of the process. But always be clear on which trumps all the rest. The writing comes first. Enjoy the book tours and author visits and interviews. But be clear that without a good story to promote, the rest will fall short.

LEE WIND (leewind.com) is a blogger and writer. His award-winning blog, "I'm Here. I'm Queer. What the Hell Do I Read?" covers LGBTQ teen books, culture and politics, and has had more than 1.25 million visits from teen readers and their allies. He is also the official blogger for the Society of Children's Book Writers and Illustrators (scbwi.blogspot.com) and the Captain of SCBWI Team Blog. Lee writes fiction (picture books, middle grade, and young adult) as well as nonfiction, and is represented by Danielle Smith at Red Fox Literary.

YOU'RE AN ILLUSTRATOR —NOW WHAT?

Tips and advice for new illustrators.

by Jodell Sadler

When we think about illustration work, we don't always think about how social media benefits us. Here's a few artists who have landed some pretty nice gigs through a variety of media channels, including how beta testing an app turned into a few TigerCreate awards and a trip to the Bologna Book Fair, how adding a quick Dot.com signature to a fun art piece as leave behind led to a great opportunity, and how a sketchbook filled with conference notes lead to a book series in a new style. Plus, these illustrators also share a few tips to illustrators just starting in:

JOSH ALVES

Online New App to Tiger Create Awards to the Bologna Book Fair

While preparing a presentation on creating interactive books, I came across TigerCreate, fell in love with their creator tool, and learned about their competition. I wanted to enter, so I pulled from my "Idea Jar," brainstormed a story that would use interactivity to complement the story, and a book about a surprise party was born.

A few weeks after entering, I learned that *Surprise!* was selected as the winner in every category, one category being "Kid's Favorite." A group of German primary students reviewed the entries and placed a sticker next to their favorite on a chart, and nearly all the stickers were on my book.

How Twitter led to Zeke Meek's 14-book series

As a marketing manager, I use social media to manage brand identity, and it includes search tools that send me Twitter alerts. A while back, I searched terms like "looking for an illustrator" and "looking for an artist" and came to a tweet that read: "Looking for an illustrator for a hilarious new chapter series." I expressed interest and provided a link to my portfolio. A couple weeks

later, I noticed the art director tweeted that she was so excited to find the illustrator and that the editor agreed! I replied, "Great! Please keep my info on file for future projects," and she replied with something like, "We're talking about you! I'm e-mailing you now!" This led to Zeke Meeks books, which turned into a 14-book series!

What advice do you have for illustrators looking to break in?

Make art. Make more art. Then put it in places where people can see it. You never know who might come across it.

What might illustrators do to activate the power of social media?

While I'm still trying to figure it out, social media connects people. It's easy to find a "tribe," or people who are pursuing similar goals. So, find those people, learn from them, and learn together.

What new projects are you working on?

I'm working on a draft of a chapter book featuring an elementary super sleuth. I'm also fleshing out a wordless concept, which places two odd characters in an exciting adventure.

For more about Alves, visit him online at joshalves.com.

RUTH MCNALLY BARSHAW

From Sketchbook to Yahoo Group to the Ellie McDoodle series

In October 2004 I heard in an SCBWI email group that my idol, Tomie dePaola, was appearing at a nearby bookstore. I met him and showed him my art. He urged me to come to the national SCBWI conference in New York. I'd been studying the industry for two years without a paycheck. My travel partner backed out, I borrowed money and had no hotel room until I was rescued by some illustrator friends. I filled a sketchbook with my adventures in New York. I left the conference educated but dismayed. I'd been hoping to get "discovered" there.

I came home, put my entire 180-page New York sketchbook on my website, and sent the link to two kidlit groups in Yahoo Groups, and it went viral. People connected to my journey, and a few insisted I create a children's book in that journal style. I did—and an agent found me. She'd been directed to my online sketchbook by a writer I didn't even know.

Within a few weeks, I had a 128-page,

fully illustrated manuscript and an agent. My book, *Ellie McDoodle: Have Pen, Will Travel*, sold quickly to Bloomsbury. In 2007, with *Diary of a Wimpy Kid*, my book helped start a new genre. But I wouldn't have pursued it if not for those online friends.

What advice do you have for illustrators looking to break in?

Create a website. It can be as simple as a blog site. Post art on it often, only your best work. Send postcards of art samples to editors and art directors. Study the market in depth so you know what works and why. Cultivate online friendships—we all share resources.

What might illustrators do to activate the power of social media?

Promote and support other writers and illustrators. Show off your best art. Others will help promote it for you.

What new projects are you working on?

As I finish the watercolor paintings for my first picture book, *Leopold*, written by Denise Brennan-Nelson for Sleeping Bear Press (September 2015), I'm excited to work on some picture books I've written on various topics: babies, music, trucks, otters, a zoo, and mice siblings. It's thrilling to see these ideas come to life in words and art.

What would you like children's lit professionals to know?

It's a small industry. People talk. Be careful what you say. Never complain on social media and always be kind and fair. There's often more to the story than what you've read.

For more about Barshaw, visit her at ruth express.com.

DREW BLOM

From Twitter to Illustration Project

Last year I was contacted via a direct message on Twitter from someone I follow to do some art. After a dozen direct messages, a phone call, and a meeting, I started working on a job that was pretty significant on my freelance books—all because I had a conversation with this person on Twitter.

I know it doesn't always work like this. Sometimes it is a job posting that someone you follow links to. Other times there is a call for submissions from an art director or editor on Twitter. So it pays to watch.

What advice do you have for illustrators looking to break in?

It's important to know your style. If you're looking to get into children's books, there are classic stories in the public domain. Pick one, illustrate a few spreads, and move a character from scene to scene. Since people are familiar with these stories, it's easy to evaluate your efforts.

What might illustrators do to activate the power of social media?

Participate in the conversations. Your portfolio should be accessible should an art director want to look you up. Social media is great for sharing tips, works in progress, or even links to helpful resources. Your social media feed should be full of personality (yours) and some thoughtfully curated links and tips.

What new projects are you working on?

Right now, I am venturing into interactive storytelling and sharing a story of a boy who lies his way into a dangerous expedition to recover a lost robot, but discovers a conspiracy that threatens the world. I'm creating illustrations to go along with a parallax scrolling mechanism as a Web app.

What would you like children's lit professionals to know?

The two spaces to watch right now are apps and indie. With funding models like Kickstarter and Indiegogo illustrators have to be open to the idea that "traditional" publishing is changing.

For more on Blom, visit drewblom.com.

LAURIE J. EDWARDS

From Facebook to Illustrator Match-Up

I took Mark Mitchell's "How to Be a Children's Book Illustrator" class online and participated in his "Illustrators' Match-Up Service." A picture book app company, ustyme, contacted Mark and requested to see student portfolios. They liked mine and offered me a job illustrating *The Teeny-Tiny Woman*. I'll be starting a second picture book app for them soon. I also was also offered two other jobs as a result of that Facebook service. I've had several people contact me after viewing my portfolio on the SCBWI site. So the majority of my recent illustration jobs have come through online contacts.

What advice do you have for illustrators looking to break in?

One of the best ways to get jobs is through social networking. Join the SCBWI and get connected to the illustration world, send out postcards, and host a website featuring your artwork. Be sure to practice your craft and get critiqued so you improve as an artist.

What might illustrators do to activate the power of social media?

Stay active on social media and join online groups of illustrators. Most share resources, contests, and job leads. Many groups offer critiques of work. Follow art directors on Twitter. Consider taking online classes to improve your skills and make connections.

What new projects are you working on?

I just finished illustrating *The Teeny-Tiny Woman* for ustyme and have three other picture book illustration jobs contracted. I'm working on a dummy for one of my own picture books as well. I'm an author, editing three books of my own books and a freelance editor as

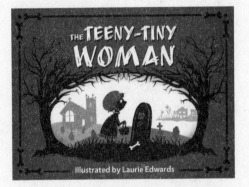

well, so I have editing jobs to complete.

What would you like children's lit professionals to know?

Have fun. Do the work because you enjoy it. Stay true to yourself. Develop your own style and remember what Scott Adams says, "Creativity is allowing yourself to make mistakes. Art is knowing which ones to keep."

For more about Edwards, visit: lauriej edwards.strikingly.com.

GREG MATUSIC

Matusic.com Signature to Museum Project

In mid-February 2014, I visited the Berkshire Museum in Pittsfield, Mass. and came to one section that offered drawing boards, paper, pencils, crayons, etc., and a few still-life exhibits. While I assumed this was for kids that never stopped me before, so I grabbed some paper and the drawing pens I cart around and drew a quick lineup of kids cheering for the Berkshire Museum, then added a "matusic.com" at the bottom, and it hung on the wall next to the terrific art created by people one-fifth my age and size.

A few days later, I received a Facebook friend request from the executive director of the Berkshire, who posted a photo of my cheering kids on Facebook. And by late fall, I was asked to illustrate an If/Then exhibit, which included a wall were visitors could hang art created at the museum. Who knew what a quick drawing and an added URL would take me.

What advice do you have for illustrators looking to break in?

Draw. Constantly. Then draw more. It will only help you get better. Also, share your work on your website and through social media. You never know who's going to see it.

What might illustrators do to activate the power of social media?

In general, be active. Post your work often. Once a day isn't too much. That will also force you to constantly create new pieces. I guarantee you'll see your work get better and better, and so will your audience. Join Facebook groups that align with your interests or weekly Tweet Chats where you can search hashtags like #kidlitart and follow/contribute to on-going discussions.

What new projects are you working on?

I'm creating portfolio pieces for SCBWI conferences and tweaking a couple of picture book dummies that I have high hopes for.

What would you like children's lit professionals to know?

Amazing podcasts answer questions about the illustration profession and industry. Do a search on iTunes for these, attend conferences, and learn your craft. Network with industry decision makers to meet your peers and illustration heroes. Aspiring children's book illustrators should also consider attending an ICON [The Illustration Conference] conference.

For more on Matusic, visit matusic.com.

STEPHANIE OLIVIERI

From Facebook to Illustration Leads

When social media came out, it was like, "Wow, I can just post on my wall that I am looking for work." After one of these posts, a friend messaged me saying that they knew someone who was looking for an artist to illustrate a children's book. I e-mailed and got my first children's book illustration job. In fact, I have gotten 99% of the jobs I have had in the last nine years from posting on social media.

Facebook connects illustrators to tons of people and has benefited my career in many ways. I can't emphasize enough the importance of social media sites like Twitter, Facebook, Tumblr, Blogger, Wordpress, Google +, Pinterest, LinkedIn, Stage 32, and Instagram. I also host portfolios on several sites: childrensillustrators.com, SCBWI, the Society of Illustrators Los Angeles (SILA), and Behance.

What advice do you have for illustrators looking to break in?

Practice, draw every day, and don't compare yourself to others. Learn

from them. Join the SCBWI—get involved, go to schmoozes, workshops, conferences, and build a website using your name as the URL on Wix, Weebly, Squarespace; these are great places to consider.

What might illustrators do to activate the power of social media?

Be active on social media and share your work. Be positive in every post and join conversations on pages, group pages, and friend pages, etc.

What new projects are you working on?

I am working on a great greeting card illustration job, revising a YA, and outlining a new story while waiting for the next children's book I am contracted to start soon.

What would you like children's lit professionals to know?

You can do it. It's a lot of work, but working in children's lit is so rewarding. There is nothing better than seeing a kid light up at one of my drawings, or a teen having an emotional reaction to something I wrote. It's the best job on the planet.

For more on Olivieri, visit stepholivieri.com.

SHAWNA JC TENNEY

Social Media to Game Illustrator to Picture Book Author-Illustrator

I have gotten several illustration jobs that link to me being active on social media. While I also send postcards to art directors, I also get jobs from people that say they found me on the Internet. There are so many ways to get your art out into the world on your own and be seen by social media outlets. Recently, CrossCut Games found me online and contracted me to create some of the artwork, including all the characters, for a game called *Wizards of the Wild* to be published by CrossCut Games, and partially funded on Kickstarter, as seen online at crosscutgames.com.

What advice do you have for illustrators looking to break in?

Don't worry if you don't get your dream job to begin with, or even for the first 10 years. Every job you get is a learning process that will take you to the next step. Enjoy the process and learn a lot along the way. Be patient, work hard, and eventually you will get where you need to be if you are persistent. My art got so much better when I decided to draw what I loved, and people started to notice.

What might illustrators do to activate the power of social media?

Social media gets your work seen by publishing professionals. Posting a picture on Facebook, Instagram, Twitter, or Tumblr will get the most attention. I hear art directors say all the time that they follow an artist's blogs. So, spend your social media time wisely. Use a program like Hootsuite and post to all social media channels at once and share cool stuff. You'll start to make some great connections!

What new projects are you working on?

Right now, I am finishing my picture book *Brunhilda's Backwards Day*, which will be published by Sky Pony Press in 2016, and really enjoying working on my own stories!

For more about Tenney, visit shawnajc tenney.com.

ILLUSTRATOR BIOS:

JOSH ALVES discovered his illustration style by mixing a love of comics (Calvin & Hobbes, The Far Side, Spider-Man) with the humor (Abbot & Costello, Dick Van Dyke, Jerry Lewis), and a pinch of pondering (C.S. Lewis, Timothy Keller) along with other odds and ends. As a husband, dad of four, graphic designer, cartooning illustrator, he spends most days doodling all sorts of fun in his studio (a.k.a. "Drawing Closet") in central Maine.

RUTH McNALLY BARSHAW wrote and illustrated The Ellie McDoodle Diaries (six books, Bloomsbury, 2007–2014). She lives with her writer husband in Michigan.

DREW BLOM is an illustrator and graphic designer instructor in Minneapolis. He's done graphic novels, children's books and character design for animation, and is also working on a couple of his own properties as well: *Calvin Hedge and the Iron Golem*, and a webcomic called *The Super-Human Resources Department*.

LAURIE J. EDWARDS, is an editor, illustrator, and author with 20 books in print or forthcoming. Some of her recent titles include *The Teeny-Tiny Woman* (ustyme, March 2015), the Wanted series writing as Erin Johnson (Switch Press, 2014-2017), *Imperial China*, *West African Kingdoms*, and *Ancient Egypt* (Cengage, 2015), *Cyber Self-Defense Manual* (Rowman & Littlefield, 2014), and a story in the YA anthology *Love & Profanity* (Capstone, 2015).

GREG MATUSIC is an Albany, NY-based illustrator and cartoonist. He routinely attends local and regional conferences, rubbing elbows with publishers, editors, art directors and especially fellow writers and illustrators. He also enjoys decaf coffee, The Clash and baseball.

STEPHANIE OLIVIERI is an illustrator and writer specializing in the children's market. She started her art career in traditional animation. She has illustrated for trade and educational markets, and continues to write MG/YA by night. Her background includes film, television and graphic novels. She's a creative consultant who loves to help writers and artists reach their dreams.

SHAWNA JC TENNEY graduated with a Bachelor of Fine Arts degree in Illustration from Brigham Young University in 2004, and has enjoyed a career as a freelance illustrator ever since. She has created artwork for many books, magazines, and games. Shawna writes picture books, and her first book, *Brunhilda's Backwards Day*, will be published by Sky Pony Press in 2016.

JODELL SADLER is the founder of Sadler Children's Literary (sadlercreativeliterary.com) as well as the author of several books on picture book writing.

DREW DAYWALT

On the art of writing and illustrating, tenacity, and connecting with your audience.

....

by Kara Gebhart Uhl

Drew Daywalt, author of *The New York Times* bestselling picture book *The Day the Crayons Quit*, graduated from Emerson College with a BFA in creative writing, and a double concentration in screenwriting and children's lit.

"It's funny, at Emerson, Newbery Award-winning Jack Gantos was my faculty advisor and favorite professor, and he always wanted me to go right into children's lit," Daywalt says. "He was my Obi Wan. Only back then, he hadn't become Newbery Award winner, he was just 'Jack, who was awesome.' I took his class a number of times, because it was creative writing and I could create new things in each semester. I loved kidlit, but back then I wanted to go off and be Quentin Tarantino, not Dr. Seuss.

"Jack was like, 'Drew, go to New York and write for kids. You have what it takes.' And I was all like, 'Jack I want to write mov-

ies! I want to be an auteur.' I laugh now at my younger, oh-so-serious self.

"I didn't listen to Jack (at that time) and off I went to Hollywood, broke, hopeful, and with a crappy compact car packed full of everything I owned. It took years to break in, but I eventually wrote and directed features and TV."

For the last 20+ years, Daywalt has focused on screenwriting, working as a writer and director in Hollywood.

"I wrote for Disney and DiC animation on shows like 'The Wacky World of Tex Avery,' 'Buzz Lightyear of Star Command,' 'Timon & Pumbaa,' and even 'Woody Woodpecker' for Universal," Daywalt says. "I've done features as well. My writing and directing debut was actually with A Band Apart, Quentin Tarrantino's company, on an indie cult film called 'Stark Raving Mad.' I also wrote for Brett Ratner, Tony Scott, Jerry Bruckheimer, and even did a zombie movie for George Romero and Tom Savini."

Here we talk with Daywalt about his switch from Hollywood screenwriter to

bestselling picture book author, as well as his venturing into illustrating. While his life work thus far has been diverse, it's still connected.

"As a writer, I've kind of done everything, but it all has one thread running through it, and that is I've always written selfishly, pursuing only the subjects and ideas that I really truly loved," Daywalt says.

How did your childhood impact your creative pursuits?

My childhood is everything, in regard to my creative pursuits. I knew I wanted to tell stories right from the beginning. I loved world building. My first experience with a world builder was Dr. Seuss. He had this amazing continuity of style and vision that was wholly singular, and simultaneously unique and other-worldly. I loved that. And in movies, I loved Star Wars because, like Seuss, Lucas created a place that I really wanted to go. And even at like, 7 years old, I knew I wanted to build worlds like that. As a kid, I did it with action figures and by drawing pictures all the time. Eventually, that grew into creative writing.

What inspired you to turn your attention to children's lit? Was The Day the Crayons Quit the first book you wrote? What inspired its particular birth?

My first feature, "Stark Raving Mad" went straight to video in 2002 and it broke my heart. Here was my first directorial and writing debut and no one responded at the studios, even though I had people like Tony Scott and Lawrence Bender championing it. It was a serious bummer in my life. At the time, I'd had a successful run in cartoons for kids, and my first foray into features didn't pan out at all. I was frustrated with screenwriting and decided to listen to Jack Gantos from 10 years earlier. I decided to sit down and write a picture book about crayons. I had a box of them on my desk, even as an adult, and I thought, *Man, if these things could only talk*. And bang, a book was born. Of course, it took six years to get purchased, and another three to be illustrated and published, but that's another story.

Please talk a little bit about your writing process and habits, and how your history with screenwriting has impacted your children's lit work.

Before I had kids, I wrote constantly, mercilessly, sacrificing a lot of other activities just to spend time writing. Since I'm a dad now, and I actually love my kids and want to be involved, my writing productivity is way down, but my dad productivity is way up, and that's how it should be. I'd rather be known as a good dad than a good writer. I love writing, but not as much as I love my kids. Oh, and there's that famous Dorothy Parker quote, "I hate writing, but I love having written." Every time I hear that I want to put a fork in her eye. My response to that is, "Well then quit writing and go do something you like! Life is too short, and there are plenty of writers who are excellent at what they do and actually love doing it. Get out of their way." I hate the whole tortured artist bullshit. I love what I do. I love writing screenplays, and I love writing for kids. I guess going through the gristmill of Hollywood screenwriting before going into kidlit tempered me. It made me tougher, edgier, and way more open to collaboration than I would have if I had gone straight into prose. I'm not sensitive. I have creative thoughts and ideas constantly, so if someone doesn't like one, no problem, let's move on. I'll make more. Like Doritos. Crunch all you want.

Michael Green at Philomel purchased *The Day the Crayons Quit* in 2009, and paired you up with illustrator Oliver Jeffers. Tell me about that day, receiving that news.

I can be such an idiot. I came into kidlit from Hollywood, so I didn't know the names, the players, the publishers, nothing. I just wanted to write creative-

ly and tell stories. I got a call from my agent at that time, Jeff Dwyer, and he gave me this great news that Philomel was publishing and that I'd been paired with Oliver Jeffers. I had no idea who either was, so I was like, "Oh that's nice. I hope the book does well." I didn't realize that, translated into movie language, that phone call was the equivalent of your agent saying "Legendary Pictures is producing for Warner Bros., and David Fincher is directing." I later realized what it all meant and just how fortunate I had been to enter picture books the way I did.

You're currently represented by Steven Malk at Writers House, but he wasn't your first agent, correct? Tell me about the querying process you went through, your first agent and the road that led you to where you are today.

Steven is one of my heroes, and a good friend. I signed with him last year. Did you know that if you cut him open, picture books fall out? Don't cut him open though. Just trust me on this one. He knows picture books like no one I've ever met. In the beginning, though, back in 2003 before I knew anyone in the business, I sent out query letters to a few kidlit agents and Jeff Dwyer responded. It was a great phone call. I love Jeff and we've since become dear friends. On that day he said he loved my writing, thought I was a natural (and I'm quoting here) "... and since you clearly know how to dot your *i's* and cross your *t's*, kid, I'll represent you." I loved that. And Jeff was so hardcore and persistent that he submitted and resubmitted *Crayons* to the publishers for six years. Six years! My rejection log is insane. It looks like a phonebook. But he believed in me and made it happen.

Your debut picture book has been a No. 1 *New York Times* bestseller, and winner of many awards including the 2014 Children's Choice Book of the Year for Kindergarten to Second Grade, winner of the 2014 E. B. White Read Aloud Award for Picture Books, and the 2015 Texas Bluebonnet Award for Best Picture Book. As such, I imagine you have found yourself quickly and deeply immersed in the world of children's lit. How does this world differ from that of screenwriting and directing? Are the road maps the same or has navigating it been a unique experience?

My ship has turned direction and is firmly plotted in the waters of kidlit now. How cheesy is that comparison? But seriously, I love the way children listen when you're reading your book to them. I get kids. And strangely, they get me. I never imagined that my arrested state of development would become my career, but I guess it always has been, only now it's more literally. I find publishing far more honest and straightforward than the movie business. No business is perfect, but I admire the passion that people have in publishing—passion to create something wonderful for children. It doesn't get any better than that to me.

Universal Pictures announced its preemptive acquisition of the film rights to *The Day the Crayons Quit*; Matt Lopez is slated to write the script and Madhouse Entertainment will produce, correct? How much involvement will you have with the movie, and given your background will sharing creative control be difficult?

In the beginning, Madhouse actually asked me if I wanted to write the screenplay for the movie and it was funny. I said, "absolutely not." I have had such an amazing personal and professional renaissance with this book that I didn't want to taint it in any way. I could totally foresee getting notes one day from some executive somewhere saying that I didn't understand the characters or the world, or what have you, and getting fired off the job. It's Hollywood and that happens every day. I didn't want to mix the two worlds. I'll have a little creative say in the film, but this is mostly their baby. The book is mine. The movie is theirs, and I like that arrangement.

Tell me about *The Day the Crayons Came Home*, which was released in August 2015 by Philomel Books. Did you always have this book in mind or was it a natural follow-up to the success of *The Day the Crayons Quit*? Did the writing process differ at all?

Actually, neither Oliver nor I planned to do a sequel. I thought it was a one-off kind of thing. So did Philomel. But then in the fall of 2013 I had an idea that really excited me, so I called everyone up and they loved it too. While *Crayons* was about conflict resolution and color study, with the universal backdrop of "how we all colored when we were kids," I decided that *Crayons 2* would be about acceptance and homecoming, with the universal backdrop of "all those crayons we lost, melted and broke when we were kids." I wanted to take a strong, important theme and apply it to something light hearted and funny and most importantly, relatable. Yes, they're just crayons, but they're also anyone who feels lost, marginalized or misunderstood. So when Duncan makes it all right in the second book, it feels even warmer than the first time. Even more from the heart. We get to dig a little deeper in

book 2, and that's been what everyone responded to.

As far as writing process, it's been a blast. In the first book, it was a typical writer never meets illustrator kind of deal, but in the second book, Oliver and I worked very closely with each other and with Michael Green, who's an incredible editor. Oliver would send me ideas he'd written, I'd send him concept sketches and he'd improve on them. It was really entertaining to intertwine and blur the lines between writer and illustrator in that way.

You've started illustrating, posting fantastic work on Facebook, and yet you seem humbled and surprised by the accolades. Clearly, though, you are an artist. What has this learning process been like for you and what inspired it?

Aw shucks … You're so nice. As a boy, I drew constantly. And in the beginning, before I knew I had a way with words, I thought for sure that I'd be an artist. My oldest brother Charlie Daywalt was a fine artist, and an incredibly talented one. He tutored me and taught me a lot, but he was also viciously critical sometimes, so much so, that by the age of like 12 or so, I gave up drawing altogether because I'd never be the artist that he was. He passed away, years ago, and only now am I returning to drawing at all, and even today, it's with an awful sense of dread that I show anyone my work. I still hear my brother calling my work "trifles and doodles, with no social relevance or importance whatsoever" and I'm attempting to get past that, so that maybe some day I can illustrate my own book. It's a personal journey that's spilling over into my professional life. And the irony is beautiful, because in this world, I'm always meeting illustrators who talk about the agony of writing. For me, it's the opposite. I can write all day long, but ask me to draw a giraffe and I'll lose sleep for two days. Stupid giraffes with their hard-to-draw heads.

Tell me about your Lost Dog and Lost Cat projects, and the importance of engaging your fans and readers, both virtually and in real life.

I saw a documentary on Banksy recently. And in it, he stayed in New York City for 30 days and created street art each day, then posted it online for people to go find it, in a sort of scavenger hunt. It fascinated me. And right now, as I'm trying to build up my own confidence as an illustrator, I thought it would be fun to do something similar, only in a kidlit fashion. I was also inspired by local "lost pet" fliers that you see around every neighborhood. So my plan was to do one lost pet a week, only I'll draw it instead of using an animal photo, and in the bottom, where fliers normally give a description and details on how to contact the owner, I decided to write little creative pieces. For instance, on the lost dog flier, I wrote, "This is my dog. He is lost. He answers to the name of Keith, even though his name is Rog-

er. I don't understand him. He's such a confusing dog."

So I'm including a little piece of art and a little piece of writing. I only print 50 or less copies, I sign and number them, and I am posting them all around different cities across America, one set per week. If you find one, just take it home. It's art, and it's free. All I ask in return is that you snap a pic and post it on twitter or Facebook and tag me or let me know. I wasn't sure how the project would go, but my first run, LOST DOG, created a fun time for a lot of people as they drove to my neighborhood to look for the fliers. I have since had great runs in Brooklyn (LOST CAT) and Manhattan (LOST GIRAFFE). I'll do 52 animals or objects, one a week, for a year. It puts art and literature in the spotlight and it involves the kidlit community.

Earlier this week a woman stopped me at my local cafe and asked if I was Drew Daywalt. When I told her yes, she informed me that she thought so, and that her son had one of my Lost Dog fliers in a plastic sleeve on his wall in his room. I was elated. That's exactly what I wanted from this project—kids chasing art and literature the way they chase video games, movies and sports.

What advice do you have for those writing and pitching picture books?

My advice for people writing picture books is the same for all writers. Write to entertain yourself. Don't dumb it down for your audience, in this case, kids. If you're dumbing things down for kids, then you've obviously never met any. Also don't sweat all the rules and regulations about what to write, what kids like, what kids don't like, all that bullshit. Just write for yourself. Entertain your inner child. Seriously. And let that be your only guide. It's a very selfish way to work, but it's the only honest way to work, too.

Rejection: What has been your experience with it and what advice do you have for hopeful authors/illustrators how are currently feeling the sting of it?

I had six years of rejections before *Crayons* sold and became a critical and financial success for all involved. If you believe in yourself and what you're writing, keep at it. I know it's a cliché, but it's so true. Just keep going. Being a writer is a long-term atrophy game. As others quit, and you hang in there, your chances grow better and better, but you have to have something worthwhile to say. Something personal. Something you believe in with all your heart.

In terms of future work do you have hopes to illustrate your next picture book? If so, how has that or will that change the creative process, in terms of conception, layout, process, etc.?

I won't illustrate my own books for a while yet, but that is the eventual goal. Like writing, illustrating is a long-term thing and you have to be in it for the long game. I think when that day comes that I'm illustrating as well as writing, I will still very likely write it first, then "bring myself on" to illustrate. I work with words and sentences so easily that it's my stronger muscle set. So I'll start there and branch outward to illustrate the characters and storyline. In the meantime though I love working with illustrators and editors as a team. I've always been collaborative, and a life in Hollywood prior to publishing has cemented that trait in me forever. I stopped being precious about my writing years ago, and it was the best thing that ever happened to me.

KARA GEBHART UHL, formerly a managing editor at *Writer's Digest* magazine, now freelance writes and edits in Fort Thomas, KY. She also blogs about parenting at pleiadesbee.com. Her essays have appeared on *The Huffington Post*, *The New York Times*' Motherlode and *TIME: Health-land*. Her parenting essay, "Apologies to the Parents I Judged Four Years Ago" was named one of *TIME*'s "Top 10 Opinions of 2012."

DAN SANTAT

On illustrating someone else's work, working in black & white, and creating for TV.

....

by Lee Wind

Dan Santat graduated with honors from the Art Center College of Design in Pasadena, California. Since then he's been busy, creating the Disney animated hit, "The Replacements," and illustrating both chapter books and picture books that other authors have written (more than twenty of them!). In 2010, he was awarded the Silver Medal from the Society of Illustrators for *Oh No! (Or How My Science Project Destroyed the World)* by Mac Barnett.

Did we say busy? Santat has also authored and illustrated his own graphic novel, *Sidekicks*, and his own picture books, the latest of which, *The Adventures of Beekle: The Unimaginary Friend*, just won him the 2015 Caldecott Medal for "the artist of the most distinguished American picture book for children" of the past year.

You can learn lots more about Santat (and check out his color and black & white portfolios) at his website, dansantat.tumblr.com

We caught up with Santat just a few weeks after he won the Caldecott Medal, and found out how he mixes technology and traditional illustration, the possibilities he sees in endpapers, his creative process, the tools illustrators have for expressing emotion, and of course, the day the Association for Library Service to Children, a division of the American Library Association, called.

You just found out that *The Adventures of Beekle: The Unimaginary Friend* won the 2015 Caldecott Medal for the best illustrated children's book of the year—congratulations! What was getting that call like?

Thank you. Getting a call like that is wonderful. I didn't know how to react because I never thought I would ever receive such an award. I never even imagined what it would be like to get a call like that because in some weird way it would feel like I felt I deserved it and feeling that way feels arrogant, if that makes any sense. When they told me I won the medal, I was filled with such a rush of emotion that I just started crying.

The art in *The Adventures of Beekle* is beautiful, and in the back you explain, "The illustrations for this book were done in pencil, crayon, watercolor, ink, and Adobe Photoshop." How do you integrate working by hand and by computer?

A lot of the traditional media I use is for textural purposes. I scan in whole sheets of watercolor washes and pencil sketches, etc. and I build a library of textures on my computer. On the computer I mask off parts of those texture layers and reveal only the parts that I need. It's sort of like collaging but without the use of scissors and using a digital paintbrush instead.

You also chose to hand-letter the text. With so many fonts out there in the world, can you talk about that choice?

I feel that integrating text with art is important for the balance of the book's aesthetic as a whole. My art is distinctly my own style, and my handwriting is also distinctly my own. You want to integrate the text and illustrations together so that it feels seamless. In *Beekle*, the writing and art feel like they belong together because it's done by the same hand. I wanted the book to feel like it was made by a child and the handwriting helped push it into that direction.

One illustration in particular struck me: It's of Beekle high in a tree with seven children around him, but none of them see Beekle. You've used so many colors to depict the different skin tones of the children, and it made me wonder, what's your take on the power illustrators have to depict diversity in their work?

I think it's important for people to be aware of it, but not to a point that it's an issue that makes it stand out, like it's a lesson that needs to be learned. Kids don't have that sort of bias. It's the adults around them who make them aware of certain differences and then indicate if those qualities are favorable or unfavorable based on their own opinions. If you present things in a way that seems natural then they simply perceive things as just they way they are. What I love about New York (where the setting of *Beekle* feels like) is that it's so densely populated that you could be shoved into a subway with over a dozen cultures and no one bats an eye. It's just the way it is. Making diversity feel like a lesson that needs to be learned, I think, adds pressure to the situation. A pressure that never would have existed if it were never brought up in the first place. Why is there a diverse group of kids climbing a tree? I don't know, as far as I'm concerned, they are just kids climbing a tree.

Looking at the body of your work, I'm struck by how every aspect of each book is customized. The endpapers

for *Oh No! (Or How My Science Project Destroyed The World)* written by Mac Barnett is a great example; the front endpapers are the blueprints for the main character's "Robot Unit Series—01" and the back endpapers are blueprints for the "Growth Ray Device—02." It's like you're keeping us in the world of that story for just a little bit longer. Does that vision come right away, or is it something that evolves over the course of doing the interior illustrations?

It depends. Sometimes I have a clear idea of what I want all the components of a book to be and other times I may have to sit and think about it for a bit and it's not until I'm fully immersed in a book where I finally figure it out. The endpapers, to me, are four pages of real estate that I can use to help further develop the story. The hardcover edi-tion of *Beekle* has endpapers whereas the paperback does not. The front pres-ents a page full of children with their imaginary friends, but Beekle is alone because he hasn't found his friend yet. You want to know what his purpose is. In the back endpapers Beekle is hold-ing up the book he made with Alice, his child. You went through a whole ad-venture and now we've completed the endpapers which, in turn, have told a story in itself. The book has a complete-ly different feel when the endpapers are removed, because I think they present the perfect opening sentence and end-ing without saying a word.

With *Oh No!* you see the robot blue-prints and you think, *Whoa. What are we getting ourselves into?*, while the back endpapers are like a final inside joke saying, *Hey, remember that growth ray from the story? Well, here's more infor-mation about it.*

A lot of people maintain that an au-thor/illustrator image should be brand-ed (and consistent) across platforms and works, but another element that you seem to customize for each book is your author photo. From your child-hood photo (with your own imaginary friend inked in next to you) for *The Ad-ventures of Beekle* to your adult self dressed up in a superhero sidekick outfit for your graphic novel, *Sidekicks*, tell us about your reasoning for chang-ing it up for each project. Oh, and nice cape, by the way.

I think my brand is my ability to diversify. You should want to treat your work as if you need to find the perfect solution to a problem, otherwise you end up trying to solve all problems with the same approach. If you are known for just doing funny dragon books then you're only going to get funny dragon book projects and so forth. Be a problem solver and brand yourself as such so that you can be someone who can be counted on to solve problems. My author photos are all part of that problem solving. If I make a superhero book, then my author photo will reflect that. I also appreciate the fact that people have come to expect something special from my author photos.

With your plate full of so many different projects in different categories and genres, how do you manage your time and workflow?

As long as I know when my due date is on a project then I budget my schedule according to what needs to be done to hit that date. For example, if I have to draw 100 illustrations for a chapter book that's due in 30 days then I know I have to draw about five finishes a day. (I try not to work on weekends and I usually dedicate my evenings to family once they get home.) I treat every day like you would for any regular job and so I always put in at least eight hours of work a day during the week (sometimes more if I have to). One of my art teachers once told me, "Why would you be willing to kill yourself working for a company in order to make them rich when you could be devoting all that time building your own career?"

Can you walk us through the process of illustrating a picture book with someone else's text?

I'll get a manuscript and read it over once. If it's a script that sort of interests me then I'll think about it for a couple of days. I'll let my brain soak in it and I basically make a loose dummy book in my head before I draw a single image. I think about the mood and tone I want it to be and then if I like what I see in my head then I agree to the project even before I draw anything. The sketch phase is actually the most important part of the book for me. That's when I figure out the pacing for page turns and type breaks. I don't take co-

one sentence. If the concept is good then I feel the rest of the story falls into place much easier. I'll write a draft of the manuscript for my editor, but there is a lot of things they don't see in my mind that the manuscript doesn't convey. I just want them to get the basic idea and I usually have to explain to them that they'll get a better understanding once I make the dummy book. When I illustrate I actually try to express as much of the story as I can in images to the point where you almost debate if it should be a wordless book. Then from there I can edit out those things in the text. If a girl is jump roping in a scene, then I'll draw that, but then I'm free to remove it from the text. It becomes redundant. Once I've drawn out the entire book I then rewrite the manuscript to say things that you don't see in the images. In other words, I let the pictures tell the superficial part of the story, but the words say something much deeper and more meaningful than what you see without being repetitive.

pious notes or sample various styles. I draw what I draw and then mold it around like clay until I come to a style that just evolves. I try to illustrate as much of the book as I can with a major emphasis on how my decisions effect the story such as page turns, or how I frame a particular scene. I'm actually thinking more about the story than I am about the style of it all. Story comes first. It's imperative that the narrative be crystal clear.

How about when you originate a picture book—are you doing the text first and then picking it up like it's someone else's words, or does the project evolve visually and the words come later?

The most important thing I look for in my books is the concept. I'll spend months thinking of a good concept. Something that sounds interesting in

Action (that the image is telling part of the story) is often cited as something that makes an illustration work—and differentiates illustration from just being a pretty picture. You play with elements and techniques like sequencing, comic book layout, even flip-the-page back and forth like in "Ricky Ricotta's Mighty Robot vs. The Mecha-Monkeys From Mars." Tell us about the

joys and challenges of capturing action in a still image.

The point of good editorial illustration is that a single image has to convey a concept, which is extremely tough. You read an entire article and you have to devise a metaphor that explains the point of that whole article. In good narrative illustration, you have to tell a story pertaining to the text, which is a different type of challenge. You have to explain a sentence, or a paragraph, in a single image, but at the same time you have to also be subtle in mood and try to elevate the narrative so that the kids understand it clearly while also possibly eluding to something more. Narrative illustration also requires consistency of drawing the same character, and maybe even whole scenes exactly the same way. Kids can sniff out those minor differences so you have to be at the top of your game. I love narrative illustration because you can tell stories just with pictures (hence the wordless picture book). I'm at a point now where I can't separate the two in craft. I have to tell stories with my pictures, now. I'm a storyteller at heart.

You created the Disney animated hit "The Replacements." Are there lessons from animation that you've brought over to the world of writing and illustrating books for kids?

Surround yourself with talented people.

Emotion (as seen on/in the characters) is another element that the best illustrations have. Even your cover image of Beekle, with Beekle's slightly crooked smile and timid 'hi there' wave are so expressive! What do you see as the tools and techniques illustrators have for expressing emotion?

Emotion depends very much on the face and body language on a character, but I use the whole page to emphasize the fact without ever showing the face. Color is an effective way to convey mood. A gray foggy day can emphasize a somberness. Maybe contrast that moment with body language and show a girl skipping in a puddle with her arms swinging about. Now, you've not only shown her being happy but you've heightened the happiness by contrasting it with a gloomy scene. Theater uses lighting very effectively to show mood. If I shine a light from below a person's face they can appear ominous. Composition is another tool. Have a completely blank page with a figure and you know they are alone, and your mind fills the blanks on the emotions that character feels because you've felt those same emotions before.

You've also done black and white illustrations for a number of chapter books, including Lisa Yee's *Bobby vs. Girls (Accidentally)* and Dan Gutman's *The Christmas Genie*. What are the different challenges of working in black and white versus color?

When working in black and white you have to be more mindful of contrast because that is the only thing helping you separate form from other objects. With color you have various other factors you can play with such as color, temperature, saturation, contrast, etc. Dark night time scenes can also be tough. You want to make everyone appear like they are in darkness but you don't want it to appear as if they have been charred because you over shaded them. It's even tougher when you have to do that same scene with various multicultural characters because then you have to be consistent with the skin tones. I'm much more aggressive when I work in color than I am in black and white.

There's a lot of discussion about writers developing a unique 'voice.' Is that a parallel concept to an illustrator having a unique 'style,' or do you think of yourself having multiple styles?

I think I have a unique voice in my work that speaks in various styles if that makes any sense. I have a serious side, a funny side, etc. but you don't paint those in the same style. You want to emphasize certain things in various sorts of work. The thoughts you express are the same, but you can tailor them into the style you deem fit for the subject matter.

Can you share your best advice for other illustrators and other author/illustrators?

When you start out, the best teacher is imitation. Copy your favorite author or authors, draw a picture in the style of your favorite artists. Once you're comfortable doing it try doing it without looking at anything. Make up your own stuff in that style. If you can nail it then you know you are capable of doing that quality of work. You've essentially trained your body with the necessary muscle and brain skills you need to create good quality work. Last but not least, the hardest step, is to stop imitating and create work in your own style. Use no references, take all the inspiration off your walls and just sit in an empty room with a blank slate and create things the way your brain tells you to do them. You have to now find it in yourself. You have to just create work and whether you realize it or not, you have to accept who you are and that is how it's going to be, but in the back of your mind, you now know that you can do it.

LEE WIND (leewind.com) is a blogger and writer. His award-winning blog, "I'm Here. I'm Queer. What the Hell Do I Read?" covers LGBTQ teen books, culture, and politics, and has had more than 1.25 million visits from teen readers and their allies. He is also the official blogger for the Society of Children's Book Writers and Illustrators (scbwi.blogspot.com) and the Captain of SCBWI Team Blog. Lee writes fiction (picture books, middle grade, and young adult) as well as nonfiction, and is represented by Danielle Smith at Red Fox Literary.

RUTA SEPETYS

On having a book published in 45 different countries.

....

by Lee Wind

Ruta Sepetys (whose name is pronounced "Roota Suh-Pettys") burst on the scene with her debut novel for young adults, *Between Shades of Gray*.

But hers is not a story of overnight success. Sepetys has written about it taking "several years, dozens of drafts, 17 rounds of revision" and "many rejections." In 2007 she won a SCBWI Work-In-Progress grant that helped give her "the courage and energy to finish the book."

Why did she need courage? Born and raised in Michigan, Sepetys is the daughter of a Lithuanian refugee. In 1941, the nations of Lithuania, Latvia, and Estonia disappeared from maps. They did not reappear until 1990. In writing about this untold part of history, Sepetys wanted to give voice to the hundreds of thousands of people who lost their lives during Stalin's cleansing of the Baltic region.

What she created is, in the words of bestselling author Laurie Halse Anderson, "a brilliant story of love and survival that will keep their memory alive for generations to come."

When *Between Shades of Gray* was published in 2012, it became a *New York Times* bestseller and a Carnegie Medal Finalist. The book won so many awards (more than 50) that it would take up too much space to list them all here. This, of course, is an excellent problem for an author to have.

Sepetys's second book, *Out of the Easy*, also hit The *New York Times* bestseller list and earned her another 30+ awards.

Writing historical fiction that is both literary and commercial, and with an international book tour schedule that doesn't quit, here Sepetys shares the secret of talking about your book with the media, how she approaches revision and opening lines, when you know you've done your research and the strategies she uses to successfully integrate fictional characters whom readers care about into history.

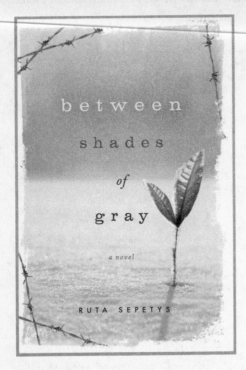

To learn more about Sepetys and her writing, visit rutasepetys.com

Your debut novel, *Between Shades of Gray*, was not only a *New York Times* bestseller, it was also an international bestseller, having been published in over 45 countries. You've written that you're "on a mission to tour all of them." This means you're talking about your book a lot, to journalists, and on radio and TV. What have you learned about talking about yourself and your book that other authors and illustrators in the fortunate position of having a media spotlight might use?

Although media varies from country to country, most journalists love a unique story. When asked about our work, we have an opportunity to "hook" a reader and plant a seed of intrigue. To make a compelling first impression, it's helpful for a writer to be able to effectively describe their project in one or two sentences. To do that, you have to distill your work into a few main points. Start by asking:

- What is unique about my project?
- What do I want this to convey?

Then weave your answers into the description.

So, given that advice, how would you encapsulate *Between Shades of Gray*?

Between Shades of Gray shares the secret history behind fifty years of Soviet terror in the Baltic countries. The story chronicles a fifteen-year old Lithuanian artist who is arrested and deported to Siberia.

After your efforts to tell this story "so this part of history won't be lost," it must have been astonishing to be bestowed "The Cross of The Knight" by the President of Lithuania for your contributions to education and culture.

Yes, it was astonishing. It also acknowledged the power of books. Through novels, readers around the world are suddenly united in story, study, and remembrance. We are not only a human community, but a global reading community, striving to learn from the past.

Tell us how you approached talking about your second novel, *Out of the Easy.*

> *Out of the Easy* is set in the French Quarter of New Orleans in 1950. Seventeen-year-old Josie Moraine is the daughter of a brothel prostitute, but dreams of building a life outside of New Orleans. She applies to college but gets tangled in a local murder investigation that threatens her life and future. The story explores identity, family, and the idea that we can all learn to fly, even if we're born with broken wings.

That's a very different story!

> As an author of historical fiction, I am particularly drawn to stories of strength through struggle. So although my characters and settings may be quite different, the goal of finding meaning within suffering is constant.

With the second novel, were you concerned about readers'—or your publisher's—expectations?

> No, I wasn't concerned. Although my first two books feature different settings and time periods, they're both historical. I specifically search for underrepresented parts of history and try to bring them to life through novels. So really, the only expectation for my books is a solid historical thread.
>
> I say write what you're most passionate about. Set your own expectations—those are the most challenging and rewarding to meet anyway.

Your opening pages of both novels are such grabbers. You pull us into the world of the main character and it's all there—tone, character, voice, enough of the plot to keep readers turning the pages. You've said you love revising—what's your approach to getting it right?

> Yes, I love revising. For me, a book truly takes shape in revision. With a first draft I decide *what* I want to say. In revision I determine *how* I want to say it.
>
> I'm considered a "crossover author" because my books are read by both adults and teens. *Between Shades of Gray,* for example, is read by sixth

graders but is also used for book clubs in retirement communities. The prose, pacing, and emotional investment has to work for an age range and demographic that spans over sixty years. Simplicity helps me achieve that.

When I revise I try to remove unnecessary words, attributions, and echoes—the goal being to convey and captivate with the fewest words possible. I'm constantly reminding myself that sometimes a bare neck is more alluring than a jeweled one.

I also apply this "less is more" concept to opening lines. I want the first line to be a story unto itself, a curling finger beckoning the reader to continue.

The following are the opening lines for my three books.

For *Between Shades of Gray*: "They took me in my nightgown."

For *Out of the Easy*: "My mother's a prostitute."

For my third novel, due out in Spring 2016: "Guilt is a hunter."

Are you a plotter or a seat-of-the-pantser when writing the first draft?

Both. I'm a plotter-pantser. With historical fiction, I'm fortunate to have a pre-existing outline. History provides framework, main plot points, and sometimes, the ending. I loosely outline the fictional aspects of my books by asking myself some general questions:

- What, exactly, does each character want?
- What is keeping each character from getting what they want?
- What are the stakes and consequences?
- What is each character hiding?

Once I answer the questions I then begin to weave fact and fiction.

I've heard it said that setting—when it's done well—is almost like another character. Both of your first two novels are so grounded in their settings, Lithuania/Siberia for *Between Shades of Gray* and New Orleans for *Out of the Easy*. Is that a result of research, or sensory details, or...?

It's a combination of both. Traveling to the setting of a novel, if possible, is an important part of research. Spending time immersed within a location allows you to communicate specifics to the reader that will transport them to the scene alongside the character. If they hear the sounds, smell the smells, and visualize the setting, the reader will feel very present in the story. If visiting the location isn't possible, another option is to interview someone who is very familiar with it.

Speaking of research, it can be wonderful, but also kind of a procrastination trap. How do you know when you've done enough research and can get writing?

Research can be thrilling, even addictive. It's like detective work. To avoid procrastination, I try to combine the writing and research process. At times, my research findings are so compelling that if I don't begin a draft I fear I'll lose the sense of excitement and immediacy. If a writer is trying to determine whether they have enough research material they might ask themselves if the information they've collected can answer and support their main plot drivers. If so, they should begin writing. Small details can always be researched during revision.

Setting stories in a different time period—historical fiction—must be full of anachronistic potholes to avoid. How do you approach getting that *time* right?

It's challenging. Modern phrasing and contemporary elements inevitably sneak their way in and you have to kick them out. Once I have a draft and a revision under my belt, I then read through for authenticity and historical consistency. I belong to an amazing writing group and they read and analyze my drafts as well before I send them to my agent or publisher. Regardless of how many times I've read through a draft, my writing group always catches things I've missed.

You've said "I look for characters that might not be classically beautiful but have a beautiful capacity to love." Does that drive the types of projects you choose to work on?

It doesn't drive the selection, but it drives the spirit of the writing.

Can you tell us how that fits into what you're writing now?

I'm finishing a novel about the greatest maritime disaster in history. Near the end of WWII, a ship sank and more than nine thousand people drowned. Five thousand were children. The sinking dwarfs the death tolls of the *Titanic* and *Lusitania*, yet it has remained hidden for 70 years.

A new novel coming out every year is an expectation that may be changing as some authors play it differently, and seem to really maximize each novel. What do you think are the top three things authors can to do maximize each novel's chance for success and readers?

1. Take time with revision. It's better to publish a strong novel every three years than a mediocre one every twelve months.

2. Understand your readership. Who will buy your books, where are they, and how can you best reach your target market?

3. Be a team player. Find ways to support your publisher's efforts. Always keep them in the loop.

Has the success your first two novels received changed your view on what success as a writer is? How do you define success now?

The global reception of my books has allowed me to write full time and I'm so grateful!

Success is an enduring love of the creative process that inspires me to take risks, face failure, and approach each day with a passionate search for story.

What advice do you have to share with writers reading this?

If you're reading *CWIM*, you're obviously serious about writing or illustrating children's books. This particular genre is not only an industry—it's a community. The authors, illustrators, agents, and publishers are colleagues and also friends. Consider joining The Society of Children's Book Writers and Illustrators (scbwi.org). Attend a conference, join a writing group, and above all—read. Good writers are good readers!

LEE WIND (leewind.com) is a blogger and writer. His award-winning blog, "I'm Here. I'm Queer. What the Hell Do I Read?" covers LGBTQ teen books, culture, and politics, and has had more than 1.25 million visits from teen readers and their allies. He is also the official blogger for the Society of Children's Book Writers and Illustrators (scbwi.blogspot.com) and the Captain of SCBWI Team Blog. Lee writes fiction (picture books, middle grade, and young adult) as well as nonfiction, and is represented by Danielle Smith at Red Fox Literary.

MARTIN WHITMORE

On illustrations, creativity, and success at using Kickstarter.

by Saranyan Vigraham

When Martin Whitmore was two years old, his parents took him to his grandparents' house for a Sunday dinner. It was a beautiful day, and his mom had taken him outside to play. There was a tree stump in the yard that he was fascinated by, which was covered in ladybugs. He watched them walk all over with curiosity and seeing that he was enjoying himself, his mom left him in the yard by the stump so she could go inside and help prepare dinner. In a little while, she came out to get him, and noticed that all the ladybugs had gone. She picked him up and said, "Marty, where did all the ladybugs go? Did they fly away?" He shook his head, opened his mouth, stuck out his tongue, and pointed into his mouth with a big smile on his face. Apparently he had eaten all the ladybugs; in his defense, he claims he thought they were candies on legs. Poison Control ensured his mom that ladybugs were harmless.

Although Whitmore no longer eats ladybugs, there is no shortage of perspectives in those illustrations of his. He and his partner, Megan Elizabeth Morris, co-founded Ideaschema, a creative growth agency aimed towards helping people spread their ideas. Whitmore's illustrations help in translating meaningful ideas into comics and art. Focusing on social impact, IdeaSchema helps people spread and manifest their ideas through creative and visual mediums. Such mission has also increased Whitmore's range as an illustrator, allowing him to experiment.

From zombies in a dystopian world to comics telling a story from his current world, he illustrates everything. He ventured into children's illustration by accident, through a commissioned work. To understand what works, Whitmore turned to Kickstarter, a popular crowdfunding platform. "Illustrators need to be in front of people, talking to them using social channels. We need to understand what works and what does not," Whitmore says. His first Kickstarter campaign was not exactly a children's book. It was an illustrated coffee table book aimed towards the young adults and adults. It was dark humor. But, it sold. His second Kickstarter project aimed to reach a much younger audience. And, it sold as well.

You can read more about Whitmore's work here: ideaschema.org/2015/02/a-tale-of-two-childrens-books/.

What is your illustrating process?

I think I must've fallen into a crack between generations, because I like a nice mix of analog and digital in my illustration process. I start my work by drawing initial pencils of the scene and characters, then I ink the pencils by hand. Next, I scan my work, and do all my clean-up and color work in Photoshop and Illustrator. I use an old Wacom tablet my dad gave me for this part of the process.

Why Kickstarter?

At the time we created the Ghastlycrud Zombies, Kickstarter was still new enough to be exciting, but tested enough that I felt like we could trust it. Megan and I had done crowdfunded artwork as far back as 2008 on a site called Fundable, and really enjoyed the community aspect of getting to interact with our backers. It was also a much less risky financial option for publishing our Ghastlycrud book—if

there wasn't enough interest to make it viable, then we simply wouldn't do it.

A children's book about zombies seems unusual. Where did you get the idea?

At SxSW Interactive, my friend Jeff Moriarty actually gave us the idea—he suggested we create a zombified homage to Edward Gorey's classic *The Gashlycrumb Tinies*. We took the idea and ran with it! Megan wrote the text, and I started in on the pencils and inks for the artwork. Megan's prose left me a lot of room to improvise and add my own spin, which I loved.

When using Kickstarter, what was the process like? How much did you have to prepare before you hit the launch button?

There was a lot of planning that happened before we launched. We spoke to our printer a lot about costs per book depending on how many we ordered (we worked with a local print shop, McCarthy Print in Austin, who were wonderful), we tried (and failed completely) to estimate how long it would take me to pack and ship all the books out to our backers, we spoke to a source for getting our magnets sculpted and cast (that fell through halfway through the campaign, and my friend Phil Hynes came through for me instead) ... and that was all before even applying for a Kickstarter account through Amazon. That was a bit of a challenge, too. Another very important step before

we launched was engaging our online community in the process. We let them know what we were planning so that they had more time to prepare to support us once the campaign went live.

And, what happened afterwards?

We exceeded our funding goals, and began the process of getting the books printed, packed, and shipped out to backers. I also had some custom painted pieces to prepare (I painted around 100 zombie head magnets, and a handful of art grenades) for the higher reward levels. I thought I would be able to ship all the orders out in a month or two after getting the books from the printer ... but it took me about a year instead. The campaign didn't actually net us much profit when compared to the work involved—most of the funds were used for printing and shipping, so I still had to be doing a lot of commissioned client work to keep us afloat. It took me a long time, but I finally managed to make the time to send out all the books. It was a humbling experience. I'm glad we did it.

If you do a Kickstarter campaign again, what would you do different? In other words, are there things that you want to go back and change?

The next Kickstarter I run will have a larger profit margin—at least enough so that I can take a couple weeks off to ship out all the rewards. I'll also offer less custom artwork options—all those handpainted magnets looked nice, but they took me so long to paint that it made it harder to fulfill the orders. Lesson learned!

For illustrators who are planning to use Kickstarter to launch/test their book idea, what will your advice be?

Really engage your community—give them an early heads-up of what's coming, lots of previews and opportunities to provide feedback about what you're offering. After all, they're the ones you're hoping will pitch in! Also, be entertaining. Give them lots of updates during the campaign that are fun and informational. I included lots of artwork with my updates, and people really enjoyed and appreciated that.

From zombies to zombie hunters, vampires to aliens, ideas to comics, your range seems to be immense. What is your favorite thing to draw/illustrate?

Characters are my favorite thing to illustrate—people (or aliens, monsters, zombies, animals, etc.) with a lot of personality are so much fun to create.

Do you laugh when you are illustrating? Do you cry? Or are you as angry as some of the zombie hunters you draw?

Sometimes I do laugh, especially when I am creating comics, or particularly ridiculous illustrations. More often than that, if you were to watch me working, you would see me making faces—I can't help but make faces like the ones I'm currently drawing. I'm sure I look quite silly. I don't tend to be angry—I'm a pretty laid back guy ... but I can make some really great angry faces.

You have done few comics. What is different about comics? When writing stories for children in comic form, what does one need to keep in mind?

I've also lately been drawing a lot of comics for Ideaschema, the company my partner and I started. There are a lot of things to keep in mind when making comics—it's a completely unique way of conveying ideas. The dialogue is very important. Continuity matters, so pay a lot of attention to that. As al-

ways, be entertaining, and remember that you can use comics to start a conversation about all sorts of really important topics. Comics can often slip under the radar for people who might not otherwise consider an idea.

Can you talk more about your two Kickstarter projects for children?

The Ghastlycrud Zombies was a purely personal project that I worked on with my partner, Megan Elizabeth Morris, and it was awesome. Zombies are a lot of fun for me, and it gave me a chance to try out a new style I had been developing in a more serious capacity. It introduced me to the way Kickstarter works, and that was a great learning tool.

Gifts From Our Father was the second children's book I created for Kickstarter, and that was commissioned by a good friend and client, Tom Wall.

It's a book of Catholic prayers for kids, which is a big departure for me, but I really enjoyed working on it with Tom. I'm not a religious person, but I really appreciate the message of love, kindness, acceptance, and generosity that we convey in this book.

Did you always want to be an illustrator?

Before I wanted to be an artist, I wanted to be a paleontologist—but then dinosaurs were so much fun to draw, I figured I might want to do that for a living instead. Since then, I've been making art constantly, and even getting paid for some of it. Bonus!

What is your greatest strength and weakness as an illustrator?

I think one of my great strengths as an illustrator is my ability to convey just about anything visually, from processes to complex abstract concepts.

I've also got a really fun graphic style that is entertaining and attention-getting. Probably my greatest weakness is that I work in a particular couple of styles almost exclusively, and they're very cartoony. I have recently been experimenting with other styles of illustration to try to be more flexible and well-rounded.

The Ghastlycrud Zombies seems like a coffee table picture book written for the adults...or rather the children hiding inside grown ups. Was that always your intention?

Yes, absolutely. *The Ghastlycrud Zombies* was never intended for very young children—it's a bit too dark and violent for that ... unless you're okay with your toddlers asking you questions about disembowelment. Older kids are probably fine reading it, but I would encourage parents to read the book first, since they'll be the best judge of what their children can handle.

But, it is still a children's book?

It is a children's book, but only in style—not in substance. It's a kid's book for your dark and twisted *inner* child.

How do you strike a balance about illustrations that are a little scary but still kid friendly?

If you can make something funny in addition to being scary, that goes a long way to making it more kid friendly. I enjoyed a lot of really gross, scary things when I was a kid—mostly because there was always a kind of humorous angle to them ... things like the Garbage Pail Kids or Goosebumps books come to mind.

Do you have final parting thoughts for aspiring illustrators or illustrators who want to use Kickstarter as a platform to launch their work?

Crowdfunding works best when you already have a crowd who's paying attention to you. It may seem counterintuitive, but your audience is probably a lot more likely to support your Kickstarter if you're giving them free, entertaining content on a regular basis. If they feel they can trust you, they're much more willing to support you. So be honest and generous with your audience, and they'll repay the kindness.

SARANYAN VIGRAHAM writes stories and builds toys. His stories sometimes have been shown to make his sons roll on the floor clutching their stomach with laughter. So, he uses this trick to disarm them when they chase him with their famous tickle claws. After spending several years building software that makes the Internet function, he now builds smart toys and apps that allow his children explore and understand the world better. He can be found on Twitter: @saranyan.

NEW AGENT SPOTLIGHTS

Learn about new reps seeking clients.

by Chuck Sambuchino

One of the most common recurring blog items I get complimented on is my "New Agent Alerts," a series where I spotlight new/newer literary reps who are open to queries and looking for clients right now.

This is due to the fact that newer agents are golden opportunities for aspiring authors because they are actively building their client lists. They're hungry to sign new clients and start the ball rolling with submissions to editors and get books sold. Whereas an established agent with 40 clients may have little to no time to consider new writers' work (let alone help them shape it), a newer agent may be willing to sign a promising writer whose work is not a guaranteed huge payday.

THE CONS AND PROS OF NEWER AGENTS

At writing conferences, a frequent question I get is "Is it OK to sign with a new agent?" The question comes about because people value experience and wonder about the skill of someone who's new to the scene. The con-cern is an interesting one, so let me try to list the downsides and upsides to choosing a rep who's in her first few years agenting.

Probable cons

- They are less experienced in contract negotiations.
- They know fewer editors at this point than a rep who's been in business a while, meaning there is a less likely chance they can help you get published. This is a big, justified point—and writers' foremost concern.
- They are in a weaker position to demand a high advance for you.
- New agents come and some go. This means if your agent is in business for a year or two and doesn't find the success for which they hoped, they could bail on the biz altogether. That leaves you without a home. If you sign with an agent who's been in business for 14 years, however, chances are they won't quit tomorrow.

Probable pros

- They are actively building their client lists—and that means they are anxious to sign new writers and lock in those first several sales.
- They are willing to give your work a longer look. They may be willing to work with you on a project to get it ready for submission, whereas a more established agent has lots of clients and no time—meaning they have no spare moments to help you with shaping your novel or proposal.
- With fewer clients under their wing, you will get more attention than you would with an established rep.
- If they've found their calling and don't seem like they're giving up any time soon (and keep in mind, most do continue on as agents), you can have a decades-long relationship that pays off with lots of books.
- They have little going against them. An established agent once told me that a new agent is in a unique position because they have no duds under their belt. Their slates are clean.

HOW CAN YOU DECIDE FOR YOURSELF?

1. Factor in if they're part of a larger agency. Agents share contacts and resources. If your agent is the new girl at an agency with five people, those other four agents will help her (and you) with submissions. In other words, she's new, but not alone.

2. Learn where the agent came from. Has she been an apprentice at the agency for two years? Was she an editor for seven years and just switched to agenting? If they already have a few years in publishing under their belt, they're not as green as you may think. Agents don't become agents overnight.

3. Ask where she will submit the work. This is a big one. If you fear the agent lacks proper contacts to move your work, ask straight out: "What editors do you see us submitting this book to, and have you sold to them before?" The question tests their plan for where to send the manuscript and get it in print.

4. Ask them, "Why should I sign with you?" This is another straight-up question that gets right to the point. If she's new and has little/no sales at that point, she can't respond with "I sell tons of books and I make it rain cash money!! Dolla dolla bills, y'all!!!" She can't rely on her track record to entice you. So what's her sales pitch? Weigh her enthusiasm, her plan for the book, her promises of hard work and anything else she tells you. In the publishing business, you want communication and enthusiasm from agents (and editors). Both are invaluable. What's the point of signing with a huge agent when they don't return your e-mails and consider your book last on their list of priorities for the day?

5. If you're not sold, you can always say no. It's as simple as that. Always query new/newer agents because, at the end of the day, just because they offer representation doesn't mean you have to accept.

NEW AGENT SPOTLIGHTS

Peppered throughout this book's large number of agency listings are sporadic "New Agent Alert" sidebars. Look them over to see if these newer reps would be a good fit for your work. Always read personal information and submission guidelines carefully. Don't let an agent reject you because you submitted work incorrectly. Wherever possible, we have included a website address for their agency, as well as their Twitter handle for those reps that tweet.

Also please note that as of when this book went to press in 2015, all these agents were still active and looking for writers. That said, I cannot guarantee every one is still in their respective position when you read this, nor that they have kept their query inboxes open. I urge you to visit agency websites and double check before you query. (This is always a good idea in any case.) Good luck!

CHUCK SAMBUCHINO (chucksambuchino.com, @chucksambuchino) edits the *Guide to Literary Agents* (guidetoliteraryagents.com/blog) as well as the *Children's Writer's & Illustrator's Market*. His pop humor books include *How to Survive a Garden Gnome Attack* (film rights optioned by Sony) and *When Clowns Attack: A Survival Guide* (Sept. 2015, Ten Speed Press). Chuck's other writing guides include *Formatting & Submitting Your Manuscript (3rd. Ed.)*, *Create Your Writer Platform*, and *Get a Literary Agent*. Besides that, he is a husband, guitarist, father, dog owner, and cookie addict.

GLOSSARY OF
INDUSTRY TERMS

AAR. Association of Authors' Representatives.

ABA. American Booksellers Association.

ABC. Association of Booksellers for Children.

ADVANCE. A sum of money a publisher pays a writer or illustrator prior to the publication of a book. It is usually paid in installments, such as one half on signing the contract, one half on delivery of a complete and satisfactory manuscript. The advance is paid against the royalty money that will be earned by the book.

ALA. American Library Association.

ALL RIGHTS. The rights contracted to a publisher permitting the use of material anywhere and in any form, including movie and book club sales, without additional payment to the creator.

ANTHOLOGY. A collection of selected writings by various authors or gatherings of works by one author.

ANTHROPOMORPHIZATION. The act of attributing human form and personality to things not human (such as animals).

ASAP. As soon as possible.

ASSIGNMENT. An editor or art director asks a writer, illustrator or photographer to produce a specific piece for an agreed-upon fee.

B&W. Black and white.

BACKLIST. A publisher's list of books not published during the current season but still in print.

BEA. BookExpo America.

BIENNIALLY. Occurring once every 2 years.

BIMONTHLY. Occurring once every 2 months.

BIWEEKLY. Occurring once every 2 weeks.

BOOK PACKAGER. A company that draws all elements of a book together, from the initial concept to writing and marketing strategies, then sells the book package to a book publisher and/or movie producer. Also known as book producer or book developer.

BOOK PROPOSAL. Package submitted to a publisher for consideration usually consisting of a synopsis and outline as well as sample chapters.

BUSINESS-SIZE ENVELOPE. Also known as a #10 envelope. The standard size used in sending business correspondence.

CAMERA-READY. Refers to art that is completely prepared for copy camera platemaking.

CAPTION. A description of the subject matter of an illustration or photograph; photo captions include persons' names where appropriate. Also called cutline.

CBC. Children's Book Council.

CLEAN-COPY. A manuscript free of errors and needing no editing; it is ready for typesetting.

CLIPS. Samples, usually from newspapers or magazines, of a writer's published work.

CONCEPT BOOKS. Books that deal with ideas, concepts and large-scale problems, promoting an understanding of what's happening in a child's world. Most prevalent are alphabet and counting books, but also includes books dealing with specific concerns facing young people (such as divorce, birth of a sibling, friendship or moving).

CONTRACT. A written agreement stating the rights to be purchased by an editor, art director or producer and the amount of payment the writer, illustrator or photographer will receive for that sale. (See the article "Running Your Business.")

CONTRIBUTOR'S COPIES. The magazine issues sent to an author, illustrator or photographer in which her work appears.

CO-OP PUBLISHER. A publisher that shares production costs with an author but, unlike subsidy publishers, handles all marketing and distribution. An author receives a high percentage of royalties until her initial investment is recouped, then standard royalties. (*Children's Writer's & Illustrator's Market* does not include co-op publishers.)

COPY. The actual written material of a manuscript.

COPYEDITING. Editing a manuscript for grammar usage, spelling, punctuation and general style.

COPYRIGHT. A means to legally protect an author's/illustrator's/photographer's work. This can be shown by writing the creator's name and the year of the work's creation.

COVER LETTER. A brief letter, accompanying a complete manuscript, especially useful if responding to an editor's request for a manuscript. May also accompany a book proposal.

CUTLINE. See caption.

DIVISION. An unincorporated branch of a company.

DUMMY. A loose mock-up of a book showing placement of text and artwork.

ELECTRONIC SUBMISSION. A submission of material by e-mail or Web form.

FINAL DRAFT. The last version of a polished manuscript ready for submission to an editor.

FIRST NORTH AMERICAN SERIAL RIGHTS. The right to publish material in a periodical for the first time, in the U.S. or Canada. (See the article "Running Your Business.")

F&GS. Folded and gathered sheets. An early, not-yet-bound copy of a picture book.

FLAT FEE. A one-time payment.

GALLEYS. The first typeset version of a manuscript that has not yet been divided into pages.

GENRE. A formulaic type of fiction, such as horror, mystery, romance, fantasy, suspense, thriller, science fiction or Western.

GLOSSY. A photograph with a shiny surface as opposed to one with a non-shiny matte finish.

GOUACHE. Opaque watercolor with an appreciable film thickness and an actual paint layer.

HALFTONE. Reproduction of a continuous tone illustration with the image formed by dots produced by a camera lens screen.

HARD COPY. The printed copy of a computer's output.

HARDWARE. Refers to all the mechanically-integrated components of a computer that are not software—circuit boards, transistors and the machines that are the actual computer.

HI-LO. High interest, low reading level.

HOME PAGE. The first page of a website.

IBBY. International Board on Books for Young People.

IMPRINT. Name applied to a publisher's specific line of books.

INTERNET. A worldwide network of computers that offers access to a wide variety of electronic resources.

IRA. International Reading Association.

IRC. International Reply Coupon. Sold at the post office to enclose with text or artwork sent to a recipient outside your own country to cover postage costs when replying or returning work.

KEYLINE. Identification of the positions of illustrations and copy for the printer.

LAYOUT. Arrangement of illustrations, photographs, text and headlines for printed material.

LINE DRAWING. Illustration done with pencil or ink using no wash or other shading.

MASS MARKET BOOKS. Paperback books directed toward an extremely large audience sold in supermarkets, drugstores, airports, newsstands, online retailers and bookstores.

MECHANICALS. Paste-up or preparation of work for printing.

MIDDLE GRADE OR MID-GRADE. See middle reader.

MIDDLE READER. The general classification of books written for readers approximately ages 9–12. Often called middle grade or mid-grade.

MS (MSS). Manuscript(s).

MULTIPLE SUBMISSIONS. See simultaneous submissions.

NCTE. National Council of Teachers of English.

ONE-TIME RIGHTS. Permission to publish a story in periodical or book form one time only. (See the article "Running Your Business.")

PACKAGE SALE. The sale of a manuscript and illustrations/photos as a "package" paid for with one check.

PAYMENT ON ACCEPTANCE. The writer, artist or photographer is paid for her work at the time the editor or art director decides to buy it.

PAYMENT ON PUBLICATION. The writer, artist or photographer is paid for her work when it is published.

PICTURE BOOK. A type of book aimed at preschoolers to 8-year-olds that tells a story using a combination of text and artwork, or artwork only.

PRINT. An impression pulled from an original plate, stone, block, screen or negative; also a positive made from a photographic negative.

PROOFREADING. Reading text to correct typographical errors.

QUERY. A letter to an editor or agent designed to capture interest in an article or book you have written or propose to write. (See the article "Before Your First Sale.")

READING FEE. Money charged by some agents and publishers to read a submitted manuscript. (*Children's Writer's & Illustrator's Market* does not include agencies that charge reading fees.)

REPRINT RIGHTS. Permission to print an already published work whose first rights have been sold to another magazine or book publisher. (See the article "Running Your Business.")

RESPONSE TIME. The average length of time it takes an editor or art director to accept or reject a query or submission, and inform the creator of the decision.

RIGHTS. The bundle of permissions offered to an editor or art director in exchange for printing a manuscript, artwork or photographs. (See the article "Running Your Business.")

ROUGH DRAFT. A manuscript that has not been checked for errors in grammar, punctuation, spelling or content.

ROUGHS. Preliminary sketches or drawings.

ROYALTY. An agreed percentage paid by a publisher to a writer, illustrator or photographer for each copy of her work sold.

SAE. Self-addressed envelope.

SASE. Self-addressed, stamped envelope.

SCBWI. The Society of Children's Book Writers and Illustrators.

SECOND SERIAL RIGHTS. Permission for the reprinting of a work in another periodical after its first publication in book or magazine form. (See the article "Running Your Business.")

SEMIANNUAL. Occurring every 6 months or twice a year.

SEMIMONTHLY. Occurring twice a month.

SEMIWEEKLY. Occurring twice a week.

SERIAL RIGHTS. The rights given by an author to a publisher to print a piece in one or more periodicals. (See the article "Running Your Business.")

SIMULTANEOUS SUBMISSIONS. Queries or proposals sent to several publishers at the same time. Also called multiple submissions. (See the article "Before Your First Sale.")

SLANT. The approach to a story or piece of artwork that will appeal to readers of a particular publication.

SLUSH PILE. Editors' term for their collections of unsolicited manuscripts.

SOFTWARE. Programs and related documentation for use with a computer.

SOLICITED MANUSCRIPT. Material that an editor has asked for or agreed to consider before being sent by a writer.

SPAR. Society of Photographers and Artists Representatives.

SPECULATION (SPEC). Creating a piece with no assurance from an editor or art director that it will be purchased or any reimbursements for material or labor paid.

SUBSIDIARY RIGHTS. All rights other than book publishing rights included in a book contract, such as paperback, book club and movie rights. (See the article "Running Your Business.")

SUBSIDY PUBLISHER. A book publisher that charges the author for the cost of typesetting, printing and promoting a book. Also called a vanity publisher. (Note: *Children's Writer's & Illustrator's Market* does not include subsidy publishers.)

SYNOPSIS. A brief summary of a story or novel. Usually a page to a page and a half, singlespaced, if part of a book proposal.

TABLOID. Publication printed on an ordinary newspaper page turned sideways and folded in half.

TEARSHEET. Page from a magazine or newspaper containing your printed art, story, article, poem or photo.

THUMBNAIL. A rough layout in miniature.

TRADE BOOKS. Books sold in bookstores and through online retailers, aimed at a smaller audience than mass market books, and printed in smaller quantities by publishers.

TRANSPARENCIES. Positive color slides; not color prints.

UNSOLICITED MANUSCRIPT. Material sent without an editor's, art director's or agent's request.

VANITY PUBLISHER. See subsidy publisher.

WORK-FOR-HIRE. An arrangement between a writer, illustrator or photographer and a company under which the company retains complete control of the work's copyright. (See the article "Running Your Business.")

YA. See young adult.

YOUNG ADULT. The general classification of books written for readers approximately ages 12–16. Often referred to as YA.

YOUNG READER. The general classification of books written for readers approximately ages 5–8.

BOOK PUBLISHERS

///

There's no magic formula for getting published. It's a matter of getting the right manuscript on the right editor's desk at the right time. Before you submit it's important to learn publishers' needs, see what kind of books they're producing, and decide which publishers your work is best suited for. *Children's Writer's & Illustrator's Market* is but one tool in this process. (Those just starting out, turn to the article "Quick Tips for Writers & Illustrators" in this book.)

To help you narrow down the list of possible publishers for your work, we've included several indexes at the back of this book. The **Subject Index** lists book and magazine publishers according to their fiction and nonfiction needs or interests. The **Age-Level Index** indicates which age groups publishers cater to. The **Photography Index** indicates which markets buy photography for children's publications. The **Poetry Index** lists publishers accepting poetry.

If you write contemporary fiction for young adults, for example, and you're trying to place a book manuscript, go first to the Subject Index. Locate the fiction categories under Book Publishers and copy the list under Contemporary. Then go to the Age-Level Index and highlight the publishers on the Contemporary list that are included under the Young Adults heading. Read the listings for the highlighted publishers to see if your work matches their needs.

Remember, *Children's Writer's & Illustrator's Market* should not be your only source for researching publishers. Here are a few other sources of information:

- The Society of Children's Book Writers and Illustrators (SCBWI) offers members an annual market survey of children's book publishers for the cost of postage or free online at www.scbwi.org. (SCBWI membership information can also be found at www.

scbwi.org.)

- The Children's Book Council website (www.cbcbooks.org) gives information on member publishers.
- If a publisher interests you, send a SASE for submission guidelines or check publishers' websites for guidelines *before* submitting. To quickly find guidelines online, visit The Colossal Directory of Children's Publishers at www.signaleader.com.
- Check publishers' websites. Many include their complete catalogs, which you can browse. Web addresses are included in many publishers' listings.
- Spend time at your local bookstore to see who's publishing what. While you're there, browse through *Publishers Weekly* and *The Horn Book*.

SUBSIDY & SELF-PUBLISHING

Some determined writers who receive rejections from royalty publishers may look to subsidy and co-op publishers as an option for getting their work into print. These publishers ask writers to pay all or part of the costs of producing a book. We strongly advise writers and illustrators to work only with publishers who pay them. For this reason, we've adopted a policy not to include any subsidy or co-op publishers in *Children's Writer's & Illustrator's Market* (or any other Writer's Digest Books market book).

If you're interested in publishing your book just to share it with friends and relatives, self-publishing is a viable option, but it involves time, energy, and money. You oversee all book production details. Check with a local printer for advice and information on cost or check online for print-on-demand publishing options (which are often more affordable).

Whatever path you choose, keep in mind that the market is flooded with submissions, so it's important for you to hone your craft and submit the best work possible. Competition from thousands of other writers and illustrators makes it more important than ever to research publishers before submitting—read their guidelines, look at their catalogs, check out a few of their titles, and visit their websites.

⊘ ABBEVILLE FAMILY

Abbeville Press, 137 Varick St., New York NY 10013. (212)366-5585. **Fax:** (212)366-6966. **E-mail:** abbeville@abbeville.com. **Website:** www.abbeville.com. "Our list is full for the next several seasons." Publishes 8 titles/year. 10% of books from first-time authors.

○ *Not accepting unsolicited book proposals at this time.*

FICTION Picture books: animal, anthology, concept, contemporary, fantasy, folktales, health, hi-lo, history, humor, multicultural, nature/environment, poetry, science fiction, special needs, sports, suspense. Average word length 300-1,000 words.

HOW TO CONTACT Please refer to website for submission policy.

ILLUSTRATION Works with approx 2-4 illustrators/year. Uses color artwork only.

PHOTOGRAPHY Buys stock and assigns work.

⊘ ABBEVILLE PRESS

137 Varick St., New York NY 10013. (212)366-5585. **Fax:** (212)366-6966. **E-mail:** abbeville@abbeville.com. **Website:** www.abbeville.com. Mainstay in the art book publishing world. "Our list is full for the next several seasons." Publishes 8 titles/year. 10% of books from first-time authors.

FICTION Picture books through imprint Abbeville Family.

HOW TO CONTACT Not accepting unsolicited book proposals at this time.

ABDO PUBLISHING CO.

8000 W. 78th St., Suite 310, Edina MN 55439. (800)800-1312. **Fax:** (952)831-1632. **E-mail:** nonfiction@abdopublishing.com. **E-mail:** fiction@abdopublishing.com; illustration@abdopublishing.com. **Website:** www.abdopub.com. **Contact:** Paul Abdo, editor-in-chief. ABDO publishes nonfiction children's books (pre-kindergarten to 8th grade) for school and public libraries—mainly history, sports, biography, geography, science, and social studies. "Please specify each submission as either nonfiction, fiction, or illustration." Publishes hardcover originals. Publishes 300 titles/year.

TERMS Guidelines online.

ABRAMS BOOKS FOR YOUNG READERS

115 W. 18th St., New York NY 10011. **Website:** www.abramsyoungreaders.com.

○ Abrams no longer accepts unsolicited mss or queries.

ILLUSTRATION Illustrations only: Do not submit original material; copies only. Contact: Chad Beckerman, art director.

Ⓐ ALADDIN

Simon & Schuster, 1230 Avenue of the Americas, 4th Floor, New York NY 10020. (212)698-7000. **Website:** www.simonandschuster.com. Aladdin also publishes Aladdin M!X, for those readers too old for kids' books, but not quite ready for adult or young adult novels. **Contact:** Acquisitions Editor. Aladdin publishes picture books, beginning readers, chapter books, middle grade, tween fiction and nonfiction, graphic novels and nonfiction in hardcover and paperback, with an emphasis on commercial, kid-friendly titles. Publishes hardcover/paperback originals and imprints of Simon & Schuster Children's Publishing Children's Division.

HOW TO CONTACT Simon & Schuster does not review, retain, or return unsolicited materials or artwork. "We suggest prospective authors and illustrators submit their mss through a professional literary agent."

⊕ ALGONQUIN YOUNG READERS

P.O. Box 2225, Chapel Hill NC 27515. **Website:** algonquinyoungreaders.com. Algonquin Young Readers is a new imprint that features books for readers 7-17. "From short illustrated novels for the youngest independent readers to timely and topical crossover young adult fiction, what ties our books together are unforgettable characters, absorbing stories, and superior writing."

FICTION Algonquin Young Readers publishes fiction and a limited number of narrative nonfiction titles for middle grade and young adult readers. "We don't publish poetry, picture books, or genre fiction."

HOW TO CONTACT Query with 15-20 sample pages and SASE.

ILLUSTRATION "At this time, we do not accept unsolicited submissions for illustration."

TERMS Guidelines online.

⊕ AMBERJACK PUBLISHING

P.O. Box 4668 #89611, New York NY 10163. (888)959-3352. **Website:** www.amberjackpublishing.com. Amberjack Publishing offers authors the freedom to write without burdening them with having to promote the work themselves. They retain all rights. "You will have no rights left to exploit, so you cannot resell, republish or use your story again."

FICTION Amberjack Publishing is always on the lookout for the next great story. "We are interested in fiction, children's books, graphic novels, science fiction, fantasy, humor, and everything in between."

HOW TO CONTACT Submit via online query form with book proposal and first 10 pages of ms.

AMERICAN PRESS

60 State St., Suite 700, Boston MA 02109. (617)247-0022. **E-mail:** americanpress@flash.net. **Website:** www.americanpresspublishers.com. **Contact:** Jana Kirk, editor. Publishes college textbooks. Publishes 25 titles/year. 50% of books from first-time authors. 90% from unagented writers.

> "Mss proposals are welcome in all subjects and disciplines."

NONFICTION "We prefer that our authors actually teach courses for which the mss are designed."

HOW TO CONTACT Query, or submit outline with tentative TOC. *No complete mss.* 350 queries received/year. 100 mss received/year. Responds in 3 months to queries. Publishes book 9 months after acceptance.

TERMS Pays 5-15% royalty on wholesale price.

AMULET BOOKS

115 W. 18th St., New York NY 10001. **Website:** www.amuletbooks.com. 10% of books from first-time authors.

> *Does not accept unsolicited mss or queries.*

FICTION Middle readers: adventure, contemporary, fantasy, history, science fiction, sports. Young adults/teens: adventure, contemporary, fantasy, history, science fiction, sports, suspense.

ILLUSTRATION Works with 10-12 illustrators/year. Uses both color and b&w. Query with samples. Contact: Chad Beckerman, art director. Samples filed.

PHOTOGRAPHY Buys stock images and assigns work.

ARBORDALE PUBLISHING

612 Johnnie Dodds, Suite A2, Mt. Pleasant SC 29464. (843)971-6722. **Fax:** (843)216-3804. **E-mail:** katie@arbordalepublishing.com. **E-mail:** donna@arbordalepublishing.com. **Website:** www.arbordalepublishing.com. **Contact:** Donna German and Katie Hall, editors. "The picture books we publish are usually, but not always, fictional stories with nonfiction woven into the story that relate to science and math and retellings of traditional cultural folklore with an underlying science theme. All books should subtly convey an educational theme through a warm story that is fun to read and that will grab a child's attention. Each book has a 4-page '*For Creative Minds*' section to reinforce the educational component. This section will have a craft and/or game as well as 'fun facts' to be shared by the parent, teacher, or other adult. Authors do not need to supply this information. Manuscripts should be less than 1,500 words and meet all of the following 4 criteria: fun to read—mostly fiction with nonfiction facts woven into the story; national or regional in scope; must tie into early elementary school curriculum; must be marketable through a niche market such as a zoo, aquarium, or museum gift shop." Publishes hardcover, trade paperback, and electronic originals. Publishes 20 titles/year. 50% of books from first-time authors. 100% from unagented writers.

FICTION Picture books: animal, folktales, nature/environment, math-related. Word length—picture books: no more than 1,500.

NONFICTION "We are not looking for mss about: pets (dogs or cats in particular); new babies; local or state-specific; magic; biographies; history-related; ABC books; poetry; series; young adult books or novels; holiday-related books. We do not consider mss. that have been previously published in any way, including e-books or self-published."

HOW TO CONTACT Accepts electronic submissions only. Snail mail submissions are discarded without being opened. Accepts electronic submissions only. Snail mail submissions are discarded without being opened. 1,000 mss received/year. Acknowledges receipt of ms submission within 1 month. Publishes book 18 months after acceptance. May hold onto mss of interest for 1 year until acceptance.

ILLUSTRATION Works with 20 illustrators/year. Prefers to work with illustrators from the US and Canada. Uses color artwork only. Submit Web link or 2-3 electronic images. Contact: Donna German. "I generally keep submissions on file until I match the mss to illustration needs."

TERMS Pays 6-8% royalty on wholesale price. Pays small advance. Book catalog and guidelines online.

TIPS "Please make sure that you have looked at our website to read our complete submission guidelines and to see if we are looking for a particular subject. Manuscripts must meet all four of our stated criteria. We look for fairly realistic, bright and colorful art-no cartoons. We want the children excited about the books. We envision the books being used at home and in the classroom."

Ⓐ ATHENEUM BOOKS FOR YOUNG READERS

Simon & Schuster, 1230 Avenue of the Americas, New York NY 10020. **Website:** kids.simonandschuster.com. Publishes hardcover originals.

FICTION All in juvenile versions. "We have few specific needs except for books that are fresh, interesting and well written. Fad topics are dangerous, as are works you haven't polished to the best of your ability. We also don't need safety pamphlets, ABC books, coloring books, and board books. In writing picture book texts, avoid the coy and 'cutesy,' such as stories about characters with alliterative names." Agented submissions only. No paperback romance-type fiction.

NONFICTION Publishes hardcover originals, picture books for young kids, nonfiction for ages 8-12 and novels for middle-grade and young adults. 100% require freelance illustration. Agented submissions only.

TERMS Guidelines for #10 SASE.

TIPS "Study our titles."

AZRO PRESS

PMB 342, 1704 Llano St. B, Santa Fe NM 87505. (505)989-3272. **Fax:** (505)989-3832. **E-mail:** books@azropress.com. **Website:** www.azropress.com.

◯ "We like to publish illustrated children's books by Southwestern authors and illustrators. We are always looking for books with a Southwestern look or theme."

FICTION Picture books: animal, history, humor, nature/environment. Young readers: adventure, animal, hi-lo, history, humor. Average word length: picture books—1,200; young readers—2,000-2,500.

NONFICTION Picture books: animal, geography, history. Young readers: geography, history.

HOW TO CONTACT Responds in 3-4 months. Publishes book 1-2 years after acceptance.

ILLUSTRATION Accepts material from international illustrators. Works with 3 illustrators/year. Uses color and b&w artwork. Reviews ms/illustration packages. Reviews work for future assignments. Query with samples. Submit samples to illustrations editor. Responds in 3-4 months. Samples not returned. Samples are filed.

TERMS Pays authors royalty of 5-10% based on wholesale price. Pays illustrators by the project ($2,000) or royalty of 5%. Catalog online.

TIPS "We are not currently accepting new mss. Please see our website for acceptance date."

BAILIWICK PRESS

309 East Mulberry St., Fort Collins CO 80524. (970)672-4878. **Fax:** (970)672-4731. **E-mail:** info@bailiwickpress.com. **E-mail:** aldozelnick@gmail.com. **Website:** www.bailiwickpress.com. "We're a micro-press that produces books and other products that inspire and tell great stories. Our motto is 'books with something to say.' We are now considering submissions, agented and unagented, for children's and young adult fiction. We're looking for smart, funny, and layered writing that kids will clamor for. Authors who already have a following have a leg up. We are only looking for humorous children's fiction. Please do not submit work for adults. Illustrated fiction is desired but not required. (Illustrators are also invited to send samples.) Make us laugh out loud, ooh and aah, and cry, 'Eureka!'"

HOW TO CONTACT "Please read the Aldo Zelnick series to determine if we might be on the same page, then fill out our submission form. Please do not send submissions via snail mail or phone calls. You must complete the online submission form to be considered. If, after completing and submitting the form, you also need to send us an e-mail attachment (such as sample illustrations or excerpts of graphics), you may e-mail them to aldozelnick@gmail.com." Responds in 6 months.

ILLUSTRATION Illustrated fiction desired but not required. Send samples.

Ⓐ BALZER & BRAY

HarperCollins Children's Books, 10 E. 53rd St., New York NY 10022. **Website:** www.harpercollinschildrens.com. "We publish bold, creative, groundbreaking picture books and novels that appeal directly to kids in a fresh way." Publishes 10 titles/year.

FICTION Picture books, young readers: adventure, animal, anthology, concept, contemporary, fantasy, history, humor, multicultural, nature/environment, poetry, science fiction, special needs, sports, suspense. Middle readers, young adults/teens: adventure, animal, anthology, contemporary, fantasy, history, humor, multicultural, nature/environment, poetry, science fiction, special needs, sports, suspense.

NONFICTION "We will publish very few nonfiction titles, maybe 1-2 per year."

HOW TO CONTACT Contact editor. Agented submissions only. Publishes book 18 months after acceptance.

ILLUSTRATION Works with 10 illustrators/year. Uses both color and b&w. Illustrations only: send tearsheets to be kept on file. Responds only if interested. Samples are not returned.

PHOTOGRAPHY Works on assignment only.

TERMS Offers advances. Pays illustrators by the project.

⊘Ⓐ BANTAM BOOKS

Imprint of Random House, Inc., 1745 Broadway, New York NY 10019. (212)782-9000. **Website:** www.bantam-dell.atrandom.com. *Not seeking mss at this time.*

BAREFOOT BOOKS

2067 Massachusettes Ave., 5th Floor, Cambridge MA 02140. (617)576-0660. **Fax:** (617)576-0049. **E-mail:** help@barefootbooks.com. **Website:** www.barefootbooks.com. "We are a small, independent publishing company that publishes high-quality picture books for children of all ages and specializes in the work of artists and writers from many cultures. We focus on themes that support independence of spirit, encourage openness to others, and foster a life-long love of learning. Prefers full ms." Publishes hardcover and trade paperback originals. Publishes 30 titles/year. 35% of books from first-time authors. 60% from un-agented writers.

FICTION "Barefoot Books only publishes children's picture books and anthologies of folktales. We do not publish novels."

HOW TO CONTACT Barefoot Books is not currently accepting ms queries or submissions. 2,000 queries received/year. 3,000 mss received/year.

ILLUSTRATION Works with 20 illustrators/year. Uses color artwork only. Reviews ms/illustration packages from artists. Send query and art samples or dummy for picture books. Query with samples or send promo sheet and tearsheets. Responds only if interested. Samples returned with SASE. Pays authors royalty of 5% based on retail price. Offers advances. Sends galleys to authors. Originals returned to artist at job's completion.

TERMS Pays advance. Book catalog for 9×12 SAE stamped with $1.80 postage.

BEHRMAN HOUSE INC.

11 Edison Place, Springfield NJ 07081. (973)379-7200. **Fax:** (973)379-7280. **E-mail:** customersupport@behrmanhouse.com. **Website:** www.behrmanhouse.com. Publishes books on all aspects of Judaism: history, cultural, textbooks, holidays. "Behrman House publishes quality books of Jewish content—history, Bible, philosophy, holidays, ethics—for children and adults." 12% of books from first-time authors.

NONFICTION All levels: Judaism, Jewish educational textbooks. Average word length: young reader—1,200; middle reader—2,000; young adult—4,000.

HOW TO CONTACT Submit outline/synopsis and sample chapters. Responds in 1 month to queries; 2 months to mss. Publishes book 18 months after acceptance.

ILLUSTRATION Works with 6 children's illustrators/year. Reviews ms/illustration packages from artists. "Query first." Illustrations only: Query with samples; send unsolicited art samples by mail. Responds to queries in 1 month; mss in 2 months.

PHOTOGRAPHY Purchases photos from freelancers. Buys stock and assigns work. Uses photos of families involved in Jewish activities. Uses color and b&w prints. Photographers should query with samples. Send unsolicited photos by mail. Submit portfolio for review.

TERMS Pays authors royalty of 3-10% based on retail price or buys ms outright for $1,000-5,000. Offers advance. Pays illustrators by the project (range: $500-5,000). Book catalog free on request. Guidelines online.

⊕ BELLEBOOKS

P.O. Box 300921, Memphis TN 38130. (901)344-9024. **E-mail:** bellebooks@bellebooks.com. **Website:** www.bellebooks.com. BelleBooks began by publishing Southern fiction. It has become a "second home" for many established authors, who also continue to publish with major publishing houses. Publishes 30-40 titles/year.

FICTION "Yes, we'd love to find the next Harry Potter, but our primary focus for the moment is publishing for the teen market."

HOW TO CONTACT Query e-mail with brief synopsis and credentials/credits with full ms attached (RTF format preferred).

TERMS Guidelines online.

TIPS "Our list aims for the teen reader and the cross-over market. If you're a 'Southern Louise Rennison,' that would catch our attention. Humor is always a plus. We'd love to see books featuring teen boys as protagonists. We're happy to see dark edgy books on serious subjects."

Ⓐ BERKLEY BOOKS

Penguin Group (USA) Inc., 375 Hudson St., New York NY 10014. **Website:** us.penguingroup.com/. **Contact:** Leslie Gelbman, president and publisher. The Berkley Publishing Group publishes a variety of general nonfiction and fiction including the traditional categories of romance, mystery and science fiction. Publishes paperback and mass market originals and reprints. Publishes 700 titles/year.

○ "Due to the high volume of mss received, most Penguin Group (USA) Inc. imprints do not normally accept unsolicited mss. The preferred and standard method for having mss considered for publication by a major publisher is to submit them through an established literary agent."

FICTION No occult fiction.

NONFICTION No memoirs or personal stories.

HOW TO CONTACT Prefers agented submissions.

BETHANY HOUSE PUBLISHERS

Division of Baker Publishing Group, 6030 E. Fulton Rd., Ada MI 49301. (616)676-9185. **Fax:** (616)676-9573. **Website:** bakerpublishinggroup.com/bethanyhouse. Bethany House Publishers specializes in books that communicate Biblical truth and assist people in both spiritual and practical areas of life. "While we do not accept unsolicited queries or proposals via telephone or e-mail, we will consider 1-page queries sent by fax and directed to adult nonfiction, adult fiction, or young adult/children." *All unsolicited mss returned unopened.* Publishes hardcover and trade paperback originals, mass market paperback reprints. Publishes 90-100 titles/year. 2% of books from first-time authors. 50% from unagented writers.

HOW TO CONTACT Responds in 3 months to queries. Publishes a book 1 year after acceptance.

TERMS Pays royalty on net price. Pays advance. Book catalog for 9×12 envelope and 5 first-class stamps. Guidelines online.

TIPS "Bethany House Publishers' publishing program relates Biblical truth to all areas of life—whether in

the framework of a well-told story, of a challenging book for spiritual growth, or of a Bible reference work. We are seeking high-quality fiction and nonfiction that will inspire and challenge our audience."

Ⓐ BLOOMSBURY CHILDREN'S BOOKS

Imprint of Bloomsbury USA, 1385 Broadway, 5th Floor, New York NY 10008. **Website:** www.bloomsbury.com/us/childrens. No phone calls or e-mails. *Agented submissions only.* Publishes 60 titles/year. 25% of books from first-time authors.

HOW TO CONTACT Agented submissions only. Responds in 6 months.

TERMS Pays royalty. Pays advance. Book catalog online. Guidelines online.

BOOKFISH BOOKS

E-mail: bookfishbooks@gmail.com. **Website:** twitter.com/bookfishbooks. BookFish Books is looking for novel and novella lengthed young adult, new adult, and middle grade works in all subgenres. Both published and unpublished, agented or unagented authors are welcome to submit.

HOW TO CONTACT Query via e-mail with a brief synopsis and first 3 chapters of ms.

TERMS Guidelines online.

TIPS "We only accept complete mss. Please do not query us with partial mss or proposals."

BOYDS MILLS PRESS

Highlights for Children, Inc., 815 Church St., Honesdale PA 18431. (570)253-1164. **Website:** www.boydsmillspress.com. Boyds Mills Press publishes picture books, nonfiction, activity books, and paperback reprints. Their titles have been named notable books by the International Reading Association, the American Library Association, and the National Council of Teachers of English. They've earned numerous awards, including the National Jewish Book Award, the Christopher Medal, the NCTE Orbis Pictus Honor, and the Golden Kite Honor. Boyds Mills Press welcomes unsolicited submissions from published and unpublished writers and artists. Submit a ms with a cover letter of relevant information, including experience with writing and publishing. Label the package "Manuscript Submission" and include an SASE. For art samples, label the package "Art Sample Submission."

FICTION Interested in picture books and middle grade fiction. Do not send a query first. Send the entire ms of picture book or the first 3 chapters and a plot summary for middle grade fiction (will request the balance of ms if interested).

NONFICTION Include a detailed bibliography with submission. Highly recommends including an expert's review of your ms and a detailed explanation of the books in the marketplace that are similar to the one you propose. References to the need for this book (by the National Academy of Sciences or by similar subject-specific organizations) will strengthen your proposal. If you intend for the book to be illustrated with photos or other graphic elements (charts, graphs, etc.), it is your responsibility to find or create those elements and to include with the submission a permissions budget, if applicable. Finally, keep in mind that good children's nonfiction has a narrative quality—a story line—that encyclopedias do not; please consider whether both the subject and the language will appeal to children.

HOW TO CONTACT Responds to mss within 3 months.

ILLUSTRATION Illustrators submitting a picture book should include the ms, a dummy, and a sample reproduction of the final artwork that reflects the style and technique you intend to use. Do not send original artwork.

TERMS Catalog online. Guidelines online.

◐⊘ BRIGHT RING PUBLISHING, INC.

P.O. Box 31338, Bellingham WA 98228. (360)592-9201. **Fax:** (360)592-4503. **E-mail:** maryann@brightring. com. **Website:** www.brightring.com. **Contact:** Mary-Ann Kohl, editor.

◑   *Bright Ring is no longer accepting ms submissions.*

CALKINS CREEK

Boyds Mills Press, 815 Church St., Honesdale PA 18431. **Website:** www.calkinscreekbooks.com. "We aim to publish books that are a well-written blend of creative writing and extensive research, which emphasize important events, people, and places in US history."

HOW TO CONTACT Submit outline/synopsis and 3 sample chapters. Submit outline/synopsis and 3 sample chapters.

ILLUSTRATION Accepts material from international illustrators. Works with 25 (for all Boyds Mills Press imprints) illustrators/year. Uses both color and b&w. Reviews ms/illustration packages. For ms/illustration packages: Submit ms with 2 pieces of final art. Submit ms/illustration packages to address above, label package "Manuscript Submission." Reviews work for future assignments. If interested in illustrating future titles, query with samples. Submit samples to address above. Label package "Art Sample Submission."

PHOTOGRAPHY Buys stock images and assigns work. Submit photos to: address above, label package "Art Sample Submission." Uses color or b&w 8×10 prints. For first contact, send promo piece (color or b&w).

TERMS Pays authors royalty or work purchased outright. Guidelines online.

TIPS "Read through our recently published titles and review our catalog. When selecting titles to publish, our emphasis will be on important events, people, and places in US history. Writers are encouraged to submit a detailed bibliography, including secondary and primary sources, and expert reviews with their submissions."

⊘⊘ ◭ CANDLEWICK PRESS

99 Dover St., Somerville MA 02144. (617)661-3330. **Fax:** (617)661-0565. **E-mail:** bigbear@candlewick. com. **Website:** www.candlewick.com. "Candlewick Press publishes high-quality, illustrated children's books for ages infant through young adult. We are a truly child-centered publisher." Publishes hardcover and trade paperback originals, and reprints. Publishes 200 titles/year. 5% of books from first-time authors.

◑   *Candlewick Press is not accepting queries or unsolicited mss at this time.*

FICTION Picture books: animal, concept, contemporary, fantasy, history, humor, multicultural, nature/environment, poetry. Middle readers, young adults: contemporary, fantasy, history, humor, multicultural, poetry, science fiction, sports, suspense/mystery.

NONFICTION Picture books: concept, biography, geography, nature/environment. Young readers: biography, geography, nature/environment.

HOW TO CONTACT "We currently do not accept unsolicited editorial queries or submissions. If you are an author or illustrator and would like us to consider your work, please read our submissions policy (online) to learn more."

ILLUSTRATION "Candlewick prefers to see a range of styles from artists along with samples showing strong characters (human or animals) in various settings with various emotions."

TERMS Pays authors royalty of 2½-10% based on retail price. Offers advance.

TIPS *"We no longer accept unsolicited mss. See our website for further information about us."*

CAPSTONE PRESS

Capstone Young Readers, 1710 Roe Crest Dr., North Mankato MN 56003. **E-mail:** nf.il.sub@capstonepub.com. **Website:** www.capstonepub.com. The Capstone Press imprint publishes nonfiction with accessible text on topics kids love to capture interest and build confidence and skill in beginning, struggling, and reluctant readers, grades pre-K-9.

FICTION Send fiction submissions via e-mail (author.sub@capstonepub.com). Include the following, in the body of the e-mail: sample chapters, résumé, and a list of previous publishing credits.

NONFICTION Send nonfiction submissions via postal mail. Include the following: résumé, cover letter, and up to 3 writing samples.

HOW TO CONTACT Responds only if submissions fit needs. Mss and writing samples will not be returned. "If you receive no reply within 6 months, you should assume the editors are not interested."

ILLUSTRATION Send fiction illustration submissions via e-mail (il.sub@capstonepub.com). Include the following, in the body of the e-mail: sample artwork, résumé, and a list of previous publishing credits. For nonfiction illustrations, send via e-mail (nf.il.sub@capstonepub.com) sample artwork (2-4 pieces) and a list of previous publishing credits.

TERMS Catalog available upon request. Guidelines online.

⊘ CAROLRHODA BOOKS, INC.

1251 Washington Ave. N., Minneapolis MN 55401. **Website:** www.lernerbooks.com. "We will continue to seek targeted solicitations at specific reading levels and in specific subject areas. The company will list these targeted solicitations on our website and in national newsletters, such as the SCBWI Bulletin." Interested in "boundary-pushing" teen fiction. *Lerner Publishing Group no longer accepts submissions to any of their imprints except for Kar-Ben Publishing.*

Ⓐ CARTWHEEL BOOKS

Imprint of Scholastic Trade Division, 557 Broadway, New York NY 10012. (212)343-6100. **Website:** www.scholastic.com. Cartwheel Books publishes innovative books for children, up to age 8. "We are looking for 'novelties' that are books first, play objects second.

Even without its gimmick, a Cartwheel Book should stand alone as a valid piece of children's literature." Publishes novelty books, easy readers, board books, hardcover and trade paperback originals.

FICTION Again, the subject should have mass market appeal for very young children. Humor can be helpful, but not necessary. Mistakes writers make are a reading level that is too difficult, a topic of no interest or too narrow, or mss that are too long.

NONFICTION Cartwheel Books publishes for the very young, therefore nonfiction should be written in a manner that is accessible to preschoolers through 2nd grade. Often writers choose topics that are too narrow or "special" and do not appeal to the mass market. Also, the text and vocabulary are frequently too difficult for our young audience.

HOW TO CONTACT *Accepts mss from agents only.*

TERMS Guidelines available free.

◯Ⓐ MARSHALL CAVENDISH

99 White Plains Rd., Tarrytown NY 10591. (914)332-8888. **Fax:** (914)332-1082. **Website:** www.marshallcavendish.us. "Marshall Cavendish is an international publisher that publishes books, directories, magazines and digital platforms. Our philosophy of enriching life through knowledge transcends boundaries of geography and culture. In line with this vision, our products reach across the globe in 13 languages, and our publishing network spans Asia and the US. Our brands have garnered international awards for educational excellence, and they include Marshall Cavendish Reference, Marshall Cavendish Benchmark, Marshall Cavendish Children, Marshall Cavendish Education and Marshall Cavendish Editions."

◖ *Marshall Cavendish is no longer accepting unsolicited mss. However, the company will continue to consider agented mss.*

CEDAR FORT, INC.

2373 W. 700 S, Springville UT 84663. (801)489-4084. **Fax:** (801)489-1097. **Website:** www.cedarfort.com. "Each year we publish well over 100 books, and many of those are by first-time authors. At the same time, we love to see books from established authors. As one of the largest book publishers in Utah, we have the capability and enthusiasm to make your book a success, whether you are a new author or a returning one. We want to publish uplifting and edifying books that help people think about what is important in life, books people enjoy reading to relax and feel better about themselves, and books to help improve lives. Although we do put out several children's books each year, we are extremely selective. Our children's books must have strong religious or moral values, and must contain outstanding writing and an excellent storyline." Publishes hardcover, trade paperback originals and reprints, mass market paperback and electronic reprints. Publishes 150 titles/year. 60% of books from first-time authors. 95% from unagented writers.

HOW TO CONTACT Submit completed ms. Query with SASE; submit proposal package, including outline, 2 sample chapters; or submit completed ms. Receives 200 queries/year; 600 mss/year. Responds in 1 month on queries; 2 months on proposals; 4 months on mss. Publishes book 10-14 months after acceptance.

TERMS Pays 10-12% royalty on wholesale price. Pays $2,000-50,000 advance. Catalog and guidelines online.

TIPS "Our audience is rural, conservative, mainstream. The first page of your ms is very important because we start reading every submission, but good writing and plot keep us reading."

○ CHARLESBRIDGE PUBLISHING

85 Main St., Watertown MA 02472. (617)926-0329. **Fax:** (617)926-5720. **E-mail:** tradeeditorial@charlesbridge.com. **Website:** www.charlesbridge.com. "Charlesbridge publishes high-quality books for children, with a goal of creating lifelong readers and lifelong learners. Our books encourage reading and discovery in the classroom, library, and home. We believe that books for children should offer accurate information, promote a positive worldview, and embrace a child's innate sense of wonder and fun. To this end, we continually strive to seek new voices, new visions, and new directions in children's literature." Publishes hardcover and trade paperback nonfiction and fiction, children's books for the trade and library markets. Publishes 30 titles/year. 10-20% of books from first-time authors; 80% from unagented writers.

FICTION Strong stories with enduring themes. Charlesbridge publishes both picture books and transitional bridge books (books ranging from early readers to middle-grade chapter books). Our fiction titles include lively, plot-driven stories with strong, engaging characters. No alphabet books, board books, coloring books, activity books, or books with audiotapes or CD-ROMs.

NONFICTION Strong interest in nature, environment, social studies, and other topics for trade and library markets.

HOW TO CONTACT *Exclusive submissions only.* "Charlesbridge accepts unsolicited mss submitted exclusively to us for a period of 3 months. 'Exclusive Submission' should be written on all envelopes and cover letters." Please submit only 1 or 2 chapters at a time. For nonfiction books longer than 30 ms pages, send a detailed proposal, a chapter outline, and 1-3 chapters of text. Responds in 3 months. Publishes ms 2-4 years after acceptance.

TERMS Pays royalty. Pays advance. Guidelines online.

TIPS "To become acquainted with our publishing program, we encourage you to review our books and visit our website where you will find our catalog."

○ CHICAGO REVIEW PRESS

814 N. Franklin St., Chicago IL 60610. (312)337-0747. **Fax:** (312)337-5110. **E-mail:** frontdesk@ipgbook.com. **Website:** www.chicagoreviewpress.com. **Contact:** Cynthia Sherry, publisher; Yuval Taylor, senior editor; Jerome Pohlen, senior editor; Lisa Reardon, senior editor. "Chicago Review Press publishes high-quality, nonfiction, educational activity books that extend the learning process through hands-on projects and accurate and interesting text. We look for activity books that are as much fun as they are constructive and informative."

NONFICTION Young readers, middle readers and young adults: activity books, arts/crafts, multicultural, history, nature/environment, science. "We're interested in hands-on, educational books; anything else probably will be rejected." Average length: young readers and young adults—144-160 pages.

HOW TO CONTACT Enclose cover letter and no more than a table of contents and 1-2 sample chapters; prefers not to receive e-mail queries. Responds in 2 months. Publishes a book 1-2 years after acceptance.

ILLUSTRATION Works with 6 illustrators/year. Uses primarily b&w artwork. Reviews ms/illustration packages from artists. Submit 1-2 chapters of ms with corresponding pieces of final art. Illustrations only: Query with samples, résumé. Responds only if interested. Samples returned with SASE.

PHOTOGRAPHY Buys photos from freelancers ("but not often"). Buys stock and assigns work.

Wants "instructive photos. We consult our files when we know what we're looking for on a book-by-book basis." Uses b&w prints.

TERMS Pays authors royalty of 7 ½-12 ½% based on retail price. Offers advances of $3,000-6,000. Pays illustrators and photographers by the project (range varies considerably). Book catalog available for $3. Ms guidelines available for $3.

TIPS "We're looking for original activity books for small children and the adults caring for them—new themes and enticing projects to occupy kids' imaginations and promote their sense of personal creativity. We like activity books that are as much fun as they are constructive. Please write for guidelines so you'll know what we're looking for."

CHILDREN'S BRAINS ARE YUMMY (CBAY) BOOKS

P.O. Box 670296, Austin TX 75367. **E-mail:** conflict submissions@gmail.com; madeline@cbaybooks.com. **Website:** www.cbaybooks.com. **Contact:** Madeline Smoot, publisher. "CBAY Books currently focuses on quality fantasy and science fiction books for the middle grade and teen markets. We are not currently accepting unsolicited submissions." Publishes 8 titles/year. 30% of books from first-time authors.

ILLUSTRATION Accepts international material. Works with 0-1 illustrators/year. Uses color artwork only. Reviews artwork. Send mss with dummy. Send résumé and tearsheets. Send samples to Madeline Smoot. Responds to queries only if interested.

PHOTOGRAPHY Buy stock images.

TERMS Pays authors royalty 10-15% based on wholesale price. Offers advances against royalties. Average amount $500. Brochure and guidelines online.

CHILD WELFARE LEAGUE OF AMERICA

1726 M St. NW, Suite 500, Washington DC 20036. **E-mail:** cwla@cwla.org. **Website:** www.cwla.org. CWLA is a privately supported, nonprofit, membership-based organization committed to preserving, protecting, and promoting the well-being of all children and their families. Publishes hardcover and trade paperback originals.

HOW TO CONTACT Submit complete ms and proposal with outline, TOC, sample chapter, intended audience, and SASE.

TERMS Book catalog and guidelines online.

TIPS "We are looking for positive, kid-friendly books for ages 3-9. We are looking for books that have a positive message—a feel-good book."

CHRONICLE BOOKS

680 Second St., San Francisco CA 94107. **E-mail:** submissions@chroniclebooks.com. **Website:** www.chroniclebooks.com. "We publish an exciting range of books, stationery, kits, calendars, and novelty formats. Our list includes children's books and interactive formats; young adult books; cookbooks; fine art, design, and photography; pop culture; craft, fashion, beauty, and home decor; relationships, mind-body-spirit; innovative formats such as interactive journals, kits, decks, and stationery; and much, much more." Publishes 90 titles/year.

FICTION Only interested in fiction for children and young adults. No adult fiction.

NONFICTION "We're always looking for the new and unusual. We do accept unsolicited mss and we review all proposals. However, given the volume of proposals we receive, we are not able to personally respond to unsolicited proposals unless we are interested in pursuing the project."

HOW TO CONTACT Submit complete ms (picture books); submit outline/synopsis and 3 sample chapters (for older readers). Will not respond to submissions unless interested. Will not consider submissions by fax, e-mail, or disk. Do not include SASE; do not send original materials. No submissions will be returned. Submit via mail or e-mail (prefers e-mail for adult submissions; only by mail for children's submissions). Submit proposal (guidelines online) and allow 3 months for editors to review and for children's submissions, allow 6 months. If submitting by mail, do not include SASE since our staff will not return materials. Responds to queries in 1 month. Publishes a book 1-3 years after acceptance.

ILLUSTRATION Works with 40-50 illustrators/year. Wants "unusual art, graphically strong, something that will stand out on the shelves. Fine art, not mass market." Reviews ms/illustration packages from artists. "Indicate if project *must* be considered jointly, or if editor may consider text and art separately." Illustrations only: Submit samples of artist's work (not necessarily from book, but in the envisioned style). Slides, tearsheets and color photocopies OK. (No original art.) Dummies helpful. Résumé helpful. Samples suited to our needs are filed for future reference. Samples not suited to our needs will be recycled. Queries and project proposals responded to in same time frame as author query/proposals."

PHOTOGRAPHY Purchases photos from freelancers. Works on assignment only.

TERMS Generally pays authors in royalties based on retail price, "though we do occasionally work on a flat fee basis." Advance varies. Illustrators paid royalty based on retail price or flat fee. Book catalog for 9×12 SAE and 8 first-class stamps. Ms guidelines for #10 SASE.

CHRONICLE BOOKS FOR CHILDREN

680 Second St., San Francisco CA 94107. (415)537-4200. **Fax:** (415)537-4460. **E-mail:** submissions@chroniclebooks.com. **Website:** www.chroniclekids.com. "Chronicle Books for Children publishes an eclectic mixture of traditional and innovative children's books. Our aim is to publish books that inspire young readers to learn and grow creatively while helping them discover the joy of reading. We're looking for quirky, bold artwork and subject matter." Publishes hardcover and trade paperback originals. Publishes 100-110 titles/year. 6% of books from first-time authors. 25% from unagented writers.

FICTION Does not accept proposals by fax, via e-mail, or on disk. When submitting artwork, either as a part of a project or as samples for review, do not send original art.

HOW TO CONTACT Query with synopsis. 30,000 queries received/year. Responds in 2-4 weeks to queries; 6 months to mss. Publishes a book 18-24 months after acceptance.

TERMS Pays variable advance. Book catalog for 9×12 envelope and 3 first-class stamps. Guidelines online.

TIPS "We are interested in projects that have a unique bent to them—be it in subject matter, writing style, or illustrative technique. As a small list, we are looking for books that will lend our list a distinctive flavor. Primarily we are interested in fiction and nonfiction picture books for children ages up to 8 years, and nonfiction books for children ages up to 12 years. We publish board, pop-up, and other novelty formats as well as picture books. We are also interested in early chapter books, middle grade fiction, and young adult projects."

⊕ CINCO PUNTOS PRESS

701 Texas Ave., El Paso TX 79901. (915)838-1625. **Fax:** (915)838-1635. **E-mail:** info@cincopuntos.com. **Web**site: www.cincopuntos.com. **Contact:** Lee Byrd, acquisitions editor. "We don't always know what we're looking for until we actually see it, but the one thing that matters to us is that the writing is good, that it is work that comes from the heart and soul of the author and that it fits well with the concerns of our press."

HOW TO CONTACT "Call our acquisitions editor; if she gives you the green light, submit the first 10 pages and we'll go from there."

CLARION BOOKS

Houghton Mifflin Co., 215 Park Ave. S., New York NY 10003. **Website:** www.hmhco.com. "Clarion Books publishes picture books, nonfiction, and fiction for infants through grade 12. Avoid telling your stories in verse unless you are a professional poet. *We are no longer responding to your unsolicited submission unless we are interested in publishing it. Please do not include a SASE. Submissions will be recycled, and you will not hear from us regarding the status of your submission unless we are interested. We regret that we cannot respond personally to each submission, but we do consider each and every submission we receive.*" Publishes hardcover originals for children. Publishes 50 titles/year.

FICTION "Clarion is highly selective in the areas of historical fiction, fantasy, and science fiction. A novel must be superlatively written in order to find a place on the list. Mss that arrive without an SASE of adequate size will *not* be responded to or returned. Accepts fiction translations."

NONFICTION No unsolicited mss.

HOW TO CONTACT Submit complete ms. No queries, please. Send to only *one* Clarion editor. Query with SASE. Submit proposal package, sample chapters, SASE. Responds in 2 months to queries. Publishes a book 2 years after acceptance.

ILLUSTRATION Pays illustrators royalty; flat fee for jacket illustration.

TERMS Pays 5-10% royalty on retail price. Pays minimum of $4,000 advance. Guidelines online.

TIPS "Looks for freshness, enthusiasm—in short, life."

CRAIGMORE CREATIONS

PMB 114, 4110 SE Hawthorne Blvd., Portland OR 97124. (503)477-9562. **E-mail:** info@craigmorecreations.com. **Website:** www.craigmorecreations.com.

NONFICTION "We publish books that make time travel seem possible: nonfiction that explores pre-history and Earth sciences for children."

HOW TO CONTACT Submit proposal package. See website for detailed submission guidelines. Submit proposal package. See website for detailed submission guidelines.

CREATIVE COMPANY

(800)445-6209. **Fax:** (507)388-2746. **E-mail:** info@thecreativecompany.us. **Website:** www.thecreativecompany.us. **Contact:** Kate Riggs, managing editor. The Creative Company has two imprints: Creative Editions (picture books), and Creative Education (nonfiction series). Publishes 140 titles/year.

○ *"We are currently not accepting fiction submissions."*

NONFICTION Picture books, young readers, young adults: animal, arts/crafts, biography, careers, geography, health, history, hobbies, multicultural, music/dance, nature/environment, religion, science, social issues, special needs, sports. Average word length: young readers—500; young adults—6,000.

HOW TO CONTACT Submit outline/synopsis and 2 sample chapters, along with division of titles within the series. Responds in 3 months. Publishes a book 2 years after acceptance.

PHOTOGRAPHY Buys stock. Contact: Donny Gettinger, photo editor. Model/property releases not required; captions required. Uses b&w prints. Submit cover letter, promo piece. Ms and photographer guidelines available for SAE.

TERMS Guidelines available for SAE.

TIPS "We are accepting nonfiction, series submissions only. Fiction submissions will not be reviewed or returned. Nonfiction submissions should be presented in series (4, 6, or 8) rather than single."

⊕ CRESTON BOOKS

P.O. Box 9369, Berkeley CA 94709. **E-mail:** submissions@crestonbooks.co. **Website:** crestonbooks.co. Creston Books is author-illustrator driven, with talented, award-winning creators given more editorial freedom and control than in a typical New York house.

HOW TO CONTACT Please paste text of picture books or first chapters of novels in the body of e-mail.

CRICKET BOOKS

Imprint of Carus Publishing, 70 E. Lake St., Suite 300, Chicago IL 60601. (603)924-7209. **Fax:** (603)924-7380. **Website:** www.cricketmag.com. **Contact:** Submissions Editor. Cricket Books publishes picture books, chapter books, and middle-grade novels. Publishes hardcover originals. Publishes 5 titles/year.

HOW TO CONTACT Publishes ms 18 months after acceptance.

ILLUSTRATION Works with 4 illustrators/year. Uses color and b&w. Illustration only: Please send artwork submissions via e-mail to: mail@cicadamag.com. Make sure "portfolio samples—cricket books" is the subject line of the e-mail. The file should be 72 dpi RGB jpg format. **Contact:** John Sandford. Responds only if interested.

TERMS Pays up to 10% royalty on retail price. Average advance: $1,500 and up. *Currently not accepting queries or mss. Check website for submissions details and updates.*

TIPS "Take a look at the recent titles to see what sort of materials we're interested in, especially for nonfiction. Please note that we aren't doing the sort of strictly educational nonfiction that other publishers specialize in."

CROSSWAY

A publishing ministry of Good News Publishing, 1300 Crescent St., Wheaton IL 60174. (630)682-4300. **Fax:** (630)682-4785. **E-mail:** info@crossway.org. **E-mail:** submissions@crossway.org. **Website:** www.crossway.org. **Contact:** Jill Carter, editorial administrator. "'Making a difference in people's lives for Christ" as its maxim, Crossway Books lists titles written from an evangelical Christian perspective." Member ECPA. Distributes titles through Christian bookstores and catalogs. Promotes titles through magazine ads, catalogs. Publishes 85 titles/year.

○ *Does not accept unsolicited mss.*

HOW TO CONTACT "Send us an e-mail query and, if your idea fits within our acquisitions guidelines, we'll invite a proposal." Publishes ms 18 months after acceptance.

TERMS Pays negotiable royalty.

CURIOSITY QUILLS

(800)998-2509. **E-mail:** editor@curiosityquills.com. **Website:** curiosityquills.com. Curiosity Quills is a publisher of hard-hitting dark sci-fi, speculative fiction, and paranormal works aimed at adults, young adults, and new adults.

FICTION Looking for "thought-provoking, mind-twisting rollercoasters—challenge our mind, turn our world upside down, and make us question. Those are the makings of a true literary marauder."

HOW TO CONTACT Submit ms using online submission form.

TERMS Pays variable royalty. Guidelines online.

KATHY DAWSON BOOKS

Penguin Group, 375 Hudson St., New York NY 10014. (212)366-2000. **Website:** kathydawsonbooks.tumblr. com. **Contact:** Kathy Dawson, vice-president and publisher. Mission statement: Publish stellar novels with unforgettable characters for children and teens that expand their vision of the world, sneakily explore the meaning of life, celebrate the written word, and last for generations. The imprint strives to publish tomorrow's award contenders: quality books with strong hooks in a variety of genres with universal themes and compelling voices—books that break the mold and the heart.

HOW TO CONTACT Accepts fiction queries via snail mail only. Include cover sheet with one-sentence elevator pitch, main themes, author version of catalog copy for book, first 10 pages of ms (double-spaced, Times Roman, 12 point type), and publishing history. No SASE needed. Responds only if interested. Responds only if interested.

TERMS Guidelines online.

Ⓐ DELACORTE PRESS

Imprint of Random House Publishing Group, 1745 Broadway, New York NY 10019. (212)782-9000. **Website:** www.randomhouse.com. Publishes middle grade and young adult fiction in hard cover, trade paperback, mass market, and digest formats.

Ⓠ   All other query letters or ms submissions must be submitted through an agent or at the request of an editor. No e-mail queries.

Ⓐ DIAL BOOKS FOR YOUNG READERS

Imprint of Penguin Group (USA), 345 Hudson St., New York NY 10014. (212)366-2000. **Website:** www. penguin.com/youngreaders. **Contact:** Lauri Hornik, president/publisher. "Dial Books for Young Readers publishes quality picture books for ages 18 months-6 years; lively, believable novels for middle readers and young adults; and occasional nonfiction for middle readers and young adults." Publishes hardcover originals. Publishes 50 titles/year. 20% of books from first-time authors.

FICTION Especially looking for lively and well-written novels for middle grade and young adult children involving a convincing plot and believable characters. The subject matter or theme should not already be overworked in previously published books. The approach must not be demeaning to any minority group, nor should the roles of female characters (or others) be stereotyped, though we don't think books should be didactic, or in any way message-y. No topics inappropriate for the juvenile, young adult, and middle grade audiences. No plays.

HOW TO CONTACT Agented queries only.

ILLUSTRATION Send nonreturnable samples, no originals, to Lily Malcolm. Show children and animals.

TERMS Pays royalty. Advance varies. Book catalog and guidelines online.

TIPS "Our readers are anywhere from preschool age to teenage. Picture books must have strong plots, lots of action, unusual premises, or universal themes treated with freshness and originality. Humor works well in these books. A very well-thought-out and intelligently presented book has the best chance of being taken on. Genre isn't as much of a factor as presentation."

Ⓐ DISNEY HYPERION BOOKS FOR CHILDREN

114 Fifth Ave., New York NY 10011-5690. **Website:** www.hyperionbooksforchildren.com.

FICTION Picture books, early readers, middle readers, young adults: adventure, animal, anthology (short stories), contemporary, fantasy, history, humor, multicultural, poetry, science fiction, sports, suspense/mystery. Middle readers, young adults: commercial fiction.

NONFICTION Narrative nonfiction for elementary schoolers.

HOW TO CONTACT *All submissions must come via an agent. Agented submissions only.*

ILLUSTRATION Works with 100 illustrators/year. "Picture books are fully illustrated throughout. All others depend on individual project." Illustrations only: Submit résumé, business card, promotional literature, or tearsheets to be kept on file. Responds only if interested. Original artwork returned at job's completion.

PHOTOGRAPHY Works on assignment only. Provide résumé, business card, promotional literature, or tearsheets to be kept on file.

DUTTON CHILDREN'S BOOKS

Penguin Group (USA), 375 Hudson St., New York NY 10014. **E-mail:** duttonpublicity@us.penguingroup.

com. **Website:** www.penguin.com. **Contact:** Julie Strauss-Gabel, vice president and publisher. Dutton Children's Books publishes high-quality fiction and nonfiction for readers ranging from preschoolers to young adults on a variety of subjects. Currently emphasizing middle grade and young adult novels that offer a fresh perspective. De-emphasizing photographic nonfiction and picture books that teach a lesson. Publishes hardcover originals as well as novelty formats. Publishes 100 titles/year. 15% of books from first-time authors.

○ "Cultivating the creative talents of authors and illustrators and publishing books with purpose and heart continue to be the mission and joy at Dutton."

FICTION Dutton Children's Books has a diverse, general interest list that includes picture books; easy-to-read books; and fiction for all ages, from first chapter books to young adult readers.

HOW TO CONTACT Query. Responds only if interested. Query.

TERMS Pays royalty on retail price. Offers advance. Pays royalty on retail price. Pays advance.

○ EDUPRESS, INC.

P.O. Box 8610, Madison WI 53708. (608)242-1201. **E-mail:** edupress@highsmith.com; lizb@demco.com. **Website:** www.edupress.com. **Contact:** Liz Bowie. Edupress, Inc., publishes supplemental curriculum resources for PK-6th grade. Currently emphasizing Common Core reading and math games and materials.

○ "Our mission is to create products that make kids want to go to school."

HOW TO CONTACT Submit complete ms via mail or e-mail with "Manuscript Submission" as the subject line. Responds in 2-4 months. Publishes ms 1-2 years after acceptance.

ILLUSTRATION Query with samples. Contact: Cathy Baker, product development manager. Responds only if interested. Samples returned with SASE.

PHOTOGRAPHY Buys stock.

TERMS Work purchased outright from authors. Catalog online.

TIPS "We are looking for unique, research-based, quality supplemental materials for Pre-K through 6th grade. We publish mainly reading and math materials in many different formats, including games. Our ma-

terials are intended for classroom and home schooling use. We do not publish picture books."

WILLIAM B. EERDMANS PUBLISHING CO.

2140 Oak Industrial Dr. NE, Grand Rapids MI 49505. (616)459-4591. **Fax:** (616)459-6540. **E-mail:** info@eerdmans.com. **Website:** www.eerdmans.com. **Contact:** Jon Pott, editor-in-chief. "The majority of our adult publications are religious and most of these are academic or semi-academic in character (as opposed to inspirational or celebrity books), though we also publish general trade books on the Christian life. Our nonreligious titles, most of them in regional history or on social issues, aim, similarly, at an educated audience." Publishes hardcover and paperback originals and reprints.

NONFICTION "We prefer that writers take the time to notice if we have published anything at all in the same category as their ms before sending it to us."

HOW TO CONTACT Query with SASE. Query with TOC, 2-3 sample chapters, and SASE for return of ms. Responds in 4 weeks.

TERMS Book catalog and ms guidelines free.

⊕ ELM BOOKS

1175 Hwy. 130, Laramie WY 82070. (610)529-0460. **E-mail:** leila.elmbooks@gmail.com. **Website:** www.elm-books.com. "We are eager to publish stories by new writers that have real stories to tell. We are looking for short stories (5,000-10,000 words) with real characters and true-to-life stories. Whether your story is fictionalized autobiography, or other stories of real-life mayhem and debauchery, we are interested in reading them!"

FICTION "We are looking for short stories (1,000-5,000 words) about kids of color that will grab readers' attentions—mysteries, adventures, humor, suspense, set in the present, near past or near future that reflect the realities and hopes of life in diverse communities." Also looking for middle grade novels (20,000-50,000 words).

HOW TO CONTACT Send complete ms for short stories; synopsis and 3 sample chapters for novels.

TERMS Pays royalties.

ENTANGLED TEEN

Website: www.entangledteen.com. "Entangled Teen and Entangled digiTeen, our young adult imprints publish the swoonworthy young adult romances readers crave. Whether they're dark and angsty or fun and sassy, contemporary, fantastical, or futuristic. We are seeking fresh voices with interesting twists on popular genres."

FICTION "We are seeking novels in the subgenres of romantic fiction for contemporary, upper young adult with crossover appeal."

HOW TO CONTACT E-mail using site. Agented and unagented submissions considered.

TERMS Pays royalty.

FACTS ON FILE, INC.

Infobase Learning, 132 W. 31st St., 17th Floor, New York NY 10001. (800)322-8755. **Fax:** (800)678-3633. **E-mail:** llikoff@factsonfile.com; custserv@factson file.com. **Website:** www.factsonfile.com. Facts on File produces high-quality reference materials on a broad range of subjects for the school library market and the general nonfiction trade. Publishes hardcover originals and reprints. Publishes 135-150 titles/year. 25% from unagented writers.

NONFICTION "We publish serious, informational books for a targeted audience. All our books must have strong library interest, but we also distribute books effectively to the trade. Our library books fit the junior and senior high school curriculum." No computer books, technical books, cookbooks, biographies (except YA), pop psychology, humor, fiction, or poetry.

HOW TO CONTACT Query or submit outline and sample chapter with SASE. No submissions returned without SASE. Responds in 2 months to queries.

ILLUSTRATION Commissions line art only.

TERMS Pays 10% royalty on retail price. Pays $5,000-10,000 advance. Book catalog available free. Guidelines online.

TIPS "Our audience is school and public libraries for our more reference-oriented books and libraries, schools and bookstores for our less reference-oriented informational titles."

FARRAR, STRAUS & GIROUX FOR YOUNG READERS

Macmillan Children's Publishing Group, 175 Fifth Ave., New York NY 10010. (212)741-6900. **Fax:** (212)633-2427. **E-mail:** childrens.editorial@fsgbooks. com. **Website:** www.fsgkidsbooks.com.

FICTION All levels, all categories. "Original and well-written material for all ages."

NONFICTION All levels, all categories. "We publish only literary nonfiction."

HOW TO CONTACT Submit cover letter, first 50 pages by mail only.

ILLUSTRATION Works with 30-60 illustrators/year. Reviews ms/illustration packages from artists. Submit ms with 1 example of final art, remainder roughs. Do not send originals. Illustrations only: Query with tearsheets. Responds if interested in 3 months. Samples returned with SASE; samples sometimes filed.

TERMS Book catalog available by request. Ms guidelines online.

TIPS "Study our catalog before submitting. We will see illustrators' portfolios by appointment. Don't ask for criticism and/or advice—due to the volume of submissions we receive, it's just not possible. Never send originals. Always enclose SASE."

Ⓐ FEIWEL AND FRIENDS

Macmillan Children's Publishing Group, 175 Fifth Ave., New York NY 10010. (646)307-5151. **Website:** us.macmillan.com/feiwelandfriends.aspx. Feiwel and Friends is a publisher of innovative children's fiction and nonfiction literature, including hardcover, paperback series, and individual titles. The list is eclectic and combines quality and commercial appeal for readers ages 0-16. The imprint is dedicated to "book by book" publishing, bringing the work of distinctive and oustanding authors, illustrators, and ideas to the marketplace. This market does not accept unsolicited mss due to the volume of submissions; they also do not accept unsolicited queries for interior art. The best way to submit a ms is through an agent.

TERMS Catalog online.

Ⓐ FIRST SECOND

Macmillan Children's Publishing Group, 175 5th Ave., New York NY 10010. **E-mail:** mail@firstsecondbooks. com. **Website:** www.firstsecondbooks.com. First Second is a publisher of graphic novels and an imprint of Macmillan Children's Publishing Group. First Second does not accept unsolicited submissions.

HOW TO CONTACT Responds in about 6 weeks.

TERMS Catalog online.

Ⓐ FLUX

Llewellyn Worldwide, Ltd., Llewellyn Worldwide, Ltd., 2143 Wooddale Dr., Woodbury MN 55125. (651)312-8613. **Fax:** (651)291-1908. **Website:** www. fluxnow.com. "Flux seeks to publish authors who see YA as a point of view, not a reading level. We look for books that try to capture a slice of teenage experience, whether in real or imagined worlds." Publishes 21 titles/year. 50% of books from first-time authors.

FICTION Young adults: adventure, contemporary, fantasy, history, humor, problem novels, religion, science fiction, sports, suspense. Average word length: 50,000.

HOW TO CONTACT *Accepts agented submissions only.*

TERMS Pays royalties of 10-15% based on wholesale price. Book catalog and guidelines online.

TIPS "Read contemporary teen books. Be aware of what else is out there. If you don't read teen books, you probably shouldn't write them. Know your audience. Write incredibly well. Do not condescend."

FREE SPIRIT PUBLISHING, INC.

217 Fifth Ave. N., Suite 200, Minneapolis MN 55401-1299. (612)338-2068. **Fax:** (612)337-5050. **E-mail:** acquisitions@freespirit.com. **Website:** www.freespirit.com. "We believe passionately in empowering kids to learn to think for themselves and make their own good choices." Publishes trade paperback originals and reprints. Publishes 12-18 titles/year. 5% of books from first-time authors. 75% from unagented writers.

Free Spirit does not accept general fiction, poetry or storybook submissions.

FICTION "We will consider fiction that relates directly to select areas of focus. Please review catalog and author guidelines (both available online) for details before submitting proposal. If you'd like material returned, enclose a SASE with sufficient postage."

NONFICTION "Many of our authors are educators, mental health professionals, and youth workers involved in helping kids and teens." No general fiction or picture storybooks, poetry, single biographies or autobiographies, books with mythical or animal characters, or books with religious or New Age content. "We are not looking for academic or religious materials, or books that analyze problems with the nation's school systems."

HOW TO CONTACT Accepts queries only—not submissions—by e-mail. Query with cover letter stating qualifications, intent, and intended audience and market analysis (how your book stands out from the field), along with your promotional plan, outline, 2 sample chapters, résumé, SASE. Do not send original copies of work. Responds to proposals in 4-6 months.

ILLUSTRATION Works with 5 illustrators/year. Submit samples to creative director for consideration. If appropriate, samples will be kept on file and artist will be contacted if a suitable project comes up. Enclose SASE if you'd like materials returned.

PHOTOGRAPHY Uses stock photos. Does not accept photography submissions.

TERMS Pays advance. Book catalog and ms guidelines online.

TIPS "Our books are issue-oriented, jargon-free, and solution-focused. Our audience is children, teens, teachers, parents, and youth counselors. We are especially concerned with kids' social and emotional well-being and look for books with ready-to-use strategies for coping with today's issues at home or in school-written in everyday language. We are not looking for academic or religious materials, or books that analyze problems with the nation's school systems. Instead, we want books that offer practical, positive advice so kids can help themselves, and parents and teachers can help kids succeed."

FULCRUM PUBLISHING

4690 Table Mountain Dr., Suite 100, Golden CO 80403. **E-mail:** acquisitions@fulcrumbooks.com. **Website:** www.fulcrum-books.com. **Contact:** T. Baker, acquisitions editor.

NONFICTION Middle and early readers: Western history, nature/ environment, Native American.

HOW TO CONTACT Submit complete ms or submit outline/synopsis and 2 sample chapters. "Publisher does not send response letters unless we are interested in publishing." Do not send SASE.

PHOTOGRAPHY Works on assignment only.

TERMS Pays authors royalty based on wholesale price. Offers advances. Catalog for SASE. Guidelines online.

TIPS "Research our line first. We look for books that appeal to the school market and trade. "

GIANT SQUID BOOKS

E-mail: editors@giantsquidbooks.com. **Website:** giantsquidbooks.com. "Our mission is to publish, support, and promote debut authors—and help them navigate the world of online publishing."

FICTION Giant Squid Books is currently open to submissions of young adult novels in any genre.

HOW TO CONTACT Query with the first 3 chapters or 50 pages of book.

TERMS Guidelines online.

TIPS "We read every submission and try to respond within two weeks but due to a high volume of submissions sometimes get behind! If it's been more than 2 weeks since you queried us, please feel free to send a follow-up e-mail."

GIBBS SMITH

P.O. Box 667, Layton UT 84041. (801)544-9800. **Fax:** (801)544-8853. **E-mail:** duribe@gibbs-smith.com. **Website:** www.gibbs-smith.com. **Contact:** Suzanne Taylor, associate publisher and creative director (children's activity books); Jennifer Grillone, art acquisitions. Publishes 3 titles/year. 50% of books from first-time authors. 50% from unagented writers.

NONFICTION Middle readers: activity, arts/crafts, cooking, how-to, nature/environment, science. Average word length: picture books—under 1,000 words; activity books—under 15,000 words.

HOW TO CONTACT Submit an outline and writing samples for activity books; query for other types of books. Responds in 2 months. Publishes ms 1-2 years after acceptance.

ILLUSTRATION Works with 2 illustrators/year. Reviews ms/illustration packages from artists. Query. Submit ms with 3-5 pieces of final art. Illustrations only: Query with samples; provide résumé, promo sheet, slides (duplicate slides, not originals). Responds only if interested. Samples returned with SASE; samples filed.

TERMS Pays illustrators by the project or royalty of 2% based on retail price. Sends galleys to authors; color proofs to illustrators. Original artwork returned at job's completion. Pays authors royalty of 2% based on retail price or work purchased outright ($500 minimum). Offers advances (average amount: $2,000). Book catalog available for 9×12 SAE and $2.30 postage. Ms guidelines available by e-mail.

TIPS "We target ages 5-11. We do not publish young adult novels or chapter books."

ⒶDAVID R. GODINE, PUBLISHER

15 Court Square, Suite 320, Boston MA 02108. (617)451-9600. **Fax:** (617)350-0250. **E-mail:** info@godine.com. **Website:** www.godine.com. "We publish books that matter for people who care." This publisher is no longer considering unsolicited mss of any type. Only interested in agented material.

HOW TO CONTACT Only interested in agented material.

ILLUSTRATION Only interested in agented material. Works with 1-3 illustrators/year. "Please do not send original artwork unless solicited. Almost all of the children's books we accept for publication come to

us with the author and illustrator already paired up. Therefore, we rarely use freelance illustrators."

ⒶⒸ GOLDEN BOOKS FOR YOUNG READERS GROUP

1745 Broadway, New York NY 10019. **Website:** www.randomhouse.com. "Random House Books aims to create books that nurture the hearts and minds of children, providing and promoting quality books and a rich variety of media that entertain and educate readers from 6 months to 12 years." *Random House-Golden Books does not accept unsolicited mss, only agented material.* They reserve the right not to return unsolicited material. 2% of books from first-time authors.

TERMS Pays authors in royalties; sometimes buys mss outright. Book catalog free on request.

GOOSEBOTTOM BOOKS

543 Trinidad Ln., Foster City CA 94404. (888)407-5286. **E-mail:** submissions@goosebottombooks.com. **Website:** goosebottombooks.com.

FICTION "We do not accept ms submissions. We accept writing and illustration samples, and then select the writers and illustrators we'd like to work with."

ILLUSTRATION Considers samples.

GREENHAVEN PRESS

27500 Drake Rd., Farmington Hills MI 48331. **Website:** www.gale.com/greenhaven. Publishes 220 young adult academic reference titles/year. 50% of books by first-time authors. Greenhaven continues to print quality nonfiction anthologies for libraries and classrooms. "Our well-known Opposing Viewpoints series is highly respected by students and librarians in need of material on controversial social issues." Greenhaven accepts no unsolicited mss. Send query, résumé, and list of published works by e-mail. Work purchased outright from authors; write-for-hire, flat fee.

NONFICTION Young adults (high school): controversial issues, social issues, history, literature, science, environment, health.

ⒶGREENWILLOW BOOKS

HarperCollins Publishers, 10 E. 53rd St., New York NY 10022. (212)207-7000. **Website:** www.greenwillowblog.com. *Does not accept unsolicited mss.* "Unsolicited mail will not be opened and will not be returned." Publishes hardcover originals, paperbacks, e-books, and reprints. Publishes 40-50 titles/year.

HOW TO CONTACT *Agented submissions only.* Publishes ms 2 years after acceptance.

TERMS Pays 10% royalty on wholesale price for first-time authors. Offers variable advance.

Ⓐ GROSSET & DUNLAP PUBLISHERS

Penguin Putnam Inc., 345 Hudson St., New York NY 10014. **Website:** www.penguin.com. **Contact:** Francesco Sedita, vice president/publisher. Grosset & Dunlap publishes children's books that show children that reading is fun, with books that speak to their interests, and that are affordable so that children can build a home library of their own. Focus on licensed properties, series, and readers. "Grosset & Dunlap publishes high-interest, affordable books for children ages 0-10 years. We focus on original series, licensed properties, readers and novelty books." Publishes hardcover (few) and mass market paperback originals. Publishes 140 titles/year.

HOW TO CONTACT *Agented submissions only.*

TERMS Pays royalty. Pays advance.

GROVE CREEK PUBLISHING

1404 W. State Rd., Suite 202, Pleasant Grove UT 84062. **E-mail:** info@grovecreekpublishing.com. **Website:** www.grovecreekpublishing.com. Grove Creek Publishing was founded to open a door into publishing for indie authors. "We are currently acquiring young adult mss for consideration. GCP does not look at any young adult project involving sex, gratuitous violence, and foul language."

HOW TO CONTACT Query first.

TERMS Guidelines online.

GRYPHON HOUSE, INC.

P.O. Box 10, 6848 Leon's Way, Lewisville NC 27023. **Website:** www.gryphonhouse.com. **Contact:** Kathy Charner, editor-in-chief. "Gryphon House publishes books that teachers and parents of young children (birth-age 8) consider essential to their daily lives." Publishes parent and teacher resource books, textbooks. Recently published *Reading Games*, by Jackie Silberg; *Primary Art*, by MaryAnn F. Kohl; *Teaching Young Children with Autism Spectrum Disorder*, by Clarissa Willis; *The Complete Resource Book for Infants*, by Pam Schiller. "At Gryphon House, our goal is to publish books that help teachers and parents enrich the lives of children from birth through age 8. We strive to make our books useful for teachers at all levels of experience, as well as for parents, caregivers, and anyone interested in working with children." Query.

Submit outline/synopsis and 2 sample chapters. Responds to queries/mss in 6 months. Publishes a book 18 months after acceptance. Will consider simultaneous submissions, e-mail submissions. Book catalog and ms guidelines available via website or with SASE. "We are looking for books of creative, participatory learning experiences that have a common conceptual theme to tie them together. The books should be on subjects that parents or teachers want to do on a daily basis." Publishes trade paperback originals. Publishes 12-15 titles/year.

NONFICTION Currently emphasizing social-emotional intelligence and classroom management; de-emphasizing literacy after-school activities.

HOW TO CONTACT "We prefer to receive a letter of inquiry and/or a proposal, rather than the entire ms. Please include: the proposed title, the purpose of the book, table of contents, introductory material, 20-40 sample pages of the actual book. In addition, please describe the book, including the intended audience, why teachers will want to buy it, how it is different from other similar books already published, and what qualifications you possess that make you the appropriate person to write the book. If you have a writing sample that demonstrates that you write clear, compelling prose, please include it with your letter." Responds in 3-6 months to queries.

ILLUSTRATION Works with 4-5 illustrators/year. Uses b&w realistic artwork only. Query with samples, promo sheet. Responds in 2 months. Samples returned with SASE; samples filed. Pays illustrators by the project.

PHOTOGRAPHY Pays photographers by the project or per photo. Sends edited ms copy to authors. Original artwork returned at job's completion.

TERMS Pays royalty on wholesale price. Guidelines available online.

Ⓐ HARLEQUIN TEEN

Harlequin, 233 Broadway, Suite 1001, New York NY 10279. **Website:** www.harlequin.com. **Contact:** Natashya Wilson, executive editor. Harlequin Teen is a single-title program dedicated to building authors and publishing unique, memorable young adult fiction.

FICTION Harlequin Teen looks for fresh, authentic fiction featuring extraordinary characters and extraordinary stories set in contemporary, paranormal, fantasy, science-fiction, and historical worlds. Wants commercial, high-concept stories that capture the teen experience and will speak to readers with power and authenticity. All subgenres are welcome, so long as the book delivers a relevant reading experience that will resonate long after the book's covers are closed. Expects that most stories will include a compelling romantic element.

HOW TO CONTACT *Agented submissions only.*

✚ HARMONY INK PRESS

5032 Capital Circle SW, Suite 2 PMB 279, Tallahassee FL 32305. (850)632-4648. **Fax:** (888)308-3739. **E-mail:** submissions@harmonyinkpress.com. **Website:** harmonyinkpress.com. Harmony Ink is accepting mss for teen and new adult fiction featuring at least one strong LGBTQ+ main character who shows significant personal growth through the course of the story.

FICTION "We are looking for stories in all subgenres, featuring primary characters across the whole LGBTQ+ spectrum between the ages of 14 and 21 that explore all the facets of young adult, teen, and new adult life. Sexual content should be appropriate for the characters and the story."

HOW TO CONTACT Submit complete ms.

TERMS Pays royalty. Pays $500-1,000 advance.

⊘ HARPERCOLLINS CHILDREN'S BOOKS/HARPERCOLLINS PUBLISHERS

195 Broadway, New York NY 10007. (212)207-7000. **Website:** www.harpercollins.com. **Contact:** Katherine Tegen, vice president and publisher; Anica Mrose Rissi, executive editor; Claudia Gabel, executive editor; Kathleen Duncan, general design assistant; Erica Dechavez, picture book assistant designer. HarperCollins, one of the largest English language publishers in the world, is a broad-based publisher with strengths in academic, business and professional, children's, educational, general interest, and religious and spiritual books, as well as multimedia titles. Publishes hardcover and paperback originals and paperback reprints. Publishes 500 titles/year.

FICTION "We look for a strong story line and exceptional literary talent."

NONFICTION *No unsolicited mss or queries.*

HOW TO CONTACT Agented submissions only. *All unsolicited mss returned.* Responds in 1 month, will contact only if interested. Does not accept any unsolicted texts.

TERMS Negotiates payment upon acceptance. Catalog online.

TIPS "We do not accept any unsolicited material."

⊘ HARPERTEEN

195 Broadway, New York NY 10007. (212)207-7000. **Website:** www.harpercollins.com. HarperTeen is a teen imprint that publishes hardcovers, paperback reprints and paperback originals. Publishes 100 titles/year.

◯   *HarperCollins Children's Books is not accepting unsolicited and/or unagented mss or queries.* Unfortunately the volume of these submissions is so large that they cannot receive the attention they deserve. Such submissions will not be reviewed or returned.

HEYDAY BOOKS

c/o Acquisitions Editor, Box 9145, Berkeley CA 94709. **Fax:** (510)549-1889. **E-mail:** heyday@heydaybooks.com. **Website:** www.heydaybooks.com. **Contact:** Gayle Wattawa, acquisitions and editorial director. "Heyday Books publishes nonfiction books and literary anthologies with a strong California focus. We publish books about Native Americans, natural history, history, literature, and recreation, with a strong California focus." Publishes hardcover originals, trade paperback originals and reprints. Publishes 12-15 titles/year. 50% of books from first-time authors. 90% from unagented writers.

FICTION Publishes picture books, beginning readers, and young adult literature.

NONFICTION Books about California only.

HOW TO CONTACT Submit complete ms for picture books; proposal with sample chapters for longer works. Mark attention: Children's Submission. Query with outline and synopsis. "Query or proposal by traditional post. Include a cover letter introducing yourself and your qualifications, a brief description of your project, a table of contents and list of illustrations, notes on the market you are trying to reach and why your book will appeal to them, a sample chapter, and a SASE if you would like us to return these materials to you." Responds in 3 months. Publishes book 18 months after acceptance.

TERMS Pays 8% royalty on net price. Book catalog online. Guidelines online.

HOLIDAY HOUSE, INC.

425 Madison Ave., New York NY 10017. (212)688-0085. **Fax:** (212)421-6134. **E-mail:** info@holiday-

house.com. **Website:** holidayhouse.com. "Holiday House publishes children's and young adult books for the school and library markets. We have a commitment to publishing first-time authors and illustrators. We specialize in quality hardcovers from picture books to young adult, both fiction and nonfiction, primarily for the school and library market." Publishes hardcover originals and paperback reprints. Publishes 50 titles/year. 5% of books from first-time authors. 50% from unagented writers.

FICTION Children's books only.

HOW TO CONTACT Query with SASE. No phone calls, please. Please send the entire ms, whether submitting a picture book or novel. "We do not accept certified or registered mail. There is no need to include a SASE. We do not consider submissions by e-mail or fax. Please note that you do not have to supply illustrations. However, if you have illustrations you would like to include with your submission, you may send detailed sketches or photocopies of the original art. Do not send original art." Responds in 4 months. Publishes 1-2 years after acceptance.

ILLUSTRATION Accepting art samples, not returned.

TERMS Pays royalty on list price, range varies. Guidelines for #10 SASE.

TIPS "We need mss with strong stories and writing."

HOUGHTON MIFFLIN HARCOURT BOOKS FOR CHILDREN

Imprint of Houghton Mifflin Trade & Reference Division, 222 Berkeley St., Boston MA 02116. (617)351-5000. **Fax:** (617)351-1111. **Website:** www.houghton mifflinbooks.com. Houghton Mifflin Harcourt gives shape to ideas that educate, inform, and above all, delight. *Does not respond to or return mss unless interested.* Publishes hardcover originals and trade paperback originals and reprints. Publishes 100 titles/year. 10% of books from first-time authors. 60% from unagented writers.

NONFICTION Interested in innovative books and subjects about which the author is passionate.

HOW TO CONTACT Submit complete ms. Query with SASE. Submit sample chapters, synopsis. 5,000 queries received/year. 14,000 mss received/year. Responds in 4-6 months to queries. Publishes ms 2 years after acceptance.

TERMS Pays 5-10% royalty on retail price. Pays variable advance. Guidelines online.

IDEALS CHILDREN'S BOOKS AND CANDYCANE PRESS

2630 Elm Hill Pike, Suite 100, Nashville TN 37214. **Website:** www.idealsbooks.com. **Contact:** Submissions.

FICTION Picture books: animal, concept, history, religion. Board books: animal, history, nature/environment, religion. Ideals publishes for ages 4-8, no longer than 800 words; CandyCane publishes for ages 2-5, no longer than 500 words.

NONFICTION Ideals publishes for ages 4-8, no longer than 800 words; CandyCane publishes for ages 2-5, no longer than 500 words.

HOW TO CONTACT Submit complete ms.

IDEALS PUBLICATIONS, INC.

2630 Elm Hill Pike, Suite 100, Nashville TN 37214. (615)333-0478. **E-mail:** idealsinfo@guideposts.org. **Website:** www.idealsbooks.com. "Ideals Publications publishes 20-25 new children's titles a year, primarily for 2-8 year-olds. Our backlist includes more than 400 titles, and we publish picture books, activity books, board books, and novelty and sound books covering a wide array of topics, such as Bible stories, holidays, early learning, history, family relationships, and values. Our bestselling titles include *The Story of Christmas, The Story of Easter, Seaman's Journal, How Do I Love You?, God Made You Special* and *A View at the Zoo*. Through our dedication to publishing high-quality and engaging books, we never forget our obligation to our littlest readers to help create those special moments with books."

FICTION Ideals Children's Books publishes fiction and nonfiction picture books for children ages 4 to 8. Subjects include holiday, inspirational, and patriotic themes; relationships and values; and general fiction. Mss should be no longer than 800 words. CandyCane Press publishes board books and novelty books for children ages 2 to 5. Subject matter is similar to Ideals Children's Books, with a focus on younger children. Mss should be no longer than 250 words.

ILLUSIO & BAQER

1827 W. Shannon Ave., Spokane WA **E-mail:** submissions@zharmae.com. **Website:** illusiobaqer.com. Illusio & Baqer publishes high-quality middle grade, young adult, and new adult fiction of all genres. "We are a young adult, new adult, and middle grade imprint of The Zharmae Publishing Press."

HOW TO CONTACT Query with synopsis and 3-5 sample chapters.

⊕ IMMORTAL INK PUBLISHING

E-mail: immortalinkpublishing@gmail.com. **Website:** www.immortalinkpublishing.com. Immortal Ink Publishing is open to most genres, but specifically wants literary fiction, women's fiction, crime/mystery/thriller, young adult, and dark and paranormal fiction that is original, character-based, and literary in flavor.

HOW TO CONTACT Submit query with first 10 pages via e-mail.

TIPS "Due to time constraints, we will not be giving reasons for our rejections (as you really shouldn't be making changes just because of something we personally didn't like anyway), but we will get back to you with either a 'no thanks' or a request for your full ms."

IMPACT PUBLISHERS, INC.

P.O. Box 6016, Atascadero CA 93423. **E-mail:** submissions@impactpublishers.com. **Website:** www.impactpublishers.com. **Contact:** Freeman Porter, submissions editor. "Our purpose is to make the best human services expertise available to the widest possible audience. We publish only popular psychology and self-help materials written in everyday language by professionals with advanced degrees and significant experience in the human services." Publishes 3-5 titles/year. 20% of books from first-time authors.

NONFICTION Young readers, middle readers, young adults: self-help.

HOW TO CONTACT Query or submit complete ms, cover letter, résumé. Responds in 3 months.

ILLUSTRATION Works with 1 illustrator/year. Not accepting freelance illustrator queries.

TERMS Pays authors royalty of 10-12%. Offers advances. Book catalog for #10 SASE with 2 first-class stamps. Guidelines for SASE.

TIPS "Please do not submit fiction, poetry, or narratives."

JEWISH LIGHTS PUBLISHING

LongHill Partners, Inc., Sunset Farm Offices, Rt. 4, P.O. Box 237, Woodstock VT 05091. (802)457-4000. **Fax:** (802)457-4004. **Website:** www.jewishlights.com. **Contact:** Acquisitions Editor. "Jewish Lights publishes books for people of all faiths and all backgrounds who yearn for books that attract, engage, educate, and spiritually inspire. Our authors are at the forefront

of spiritual thought and deal with the quest for the self and for meaning in life by drawing on the Jewish wisdom tradition. Our books cover topics including history, spirituality, life cycle, children, self-help, recovery, theology, and philosophy. We do not publish autobiography, biography, fiction, haggadot, poetry, or cookbooks. At this point we plan to do only two books for children annually, and one will be for younger children (ages 4-10)." Publishes hardcover and trade paperback originals, trade paperback reprints. Publishes 30 titles/year. 50% of books from first-time authors. 75% from unagented writers.

FICTION Picture books, young readers, middle readers: spirituality. "We are not interested in anything other than spirituality."

NONFICTION Picture book, young readers, middle readers: activity books, spirituality. "We do *not* publish haggadot, biography, poetry, or cookbooks."

HOW TO CONTACT Query with outline/synopsis and 2 sample chapters; submit complete ms for picture books. Query. Responds in 3 months to queries. Publishes ms 1 year after acceptance.

TERMS Pays authors royalty of 10% of revenue received; 15% royalty for subsequent printings. Book catalog and guidelines online.

TIPS "We publish books for all faiths and backgrounds that also reflect the Jewish wisdom tradition. Explain in your cover letter why you're submitting your project to us in particular. Make sure you know what we publish."

JOLLY FISH BOOKS

P.O. Box 1773, Provo UT 84603. **E-mail:** submit@jollyfishpress.com. **Website:** jollyfishpress.com.

FICTION "We accept literary fiction, fantasy, sci-fi, mystery, suspense, horror, thriller, children's literature, young adult, trade."

NONFICTION Nonfiction mss do not have to be completed, but the status of the ms should be noted.

HOW TO CONTACT Submit query with synopsis and first 3 chapters. Submit query and proposal.

TERMS Guidelines online.

JOURNEYFORTH

Imprint of BJU Press, 1700 Wade Hampton Blvd., Greenville SC 29614. (864)242-5100, ext. 4350. **Fax:** (864)298-0268. **E-mail:** journeyforth@bjupress.com. **Website:** www.journeyforth.com. "Small independent publisher of trustworthy novels and biographies for readers pre-school through high school from a conservative Christian perspective, Christian living books, and Bible studies for adults." Publishes paperback originals. Publishes 25 titles/year. 10% of books from first-time authors. 8% from unagented writers.

FICTION "Our fiction is all based on a moral and Christian worldview." Does not want short stories.

NONFICTION Christian living, Bible studies, church and ministry, church history. "We produce books for the adult Christian market that are from a conservative Christian worldview."

HOW TO CONTACT Submit 5 sample chapters, synopsis, SASE. Responds in 1 month to queries; 3 months to mss. Publishes book 12-18 months after acceptance.

ILLUSTRATION Works with 2-4 illustrators/year. Query with samples. Send promo sheet; will review website portfolio if applicable. Responds only if interested. Samples returned with SASE; samples filed.

TERMS Pays authors royalty based on wholesale price. Pays illustrators by the project. Originals returned to artist at job's completion. Pays royalty. Book catalog available free. Guidelines online.

TIPS "Study the publisher's guidelines. No picture books and no submissions by e-mail."

KANE/MILLER BOOK PUBLISHERS

4901 Morena Blvd., Suite 213, San Diego CA 92117. (858)456-0540. **Fax:** (858)456-9641. **E-mail:** submissions@kanemiller.com. **Website:** www.kanemiller.com. **Contact:** Editorial Department. "Kane/Miller Book Publishers is a division of EDC Publishing, specializing in award-winning children's books from around the world. Our books bring the children of the world closer to each other, sharing stories and ideas, while exploring cultural differences and similarities. Although we continue to look for books from other countries, we are now actively seeking works that convey cultures and communities within the US. We are looking for picture book fiction and nonfiction on those subjects that may be defined as particularly American: sports such as baseball, historical events, American biographies, American folk tales, etc. We are committed to expanding our early and middlegrade fiction list. We're interested in great stories with engaging characters in all genres (mystery, fantasy, adventure, historical, etc.) and, as with picture books, especially those with particularly American subjects."

FICTION Picture Books: concept, contemporary, health, humor, multicultural. Young Readers: contemporary, multicultural, suspense. Middle Readers: contemporary, humor, multicultural, suspense.

HOW TO CONTACT Responds in 90 days to queries.

TIPS "We like to think that a child reading a Kane/Miller book will see parallels between his own life and what might be the unfamiliar setting and characters of the story. And that by seeing how a character who is somehow or in some way dissimilar—an outsider—finds a way to fit comfortably into a culture or community or situation while maintaining a healthy sense of self and self-dignity, she might be empowered to do the same."

KAR-BEN PUBLISHING

Lerner Publishing Group, 241 First Ave. N, Minneapolis MN 55401. (612)215-6229. **Fax:** 612-332-7615. **E-mail:** Editorial@Karben.com. **Website:** www.karben.com. Publishes hardcover, trade paperback, and electronic originals. Publishes 10-15 titles/year. 20% of books from first-time authors. 70% from unagented writers.

FICTION "We seek picture book mss of about 1,000 words on Jewish-themed topics for children." Picture books: Adventure, concept, folktales, history, humor, multicultural, religion, special needs; must be on a Jewish theme. Average word length: picture books–1,000. Recently published titles: *The Count's Hanukkah Countdown, Sammy Spider's First Book of Jewish Holidays, The Cats of Ben Yehuda Street.*

NONFICTION "In addition to traditional Jewish-themed stories about Jewish holidays, history, folktales and other subjects, we especially seek stories that reflect the rich diversity of the contemporary Jewish community." Picture books, young readers: activity books, arts/crafts, biography, careers, concept, cooking, history, how-to, multicultural, religion, social issues, special needs; must be of Jewish interest. No textbooks, games, or educational materials.

HOW TO CONTACT Submit full ms of picture books only. Submit completed ms. 800 mss received/year. Responds in 6 weeks. Most mss published within 2 years.

TERMS Pays 5% royalty on net sale. Pays $500-2,500 advance. Book catalog available online; free upon request. Guidelines available online.

TIPS "Authors: Do a literature search to make sure similar title doesn't already exist. Illustrators: Look at our online catalog for a sense of what we like—bright colors and lively composition."

KREGEL PUBLICATIONS

2450 Oak Industrial Dr. NE, Grand Rapids MI 49505. (616)451-4775. **Fax:** (616)451-9330. **E-mail:** kregel books@kregel.com. **Website:** www.kregelpublica tions.com. **Contact:** Dennis R. Hillman, publisher. "Our mission as an evangelical Christian publisher is to provide—with integrity and excellence—trusted, Biblically based resources that challenge and encourage individuals in their Christian lives. Works in theology and Biblical studies should reflect the historic, orthodox Protestant tradition." Publishes hardcover and trade paperback originals and reprints. Publishes 90 titles/year. 20% of books from first-time authors. 35% from unagented writers.

FICTION Fiction should be geared toward the evangelical Christian market. Wants books with fast-paced, contemporary storylines presenting a strong Christian message in an engaging, entertaining style.

NONFICTION "We serve evangelical Christian readers and those in career Christian service."

HOW TO CONTACT Finds works through The Writer's Edge and Christian Manuscript Submissions ms screening services. Publishes ms 16 months after acceptance.

TERMS Pays royalty on wholesale price. Pays negotiable advance. Guidelines online.

TIPS "Our audience consists of conservative, evangelical Christians, including pastors and ministry students."

LEE & LOW BOOKS

95 Madison Ave., #1205, New York NY 10016. (212)779-4400. **E-mail:** general@leeandlow.com. **Website:** www.leeandlow.com. **Contact:** Louise May, vice president/editorial director (multicultural children's fiction/nonfiction). "Our goals are to meet a growing need for books that address children of color, and to present literature that all children can identify with. We only consider multicultural children's books. Sponsors a yearly New Voices Award for first-time picture book authors of color. Contest rules online at website or for SASE." Publishes hardcover originals and trade paperback reprints. Publishes 12-14 titles/year. 20% of books from first-time authors. 50% from unagented writers.

FICTION Picture books, young readers: anthology, contemporary, history, multicultural, poetry. Picture book, middle reader: contemporary, history, multicultural, nature/environment, poetry, sports. Average word length: picture books—1,000-1,500 words. "We do not publish folklore or animal stories."

NONFICTION Picture books: concept. Picture books, middle readers: biography, history, multicultural, science and sports. Average word length: picture books-1,500-3,000.

HOW TO CONTACT Submit complete ms. Submit complete ms. Receives 100 queries/year; 1,200 mss/year. Responds in 6 months to mss if interested. Publishes book 2 years after acceptance.

ILLUSTRATION Works with 12-14 illustrators/year. Uses color artwork only. Reviews ms/illustration packages from artists. Contact: Louise May. Illustrations only: Query with samples, résumé, promo sheet, and tearsheets. Responds only if interested. Samples returned with SASE; samples filed. Original artwork returned at job's completion.

PHOTOGRAPHY Buys photos from freelancers. Works on assignment only. Model/property releases required. Submit cover letter, résumé, promo piece and book dummy.

TERMS Pays net royalty. Pays authors advances against royalty. Pays illustrators advance against royalty. Photographers paid advance against royalty. Book catalog available online. Guidelines available online or by written request with SASE.

TIPS "Check our website to see the kinds of books we publish. Do not send mss that don't fit our mission."

LEGACY PRESS

P.O. Box 261129, San Diego CA 92196. (858)277-1167. **E-mail:** john.gregory@rainbowpublishers.com. **Website:** www.rainbowpublishers.com. Publishes 4 young readers/year; 4 middle readers/year; 4 young adult titles/year. 50% of books by first-time authors. "Our mission is to publish Bible-based, teacher resource materials that contribute to and inspire spiritual growth and development in kids ages 2-12."

NONFICTION Young readers, middle readers, young adult/teens: activity books, arts/crafts, how-to, reference, religion.

HOW TO CONTACT Responds to queries in 6 weeks, mss in 3 months.

TERMS For authors work purchased outright (range: $500 and up). Pays illustrators by the project (range: $300 and up). Sends galleys to authors.

TIPS "Our Rainbow imprint publishes reproducible books for teachers of children in Christian ministries, including crafts, activities, games and puzzles. Our Legacy imprint publishes titles for children such as devotionals, fiction and Christian living. Please see website and study the market before submitting material."

LERNER PUBLISHING GROUP

1251 Washington Ave. N., Minneapolis MN 55401. (800)452-7236; (612)332-3344. **Fax:** (612)337-7615. **E-mail:** editorial@karben.com. **Website:** www.karben.com; www.lernerbooks.com. Primarily publishes books for children ages 7-18. List includes titles in geography, natural and physical science, current events, ancient and modern history, high interest, sports, world cultures, and numerous biography series.

Starting in 2007, Lerner Publishing Group no longer accepts submission in any of their imprints except for Kar-Ben Publishing.

HOW TO CONTACT "We will continue to seek targeted solicitations at specific reading levels and in specific subject areas. The company will list these targeted solicitations on our website and in national newsletters, such as the SCBWI *Bulletin*."

ARTHUR A. LEVINE BOOKS

Scholastic, Inc., 557 Broadway, New York NY 10012. (212)343-4436. **Fax:** (212)343-6143. **Website:** www.arthuralevinebooks.com. **Contact:** Arthur A. Levine, VP/publisher. Publishes hardcover, paperback, and e-book editions.

FICTION "Arthur A. Levine is looking for distinctive literature, for children and young adults, for whatever's extraordinary." Averages 18-20 total titles/year.

HOW TO CONTACT Query. Please follow submission guidelines. Responds in 1 month to queries; 5 months to mss. Publishes a book 18 months after acceptance.

TERMS Guidelines online.

LITTLE, BROWN BOOKS FOR YOUNG READERS

Hachette Book Group USA, 1290 Avenue of the Americas, New York NY 10104. (212)364-1100. **Fax:** (212)364-0925. **E-mail:** publicity@lbchildrens.com. **Website:** hachettebookgroup.com. "Little, Brown and Co. Children's Publishing publishes all formats including board books, picture books, middle grade fiction, and nonfiction YA titles. We are looking for strong writing and presentation, but no predeter-

mined topics." *Only interested in solicited agented material.* Publishes 100-150 titles/year.

FICTION Average word length: picture books—1,000; young readers—6,000; middle readers—15,000-50,000; young adults—50,000 and up.

NONFICTION "Writers should avoid looking for the 'issue' they think publishers want to see, choosing instead topics they know best and are most enthusiastic about/inspired by."

HOW TO CONTACT *Agented submissions only.* Responds in 1-2 months. Publishes ms 2 years after acceptance.

ILLUSTRATION Works with 40 illustrators/year. Illustrations only: Query art director with b&w and color samples; provide résumé, promo sheet, or tearsheets to be kept on file. Does not respond to art samples. Do not send originals; copies only. Accepts illustration samples by postal mail or e-mail.

PHOTOGRAPHY Works on assignment only. Model/property releases required; captions required. Publishes photo essays and photo concept books. Uses 35mm transparencies. Photographers should provide résumé, promo sheets, or tearsheets to be kept on file.

TERMS Pays authors royalties based on retail price. Pays illustrators and photographers by the project or royalty based on retail price. Sends galleys to authors; dummies to illustrators. Pays negotiable advance.

TIPS "In order to break into the field, authors and illustrators should research their competition and try to come up with something outstandingly different."

LITTLE PICKLE PRESS

3701 Sacramento St., #494, San Francisco CA 94118. (415)340-3344. **Fax:** (415)366-1520. **Website:** www.littlepicklepress.com. Little Pickle Press is a 21st Century publisher dedicated to helping parents and educators cultivate conscious, responsible little people by stimulating explorations of the meaningful topics of their generation through a variety of media, technologies, and techniques. Submit through submission link on site.

TIPS "We have lots of mss to consider, so it will take up to 8 weeks before we get back to you."

LITTLE SIMON

Imprint of Simon & Schuster, 1230 Avenue of the Americas, New York NY 10020. (212)698-1295. **Fax:** (212)698-2794. **Website:** www.simonsayskids.com. "Our goal is to provide fresh material in an innovative format for preschool to age 8. Our books are often, if not exclusively, format driven." Publishes novelty and branded books only.

FICTION Novelty books include many things that do not fit in the traditional hardcover or paperback format, such as pop-up, board book, scratch and sniff, glow in the dark, lift the flap, etc. Children's/juvenile. No picture books. Large part of the list is holiday-themed.

NONFICTION "We publish very few nonfiction titles." No picture books.

HOW TO CONTACT *Currently not accepting unsolicited mss.*

TERMS Offers advance and royalties.

LUCKY MARBLE BOOKS

PageSpring Publishing, P.O. Box 21133, Columbus OH 43221. **E-mail:** yaeditor@pagespringpublishing.com. **Website:** www.luckymarblebooks.com. "Lucky Marble Books publishes novel-length young adult and middle grade fiction. We are looking for engaging characters and well-crafted plots that keep our readers turning the page. We accept e-mail queries only; see our website for details." Publishes trade paperback and electronic originals.

FICTION Does not want picture books.

HOW TO CONTACT Submit proposal package via e-mail. Include synopsis and 30 sample pages. Responds in 3 months. Publishes ms 9-12 months after acceptance.

TERMS Pays royalty. Guidelines online.

TIPS "We are particularly interested in books that integrate education content into a great story with vivid characters."

MAGINATION PRESS

750 First St. NE, Washington DC 20002. (202)336-5618. **Fax:** (202)336-5624. **E-mail:** magination@apa.org. **Website:** www.apa.org. Magination Press is an imprint of the American Psychological Association. "We publish books dealing with the psycho/therapeutic resolution of children's problems and psychological issues with a strong self-help component." Submit complete ms. Materials returned only with SASE. Publishes 12 titles/year. 75% of books from first-time authors.

FICTION All levels: psychological and social issues, self-help, health, parenting concerns and, special needs. Picture books, middle school readers.

NONFICTION All levels: psychological and social issues, self-help, health, multicultural, special needs.

HOW TO CONTACT Responds to queries in 1-2 months; mss in 2-6 months. Publishes a book 18-24 months after acceptance.

ILLUSTRATION Works with 10-15 illustrators/year. Reviews ms/illustration packages. Will review artwork for future assignments. Responds only if interested, or immediately if SASE or response card is included. "We keep samples on file."

MARTIN SISTERS PUBLISHING, LLC

P.O. Box 1154, Barbourville KY 40906-1499. **E-mail:** submissions@martinsisterspublishing.com. **Website:** www.martinsisterspublishing.com. **Contact:** Melissa Newman, publisher/editor (fiction/nonfiction). Firm/imprint publishes trade and mass market paperback originals; electronic originals. Publishes 12 titles/year. 75% of books from first-time authors. 100% from unagented writers.

HOW TO CONTACT Send query letter only. Send query letter only. Responds in 1 month on queries, 2 months on proposals, 3-6 months on mss. Publishes ms 6 months after acceptance.

TERMS Pays 7.5% royalty/max on retail price. No advance offered. Catalog and guidelines online.

○ MASTER BOOKS

P.O. Box 726, Green Forest AR 72638. (870)438-5288. **Fax:** (870)438-5120. **E-mail:** submissions@newleafpress.net. **Website:** www.masterbooks.net. **Contact:** Craig Froman, acquisitions editor. Publishes 3 middle readers/year; 2 young adult nonfiction titles/year; 10 homeschool curriculum titles; 20 adult trade books/year. 10% of books from first-time authors.

NONFICTION Picture books: activity books, animal, nature/environment, creation. Young readers, middle readers, young adults: activity books, animal, biography Christian, nature/environment, science, creation.

HOW TO CONTACT Submission guidelines on website. Responds in 6 months. Publishes book 1 year after acceptance.

TERMS Pays authors royalty of 3-15% based on wholesale price. Book catalog available upon request. Guidelines online.

TIPS "All of our children's books are creation-based, including topics from the Book of Genesis. We look also for home school educational material that would be supplementary to a home school curriculum, especially elementary material."

MARGARET K. MCELDERRY BOOKS

Imprint of Simon & Schuster Children's Publishing Division, 1230 Sixth Ave., New York NY 10020. (212)698-7200. **Website:** www.simonsayskids.com. "Margaret K. McElderry Books publishes hardcover and paperback trade books for children from preschool age through young adult. This list includes picture books, middle grade and teen fiction, poetry, and fantasy. The style and subject matter of the books we publish is almost unlimited. We do not publish textbooks, coloring and activity books, greeting cards, magazines, pamphlets, or religious publications." Publishes 30 titles/year. 15% of books from first-time authors. 50% from unagented writers.

FICTION No unsolicited mss.

NONFICTION No unsolicited mss. Agented submissions only.

HOW TO CONTACT Agented submissions only.

TERMS Pays authors royalty based on retail price. Pays illustrator royalty of by the project. Pays photographers by the project. Original artwork returned at job's completion. Offers $5,000-8,000 advance for new authors. Guidelines for #10 SASE.

TIPS "Read! The children's book field is competitive. See what's been done and what's out there before submitting. We look for high quality: an originality of ideas, clarity and felicity of expression, a well organized plot, and strong character-driven stories. We're looking for strong, original fiction, especially mysteries and middle grade humor. We are always interested in picture books for the youngest age reader. Study our titles."

MEDALLION MEDIA GROUP

4222 Meridian Pkwy., Aurora IL 60504. (630)513-8316. **E-mail:** emily@medallionmediagroup.com. **E-mail:** submissions@medallionmediagroup.com. **Website:** medallionmediagroup.com. **Contact:** Emily Steele, editorial director. "We are an independent, innovative publisher looking for compelling, memorable stories told in distinctive voices." Publishes trade paperback, hardcover, e-book originals, book apps, and TREEbook.

FICTION Word count: 40,000-90,000 for YA; 60,000-120,000 for all others. No short stories, anthologies, erotica.

NONFICTION Agented only.

HOW TO CONTACT Submit first 3 consecutive chapters and a synopsis through our online submission form. Please query. Responds in 2-3 months to mss. Publishes ms 1-2 years after acceptance.

TERMS Offers advance. Guidelines online.

TIPS "We are not affected by trends. We are simply looking for well-crafted, original, compelling works of fiction and nonfiction. Please visit our website for the most current guidelines prior to submitting anything to us."

MILKWEED EDITIONS

1011 Washington Ave. S., Suite 300, Minneapolis MN 55415. (612)332-3192. **Fax:** (612)215-2550. **Website:** www.milkweed.org. Publishes 3-4 middle readers/year. 25% of books by first-time authors. **Contact:** Patrick Thomas, editor and program director. "Milkweed Editions publishes with the intention of making a humane impact on society, in the belief that literature is a transformative art uniquely able to convey the essential experiences of the human heart and spirit. To that end, Milkweed Editions publishes distinctive voices of literary merit in handsomely designed, visually dynamic books, exploring the ethical, cultural, and esthetic issues that free societies need continually to address." Publishes hardcover, trade paperback, and electronic originals; trade paperback and electronic reprints. Publishes 15-20 titles/year. 25% of books from first-time authors. 75% from unagented writers.

FICTION Novels for adults and for readers 8-13. High literary quality. For adult readers: literary fiction, nonfiction, poetry, essays. Middle readers: adventure, contemporary, fantasy, multicultural, nature/environment, suspense/mystery. Average length: middle readers—90-200 pages. No romance, mysteries, science fiction.

HOW TO CONTACT Query with SASE, submit completed ms. Responds in 6 months. Publishes book in 18 months.

TERMS Pays authors variable royalty based on retail price. Offers advance against royalties. Pays varied advance from $500-10,000. Book catalog online. Guidelines online.

TIPS "We are looking for excellent writing with the intent of making a humane impact on society. Please read submission guidelines before submitting and acquaint yourself with our books in terms of style and quality before submitting. Many factors influence our selection process, so don't get discouraged. Nonfiction is focused on literary writing about the natural world, including living well in urban environments."

THE MILLBROOK PRESS

Lerner Publishing Group, 1251 Washington Ave N, Minneapolis MN 55401. **Website:** www.lernerbooks.com. "Millbrook Press publishes informative picture books, illustrated nonfiction titles, and inspiring photo-driven titles for grades K–5. Our authors approach curricular topics with a fresh point of view. Our fact-filled books engage readers with fun yet accessible writing, high-quality photographs, and a wide variety of illustration styles. We cover subjects ranging from the parts of speech and other language arts skills; to history, science, and math; to art, sports, crafts, and other interests. Millbrook Press is the home of the bestselling Words Are CATegorical® series and Bob Raczka's Art Adventures. We do not accept unsolicited mss from authors. Occasionally, we may put out a call for submissions, which will be announced on our website."

MITCHELL LANE PUBLISHERS, INC.

P.O. Box 196, Hockessin DE 19707. (302)234-9426. **Fax:** (866)834-4164. **E-mail:** barbaramitchell@mitchelllane.com. **Website:** www.mitchelllane.com. **Contact:** Barbara Mitchell, publisher. Publishes hardcover and library bound originals. Publishes 80 titles/year. 0% of books from first-time authors. 90% from unagented writers.

NONFICTION Young readers, middle readers, young adults: biography, nonfiction, and curriculum-related subjects. Average word length: 4,000-50,000 words. Recently published: *My Guide to US Citizenship*, *Rivers of the World* and *Vote America*.

HOW TO CONTACT Query with SASE. *All unsolicited mss discarded.* 100 queries received/year. 5 mss received/year. Responds only if interested to queries. Publishes ms 1 year after acceptance.

ILLUSTRATION Works with 2-3 illustrators/year. Reviews ms/illustration packages from artists. Query. Illustration only: Query with samples; send résumé, portfolio, slides, tearsheets. Responds only if interested. Samples not returned; samples filed.

PHOTOGRAPHY Buys stock images. Needs photos of famous and prominent minority figures. Captions required. Uses color prints or digital images. Submit cover letter, résumé, published samples, stock photo list.

TERMS Work purchased outright from authors (range: $350-2,000). Pays illustrators by the project (range: $40-400). Book catalog available free.

TIPS "We hire writers on a 'work-for-hire' basis to complete book projects we assign. Send résumé and writing samples that do not need to be returned."

MONTH9BOOKS

454 W. 44th St., New York NY 10036. (212)713-1633. **Fax:** (212)581-8830. **Website:** month9booksblog.com. "We accept science fiction, fantasy, horror, supernatural fiction, superhero fiction, utopian, dystopian, apocalyptic, post-apocalyptic, and alternate history fiction for teens."

HOW TO CONTACT Submit via submittable page.

TERMS Pays variable royalty. Offers advances starting at $200. Guidelines online.

TIPS "We are especially interested in books with male main characters!"

MOODY PUBLISHERS

Moody Bible Institute, 820 N. LaSalle Blvd., Chicago IL 60610. (800)678-8812. **Fax:** (312)329-4157. **E-mail:** authors@moody.edu. **Website:** www.moodypublishers.org. "The mission of Moody Publishers is to educate and edify the Christian and to evangelize the non-Christian by ethically publishing conservative, evangelical Christian literature and other media for all ages around the world, and to help provide resources for Moody Bible Institute in its training of future Christian leaders." Publishes hardcover, trade, and mass market paperback originals. Publishes 60 titles/year. 1% of books from first-time authors. 80% from unagented writers.

NONFICTION "We are no longer reviewing queries or unsolicited mss unless they come to us through an agent. Unsolicited proposals will be returned only if proper postage is included. We are not able to acknowledge the receipt of your unsolicited proposal."

HOW TO CONTACT "Please query us at month-9books.submittable.com. We look forward to reading your work of middle grade or young adult speculative fiction."

TERMS Royalty varies. Book catalog for 9×12 envelope and 4 first-class stamps. Guidelines online.

TIPS "In our fiction list, we're looking for Christian storytellers rather than teachers trying to present a message. Your motivation should be to delight the reader. Using your skills to create beautiful works is glorifying to God."

ⓐ NATIONAL GEOGRAPHIC CHILDREN'S BOOKS

1145 17th St. NW, Washington DC 20090-8199. (800)647-5463. **Website:** www.ngchildrensbooks. org. National Geographic CHildren's Books provides quality nonfiction for children and young adults by award-winning authors. *This market does not currently accept unsolicited mss.*

ⓐ TOMMY NELSON

Imprint of Thomas Nelson, Inc., P.O. Box 141000, Nashville TN 37214-1000. (615)889-9000. **Fax:** (615)902-2219. **Website:** www.tommynelson.com. "Tommy Nelson publishes children's Christian nonfiction and fiction for boys and girls up to age 14. We honor God and serve people through books, videos, software and Bibles for children that improve the lives of our customers." Publishes hardcover and trade paperback originals. Publishes 50-75 titles/year.

FICTION No stereotypical characters.

HOW TO CONTACT *Does not accept unsolicited mss.*

TERMS Guidelines online.

TIPS "Know the Christian Booksellers Association market. Check out the Christian bookstores to see what sells and what is needed."

NIGHTSCAPE PRESS

P.O. Box 1948, Smyrna TN 37167. **E-mail:** submissions@nightscapepress.com. **Website:** www.nightscapepress.com. Nightscape Press is seeking quality book-length words of at least 50,000 words (40,000 for young adult).

HOW TO CONTACT Query.

TERMS Pays monthly royalties. Offers advance. Guidelines online.

NOMAD PRESS

2456 Christain St., White River Junction VT 05001. (802)649-1995. **Fax:** (802)649-2667. **E-mail:** rachel@nomadpress.net; info@nomadpress.net. **Website:** www.nomadpress.net. **Contact:** Alex Kahan, publisher. "We produce nonfiction children's activity books that bring a particular science or cultural topic into sharp focus. Nomad Press does not accept unsolicited mss. If authors are interested in contributing to our children's series, please send a writing resume that includes relevant experience/expertise and publishing credits."

Nomad Press does not accept picture books or fiction.

NONFICTION Middle readers: activity books, history, science. Average word length: middle readers—30,000.

HOW TO CONTACT Responds to queries in 3-4 weeks. Publishes book 1 year after acceptance.

TERMS Pays authors royalty based on retail price or work purchased outright. Offers advance against royalties. Catalog online.

TIPS "We publish a very specific kind of nonfiction children's activity book. Please keep this in mind when querying or submitting."

NORTH ATLANTIC BOOKS

2526 MLK Jr. Way, Berkeley CA 94704. **Website:** www.northatlanticbooks.com. **Contact:** Acquisitions Board. Publishes hardcover, trade paperback, and electronic originals; trade paperback and electronic reprints. Publishes 60 titles/year. 50% of books from first-time authors. 75% from unagented writers.

FICTION "We only publish fiction on rare occasions."

HOW TO CONTACT Submit proposal package including an outline, 3-4 sample chapters, and "a 75-word statement about the book, your qualifications as an author, marketing plan/audience, for the book, and comparable titles." Receives 200 mss/year. Responds in 3-6 months. Publishes ms 14 months after acceptance.

TERMS Pays royalty percentage on wholesale price. Book catalog free on request (if available). Guidelines online.

NORTH-SOUTH BOOKS

600 Third Ave., 2nd Floor, New York NY 10016. (917)210-5868. **E-mail:** hlennon@northsouth.com. **E-mail:** bterrill@northsouthbooks.us. **Website:** www.northsouth.com.

FICTION Looking for fresh, original fiction with universal themes that could appeal to children ages 3-8. "NorthSouth Books is very happy to announce that we're now accepting picture book submissions from US-based authors and illustrators."

HOW TO CONTACT Submit picture book mss (1,000 words or less) via e-mail.

TERMS Guidelines online.

ⓞ ONSTAGE PUBLISHING

190 Lime Quarry Rd., Suite 106-J, Madison AL 35758-8962. (256)461-0661. **E-mail:** onstage123@knology.

net. **Website:** www.onstagepublishing.com. **Contact:** Dianne Hamilton, senior editor. "At this time, we only produce fiction books for ages 8-18. We have added an eBook only side of the house for mysteries for grades 6-12. See our website for more information. We will not do anthologies of any kind. Query first for nonfiction projects as nonfiction projects must spark our interest. Now accepting e-mail queries and submissions. For submissions: Put the first 3 chapters in the body of the e-mail. Do not use attachments! We will no longer return any mss. Only an SASE envelope is needed. Send complete ms if under 20,000 words, otherwise send synopsis and first 3 chapters." 80% of books from first-time authors.

○ "To everyone who has submitted a ms, we are currently about 4 months behind. We should get back on track soon. Please feel free to submit your ms to other houses. OnStage Publishing understands that authors work very hard to produce the finished ms and we do not have to have exclusive submission rights. Please let us know if you sell your ms. Meanwhile, keep writing and we'll keep reading for our next acquisitions."

FICTION Middle readers: adventure, contemporary, fantasy, history, nature/environment, science fiction, suspense/mystery. Young adults: adventure, contemporary, fantasy, history, humor, science fiction, suspense/mystery. Average word length: chapter books—4,000-6,000 words; middle readers—5,000 words and up; young adults—25,000 and up. Recently published *Mission: Shanghai* by Jamie Dodson (an adventure for boys ages 12+); *Birmingham, 1933: Alice* (a chapter book for grades 3-5). "We do not produce picture books."

ILLUSTRATION Reviews ms/illustration packages from artists. Submit with 3 pieces of final art. **Contact:** Dianne Hamilton, senior editor. Illustrations only. Samples not returned.

TERMS Pays authors/illustrators/photographers advance plus royalties.

TIPS "Study our titles and get a sense of the kind of books we publish, so that you know whether your project is likely to be right for us."

Ⓐ ORCHARD BOOKS

557 Broadway, New York NY 10012. **E-mail:** mcroland@scholastic.com. **Website:** www.scholastic.com. **Contact:** Ken Geist, vice president/editorial director;

David Saylor, vice president/creative director. *Orchard is not accepting unsolicited mss.* Publishes 20 titles/year. 10% of books from first-time authors.

FICTION Picture books, early readers, and novelty: animal, contemporary, history, humor, multicultural, poetry.

TERMS Most commonly offers an advance against list royalties.

○ OUR SUNDAY VISITOR, INC.

200 Noll Plaza, Huntington IN 46750. **E-mail:** jlindsey@osv.com. **Website:** www.osv.com. **Contact:** Jacquelyn Lindsey; David Dziena; Bert Ghezzi; Cindy Cavnar; Tyler Ottinger, art director. "We are a Catholic publishing company seeking to educate and deepen our readers in their faith. Currently emphasizing devotional, inspirational, Catholic identity, apologetics, and catechetics." Publishes paperback and hardbound originals. Publishes 40-50 titles/year.

○ Our Sunday Visitor, Inc. is publishing only those children's books that are specifically Catholic. See website for submission guidelines.

NONFICTION Prefers to see well-developed proposals as first submission with annotated outline and definition of intended market; Catholic viewpoints on family, prayer, and devotional books, and Catholic heritage books. Picture books, middle readers, young readers, young adults.

HOW TO CONTACT Query, submit complete ms, or submit outline/synopsis and 2-3 sample chapters. Responds in 2 months. Publishes ms 1-2 years after acceptance.

TERMS Pays authors royalty of 10-12% net. Pays illustrators by the project (range: $25-1,500). Book catalog for 9×12 envelope and first-class stamps; ms guidelines available online.

TIPS "Stay in accordance with our guidelines."

THE OVERMOUNTAIN PRESS

P.O. Box 1261, Johnson City TN 37605. (423)926-2691. **Fax:** (423)232-1252. **E-mail:** submissions@overmtn.com. **Website:** www.overmtn.com. "The Overmountain Press publishes primarily Appalachian history. Audience is people interested in history of Tennessee, Virginia, North Carolina, Kentucky, and all aspects of this region--Revolutionary War, Civil War, county histories, historical biographies, etc." Publishes hardcover and trade paperback originals and reprints.

NONFICTION Regional works only.

HOW TO CONTACT Submit complete ms. Submit proposal package, outline, 3 sample chapters, marketing suggestions. Responds in 3-6 months to mss. Publishes ms 1-2 years after acceptance.

TERMS Book catalog available free. Guidelines online.

RICHARD C. OWEN PUBLISHERS, INC.

P.O. Box 585, Katonah NY 10536. (914)232-3903; (800)262-0787. **E-mail:** richardowen@rcowen.com. **Website:** www.rcowen.com. **Contact:** Richard Owen, publisher. "We publish child-focused books, with inherent instructional value, about characters and situations with which 5, 6, and 7-year-old children can identify—books that can be read for meaning, entertainment, enjoyment and information. We include multicultural stories that present minorities in a positive and natural way. Our stories show the diversity in America." Not interested in lesson plans, or books of activities for literature studies or other content areas. Submit complete ms and cover letter.

○ "Due to high volume and long production time, we are currently limiting to nonfiction submissions only."

NONFICTION "Our books are for kindergarten, first- and second-grade children to read on their own. The stories are very brief—up to 2,000 words—yet well structured and crafted with memorable characters, language, and plots. Picture books, young readers: animals, careers, history, how-to, music/dance, geography, multicultural, nature/environment, science, sports. Multicultural needs include: Good stories respectful of all heritages, races, cultural—African-American, Hispanic, American Indian, Asian, European, Middle Eastern." Wants lively stories. No "encyclopedic" type of information stories. Average word length: under 500 words.

HOW TO CONTACT Responds to mss in 1 year. Publishes book 2-3 years after acceptance.

ILLUSTRATION Works with 20 illustrators/year. Uses color artwork only. Illustration only: Send color copies/reproductions or photos of art or provide tearsheets; do not send slides or originals. Include SASE and cover letter. Responds only if interested; samples filed.

TERMS Pays authors royalty of 5% based on net price or outright purchase (range: $25-500). Offers no advances. Pays illustrators by the project (range: $100-2,000) or per photo (range: $50-150). Book catalog available with SASE. Ms guidelines with SASE or online.

PAGESPRING PUBLISHING

P.O. Box 2113, Columbus OH 43221. **E-mail:** ps@pagespringpublishing.com. **E-mail:** yaeditor@pagespringpublishing.com; weditor@pagespringpublishing.com. **Website:** www.pagespringpublishing.com. "PageSpring Publishing publishes young adult and middle grade titles under the Lucky Marble Books imprint and women's fiction under the Cup of Tea imprint. See imprint websites for submission details." Publishes trade paperback and electronic originals. Publishes 10-20 titles/year.

HOW TO CONTACT Submit proposal package including synopsis and 3 sample chapters. Responds to queries in 1 month. Publishes ms 6 months after acceptance.

TERMS Pays royalty on wholesale price. Guidelines online.

PANTS ON FIRE PRESS

2062 Harbor Cove Way, Winter Garden FL 34787. **E-mail:** editor@pantsonfirepress.com. **E-mail:** submission@pantsonfirepress.com. **Website:** www.pantsonfirepress.com. **Contact:** Becca Goldman, senior editor; Emily Gerety, editor. Pants On Fire Press is an award-winning book publisher of picture, middle-grade, young adult, and adult books. They are a digital-first book publisher, striving to follow a high degree of excellence while maintaining quality standards. Publishes hardcover originals and reprints, trade paperback originals and reprints, and electronic originals and reprints. Publishes 10-15 titles/year. 60% of books from first-time authors. 80% from unagented writers.

FICTION Publishes big story ideas with high concepts, new worlds, and meaty characters for children, teens, and discerning adults. Always on the lookout for action, adventure, animals, comedic, dramatic, dystopian, fantasy, historical, paranormal, romance, sci-fi, supernatural, and suspense stories.

HOW TO CONTACT Submit a proposal package including a synopsis, 3 sample chapters, and a query letter via e-mail. Receives 2,500 queries and mss per year. Responds in 3 months to queries, proposals, and mss. Publishes ms approximately 7 months after acceptance.

TERMS Pays 10-50% royalties on wholesale price. Catalog available on website. Mss guidelines available on website.

PAUL DRY BOOKS

1700 Sansom St., Suite 700, Philadelphia PA 19103. (215)231-9939. **Fax:** (215)231-9942. **E-mail:** pdry@pauldrybooks.com; editor@pauldrybooks.com. **Website:** pauldrybooks.com. "We publish fiction, both novels and short stories, and nonfiction, biography, memoirs, history, and essays, covering subjects from Homer to Chekhov, bird watching to jazz music, New York City to shogunate Japan." Hardcover and trade paperback originals, trade paperback reprints.

○ "Take a few minutes to familiarize yourself with the books we publish. Then if you think your book would be a good fit in our line, we invite you to submit the following: A 1- or 2-page summary of the work. Be sure to tell us how many pages or words the full book will be; a sample of 20-30 pages; your bio. A brief description of how you think the book (and you, the author) could be marketed."

HOW TO CONTACT Submit sample chapters, clips, bio. Submit proposal package.

TERMS Book catalog available online. Guidelines available online.

TIPS "Our aim is to publish lively books 'to awaken, delight, and educate'—to spark conversation."

PAULINE BOOKS & MEDIA

50 St. Paul's Ave., Boston MA 02130. (617)522-8911. **Fax:** (617)541-9805. **E-mail:** design@paulinemedia.com; editorial@paulinemedia.com. **Website:** www.pauline.org. "Submissions are evaluated on adherence to Gospel values, harmony with the Catholic faith tradition, relevance of topic, and quality of writing." For board books and picture books, the entire ms should be submitted. For easy-to-read, young readers, and middle reader books and teen books, please send a cover letter accompanied by a synopsis and two sample chapters. "Electronic submissions are encouraged. We make every effort to respond to unsolicited submissions within 2 months." Publishes trade paperback originals and reprints. Publishes 40 titles/year.

FICTION Children's and teen fiction only. We are now accepting submissions for easy-to-read and middle reader chapter, and teen well documented historical fiction. We would also consider well-written fantasy, fairy tales, myths, science fiction, mysteries, or romance if approached from a Catholic perspective and consistent with church teaching. Please see our Writer's Guidelines.

NONFICTION Picture books, young readers, middle readers, teen: religion and fiction. Average word length: picture books—500-1,000; young readers—8,000-10,000; middle readers—15,000-25,000; teen—30,000-50,000. Recently published children's titles: *Bible Stores for Little Ones* by Genny Monchapm; *I Forgive You: Love We Can Hear, Ask For and Give* by Nicole Lataif; *Shepherds To the Rescue* (first place Catholic Book Award Winner) by Maria Grace Dateno; *FSP*; *Jorge from Argentina*; *Prayers for Young Catholics*. Teen Titles: *Teens Share the Mission* by Teens; *Martyred: The Story of Saint Lorenzo Ruiz*; *Ten Commandmenst for Kissing Gloria Jean* by Britt Leigh; *A.K.A. Genius* (2nd Place Catholic Book Award Winner) by Marilee Haynes; *Tackling Tough Topics* with Faith and Fiction by Diana Jenkins. No memoir/autobiography, poetry, or strictly nonreligious works currently considered.

HOW TO CONTACT "Submit proposal package, including synopsis, 2 sample chapters, and cover letter; also include intended audience and proposed length. Responds in 2 months to queries, proposals, and mss. Publishes a book approximately 11-18 months after acceptance.

ILLUSTRATION Works with 10-15 illustrators/year. Uses color and black-and-white- artwork. Samples and résumés will be kept on file unless return is requested and SASE provided.

TERMS Varies by project, but generally are royalties with advance. Flat fees sometimes considered for smaller works. Book catalog available online. Guidelines available online & by e-mail.

TIPS "Manuscripts may or may not be explicitly catechetical, but we seek those that reflect a positive worldview, good moral values, awareness and appreciation of diversity, and respect for all people. All material must be relevant to the lives of readers and must conform to Catholic teaching and practice."

PAULIST PRESS

997 MacArthur Blvd., Mahwah NJ 07430. (201)825-7300. **Fax:** (201)825-8345. **Website:** www.paulistpress.com. **Contact:** Trace Murphy, editorial director. "Paulist Press publishes ecumenical theology, Roman Catholic studies, and books on scripture,

liturgy, spirituality, church history, and philosophy, as well as works on faith and culture. Our publishing is oriented toward adult-level nonfiction. We do not publish poetry or works of fiction, and we have scaled back our involvement in children's publishing."

HOW TO CONTACT Accepts submissions via e-mail. Hard copy submissions returned only if accompanied by self-addressed envelope with adequate postage. Receives 250 submissions/year. Responds in 3 months to queries and proposals; 3-4 months on mss. Publishes a book 18-24 months after acceptance.

TERMS Royalties and advances are negotible. Illustrators sometimes receive a flat fee when all we need are spot illustrations. Book catalog available online. Guidelines available online and by e-mail.

PEACE HILL PRESS

Affiliate of W.W. Norton, 18021 The Glebe Ln., Charles City VA 23030. (804)829-5043. **Fax:** (804)829-5704. **E-mail:** info@peacehillpress.com. **Website:** www.peacehillpress.com. Publishes hardcover and trade paperback originals. Publishes 4-8 titles/year.

HOW TO CONTACT Does not take submissions. Publishes a book 18 months after acceptance.

TERMS Pays 6-10% royalty on retail price. Pays $500-1,000 advance.

PEACHTREE CHILDREN'S BOOKS

Peachtree Publishers, Ltd., 1700 Chattahoochee Ave., Atlanta GA 30318-2112. (404)876-8761. **Fax:** (404)875-2578. **E-mail:** hello@peachtree-online.com. **Website:** www.peachtree-online.com. **Contact:** Helen Harriss, submissions editor. "We publish a broad range of subjects and perspectives, with emphasis on innovative plots and strong writing." Publishes hardcover and trade paperback originals. Publishes 30 titles/year. 25% of books from first-time authors. 25% from unagented writers.

FICTION Looking for very well-written middle grade and young adult novels. No adult fiction. No collections of poetry or short stories; no romance or science fiction.

NONFICTION No e-mail or fax queries of mss.

HOW TO CONTACT Submit complete ms with SASE. Submit complete ms with SASE, or summary and 3 sample chapters with SASE. Responds in 6 months and mss. Publishes ms 1 year after acceptance.

TERMS Pays royalty on retail price. Book catalog for 6 first-class stamps. Guidelines online.

PEACHTREE PUBLISHERS, LTD.

1700 Chattahoochee Ave., Atlanta GA 30318. (404)876-8761. **Fax:** (404)875-2578. **E-mail:** hello@peachtree-online.com. **Website:** www.peachtree-online.com. **Contact:** Helen Harriss, acquisitions editor; Loraine Joyner, art director; Melanie McMahon Ives, production manager. Publishes 30-35 titles/year.

FICTION Picture books, young readers: adventure, animal, concept, history, nature/environment. Middle readers: adventure, animal, history, nature/environment, sports. Young adults: fiction, mystery, adventure. Does not want to see science fiction, romance.

NONFICTION Picture books: animal, history, nature/environment. Young readers, middle readers, young adults: animal, biography, nature/environment. Does not want to see religion.

HOW TO CONTACT Submit complete ms or 3 sample chapters by postal mail only. Submit complete ms or 3 sample chapters by postal mail only. Responds in 6-7 months. Publishes book 1-2 years after acceptance.

ILLUSTRATION Works with 8-10 illustrators/year. Illustrations only: Query production manager or art director with samples, résumé, slides, color copies to keep on file. Responds only if interested. Samples returned with SASE; samples filed.

PELICAN PUBLISHING COMPANY

1000 Burmaster St., Gretna LA 70053. (504)368-1175. **Fax:** (504)368-1195. **E-mail:** editorial@pelicanpub.com. **Website:** www.pelicanpub.com. "We believe ideas have consequences. One of the consequences is that they lead to a bestselling book. We publish books to improve and uplift the reader. Currently emphasizing business and history titles." Publishes 20 young readers/year; 1 middle reader/year. "Our children's books (illustrated and otherwise) include history, biography, holiday, and regional. Pelican's mission is to publish books of quality and permanence that enrich the lives of those who read them." Publishes hardcover, trade paperback, and mass market paperback originals and reprints.

FICTION We publish no adult fiction. Young readers: history, holiday, science, multicultural and regional. Middle readers: Louisiana history. Multicultural needs include stories about African-Americans, Irish-Americans, Jews, Asian-Americans, and Hispanics. Does not want animal stories, general Christmas stories, "day at school" or "accept yourself" stories. Maximum word length: young readers—1,100; middle readers—40,000. No young adult, romance, science fiction, fantasy, gothic, mystery, erotica, confession, horror, sex, or violence. Also no psychological novels.

NONFICTION "We look for authors who can promote successfully. We require that a query be made first. This greatly expedites the review process and can save the writer additional postage expenses." Young readers: biography, history, holiday, multicultural. Middle readers: Louisiana history, holiday, regional. No multiple queries or submissions.

HOW TO CONTACT Query with SASE. Submit outline, clips, 2 sample chapters. Responds in 1 month to queries; 3 months to mss. Publishes a book 9-18 months after acceptance.

ILLUSTRATION Works with 20 illustrators/year. Reviews ms/illustration packages from artists. Query first. Illustrations only: Query with samples (no originals). Responds only if interested. Samples returned with SASE; samples kept on file.

TERMS Pays authors in royalties; buys ms outright "rarely." Illustrators paid by "various arrangements." Advance considered. Book catalog and ms guidelines online.

TIPS "We do extremely well with cookbooks, popular histories, and business. We will continue to build in these areas. The writer must have a clear sense of the market and knowledge of the competition. A query letter should describe the project briefly, give the author's writing and professional credentials, and promotional ideas."

PERSEA BOOKS

277 Broadway, Suite 708, New York NY 10007. (212)260-9256. **Fax:** (212)267-3165. **E-mail:** info@perseabooks.com. **Website:** www.perseabooks.com. The aim of Persea is to publish works that endure by meeting high standards of literary merit and relevance. "We have often taken on important books other publishers have overlooked, or have made significant discoveries and rediscoveries, whether of a single work or writer's entire oeuvre. Our books cover a wide range of themes, styles, and genres. We have published poetry, fiction, essays, memoir, biography, titles of Jewish and Middle Eastern interest, women's studies, American Indian folklore, and revived classics, as well as a notable selection of works in translation."

HOW TO CONTACT Queries should include a cover letter, author background and publication history, a detailed synopsis of the proposed work, and a sample chapter. Please indicate if the work is simultaneously submitted. Queries should include a cover letter, author background and publication history, a detailed synopsis of the proposed work, and a sample chapter. Please indicate if the work is simultaneously submitted. Responds in 8 weeks to proposals; 10 weeks to mss.

TERMS Guidelines online.

PHILOMEL BOOKS

Imprint of Penguin Group (USA), Inc., 375 Hudson St., New York NY 10014. (212)414-3610. **Website:** www.penguin.com. **Contact:** Michael Green, president/publisher. "We look for beautifully written, engaging manuscripts for children and young adults." Publishes hardcover originals. Publishes 8-10 titles/year. 5% of books from first-time authors. 20% from unagented writers.

NONFICTION Picture books.

HOW TO CONTACT *No unsolicited mss. Agented submissions only.*

ILLUSTRATION Works with 8-10 illustrators/year. Reviews ms/illustration packages from artists. Query with art sample first. Illustrations only: Query with samples. Send résumé and tearsheets. Responds to art samples in 1 month. Original artwork returned at job's completion. Samples returned with SASE or kept on file.

TERMS Pays authors in royalties. Average advance payment "varies." Illustrators paid by advance and in royalties. Pays negotiable advance.

PIANO PRESS

P.O. Box 85, Del Mar CA 92014. (619)884-1401. **Fax:** (858)755-1104. **E-mail:** pianopress@pianopress.com. **Website:** www.pianopress.com. **Contact:** Elizabeth C. Axford, editor. "We publish music-related books, either fiction or nonfiction, coloring books, songbooks, and poetry."

FICTION Picture books, young readers, middle readers, young adults: folktales, multicultural, poetry, music. Average word length: picture books—1,500-2,000.

NONFICTION Picture books, young readers, middle readers, young adults: multicultural, music/dance. Average word length: picture books—1,500-2,000.

HOW TO CONTACT Responds to queries in 3 months; mss in 6 months. Publishes book 1 year after acceptance.

ILLUSTRATION Works with 1 or 2 illustrators/year. Reviews ms/illustration packages from artists. Query. Illustrations only: Query with samples. Responds in 3 months. Samples returned with SASE; samples filed.

PHOTOGRAPHY Buys stock and assigns work. Looking for music-related, multicultural. Model/property releases required. Uses glossy or flat, color or b&w prints. Submit cover letter, résumé, client list, published samples, stock photo list.

TERMS Pays authors, illustrators, and photographers royalty of 5-10% based on retail price. Book catalog available for #10 SASE and 2 first-class stamps.

TIPS "We are looking for music-related material only for any juvenile market. Please do not send non-music-related materials. Query first before submitting anything."

PIÑATA BOOKS

Imprint of Arte Publico Press, University of Houston, 4902 Gulf Fwy., Bldg. 19, Room 100, Houston TX 77204-2004. (713)743-2845. **Fax:** (713)743-3080. **E-mail:** submapp@uh.edu. **Website:** www.artepublicopress.com. "Piñata Books is dedicated to the publication of children's and young adult literature focusing on US Hispanic culture by US Hispanic authors. Arte Publico's mission is the publication, promotion and dissemination of Latino literature for a variety of national and regional audiences, from early childhood to adult, through the complete gamut of delivery systems, including personal performance as well as print and electronic media." Publishes hardcover and trade paperback originals. Publishes 10-15 titles/year. 80% of books from first-time authors.

NONFICTION Piñata Books specializes in publication of children's and young adult literature that authentically portrays themes, characters and customs unique to US Hispanic culture.

HOW TO CONTACT Submissions made through online submission form. Responds in 2-3 months to queries; 4-6 months to mss. Publishes book 2 years after acceptance.

ILLUSTRATION Works with 6 illustrators/year. Uses color artwork only. Reviews ms/illustration packages from artists. Query or send portfolio (slides, color copies). Illustrations only: Query with samples or send résumé, promo sheet, portfolio, slides, client list and tearsheets. Responds only if interested. Samples not returned; samples filed.

TERMS Pays 10% royalty on wholesale price. Pays $1,000-3,000 advance. Book catalog and guidelines online.

TIPS "Include cover letter with submission explaining why your ms is unique and important, why we should publish it, who will buy it, etc."

PINEAPPLE PRESS, INC.

P.O. Box 3889, Sarasota FL 34230. (941)706-2507. **Fax:** (800)746-3275. **E-mail:** info@pineapplepress.com. **Website:** www.pineapplepress.com. **Contact:** June Cussen, executive editor. "We are seeking quality nonfiction on diverse topics for the library and book trade markets. Our mission is to publish good books about Florida." Publishes hardcover and trade paperback originals. Publishes 25 titles/year. 50% of books from first-time authors. 95% from unagented writers.

FICTION Picture books, young readers, middle readers, young adults: animal, folktales, history, nature/environment.

NONFICTION Picture books: animal, history, nature/environmental, science. Young readers, middle readers, young adults: animal, biography, geography, history, nature/environment, science.

HOW TO CONTACT Query or submit outline/synopsis and 3 sample chapters. Query or submit outline/synopsis and intro and 3 sample chapters. 1,000 queries received/year. 500 mss received/year. Responds in 2 months. Publishes a book 1 year after acceptance.

ILLUSTRATION Works with 2 illustrators/year. Reviews ms/illustration packages from artists. Query with nonreturnable samples. Contact: June Cussen, executive editor. Illustrations only: Query with brochure, nonreturnable samples, photocopies, résumé. Responds only if interested. Samples returned with SASE, but prefers nonreturnable; samples filed.

TERMS Pays authors royalty of 10-15%. Book catalog for 9×12 SAE with $1.25 postage. Guidelines online.

TIPS "Quality first novels will be published, though we usually only do one or two novels per year and they must be set in Florida. We regard the author/editor relationship as a trusting relationship with communication open both ways. Learn all you can about the publishing process and about how to promote your book once it is published. A query on a novel without a brief sample seems useless."

THE POISONED PENCIL

Poisoned Pen Press, 6962 E. 1st Ave., Suite 103, Scottsdale AZ 85251. (480)945-3375. **Fax:** (480)949-1707. **E-mail:** info@thepoisonedpencil.com. **E-mail:** ellen@thepoisonedpencil.com. **Website:** www.thepoisonedpencil.com. **Contact:** Ellen Larson, editor. Publishes trade paperback and electronic originals. Publishes 4-6 titles/year.

○ *Accepts young adult mysteries only.*

FICTION "We publish only young adult mystery novels, 45,000 to 90,000 words in length. For our purposes, a young adult book is a book with a protagonist between the ages of 13 and 18. We are looking for both traditional and cross-genre young adult mysteries. We encourage off-beat approaches and narrative choices that reflect the complexity and ambiguity of today's world. Submissions from teens are very welcome. Avoid serial killers, excessive gore, and vampires (and other heavy supernatural themes). We only consider authors who live in the US or Canada, due to practicalities of marketing promotion. Avoid coincidence in plotting. Avoid having your sleuth leap to conclusions rather than discover and deduce. Pay attention to the resonance between character and plot; between plot and theme; between theme and character. We are looking for clean style, fluid storytelling, and solid structure. Unrealistic dialogue is a real turn-off."

HOW TO CONTACT Submit proposal package including synopsis, complete ms, and cover letter. 150 submissions received/year. Responds in 6 weeks to mss. Publishes ms 15 months after acceptance.

TERMS Pays 9-15% for trade paperback; 25-35% for e-books. Pays advance of $1,000. Guidelines online.

TIPS "Our audience includes young adults and adults who love YA mysteries."

⊕ POLIS BOOKS

E-mail: info@polisbooks.com. **E-mail:** submissions@polisbooks.com. **Website:** www.polisbooks.com. "Polis Books is an independent digital publishing company actively seeking new and established authors for our growing list. We are actively acquiring titles in young adult, mystery, thriller, suspense, procedural, traditional crime, science fiction, fan-

tasy, horror, supernatural, urban fantasy, romance, erotica, and commercial women's fiction."

HOW TO CONTACT Query with 3 sample chapters and bio via e-mail.

TERMS Offers advance against royalties. Guidelines online.

Ⓐ PRICE STERN SLOAN, INC.

Penguin Group, 375 Hudson St., New York NY 10014. (212)366-2000. **Website:** www.penguin.com. **Contact:** Francesco Sedita, vice-president/publisher. "Price Stern Sloan publishes quirky mass market novelty series for childrens as well as licensed movie tie-in books." Price Stern Sloan only responds to submissions it's interested in publishing.

FICTION Publishes picture books and novelty/board books.

HOW TO CONTACT *Agented submissions only.*

TERMS Book catalog online.

TIPS "Price Stern Sloan publishes unique, fun titles."

Ⓐ PUFFIN BOOKS

Imprint of Penguin Group (USA), Inc., 375 Hudson St., New York NY 10014. (212)366-2000. **Website:** www.penguin.com. **Contact:** Eileen Bishop Kreit, publisher. "Puffin Books publishes high-end trade paperbacks and paperback reprints for preschool children, beginning and middle readers, and young adults." Publishes trade paperback originals and reprints. Publishes 175-200 titles/year.

NONFICTION "Women in history books interest us."

HOW TO CONTACT *No unsolicited mss. Agented submissions only.* Publishes book 1 year after acceptance.

ILLUSTRATION Reviews artwork. Send color copies.

PHOTOGRAPHY Reviews photos. Send color copies.

TIPS "Our audience ranges from little children 'first books' to young adult (ages 14-16). An original idea has the best luck."

Ⓐ PUSH

Scholastic, 557 Broadway, New York NY 10012. **E-mail:** dlevithan@scholastic.com. **Website:** www.thisispush.com. PUSH publishes new voices in teen literature. PUSH does not accept unsolicited mss or queries, only agented or referred fiction/memoir. Publishes 6-9 titles/year. 50% of books from first-time authors.

HOW TO CONTACT *Does not accept unsolicited mss.*

Ⓐ G.P. PUTNAM'S SONS HARDCOVER

Imprint of Penguin Group (USA), Inc., 375 Hudson, New York NY 10014. (212)366-2000. **Fax:** (212)366-2664. **Website:** www.penguinputnam.com. **Contact:** Christine Pepe, vice president/executive editor; Kerri Kolen, executive editor. Publishes hardcover originals.

HOW TO CONTACT *Agented submissions only. No unsolicited mss.*

TERMS Pays variable royalties on retail price. Pays varies advance. Request book catalog through mail order department.

RAINBOW PUBLISHERS

P.O. Box 261129, San Diego CA 92196. (858)277-1167. **E-mail:** editor@rainbowpublishers.com. **Website:** www.rainbowpublishers.com; www.legacypresskids.com. "Our mission is to publish Bible-based, teacher resource materials that contribute to and inspire spiritual growth and development in kids ages 2-12."

NONFICTION Young readers, middle readers, young adult/teens: activity books, arts/crafts, how-to, reference, religion.

HOW TO CONTACT Responds to queries in 6 weeks; mss in 3 months.

ILLUSTRATION Works with 25 illustrators/year. Reviews ms/illustration packages from artists. Submit ms with 2-5 pieces of final art. Illustrations only: Query with samples. Responds in 6 weeks. Samples returned with SASE; samples filed.

TERMS Pays illustrators by the project (range: $300 and up). For authors work purchased outright (range: $500 and up).

TIPS "Our Rainbow imprint publishes reproducible books for teachers of children in Christian ministries, including crafts, activities, games and puzzles. Our Legacy imprint publishes titles for children such as devotionals, fiction and Christian living. Please write for guidelines and study the market before submitting material."

Ⓐ RANDOM HOUSE CHILDREN'S BOOKS

1745 Broadway, New York NY 10019. (212)782-9000. **Website:** www.randomhouse.com. "Producing books for preschool children through young adult readers, in all formats from board to activity books to picture books and novels, Random House Children's Books brings together world-famous franchise characters, multimillion-copy series and top-flight, award-winning authors, and illustrators." Submit mss through a literary agent.

FICTION "Random House publishes a select list of first chapter books and novels, with an emphasis on fantasy and historical fiction." Chapter books, middle-grade readers, young adult.

HOW TO CONTACT *Does not accept unsolicited mss.*

ILLUSTRATION The Random House publishing divisions hire their freelancers directly. To contact the appropriate person, send a cover letter and résumé to the department head at the publisher as follows: "Department Head" (e.g., Art Director, Production Director), "Publisher/Imprint" (e.g., Knopf, Doubleday, etc.), 1745 Broadway New York, NY 10019. Works with 100-150 freelancers/year. Works on assignment only. Send query letter with résumé, tearsheets and printed samples; no originals. Samples are filed. Negotiates rights purchased. Assigns 5 freelance design jobs/year. Pays by the project.

TIPS "We look for original, unique stories. Do something that hasn't been done before."

RAZORBILL

Penguin Young Readers Group, 375 Hudson St., New York NY 10014. (212)414-3600. **Fax:** (212)414-3343. **E-mail:** mgrossman@penguinrandomhouse.com; bschrank@penguinrandomhouse.com. **Website:** www.razorbillbooks.com. **Contact:** Gillian Levinson, editor; Jessica Almon, editor; Elizabeth Tingue, associate editor; Casey McIntyre, associate publisher; Deborah Kaplan, vice president and executive art director. "This division of Penguin Young Readers is looking for the best and the most original of commercial contemporary fiction titles for middle grade and YA readers. A select quantity of nonfiction titles will also be considered." Publishes 30 titles/year.

FICTION Middle Readers: adventure, contemporary, graphic novels, fantasy, humor, problem novels. Young adults/teens: adventure, contemporary, fantasy, graphic novels, humor, multicultural, suspense, paranormal, science fiction, dystopian, literary, romance. Average word length: middle readers—40,000; young adult—60,000.

NONFICTION Middle readers and young adults/teens: concept.

HOW TO CONTACT Submit cover letter with up to 30 sample pages. Submit cover letter with up to 30 sample pages. Responds in 1-3 months. Publishes book 1-2 after acceptance.

TERMS Offers advance against royalties.

TIPS "New writers will have the best chance of acceptance and publication with original, contemporary material that boasts a distinctive voice and well-articulated world. Check out website to get a better idea of what we're looking for."

⊕ REDLEAF LANE

10 Yorktown Ct., St. Paul MN 55117. (800)423-8309. **Website:** www.redleafpress.org. Redleaf Lane publishes engaging, high-quality picture books for children. "Our books are unique because they take place in group-care settings and reflect developmentally appropriate practices and research-based standards."

TERMS Guidelines online.

RENAISSANCE HOUSE

465 Westview Ave., Englewood NJ 07631. (201)408-4048. **E-mail:** info@renaissancehouse.net. **Website:** www.renaissancehouse.net. "We specialize in the development and management of educational and multicultural materials for young readers, Bilingual and Spanish. Our titles are suitable for the school, library, trade markets and reading programs. Publishes biographies, legends and multicultural with a focus on the Hispanic market. Specializes in multicultural and bilingual titles, Spanish-English." Submit ms; e-mail submissions. Children's, educational, and multicultural. Represents 80 illustrators. 95% of artwork handled is children's book illustration. Currently open to illustrators seeking representation. Open to both new and established illustrators.

HOW TO CONTACT Responds to queries/mss in 2 weeks. Publishes ms 1 year after acceptance.

ILLUSTRATION Works with 25 illustrators/year. Uses color and b&w artwork. Reviews ms/illustration packages from artists. Send ms with dummy. Contact: Sam Laredo. Contact: Raquel Benatar. Responds in 3 weeks. Samples not returned; samples filed.

RIPPLE GROVE PRESS

P.O. Box 86740, Portland OR 97286. **E-mail:** submit@ripplegrovepress.com. **Website:** www.ripplegrovepress.com. "We started Ripple Grove Press because we have a passion for well-written and beautifully illustrated children's picture books. Each story selected has been read dozens of times, then slept on, then walked away from, then talked about again and again. If the story has the same intrigue and the same interest that it had when we first read it, we move for-

ward." Publishes hardcover originals. Publishes 3-6 titles/year.

FICTION "Our focus is picture books for children age 2-6. We want something unique, sweet, funny, touching, offbeat, colorful, surprising, charming, different, and creative."

HOW TO CONTACT Submit completed ms. Accepts submissions by mail and e-mail. Please submit a cover letter including a summary of your story, the age range of the story, a brief biography of yourself, and contact information. Submit completed mss only. Accepts submissions by mail and e-mail. Please submit a cover letter including a summary of your story, the age range of the story, a brief biography of yourself, and contact information. Responds to queries within 4 months. Average length of time between acceptance of a book-length ms and publication is 12-18 months.

TERMS Authors receive between 10-12% royalty on net receipt. Guidelines online.

TIPS Also targeting the adults reading to the children. "We create books that children and adults want to read over and over again. Our books showcase art as well as stories and tie them together to create a unique and creative product."

Ⓐ ROARING BROOK PRESS

Macmillan Children's Publishing Group, 175 Fifth Ave., New York NY 10010. (646)307-5151. **Website:** us.macmillan.com. Roaring Brook Press is an imprint of MacMillan, a group of companies that includes Henry Holt and Farrar, Straus & Giroux. *Roaring Brook is not accepting unsolicited mss.*

SEEKS Picture books, young readers, middle readers, young adults: adventure, animal, contemporary, fantasy, history, humor, multicultural, nature/environment, poetry, religion, science fiction, sports, suspense/mystery.

HOW TO CONTACT *Not accepting unsolicited mss or queries.*

ILLUSTRATION Works with 25 illustrators/year. Illustrations only: Query with samples. Do not send original art; copies only through the mail. Samples returned with SASE.

TERMS Pays authors royalty based on retail price.

TIPS "You should find a reputable agent and have him/her submit your work."

ROSEN PUBLISHING

29 E. 21st St., New York NY 10010. (800)237-9932. **Fax:** (888)436-4643. **Website:** www.rosenpublishing.

com. Artists and writers should contact customer service team through online form for information about contributing to Rosen Publishing. Rosen Publishing is an independent educational publishing house, established to serve the needs of students in grades Pre-K-12 with high interest, curriculum-correlated materials. Rosen publishes more than 700 new books each year and has a backlist of more than 7,000.

⊕ SADDLEBACK EDUCATIONAL PUBLISHING

3120-A Pullman St., Costa Mesa CA 92626. (888)735-2225. **Website:** www.sdlback.com. Saddleback is always looking for fresh, new talent. "Please note that we primarily publish books for kids ages 12-18."

FICTION "We look for diversity for our characters and content."

HOW TO CONTACT Mail typed submission along with a query letter describing the work simply and where it fits in with other titles.

SASQUATCH BOOKS

1904 Third Ave., Suite 710, Seattle WA 98101. (206)467-4300. **Fax:** (206)467-4301. **E-mail:** custserv@sasquatchbooks.com. **Website:** www.sasquatchbooks.com. "Sasquatch Books publishes books for and from the Pacific Northwest, Alaska, and California is the nation's premier regional press. Sasquatch Books' publishing program is a veritable celebration of regionally written words. Undeterred by political or geographical borders, Sasquatch defines its region as the magnificent area that stretches from the Brooks Range to the Gulf of California and from the Rocky Mountains to the Pacific Ocean. Our top-selling Best Places® travel guides serve the most popular destinations and locations of the West. We also publish widely in the areas of food and wine, gardening, nature, photography, children's books, and regional history, all facets of the literature of place. With more than 200 books brimming with insider information on the West, we offer an energetic eye on the lifestyle, landscape, and worldview of our region. Considers queries and proposals from authors and agents for new projects that fit into our West Coast regional publishing program. We can evaluate query letters, proposals, and complete mss." Publishes regional hardcover and trade paperback originals. Publishes 30 titles/year. 20% of books from first-time authors. 75% from unagented writers.

FICTION Young readers: adventure, animal, concept, contemporary, humor, nature/environment.

NONFICTION "We are seeking quality nonfiction works about the Pacific Northwest and West Coast regions (including Alaska to California). The literature of place includes how-to and where-to as well as history and narrative nonfiction." Picture books: activity books, animal, concept, nature/environment.

HOW TO CONTACT Query first, then submit outline and sample chapters with SASE. Send submissions to The Editors. E-mailed submissions and queries are not recommended. Please include return postage if you want your materials back. Responds to queries in 3 months. Publishes book 6-9 months after acceptance.

ILLUSTRATION Accepts material from international illustrators. Works with 5 illustrators/year. Uses both color and b&w. Reviews ms/illustration packages. For ms/illustration packages: Query. Submit ms/illustration packages to The Editors. Reviews work for future assignments. If interested in illustrating future titles, query with samples. Samples returned with SASE. Samples filed.

TERMS Pays royalty on cover price. Pays wide range advance. Guidelines online.

TIPS "We sell books through a range of channels in addition to the book trade. Our primary audience consists of active, literate residents of the West Coast."

ⓐ SCHOLASTIC LIBRARY PUBLISHING

90 Old Sherman Turnpike, Danbury CT 06816. (203)797-3500. **Fax:** (203)797-3197. **E-mail:** slpservice@scholastic.com. **Website:** www.scholastic.com/librarypublishing. **Contact:** Phil Friedman, vice president/publisher; Kate Nunn, editor-in-chief; Marie O'Neil, art director. "Scholastic Library is a leading publisher of reference, educational, and children's books. We provide parents, teachers, and librarians with the tools they need to enlighten children to the pleasure of learning and prepare them for the road ahead. Publishes informational (nonfiction) for K-12; picture books for young readers, grades 1-3." Publishes hardcover and trade paperback originals.

◖ *Accepts agented submissions only.*

FICTION Publishes 1 picture book series, Rookie Readers, for grades 1-2. Does not accept unsolicited mss.

NONFICTION Photo-illustrated books for all levels: animal, arts/crafts, biography, careers, concept, geography, health, history, hobbies, how-to, multicultural, nature/environment, science, social issues, special needs, sports. Average word length: young readers—2,000; middle readers—8,000; young adult—15,000.

HOW TO CONTACT *Does not accept fiction proposals.* Query; submit outline/synopsis, résumé, and/or list of publications, and writing sample. SASE required for response.

ILLUSTRATION Works with 15-20 illustrators/year. Uses color artwork and line drawings. Illustrations only: Query with samples or arrange personal portfolio review. Responds only if interested. Samples returned with SASE. Samples filed. Do not send originals. No phone or e-mail inquiries; contact only by mail.

TERMS Pays authors royalty based on net or work purchased outright. Pays illustrators at competitive rates.

Ⓐ SCHOLASTIC PRESS

Imprint of Scholastic, Inc., 557 Broadway, New York NY 10012. (212)343-6100. **Fax:** (212)343-4713. **Website:** www.scholastic.com. Scholastic Press publishes fresh, literary picture book fiction and nonfiction; fresh, literary nonseries or nongenre-oriented middle grade and young adult fiction. Currently emphasizing subtly handled treatments of key relationships in children's lives; unusual approaches to commonly dry subjects, such as biography, math, history, or science. De-emphasizing fairy tales (or retellings), board books, genre, or series fiction (mystery, fantasy, etc.). Publishes hardcover originals. Publishes 60 titles/year. 1% of books from first-time authors.

FICTION Looking for strong picture books, young chapter books, appealing middle grade novels (ages 8-11) and interesting and well-written young adult novels. Wants fresh, exciting picture books and novels—inspiring, new talent.

HOW TO CONTACT *Agented submissions and previously published authors only.* 2,500 queries received/year. Responds in 3 months to queries; 6-8 months to mss. Publishes book 2 years after acceptance.

ILLUSTRATION Works with 30 illustrators/year. Uses both b&w and color artwork. Illustrations only: Query with samples; send tearsheets. Responds only if interested. Samples returned with SASE. Original artwork returned at job's completion.

TERMS Pays royalty on retail price. Pays variable advance.

TIPS "Read *currently* published children's books. Revise, rewrite, rework, and find your own voice, style, and subject. We are looking for authors with a strong and unique voice who can tell a great story and have the ability to evoke genuine emotion. Children's publishers are becoming more selective, looking for irresistible talent and fairly broad appeal, yet still very willing to take risks, just to keep the game interesting."

SEEDLING CONTINENTAL PRESS

520 E. Bainbridge St., Elizabethtown PA 17022. **Website:** www.continentalpress.com. Publishes books for classroom use only for the beginning reader in English. "Natural language and predictable text are requisite. Patterned text is acceptable, but must have a unique story line. Poetry, books in rhyme and full-length picture books are not being accepted. Illustrations are not necessary."

FICTION Young readers: adventure, animal, folktales, humor, multicultural, nature/environment. Does not accept texts longer than 12 pages or over 300 words. Average word length: young readers—100.

NONFICTION Young readers: animal, arts/crafts, biography, careers, concept, multicultural, nature/environment, science. Does not accept texts longer than 12 pages or over 300 words. Average word length: young readers—100.

HOW TO CONTACT Submit complete ms. Submit complete ms. Responds to mss in 6 months. Publishes book 1-2 years after acceptance.

ILLUSTRATION Works with 8-10 illustrators/year. Uses color artwork only. Reviews ms/illustration packages from artists. Submit ms with dummy. Illustrations only: Color copies or line art. Responds only if interested. Samples returned with SASE only; samples filed if interested.

PHOTOGRAPHY Buys photos from freelancers. Works on assignment only. Model/property releases required. Uses color prints and 35mm transparencies. Submit cover letter and color promo piece.

TERMS Work purchased outright from authors.

TIPS "See our website. Follow writers' guidelines carefully and test your story with children and educators."

⊕ SILVER DOLPHIN BOOKS

E-mail: infosilverdolphin@baker-taylor.com. **Website:** www.silverdolphinbooks.com. Silver Dolphin

Books publishes activity, novelty, and educational nonfiction books for preschoolers to 12-year-olds. Highly interactive formats such as the Field Guides and Uncover series both educate and entertain older children. "We will consider submissions only from authors with previously published works."

HOW TO CONTACT Submit cover letter with full proposal and SASE.

Ⓐ SIMON & SCHUSTER BOOKS FOR YOUNG READERS

Imprint of Simon & Schuster Children's Publishing, 1230 Avenue of the Americas, New York NY 10020. (212)698-7000. **Fax:** (212)698-2796. **Website:** www.simonsayskids.com. "Simon and Schuster Books For Young Readers is the Flagship imprint of the S&S Children's Division. We are committed to publishing a wide range of contemporary, commercial, award-winning fiction and nonfiction that spans every age of children's publishing. BFYR is constantly looking to the future, supporting our foundation authors and franchises, but always with an eye for breaking new ground with every publication. We publish high-quality fiction and nonfiction for a variety of age groups and a variety of markets. Above all, we strive to publish books that we are passionate about." *No unsolicited mss.* All unsolicited mss returned unopened. Publishes hardcover originals. Publishes 75 titles/year.

NONFICTION Picture books: concept. All levels: narrative, current events, biography, history. "We're looking for picture books or middle grade nonfiction that have a retail potential. No photo essays."

HOW TO CONTACT *Agented submissions only.* Publishes ms 2-4 years after acceptance.

ILLUSTRATION Works with 70 illustrators/year. Do not submit original artwork. Does not accept unsolicited or unagented illustration submissions.

TERMS Pays variable royalty on retail price. Guidelines online.

TIPS "We're looking for picture books centered on a strong, fullydeveloped protagonist who grows or changes during the course of the story; YA novels that are challenging and psychologically complex; also imaginative and humorous middle-grade fiction. And we want nonfiction that is as engaging as fiction. Our imprint's slogan is 'Reading You'll Remember.' We aim to publish books that are fresh,

accessible and familyoriented; we want them to have an impact on the reader."

SKINNER HOUSE BOOKS

The Unitarian Universalist Association, 24 Farnsworth St., Boston MA 02210. (617)742-2100 ext. 603. **Fax:** (617)948-6466. **E-mail:** bookproposals@uua.org. **Website:** www.uua.org/publications/skinnerhouse. **Contact:** Betsy Martin. "We publish titles in Unitarian Universalist faith, liberal religion, history, biography, worship, and issues of social justice. Most of our children's titles are intended for religious education or worship use. They reflect Unitarian Universalist values. We also publish inspirational titles of poetic prose and meditations. Writers should know that Unitarian Universalism is a liberal religious denomination committed to progressive ideals. Currently emphasizing social justice concerns." Publishes trade paperback originals and reprints. Publishes 10-20 titles/year. 30% of books from first-time authors. 100% from unagented writers.

FICTION Only publishes fiction for children's titles for religious instruction.

NONFICTION All levels: activity books, multicultural, music/dance, nature/environment, religion.

HOW TO CONTACT Query or submit proposal with cover letter, TOC, 2 sample chapters. Responds to queries in 1 month. Publishes book 1 year after acceptance.

ILLUSTRATION Works with 2 illustrators/year. Uses both color and b&w. Reviews ms/illustration packages from artists. Query. Contact: Suzanne Morgan, design director. Responds only if interested. Samples returned with SASE.

PHOTOGRAPHY Buys stock images and assigns work. Contact: Suzanne Morgan, design director. Uses inspirational types of photo's. Model/property releases required; captions required. Uses color, b&w. Submit cover letter, résumé.

TERMS Book catalog for 6×9 SAE with 3 first-class stamps. Guidelines online.

TIPS "From outside our denomination, we are interested in manuscripts that will be of help or interest to liberal churches, Sunday School classes, parents, ministers, and volunteers. Inspirational/spiritual and children's titles must reflect liberal Unitarian Universalist values."

🅐 LIZZIE SKURNICK BOOKS

Ig Publishing, 392 Clinton Ave., Brooklyn NY 11238. (718)797-0676. **Website:** lizzieskurnickbooks.com. Lizzie Skurnick Books, an imprint of Ig Publishing, is devoted to reissuing the very best in young adult literature, from the classics of the 1930s and 1940s to the social novels of the 1970s and 1980s. Ig does not accept unsolicited mss, either by e-mail or regular mail. If you have a ms that you would like Ig to take a look at, send a query throught online contact form. If interested, they will contact. All unsolicited mss will be discarded.

⊕ SKY PONY PRESS

307 W. 36th St., 11th Floor, New York NY 10018. (212)643-6816. **Fax:** (212)643-6819. **E-mail:** skyponysubmissions@skyhorsepublishing.com. **Website:** skyponypress.com. Sky Pony Press is the children's book imprint of Skyhorse Publishing. "Following in the footsteps of our parent company, our goal is to provide books for readers with a wide variety of interests."

FICTION "We will consider picture books, early readers, mid-grade novels, novelties, and informational books for all ages."

NONFICTION "Our parent company publishes many excellent books in the fields of ecology, independent living, farm living, wilderness living, recycling, and other green topics, and this will be a theme in our children's books. We are also searching for books that have strong educational themes and that help inform children of the world in which they live."

HOW TO CONTACT Submit ms or proposal. Submit proposal via e-mail.

TERMS Guidelines online.

SLEEPING BEAR PRESS

315 E. Eisenhower Pkwy., Suite 200, Ann Arbor MI 48108. (800)487-2323. **Fax:** (734)794-0004. **E-mail:** submissions@sleepingbearpress.com. **Website:** www.sleepingbearpress.com. **Contact:** Manuscript Submissions.

FICTION Picture books: adventure, animal, concept, folktales, history, multicultural, nature/environment, religion, sports. Young readers: adventure, animal, concept, folktales, history, humor, multicultural, nature/environment, religion, sports. Average word length: picture books—1,800.

HOW TO CONTACT Query with sample of work (up to 15 pages) and SASE.

TERMS Book catalog available via e-mail.

⊕ SOURCEBOOKS FIRE

1935 Brookdale Rd., Suite 139, Naperville IL 60563. (630)961-3900. **Fax:** (630)961-2168. **E-mail:** submissions@sourcebooks.com. **Website:** www.sourcebooks.com. "We're actively acquiring knockout books for our YA imprint. We are particularly looking for strong writers who are excited about promoting and building their community of readers, and whose books have something fresh to offer the ever-growing young adult audience."

HOW TO CONTACT Query with the full ms attached in Word doc.

⊕ SPENCER HILL PRESS

P.O. Box 243, Marlborough CT 06447. (860)207-2206. **E-mail:** submissions@spencerhillpress.com. **Website:** www.spencerhillpress.com. **Contact:** Jennifer Carson. Spencer Hill Press is an independent publishing house specializing in sci-fi, urban fantasy, and paranormal romance for young adult readers. "Our books have that 'I couldn't put it down!' quality."

FICTION "We are interested in young adult, new adult, and middle grade sci-fi, psych-fi, paranormal, or urban fantasy, particularly those with a strong and interesting voice."

HOW TO CONTACT Check website for open submission periods.

TERMS Guidelines online.

SPINNER BOOKS

University Games, 2030 Harrison St., San Francisco CA 94110. (415)503-1600. **Fax:** (415)503-0085. **E-mail:** info@ugames.com. **Website:** www.ugames.com. "Spinners Books publishes books of puzzles, games and trivia."

NONFICTION Picture books: games and puzzles.

HOW TO CONTACT Query. Responds to queries in 3 months; mss in 2 months only if interested. Publishes book 6 months after acceptance.

ILLUSTRATION Only interested in agented material. Uses both color and b&w. Illustrations only: Query with samples. Responds in 3 months only if interested. Samples not returned.

⊕ SPLASHING COW BOOKS

P.O. Box 867, Manchester VT 05254. **Website:** www.splashingcowbooks.com. **Contact:** Gordon McClellan, publisher. Splashing Cow Books publishes books for children. Publishes mass market paperback and electronic originals. Publishes 10 titles/year. 100% of books from first-time authors. 100% from unagented writers.

FICTION Interested in a wide range of subject matter for children.

NONFICTION Open to any topic that would be of interest to children (or to women, for Blue Boot Books). Query with completed ms and SASE.

HOW TO CONTACT Query with completed ms and SASE. Responds in 1 month to mss.

TERMS Pays royalties on retail price. Does not offer an advance. Catalog available online. Guidelines available online.

STANDARD PUBLISHING

Standex International Corp., 8805 Governor's Hill Dr., Suite 400, Cincinnati OH 45249. (800)543-1353. **E-mail:** customerservice@standardpub.com. **Website:** www.standardpub.com. Publishes resources that meet church and family needs in the area of children's ministry.

TERMS Guidelines online.

✛ STAR BRIGHT BOOKS

13 Landsdowne St., Cambridge MA 02139. (617)354-1300. **Fax:** (617)354-1399. **E-mail:** info@starbrightbooks.com. **Website:** www.starbrightbooks.com. Star Bright Books does accept unsolicited mss and art submissions. "We welcome submissions for picture books and longer works, both fiction and nonfiction." Query first.

STERLING PUBLISHING CO., INC.

1166 Avenue of the Americas, 17th Floor, New York NY 10036. (212)532-7160. **Fax:** (212)981-0508. **Website:** www.sterlingpublishing.com. "Sterling publishes highly illustrated, accessible, hands-on, practical books for adults and children. Our mission is to publish high-quality books that educate, entertain, and enrich the lives of our readers." Publishes hardcover and paperback originals and reprints. 15% of books from first-time authors.

FICTION Publishes fiction for children.

NONFICTION Proposals on subjects such as crafting, decorating, outdoor living, and photography should be sent directly to Lark Books at their Asheville, North Carolina offices. Complete guidelines can be found on the Lark site: www.larkbooks.com/submissions. Publishes nonfiction only.

HOW TO CONTACT Submit to attention of "Children's Book Editor." Submit outline, publishing history, 1 sample chapter (typed and double-spaced), SASE. "Explain your idea. Send sample illustrations where applicable. For children's books, please submit full mss. We do not accept electronic (e-mail) submissions. Be sure to include information about yourself with particular regard to your skills and qualifications in the subject area of your submission. It is helpful for us to know your publishing history—whether or not you've written other books and, if so, the name of the publisher and whether those books are currently in print."

ILLUSTRATION Works with 50 illustrators/year. Reviews ms/illustration packages from artists. Illustrations only: Send promo sheet. Contact: Karen Nelson, creative director. Responds in 6 weeks. Samples returned with SASE; samples filed.

PHOTOGRAPHY Buys stock and assigns work. Contact: Karen Nelson.

TERMS Pays royalty or work purchased outright. Offers advances (average amount: $2,000). Catalog online. Guidelines online.

TIPS "We are primarily a nonfiction activities-based publisher. We have a picture book list, but we do not publish chapter books or novels. Our list is not trend-driven. We focus on titles that will backlist well. "

STONE ARCH BOOKS

1710 Roe Crest Rd., North Mankato MN 56003. **E-mail:** author.sub@capstonepub.com. **Website:** www.stonearchbooks.com.

FICTION Young readers, middle readers, young adults: adventure, contemporary, fantasy, humor, light humor, mystery, science fiction, sports, suspense. Average word length: young readers—1,000-3,000; middle readers and early young adults—5,000-10,000.

HOW TO CONTACT Submit outline/synopsis and 3 sample chapters. Electronic submissions preferred.

ILLUSTRATION Works with 35 illustrators/year. Uses both color and b&w.

TERMS Work purchased outright from authors. Catalog online.

TIPS "A high-interest topic or activity is one that a young person would spend their free time on without adult direction or suggestion."

STOREY PUBLISHING

210 MASS MoCA Way, North Adams MA 01247. (800)793-9396. **Fax:** (413)346-2196. **E-mail:** feed

back@storey.com. **Website:** www.storey.com. **Contact:** Deborah Balmuth, editorial director (building and mind/body/spirit). "The mission of Storey Publishing is to serve our customers by publishing practical information that encourages personal independence in harmony with the environment. We seek to do this in a positive atmosphere that promotes editorial quality, team spirit, and profitability. The books we select to carry out this mission include titles on gardening, small-scale farming, building, cooking, homebrewing, crafts, part-time business, home improvement, woodworking, animals, nature, natural living, personal care, and country living. We are always pleased to review new proposals, which we try to process expeditiously. We offer both work-for-hire and standard royalty contracts." Publishes hardcover and trade paperback originals and reprints. Publishes 40 titles/year. 25% of books from first-time authors. 60% from unagented writers.

HOW TO CONTACT Submit a proposal. 600 queries received/year. 150 mss received/year. Responds in 1-3 months. Publishes book 2 years after acceptance.

TERMS We offer both work-for-hire and standard royalty contracts. Pays advance. Book catalog available free. Guidelines online.

SUNSTONE PRESS

Box 2321, Santa Fe NM 87504. (800)243-5644. **Website:** www.sunstonepress.com. **Contact:** Submissions Editor. Sunstone's original focus was on nonfiction subjects that preserved and highlighted the richness of the American Southwest but it has expanded its view over the years to include mainstream themes and categories—both nonfiction and fiction—that have a more general appeal.

HOW TO CONTACT Query with 1 sample chapter. Query with 1 sample chapter.

TERMS Guidelines online.

KATHERINE TEGEN BOOKS

HarperCollins, 10 E. 53rd St., New York NY 10022. **Website:** www.harpercollins.com. **Contact:** Katherine Tegen, vice-president and publisher. Katherine Tegen Books publishes high-quality, commercial literature for children of all ages, including teens. Talented authors and illustrators who offer powerful narratives that are thought-provoking, well-written, and entertaining are the core of the Katherine Tegen

Books imprint. *Katherine Tegen Books accepts agented work only.*

THUNDERSTONE BOOKS

6575 Horse Dr., Las Vegas NV 89131. **E-mail:** info@thunderstonebooks.com. **Website:** www.thunderstonebooks.com. **Contact:** Rachel Noorda, editorial director. "At ThunderStone Books, we aim to publish children's books that have an educational aspect. We are not looking for curriculum for learning certain subjects, but rather stories that encourage learning for children, whether that be learning about a new language/culture or learning more about science and math in a fun, fictional format. We want to help children to gain a love for other languages and subjects so that they are curious about the world around them. We are currently accepting fiction and nonfiction submissions." Publishes hardcover, trade paperback, mass market paperback, and electronic originals. Publishes 2-5 titles/year. 100% of books from first-time authors. 100% from unagented writers.

FICTION Interested in multicultural stories with an emphasis on authentic culture and language (these may include mythology).

NONFICTION Looking for engaging educational materials, not a set curriculum, but books that teach as well as have some fun. Open to a variety of educational subjects, but specialty and main interest lies in language exposure/learning, science, math, and history.

HOW TO CONTACT Query with SASE. Query with SASE. Receives 30 queries and mss/year. Responds in 3 months to queries, proposals, and mss. Publishes ms 6 months after acceptance.

TERMS Pays 5-15% royalties on retail price. Pays $300-1,000 advance. Catalog available for SASE. Guidelines available on website.

TILBURY HOUSE PUBLISHERS

WordSplice Studio, Inc., 12 Starr St., Thomaston ME 04861. (800)582-1899. **Fax:** (207)582-8772. **E-mail:** tilbury@tilburyhouse.com. **Website:** www.tilburyhouse.com. **Contact:** Audrey Maynard, children's book editor; Jonathan Eaton, publisher. Publishes 10 titles/year.

FICTION Picture books: multicultural, nature/environment. Special needs include books that teach children about tolerance and honoring diversity.

NONFICTION Regional adult biography/history/maritime/nature, and children's picture books that deal with issues, such as bullying, multiculturalism, etc., science/nature.

HOW TO CONTACT Send art/photography samples and/or complete ms to Audrey Maynard, children's book editor. Submit complete ms for picture books or outline/synopsis for longer works. Responds to mss in 3 months. Publishes ms 1 year after acceptance.

ILLUSTRATION Works with 2-3 illustrators/year. Illustrations only: Query with samples. Responds in 1 month. Samples returned with SASE. Original artwork returned at job's completion.

PHOTOGRAPHY Buys photos from freelancers. Works on assignment only.

TERMS Pays royalty based on wholesale price. Guidelines and catalog online.

TIPS "We are always interested in stories that will encourage children to understand the natural world and the environment, as well as stories with social justice themes. We really like stories that engage children to become problem solvers as well as those that promote respect, tolerance and compassion." We do not publish books with personified animal characters; historical fiction; YA or middle grade fiction or chapter books; fantasy."

TOR BOOKS

Tom Doherty Associates, 175 Fifth Ave., New York NY 10010. **Website:** www.tor-forge.com. Tor Books is the "world's largest publisher of science fiction and fantasy, with strong category publishing in historical fiction, mystery, western/Americana, thriller, YA." Publishes 10-20 titles/year.

HOW TO CONTACT Submit first 3 chapters, 3-10 page synopsis, dated cover letter, SASE.

TERMS Pays author royalty. Pays illustrators by the project. Book catalog available. Guidelines online.

TRIANGLE SQUARE

Seven Stories Press, 140 Watts St., New York NY 10013. (212)226-8760. **Fax:** (212)226-1411. **Website:** www.sevenstories.com/trianglesquare/. Triangle Square is a children's and young adult imprint of Seven Story Press.

HOW TO CONTACT Send a cover letter with 2 sample chapters and SASE.

TU BOOKS

Lee & Low Books, 95 Madison Ave., Suite #1205, New York NY 10016. (212)779-4400. **Fax:** (212)683-1894. **Website:** www.leeandlow.com/imprints/3. **Contact:** Stacy Whitman, publisher. The Tu imprint spans many genres: science fiction, fantasy, mystery, and more. "We don't believe in labels or limits, just great stories. Join us at the crossroads where fantasy and real life collide. You'll be glad you did."

FICTION Focuses on well-told, exciting, adventurous fantasy, science fiction, and mystery novels featuring people of color and/or set in worlds inspired by non-Western folklore or culture. Looking specifically for stories for both middle grade (ages 8-12) and young adult (ages 12-18) readers.

HOW TO CONTACT Mss should be sent through postal mail only. Mss should be accompanied by a cover letter that includes a brief biography of the author, including publishing history. The letter should also state if the ms is a simultaneous or an exclusive submission. Include a synopsis and the first 3 chapters of the novel. Include full contact information on the cover letter and the first page of the ms. Responds only if interested.

ILLUSTRATION Tu Books will consider fantasy, science fiction, and mystery artwork for book covers and spot illustrations, for novels aimed at older readers (ages 8-18). Artists should send a postcard sample with the address of their website portfolio, along with a résumé and/or cover letter as well as color copies, tear sheets, or other non-returnable illustration samples.

TERMS Guidelines online. Electronic submissions can be submitted here (only): https://tubooks.submittable.com/submit.

⊕ TUMBLEHOME LEARNING

P.O. Box 71386, Boston MA 02117. **E-mail:** info@tumblehomelearning.com. **Website:** www.tumblehomelearning.com. **Contact:** Pendred Noyce, editor. Tumblehome Learning helps kids imagine themselves as young scientists or engineeers and encourages them to experience science through adventure and discovery. "We do this with exciting mystery and adventure tales as well as experiments carefully designed to engage students from ages 8 and up." Publishes hardcover, trade paperback, and electronic originals. Publishes 8-10 titles/year. 50% of books from first-time authors. 100% from unagented writers.

FICTION "All our fiction has science at its heart. This can include using science to solve a mystery (see *The Walking Fish* by Rachelle Burk or *Something Stinks!* by Gail Hedrick), realistic science fiction, books in our Galactic Academy of Science series, science-based adventure tales, and the occasional picture book with a science theme, such as appreciation of the stars and constellations in *Elizabeth's Constellation Quilt* by Olivia Fu. A graphic novel about science would also be welcome."

NONFICTION Rarely publishes nonfiction. Book would need to be sold to trade, not just the school market.

HOW TO CONTACT Submit completed ms electronically. Receives 20 queries and 20 mss/year. Responds in 1 month to queries and proposals, and 2 months to mss. Publishes ms 8 months after acceptance.

TERMS Pays authors 8-12% royalties on retail price. Pays $500 advance. Catalog available online. Guidelines available on request for SASE.

TIPS "Please don't submit to us if your book is not about science. We don't accept generic books about animals or books with glaring scientific errors in the first chapter. That said, the book should be fun to read and the science content can be subtle. We work closely with authors, including first-time authors, to edit and improve their books. As a small publisher, the greatest benefit we can offer is this friendly and respectful partnership with authors."

Ⓐ TYNDALE HOUSE PUBLISHERS, INC.

351 Executive Dr., Carol Stream IL 60188. (800)323-9400. **Fax:** (800)684-0247. **Website:** www.tyndale.com. **Contact:** Katara Washington Patton, acquisitions; Talinda Iverson, art acquisitions. "Tyndale House publishes practical, user-friendly Christian books for the home and family." Publishes hardcover and trade paperback originals and mass paperback reprints. Publishes 15 titles/year.

FICTION "Christian truths must be woven into the story organically. No short story collections. Youth books: character building stories with Christian perspective. Especially interested in ages 10-14. We primarily publish Christian historical romances, with occasional contemporary, suspense, or standalones."

HOW TO CONTACT *Agented submissions only. No unsolicited mss.*

ILLUSTRATION Uses full-color for book covers, b&w or color spot illustrations for some nonfiction. Illustrations only: Query with photocopies (color or b&w) of samples, résumé.

PHOTOGRAPHY Buys photos from freelancers. Works on assignment only.

TERMS Pays negotiable royalty. Pays negotiable advance. Guidelines online.

TIPS "All accepted mss will appeal to Evangelical Christian children and parents."

URJ PRESS

633 Third Ave., 7th Floor, New York NY 10017. (212)650-4120. **Fax:** (212)650-4119. **E-mail:** press@urj.org. **Website:** www.urjbooksandmusic.com. **Contact:** Michael H. Goldberg, editor-in-chief. "URJ publishes textbooks for the religious classroom, children's tradebooks and scholarly work of Jewish education import—no adult fiction and no YA fiction." *URJ Press publishes books related to Judaism.* Publishes hardcover and trade paperback originals. Publishes 22 titles/year. 70% of books from first-time authors. 90% from unagented writers.

NONFICTION Picture books, young readers, middle readers: religion. Average word length: picture books—1,500.

HOW TO CONTACT Submit proposal package, outline, bio, 1-2 sample chapters. 500 queries received/year. 400 mss received/year. Responds in 4 months. Publishes book 18-24 months after acceptance.

ILLUSTRATION Works with 5 illustrators/year. Reviews ms/illustration packages from artists. Send ms with dummy. Illustrations only: Send portfolio to be kept on file. Responds in 2 months. Samples returned with SASE. Looking specifically for Jewish themes.

PHOTOGRAPHY Buys stock and assigns work. Uses photos with Jewish content. Prefers modern settings. Submit cover letter and promo piece.

TERMS Pays 3-5% royalty on retail price. Makes outright purchase of $500-2,000. Pays $500-2,000 advance. Book catalog and ms guidelines online.

TIPS "Look at some of our books. Have an understanding of the Reform Judaism community. In addition to bookstores, we sell to Jewish congregations and Hebrew day schools."

Ⓐ VIKING CHILDREN'S BOOKS

375 Hudson St., New York NY 10014. **Website:** www.penguin.com. **Contact:** Kenneth Wright, publisher. "Viking Children's Books is known for humorous, quirky picture books, in addition to more traditional fiction. We publish the highest quality fiction, nonfiction, and picture books for pre-schoolers through young adults." *Does not accept unsolicited submissions.* Publishes hardcover originals. Publishes 70 titles/year.

FICTION All levels: adventure, animal, contemporary, fantasy, history, humor, multicultural, nature/environment, poetry, problem novels, romance, science fiction, sports, suspense/mystery.

NONFICTION All levels: biography, concept, history, multicultural, music/dance, nature/environment, science, and sports.

HOW TO CONTACT *Agented submissions only.* Responds in 6 months. Publishes book 1-2 years after acceptance.

ILLUSTRATION Works with 30 illustrators/year. Responds to artist's queries/submissions only if interested. Samples returned with SASE only or samples filed. Originals returned at job's completion.

TERMS Pays 2-10% royalty on retail price or flat fee. Pays negotiable advance.

TIPS "No 'cartoony' or mass-market submissions for picture books."

WANNABEE BOOKS

750 Pinehurst Dr., Rio Vista CA 94571-9757. **E-mail:** books@wannabeebooks.com. **Website:** www.wannabeebooks.com. **Contact:** Joanne McCoy, senior editor. Wannabee Books publishes full-color, digitally enhanced, and acoustically supplemented children's picture books on CDs that explore exciting subjects that stimulate young minds. Publishes trade paperback originals. Publishes 6 titles/year. 100% of books from first-time authors. 100% from unagented writers.

NONFICTION Interested in topics that explore exciting subjects that stimulate young minds. Wannabee Books helps kids decide what they "wannabee." Do they "wannabee" astronauts, chemists, architects, engineers, etc.?

HOW TO CONTACT Submit completed ms. Receives 12-20 queries/year. Receives 12 mss/year. Responds in 1 month to queries, proposals, and mss. Publishes mss in 3-4 months upon acceptance.

TERMS Pays 15% royalties or makes an outright purchase between $250-500. Catalog available online. Guidelines available online or by e-mail.

WHITE MANE KIDS

73 W. Burd St., P.O. Box 708, Shippensburg PA 17257. (717)532-2237. **Fax:** (717)532-6110. **E-mail:** marketing@whitemane.com. **Website:** www.whitemane.com. **Contact:** Harold Collier, acquisitions editor.

FICTION Middle readers, young adults: history (primarily American Civil War). Average word length: middle readers—30,000. Does not publish picture books.

NONFICTION Middle readers, young adults: history. Average word length: middle readers—30,000. Does not publish picture books.

HOW TO CONTACT Query. Submit outline/synopsis and 2-3 sample chapters. Responds to queries in 1 month, mss in 6-9 months. Publishes book 18 months after acceptance.

ILLUSTRATION Works with 4 illustrators/year. Illustrations used for cover art only. Responds only if interested. Samples returned with SASE.

PHOTOGRAPHY Buys stock and assigns work. Submit cover letter and portfolio.

TERMS Pays authors royalty of 7-10%. Pays illustrators and photographers by the project. Book catalog and writer's guidelines available for SASE.

TIPS "Make your work historically accurate. We are interested in historically accurate fiction for middle and young adult readers. We do *not* publish picture books. Our primary focus is the American Civil War and some America Revolution topics."

ALBERT WHITMAN & COMPANY

250 S. Northwest Hwy., Suite 320, Park Ridge IL 60068. (800)255-7675. **Fax:** (847)581-0039. **E-mail:** submissions@awhitmanco.com. **Website:** www.albertwhitman.com. Albert Whitman & Company publishes books for the trade, library, and school library market. Interested in reviewing the following types of projects: Picture book mss for ages 2-8; novels and chapter books for ages 8-12; young adult novels; nonfiction for ages 3-12 and YA; art samples showing pictures of children. Best known for the classic series The Boxcar Children® Mysteries. "We are no longer reading unsolicited queries and mss sent through the US mail. We now require these submissions to be sent by e-mail. You must visit our website for our guidelines, which include instructions for formatting your e-mail. E-mails that do not follow this format may not be read. We read every submission within 4 months of receipt, but we can no longer respond to every one. If you do not receive a response from us after four months, we have declined to publish your submission." Publishes in original hardcover, paperback, boardbooks. Publishes 60 titles/year. 10% of books from first-time authors. 50% from unagented writers.

FICTION Picture books (up to 1,000 words); middle grade (up to 35,000 words); young adult (up to 70,000 words).

NONFICTION Picture books up to 1,000 words.

HOW TO CONTACT For picture books, submit cover letter and brief description. For middle grade and young adult, send query, synopsis, and first 3 chapters. Submit cover letter, brief description.

TERMS Guidelines online.

WILLIAMSON BOOKS

2630 Elm Hill Pike, Suite 100, Nashville TN 37214. **Website:** www.idealsbooks.com. Publishes "very successful nonfiction series (Kids Can! Series) on subjects such as history, science, arts/crafts, geography, diversity, multiculturalism. Little Hands series for ages 2-6, Kaleidoscope Kids series (age 7 and up) and Quick Starts for Kids! series (ages 8 and up). Our goal is to help every child fulfill his/her potential and experience personal growth."

NONFICTION Hands-on active learning books, animals, African-American, arts/crafts, Asian, biography, diversity, careers, geography, health, history, hobbies, how-to, math, multicultural, music/dance, nature/environment, Native American, science, writing and journaling. Does not want to see textbooks, picture books, fiction. "Looking for all things African American, Asian American, Hispanic, Latino, and Native American including crafts and traditions, as well as their history, biographies, and personal retrospectives of growing up in US for grades pre K-8th. We are looking for books in which learning and doing are inseparable."

HOW TO CONTACT Query with annotated TOC/synopsis and 1 sample chapter. Responds in 4 months. Publishes book 1 year after acceptance.

ILLUSTRATION Works with at least 2 illustrators and 2 designers/year. "We're interested in expanding our illustrator and design freelancers." Uses primarily 2-color and 4-color artwork. Responds only if interested. Samples returned with SASE; samples filed.

PHOTOGRAPHY Buys photos from freelancers; uses archival art and photos.

TERMS Pays authors advance against future royalties based on wholesale price or purchases outright.

Pays illustrators by the project. Pays photographers per photo. Guidelines online.

Ⓐ PAULA WISEMAN BOOKS

1230 Sixth Ave., New York NY 10020. (212)698-7272. **Fax:** (212)698-2796. **E-mail:** paula.wiseman@simonandschuster.com; sylvie.frank@simonandschuster.com; sarahjane.abbott@simonandschuster.com. **Website:** kids.simonandschuster.com. Publishes 30 titles/year. 15% of books from first-time authors.

FICTION Considers all categories. Average word length: picture books—500; others standard length.

NONFICTION Picture books: animal, biography, concept, history, nature/environment. Young readers: animal, biography, history, multicultural, nature/environment, sports. Average word length: picture books—500; others standard length.

HOW TO CONTACT Does not accept unsolicited or unagented mss.

ILLUSTRATION Works with 15 illustrators/year. Does not accept unsolicited or unagented illustrations or submissions.

Ⓐ WORDSONG

815 Church St., Honesdale PA 18431. **Fax:** (570)253-0179. **Website:** www.wordsongpoetry.com. "We publish fresh voices in contemporary poetry."

HOW TO CONTACT Responds to mss in 3 months.

ILLUSTRATION Works with 7 illustrators/year. Reviews ms/illustration packages from artists. Submit complete ms with 1 or 2 pieces of art. Illustrations only: Query with samples best suited to the art (postcard, 8½× 1, etc.). Label package "Art Sample Submission." Responds only if interested. Samples returned with SASE.

PHOTOGRAPHY Assigns work.

TERMS Pays authors royalty or work purchased outright.

TIPS "Collections of original poetry, not anthologies, are our biggest need at this time. Keep in mind that the strongest collections demonstrate a facility with multiple poetic forms and offer fresh images and insights. Check to see what's already on the market and on our website before submitting."

WORLD BOOK, INC.

233 N. Michigan Ave., Suite 2000, Chicago IL 60601. (312)729-5800. **Fax:** (312)729-5600. **Website:** www.worldbook.com. World Book, Inc. (publisher of The World Book Encyclopedia), publishes refer-

ence sources and nonfiction series for children and young adults in the areas of science, mathematics, English-language skills, basic academic and social skills, social studies, history, and health and fitness. "We publish print and non-print material appropriate for children ages 3-14. WB does not publish fiction, poetry, or wordless picture books."

NONFICTION Young readers: animal, arts/crafts, careers, concept, geography, health, reference. Middle readers: animal, arts/crafts, careers, geography, health, history, hobbies, how-to, nature/environment, reference, science. Young adult: arts/crafts, careers, geography, health, history, hobbies, how-to, nature/environment, reference, science.

HOW TO CONTACT Query. Responds to queries in 2 months. Publishes book 18 months after acceptance.

ILLUSTRATION Works with 10-30 illustrators/year. Illustrations only: Query with samples. Responds only if interested. Samples returned with SASE; samples filed "if extra copies and if interested."

PHOTOGRAPHY Buys stock and assigns work. Needs broad spectrum; editorial concept, specific natural, physical and social science spectrum. Model/property releases required; captions required. Submit cover letter, résumé, promo piece (color and b&w).

TERMS Payment negotiated on project-by-project basis.

⊕ WORLD WEAVER PRESS

E-mail: submissions@worldweaverpress.com. **Website:** www.worldweaverpress.com. **Contact:** WWP Editors. World Weaver Press publishes digital and print editions of speculative fiction at various lengths for adult, young adult, and new adult audiences.

HOW TO CONTACT Query with first 5,000 words.

TERMS Guidelines online.

TIPS "Use your letter to pitch us the story, not talk about its themes or inception."

ZEST BOOKS

35 Stillman St., Suite 121, San Francisco CA 94107. (415)777-8654. **Fax:** (415)777-8653. **E-mail:** info@zestbooks.net. **E-mail:** dan@zestbooks.net. **Website:** zestbooks.net. **Contact:** Dan Harmon, editor. Zest Books is a leader in young adult nonfic-

tion, publishing books on entertainment, history, science, health, fashion, and lifestyle advice since 2006. Zest Books is distributed by Houghton Mifflin Harcourt.

HOW TO CONTACT Submit proposal.

ILLUSTRATION "If you are interested in becoming part of our team of illustrators, please send examples of printed work to adam@zestbooks.net."

TERMS Guidelines online.

TIPS "If you're interested in becoming a member of our author pool, send a cover letter stating why you are interested in young adult nonfiction, plus your specific areas of interest and specialties, your résumé, 3-5 writing samples."

ZUMAYA PUBLICATIONS, LLC

3209 S. Interstate 35, Austin TX 78741. **E-mail:** business@zumayapublications.com. **E-mail:** acquisitions@zumayapublications.com. **Website:** www.zumayapublications.com. **Contact:** Rie Sheridan Rose, acquisitions editor. Publishes trade paperback and electronic originals and reprints. Publishes 20-25 titles/year. 5% of books from first-time authors. 98% from unagented writers.

> ○ "We accept only electronic queries; all others will be discarded unread. A working knowledge of computers and relevant software is a necessity, as our production process is completely digital."

FICTION "We are currently oversupplied with speculative fiction and are reviewing submissions in SF, fantasy and paranormal suspense by invitation only. We are much in need of GLBT and YA/middle grade, historical and western, New Age/inspirational (no overtly Christian materials, please), non-category romance, thrillers. As with nonfiction, we encourage people to review what we've already published so as to avoid sending us more of the same, at least, insofar as the plot is concerned. While we're always looking for good specific mysteries, we want original concepts rather than slightly altered versions of what we've already published."

NONFICTION "The easiest way to figure out what we're looking for is to look at what we've already done. Our main nonfiction interests are in collections of true ghost stories, ones that have been investigated or thoroughly documented, memoirs that address specific regions and eras from a 'normal person' viewpoint and books on the craft of writing. That doesn't mean we won't consider something else."

HOW TO CONTACT Electronic query only. 1,000 queries received/year. 100 mss received/year. Responds in 6 months to queries and proposals; 9 months to mss. Publishes book 2 years after acceptance.

TERMS Guidelines online.

TIPS "We're catering to readers who may have loved last year's best seller but not enough to want to read 10 more just like it. Have something different. If it does not fit standard pigeonholes, that's a plus. On the other hand, it has to have an audience. And if you're not prepared to work with us on promotion and marketing, particularly via social media, it would be better to look elsewhere."

CANADIAN & INTERNATIONAL BOOK PUBLISHERS

///

While the United States is considered the largest market in children's publishing, the children's publishing world is by no means strictly dominated by the United States. After all, the most prestigious children's book extravaganza in the world occurs each year in Bologna, Italy, at the Bologna Children's Book Fair and some of the world's most beloved characters were born in the United Kingdom (i.e., Winnie-the-Pooh and Mr. Potter).

In this section you'll find book publishers from English-speaking countries around the world from Canada, Australia, New Zealand, and the United Kingdom. The listings in this section look just like the United States. Book Publishers section; and the publishers listed are dedicated to the same goal—publishing great books for children.

Like always, be sure to study each listing and research each publisher carefully before submitting material. Determine whether a publisher is open to United States or international submissions, as many publishers accept submissions only from residents of their own country. Some publishers accept illustration samples from foreign artists, but do not accept manuscripts from foreign writers. Illustrators do have a slight edge in this category as many illustrators generate commissions from all around the globe. Visit publishers' websites to be certain they publish the sort of work you do. Visit online bookstores to see if publishers' books are available there. Write or e-mail to request catalogs and submission guidelines.

When mailing requests or submissions out of the United States, remember that United States postal stamps are useless on your SASE. Always include International Reply Coupons (IRCs) with your SAE. Each IRC is good for postage for one letter. So if you want the publisher to return your manuscript or send a catalog, be sure to enclose enough IRCs to pay the postage. For more help visit the United State Postal Service website at www.usps.com/global. Visit www.timeanddate.com/worldclock and American Computer Resources,

Inc.'s International Calling Code Directory at www.the-acr.com/codes/cntrycd.htm before calling or faxing internationally to make sure you're calling at a reasonable time and using the correct numbers.

As in the rest of *Children's Writer's & Illustrator's Market*, the maple leaf ☽ symbol identifies Canadian markets. Look for International ☽ symbol throughout *Children's Writer's & Illustrator's Market* as well. Several of the Society of Children's Book Writers and Illustrator's (SCBWI) international conferences are listed in the Conferences & Workshops section along with other events in locations around the globe. Look for more information about SCBWI's international chapters on the organization's website, www.scbwi.org.

⊕ ☺ ALLEN & UNWIN

406 Albert St., East Melbourne VIC 3002, Australia. (61)(3)9665-5000. **E-mail:** fridaypitch@allenandunwin.com. **Website:** www.allenandunwin.com. Allen & Unwin publish over 80 new books for children and young adults each year, many of these from established authors and illustrators. "However, we know how difficult it can be for new writers to get their work in front of publishers, which is why we've decided to extend our innovative and pioneering Friday Pitch service to emerging writers for children and young adults. The Friday Pitch allows for writers of all genres to have their work considered by one of our in-house Submission Editors."

TERMS Guidelines online.

⊕ ☺ ANDERSEN PRESS

20 Vauxhall Bridge Rd., London SW1V 2SA, United Kingdom. **Website:** www.andersenpress.co.uk. Andersen Press is a specialist children's publisher. "We publish picture books, for which the required text would be approximately 500 words (maximum 1,000), juvenile fiction for which the text would be approximately 3,000-5,000 words and older fiction up to 75,000 words. We do not publish adult fiction, nonfiction, poetry, or short story anthologies."

HOW TO CONTACT Send all submissions by post: Query and full ms for picture books; synopsis and 3 chapters for longer fiction.

TERMS Guidelines online.

☻ ANNICK PRESS, LTD.

15 Patricia Ave., Toronto ON M2M 1H9, Canada. (416)221-4802. **Fax:** (416)221-8400. **Website:** www.annickpress.com. **Contact:** The Editors. "Annick Press maintains a commitment to high quality books that entertain and challenge. Our publications share fantasy and stimulate imagination, while encouraging children to trust their judgment and abilities." *Does not accept unsolicited mss.* Publishes picture books, juvenile and YA fiction and nonfiction; specializes in trade books. Publishes 25 titles/year. 20% of books from first-time authors. 80-85% from unagented writers.

FICTION Publisher of children's books. Not accepting picture books at this time.

HOW TO CONTACT 5,000 queries received/year. 3,000 mss received/year. Publishes a book 2 years after acceptance.

TERMS Pays authors royalty of 5-12% based on retail price. Offers advances (average amount: $3,000). Pays illustrators royalty of 5% minimum. Book catalog and guidelines online.

☻ BOREALIS PRESS, LTD.

8 Mohawk Crescent, Napean ON K2H 7G6, Canada. (613)829-0150. **Fax:** (613)829-7783. **E-mail:** drt@borealispress.com. **Website:** www.borealispress.com. "Our mission is to publish work that will be of lasting interest in the Canadian book market." Currently emphasizing Canadian fiction, nonfiction, drama, poetry. De-emphasizing children's books. Publishes hardcover and paperback originals and reprints. Publishes 20 titles/year. 80% of books from first-time authors. 95% from unagented writers.

FICTION Only material Canadian in content and dealing with significant aspects of the human situation.

NONFICTION Only material Canadian in content. Looks for style in tone and language, reader interest, and maturity of outlook.

HOW TO CONTACT Query with SASE. Submit clips, 1-2 sample chapters, ouline. *No unsolicited mss.* Responds in 2 months to queries; 4 months to mss. Publishes book 18 months after acceptance.

TERMS Pays 10% royalty on net receipts; plus 3 free author's copies. Book catalog online. Guidelines online.

☻ THE BRUCEDALE PRESS

P.O. Box 2259, Port Elgin ON N0H 2C0, Canada. (519)832-6025. **E-mail:** info@brucedalepress.ca. **Website:** brucedalepress.ca. The Brucedale Press publishes books and other materials of regional interest and merit, as well as literary, historical, and/or pictorial works. Publishes hardcover and trade paperback originals. Publishes 3 titles/year. 75% of books from first-time authors. 100% from unagented writers.

💬 *Accepts works by Canadian authors only. Book submissions reviewed November to January. Submissions to The Leaf Journal accepted in September and March only.*

HOW TO CONTACT 50 queries received/year. 30 mss received/year. Publishes book 1 year after acceptance.

TERMS Pays royalty. Book catalog online. Guidelines online.

TIPS "Our focus is very regional. In reading submissions, I look for quality writing with a strong connection to the Queen's Bush area of Ontario. All authors should visit our website, get a catalog, and read our books before submitting."

BUSTER BOOKS

9 Lion Yard, Tremadoc Rd., London WA SW4 7NQ, United Kingdom. (020)7720-8643. **Fax:** (022)7720-8953. **E-mail:** enquiries@mombooks.com. **Website:** www.busterbooks.co.uk. "We are dedicated to providing irresistible and fun books for children of all ages. We typically publish black & white nonfiction for children aged 8-12 novelty titles-including doodle books."

HOW TO CONTACT Submit synopsis and sample text. Prefers synopsis and sample text over complete ms.

TIPS "We do not accept fiction submissions. Please do not send original artwork as we cannot guarantee its safety." Visit website before submitting.

CHILD'S PLAY (INTERNATIONAL) LTD.

Child's Play, Ashworth Rd. Bridgemead, Swindon, Wiltshire SN5 7YD, United Kingdom. **E-mail:** neil@childs-play.com; office@childs-play.com. **Website:** www.childs-play.com. **Contact:** Sue Baker, Neil Burden, manuscript acquisitions. Specializes in nonfiction, fiction, educational material, multicultural material. Produces 30 picture books/year; 10 young readers/year. "A child's early years are more important than any other. This is when children learn most about the world around them and the language they need to survive and grow. Child's Play aims to create exactly the right material for this all-important time." Publishes 40 titles/year.

○ "Due to a backlog of submissions, Child's Play is currently no longer able to accept anymore mss."

FICTION Picture books: adventure, animal, concept, contemporary, folktales, multicultural, nature/environment. Young readers: adventure, animal, anthology, concept, contemporary, folktales, humor, multicultural, nature/environment, poetry. Average word length: picture books—1,500; young readers—2,000.

NONFICTION Picture books: activity books, animal, concept, multicultural, music/dance, nature/environment, science. Young readers: activity books, animal, concept, multicultural, music/dance, nature/environment, science. Average word length: picture books—2,000; young readers—3,000.

HOW TO CONTACT Publishes book 2 years after acceptance.

ILLUSTRATION Accepts material from international illustrators. Works with 10 illustrators/year. Uses color artwork only. Reviews ms/illustration packages. For ms/illustration packages: Query or submit ms/illustration packages to Sue Baker, editor. Reviews work for future assignments. If interested in illustrating future titles, query with samples, CD, website address. Submit samples to Annie Kubler, art director. Responds in 10 weeks. Samples not returned. Samples filed.

TIPS "Look at our website to see the kind of work we do before sending. Do not send cartoons. We do not publish novels. We do publish lots of books with pictures of babies/toddlers."

CHRISTIAN FOCUS PUBLICATIONS

Geanies House, Fearn, Tain Ross-shire Scotland IV20 1TW, United Kingdom. (44)1862-871-011. **Fax:** (44)1862-871-699. **E-mail:** submissions@christianfocus.com. **Website:** www.christianfocus.com. **Contact:** Director of Publishing. Specializes in Christian material, nonfiction, fiction, educational material. Publishes 22-32 titles/year. 2% of books from first-time authors.

FICTION Picture books, young readers, adventure, history, religion. Middle readers: adventure, problem novels, religion. Young adult/teens: adventure, history, problem novels, religion. Average word length: young readers—5,000; middle readers—max 10,000; young adult/teen—max 20,000.

NONFICTION All levels: activity books, biography, history, religion, science. Average word length: picture books—5,000; young readers—5,000; middle readers—5,000-10,000; young adult/teens—10,000-20,000.

HOW TO CONTACT Query or submit outline/synopsis and 3 sample chapters. Will consider electronic submissions and previously published work. Query or submit outline/synopsis and 3 sample chapters. Will consider electronic submissions and previously published work. Responds to queries in 2 weeks; mss in 3 months. Publishes book 1 year after acceptance.

ILLUSTRATION Works on 15-20 potential projects. "Some artists are chosen to do more than one. Some projects just require a cover illustration, some require full color spreads, others black and white line art." **Contact:** Catherine Mackenzie, children's editor. Responds in 2 weeks only if interested. Samples are not returned.

PHOTOGRAPHY "We only purchase royalty free photos from particular photographic associations. However portfolios can be presented to our designer." **Contact:** Daniel van Straaten. Photographers should send cover letter, résumé, published samples, client list, portfolio.

TIPS "Be aware of the international market as regards to writing style/topics as well as illustration styles. Our company sells rights to European as well as Asian countries. Fiction sales are not as good as they were. Christian fiction for youngsters is not a product that is performing well in comparison to nonfiction such as Christian biography/Bible stories/church history, etc."

☼ COTEAU BOOKS

Thunder Creek Publishing Co-operative Ltd., 2517 Victoria Ave., Regina SK S4P 0T2, Canada. (306)777-0170. **Fax:** (306)522-5152. **E-mail:** coteau@coteaubooks.com. **Website:** www.coteaubooks.com. **Contact:** Geoffrey Ursell, publisher. "Our mission is to publish the finest in Canadian fiction, nonfiction, poetry, drama, and children's literature, with an emphasis on Saskatchewan and prairie writers. De-emphasizing science fiction, picture books." Publishes trade paperback originals and reprints. Publishes 12 titles/year. 25% of books from first-time authors. 90% from unagented writers.

FICTION *Canadian authors only.* No science fiction. No children's picture books.

NONFICTION *Canadian authors only.*

HOW TO CONTACT Query. Submit hard copy query, bio, 3-4 sample chapters, SASE. 200 queries received/year. 40 mss received/year. Responds in 3 months. Publishes book 1 year after acceptance.

TERMS Pays 10% royalty on retail price. Book catalog available free. Guidelines online.

TIPS "Look at past publications to get an idea of our editorial program. We do not publish romance, horror, or picture books but are interested in juvenile and teen fiction from Canadian authors. Submissions, even queries, must be made in hard copy only. We do not accept simultaneous/multiple submissions. Check our website for new submission timing guidelines."

✚☻ CURIOUS FOX

Brunel Rd., Houndmills, Basingstoke Hants RG21 6XS, United Kingdom. **E-mail:** submissions@curious-fox.com. **Website:** www.curious-fox.com. "Do you love telling good stories? If so, we'd like to hear from you. Curious Fox is on the lookout for UK-based authors, whether new talent or established authors with exciting ideas. We take submissions for books aimed at ages 3-young adult. If you have story ideas that are bold, fun, and imaginative, then please do get in touch!"

HOW TO CONTACT "We prefer submissions by e-mail. Please submit a synopsis, with a chapter-by-chapter breakdown, and the full ms, double-spaced."

ILLUSTRATION Please submit any illustrations/artwork by e-mail.

TERMS Guidelines online.

☼ DUNDURN PRESS, LTD.

3 Church St., Suite 500, Toronto ON M5E 1M2, Canada. (416)214-5544. **E-mail:** info@dundurn.com. **Website:** www.dundurn.com. **Contact:** Acquisitions Editor. Dundurn publishes books by Canadian authors. Publishes hardcover, trade paperback, and e-book originals and reprints. 25% of books from first-time authors. 50% from unagented writers.

FICTION No romance, science fiction, or experimental.

HOW TO CONTACT "Until further notice, we will not be accepting any unsolicited fiction mss." Submit cover letter, synopsis, cv, TOC, writing sample, e-mail contact. Accepts submissions via postal mail only. Do not submit original materials. Submissions will not be returned. 600 queries received/year. Responds in 3 months to queries. Publishes ms 1-2 year after acceptance.

TERMS Guidelines online.

✚☻ FAT FOX BOOKS

The Fox's Den, Wickets, Frittenden Rd., Staplehurst, Kent TN12 0DH, United Kingdom. (44)(0)1580-857249. **E-mail:** hello@fatfoxbooks.com. **E-mail:** submissions@fatfoxbooks.com. **Website:** fatfoxbooks.com. "Can you write engaging, funny, original and brilliant stories? We are looking for fresh new talent as well as exciting new ideas from established writers and illustrators. We publish books for children from 3-14, and if we think the story is brilliant and fits our list, then as one of the few publishers who accepts unsolicited material, we will take it seriously. We will consider books of all genres."

HOW TO CONTACT For picture books, send complete ms; for longer works, send first 3 chapters and estimate of final word count.

ILLUSTRATION "We are looking for beautiful, original, distinctive illustration that stands out."

TERMS Guidelines online.

DAVID FICKLING BOOKS

31 Beamont St., Oxford OX1 2NP, United Kingdom. (018)65-339000. **Fax:** (018)65-339009. **E-mail:** submissions@davidficklingbooks.com. **Website:** www.davidficklingbooks.co.uk. **Contact:** Simon Mason, managing editor. David Fickling Books is a story house. Publishes 12-20 titles/year.

FICTION Considers all categories.

HOW TO CONTACT Submit cover letter and 3 sample chapters as PDF attachment saved in format "Author Name_Full Title." Responds to mss in 3 months, if interested.

ILLUSTRATION Reviews ms/illustration packages from artists. Illustrations only: query with samples.

PHOTOGRAPHY Submit cover letter, résumé, promo pieces.

TERMS Guidelines online.

TIPS "We adore stories for all ages, in both text and pictures. Quality is our watch word."

FITZHENRY & WHITESIDE LTD.

195 Allstate Pkwy., Markham ON L3R 4T8, Canada. (905)477-9700. **Fax:** (905)477-9179. **E-mail:** fitzkids@fitzhenry.ca; godwit@fitzhenry.ca; charkin@fitzhenry.ca. **Website:** www.fitzhenry.ca/. **Contact:** Sharon Fitzhenry (adult books); Cheryl Chen (children's books). Emphasis on Canadian authors and illustrators, subject or perspective. Publishes 15 titles/year. 10% of books from first-time authors.

HOW TO CONTACT Publishes book 1-2 years after acceptance.

ILLUSTRATION Works with approximately 10 illustrators/year. Reviews ms/illustration packages from artists. Submit outline and sample illustration (copy). Illustrations only: Query with samples and promo sheet. Samples not returned unless requested.

PHOTOGRAPHY Buys photos from freelancers. Buys stock and assigns work. Captions required. Uses b&w 8×10 prints; 35mm and 4×5 transparencies, 300+ dpi digital images. Submit stock photo list and promo piece.

TERMS Pays authors 8-10% royalty with escalations. Offers "respectable" advances for picture books, split 50/50 between author and illustrator. Pays illustrators by project and royalty. Pays photographers per photo.

TIPS "We respond to quality."

FLAME LILY BOOKS

13 Stapleton Rd., Meole Brace, Shrewsbury SY3 9LY, United Kingdom. **E-mail:** submissions@flamelilybooks.co.uk. **Website:** www.flamelilybooks.co.uk. "We are a small publisher and bring out only a few books every year. We want all our books to make very good reads, therefore we spend a lot of our own time, money, and effort into bringing a book to life, and we would like to enjoy what we do. For this reason, we only publish books that we really like."

FICTION "Of particular interest are books aimed at children and early teens especially science fiction and fantasy but not exclusively."

HOW TO CONTACT Submit ms in RTF or PDF format via e-mail.

FLYING EYE BOOKS

62 Great Eastern St., London EC2A 3QR, United Kingdom. (44)(0)207-033-4430. **E-mail:** picturbksubs@nobrow.net. **Website:** www.flyingeyebooks.com. Flying Eye Books is the children's imprint of award-winning visual publishing house Nobrow. FEB seeks to retain the same attention to detail and excellence in illustrated content as its parent publisher, but with a focus on the craft of children's storytelling and nonfiction.

TERMS Guidelines online.

FRANCES LINCOLN BOOKS

74-77 White Lion St., Islington, London N1 9PF, United Kingdom. (44)(20)7284-4009. **E-mail:** fl@franceslincoln.com. **Website:** www.franceslincoln.com. Publishes 100 titles/year. 6% of books from first-time authors.

HOW TO CONTACT Query by e-mail. Responds in 6 weeks to mss. Publishes book 18 months after acceptance.

FRANCES LINCOLN CHILDREN'S BOOKS

Frances Lincoln, 74-77 White Lion St., Islington, London N1 9PF, United Kingdom. (44)(20)7284-4009. **E-mail:** fl@franceslincoln.com. **Website:** www.franceslincoln.com. "Our company was founded by Frances Lincoln in 1977. We published our first books two years later, and we have been creating illustrated books of the highest quality ever since, with special emphasis on gardening, walking and the outdoors, art, architecture, design, and landscape. In 1983, we started to publish illustrated books for children. Since then we have won many awards and prizes with both fiction and nonfiction children's books." Publishes 100 titles/year. 6% of books from first-time authors.

FICTION Average word length: picture books--1,000; young readers—9,788; middle readers—20,653; young adults—35,407.

NONFICTION Average word length: picture books—1,000; middle readers—29,768.

HOW TO CONTACT Query by e-mail. Query by e-mail. Responds in 6 weeks to mss. Publishes book 18 months after acceptance.

ILLUSTRATION Works with approx 56 illustrators/year. Uses both color and b&w. Reviews ms/illustration packages from artist. Sample illustrations. Illustrations only: Query with samples. Responds only if interested. Samples are returned with SASE. Samples are kept on file only if interested.

PHOTOGRAPHY Buys stock images and assign work. Uses children, multicultural photos. Submit cover letter, published samples, or portfolio.

ⒶⓈ FRANKLIN WATTS

338 Euston Rd., London NW1 3BH, United Kingdom. (44)(20)7873-6000. **Fax:** (44)(20)7873-6024. **E-mail:** ad@hachettechildrens.co.uk. **Website:** www.franklinwatts.co.uk. Franklin Watts is well known for its high quality and attractive information books, which support the National Curriculum and stimulate children's enquiring minds. *Generally does not accept unsolicited mss.*

◯ GROUNDWOOD BOOKS

110 Spadina Ave., Suite 801, Toronto Ontario M5V 2K4, Canada. (416)363-4343. **Fax:** (416)363-1017. **E-mail:** ssutherland@groundwoodbooks.com. **Website:** www.groundwoodbooks.com. Publishes 19 picture books/year; 2 young readers/year; 3 middle readers/year; 3 young adult titles/year, approximately 2 nonfiction titles/year.

FICTION Recently published: *Lost Girl Found*, by Leah Bassoff and Laura Deluca; *A Simple Case of Angels*, by Carolnie Adderson; *This One Summer*, by Mariko Tamaki and Jillian Tamaki.

NONFICTION Recently published: *The Amazing Travels of IBN Batutta*, by Fatima Sharafeddine, Illustrated by Intelaq Mohammed Ali. Picture books recently published: *Mr. Frank*, by Irene Luxbacher; *The Tweedles Go Electric*, by Monica Kulling, illustrated by Marie LaFrance; *Morris Micklewhite and the Tangerine Dress*, by Christine Baldacchino, illustrated

by Isabelle Malenfant; *Why Are You Doing That?*, by Elisa Amado, illustrated by Manuel Monroy; *Don't*, by Litsa Trochatos, illustrated by Virginia Johnson.

HOW TO CONTACT Submit synopsis and sample chapters via e-mail. Responds to mss in 6-8 months.

TERMS Offers advances. Visit website for guidelines: www.houseofanansi.com/Groundwoodsubmissions.aspx.

◯ KIDS CAN PRESS

25 Dockside Dr., Toronto ON M5A 0B5, Canada. (416)479-7000. **Fax:** (416)960-5437. **Website:** www.kidscanpress.com. **Contact:** Corus Quay, acquisitions.

◯ *Kids Can Press is currently accepting unsolicited mss from Canadian adult authors only.*

FICTION Picture books, young readers: concepts. "We do not accept young adult fiction or fantasy novels for any age." Adventure, animal, contemporary, folktales, history, humor, multicultural, nature/environment, special needs, sports, suspense/mystery. Average word length: picture books 1,000-2,000; young readers 750-1,500; middle readers 10,000-15,000; young adults over 15,000.

NONFICTION Picture books: activity books, animal, arts/crafts, biography, careers, concept, health, history, hobbies, how-to, multicultural, nature/environment, science, social issues, special needs, sports. Young readers: activity books, animal, arts/crafts, biography, careers, concept, history, hobbies, how-to, multicultural. Middle readers: cooking, music/dance. Average word length: picture books 500-1,250; young readers 750-2,000; middle readers 5,000-15,000.

HOW TO CONTACT Submit outline/synopsis and 2-3 sample chapters. For picture books submit complete ms. Submit outline/synopsis and 2-3 sample chapters. For picture books submit complete ms. Responds in 6 months only if interesed. Publishes book 18-24 months after acceptance.

ILLUSTRATION Works with 40 illustrators/year. Reviews ms/illustration packages from artists. Send color copies of illustration portfolio, cover letter outlining other experience. Contact: Art Director. Illustrations only: Send tearsheets, color photocopies. Responds only if interested.

⊕Ⓢ LANTANA PUBLISHING

United Kingdom. **E-mail:** info@lantanapublishing.com. **E-mail:** submissions@lantanapublishing.com. **Website:** www.lantanapublishing.com. "We mainly publish picture books for 4 to 8 year olds but will consider longer narratives written for older children (9-13) and young adults (14-18) if the stories really resonate with the themes and ideas we love."

FICTION "We love quirky retellings of folktales or fairy tales that blend modern values with traditional storytelling. We particularly love stories that pack a punch with strong role models, positive relationships between communities and the environment, and evocative storylines that can provide a glimpse into the belief systems of other cultures." No nonfiction.

HOW TO CONTACT Picture book authors should submit complete ms. Query with 3 sample chapters for longer works.

TERMS Guidelines online.

○ LES ÉDITIONS DU VERMILLON

305 Saint Patrick St., Ottawa ON K1N 5K4, Canada. (613)241-4032. **Fax:** (613)241-3109. **E-mail:** lesedition sduvermillon@rogers.com. **Website:** www.lesedition sduvermillon.ca. **Contact:** Jacques Flamand, editorial director. Publishes trade paperback originals. Publishes 15-20 titles/year.

HOW TO CONTACT Responds in 6 months to mss. Publishes ms 18 months after acceptance.

TERMS Pays 10% royalty. Book catalog available free.

○ LITTLE TIGER PRESS

1 The Coda Centre, 189 Munster Rd., London SW6 6AW, United Kingdom. (44)(20)7385-6333. **Website:** www.littletigerpress.com. Little Tiger Press is a dynamic and busy independent publisher.

FICTION Picture books: animal, concept, contemporary, humor. Average word length: picture books–750 words or less.

ILLUSTRATION Digital submissions preferred please send in digital samples as pdf or jpeg attachments to artsubmissions@littletiger.co.uk. Files should be flattened and no bigger than 1mb per attachment. Include name and contact details on any attachments. Printed submissions please send in printed color samples as A4 printouts. Do not send in original artwork as we cannot be held responsible for unsolicited original artwork being lost or damaged in the post. We aim to acknowledge unsolicited material and to return material if so requested within 3 months. Please include SAE if return of material is requested.

TIPS "Every reasonable care is taken of the mss and samples we receive, but we cannot accept responsibility for any loss or damage. Try to read or look at as many books on the Little Tiger Press list before send-

ing in your material. Refer to our website for further details."

○ MANOR HOUSE PUBLISHING, INC.

452 Cottingham Crescent, Ancaster ON L9G 3V6, Canada. **E-mail:** mbdavie@manor-house.biz. **Website:** www.manor-house.biz. **Contact:** Mike Davie, president (novels, poetry, and nonfiction). Publishes hardcover, trade paperback, and mass market paperback originals reprints. Publishes 5-6 titles/year. 90% of books from first-time authors. 90% from unagented writers.

FICTION Stories should have Canadian settings and characters should be Canadian, but content should have universal appeal to wide audience.

NONFICTION "We are a Canadian publisher, so mss should be Canadian in content and aimed as much as possible at a wide, general audience. At this point in time, we are only publishing books by Canadian citizens residing in Canada."

HOW TO CONTACT Query via e-mail. Submit proposal package, clips, bio, 3 sample chapters. Submit complete ms. Query via e-mail. Submit proposal package, outline, bio, 3 sample chapters. Submit complete ms. 30 queries received/year; 20 mss received/year. Queries and mss to be sent by e-mail only. "We will respond in 30 days if interested-if not, there is no response. Do not follow up unless asked to do so." Publishes book 1 year after acceptance.

TERMS Pays 10% royalty on retail price. Book catalog online. Guidelines available via e-mail.

TIPS "Our audience includes everyone-the general public/mass audience. Self-edit your work first, make sure it is well written with strong Canadian content."

○○ MOGZILLA

8 Maud Jane's Close, Ivinghoe, Bucks LU7 9ED, United Kingdom. (44)(0)845-838-5526. **E-mail:** info@ mogzilla.co.uk. **Website:** mogzilla.co.uk. Mogzilla is an independent company on a mission. "We want to get children into history through storytelling and fire their imagination with brilliant books and graphic novels."

FICTION "Mogzilla started off specializing in fiction for pre-teens and younger teenagers, although we are also getting into color books for younger readers and graphic novels too. As a rough guide, a novel for this age range would be between 45,000 and 75,000 words."

HOW TO CONTACT Query by mail or e-mail.

TERMS Guidelines online.

TIPS "If we do not respond to your e-mail, please assume that we are not interested. We receive a great deal of proposals every week, and we regret that we cannot get into correspondence about why we did not want to progress your proposal."

❁❀ NOSY CROW PUBLISHING

The Crow's Nest, 10a Lant St., London SE1 1QR, United Kingdom. (44)(0)207-089-7575. **Fax:** (44)(0)207-089-7576. **E-mail:** hello@nosycrow.com. **E-mail:** adrian@nosycrow.com. **Website:** nosycrow.com. "We publish books for children 0-14. We're looking for 'parent-friendly' books, and we don't publish books with explicit sex, drug use, or serious violence, so no edgy YA or edgy cross-over. And whatever New Adult is, we don't do it. We also publish apps for children from 2-7, and may publish apps for older children if the idea feels right."

FICTION "As a rule, we don't like books with 'issues' that are in any way overly didactic."

HOW TO CONTACT Prefers submissions by e-mail, but post works if absolutely necessary.

TERMS Guidelines online.

TIPS "Please don't be too disappointed if we reject your work! We're a small company and can only publish a few new books and apps each year, so do try other publishers and agents: publishing is necessarily a hugely subjective business. We wish you luck!"

❀ ORCA BOOK PUBLISHERS

P.O. Box 5626, Stn. B, Victoria BC V8R 6S4, Canada. **Fax:** (877)408-1551. **E-mail:** orca@orcabook.com. **Website:** www.orcabook.com. **Contact:** Amy Collins, editor (picture books); Sarah Harvey, editor (young readers); Andrew Wooldridge, editor (juvenile and teen fiction); Bob Tyrrell, publisher (YA, teen); Ruth Linka, associate editor (rapid reads). Publishes hardcover and trade paperback originals, and mass market paperback originals and reprints. Publishes 30-50 titles/year. 20% of books from first-time authors. 75% from unagented writers.

❁ Only publishes Canadian authors.

FICTION Picture books: animals, contemporary, history, nature/environment. Middle readers: contemporary, history, fantasy, nature/environment, problem novels, graphic novels. Young adults: adventure, contemporary, hi-lo (Orca Soundings), history, multicultural, nature/environment, problem novels, suspense/mystery, graphic novels. Average word length: picture books—500-1,500; middle readers—20,000-35,000;

young adult—25,000-45,000; Orca Soundings—13,000-15,000; Orca Currents—13,000-15,000. No romance, science fiction.

NONFICTION Only publishes Canadian authors.

HOW TO CONTACT Query with SASE. Submit proposal package, outline, clips, 2-5 sample chapters, SASE. Query with SASE. 2,500 queries received/year. 1,000 mss received/year. Responds in 1 month to queries; 2 months to proposals and mss. Publishes book 12-18 months after acceptance.

ILLUSTRATION Works with 8-10 illustrators/year. Reviews ms/illustration packages from artists. Submit ms with 3-4 pieces of final art. "Reproductions only, no original art please." Illustrations only: Query with samples; provide résumé, online portfolio. Responds in 2 months. Samples returned with SASE; samples filed.

TERMS Pays 10% royalty. Book catalog for 8½×11 SASE. Guidelines online.

TIPS "Our audience is students in grades K-12. Know our books, and know the market."

❁❀ PAJAMA PRESS

181 Carlaw Ave., Suite 207, Toronto ON M4M 2S1, Canada. **E-mail:** info@pajamapress.ca. **Website:** pajamapress.ca. "We publish picture books—both for the very young and for school-aged readers—as well as novels for middle grade readers and for young adults aged 12+. Our nonfiction titles typically contain a strong narrative element."

HOW TO CONTACT Query with an excerpt.

❁❀ RANDOM HOUSE CHILDREN'S PUBLISHERS UK

61-63 Uxbridge Rd., London En W5 5SA, United Kingdom. (44)(208)579-2652. **Fax:** (44)(208)231-6737. **E-mail:** enquiries@randomhouse.co.uk. **Website:** www.kidsatrandomhouse.co.uk. **Contact:** Francesca Dow, managing director. Publishes 250 titles/year.

❀ *Only interested in agented material.*

FICTION Picture books: adventure, animal, anthology, contemporary, fantasy, folktales, humor, multicultural, nature/environment, poetry, suspense/mystery. Young readers: adventure, animal, anthology, contemporary, fantasy, folktales, humor, multicultural, nature/environment, poetry, sports, suspense/mystery. Middle readers: adventure, animal, anthology, contemporary, fantasy, folktales, humor, multicultural, nature/environment, problem novels, romance, sports, suspense/mystery. Young adults: adventure, contemporary, fantasy, humor, multicultural, nature/environment, problem novels, romance, science fiction, suspense/mystery. Average word length: picture books—800; young readers—1,500-6,000; middle readers—10,000-15,000; young adults—20,000-45,000.

ILLUSTRATION Works with 50 illustrators/year. Reviews ms/illustration packages from artists. Query with samples. Contact: Margaret Hope. Samples are returned with SASE (IRC).

PHOTOGRAPHY Buys photos from freelancers. Contact: Margaret Hope. Photo captions required. Uses color or b&w prints. Submit cover letter, published samples.

TERMS Pays authors royalty. Offers advances.

TIPS "Although Random House is a big publisher, each imprint only publishes a small number of books each year. Our lists for the next few years are already full. Any book we take on from a previously unpublished author has to be truly exceptional. Manuscripts should be sent to us via literary agents."

REBELIGHT PUBLISHING, INC.

23-845 Dakota St., Suite 314, Winnipeg Manitoba R2M 5M3, Canada. **E-mail:** submit@rebelight.com. **Website:** www.rebelight.com. **Contact:** Editor. Rebelight Publishing is interested in mss for middle grade, young adult and new adult novels. Publishes trade paperback and electronic originals. Publishes 10-15 titles/year. 25% of books from first-time authors. 100% from unagented writers.

Only considers submissions from Canadian writers.

FICTION All genres are considered, providered they are for a middle grade, young adult, or new adult audience. "Become familiar with our books. Study our website. Stick within the guidelines. Our tag line is 'crack the spine, blow your mind'—we are looking for well-written, powerful, fresh, fast-paced fiction. Keep us turning the pages. Give us something we just have to spread the word about."

HOW TO CONTACT Submit proposal package, including a synopsis and 3 sample chapters. Read guidelines carefully. Receives 520 queries/year, 35 mss/year. Responds in 3 months to queries and mss. Publishes ms 12 months after acceptance.

TERMS Pays 12-30% royalties on retail price. Does not offer an advance. Catalog available online. Guidelines available online.

RONSDALE PRESS

3350 W. 21st Ave., Vancouver BC V6S 1G7, Canada. (604)738-4688. **Fax:** (604)731-4548. **E-mail:** ronsdale@shaw.ca. **Website:** ronsdalepress.com. **Contact:** Ronald B. Hatch (fiction, poetry, nonfiction, social commentary); Veronica Hatch (YA novels and short stories). "Ronsdale Press is a Canadian literary publishing house that publishes 12 books each year, four of which are young adult titles. Of particular interest are books involving children exploring and discovering new aspects of Canadian history." Publishes trade paperback originals. Publishes 12 titles/year. 40% of books from first-time authors. 95% from unagented writers.

FICTION Young adults: Canadian novels. Average word length: middle readers and young adults—50,000.

NONFICTION Middle readers, young adults: animal, biography, history, multicultural, social issues. Average word length: young readers—90; middle readers—90. "We publish a number of books for children and young adults in the age 10 to 15 range. We are especially interested in YA historical novels. We regret that we can no longer publish picture books."

HOW TO CONTACT Submit complete ms. Submit complete ms. 40 queries received/year. 800 mss received/year. Responds to queries in 2 weeks; mss in 2 months. Publishes book 1 year after acceptance.

ILLUSTRATION Works with 2 illustrators/year. Reviews ms/illustration packages from artists. Requires only cover art. Responds in 2 weeks. Samples returned with SASE. Originals returned to artist at job's completion.

TERMS Pays 10% royalty on retail price. Book catalog for #10 SASE. Guidelines online.

TIPS "Ronsdale Press is a literary publishing house, based in Vancouver, and dedicated to publishing books from across Canada, books that give Canadians new insights into themselves and their country. We aim to publish the best Canadian writers."

SCHOLASTIC CHILDREN'S BOOKS UK

Website: www.scholastic.co.uk.

Scholastic UK does not accept unsolicited submissions. Unsolicited illustrations are accepted, but please do not send any original artwork as it will not be returned.

TIPS "Getting work published can be a frustrating process, and it's often best to be prepared for disappointment, but don't give up."

⟲ SECOND STORY PRESS

20 Maud St., Suite 401, Toronto ON M5V 2M5, Canada. (416)537-7850. **Fax:** (416)537-0588. **E-mail:** info@secondstorypress.ca. **Website:** www.secondstorypress.ca.

FICTION Considers non-sexist, non-racist, and nonviolent stories, as well as historical fiction, chapter books, picture books.

NONFICTION Picture books: biography.

HOW TO CONTACT Accepts appropriate material from residents of Canada only. Submit complete ms or submit outline and sample chapters by postal mail only. No electronic submissions or queries.

⊕ ⟲ SIMPLY READ BOOKS

501-5525 W. Blvd., Vancouver BC V6M 3W6, Canada. **Website:** www.simplyreadbooks.com. Simply Read Books is current seeking mss in picture books, early readers, early chapter books, middle grade fiction, and graphic novels.

HOW TO CONTACT Query or submit complete ms.

⊕ ⟳ SWEET CHERRY PUBLISHING

Unit E, Vulcan Business Complex, Vulcan Rd., Leicester LE5 3EB, United Kingdom. **E-mail:** info@sweetcherrypublishing.com. **E-mail:** submissions@sweetcherrypublishing.com. **Website:** www.sweetcherrypublishing.com. Sweet Cherry is looking for talented new authors of children's series and collections. "If you have written an original series with strong themes and characters, we would love to hear from you."

HOW TO CONTACT Submit cover letter and synopsis with 3 sample chapters via post or e-mail.

ILLUSTRATION Submissions may include illustrations, but Sweet Cherry employs in-house illustrators and would therefore by unlikely to utilize them in the event of publication.

TERMS Offers a one-time fee for work that is accepted. Guidelines online.

TIPS "If your work is accepted, Sweet Cherry may consider commissioning you for future series."

⟳ TAFELBERG PUBLISHERS

Imprint of NB Publishers, P.O. Box 879, Cape Town 8000, South Africa. (27)(21)406-3033. **Fax:** (27) (21)406-3812. **E-mail:** kristin@nb.co.za. **Website:** www.tafelberg.com. **Contact:** Kristin Paremoer. General publisher best known for Afrikaans fiction, authoritative political works, children's/youth literature, and a variety of illustrated and nonillustrated nonfiction. Publishes 10 titles/year.

FICTION Picture books, young readers: animal, anthology, contemporary, fantasy, folktales, hi-lo, humor, multicultural, nature/environment, scient fiction, special needs. Middle readers, young adults: animal (middle reader only), contemporary, fantasy, hi-lo, humor, multicultural, nature/environment, problem novels, science fiction, special needs, sports, suspense/mystery. Average word length: picture books—1,500-7,500; young readers—25,000; middle readers—15,000; young adults—40,000.

HOW TO CONTACT Submit complete ms. Submit outline, information on intended market, bio, and 1-2 sample chapters. Responds to queries in 2 weeks; mss in 6 months. Publishes book 1 year after acceptance.

ILLUSTRATION Works with 2-3 illustrators/year. Reviews ms/illustration packages from artists. Send ms with dummy or e-mail and jpegs. Contact: Louise Steyn, publisher. Illustrations only: Query with brochure, photocopies, résumé, URL, JPEGs. Responds only if interested. Samples not returned.

TERMS Pays authors royalty of 15-18% based on wholesale price.

TIPS "Writers: Story needs to have a South African or African style. Illustrators: I'd like to look, but the chances of getting commissioned are slim. The market is small and difficult. Do not expect huge advances. Editorial staff attended or plans to attend the following conferences: IBBY, Frankfurt, SCBWI Bologna."

⟲ THISTLEDOWN PRESS LTD.

410 2nd Ave., Saskatoon SK S7K 2C3, Canada. (306)244-1722. **Fax:** (306)244-1762. **E-mail:** editorial@thistledownpress.com. **Website:** www.thistledownpress.com. **Contact:** Allan Forrie, publisher. "Thistledown originates books by Canadian authors only, although we have co-published titles by authors outside Canada. We do not publish children's picture books."

FICTION Middle readers, young adults: adventure, anthology, contemporary, fantasy, humor, poetry, romance, science fiction, suspense/mystery, short stories. Average word length: young adults—40,000.

HOW TO CONTACT Submit outline/synopsis and sample chapters. *Does not accept mss.* Do not query by e-mail. Responds to queries in 4 months. Publishes book 1 year after acceptance.

ILLUSTRATION Prefers agented illustrators but "not mandatory." Works with few illustrators. Illustrations only: Query with samples, promo sheet, slides, tearsheets. Responds only if interested. Samples returned with SASE; samples filed.

TERMS Pays authors royalty of 10-12% based on net dollar sales. Pays illustrators and photographers by the project (range: $250-750). Book catalog free on request.

TIPS "Send cover letter including publishing history and SASE."

TIGHTROPE BOOKS

#207-2 College St., Toronto ON M5G 1K3, Canada. (416)928-6666. **E-mail:** tightropeasst@gmail.com. **Website:** www.tightropebooks.com. **Contact:** Jim Nason, publisher. Publishes hardcover and trade paperback originals. Publishes 12 titles/year. 70% of books from first-time authors. 100% from unagented writers.

Accepting submissions for new mystery imprint, Mysterio.

HOW TO CONTACT Responds if interested. Publishes book 1 year after acceptance.

TERMS Pays 5-15% royalty on retail price. Pays advance of $200-300. Catalog and guidelines online.

TIPS "Audience is young, urban, literary, educated, unconventional."

TRADEWIND BOOKS

202-1807 Maritime Mews, Granville Island, Vancouver BC V6H 3W7, Canada. (604)662-4405. **Website:** www.tradewindbooks.com. **Contact:** R. David Stephens, senior editor. "Tradewind Books publishes juvenile picture books and young adult novels. Requires that submissions include evidence that author has read at least 3 titles published by Tradewind Books." Publishes hardcover and trade paperback originals. Publishes 5 titles/year. 15% of books from first-time authors. 50% from unagented writers.

FICTION Average word length: 900 words.

HOW TO CONTACT Send complete ms for picture books. *YA novels by Canadian authors only. Chapter books by US authors considered.* Responds to mss in 2 months. Publishes book 3 years after acceptance.

ILLUSTRATION Works with 3-4 illustrators/year. Reviews ms/illustration packages from artists. Send

illustrated ms as dummy. Illustrations only: Query with samples. Responds only if interested. Samples returned with SASE; samples filed.

TERMS Pays 7% royalty on retail price. Pays variable advance. Book catalog and ms guidelines online.

USBORNE PUBLISHING

83-85 Saffron Hill, London En EC1N 8RT, United Kingdom. (44)207430-2800. **Fax:** (44)207430-1562. **E-mail:** mail@usborne.co.uk. **Website:** www.usborne.com. "Usborne Publishing is a multiple-award winning, world-wide children's publishing company publishing almost every type of children's book for every age from baby to young adult."

FICTION Young readers, middle readers: adventure, contemporary, fantasy, history, humor, multicultural, nature/environment, science fiction, suspense/mystery, strong concept-based or character-led series. Average word length: young readers—5,000-10,000; middle readers—25,000-50,000; young adult—50,000-100,000.

HOW TO CONTACT *Agented submissions only.*

ILLUSTRATION Works with 100 illustrators per year. Illustrations only: Query with samples. Samples not returned; samples filed.

PHOTOGRAPHY Contact: Usborne Art Department. Submit samples.

TERMS Pays authors royalty.

TIPS "Do not send any original work and, sorry, but we cannot guarantee a reply."

WHITECAP BOOKS, LTD.

210 - 314 W. Cordova St., Vancouver BC V6B 1 E8, Canada. (604)681-6181. **Fax:** (905)477-9179. **E-mail:** steph@whitecap.ca. **Website:** www.whitecap.ca. "Whitecap Books is a general trade publisher with a focus on food and wine titles. Although we are interested in reviewing unsolicited ms submissions, please note that we only accept submissions that meet the needs of our current publishing program. Please see some of most recent releases to get an idea of the kinds of titles we are interested in." Publishes hardcover and trade paperback originals. Publishes 30 titles/year. 20% of books from first-time authors. 90% from unagented writers.

FICTION No children's picture books or adult fiction.

NONFICTION Young children's and middle reader's nonfiction focusing mainly on nature, wildlife and animals. "Writers should take the time to research our list and read the submission guidelines on our website. This is especially important for children's writers and cookbook authors. We will only consider submissions that fall into these categories: cookbooks, wine and spirits, regional travel, home and garden, Canadian history, North American natural history, juvenile series-based fiction. At this time, we are not accepting the following categories: self-help or inspirational books, political, social commentary, or issue books, general how-to books, biographies or memoirs, business and finance, art and architecture, religion, and spirituality."

HOW TO CONTACT Submit cover letter, synopsis, SASE via ground mail. See guidelines online. 500 queries received/year; 1,000 mss received/year. Responds in 2-3 months to proposals. Publishes book 1 year after acceptance.

ILLUSTRATION Works with 1-2 illustrators/year. Uses color artwork only. Reviews ms/illustration packages from artists. Query. Contact: Rights and Acquisitions. Illustrations only: Send postcard sample with tearsheets. Contact: Michelle Furbacher, art director. Responds only if interested.

PHOTOGRAPHY Only accepts digital photography. Submit stock photo list. Buys stock and assigns work. Model/property releases required.

TERMS Pays royalty. Pays negotiated advance. Catalog and guidelines online.

TIPS "We want well-written, well-researched material that presents a fresh approach to a particular topic."

MAGAZINES

///

Children's magazines are a great place for unpublished writers and illustrators to break into the market. Writers, illustrators and photographers alike may find it easier to get book assignments if they have tearsheets from magazines. Having magazine work under your belt shows you're professional and have experience working with editors and art directors and meeting deadlines.

But magazines aren't merely a breaking-in point. Writing, illustration and photo assignments for magazines let you see your work in print quickly, and the magazine market can offer steady work and regular paychecks (a number of them pay on acceptance). Book authors and illustrators may have to wait a year or two before receiving royalties from a project. The magazine market is also a good place to use research material that didn't make it into a book project you're working on. You may even work on a magazine idea that blossoms into a book project.

TARGETING YOUR SUBMISSIONS

It's important to know the topics typically covered by different children's magazines. To help you match your work with the right publications, we've included several indexes in the back of this book. The **Subject Index** lists both book and magazine publishers by the fiction and nonfiction subjects they're seeking.

If you're a writer, use the Subject Index in conjunction with the **Age-Level Index** to narrow your list of markets. Targeting the correct age group with your submission is an important consideration. Many rejection slips are sent because a writer has not targeted a manuscript to the correct age. Few magazines are aimed at children of all ages, so you must be certain your manuscript is written for the audience level of the particular magazine you're submitting to. Magazines for children (just as magazines for adults) may also target a specific gender.

If you're a poet, refer to the **Poetry Index** to find which magazines publish poems.

Each magazine has a different editorial philosophy. Language usage also varies between periodicals, as does the length of feature articles and the use of artwork and photographs. Reading magazines *before* submitting is the best way to determine if your material is appropriate. Also, because magazines targeted to specific age groups have a natural turnover in readership every few years, old topics (with a new slant) can be recycled.

If you're a photographer, the **Photography Index** lists children's magazines that use photos from freelancers. Using it in combination with the subject index can narrow your search. For instance, if you photograph sports, compare the Magazine list in the Photography Index with the list under Sports in the Subject Index. Highlight the markets that appear on both lists, then read those listings to decide which magazines might be best for your work.

Because many kids' magazines sell subscriptions through direct mail or schools, you may not be able to find a particular publication at bookstores or newsstands. Check your local library, or send for copies of the magazines you're interested in. Most magazines in this section have sample copies available and will send them for a SASE or small fee.

Also, many magazines have submission guidelines and theme lists available for a SASE. Check magazines' websites, too. Many offer excerpts of articles, submission guidelines, and theme lists and will give you a feel for the editorial focus of the publication.

Watch for the Canadian ✪ and International ✪ symbols. These publications' needs and requirements may differ from their United States. counterparts.

ADVOCATE, PKA'S PUBLICATION

1881 Little Westkill Rd., Prattsville NY 12468. (518)299-3103. **Website:** advocatepka.weebly.com; www.facebook.com/Advocate/PKAPublications; www.facebook.com/GaitedHorseAssociation. advoad@localnet.com. **Contact:** Patricia Keller, publisher. *Advocate, PKA's Publication*, published bimonthly, is an advertiser-supported tabloid using "original, previously unpublished works, such as feature stories, essays, 'think' pieces, letters to the editor, profiles, humor, fiction, poetry, puzzles, cartoons, or line drawings. Advocates for good writers and quality writings. We publish art, fiction, photos and poetry. *Advocate*'s submitters are talented people of all ages who do not earn their livings as writers. We wish to promote the arts and to give those we publish the opportunity to be published." Estab. 1987. Circ. 7,000.

○ "This publication has a strong horse orientation." Includes Gaited Horse Association newsletter. Horse-oriented stories, poetry, art, and photos are currently needed.

FICTION Looks for "well-written, entertaining work, whether fiction or nonfiction." Wants to see more humorous material, nature/environment, and romantic comedy. middle readers, young adults/teens, adults: adventure, animal, contemporary, fantasy, folktales, health, humorous, nature/environment, problem-solving, romance, science fiction, sports, suspense/mystery. "Nothing religious, pornographic, violent, erotic, pro-drug, or anti-enviroment." Send complete ms. Length: up to 1,500 words. Pays contributor copies.

NONFICTION Middle readers, young adults/teens: animal, arts/crafts, biography, careers, concept, cooking, fashion, games/puzzles, geography, history, hobbies, how-to, humorous, interview/profile, nature/environment, problem-solving, science, social issues, sports, travel. Send complete ms. Length: up to 1,500 words. Pays contributors copies.

POETRY "Poetry ought to speak to people and not be so oblique as to have meaning only to the poet. If I had to be there to understand the poem, don't send it. Also looking for horse-related poems, stories, drawings, and photos." Considers poetry by children and teens (when included with release form signed by adult). Accepts about 25% of poems received. Wants "nearly any kind of poetry, any length." Occasionally comments on rejected poems. Submit any number of poems at a time. No religious or pornographic poetry. Pays contributors copies.

HOW TO CONTACT Responds to queries in 6 weeks; mss in 2 months. Publishes ms 2-18 months after acceptance.

ILLUSTRATION Uses b&w artwork only. Uses cartoons. Reviews ms/illustration packages from artists. Submit a photo print (b&w or color), an excellent copy of work (no larger than 8×10) or original. Prints in b&w but accepts color work that converts well to gray scale. Illustrations only: "Send previous unpublished art with SASE, please." Responds in 2 months. Samples returned with SASE; samples not filed. Credit line given.

PHOTOS Buys photos from freelancers. Model/property releases required. Uses color and b&w prints (no slides). Send unsolicited photos by mail with SASE. Wants nature, artistic, and humorous photos.

TERMS Acquires first rights for mss, artwork, and photographs. Pays on publication with contributors copies. Sample copy: $5 (includes guidelines). Subscription: $18.50 (6 issues). Previous 6 issues are on our website.

TIPS "Please, no simultaneous submissions, work that has appeared on the Internet, pornography, overt religiousity, anti-environmentalism, or gratuitous violence. Artists and photographers should keep in mind that we are a b&w paper. Please do not send postcards. Use envelope with SASE."

AMERICAN CAREERS

Career Communications, Inc., 6701 W. 64th St., Suite 210, Overland Park KS 66202. (800)669-7795. **E-mail:** ccinfo@carcom.com. **Website:** www.carcom.com; www.americancareersonline.com. **Contact:** Mary Pitchford, editor-in-chief; Jerry Kanabel, art director. *American Careers* provides career, salary, and education information to middle school and high school students. Self-tests help them relate their interests and abilities to future careers. Estab. 1989. Circ. 500,000.

NONFICTION Query by mail only with published clips. Length: 300-1,000 words. Pays $100-450.

HOW TO CONTACT Accepts queries by mail.

PHOTOS State availability. Captions, identification of subjects, model releases required. Negotiates payment individually.

TERMS Buys all rights. Makes work-for-hire assignments. Byline given. Pays 1 month after acceptance.

No kill fee. 10% freelance written. Sample copy for $4. Guidelines for #10 SASE.

TIPS "Letters of introduction or query letters with samples and résumés are ways we get to know writers. Samples should include how-to articles and career-related articles. Articles written for teenagers also would make good samples. Short feature articles on careers, career-related how-to articles, and self-assessment tools (10-20 point quizzes with scoring information) are primarily what we publish."

AMERICAN CHEERLEADER

Macfadden Performing Arts Media LLC, 110 William St., 23rd Floor, New York NY 10038. (646)459-4800. **Fax:** (646)459-4900. **E-mail:** editors@americancheerleader.com. **Website:** www.americancheerleader.com. **Contact:** Marisa Walker, editor-in-chief. Bimonthly magazine covering high school, college, and competitive cheerleading. "We try to keep a young, informative voice for all articles—'for cheerleaders, by cheerleaders.'" Estab. 1995. Circ. 200,000.

NONFICTION Needs young adults: biography, interview/profile (sports personalities), careers, fashion, beauty, health, how-to (cheering techniques, routines, pep songs, etc.), problem-solving, sports, cheerleading-specific material. Query by e-mail; provide résumé, business card, and tearsheets to be kept on file. "We're looking for authors who know cheerleading." Length: 750-2,000 words. Pays $100-250 for assigned articles; $100 maximum for unsolicited articles.

HOW TO CONTACT Editorial lead time 3 months. Responds in 4 weeks to queries. Responds in 2 months to mss. Publishes ms an average of 4 months after acceptance. Accepts queries by mail, e-mail, online submission form.

ILLUSTRATION Reviews ms/illustration packages from artists. Illustrations only: Query with samples; arrange portfolio review. Responds only if interested. Samples filed. Originals not returned at job's completion. Credit line given.

PHOTOS State availability. Model releases required. Reviews transparencies, 5x7 prints. Offers $50/photo.

TERMS Buys all rights. Byline given. Pays on publication. Offers 25% kill fee. 30% freelance written. Sample copy for $2.95. Guidelines free.

TIPS "We invite proposals from freelance writers who are involved in or have been involved in cheerleading—i.e., coaches, sponsors, or cheerleaders. Our writing style is upbeat and 'sporty' to catch and hold

the attention of our teenaged readers. Articles should be broken down into lots of sidebars, bulleted lists, Q&As, etc."

APPLESEEDS

E-mail: mlusted@cricketmedia.com. **Website:** www.cricketmag.com. **Contact:** Marcia Amidon Lusted, editor. *AppleSeeds* is a 36-page, multidisciplinary, nonfiction social studies magazine from Cobblestone Publishing for ages 6-9 (primarily grades 3 and 4). Each issue focuses on 1 theme.

Does not accept unsolicited mss.

NONFICTION Query only (via e-mail). See website for submission guidelines and theme list.

HOW TO CONTACT Accepts queries by e-mail only.

TERMS Buys all rights. Sample copy for $6.95 + $2 s&h. Guidelines available on website.

TIPS "Submit queries specifically focused on the theme of an upcoming issue. We generally work 6 months ahead on themes. We look for unusual perspectives, original ideas, and excellent scholarship. Writers should check our website for current guidelines, topics, and query deadlines. We use very little fiction. Illustrators should not submit unsolicited art."

AQUILA

Studio 2, 67A Willowfield Rd., Eastbourne BN22 8AP, United Kingdom. (44)(132)343-1313. **Fax:** (44)(132)373-1136. **E-mail:** info@aquila.co.uk. **Website:** www.aquila.co.uk. **Contact:** Jackie Berry, editor. "*Aquila* is an educational magazine for readers ages 8-13 including factual articles (no pop/celebrity material), arts/crafts, and puzzles." Entire publication aimed at juvenile market. Estab. 1993. Circ. 40,000.

FICTION Young Readers: animal, contemporary, fantasy, folktales, health, history, humorous, multicultural, nature/environment, problem solving, religious, science fiction, sports, suspense/mystery. Middle Readers: animal, contemporary, fantasy, folktales, health, history, humorous, multicultural, nature/environment, problem solving, religious, romance, science fiction, sports, suspense/mystery. Query with published clips. Length: 1,000-1,150 words. Pays £90/short story and £80/episode for serial.

NONFICTION Young Readers: animal, arts/crafts, concept, cooking, games/puzzles, health, history, how-to, interview/profile, math, nature/environment, science, sports. Middle Readers: animal, arts/crafts, concept, cooking, games/puzzles, health, history, interview/profile, math, nature/environment, science, sports. Query. Length: 600-800 words. Pays £50-75.

HOW TO CONTACT Editorial lead time is 1 year. Responds to queries in 6-8 weeks. Publishes ms 1 year after acceptance.

ILLUSTRATION Color artwork only.Works on assignment only. For first contact, query with samples. Submit samples to Jackie Berry, editor. Responds only if interested. Samples not returned. Samples filed.

TERMS Buys exclusive magazine rights. Pays on publication. Sample copy: £5. Guidelines online.

TIPS "We only accept a high level of educational material for children ages 8-13 with a good standard of literacy and ability."

○ ASK

Cricket Magazine Group, 70 E. Lake St., Suite 800, Chicago IL 60601. **E-mail:** ask@askmagkids.com. **Website:** www.cricketmag.com. **Contact:** Liz Huyck, editor. Magazine published 9 times/year covering science for children ages 7-10. *"Ask* is a magazine of arts and sciences for curious kids who like to find out how the world works." Estab. 2002.

NONFICTION Needs young readers, middle readers: science, engineering, invention, machines, archaeology, animals, nature/environment, history, history of science. *"ASK* commissions most articles but welcomes queries from authors on all nonfiction subjects. Particularly looking for odd, unusual, and interesting stories likely to interest science-oriented kids. Writers interested in working for *ASK* should send a résumé and writing sample (including at least 1 page unedited) for consideration." Average word length: 150-1,600.

ILLUSTRATION Buys 10 illustrations/issue; 60 illustrations/year. Works on assignment only. For illustrations, send query with samples.

PHOTOS Buys 10 illustrations/issue; 60 illustrations/year. Works on assignment only. For illustrations, send query with samples.

TERMS Byline given. Visit www.cricketmag.com/19-Submission-Guidelines-for-ASK-magazine-for-children-ages-6-9 or cricketmag.submittable.com for current issue theme list and calendar.

BABAGANEWZ

Behrman House, 11 Edison Pl., Springfield NJ 07081. **E-mail:** customersupport@behrmanhouse.com. **Website:** www.babaganewz.com. **Contact:** Mark Levine, articles editor; Jean Max, managing editor.

"Babaganewz helps middle school students explore Jewish values that are at the core of Jewish beliefs and practices." Estab. 2001.

FICTION Middle readers: religious, Jewish themes. Query. Average word length: 1,000-1,500.

NONFICTION Middle readers: arts/crafts, concept, games/puzzles, geography, history, humorous, interview/profile, nature/environment, religion, science, social issues. Most articles are written by assignment. Submit complete ms. Average word length: 350-1,000.

HOW TO CONTACT Responds in 3 months. Accepts queries by mail, e-mail.

ILLUSTRATION Uses color artwork only. Works on assignment only. Illustrations only: Send postcard sample with promo sheet, résumé, URL. Responds only if interested. Credit line given.

PHOTOS Photos by assignment.

TERMS Byline given. Pays on acceptance. Sample copy for 9x12 SAE and 4 first-class stamps.

TIPS "Most work is done on assignment. We are looking for freelance writers with experience writing nonfiction for 9- to 13-year-olds, especially on Jewish-related themes. No unsolicited mss."

BABYBUG

Cricket Magazine Group, 70 East Lake St., Suite 800, Chicago IL 60601. **E-mail:** babybug@babybugmagkids.com. **Website:** www.cricketmag.com/babybug; www.babybugmagkids.com. **Contact:** Submissions editor. *Babybug* is a look-and-listen magazine for babies and toddlers ages 6 months-3 years. Publishes 9 issues per year. Estab. 1994. Circ. 45,000.

FICTION Wants very short, clear fiction. Length: up to 6 sentences. Up to 25¢/word.

NONFICTION Submit through online submissions manager: submittable.cricketmag.com. Length: up to 6 sentences. Pays up to 25¢ per word.

POETRY "We are especially interested in rhythmic and rhyming poetry. Poems may explore a baby's day, or they may be more whimsical." Pays up to $3/line; $25 minimum.

HOW TO CONTACT Responds in 3-6 months to mss.

ILLUSTRATION Uses color artwork only. Works on assignment only. Reviews ms/illustration packages from artists. "The mss will be evaluated for quality of concept and text before the art is considered." Illustrations only: Send tearsheets or photo prints/photocopies with SASE. "Submissions without SASE will be discarded." Responds in 3 months. Samples filed.

PHOTOS Pays $500/spread; $250/page.

TERMS Rights vary. Byline given. Pays on publication. 50% freelance written. Guidelines available online: www.cricketmag.com/submissions.

TIPS "Imagine having to read your story or poem—out loud—50 times or more! That's what parents will have to do. Babies and toddlers demand, 'Read it again!' Your material must hold up under repetition. And humor is much appreciated by all."

BOYS' LIFE

Boy Scouts of America, P.O. Box 152079, 1325 W. Walnut Hill Ln., Irving TX 75015. **Website:** www. boyslife.org. **Contact:** Paula Murphey, senior editor; Clay Swartz, associate editor. *Boys' Life* is a monthly 4-color general interest magazine for boys 7-18, most of whom are Cub Scouts, Boy Scouts, or Venturers. Estab. 1911. Circ. 1.1 million.

FICTION All fiction is assigned.

NONFICTION Needs scouting activities and general interests. Query senior editor with SASE. No phone or e-mail queries. Length: 500-1,500 words. Pay ranges from $400-1,500.

HOW TO CONTACT Responds to queries/mss in 2 months. Publishes ms approximately 1 year after acceptance. Accepts queries by mail.

ILLUSTRATION Buys 10-12 illustrations/issue; 100-125 illustrations/year. Works on assignment only. Reviews ms/illustration packages from artists. "Query first." Illustrations only: Send tearsheets. Responds to art samples only if interested. Samples returned with SASE. Original artwork returned at job's completion. Works on assignment only.

PHOTOS Photo guidelines free with SASE. Pays $500 base editorial day rate against placement fees, plus expenses. **Pays on acceptance.** Buys one-time rights.

TERMS Buys one-time rights. Byline given. Pays on acceptance. 75% freelance written. Prefers to work with published/established writers; works with small number of new/unpublished writers each year. Sample copy: $3.95 plus 9x12 SASE. Guidelines online.

TIPS "We strongly recommend reading at least 12 issues of the magazine before submitting queries. We are a good market for any writer willing to do the necessary homework. Write for a boy you know who is 12. Our readers demand punchy writing in relatively short, straightforward sentences. The editors demand well-reported articles that demonstrate high standards of journalism. We follow the *Associated*

Press manual of style and usage. Learn and read our publications before submitting anything."

BOYS' QUEST

P.O. Box 227, Bluffton OH 45817-0227. (419)358-4610, ext. 101. **Fax:** (419)358-8020. **Website:** www.fun forkidzmagazines.com. **Contact:** Marilyn Edwards, editor. Bimonthly magazine. "*Boys' Quest* is a magazine created for boys from 5 to 14 years, with youngsters 8, 9 and 10 the specific target age. Our point of view is that every young boy deserves the right to be a young boy for a number of years before he becomes a young adult." Estab. 1995. Circ. 10,000.

FICTION Picture-oriented material, young readers, middle readers: adventure, animal, history, humorous, multicultural, nature/environment, problem-solving, sports. Does not want to see violence, teenage themes. Buys 30 mss/year. Query or send complete ms (preferred). Send SASE with correct postage. No faxed or e-mailed material. Length: 350 words per page

NONFICTION Needs nonfiction pieces that are accompanied by clear photos. Articles accompanied by photos with high resolution are far more likely to be accepted than those that need illustrations. Query or send complete ms (preferred). Send SASE with correct postage. No faxed or e-mailed material. Length: 350 words per page.

POETRY Reviews poetry. Limit submissions to 6 poems. Length: 21 lines maximum.

HOW TO CONTACT Responds to queries in 2 weeks; mss in 2 weeks (if rejected); 6 weeks (if scheduled). Accepts queries by mail.

ILLUSTRATION Buys 10 illustrations/issue; 60-70 illustrations/year. Uses b&w artwork only. Works on assignment only. Reviews ms/illustration packages from artists. Illustrations only: Query with samples, tearsheets. Responds in 1 month only if interested and a SASE. Samples returned with SASE; samples filed. Credit line given.

PHOTOS Photos used for support of nonfiction. "Excellent photographs included with a nonfiction story is considered very seriously." Model/property releases required. Uses b&w, 5×7 or 3×5 prints. Query with samples; send unsolicited photos by mail. Responds in 3 weeks. "We use a number of photos, printed in b&w, inside the magazine. These photos support the articles." $5/photo.

TERMS Buys first North American serial rights for mss. Byline given. Pays on publication. Guidelines and open themes available for SASE, or visit www. funforkidz.com and click on 'Writers' at the bottom of the homepage.

TIPS "First be familiar with our magazines. We are looking for lively writing, most of it from a young boy's point of view—with the boy or boys directly involved in an activity that is both wholesome and unusual. We need nonfiction with photos and fiction stories—around 500 words—puzzles, poems, cooking, carpentry projects, jokes and riddles. Nonfiction pieces that are accompanied by b&w photos are far more likely to be accepted than those that need illustrations. We will entertain simultaneous submissions as long as that fact is noted on the ms."

BREAD FOR GOD'S CHILDREN

P.O. Box 1017, Arcadia FL 34265. (863)494-6214. **E-mail:** bread@breadministries.org. **Website:** www.breadministries.org. **Contact:** Judith M. Gibbs, editor. An interdenominational Christian teaching publication published 6-8 times/year written to aid children and youth in leading a Christian life. Estab. 1972. Circ. 10,000 (US and Canada).

FICTION "We are looking for writers who have a solid knowledge of Biblical principles and are concerned for the youth of today living by those principles. Stories must be well written, with the story itself getting the message across—no preaching, moralizing, or tag endings." Young readers, middle readers, young adult/teen: adventure, religious, problem-solving, sports. Looks for "teaching stories that portray Christian lifestyles without preaching." Send complete ms. Length: 600-800 words for young children; 900-1,500 words for older children. Pays $40-50.

NONFICTION All levels: how-to. "We do not want anything detrimental to solid family values. Most topics will fit if they are slanted to our basic needs." Send complete ms. Length: 500-800 words.

HOW TO CONTACT Responds in 6 months to mss. Publishes ms an average of 6 months after acceptance. Accepts queries by mail.

ILLUSTRATION "The only illustrations we purchase are those occasional good ones accompanying an accepted story."

TERMS Pays on publication. Pays $30-50 for stories; $30 for articles. Sample copies free for 9×12 SAE and 5 first-class stamps (for 2 copies). Buys first rights. Byline given. No kill fee. 10% freelance written. Sample

copy for 9×12 SAE and 5 first-class stamps. Guidelines for #10 SASE.

TIPS "We want stories or articles that illustrate overcoming obstacles by faith and living solid, Christian lives. Know our publication and what we have used in the past. Know the readership and publisher's guidelines. Stories should teach the value of morality and honesty without preaching. Edit carefully for content and grammar."

☺ BRILLIANT STAR

1233 Central St., Evanston IL 60201. (847)853-2354. **E-mail:** brilliant@usbnc.org; sengle@usbnc.org. **Website:** www.brilliantstarmagazine.org. **Contact:** Susan Engle, associate editor. "*Brilliant Star* presents Bahá'í history and principles through fiction, nonfiction, activities, interviews, puzzles, cartoons, games, music, and art. Universal values of good character, such as kindness, courage, creativity, and helpfulness are incorporated into the magazine." Estab. 1969.

FICTION Needs middle readers: contemporary, fantasy, folktale, multicultural, nature/environment, problem-solving, religious. Submit complete ms. Length: 700-1,400 words.

NONFICTION Middle readers: arts/crafts, games/puzzles, geography, how-to, humorous, multicultural, nature/environment, religion, social issues. Query. Length: 300-700 words.

POETRY "We only publish poetry written by children at the moment."

ILLUSTRATION Reviews ms/illustration packages from artists. Illustrations only; query with samples. Contact: Aaron Kreader, graphic designer, at brilliant@usbnc.org. Responds only if interested. Samples kept on file. Credit line given.

PHOTOS Buys photos with accompanying ms only. Model/property release required; captions required. Responds only if interested.

TERMS Buys first rights and reprint rights for mss, artwork, and photos. Byline given. Pays 2 contributors copies. Guidelines available for SASE or via e-mail.

TIPS "*Brilliant Star*'s content is developed with a focus on children in their 'tween' years, ages 8-12. This is a period of intense emotional, physical, and psychological development. Familiarize yourself with the interests and challenges of children in this age range. Protagonists in our fiction are usually in the upper part of our age range: 10-12 years old. They solve their problems without adult intervention. We appreciate seeing a sense of humor but not related to bodily functions or put-downs. Keep your language and concepts age-appropriate. Use short words, sentences, and paragraphs. Activities and games may be submitted in rough or final form. Send us a description of your activity along with short, simple instructions. We avoid long, complicated activities that require adult supervision. If you think they will be helpful, please try to provide step-by-step rough sketches of the instructions. You may also submit photographs to illustrate the activity."

CADET QUEST MAGAZINE

P.O. Box 7259, Grand Rapids MI 49510-7259. (616)241-5616. **Fax:** (616)241-5558. **E-mail:** submissions@calvinistcadets.org. **Website:** www.calvinistcadets.org. **Contact:** G. Richard Broene, editor. Magazine published 7 times/year. *Cadet Quest Magazine* shows boys 9-14 how God is at work in their lives and in the world around them. Estab. 1958. Circ. 6,000.

FICTION "Fast-moving, entertaining stories that appeal to a boy's sense of adventure or to his sense of humor are welcomed. Stories must present Christian life realistically and help boys relate Christian values to their own lives. Stories must have action without long dialogues. Favorite topics for boys include sports and athletes, humor, adventure, mystery, friends, etc. They must also fit the theme of that issue of *Cadet Quest*. Stories with preachiness and/or clichés are not of interest to us." middle readers, boys/early teens: adventure, arts/craft, games/puzzles, hobbies, humorous, multicultural, religious, science, sports. No fantasy, science fiction, fashion, horror, or erotica. Send complete ms by postal mail or e-mail (in body of e-mail; no attachments). Length: 1,000-1,300 words. Pays 5¢/word and 1 contributors copy.

NONFICTION Needs how-to, humor, inspirational, interview, personal experience. informational. Send complete ms via postal mail or e-mail (in body of e-mail; no attachments). Length: up to 1,500 words. Pays 5¢/word and 1 contributors copy.

HOW TO CONTACT Responds in 2 months to mss. Publishes ms an average of 4-11 months after acceptance.

ILLUSTRATION Works on assignment only. Reviews ms/illustration packages from artists.

PHOTOS Pays $5 each for photos purchased with ms.

TERMS Buys all rights, first rights, and second rights. Rights purchased vary with author and material. Byline given. Pays on acceptance. No kill fee. Sample copy for 9×12 SASE and $1.45 postage. Guidelines online.

TIPS "The best time to submit stories/articles is early in the year (January-April). Also remember readers are boys ages 9-14. Stories must reflect or add to the theme of the issue and be from a Christian perspective."

CALLIOPE

30 Grove St., Suite C, Peterborough NH 03458-1454. (603)924-7209. **Fax:** (603)924-7380. **E-mail:** customerservice@caruspub.com. **Website:** www.cobblestonepub.com. **Contact:** Rosalie Baker and Charles Baker, co-editors; Lou Waryncia, editorial director; Ann Dillon, art director. Magazine published 9 times/year covering world history (East and West) through 1800 AD for 9- to 14-year-old kids.. Estab. 1990. Circ. 13,000.

◗ Articles must relate to the issue's theme. Lively, original approaches to the subject are the primary concerns of the editors in choosing material.

FICTION Material must relate to forthcoming themes. authentic historical and biographical fiction, adventure, retold legends, all relating to theme. Query with cover letter, one-page outline, bibliography, SASE. Length: no more than 800 words. Pays 20-25¢/word.

NONFICTION In-depth nonfiction, plays, biographies. Query with cover letter, one-page outline, bibliography, SASE. Length: 700-800 words for feature articles; 300-600 words for supplemental nonfiction. Pays 20-25¢/word.

HOW TO CONTACT If interested, responds 5 months before publication date. Accepts queries by mail.

PHOTOS "Illustrations only: Send tearsheets, photocopies. Original work returned upon job's completion (upon written request). Buys photos from freelancers. Wants photos pertaining to any upcoming themes. Uses b&w/color prints, 35mm transparencies, and 300 DPI digital images. Send unsolicited photos by mail (on speculation). Buys all rights for mss and artwork." If you have photographs pertaining to any upcoming theme, please contact the editor by mail or fax, or send them with your query. You may also send images on speculation. Model/property release preferred. Reviews b&w prints, color slides. Reviews photos with or without accompanying ms. "We buy one-time use. Our suggested fee range for professional quality photographs follows: ¼ page to full page b&w, $15-100; color, $25-100. Please note that fees for nonprofessional quality photographs are negotiated. Cover fees are set on an individual basis for one-time use, plus promotional use. All cover images are color. Prices set by museums, societies, stock photography houses, etc., are paid or negotiated. Photographs that are promotional in nature (e.g., from tourist agencies, organizations, special events, etc.) are usually submitted at no charge." Pays on publication. Credit line given.

TERMS "Covers are assigned and paid on an individual basis." Pays photographers per photo ($15-100 for b&w; $25-100 for color). Buys all rights. Byline given. Pays on publication. Kill fee. 50% freelance written. Sample copy for $5.95, $2 shipping and handling, and 10×13 SASE. Guidelines available online.

CARUS PUBLISHING COMPANY

30 Grove St., Suite C, Peterborough NH 03458. **Website:** www.cricketmag.com. See listings for *Babybug*, *Cicada*, *Click*, *Cricket*, *Ladybug*, *Muse*, *Spider*, and *Ask*. Carus Publishing owns Cobblestone Publishing, publisher of *AppleSeeds*, *Calliope*, *Cobblestone*, *Dig*, *Faces*, and *Odyssey*.

◎ CHEMMATTERS

1155 16th St., NW, Washington DC 20036. (202)872-6164. **Fax:** (202)833-7732. **E-mail:** chemmatters@acs.org. **Website:** www.acs.org/chemmatters. **Contact:** Patrice Pages, editor; Cornithia Harris, art director. Covers content covered in a standard high school chemistry textbook. *ChemMatters*, published 4 times/year, is a magazine that helps high school students find connections between chemistry and the world around them. Estab. 1983.

NONFICTION Query with published clips. Pays $500-1,000 for article. Additional payment for mss/illustration packages and for photos accompanying articles.

HOW TO CONTACT Responds to queries/mss in 4 weeks. Publishes ms 6 months after acceptance. Accepts queries by mail, e-mail.

ILLUSTRATION Buys 3 illustrations/issue; 12 illustrations/year. Uses color artwork only. Works on assignment only. Reviews ms/illustration packages from artists. Query. Illustrations only: Query with promo sheet, résumé. Samples returned with self-addressed stamped envelope; samples not filed. Credit line given.

PHOTOS Looking for photos of high school students engaged in science-related activities. Model/property release required; captions required. Uses color prints, but prefers high-resolution PDFs. Query with samples. Responds in 2 weeks.

TERMS Minimally buys first North American serial rights, but prefers to buy all rights, reprint rights, electronic rights for mss. Buys all rights for artwork; nonexclusive first rights for photos. Pays on acceptance. Sample copies free for 10×13 SASE and 3 first-class stamps. Writer's guidelines free for SASE (available as e-mail attachment upon request).

TIPS "Be aware of the content covered in a standard high school chemistry textbook. Choose themes and topics that are timely, interesting, fun, *and* that relate to the content and concepts of the first-year chemistry course. Articles should describe real people involved with real science. Best articles feature young people making a difference or solving a problem."

CICADA MAGAZINE

Cricket Magazine Group, 70 E. Lake St., Suite 800, Chicago IL 60601. **E-mail:** cicada@cicadamag.com. **Website:** www.cricketmag.com/cicada. **Contact:** submissions editor. "*Cicada* is a YA lit/comics magazine fascinated with the lyric and strange and committed to work that speaks to teens' truths. We publish poetry, realistic and genre fiction, essay, and comics by adults and teens. (We are also inordinately fond of Viking jokes.) Our readers are smart and curious; submissions are invited but not required to engage young adult themes." Bimonthly literary magazine for ages 14 and up. Publishes 6 issues/year. Estab. 1998. Circ. 6,000.

FICTION realism, science fiction, fantasy, historical fiction. Wants everything from flash fiction to novellas. Length: up to 9,000 words. Pays up to 25¢/word.

NONFICTION narrative nonfiction (especially teen-written), essays on literature, culture, and the arts. Prefers online submissions (submittable.cricketmag.com; www.cricketmag.com/submissions). Length: up to 5,000 words. Pays up to 25¢/word.

POETRY Reviews serious, humorous, free verse, rhyming. Length: up to 25 lines/poem. Pays up to $3/line ($25 minimum).

HOW TO CONTACT Responds in 3-6 months to mss.

ILLUSTRATION Buys 4 illustrations/issue; 24 illustrations/year. Uses color artwork for cover; b&w for interior. Works on assignment only. Reviews ms/illustration packages from artists. "To submit samples, e-mail a link to your online portfolio to: cicada@ci cadamag.com. You may also e-mail a sample up to a maximum attachment size of 50 KB. We will keep your samples on file and contact you if we find an assignment that suits your style."

PHOTOS Wants documentary photos (clear shots that illustrate specific artifacts, persons, locations, phenomena, etc., cited in the text) and "art" shots of teens in photo montage/lighting effects etc.

TERMS Pays after publication. Guidelines available online at submittable.cricketmag.com or www.cricketmag.com/submissions.

TIPS "Favorite writers, YA and otherwise: Bennett Madison, Sarah McCarry, Leopoldine Core, J. Hope Stein, José Olivarez, Sofia Samatar, Erica Lorraine Scheidt, David Levithan, Sherman Alexie, Hilary Smith, Nnedi Okorafor, Teju Cole, Anne Boyer, Malory Ortberg. @cicadamagazine; cicadamagazine.tumblr.com."

CLICK

Cricket Magazine Group, 70 E. Lake St., Suite 800, Chicago IL 60601. **Website:** www.cricketmag.com. **Contact:** Submissions editor. Magazine covering areas of interest for children ages 3-7. "*Click* is a science and exploration magazine for children ages 3-6. Designed and written with the idea that it's never too early to encourage a child's natural curiosity about the world, *Click*'s 40 full-color pages are filled with amazing photographs, beautiful illustrations, and stories and articles that are both entertaining and thought-provoking."

◯ *Does not accept unsolicited mss.*

FICTION Wants short stories suitable for children 3-6. "*Click* seeks stories that contain and explain nonfiction concepts within them. Since it is part of *Click*'s mission to encourage children to question, observe, and explore, successful stories often show children engaged in finding out about their universe—with the help of supportive, but not all-knowing, adults." Query. Length: 600-1,000 words.

NONFICTION Query with résumé and published clips. Length: 200-400 words.

POETRY Wants poems suitable for ages 3-6. Query.

ILLUSTRATION Buys 10 illustrations/issue; 100 illustrations/year. Works on assignment only. Query with samples. Responds only if interested. Credit line given.

TERMS Guidelines online.

TIPS "The best way for writers to understand what *Click* is looking for is to read the magazine. Writers are encouraged to examine several past copies before submitting an article or story."

COBBLESTONE

Cobblestone Publishing, 30 Grove St., Suite C, Peterborough NH 03458. **Website:** www.cobblestonepub.com. **Contact:** Meg Chorlian. "*Cobblestone* is interested in articles of historical accuracy and lively, original approaches to the subject at hand." American history magazine for ages 8-14. Circ. 15,000.

◯ "*Cobblestone* stands apart from other children's magazines by offering a solid look at one subject and stressing strong editorial content, color photographs throughout, and original illustrations." *Cobblestone* themes and deadline are available on website or with SASE.

FICTION Needs adventure, historical, biographical, retold legends, folktales, multicultural. Query. Length: up to 800 words. Pays 20-25¢/word.

NONFICTION Needs historical, humor, interview, personal experience, photo feature, travel, crafts, recipes, activities. Query with writing sample, one-page outline, bibliography, SASE. Length: 700-800 words for feature articles; 300-600 words for supplemental nonfiction; up to 700 words for activities. Pays 20-25¢/word.

POETRY Serious and light verse considered. Must have clear, objective imagery. Length: up to 100 lines/poem. Pays on an individual basis.

HOW TO CONTACT Accepts queries by mail.

ILLUSTRATION Reviews ms/illustration packages from artists. Query. Illustrations only: Send photocopies, tearsheets, or other nonreturnable samples. "Illustrators should consult issues of *Cobblestone* to familiarize themselves with our needs." Responds to art samples in 1 month. Samples are not returned; samples filed. Original artwork returned at job's completion (upon written request). Credit line given. Illustrators: "Submit color samples, not too juvenile. Study past issues to know what we look for. The illustration we use is generally for stories, recipes, and activities."

PHOTOS Photos must relate to upcoming themes. Send transparencies and/or color prints. Submit on speculation. Captions, identification of subjects, model release required. Reviews contact sheets, transparencies, prints. Pays $15-100/b&w. Pays on publication. Credit line given. Buys one-time rights. "Our suggested fee range for professional-quality photographs follows: ¼ page to full page b&w, $15-100; color, $25-100.

Please note that fees for non-professional-quality photographs are negotiated."

TERMS Buys all rights. Byline given. Pays on publication. Offers 50% kill fee. 50% freelance written. Sample copy: $6.95, plus $2 s&h. Guidelines online.

TIPS "Review theme lists and past issues to see what we're looking for."

COLLEGEXPRESS MAGAZINE

Carnegie Communications, LLC, 2 LAN Dr., Suite 100, Westford MA 01886. **E-mail:** info@carnegiecomm.com. **Website:** www.collegexpress.com. *CollegeXpress Magazine*, formerly *Careers and Colleges*, provides juniors and seniors in high school with editorial, tips, trends, and websites to assist them in the transition to college, career, young adulthood, and independence.

○ Distributed to 760,000 homes of 15- to 17-year-olds and college-bound high school graduates, and 10,000 high schools.

NONFICTION Needs young adults/teens: careers, college, health, how-to, humorous, interview/profile, personal development, problem-solving, social issues, sports, travel. Query. Length: 1,000-1,500 words.

HOW TO CONTACT Responds to queries in 6 weeks. Accepts queries by mail, e-mail.

TERMS Buys all rights. Byline given. Pays on acceptance plus 45 days. Guidelines online.

TIPS "Articles with great quotes, good reporting, good writing. Rich with examples and anecdotes. Must tie in with the objective to help teenaged readers plan for their futures. Current trends, policy changes and information regarding college admissions, financial aid, and career opportunities."

CRICKET

Cricket Magazine Group, 70 E. Lake St., Suite 800, Chicago IL 60601. **Website:** www.cricketmag.com/ckt-cricket-magazine-for-kids-ages-9-14; www.cricketmagkids.com. **Contact:** Submissions editor. Monthly magazine for children ages 9-14. *Cricket* is a monthly literary magazine for ages 9-14. Publishes 9 issues per year. Estab. 1973. Circ. 73,000.

FICTION Needs realistic, contemporary, historic, humor, mysteries, fantasy, science fiction, folk/fairy tales, legend, myth. No didactic, sex, religious, or horror stories. Submit complete ms. *Cricket* readers want to read about characters who are actively meeting their own challenges-not passively relying on the intervention of adults to solve problems of friends, family,

and school. Even if not fully successful, characters in *Cricket* at least progress in coming to terms with themselves and life. Length: 1,200-1,800 words. Pays up to 25¢/word.

NONFICTION *Cricket* publishes thought-provoking nonfiction articles on a wide range of subjects: history, biography, true adventure, science and technology, sports, inventors and explorers, architecture and engineering, archaeology, dance, music, theater, and art. Articles should be carefully researched and include a solid bibliography that shows that research has gone beyond reviewing websites. Length: 1,200-1,800 words. Pays up to 25¢/word.

POETRY *Cricket* publishes both serious and humorous poetry. Poems should be well-crafted, with precise and vivid language and images. Poems can explore a variety of themes, from nature, to family and friendships, to whatever you can imagine that will delight our readers and invite their wonder and emotional response. Length: 35 lines maximum. Most poems run 8-15 lines. Pays up to $3/line.

HOW TO CONTACT Responds in 3-6 months to mss. Accepts queries by mail.

ILLUSTRATION Buys 22 illustrations (7 separate commissions)/issue; 198 illustrations/year. Preferred theme for style: "stylized realism; strong people, especially kids; good action illustration; whimsical and humorous. All media, generally full color." Reviews ms/illustration packages from artists, "but reserves option to re-illustrate." Send complete ms with sample and query. Illustrations only: Provide link to website or tearsheets and good quality photocopies to be kept on file. SASE required for response/return of samples.

TERMS Byline given. Pays on publication. Guidelines available online at submittable.cricketmag.com or www.cricketmag.com/submissions.

TIPS Writers: "Read copies of back issues and current issues. Adhere to specified word limits. *Please* do not query." Would currently like to see more fantasy and science fiction. Illustrators: "Send only your best work and be able to reproduce that quality in assignments. Put name and address on *all* samples. Know a publication before you submit."

DAVEY AND GOLIATH'S DEVOTIONS

Evangelical Lutheran Church in America, ELCA Churchwide Ministries, 8765 W. Higgins Rd., Chicago IL 60631. **E-mail:** daveyandgoliath@elca.org. **E-mail:** cllsub@augsburgfortress.org. **Website:** www.

daveyandgoliath.org. "*Davey and Goliath's Devotions* is a magazine with concrete ideas that families can use to build Biblical literacy and share faith and serve others. It includes Bible stories, family activities, crafts, games, and a section of puzzles and mazes."

○ A booklet of interactive conversations and activities related to weekly devotional material. Used primarily by Lutheran families with elementary school-age children.

NONFICTION Needs religious. If you are interested in writing weekly content or puzzles or games, query with samples. Follow Weekly Content or Puzzles and Games Content guidelines, available online. Length: 350-400 words for Weekly Content.

TERMS Buys all rights. Pays on acceptance.

TIPS "Pay attention to details in the sample devotional. Follow the process laid out in the information for prospective writers. Ability to interpret Bible texts appropriately for children is required. Content must be doable and fun for families on the go."

DIG INTO HISTORY

Cobblestone Publishing, Editorial Dept., 30 Grove St., Suite C, Peterborough NH 03458. **Website:** www.cobblestonepub.com. **Contact:** Rosalie Baker, editor. *Dig into History* is an archaeology magazine for kids ages 10-14. Publishes entertaining and educational stories about discoveries, artifacts, and archaeologists. Estab. 1999.

FICTION Query. "Writers new to *Dig* should send a writing sample with query." Multiple queries accepted but may not be answered for many months. Length: up to 800 words. Pays 20-25¢/printed word.

NONFICTION Query. "A query must consist of all of the following to be considered: a brief cover letter stating the subject and word length of the proposed article, a detailed 1-page outline explaining the information to be presented in the article, a bibliography of materials the author intends to use in preparing the article, and a SASE. Writers new to *Dig* should send a writing sample with query." Multiple queries accepted; may not be answered for many months. Length: 700-800 words for feature articles; 300-600 words for supplemental nonfiction; up to 700 words for activities. Pays 20-25¢/printed word for feature articles and supplemental nonfiction. Pays activities, puzzles, and games on an individual basis.

ILLUSTRATION Buys 10-15 illustrations/issue; 60-75 illustrations/year. Prefers color artwork. Works on assignment only. Reviews ms/illustration packages from artists. Query. Illustrations only: Query with samples. Arrange portfolio review. Send tearsheets. Responds in 2 months only if interested. Samples not returned; samples filed. Credit line given.

PHOTOS Uses anything related to archaeology, history, artifacts, and current archaeological events that relate to kids. Uses color prints and 35mm transparencies, and 300 dpi digital images. Provide résumé, promotional literature, or tearsheets to be kept on file. Responds only if interested.

TERMS Buys all rights for mss. Buys first North American rights for photos. Pays on publication. Sample copy for $6.95 + $2 s&h.

TIPS "We are looking for writers who can communicate archaeological concepts in a conversational, interesting, informative, and *accurate* style for kids. Writers should have some idea of where photography can be located to support their articles."

DRAMATICS MAGAZINE

Educational Theatre Association, 2343 Auburn Ave., Cincinnati OH 45219. (513)421-3900. **E-mail:** dcorathers@schooltheatre.org. **Website:** http://schooltheatre.org. **Contact:** Don Corathers, editor. *Dramatics* is for students (mainly high school age) and teachers of theater. Mix includes how-to (tech theater, acting, directing, etc.), informational, interview, photo feature, humorous, profile, technical. *Dramatics* wants student readers to grow as theater artists and become a more discerning and appreciative audience. Material is directed to both theater students and their teachers, with strong student slant. Tries to portray the theater community in all its diversity. Estab. 1929. Circ. 45,000.

FICTION Young adults: drama (one-act and full-length plays). "We prefer unpublished scripts that have been produced at least once." Does not want to see plays that show no understanding of the conventions of the theater. No plays for children, no Christmas or didactic "message" plays. Submit complete ms. Buys 5-9 plays/year. Emerging playwrights have better chances with résumé of credits. Length: 10 minutes to full length. Pays $100-500 for plays.

NONFICTION Needs young adults: arts/crafts, careers, how-to, interview/profile, multicultural (all theater-related). Submit complete ms. Length: 750-3,000 words. Pays $50-500 for articles.

HOW TO CONTACT Publishes ms 3 months after acceptance.

ILLUSTRATION Buys 3-8 illustrations/year. Works on assignment only. Arrange portfolio review; send résumé, promo sheets, and tearsheets. Responds only if interested. Samples returned with SASE; sample not filed. Credit line given. Pays up to $300 for illustrations.

PHOTOS Buys photos with accompanying ms only. Looking for "good-quality production or candid photography to accompany article. We very occasionally publish photo essays." Model/property release and captions required. Prefers hi-res JPG files. Will consider prints or transparencies. Query with résumé of credits. Responds only if interested.

TERMS Byline given. Pays on acceptance. Sample copy available for 9x12 SAE with 4-ounce first-class postage. Guidelines available for SASE.

TIPS "Obtain our writer's guidelines and look at recent back issues. The best way to break in is to know our audience—drama students, teachers, and others interested in theater—and write for them. Writers who have some practical experience in theater, especially in technical areas, have an advantage, but we'll work with anybody who has a good idea. Some freelancers have become regular contributors."

FACES

Cobblestone Publishing, 30 Grove St., Peterborough NH 03458. **E-mail:** ecarpentiere@caruspub.com. **Website:** www.cobblestonepub.com. **Contact:** Elizabeth Crooker Carpentiere. "Published 9 times/year, *Faces* covers world culture for ages 9-14. It stands apart from other children's magazines by offering a solid look at 1 subject and stressing strong editorial content, color photographs throughout, and original illustrations. *Faces* offers an equal balance of feature articles and activities, as well as folktales and legends." Estab. 1984. Circ. 15,000.

FICTION Needs ethnic, historical, retold legends and folktales, original plays. Query. Length: up to 800 words. Pays 20-25¢/word.

NONFICTION Needs historical, humor, interview, personal experience, photo feature, travel, recipes, activities, crafts. Query with writing sample, one-page outline, bibliography, SASE. Length: 800 words for feature articles; 300-600 for supplemental nonfiction; up to 700 words for activities. Pays 20-25¢/word.

POETRY Serious and light verse considered. Must have clear, objective imagery. Length: up to 100 lines/poem. Pays on an individual basis.

HOW TO CONTACT Accepts queries by mail, e-mail.

ILLUSTRATION "Submit b&w samples, not too juvenile. Study past issues to know what we look for. The illustration we use is generally for retold legends, recipes, and activities." Buys 3 illustrations/issue; 27 illustrations/year. Preferred theme or style: material that is meticulously researched (most articles are written by professional anthropologists); simple, direct style preferred, but not too juvenile. Works on assignment only. Roughs required. Reviews ms/illustration packages from artists. Illustrations only: Send samples of b&w work. "Illustrators should consult issues of *Faces* to familiarize themselves with our needs." Responds to art samples only if interested. Samples returned with SASE. Original artwork returned at job's completion (upon written request). Credit line given.

PHOTOS Wants photos relating to forthcoming themes. "Contact the editor by mail or e-mail, or send photos with your query. You may also send images on speculation." Captions, identification of subjects, model releases required. Reviews contact sheets, transparencies, prints. Pays $15-100 for b&w; $25-100 for color; cover fees are negotiated.

TERMS Buys all rights. Byline given. Pays on publication. Offers 50% kill fee. 90-100% freelance written. Sample copy: $6.95, plus $2 s&h. Guidelines online.

TIPS "Writers are encouraged to study past issues of the magazine to become familiar with our style and content. Writers with anthropological and/or travel experience are particularly encouraged; *Faces* is about world cultures. All feature articles, recipes, and activities are freelance contributions."

FCA MAGAZINE

Fellowship of Christian Athletes, 8701 Leeds Rd., Kansas City MO 64129. (816)921-0909; (800)289-0909. **Fax:** (816)921-8755. **E-mail:** mag@fca.org. **Website:** www.fca.org/mag. **Contact:** Clay Meyer, editor; Matheau Casner, creative director. Published 6 times/year. *FCA Magazine*'s mission is to serve as a ministry tool of the Fellowship of Christian Athletes by informing, inspiring and involving coaches, athletes and all whom they influence, that they may make an impact for Jesus Christ. Estab. 1959. Circ. 75,000.

NONFICTION Needs inspirational, interview (with name athletes and coaches solid in their faith), personal experience, photo feature. Articles should be accompanied by at least 3 quality photos. Query and submit via e-mail. Length: 1,000-2,000 words. Pays $150-400 for assigned and unsolicited articles.

HOW TO CONTACT Responds to queries/mss in 3 months. Publishes ms an average of 4 months after acceptance.

PHOTOS Purchases photos separately. Looking for photos of sports action. Uses color prints and high resolution electronic files of 300 dpi or higher. State availability. Reviews contact sheets. Payment based on size of photo.

TERMS Buys first rights and second serial (reprint) rights. Byline given. Pays on publication. No kill fee. 50% freelance written. Prefers to work with published/established writers, but works with a growing number of new/unpublished writers each year. Sample copy for $2 and 9×12 SASE with 3 first-class stamps. Guidelines available at www.fca.org/mag/media-kit.

TIPS "Profiles and interviews of particular interest to coed athlete, primarily high school and college age. Our graphics and editorial content appeal to youth. The area most open to freelancers is profiles on or interviews with well-known athletes or coaches (male, female, minorities) who have been or are involved in some capacity with FCA."

THE FRIEND MAGAZINE

The Church of Jesus Christ of Latter-day Saints, 50 E. North Temple St., Salt Lake City UT 84150. (801)240-2210. **Fax:** (801)240-2270. **E-mail:** friend@ldschurch.org. **Website:** www.lds.org/friend. **Contact:** Paul B. Pieper, editor; Mark W. Robison, art director. Monthly magazine for 3-12 year olds. "The *Friend* is published by The Church of Jesus Christ of Latter-day Saints for boys and girls up to 3-12 years of age." Estab. 1971. Circ. 275,000.

FICTION Wants illustrated stories and "For Little Friends" stories. See guidelines online.

NONFICTION Needs historical, humor, inspirational, religious, adventure, ethnic, nature, family- and gospel-oriented puzzles, games, cartoons. Send complete ms by mail or e-mail. Length: up to 1,000 words. Pays $100-150 (400 words and up) for stories; $20 minimum for activities and games.

POETRY "We are looking for easy-to-illustrate poems with catchy cadences. Poems should convey a sense of joy and reflect gospel teachings. Also brief poems that will appeal to preschoolers." Pays $30 for poems.

HOW TO CONTACT Responds in 2 months to mss.

ILLUSTRATION Illustrations only: Query with samples; arrange personal interview to show portfolio; provide résumé and tearsheets for files.

TERMS Buys all rights. "Authors may request rights to have their work reprinted after their ms is published." Pays on acceptance. Sample copy for $1.50, 9×12 envelope, and 4 first-class stamps.

FUN FOR KIDZ

P.O. Box 227, Bluffton OH 45817. (419)358-4610. **Website:** funforkidz.com. **Contact:** Marilyn Edwards, articles editor. "*Fun for Kidz* is a magazine created for boys and girls ages 6-13, with youngsters 8, 9, and 10 the specific target age. The magazine is designed as an activity publication to be enjoyed by both boys and girls on the alternative months of *Hopscotch* and *Boys' Quest* magazines." Estab. 2002.

NONFICTION Needs picture-oriented material, young readers, middle readers: animal, arts/crafts, cooking, games/puzzles, history, hobbies, how-to, humorous, problem-solving, sports, carpentry projects. Submit complete ms with SASE, contact info, and notation of which upcoming theme your content should be considered for. Length: 300-750 words. Pays minimum 5¢/word for articles; variable rate for games and projects, etc.

HOW TO CONTACT Responds in 2 weeks to queries; 6 weeks to mss. Accepts queries by mail.

ILLUSTRATION Works on assignment mostly. "We are anxious to find artists capable of illustrating stories and features. Our inside art is pen and ink." Query with samples. Samples kept on file. Pays $35 for full page and $25 for partial page.

PHOTOS "We use a number of b&w photos inside the magazine; most support the articles used."

TERMS Buys first North American serial rights. Byline given. Pays on acceptance. Sample copy: $6 in US, $9 in Canada, and $12.25 internationally. Guidelines online.

TIPS "Our point of view is that every child deserves the right to be a child for a number of years before he or she becomes a young adult. As a result, *Fun for Kidz* looks for activities that deal with timeless topics, such as pets, nature, hobbies, science, games, sports, careers, simple cooking, and anything else likely to interest a child."

GIRLS' LIFE

Monarch Publishing, 3 S. Frederick St., Suite 806, Baltimore MD 21202. (410)426-9600. **Fax:** (866)793-1531. **E-mail:** writeforGL@girlslife.com. **Website:** www.girlslife.com. **Contact:** Karen Bokram, founding editor and publisher; Jessica D'Argenio Waller, fashion editor; Chun Kim, art director. Bimonthly magazine covering girls ages 9-15.. Estab. 1994. Circ. 2.16 million.

FICTION "We accept short fiction. They should be stand-alone stories and are generally 2,500-3,500 words."

NONFICTION Needs book excerpts, essays, general interest, how-to, humor, inspirational, interview, new product, travel. Query by mail with published clips. Submit complete mss on spec only. "Features and articles should speak to young women ages 10-15 looking for new ideas about relationships, family, friends, school, etc. with fresh, savvy advice. Front-of-the-book columns and quizzes are a good place to start." Length: 700-2,000 words. Pays $350/regular column; $500/feature.

HOW TO CONTACT Editorial lead time 4 months. Responds in 1 month to queries. Publishes ms an average of 3 months after acceptance. Accepts queries by mail, e-mail.

PHOTOS State availability with submission if applicable. Reviews contact sheets, negatives, transparencies. Negotiates payment individually. Captions, identification of subjects, model releases required. State availability. Captions, identification of subjects, model releases required. Reviews contact sheets, negatives, transparencies. Negotiates payment individually.

TERMS Buys all rights. Byline given. Pays on publication. Sample copy for $5 or online. Guidelines available online.

TIPS "Send thought-out queries with published writing samples and detailed résumé. Have fresh ideas and a voice that speaks to our audience-not down to them. And check out a copy of the magazine or visit girlslife. com before submitting."

☻ GREEN TEACHER

Green Teacher, 95 Robert St., Toronto ON M2S 2K5, Canada. (416)960-1244. **Fax:** (416)925-3474. **E-mail:** tim@greenteacher.com; info@greenteacher.com. **Website:** www.greenteacher.com. **Contact:** Tim Grant, co-editor; Amy Stubbs, editorial assistant. "We're a nonprofit organization dedicated to helping educators, both inside and outside of schools, promote environmental awareness among young people aged 6-19." Estab. 1991. Circ. 15,000.

NONFICTION multicultural, nature, environment Query. Submit one-page summary or outline. Length: 1,500-3,500 words.

HOW TO CONTACT Responds to queries in 1 week. Publishes ms 8 months after acceptance. Accepts queries by mail, e-mail.

ILLUSTRATION Buys 3 illustrations/issue from freelancers; 10 illustrations/year from freelancers. B&w artwork only. Works on assignment only. Reviews ms/illustration packages from artists. Query with samples; tearsheets. Responds only if interested. Samples not returned. Samples filed. Credit line given.

PHOTOS Purchases photos both separately and with accompanying mss. "Activity photos, environmental photos." Uses b&w prints. Query with samples. Responds only of interested.

TERMS Pays on acceptance.

GUIDE

Pacific Press Publishing Association, P.O. Box 5353, Nampa ID 83653. (301)393-4037. **Fax:** (301)393-4055. **E-mail:** guide@pacificpress.com. **Website:** www. guidemagazine.org. **Contact:** Randy Fishell, editor; Brandon Reese, designer. *Guide* is a Christian story magazine for young people ages 10-14. The 32-page, 4-color publication is published weekly by the Pacific Press. Their mission is to show readers, through stories that illustrate Bible truth, how to walk with God now and forever. Estab. 1953.

NONFICTION Send complete ms. "Each issue includes 3-4 true stories. *Guide* does not publish fiction, poetry, or articles (devotionals, how-to, profiles, etc.). However, we sometimes accept quizzes and other unique nonstory formats. Each piece should include a clear spiritual element." Looking for pieces on adventure, personal growth, Christian humor, inspiration, biography, story series, and nature. Length: 1,000-1,200 words. Pays 7-10¢/word.

HOW TO CONTACT Responds in 6 weeks to mss. Accepts queries by mail, e-mail.

TERMS Buys first serial rights. Byline given. Pays on acceptance. Sample copy free with 6×9 SAE and 2 first-class stamps. Guidelines available on website.

TIPS "Children's magazines want mystery, action, discovery, suspense, and humor—no matter what the topic. For us, truth is stronger than fiction."

HIGHLIGHTS FOR CHILDREN

803 Church St., Honesdale PA 18431. (570)253-1080. **Fax:** (570)251-7847. **Website:** www.highlights.com. **Contact:** Christine French Cully, editor-in-chief. Monthly magazine for children up to ages 6-12. "This book of wholesome fun is dedicated to helping children grow in basic skills and knowledge, in creativeness, in ability to think and reason, in sensitivity to others, in high ideals, and worthy ways of living—for children are the world's most important people. We publish stories for beginning and advanced readers. Up to 500 words for beginning readers, up to 800 words for advanced readers." Estab. 1946. Circ. approximately 1.5 million.

FICTION Meaningful stories appealing to both girls and boys, up to age 12. Vivid, full of action. Engaging plot, strong characterization, lively language. Prefers stories in which a child protagonist solves a dilemma through his or her own resources. Seeks stories that the child ages 8-12 will eagerly read, and the younger child will like to hear when read aloud (500-800 words). Stories require interesting plots and a number of illustration possiblities. Also need rebuses (picture stories 100 words), stories with urban settings, stories for beginning readers (100-500 words), sports and humorous stories, adventures, holiday stories, and mysteries. We also would like to see more material of 1-page length (300 words), both fiction and factual. Needs adventure, fantasy, historical, humorous. animal, contemporary, folktales, multi-cultural, problem-solving, sports No stories glorifying war, crime or violence. Send complete ms. Pays $150 minimum plus 2 contributors copies.

NONFICTION "Generally we prefer to see a manuscript rather than a query. However, we will review queries regarding nonfiction." Length: 800 words maximum. Pays $25 for craft ideas and puzzles; $25 for fingerplays; $150 and up for articles.

POETRY Lines/poem: 16 maximum ("most poems are shorter"). Considers simultaneous submissions ("please indicate"); no previously published poetry. No e-mail submissions. "Submit typed ms with very brief cover letter." Occasionally comments on submissions "if ms has merit or author seems to have potential for our market." Guidelines available for SASE.

Responds "generally within 2 months." Always sends prepublication galleys. Pays 2 contributor's copies; "money varies." Acquires all rights.

HOW TO CONTACT Responds in 2 months to queries. Accepts queries by mail.

PHOTOS Reviews electronic files, color 35mm slides, photos.

TERMS Buys all rights. Pays on acceptance. 80% freelance written. Sample copy free. Guidelines on website in "Company" area.

TIPS "Know the magazine's style before submitting. Send for guidelines and sample issue if necessary." Writers: "At *Highlights* we're paying closer attention to acquiring more nonfiction for young readers than we have in the past." Illustrators: "Fresh, imaginative work encouraged. Flexibility in working relationships a plus. Illustrators presenting their work need not confine themselves to just children's illustrations as long as work can translate to our needs. We also use animal illustrations, real and imaginary. We need crafts, puzzles and any activity that will stimulate children mentally and creatively. Know our publication's standards and content by reading sample issues, not just the guidelines. Avoid tired themes, or put a fresh twist on an old theme so that its style is fun and lively. Write what inspires you, not what you think the market needs. We are pleased that many authors of children's literature report that their first published work was in the pages of *Highlights*. It is not our policy to consider fiction on the strength of the reputation of the author. We judge each submission on its own merits. Query with simple letter to establish whether the nonfiction subject is likely to be of interest. Expert reviews and complete bibliography required for nonfiction. A beginning writer should first become familiar with the type of material that *Highlights* publishes. Include special qualifications, if any, of author. Write for the child, not the editor. Write in a voice that children understand and relate to. Speak to today's kids, avoiding didactic, overt messages. Even though our general principles haven't changed over the years, we are contemporary in our approach to issues. Avoid worn themes."

HOPSCOTCH

Fun for Kidz Magazines, P.O. Box 227, Bluffton OH 45817. (419)358-4610. **Website:** www.hopscotch magazine.com. **Contact:** Marilyn Edwards, editor. "For girls from ages 6-13, featuring traditional subjects—pets, games, hobbies, nature, science, sports, etc.—with an emphasis on articles that show girls actively involved in unusual and/or worthwhile activities." Estab. 1989. Circ. 14,000.

FICTION Query or submit complete ms with SASE, contact info, and notation of which upcoming theme the content should be considered for. Length: 350-750 words. Pays minimum 5¢/word.

NONFICTION Needs picture-oriented material, young readers, middle readers: animal, arts/crafts, biography, cooking, games/puzzles, geography, hobbies, how-to, humorous, math, nature/environment, science. "Need more nonfiction with quality photos about a *Hopscotch*-age girl involved in a worthwhile activity." Query or submit complete ms with SASE, contact info, and notation of which upcoming theme the content should be considered for. Length: 350-750 words. Pays minimum 5¢/word; pays minimum $10/puzzle; pays variable rate for games, crafts, cartoons, etc.

POETRY Query or submit poems with SASE, contact info, and notation of which upcoming theme the content should be considered for. Pays minimum $10/poem.

HOW TO CONTACT Responds in 2 weeks to queries; 5 weeks to mss.

ILLUSTRATION Buys approximately 10 illustrations/issue. "Generally, the illustrations are assigned after we have purchased a piece (usually fiction). Occasionally, we will use a painting—in any given medium—for the cover, and these are usually seasonal." Uses b&w artwork only for inside; color for cover. Reviews ms/illustration packages from artists. Query first or send complete ms with final art. Illustrations only: Send résumé, portfolio, client list, and tearsheets. Responds to art samples only if interested in 1 month. Samples returned with SASE. Credit line given. Pays $35 for full page and $25 for partial page.

PHOTOS Purchases photos separately (cover only) and with accompanying ms only. Looking for photos to accompany article. Model/property releases required. Uses 5×7, b&w prints; 35mm transparencies. B&w photos should go with ms. Should show girl or girls ages 6-12. Pays $5/photo.

TERMS Byline given. Pays on publication. Sample copy: $6 in US; $9 in Canada; $12.25 internationally.

TIPS "Remember that we publish only 6 issues a year, which means our editorial needs are extremely limited. Please look at our guidelines and our magazine.

Remember, we use far more nonfiction than fiction. Guidelines and current theme list can be downloaded from our website. If decent photos accompany the piece, it stands an even better chance of being accepted. We believe it is the responsibility of the contributor to come up with photos. Please remember, our readers are 6-12 years—most are 8-10—and your text should reflect that. Many magazines try to entertain first and educate second. We try to do the reverse. Our magazine is more simplistic, like a book to be read from cover to cover. We are looking for wholesome, nondated material."

☺ HORSEPOWER

Box 670, Aurora ON L4G 4J9, Canada. (800)505-7428. **Fax:** (905)841-1530. **E-mail:** ftdesk@horse-canada. com. **Website:** www.horse-canada.com. **Contact:** Susan Stafford-Pooley, managing editor. Bimonthly 16-page magazine, bound into *Horse Canada*, a bimonthly family horse magazine. "*Horsepower* offers how-to articles and stories relating to horse care for kids ages 6-16, with a focus on safety." Estab. 1988. Circ. 17,000.

○ *Horsepower* no longer accepts fiction.

NONFICTION Needs Middle grade readers, young adults: arts/crafts, biography, careers, fashion, games/puzzles, health, history, hobbies, how-to, humorous, interview/profile, problem-solving, travel. Submit complete ms. Length: 500-1,200 words.

HOW TO CONTACT Responds to mss in 3 months.

ILLUSTRATION Buys 3 illustrations/year. Reviews ms/illustration packages from artists. Contact: Editor. Query with samples. Responds only if interested. Samples returned with SASE; samples kept on file. Credit line given.

PHOTOS Looks for photos of kids and horses, instructional/educational, relating to riding or horse care. Uses color matte or glossy prints. Query with samples. Responds only if interested. Accepts TIFF or JPEG 300 dpi, disk or e-mail. Children on horseback must be wearing riding helmets or photos cannot be published.

TERMS Buys one-time rights for mss. Pays on publication. Guidelines available for SASE.

TIPS "Articles must be easy to understand, yet detailed and accurate. How-to or other educational features must be written by, or in conjunction with, a riding/teaching professional. Fiction is not encouraged, unless it is outstanding and teaches a moral or practical lesson. Note: Preference will be given to Canadian writers and photographers due to Canadian content laws. Non-Canadian contributors accepted on a very limited basis."

⬤☺⊕ HUNGER MOUNTAIN

Vermont College of Fine Arts, 36 College St., Montpelier VT 05602. (802)828-8517. **E-mail:** hungermtn@vcfa.edu. **Website:** www.hungermtn.org. "We accept picture book, middle grade, YA, and YA crossover work (text only—for now). We're looking for polished pieces that entertain, that show the range of adolescent experience, and that are compelling, creative, and will appeal to the devoted followers of the kid-lit craft, as well as the child inside us all." **Contact:** Miciah Bay Gault, editor. Monthly online publication and annual perfect-bound journal covering high-quality fiction, poetry, creative nonfiction, craft essays, writing for children, and artwork. Accepts high-quality work from unknown, emerging, or successful writers. No genre fiction, drama, or academic articles, please. Estab. 2002.

○   *Hunger Mountain* is about 200 pages, 7×10, professionally printed, perfect-bound, with full-bleed color artwork on cover. Press run is 1,000; 10,000 visits online monthly. Uses online submissions manager. Member: CLMP.

FICTION "We look for work that is beautifully crafted and tells a good story, with characters that are alive and kicking, storylines that stay with us long after we've finished reading, and sentences that slay us with their precision." Needs adventure, high-quality short stories, short shorts. No genre fiction, meaning science fiction, fantasy, horror, erotic, etc. Submit ms using online submissions manager. Length: up to 10,000 words. Pays $25-100.

NONFICTION "We welcome an array of traditional and experimental work, including, but not limited to, personal, lyrical, and meditative essays, memoirs, collages, rants, and humor. The only requirements are recognition of truth, a unique voice with a firm command of language, and an engaging story with multiple pressure points." Submit complete ms using online submissions manager. Length: up to 10,000 words.

POETRY Submit 3-10 poems at a time. All poems should be in 1 file. "We look for poetry that is as much about the world as about the self, that's an invitation, an opening out, a hand beckoning. We like poems that name or identify something essential that we may

have overlooked. We like poetry with acute, precise attention to both content and diction." Submit using online submissions manager. No light verse, humor/quirky/catchy verse, greeting card verse.

HOW TO CONTACT Responds in 4 months to mss. Publishes ms an average of 1 year after acceptance. Accepts queries by online submission form.

PHOTOS Send photos. Reviews contact sheets, transparencies, prints, GIF/JPEG files. Slides preferred. Negotiates payment individually.

TERMS Buys first worldwide serial rights. Byline given. Pays on publication. No kill fee. Single copy: $10; subscription: $12/year, $22 for 2 years. Make checks payable to Vermont College of Fine Arts. Guidelines online.

TIPS "Mss must be typed, prose double-spaced. Poets submit at least 3 poems. No multiple genre submissions. Fresh viewpoints and human interest are very important, as is originality. We are committed to publishing an outstanding journal of the arts. Do not send entire novels, mss, or short story collections. Do not send previously published work."

INSIGHT

Pacific Press Publishing Association, P.O. Box 5353, Nampa ID 83653. (208)465-2579. **E-mail:** insight@rhpa.org. **E-mail:** insight@pacificpress.com. **Website:** www.insightmagazine.org. Weekly 16-page magazine covering spiritual life of teenagers. *Insight* publishes true dramatic stories, interviews, and community and mission service features that relate directly to the lives of Christian teenagers, particularly those with a Seventh-day Adventist background. Estab. 1970. Circ. 8,000.

NONFICTION Needs how-to, teen relationships and experiences, humor, interview, personal experience, photo feature, religious. Send complete ms. Articles should address topics of interest to today's teenagers from a Christian perspective. An article should begin with a story or several anecdotes to introduce the topic. The story or anecdotes should be true and involve teenagers. Length: 500-1,000 words. Pays $25-150 for assigned articles. Pays $25-125 for unsolicited articles.

HOW TO CONTACT Editorial lead time 6 months. Responds in 1 month to mss. Publishes ms an average of 4 months after acceptance. Accepts queries by mail, e-mail, fax.

PHOTOS State availability. Model releases required. Reviews contact sheets, negatives, transparencies, prints. Negotiates payment individually.

TERMS Buys first rights, buys second serial (reprint) rights. Byline given. Pays on publication. No kill fee. 80% freelance written. Sample copy for $2 and #10 SASE. Guidelines available online.

TIPS "Skim 2 months of *Insight*. Write about your teen experiences. Use informed, contemporary style and vocabulary. Follow Jesus' life and example."

JUNIOR BASEBALL

(203)210-5726. **E-mail:** publisher@juniorbaseball. com. **Website:** www.juniorbaseball.com. **Contact:** Jim Beecher, publisher. Bimonthly magazine focused on youth baseball players ages 7-17 (including high school) and their parents/coaches. Edited to various reading levels, depending upon age/skill level of feature. Estab. 1996. Circ. 20,000.

NONFICTION Needs skills, tips, features, how to play better baseball, etc., interview with major league players (only on assignment), personal experience from coaches' or parents' perspective. Query. Length: 500-1,000 words. Pays $50-100.

HOW TO CONTACT Editorial lead time 3 months. Responds in 2 weeks to queries; 1 month to mss. Publishes ms an average of 4 months after acceptance.

PHOTOS Photos can be e-mailed in 300 dpi JPEGs. State availability. Captions, identification of subjects required. Reviews 35mm transparencies, 3×5 prints. Offers $10-100/photo; negotiates payment individually.

TERMS Buys all rights. Byline given. Pays on publication. No kill fee. 25% freelance written. Sample copy: $5 or free online.

TIPS "Must be well-versed in baseball! Have a child who is very involved in the sport, or have extensive hands-on experience in coaching baseball, at the youth, high school, or higher level. We can always use accurate, authoritative skills information, and good photos to accompany is a big advantage! This magazine is read by experts. No fiction, poems, games, puzzles, etc." Does not want first-person articles about your child.

KEYS FOR KIDS

Box 1001, Grand Rapids MI 49501-1001. (616)647-4500. **Fax:** (616)647-4950. **E-mail:** editorial@ keysforkids.org. **Website:** www.cbhministries.org. **Contact:** Hazel Marett, fiction editor. *Keys for Kids*, published by CBH Ministries, features stories and Key Verses of the Day for children ages 6-12 teaching about God's love. Estab. 1982.

FICTION "Propose a title and suggest an appropriate Scripture passage, generall 3-10 verses, to reinforce the theme of your story. Tell a story (not a Bible story) with a spiritual application. Avoid Pollyanna-type children—make them normal, ordinary kids, not goody-goodies. Avoid fairy-tale endings and minced oaths (gee, golly, gosh, darn). Include some action—not conversation only. Some humor is good." Needs religious. Submit complete ms. Length: up to 350 words. Pays $25.

TERMS Buys all rights. Pays on acceptance. Sample copy for 6x9 SAE and 3 first-class stamps. Guidelines online.

TIPS "Be sure to follow guidelines after studying sample copy of the publication."

KIDS LIFE MAGAZINE

1426 22nd Ave., Tuscaloosa AL 35401. (205)345-1193. **E-mail:** kidslife@comcast.net. **Website:** www.kid slifemagazine.com. **Contact:** Mary Jane Turner, publisher. "*Kids Life Magazine*, established in 2000, prides itself in bringing you a publication that showcases all the Tuscaloosa area has to offer its families. Not only does our community offer many activities and family-oriented events, we also have wonderful shopping and dining!" Estab. 2000. Circ. 30,000.

KIDZ CHAT

8805 Governor's Hill Dr., Suite 400, Cincinnati OH 45249. (513)931-4050. **Fax:** (877)867-5751. **E-mail:** lnickelson@standardpub.com. **Website:** www.stan dardpub.com. **Contact:** Lu Ann Nickelson, editor. Circ. 55,000.

Kidz Chat has decided to reuse much of the material that was a part of the first publication cycle. They will not be sending out theme lists, sample copies, or writers guidelines or accepting any unsolicited material because of this policy.

LADYBUG

Cricket Magazine Group, 700 E. Lake St., Suite 800, Chicago IL 60601. **Website:** www.cricketmag.com/ ladybug; ladybugmagkids.com. **Contact:** submissions editor. Monthly magazine for children ages 3-6. *Ladybug* magazine is an imaginative magazine with art and literature for young children (ages 3-6). Publishes 9 issues per year. Estab. 1990. Circ. 125,000.

FICTION Needs imaginative contemporary stories, original retellings of fairy and folk tales, multicultural stories. Submit via online submissions manager: cricket.submittable.com. Length: up to 800 words. Pays up to 25¢/word.

NONFICTION Needs gentle nonfiction, action rhymes, finger plays, crafts and activities. Submit via online submissions manager: cricketmag.submittable.com. Length: up to 400 words. Pays up to 25¢/word.

POETRY Wants poetry that is "rhythmic, rhyming; serious, humorous." Submit via online submissions manager: cricket.submittable.com. Length: up to 20 lines/poem. Pays up to $3/line ($25 minimum).

HOW TO CONTACT Responds in 6 months to mss.

ILLUSTRATION Prefers "bright colors; all media, but uses watercolor and acrylics most often; same size as magazine is preferred but not required." To be considered for future assignments: Submit promo sheet, slides, tearsheets, color and b&w photocopies. Responds to art samples in 3 months. Submissions without SASE will be discarded.

TERMS Byline given. Pays on publication. Guidelines available online at submittable.cricketmag.com or www.cricketmag.com/submissions.

LEADING EDGE

4087 JKB, Provo UT 84602. **E-mail:** editor@leadingedgemagazine.com; fiction@leadingedgemagazine.com; art@leadingedgemagazine.com. **Website:** www.leadingedgemagazine.com. **Contact:** Kenna Blaylock, editor in chief. Semiannual magazine covering science fiction and fantasy.. "*Leading Edge* is a magazine dedicated to new and upcoming talent in the fields of science fiction and fantasy. We strive to encourage developing and established talent and provide high-quality speculative fiction to our readers." Does not accept mss with sex, excessive violence, or profanity. Estab. 1981. Circ. 200.

○ Accepts unsolicited submissions.

FICTION Needs fantasy, science fiction. Send complete ms with cover letter and SASE. Include estimated word count. Length: 15,000 words maximum. Pays 1¢/word; $10 minimum.

POETRY "Publishes 2-4 poems per issue. Poetry should reflect both literary value and popular appeal and should deal with science fiction- or fantasy-related themes." Submit 1 or more poems at a time. No e-mail submissions. Cover letter is preferred. Include name, address, phone number, length of poem, title, and type of poem at the top of each page. Please include SASE with every submission." Pays $10 for first 4 pages; $1.50/each subsequent page.

HOW TO CONTACT Responds in 2-4 months to mss. Publishes ms an average of 2-4 months after acceptance.

ILLUSTRATION Buys 24 illustrations/issue; 48 illustrations/year. Uses b&w artwork only. Works on assignment only. Contact: Art Director. Illustrations only: Send postcard sample with portfolio, samples, URL. Responds only if interested. Samples filed. Credit line given.

TERMS Buys first North American serial rights. Byline given. Pays on publication. No kill fee. 90% freelance written. Single copy: $5.95. "We no longer provide subscriptions, but *Leading Edge* is now available on Amazon Kindle, as well as print-on-demand." Guidelines available online at website.

TIPS "Buy a sample issue to know what is currently selling in our magazine. Also, make sure to follow the writer's guidelines when submitting."

LIVE WIRE

8805 Governor's Hill Dr., Suite 400, Cincinnati OH 45249. (513)931-4050. **Fax:** (877)867-5751. **E-mail:** lnickelson@standardpub.com. **Website:** www.standardpub.com. **Contact:** Lu Ann Nickelson, editor. Estab. 1949.

○ *Live Wire* has decided to reuse much of the material that was a part of the first publication cycle. They will not be sending out theme lists, sample copies, or writers guidelines or accepting any unsolicited material because of this policy.

THE LOUISVILLE REVIEW

Spalding University, 851 S. Fourth St., Louisville KY 40203. (502)873-4398. **Fax:** (502)992-2409. **E-mail:** louisvillereview@spalding.edu. **Website:** www.louisvillereview.org. **Contact:** Ellyn Lichvar, assistant managing editor. *The Louisville Review*, published twice/year, prints all kinds of poetry. Has a section devoted to poetry by children and teens (grades K-12) called The Children's Corner. Estab. 1976.

○ *The Louisville Review* is 150 pages, digest-sized, flat-spined. Receives about 700 submissions/year, accepts about 10%.

POETRY Accepts submissions via online manager; please see website for more information. "Poetry by children must include permission of parent to publish if accepted. Address those submissions to The Children's Corner." Reads submissions year round. Has published poetry by Wendy Bishop, Gary Fincke, Michael Burkard, and Sandra Kohler. Pays in contributors copies.

TERMS Sample: $5. Single copy: $8. Subscription: $14/year, $27/2 years, $40/3 years (foreign subscribers add $6/year for s&h).

MUSE

Cricket Magazine Group, 70 E. Lake St., Suite 800, Chicago IL 60601. **E-mail:** muse@musemagkids. com. **Website:** www.cricketmag.com. **Contact:** submissions editor. "The goal of *Muse* is to give as many children as possible access to the most important ideas and concepts underlying the principal areas of human knowledge. Articles should meet the highest possible standards of clarity and transparency, aided, wherever possible, by a tone of skepticism, humor, and irreverence." All articles are commissioned. To be considered for assignments, experienced science writers may send a résumé and 3 published clips. Estab. 1996. Circ. 40,000.

○ *Muse is not accepting unsolicited mss.*

NONFICTION middle readers, young adult: animal, arts, history, math, nature/environment, problem-solving, science, social issues. Query with published clips.

HOW TO CONTACT Accepts queries by mail, e-mail.

ILLUSTRATION Works on assignment only. Credit line given. Send prints or tearsheets, but please, no portfolios or original art, and above all, *do not send samples that need to be returned.*

PHOTOS Needs vary. Query with samples to photo editor.

NATIONAL GEOGRAPHIC KIDS

National Geographic Society, 1145 17th St. NW, Washington DC 20036. **E-mail:** ashaw@ngs.org. **E-mail:** chughes@ngs.org; asilen@ngs.org; kboatner@ngs.org. **Website:** www.kids.nationalgeographic.com. **Contact:** Catherine Hughes, science editor; Andrea Silen, associate editor; Kay Boatner, associate editor; Jay Sumner, photo director. Magazine published 10 times/year. "It's our mission to find fresh ways to entertain children while educating and exciting them about their world." Estab. 1975. Circ. 1.3 million.

○ "We do not want poetry, sports, fiction, or story ideas that are too young—our audience is between ages 6-14."

NONFICTION Needs general interest, humor, interview, technical, travel, animals, human interest, science, technology, entertainment, archaeology, pets, history, paleontology. Query with published clips and résumé. Length: 100-1,000 words. Pays $1/word for assigned articles.

HOW TO CONTACT Editorial lead time 6+ months. Publishes ms an average of 6 months after acceptance. Accepts queries by mail.

PHOTOS State availability. Captions, identification of subjects, model releases required. Reviews contact sheets, negatives, transparencies, prints. Negotiates payment individually.

TERMS Buys all rights. Makes work-for-hire assignments. Byline given. Pays on acceptance. Offers 10% kill fee. 70% freelance written. Sample copy for #10 SASE. Guidelines online.

TIPS "Submit relevant clips. Writers must have demonstrated experience writing for kids. Read the magazine before submitting."

NATURE FRIEND MAGAZINE

4253 Woodcock Lane, Dayton VA 22821. (540)867-0764. **E-mail:** info@naturefriendmagazine.com; editor@naturefriendmagazine.com; photos@naturefriendmagazine.com. **Website:** www.naturefriendmagazine.com. **Contact:** Kevin Shank, editor. Monthly children's magazine covering creation-based nature.. "*Nature Friend* includes stories, puzzles, science experiments, nature experiments—all submissions need to honor God as creator." Estab. 1982. Circ. 13,000.

○ Picture-oriented material and conversational material needed.

NONFICTION Needs how-to, nature, photo feature, science experiments (for ages 8-12), articles about interesting/unusual animals. Send complete ms. Length: 250-900 words. Pays 5¢/word.

HOW TO CONTACT Editorial lead time 4 months. Responds in 6 months to mss.

PHOTOS Send photos. Captions, identification of subjects required. Reviews prints. Offers $20-75/photo.

TERMS Buys first rights, buys one-time rights. Byline given. Pays on publication. No kill fee. 80% freelance written. Sample copy: $5, postage paid. Guidelines available on website.

TIPS "We want to bring joy and knowledge to children by opening the world of God's creation to them.

We endeavor to create a sense of awe about nature's Creator and a respect for His creation. We'd like to see more submissions on hands-on things to do with a nature theme (not collecting rocks or leaves—real stuff). Also looking for good stories that are accompanied by good photography."

NEW MOON GIRLS

New Moon Girl Media, P.O. Box 161287, Duluth MN 55816. (218)728-5507. **Fax:** (218)728-0314. **E-mail:** submissions@newmoon.com. **Website:** www.new moon.com. Bimonthly magazine covering girls ages 8-14, edited by girls ages 8-14. "*New Moon Girls* is for every girl who wants her voice heard and her dreams taken seriously. *New Moon* celebrates girls, explores the passage from girl to woman, and builds healthy resistance to gender inequities. The *New Moon* girl is true to herself, and *New Moon Girls* helps her as she pursues her unique path in life, moving confidently into the world." Estab. 1992. Circ. 30,000.

◌ In general, all material should be pro-girl and feature girls and women as the primary focus.

FICTION Prefers girl-written material. All girl-centered. Needs adventure, fantasy, historical, humorous, slice-of-life vignettes. Send complete ms by e-mail. Length: 900-1,600 words. Pays 6-12¢/word.

NONFICTION Needs essays, general interest, humor, inspirational, interview, opinion, personal experience, written by girls, photo feature, religious, travel, multicultural/girls from other countries. Send complete ms by e-mail. Publishes nonfiction by adults in Herstory and Women's Work departments only. Length: 600 words. Pays 6-12¢/word.

POETRY No poetry by adults.

HOW TO CONTACT Editorial lead time 6 months. Responds in 2 months to mss. Publishes ms an average of 6 months after acceptance. Accepts queries by mail, e-mail, fax.

ILLUSTRATION Buys 6-12 illustrations/year from freelancers. *New Moon* seeks 4-color cover illustrations. Reviews ms/illustrations packages from artists. Query. Submit ms with rough sketches. Illustration only: Query; send portfolio and tearsheets. Samples not returned; samples filed. Responds in 6 months only if interested. Credit line given.

PHOTOS State availability. Captions, identification of subjects required. Negotiates payment individually.

TERMS Buys all rights. Byline given. Pays on publication. 25% freelance written. Sample copy: $7.50 or online. Guidelines available at website.

TIPS "We'd like to see more girl-written feature articles that relate to a theme. These can be about anything the girl has done personally, or she can write about something she's studied. Please read *New Moon Girls* before submitting to get a sense of our style. Writers and artists who comprehend our goals have the best chance of publication. We love creative articles—both nonfiction and fiction—that are not condescending to our readers. Keep articles to suggested word lengths; avoid stereotypes. Refer to our guidelines and upcoming themes online."

POCKETS

The Upper Room, P.O. Box 340004, Nashville TN 37203. (615)340-7333. **E-mail:** pockets@upperroom. org. **Website:** pockets.upperroom.org. **Contact:** Lynn W. Gilliam, editor. Magazine published 11 times/year. "*Pockets* is a Christian devotional magazine for children ages 6-12. All submissions should address the broad theme of the magazine. Each issue is built around a theme with material which can be used by children in a variety of ways. Scripture stories, fiction, poetry, prayers, art, graphics, puzzles and activities are included. Submissions do not need to be overtly religious. They should help children experience a Christian lifestyle that is not always a neatly wrapped moral package but is open to the continuing revelation of God's will. Seasonal material, both secular and liturgical, is desired." Estab. 1981.

◌ Does not accept e-mail or fax submissions.

FICTION "Stories should contain lots of action, use believable dialogue, be simply written, and be relevant to the problems faced by this age group in everyday life." Submit complete ms by mail. No e-mail submissions. Length: 600-1,000 words.

NONFICTION Picture-oriented, young readers, middle readers: cooking, games/puzzles. Submit complete ms by mail. No e-mail submissions. Length: 400-1,000 words. Pays 14¢/word.

POETRY Both seasonal and theme poems needed. Considers poetry by children. Length: up to 20 lines. Pays $25 minimum.

HOW TO CONTACT Responds in 8 weeks to mss. Publishes ms an average of 1 year after acceptance.

PHOTOS Send 4-6 close-up photos of children actively involved in peacemakers at work activities. Send photos, contact sheets, prints, or digital images. Must be 300 dpi. Pays $25/photo.

TERMS Buys first North American serial rights. Byline given. Pays on acceptance. No kill fee. 60% freelance written. Each issue reflects a specific theme. Guidelines online.

TIPS "Theme stories, role models, and retold scripture stories are most open to freelancers. Poetry is also open. It is very helpful if writers read our writers' guidelines and themes on our website."

RAINBOW RUMPUS

P.O. Box 6881, Minneapolis MN 55406. **Website:** www.rainbowrumpus.org. **Contact:** Beth Wallace, editor in chief and fiction editor. *"Rainbow Rumpus* is the world's only online literary magazine for children and youth with lesbian, gay, bisexual, and transgender (LGBT) parents. We are creating a new genre of children's and young adult fiction. Please carefully read and observe the guidelines on our website." Estab. 2005. Circ. 300 visits/day.

FICTION "Stories should be written from the point of view of children or teens with lesbian, gay, bisexual, or transgender parents or other family members, or who are connected to the LGBT community. Stories featuring families of color, bisexual parents, transgender parents, family members with disabilities, and mixed-race families are particularly welcome." Needs all levels: adventure, animal, contemporary, fantasy, folktales, history, humorous, multicultural, nature/environment, problem solving, science fiction, sports, suspense/mystery. Query editor through website's Contact page. Be sure to select the Submissions category. Length: 800-2,500 words for stories for 4- to 12-year-olds; up to 5,000 words for stories for 13- to 18-year-olds. Pays $300/story.

ILLUSTRATION Buys 1 illustration/issue. Uses both b&w and color artwork. Reviews ms/illustration packages from artists: Query. Illustrations only: Query with samples. Contact: Beth Wallace, fiction editor. Samples not returned; samples filed depending on the level of interest. Credit line given.

TERMS Buys first North American online rights for mss; may request print anthology and audio or recording rights. Byline given. Pays on publication. Guidelines online.

TIPS "Emerging writers encouraged to submit. You do not need to be a member of the LGBT community to participate."

SCIENCE WEEKLY

P.O. Box 70638, Chevy Chase MD 20813. (301)680-8804. **E-mail:** info@scienceweekly.com. **Website:** www.scienceweekly.com. **Contact:** Dr. Claude Mayberry, publisher. *Science Weekly* uses freelance writers to develop and write an entire issue on a single science topic. Send résumé only, not submissions. Authors preferred within the greater D.C./Virginia/Maryland area. *Science Weekly* works on assignment only. Estab. 1984. Circ. 200,000.

🔘 Submit résumé only.

NONFICTION young readers, middle readers (K-6th grade): science/math education, education, problem-solving.

TERMS Pays on publication. Sample copy free online.

SEVENTEEN MAGAZINE

300 W. 57th St., 17th Floor, New York NY 10019. (917)934-6500. **Fax:** (917)934-6574. **E-mail:** mail@seventeen.com. **Website:** www.seventeen.com. **Contact:** Consult masthead to contact appropriate editor. Monthly magazine covering topics geared toward young adult American women. "We reach 14.5 million girls each month. Over the past 6 decades, *Seventeen* has helped shape teenage life in America. We represent an important rite of passage, helping to define, socialize, and empower young women. We create notions of beauty and style, proclaim what's hot in popular culture, and identify social issues." Estab. 1944. Circ. 2,000,000.

🔘 *Seventeen* no longer accepts fiction submissions.

NONFICTION Needs young adults: careers, cooking, hobbies, how-to, humorous, interview/profile, multicultural, social issues. Query by mail. Consult masthead to pitch appropriate editor. Length: 200-2,000 words.

HOW TO CONTACT Accepts queries by mail.

ILLUSTRATION *Only interested in agented material.* Buys 10 illustrations/issue; 120 illustrations/year. Works on assignment only. Reviews ms/illustration packages. Illustrations only: Query with samples. Responds only if interested. Samples not returned; samples filed. Credit line given.

PHOTOS Looking for photos to match current stories. Model/property releases required; captions required.

Uses color, 8×10 prints; 35mm, 2¼×2¼, 4×5, or 8×10 transparencies. Query with samples or résumé of credits, or submit portfolio for review. Responds only if interested.

TERMS Buys first North American serial rights, first rights, or all rights. Buys exclusive rights for 3 months. Byline sometimes given. Pays on publication. Writer's guidelines for SASE.

TIPS "Send for guidelines before submitting."

SHINE BRIGHTLY

GEMS Girls' Clubs, 1333 Alger St., SE, Grand Rapids MI 49507. (616)241-5616. **Fax:** (616)241-5558. **E-mail:** shinebrightly@gemsgc.org. **Website:** www.gemsgc. org. **Contact:** Kristine Palosaari, executive director; Kelli Gilmore, managing editor. Monthly magazine (with combined June/July, August summer issue).. "Our purpose is to lead girls into a living relationship with Jesus Christ and to help them see how God is at work in their lives and the world around them. Puzzles, crafts, stories, and articles for girls ages 9-14." Estab. 1970. Circ. 17,000.

FICTION Does not want "unrealistic stories and those with trite, easy endings. We are interested in mss that show how girls can change the world." Needs adventure experiences girls could have in their hometowns or places they might realistically visit, ethnic, historical, humorous, mystery, religious, omance, slice-of-life vignettes, suspense,. Believable only. Nothing too preachy. Submit complete ms in body of e-mail. No attachments. Length: 700-900 words. Pays up to $35, plus 2 copies.

NONFICTION Needs humor, inspirational, seasonal and holiday, interview, personal experience, photo feature, religious, travel. adventure, mystery Submit complete ms in body of e-mail. No attachments. Length: 100-800 words. Pays up to $35, plus 2 copies.

POETRY Limited need for poetry. Pays $5-15.

HOW TO CONTACT Responds in 2 months to mss. Publishes ms an average of 1 year after acceptance.

ILLUSTRATION Samples returned with SASE. Credit line given.

PHOTOS Purchased with or without ms. Appreciate multicultural subjects. Reviews 5×7 or 8×10 clear color glossy prints. Pays $25-50 on publication.

TERMS Buys first North American serial rights, buys second serial (reprint) rights, buys simultaneous rights. Byline given. Pays on publication. No kill fee. 80% freelance written. Works with new and pub-

lished/established writers. Sample copy with 9×12 SASE with 3 first class stamps and $1. Guidelines available online.

TIPS Writers: "Please check our website before submitting. We have a specific style and theme that deals with how girls can impact the world. The stories should be current, deal with pre-adolescent problems and joys, and help girls see God at work in their lives through humor as well as problem-solving." Prefers not to see anything on the adult level, secular material, or violence. Writers frequently oversimplify the articles and often write with a Pollyanna attitude. An author should be able to see his/her writing style as exciting and appealing to girls ages 9-14. The style can be fun, but also teach a truth. Subjects should be current and important to *SHINE brightly* readers. Use our theme update as a guide. We would like to receive material with a multicultural slant."

SKIPPING STONES: A MULTICULTURAL LITERARY MAGAZINE

P.O. Box 3939, Eugene OR 97403-0939. (541)342-4956. **E-mail:** editor@skippingstones.org. **Website:** www.skippingstones.org. **Contact:** Arun Toké, editor. "*Skipping Stones* is an award-winning multicultural, nonprofit magazine designed to promote cooperation, creativity and celebration of cultural and ecological richness. We encourage submissions by children of color, minorities and under-represented populations. We want material meant for children and young adults/teenagers with multicultural or ecological awareness themes. Think, live and write as if you were a child, tween or teen. We want material that gives insight to cultural celebrations, lifestyle, customs and traditions, glimpse of daily life in other countries and cultures. Photos, songs, artwork are most welcome if they illustrate/highlight the points. Translations are invited if your submission is in a language other than English." Themes may include cultural celebrations, living abroad, challenging disability, hospitality customs of various cultures, cross-cultural understanding, African, Asian and Latin American cultures, humor, international understanding, turning points and magical moments in life, caring for the earth, spirituality, and multicultural awareness. *Skipping Stones* is magazine-sized, saddle-stapled, printed on recycled paper. Published quarterly during the school year (4 issues). Estab. 1988. Circ. 1,400 print, plus Web.

FICTION Middle readers, young adult/teens: contemporary, meaningful, humorous. All levels: folktales, multicultural, nature/environment. Multicultural needs include: bilingual or multilingual pieces; use of words from other languages; settings in other countries, cultures or multi-ethnic communities. Needs adventure, ethnic, historical, humorous. multicultural, international, social issues No suspense or romance stories. Send complete ms. Length: 1,000 words maximum. Pays 6 contributors copies.

NONFICTION Needs essays, general interest, humor, inspirational, interview, opinion, personal experience, photo feature, travel. All levels: animal, biography, cooking, games/puzzles, history, humorous, interview/profile, multicultural, nature/environment, creative problem-solving, religion and cultural celebrations, sports, travel, social and international awareness. Does not want to see preaching, violence or abusive language. Send complete ms. Length: 1,000 words maximum. Pays 6 contributors copies.

POETRY Submit up to 5 poems at a time. Considers simultaneous submissions; no previously published poems. Accepts e-mail submissions. Cover letter is preferred. "Include your cultural background, experiences, and the inspiration behind your creation." Time between acceptance and publication is 6-9 months. "A piece is chosen for publication when most of the editorial staff feel good about it." Seldom comments on rejected poems. Publishes multi-theme issues. Responds in up to 4 months. Length: 30 lines maximum. Pays 2 contributors copies, offers 40% discount for more copies and subscription, if desired.

HOW TO CONTACT Editorial lead time 3-4 months. Responds only if interested. Send nonreturnable samples. Publishes ms an average of 4-8 months after acceptance. Accepts queries by mail, e-mail.

ILLUSTRATION Prefers illustrations by teenagers and young adults. Will consider all illustration packages. Manuscript/illustration packages: Query; submit complete ms with final art; submit tearsheets. Responds in 4 months. Credit line given.

PHOTOS Black & white photos preferred, but color photos with good contrast are welcome. Needs: youth 7-17, international, nature, celebrations. Send photos. Captions required. Reviews 4×6 prints, low-res JPEG files. Offers no additional payment for photos.

TERMS Buys first North American serial rights, non-exclusive reprint, and electronic rights. Byline given. No kill fee. 80% freelance written. Sample: $7. Subscription: $25. Guidelines available online or for SASE.

TIPS "Be original and innovative. Use multicultural, nature, or cross-cultural themes. Multilingual submissions are welcome."

SPARKLE

GEMS Girls' Clubs, 1333 Alger St. SE, Grand Rapids MI 49507. (616)241-5616. **Fax:** (616)241-5558. **E-mail:** kelli@gemsgc.org. **Website:** www.gemsgc.org. **Contact:** Kelli Gilmore, managing editor; Lisa Hunter, art director/photo editor. Bimonthly magazine for girls ages 6-9. Mission is to prepare young girls to live out their faith and become world-changers. Strives to help girls make a difference in the world. Looks at the application of scripture to everyday life. Also strives to delight the reader and cause the reader to evalute her own life in light of the truth presented. Finally, attempts to teach practical life skills. Estab. 2002. Circ. 9,000.

FICTION Needs young readers: adventure, animal, contemporary, ethnic/multicultural, fantasy, folktale, health, history, humorous, music and musicians, mystery, nature/environment, problem-solving, religious, recipes, service projects, slice-of-life, sports, suspense/mystery, vignettes, interacting with family and friends. Send complete ms. Length: 100-400 words. Pays $35 maximum.

NONFICTION Needs young readers: animal, arts/crafts, biography, careers, cooking, concept, games/puzzles, geography, health, history, hobbies, how-to, humor, inspirational, interview/profile, math, multicultural, music/drama/art, nature/environment, personal experience, photo feature, problem-solving, quizzes, recipes, religious, science, social issues, sports, travel. Looking for inspirational biographies, stories from Zambia, and ideas on how to live a green lifestyle Send complete ms. Length: 100-400 words. Pays $35 maximum.

POETRY Prefers rhyming. "We do not wish to see anything that is too difficult for a first grader to read. We wish it to remain light. The style can be fun but should also teach a truth." No violence or secular material.

HOW TO CONTACT Editorial lead time 3 months. Responds in 3 weeks to queries; 3 months to mss. Accepts queries by mail, e-mail.

ILLUSTRATION Buys 1-2 illustrations/issue; 8-10 illustrations/year. Uses color artwork only. Works on assignment only. Reviews ms/illustration packages from artists. Send ms with dummy. Illustrations only:

send promo sheet. Contact: Sara DeRidder. Responds in 3 weeks only if interested. Samples returned with SASE; samples filed. Credit line given.

PHOTOS Send photos. Identification of subjects required. Reviews at least 5×7 clear color glossy prints, GIF/JPEG files on CD. Offers $25-50/photo.

TERMS Buys first North American serial rights, first rights, one-time rights, second serial (reprint) rights, simultaneous rights. Byline given. Pays on publication. Offers $20 kill fee. 80% freelance written. Sample copy for 9×13 SAE, 3 first-class stamps, and $1 for coverage/publication cost. Writer's guidelines for #10 SASE or online.

TIPS "Keep it simple. We are writing to first to third graders. It must be simple yet interesting. Mss should build girls up in Christian character but not be preachy. They are just learning about God and how He wants them to live. Manuscripts should be delightful as well as educational and inspirational. Writers should keep stories simple but not write with a 'Pollyanna' attitude. Authors should see their writing style as exciting and appealing to girls ages 6-9. Subjects should be current and important to *Sparkle* readers. Use our theme as a guide. We would like to receive material with a multicultural slant."

SPIDER

Cricket Magazine Group, 70 East Lake St., Suite 300, Chicago IL 60601. **Website:** www.cricketmag.com. **Contact:** Marianne Carus, editor in chief; Suzanne Beck, managing art director. Monthly reading and activity magazine for children ages 6-9. "*Spider* introduces children to the highest-quality stories, poems, illustrations, articles, and activities. It was created to foster in beginning readers a love of reading and discovery that will last a lifetime. We're looking for writers who respect children's intelligence." Estab. 1994. Circ. 70,000.

FICTION Stories should be easy to read. Has published work by Polly Horvath, Andrea Cheng, and Beth Wagner Brust. Needs fantasy, humorous, science fiction, folk tales, fairy tales, fables, myths. No romance, horror, religious. Submit complete ms via online submissions manager (cricketmag.submittable.com). Length: 300-1,000 words. Pays up to 25¢/word.

NONFICTION Submit complete ms via online submissions manager (cricketmag.submittable.com). Length: 300-800 words. Pays up to 25¢/word.

POETRY Submit up to 5 poems via online submissions manager (cricketmag.submittable.com). Length: up to 20 lines/poem. Pays up to $3/line.

HOW TO CONTACT Responds in 6 months to mss.

ILLUSTRATION Buys 5-10 illustrations/issue; 45-90 illustrations/year. Uses color artwork only. "We prefer that you work on flexible or strippable stock, no larger than 20×22 (image area 19×21). This will allow us to put the art directly on the drum of our separator's laser scanner. Art on disk CMYK, 300 dpi. We use more realism than cartoon-style art." Works on assignment only. Reviews ms/illustration packages from artists. Illustrations only: Send promo sheet and tearsheets. Responds in 3 months. Samples returned with SASE; samples filed. Credit line given.

PHOTOS Buys photos from freelancers. Buys photos with accompanying ms only. Model/property releases and captions required. Uses 35mm, 2¼×2¼ transparencies or digital files. Send unsolicited photos by mail; provide résumé and tearsheets. Responds in 3 months. For art samples, it is especially helpful to see pieces showing children, animals, action scenes, and several scenes from a narrative showing a character in different situations. Send photocopies/tearsheets. Also considers photo essays (prefers color, but b&w is also accepted). Captions, identification of subjects, model releases required. Reviews contact sheets, transparencies, 8×10 prints.

TERMS Rights purchased vary. Byline given. Pays on publication. 85% freelance written. Guidelines online.

TIPS "We'd like to see more of the following: engaging nonfiction, fillers, and 'takeout page' activities; folktales, fairy tales, science fiction, and humorous stories. Most importantly, do not write down to children."

STONE SOUP

Children's Art Foundation, P.O. Box 83, Santa Cruz CA 95063-0083. (831)426-5557. **E-mail:** editor@stonesoup.com. **Website:** http://stonesoup.com. **Contact:** Ms. Gerry Mandel, editor. Bimonthly magazine of writing and art by children age 13 under, including fiction, poetry, book reviews, and art. *Stone Soup* is 48 pages, 7×10, professionally printed in color on heavy stock, saddle-stapled, with coated cover with full-color illustration. Receives 5,000 poetry submissions/year, accepts about 12. Press run is 15,000. Subscription: $37/year (US). "We have a preference for writing and art based on real-life experiences; no formula stories or poems. We only publish writing by children ages 8 to 13. We do not publish writing by adults." Estab. 1973.

○ "Stories and poems from past issues are available online."

FICTION Needs adventure, ethnic, experimental, fantasy, historical, humorous, mystery, science fiction, slice-of-life vignettes, suspense. "We do not like assignments or formula stories of any kind." Send complete ms; no SASE. Length: 150-2,500 words. Pays $40 for stories, a certificate and 2 contributors copies, plus discounts.

NONFICTION Needs historical, personal experience. book reviews Submit complete ms; no SASE. Pays $40, a certificate and 2 contributors copies, plus discounts.

POETRY Wants free verse poetry. Does not want rhyming poetry, haiku, or cinquain. Pays $40/poem, a certificate, and 2 contributors copies, plus discounts.

HOW TO CONTACT Publishes ms an average of 4 months after acceptance.

TERMS Buys all rights. Pays on publication. 100% freelance written. Sample copy by phone only. Guidelines available online.

TIPS "All writing we publish is by young people ages 13 and under. We do not publish any writing by adults. We can't emphasize enough how important it is to read a couple of issues of the magazine. You can read stories and poems from past issues online. We have a strong preference for writing on subjects that mean a lot to the author. If you feel strongly about something that happened to you or something you observed, use that feeling as the basis for your story or poem. Stories should have good descriptions, realistic dialogue, and a point to make. In a poem, each word must be chosen carefully. Your poem should present a view of your subject, and a way of using words that are special and all your own."

◐ TC MAGAZINE (TEENAGE CHRISTIAN)

HU Box 10750, Searcy AR 72149. (501)279-4530. **E-mail:** season@harding.edu. **Website:** www.tcmagazine.org. "*TC Magazine* is published by the Mitchell Center for Leadership & Ministry. We are dedicated to the idea that it is not only possible but entirely excellent to live in this world with a vibrant and thriving faith. That, and an awesome magazine." Estab. 1961.

NONFICTION Query or submit complete ms.

HOW TO CONTACT Accepts queries by e-mail.

ILLUSTRATION Works on assignment only. Send ms with dummy. Illustrations only. Responds only if interested.

PHOTOS Buys photos separately. Model/property release required. Uses hi-res color digital photos. E-mail. Responds only if interested.

TERMS Pays on publication. Guidelines online.

YOUNG RIDER

P.O. Box 8237, Lexington KY 40533. (859)260-9800. **Fax:** (859)260-9814. **E-mail:** yreditor@i5publishing. com. **Website:** www.youngrider.com. "*Young Rider* magazine teaches young people, in an easy-to-read and entertaining way, how to look after their horses properly, and how to improve their riding skills safely." Estab. 1994.

FICTION young adults: adventure, animal, horses. "We would prefer funny stories, with a bit of conflict, which will appeal to the 13-year-old age group. They should be written in the third person, and about kids." Query. Length: 800-1,000 words. Pays $150.

NONFICTION young adults: animal, careers, famous equestrians, health (horse), horse celebrities, riding. Query with published clips. Length: 800-1,000 words. Pays $200/story.

HOW TO CONTACT Rsponds in 2 weeks to queries. Publishes ms 6-12 months after acceptance.

ILLUSTRATION Buys 2 illustrations/issue; 10 illustrations/year. Works on assignment only. Reviews ms/illustration packages from artists. Illustrations only: Query with samples. Responds in 2 weeks. Samples returned with SASE. Credit line given.

PHOTOS Buys photos with accompanying ms only. Uses high-res digital images only—in focus, good light. Model/property release required; captions required. Query with samples. Responds in 2 weeks.

TERMS Buys first North American serial rights. Byline given. Pays on publication. Sample copy: $3.50. Guidelines online.

TIPS "Fiction must be in third person. Read magazine before sending in a query. No 'true story from when I was a youngster.' No moralistic stories. Fiction must be up-to-date and humorous, teen-oriented. No practical or how-to articles—all done in-house."

AGENTS & ART REPS

//

This section features listings of literary agents and art reps who either specialize in, or represent a good percentage of, children's writers and/or illustrators. While there are a number of children's publishers who are open to non-agented material, using the services of an agent or rep can be beneficial to a writer or artist. Agents and reps can get your work seen by editors and art directors more quickly. They are familiar with the market and have insights into which editors and art directors would be most interested in your work. Also, they negotiate contracts and will likely be able to get you a better deal than you could get on your own.

Agents and reps make their income by taking a percentage of what writers and illustrators receive from publishers. The standard percentage for agents is 10 to 15 percent; art reps generally take 25 to 30 percent. We have not included any agencies in this section that charge reading fees.

WHAT TO SEND

When putting together a package for an agent or rep, follow the guidelines given in their listings. Most agents open to submissions prefer initially to receive a query letter describing your work. For novels and longer works, some agents ask for an outline and a number of sample chapters, but you should send these only if you're asked to do so. Never fax or e-mail query letters or sample chapters to agents without their permission. Just as with publishers, agents receive a large volume of submissions. It may take them a long time to reply, so you may want to query several agents at one time. It's best, however, to have a complete manuscript considered by only one agent at a time. Always include a self-addressed, stamped envelope (SASE).

For initial contact with art reps, send a brief query letter and self-promo pieces, following the guidelines given in the listings. If you don't have a flier or brochure, send photocopies. Always include a SASE.

For those who both write and illustrate, some agents listed will consider the work of author/illustrators. Read through the listings for details.

As you consider approaching agents and reps with your work, keep in mind that they are very choosy about who they take on to represent. Your work must be high quality and presented professionally to make an impression on them. For more information on approaching agents and additional listings, see *Guide to Literary Agents* (Writer's Digest Books). For additional listings of art reps see *Artist's & Graphic Designer's Market* (Writer's Digest Books).

AN ORGANIZATION FOR AGENTS

In some listings of agents you'll see references to AAR (The Association of Authors' Representatives). This organization requires its members to meet an established list of professional standards and code of ethics.

The objectives of AAR include keeping agents informed about conditions in publishing and related fields; encouraging cooperation among literary organizations; and assisting agents in representing their author-clients' interests. Officially, members are prohibited from directly or indirectly charging reading fees. They offer writers a list of member agents on their website. They also offer a list of recommended questions an author should ask an agent and other FAQs, all found on their website. They can be contacted at AAR, 676A 9th Ave. #312, New York NY 10036. (212)840-5777. E-mail: aarinc@mindspring.com. Website: www.aar-online.org.

AGENTS

ADAMS LITERARY

7845 Colony Rd., C4 #215, Charlotte NC 28226. (704)542-1440. **Fax:** (704)542-1450. **E-mail:** info@adamsliterary.com. **Website:** www.adamsliterary.com. **Contact:** Tracey Adams, Josh Adams. Member of AAR. Other memberships include SCBWI and WNBA. Currently handles: juvenile books.

MEMBER AGENTS Tracey Adams, Josh Adams, Samantha Bagood (assistant).

REPRESENTS Considers these fiction areas: middle grade, picture books, young adult.

8—⚓ Represents "the finest children's book authors and artists."

HOW TO CONTACT Contact through online form on website only. Send e-mail if that is not operating correctly. All submissions and queries should first be made through the online form on website. Will not review—and will promptly recycle—any unsolicited submissions or queries received by mail. Before submitting work for consideration, review complete guidelines online, as the agency sometimes shuts off to new submissions. "While we have an established client list, we do seek new talent—and we accept submissions from both published and aspiring authors and artists."

TERMS Agent receives 15% commission on domestic sales; 20% on foreign sales. Offers written contract.

RECENT SALES *Exposed*, by Kimberly Marcus (Random House); *The Lemonade Crime*, by Jacqueline Davies (Houghton Mifflin); *Jane Jones: Worst Vampire Ever*, by Caissie St. Onge (Random House).

TIPS "Guidelines are posted (and frequently updated) on our website."

INTERESTS, IT'S BEST to approach with a professional recommendation from a client.

ⓘ AZANTIAN LITERARY AGENCY

E-mail: queries@azantianlitagency.com. **Website:** www.azantianlitagency.com. Estab. 2014.

◯ Prior to her current position, Jennifer Azantian was with Sandra Dijkstra Literary Agency.

8—⚓ Actively seeking fantasy, science fiction and psychological horror for adult, young adult, and middle grade readers. Does not want to receive nonfiction or picture books.

HOW TO CONTACT To submit, send your query letter, 1-2 page synopsis, and first 10-15 pages all pasted in an e-mail (no attachments) to queries@azantianlitagency.com. Please note in the e-mail subject line if your work was requested at a conference, is an exclusive submission, or if your work was referred by a current client. Accepts simultaneous submissions. Responds within 6 weeks. Check the website before submitting to make sure Jennifer is currently open to queries.

BOOKSTOP LITERARY AGENCY

67 Meadow View Rd., Orinda CA 94563. (925)254-2664. **Fax:** (925)254-2668. **E-mail:** kendra@bookstopliterary.com; info@bookstopliterary.com. **Website:** www.bookstopliterary.com. Estab. 1983.

8—⚓ "Special interest in Hispanic, Asian American, African American, and multicultural writers; quirky picture books; clever adventure/mystery novels; eye-opening nonfiction; heartfelt middle grade; unusual teen romance."

HOW TO CONTACT Send: cover letter, entire ms for picture books; first 10 pages of novels; proposal and sample chapters OK for nonfiction. E-mail submissions: Paste cover letter and first 10 pages of ms into body of e-mail, send to info@bookstopliterary.com. Send sample illustrations only if you are an illustrator. Illustrators: send postcard or link to online portfolio. Do not send original artwork.

TERMS Agent receives 15% commission on domestic sales. Offers written contract, binding for 1 year. *Exile to Leadership* (Overlook).

ⓘ BRADFORD LITERARY AGENCY

5694 Mission Center Rd., #347, San Diego CA 92108. (619)521-1201. **E-mail:** queries@bradfordlit.com. **Website:** www.bradfordlit.com. **Contact:** Laura Bradford, Natalie Lakosil, Sarah LaPolla; Monica Odom. Estab. 2001. Member of AAR. RWA, SCBWI, ALA Represents 50 clients. 20% of clients are new/unpublished writers. Currently handles: nonfiction books 5%, novels 95%.

REPRESENTS Considers these nonfiction areas: biography, business, creative nonfiction, humor, memoirs, parenting, self-help. **Considers these fiction areas:** erotica, middle grade, mystery, paranormal, picture books, romance, thriller, women's, young adult.

8—⚓ Actively seeking many types of romance (historical, romantic suspense, paranormal, category, contemporary, erotic). Does not want to receive poetry, screenplays, short stories, westerns, horror, new age, religion, crafts, cookbooks, gift books.

HOW TO CONTACT Accepts e-mail queries only; send to queries@bradfordlit.com (or sarah@bradfordlit if contacting Sarah LaPolla). The entire submission must appear in the body of the e-mail and not as an attachment. The subject line should begin as follows: QUERY: (the title of the ms or any short message that is important should follow). For fiction: e-mail a query letter along with the first chapter of ms and a synopsis. Include the genre and word count in cover letter. Nonfiction: e-mail full nonfiction proposal including a query letter and a sample chapter. Accepts simultaneous submissions. Responds in 2-4 weeks to queries. Responds in 10 weeks to mss. Obtains most new clients through solicitations.

TERMS Agent receives 15% commission on domestic sales. Agent receives 20% commission on foreign sales. Offers written contract. Charges for extra copies of books for foreign submissions.

RECENT SALES Sold 93 titles in the last year. *The Sweetness of Honey*, by Alison Kent (Montlake); *Weave of Absence*, by Carol Ann Martin (NAL); *Pushing the Limit*, by Emmy Curtis (Forever Yours); *Voyage of the Heart*, by Soraya Lane (Amazon); *The Last Cowboy in Texas*, by Katie Lane (Grand Central); *Broken Open*, by Lauren Dane (HQN); *Lovely Wild*, by Megan Hart (Mira).

WRITERS CONFERENCES RWA National Conference; Romantic Times Booklovers Convention.

ⓘ ANDREA BROWN LITERARY AGENCY, INC.

1076 Eagle Dr., Salinas CA 93905. (831)422-5925. **E-mail:** andrea@andreabrownlit.com; caryn@andreabrownlit.com; lauraqueries@gmail.com; jennifer@andreabrownlit.com; kelly@andreabrownlit.com; jennL@andreabrownlit.com; jamie@andreabrownlit.com; jmatt@andreabrownlit.com; lara@andreabrownlit.com. **Website:** www.andreabrownlit.com. Member of AAR. 10% of clients are new/unpublished writers.

💬 Prior to opening her agency, Ms. Brown served as an editorial assistant at Random House and Dell Publishing and as an editor with Knopf.

MEMBER AGENTS Andrea Brown (president); **Laura Rennert** (senior agent); **Caryn Wiseman** (senior agent); **Kelly Sonnack** (agent); **Jennifer Rofé** (agent); **Jennifer Laughran** (agent); **Jamie Weiss Chilton** (agent); **Jennifer Mattson** (agent); **Lara Perkins** (associate agent, digital manager).

REPRESENTS nonfiction, fiction, juvenile books. **Considers these nonfiction areas:** juvenile nonfiction, memoirs, young adult, narrative. **Considers these fiction areas:** juvenile, literary, picture books, women's, young adult, middle grade, all juvenile genres.

⚲ Specializes in "all kinds of children's books—illustrators and authors." 98% juvenile books. Considers: nonfiction, fiction, picture books, young adult.

HOW TO CONTACT For picture books, submit complete ms. For fiction, submit query letter, first 10 pages. For nonfiction, submit proposal, first 10 pages. Illustrators: submit a query letter and 2-3 illustration samples (in jpeg format), link to online portfolio, and text of picture book, if applicable. "We only accept queries via e-mail. No attachments, with the exception of jpeg illustrations from illustrators." Visit the agents' bios on our website and choose only *one* agent to whom you will submit your e-query. Send a short e-mail query letter to that agent with QUERY in the subject field. Accepts simultaneous submissions. If we are interested in your work, we will certainly follow up by e-mail or by phone. However, if you haven't heard from us within 6 to 8 weeks, please assume that we are passing on your project. Obtains most new clients through referrals from editors, clients and agents. Check website for guidelines and information.

TERMS Agent receives 15% commission on domestic sales. Agent receives 25% commission on foreign sales. Offers written contract.

RECENT SALES *The Scorpio Races*, by Maggie Stiefvater (Scholastic); *The Raven Boys*, by Maggie Stiefvater (Scholastic); *Wolves of Mercy Falls* series, by Maggie Stiefvater (Scholastic); *The Future of Us*, by Jay Asher; *Triangles*, by Ellen Hopkins (Atria); *Crank*, by Ellen Hopkins (McElderry/S&S); *Burned*, by Ellen Hopkins (McElderry/S&S); *Impulse*, by Ellen Hopkins (McElderry/S&S); *Glass*, by Ellen Hopkins (McElderry/S&S); *Tricks*, by Ellen Hopkins (McElderry/S&S); *Fallout*, by Ellen Hopkins (McElderry/S&S); *Perfect*, by Ellen Hopkins (McElderry/S&S); *The Strange Case of Origami Yoda*, by Tom Angleberger (Amulet/Abrams); *Darth Paper Strikes Back*, by Tom Angleberger (Amulet/Abrams); *Becoming Chloe*, by Catherine Ryan Hyde (Knopf); Sasha Cohen autobiography (HarperCollins); *The Five Ancestors*, by Jeff Stone (Random House); *Thir-*

HEATHER ALEXANDER
PIPPIN PROPERTIES

Pippinproperties.com

@HeatherAlexand

ABOUT HEATHER: Heather came into publishing through editorial at Dial, working with such authors as Jenny Martin, Vin Vogel, Scott McCormick, and Jeanne Ryan. After six years at Penguin, she was asked a very interesting question: Had she ever considered becoming an agent? Many discussions later, she accepted a position at Pippin Properties, where she is building her roster of authors and illustrators, including A. N. Kang, Darren Farrell, and Jennifer Goldfinger.

SHE IS SEEKING: Picture books, middle grade, young adult, and literary graphic novels. She specifically seeks quirky picture books with a strong emotional core, middle grade about a moment that changes a kid forever, and beautifully written YA. She enjoys contemporary, historical, funny, high stakes, gothic style horror, and magical realism, but not high fantasy, medieval, or time travel. She favors literary over commercial and as an agent, she is excited to develop new talent and help shape careers, which is what she loves to do best.

HOW TO SUBMIT: Send a query addressed to Heather via e-mail along with your first chapter of your manuscript or the entire picture book in the body of the e-mail to info@pippinproperties.com. Please include a short synopsis of the work, your background and/or publishing history, and anything else you think is relevant. No attachments, please.

teen *Reasons Why*, by Jay Asher (Penguin); *Identical*, by Ellen Hopkins (S&S).
WRITERS CONFERENCES SCBWI; Asilomar; Maui Writers' Conference; Southwest Writers' Conference; San Diego State University Writers' Conference; Big Sur Children's Writing Workshop; William Saroyan Writers' Conference; Columbus Writers' Conference; Willamette Writers' Conference; La Jolla Writers' Conference; San Francisco Writers' Conference; Hilton Head Writers' Conference; Pacific Northwest Conference; Pikes Peak Conference.

BROWNE & MILLER LITERARY ASSOCIATES, LLC
410 S. Michigan Ave., Suite 460, Chicago IL 60605. (312)922-3063. **Fax:** (312)922-1905. **E-mail:** mail@browneandmiller.com. **Website:** www.browneandmiller.com. Estab. 1971. Member of AAR, RWA, MWA.

◯ Prior to opening the agency, Danielle Egan-Miller worked as an editor.

MEMBER AGENTS Danielle Egan-Miller (heavy emphasis on commercial adult fiction); **Abby Saul** (runs the gamut from literary newbies and classics, to cozy mysteries, to sappy women's fiction, to dark and twisted thrillers); **Joanna MacKenzie** (women's fiction, thrillers, new adult, and young adult genres).

❧ Browne & Miller is most interested in literary/commercial fiction/women's fiction, women's historical fiction, literary-leaning crime fiction, romance, and Amish fiction. We are also interested in time travel stories; Christian/inspirational fiction by established authors; literary and commercial young adult fiction; a broad array of nonfiction by nationally-recognized, platformed author/experts. "We do not represent children's picture books, horror or sci-fi novels, short stories, poetry, original screenplays, articles, or software."

HOW TO CONTACT E-query. No attachments. Responds in 2-4 weeks to queries; 4-6 months to mss. Obtains clients through recommendations from others.

TERMS Agent receives 15% commission on domestic sales; 20% on foreign sales. Offers written contract. Offers written contract, binding for 2 years. 30 days notice must be given to terminate contract.

RECENT SALES Sold 10 books for young readers in the last year.

TIPS "WE are very hands-on and do much editorial work with our clients. We are passionate about the books we represent and work hard to help clients reach their publishing goals."

🌓 KIMBERLEY CAMERON & ASSOCIATES

1550 Tiburon Blvd., #704, Tiburon CA 94920. **Fax:** (415)789-9191. **Website:** www.kimberleycameron. com. **Contact:** Kimberley Cameron. Member of AAR.

💬 Kimberley Cameron & Associates (formerly The Reece Halsey Agency) has had an illustrious client list of established writers, including the estate of Aldous Huxley, and has represented Upton Sinclair, William Faulkner, and Henry Miller.

MEMBER AGENTS Kimberley Cameron; **Elizabeth Kracht**, liz@kimberleycameron.com (literary, commercial, women's, thrillers, mysteries, and YA with crossover appeal); **Pooja Menon**, pooja@kimber leycameron.com (international stories, literary, historical, commercial, fantasy and high-end women's fiction; in nonfiction, she's looking for adventure & travel memoirs, journalism and human-interest stories, and self-help books addressing relationships and the human psychology from a fresh perspective); **Amy Cloughley**, amyc@kimberleycameron.com (literary and upmarket fiction, women's, mystery, narrative nonfiction); **Mary C. Moore** (literary fiction; she also loves a good commercial book; commercially she is looking for unusual fantasy, grounded science fiction, and atypical romance; strong female characters and unique cultures especially catch her eye).

REPRESENTS Considers these nonfiction areas: creative nonfiction, psychology, self-help, travel. **Considers these fiction areas:** commercial, fantasy, historical, literary, mystery, romance, science fiction, thriller, women's, young adult.

❧ "We are looking for a unique and heartfelt voice that conveys a universal truth."

HOW TO CONTACT "We accept e-mail queries only. Please address all queries to one agent only. Please send a query letter in the body of the e-mail, written in a professional manner and clearly addressed to the agent of your choice. Attach a one-page synopsis and the first 50 pages of your ms as separate Word or PDF documents. We have difficulties opening other file formats. Include 'Author Submission' in the subject line. If submitting nonfiction, attach a nonfiction proposal." Obtains new clients through recommendations from others, solicitations.

TERMS Agent receives 15% on domestic sales; 10% on film sales. Offers written contract, binding for 1 year.

TIPS "Please consult our submission guidelines and send a polite, well-written query to our e-mail address."

🎯 COMPASS TALENT

6 East 32nd Street, 6th Floor, New York NY 10016. (646)376-7718. **E-mail:** query@compasstalent.com. **Website:** www.compasstalent.com. **Contact:** Heather Schroder.

REPRESENTS Considers these nonfiction areas: cooking, creative nonfiction, foods, history, memoirs, science. **Considers these fiction areas:** commercial, juvenile, literary, mainstream.

AMANDA PANITCH
LIPPINCOTT MASSIE MCQUILKIN

Lmqlit.com

@AmandaPanitch

ABOUT AMANDA: Before joining LMQ in 2012, Amanda interned at Writers House and attended The George Washington University and New York University's Summer Publishing Institute. A writer herself, her first novel, *Damage Done*, was released in July 2015 from Random House Books for Young Readers.

SHE IS SEEKING: Young adult and middle grade only. In particular, she'd love to find a high fantasy set in a non-Western inspired setting. Other concepts she'd love to see in her inbox include a dark psychological thriller, a quirky mystery, a gorgeous literary contemporary, historical fiction set in a place or time not often explored in fiction, or anything featuring food as a main element. She is also drawn to generational spaceships, unreliable narrators, magical realism, the pre-Columbian Americas, the Amazon, close sibling relationships, and slow-burning romances.

HOW TO SUBMIT: Submit your query, including the first 5–10 pages of your manuscript pasted into the body of the email (no attachments) to Amanda@lmqlit.com. Include the word "Query" in the subject line.

HOW TO CONTACT This agency is currently closed to unsolicited submissions.

RECENT SALES A full list of agency clients is available on the website.

⊙⊙ JILL CORCORAN LITERARY AGENCY

P.O. Box 4116, Palos Verdes Peninsula CA 90274. **Website:** http://jillcorcoranliteraryagency.com; http://jillcorcoran.blogspot.com. **Contact:** Jill Corcoran. Estab. 2013.

REPRESENTS Considers these fiction areas: juvenile, middle grade, picture books, young adult.

HOW TO CONTACT Jill is closed to submissions. New assistant Eve Porinchak is open to submissions for picture books, middle grade and young adult: eve@jillcorcoranliteraryagency.com.

RECENT SALES Recent titles: *Guy-Write: What Every Guy Writer Needs to Know*, by Ralph Fletcher; *Kiss, Kiss Good Night*, by Kenn Nesbitt; *The Plot Whisperer: Secrets of Story Structure Any Writer Can Master*, by Martha Alderson; *Blind Spot*, by Laura Ellen; *How I Lost You*, by Janet Gurtler.

⊙ CORVISIERO LITERARY AGENCY

275 Madison Ave., 14th Floor, New York NY 10016. (646)942-8396. **Fax:** (646)217-3758. **E-mail:** contact@corvisieroagency.com. **E-mail:** query@corvisieroagency.com. **Website:** www.corvisieroagency.com. **Contact:** Marisa A. Corvisiero, senior agent and literary attorney.

MEMBER AGENTS Marisa A. Corvisiero, senior agent and literary attorney (nonfiction, picture books, middle grade, new adult, young adult, romance, thrillers, adventure, paranormal, fantasy, science fiction, and Christmas themes; **Saritza Hernandez**, senior agent (all kinds of romance, GLBT young adult, erotica); **Sarah Negovetich** (young adult, middle grade); **Doreen McDonald** (do not query); **Cate Hart** (YA, MG, historical romance, erotica, LGBTQ, romance, steampunk, clockpunk, candlepunk); **Samantha Bremekamp** (children's, middle grade, young adult, and new adult); **Ella Kennen** (picture books, MG, YA, some nonfiction).

REPRESENTS Considers these fiction areas: adventure, commercial, erotica, fantasy, gay, historical, lesbian, middle grade, multicultural, mystery, new adult, paranormal, picture books, science fiction, thriller, urban fantasy, young adult.

HOW TO CONTACT Accepts submissions via e-mail only. Include 5 pages of complete and polished ms pasted into the body of an e-mail, and a 1-2 page synopsis. For nonfiction, include a proposal instead of the synopsis. Put "Query for [Agent]" in the e-mail subject line.

TIPS "For tips and discussions on what we look for in query letters and submissions, please take a look at Marisa A. Corvisiero's blog: Thoughts From A Literary Agent."

CURTIS BROWN, LTD.

10 Astor Place, New York NY 10003-6935. (212)473-5400. **Website:** www.curtisbrown.com. **Contact:** Ginger Knowlton. Alternate address: Peter Ginsberg, president at CBSF, 1750 Montgomery St., San Francisco CA 94111; (415)954-8566. Member of AAR. Signatory of WGA.

MEMBER AGENTS Ginger Clark (science fiction, fantasy, paranormal romance, literary horror, and young adult and middle grade fiction); **Katherine Fausset** (adult fiction and nonfiction, including literary and commercial fiction, journalism, memoir, lifestyle, prescriptive and narrative nonfiction); **Holly Frederick**; **Peter Ginsberg**, president; **Elizabeth Harding**, vice president (represents authors and illustrators of juvenile, middle grade, and young adult fiction); **Steve Kasdin** (commercial fiction, including mysteries/thrillers, romantic suspense—emphasis on the suspense, and historical fiction; narrative nonfiction, including biography, history, and current affairs; and young adult fiction, particularly if it has adult crossover appeal); **Ginger Knowlton**, executive vice president (authors and illustrators of children's books in all genres); **Timothy Knowlton**, chief executive officer; **Jonathan Lyons** (biographies, history, science, pop culture, sports, general narrative nonfiction, mysteries, thrillers, science fiction and fantasy, and young adult fiction); **Laura Blake Peterson**, vice president (memoir and biography, natural history, literary fiction, mystery, suspense, women's fiction, health and fitness, children's and young adult, faith issues and popular culture); **Maureen Walters**, senior vice president (working primarily in women's fiction and nonfiction projects on subjects as eclectic as parenting & child care, popular psychology, inspirational/motivational volumes as well as a few medical/nutritional book); **Mitchell Waters** (literary and commercial fiction and nonfiction, including mystery, history, biography, memoir, young adult, cookbooks, self-help, and popular culture); **Kerry D'Agostino** (a wide range of literary and commercial fiction, as well as narrative nonfiction and memoir); **Noah Ballard** (literary debuts, upmarket thrillers and narrative nonfiction, and he is always on the look-out for honest and provocative new writers).

REPRESENTS nonfiction books, novels, short story collections, juvenile. **Considers these nonfiction areas:** animals, anthropology, art, biography, business, computers, cooking, crafts, creative nonfiction, current affairs, education, ethnic, film, gardening, government, health, history, how-to, humor, language, memoirs, military, money, multicultural, music, New Age, philosophy, photography, popular culture, psychology, recreation, regional, science, self-help, sex, sociology, software, spirituality, sports, translation, travel, true crime. **Considers these fiction areas:** adventure, confession, detective, erotica, ethnic, experimental, fantasy, feminist, gay, historical, horror, humor, juvenile, literary, mainstream, middle grade, military, multicultural, multimedia, mystery, New Age, occult, picture books, regional, religious, romance, spiritual, sports, thriller, translation, women's, young adult.

HOW TO CONTACT "Send us a query letter, a synopsis of the work, a sample chapter and a brief resume. Illustrators should send 1-2 samples of published work, along with 6-8 color copies (no original art). Please send all book queries to our address, Attn: Query Department. Please enclose a stamped, self-addressed envelope for our response and return postage if you wish to have your materials returned to you. We typi-

HEATHER FLAHERTY
THE BENT AGENCY

Thebentagency.com

@heddaflaherty

ABOUT HEATHER: "I grew up in Massachusetts, between Boston and the Cape, and started working in New York City as a playwright during college. This pushed me towards English as a focus, and I wound up finally beginning my publishing career in editorial, specifically at Random House in the UK. That's also where I became a YA and children's literary scout, which finally landed me back in NYC, consulting with foreign publishers and Hollywood regarding what the next big book will be. Now as an agent, I'm thrilled to turn my focus on growing authors for that same success."

SHE IS SEEKING: Authors who write children's, middle grade, and young adult fiction and nonfiction. "Currently I'm looking for YA fiction across-the-board, though my heart does sway towards issue-related YA with humor and heart—not depressing, or mopey. I also love hard, punchy, contemporary YA that's got no hesitations when it comes to crazy. I'm also always up for seeing contemporary stories with sci-fi or fantasy elements, as well as a clever respin of an old or classic tale. And then, I seek lastly, really good horror and ghost stories. As for the middle grade I'm looking for, I want it stark, honest, and even dark; either contemporary or period, as long as it's accessible. Coming-of-age stories, dealing-with-difficulty stories, witness stories (adult issues seen through the child's POV kinda thing), anything that makes you want to hold the narrator's hand. On the nonfiction side, I'm looking for strong teen memoirs about overcoming crushing situations."

HOW TO SUBMIT: Review The Bent Agency's updated submissions guidelines online, and then e-mail flahertyqueries@thebentagency.com.

cally respond to queries within 6 to 8 weeks." Note that some agents list their e-mail on the agency website and are fine with e-mail submissions. Note in your submission if the query is being considered elsewhere. Responds in 3 weeks to queries; 5 weeks to mss. Ob-

tains most new clients through recommendations from others, solicitations, conferences.

TERMS Agent receives 15% commission on domestic sales; 20% on foreign sales. Offers written contract. 75-day notice must be given to terminate contract.

Offers written contract. Charges for some postage (overseas, etc.).

RECENT SALES This agency prefers not to share information on specific sales.

D4EO LITERARY AGENCY

7 Indian Valley Rd., Weston CT 06883. (203)544-7180. **Fax:** (203)544-7160. **Website:** www.d4eoliteraryagency.com. **Contact:** Bob Diforio.

○ Prior to opening his agency, Mr. Diforio was a publisher.

MEMBER AGENTS Bob Diforio (prefers referrals); **Mandy Hubbard** (middle grade, young adult, and genre romance); **Kristin Miller** (closed to queries); **Bree Odgen** (children's, young adult, juvenile nonfiction, graphic novels, pop culture, art books, genre horror, noir, genre romance, historical, hard sci-fi); **Joyce Holland**; **Pam van Hycklama Vlieg**.

REPRESENTS nonfiction books, novels. **Considers these nonfiction areas:** juvenile, art, biography, business, child, current affairs, gay, health, history, how-to, humor, memoirs, military, money, psychology, religion, science, self help, sports, true crime, women's. **Considers these fiction areas:** adventure, detective, erotica, historical, horror, humor, juvenile, literary, mainstream, middle grade, mystery, picture books, romance, sports, thriller.

HOW TO CONTACT Each of these agents has a different submission e-mail and different tastes regarding how they review material. See all on their individual agent pages on the agency website. Responds in 1 week to queries if interested. Obtains most new clients through recommendations from others.

TERMS Offers written contract, binding for 2 years; automatic renewal unless 60 days notice given prior to renewal date. Charges for photocopying and submission postage.

◑ THE JENNIFER DECHIARA LITERARY AGENCY

31 East 32nd St., Suite 300, New York NY 10016. (212)481-8484. **Fax:** (212)481-9582. **Website:** www.jdlit.com.

MEMBER AGENTS Jennifer DeChiara, jenndec@aol.com (literary, commercial, women's fiction (no bodice-rippers, please), chick-lit, mysteries, suspense, thrillers, funny/quirky picture books, middle grade and young adult; for nonfiction: celebrity memoirs and biographies, GLBTQ, memoirs, books about the arts and performing arts, behind-the-scenes-type books, and books about popular culture); **Stephen Fraser**, fraserstephena@gmail.com (one-of-a-kind picture books; strong chapter book series; whimsical, dramatic, or humorous middle grade; dramatic or high-concept young adult; powerful and unusual nonfiction; nonfiction with a broad audience on topics as far reaching as art history, theater, film, literature, and travel); **Marie Lamba**, marie.jdlit@gmail.com (young adult and middle grade fiction, along with general and women's fiction, and some memoir; interested in established illustrators and picture book authors); **Linda Epstein**, linda.p.epstein@gmail.com (young adult, middle grade, literary fiction, quality upscale commercial fiction, vibrant narrative nonfiction, compelling memoirs, health and parenting books, cookbooks); **Roseanne Wells**, queryroseanne@gmail.com (literary fiction, YA, middle grade, narrative nonfiction, select memoir, science (popular or trade, not academic), history, religion (not inspirational), travel, humor, food/cooking, and similar subjects); **Victoria Selvaggio**, vselvaggio@windstream.net (lyrical picture books, middle grade and young adult fiction, mysteries, suspense, thrillers, paranormal, fantasy, narrative nonfiction).

REPRESENTS nonfiction books, novels, juvenile. **Considers these nonfiction areas:** art, cooking, creative nonfiction, film, foods, gay/lesbian, health, history, humor, literature, memoirs, parenting, popular culture, religious, science, theater, travel. **Considers these fiction areas:** commercial, literary, middle grade, mystery, picture books, suspense, thriller, women's, young adult.

HOW TO CONTACT Each agent has their own e-mail submission address and submission instructions. Accepts simultaneous submissions. Obtains most new clients through recommendations from others, conferences, query letters.

TERMS Agent receives 15% commission on domestic sales. Agent receives 20% commission on foreign sales. Offers written contract.

◑ LIZA DAWSON ASSOCIATES

350 Seventh Ave., Suite 2003, New York NY 10001. (212)465-9071. **Website:** www.lizadawsonassociates.com. **Contact:** Caitie Flum. Member of AAR. Other memberships include MWA, Women's Media Group. Represents 50+ clients. 30% of clients are new/unpublished writers.

VICTORIA SELVAGGIO
JENNIFER DE CHIARA LITERARY AGENCY

Jdlit.com

@vselvaggio1

ABOUT VICTORIA: Victoria joins The Jennifer De Chiara Literary Agency as an Associate Agent with a strong background in business ownership and over six years of actively working as a volunteer and Regional Advisor for SCBWI: Northern Ohio.

SHE IS SEEKING: "I am currently looking for lyrical picture books, middle grade and young adult fiction. If it's out of the box, and it will make me think and think, long after I'm done reading, send it to me. On the flip side, I yearn for books that make me laugh, cry and wonder about the world."

HOW TO SUBMIT: Please e-query vselvaggio@windstream.net. Put "Query" in the subject line of your e-mail. For queries regarding children's and adult fiction, please send the first 20 pages in the body of your e-mail, along with a one-paragraph bio and a one-paragraph pitch. "I usually respond within three to six months. If you haven't received a response after six months, feel free to query me again."

Prior to becoming an agent, Ms. Dawson was an editor for 20 years, spending 11 years at William Morrow as vice president and 2 years at Putnam as executive editor. Ms. Blasdell was a senior editor at HarperCollins and Avon.

MEMBER AGENTS Liza Dawson, queryliza@LizaDawsonAssociates.com (plot-driven literary and popular fiction, historicals, thrillers, suspense, history,psychology [both popular and clinical], politics, narrative nonfiction and memoirs); **Caitlin Blasdell**, queryCaitlin@LizaDawsonAssociates.com (science fiction, fantasy [both adult and young adult], parenting, business, thrillers and women's fiction; **Hannah Bowman**, queryHannah@LizaDawsonAssociates.com, West coast office; (commercial fiction—especially science fiction and fantasy, women's fiction, cozy mysteries, romance, young adult, also nonfiction in the areas of mathematics, science, and spirituality); **Caitie Flum**, querycaitie@LizaDawsonAssociates.com (commercial fiction, especially historical, women's fiction, mysteries, new adult and young adult, nonfiction in the areas of theater, memoir, current affairs and pop culture).

This agency specializes in readable literary fiction, thrillers, mainstream historicals, women's fiction, academics, historians, journalists, and psychology.

HOW TO CONTACT Query by e-mail only. No phone calls. Each of these agents has their own specific submission requirements, which you can find online at their website. queryHannah@LizaDawsonAssociates.com; query-havis@LizaDawsonAssociates.com; queryanna@LizaDawsonAssociates.com; queryCaitlin@LizaDawsonAssociates.com; queryliza@LizaDawsonAssociates.com. Responds in 4 weeks to queries; 8 weeks to mss. Obtains most new clients through recommendations from others, conferences.

TERMS Agent receives 15% commission on domestic sales. Agent receives 20% commission on foreign sales. Offers written contract.

ⓓ DEFIORE & CO.

47 E. 19th St., 3rd Floor, New York NY 10003. (212)925-7744. **Fax:** (212)925-9803. **E-mail:** brian@defliterary.com. **E-mail:** info@defliterary.com; submissions@defliterary.com. **Website:** www.defioreandco.com. Member of AAR.

○ Prior to becoming an agent, Mr. DeFiore was publisher of Villard Books (1997-1998), editor-in-chief of Hyperion (1992-1997), and editorial director of Delacorte Press (1988-1992).

MEMBER AGENTS Brian DeFiore (popular nonfiction, business, pop culture, parenting, commercial fiction); **Laurie Abkemeier** (memoir, parenting, business, how-to/self-help, popular science); **Kate Garrick** (literary fiction, memoir, popular nonfiction); **Matthew Elblonk** (young adult, popular culture, narrative nonfiction); **Caryn Karmatz-Rudy** (popular fiction, self-help, narrative nonfiction); **Adam Schear** (commercial fiction, humor, YA, smart thrillers, historical fiction, and quirky debut literary novels. For nonfiction: popular science, politics, popular culture, and current events); **Meredith Kaffel** (smart upmarket women's fiction, literary fiction [especially debut] and literary thrillers, narrative nonfiction, nonfiction about science and tech, sophisticated pop culture/humor books); **Rebecca Strauss** (literary and commercial fiction, women's fiction, urban fantasy, romance, mystery, YA, memoir, pop culture, and select nonfiction); **Debra Goldstein** (nonfiction books on how to live better).

REPRESENTS nonfiction books, novels. **Considers these nonfiction areas:** autobiography, biography, business, child guidance, cooking, economics, foods, how-to, inspirational, money, multicultural, parenting, popular culture, politics, psychology, religious, science, self-help, sports, young adult. **Considers these fiction areas:** ethnic, literary, mainstream, middle grade, mystery, paranormal, romance, short story collections, suspense, thriller, women's, young adult.

☞ "Please be advised that we are not considering poetry, adult science fiction and fantasy, or dramatic projects at this time."

HOW TO CONTACT Query with SASE or e-mail to submissions@defliterary.com. "Please include the word 'Query' in the subject line. All attachments will be deleted; please insert all text in the body of the e-mail. For more information about our agents, their individual interests, and their query guidelines, please visit our 'About Us' page on our website." There is more information (details, sales) for each agent on the agency website. Accepts simultaneous submissions. Obtains most new clients through recommendations from others.

TERMS Agent receives 15% commission on domestic sales. Agent receives 20% commission on foreign sales. Offers written contract; 10-day notice must be given to terminate contract. Charges clients for photocopying and overnight delivery (deducted only after a sale is made).

ⓓ SANDRA DIJKSTRA LITERARY AGENCY

1155 Camino del Mar, PMB 515, Del Mar CA 92014. (858)755-3115. **Fax:** (858)794-2822. **E-mail:** elise@dijkstraagency.com. **Website:** www.dijkstraagency.com. Member of AAR. Other memberships include Authors Guild, PEN West, PEN USA, Organization of American Historians, Poets and Editors, MWA. Represents 100+ clients. 30% of clients are new/unpublished writers.

MEMBER AGENTS Sandra Dijkstra, president (adult only). Acquiring Sub-agents: **Elise Capron** (adult only), **Jill Marr** (adult only), **Thao Le** (adult and YA), **Roz Foster** (adult and YA), **Jessica Watterson** (subgenres of adult and new adult romance, and women's fiction).

REPRESENTS nonfiction books, novels. **Considers these nonfiction areas:** biography, business, creative nonfiction, design, history, memoirs, psychology, science, self-help, narrative. **Considers these fiction areas:** commercial, horror, literary, middle grade, new adult, romance, science fiction, suspense, thriller, women's, young adult.

HOW TO CONTACT "Please see guidelines on our website, and note that we only accept e-mail submissions. Due to the large number of unsolicited submissions we receive, we are only able to respond those

NEW AGENT SPOTLIGHT

VICTORIA SELVAGGIO
JENNIFER DE CHIARA LITERARY AGENCY

Jdlit.com

@vselvaggio1

ABOUT VICTORIA: Victoria joins The Jennifer De Chiara Literary Agency as an Associate Agent with a strong background in business ownership and over six years of actively working as a volunteer and Regional Advisor for SCBWI: Northern Ohio.

SHE IS SEEKING: "I am currently looking for lyrical picture books, middle grade and young adult fiction. If it's out of the box, and it will make me think and think, long after I'm done reading, send it to me. On the flip side, I yearn for books that make me laugh, cry and wonder about the world."

HOW TO SUBMIT: Please e-query vselvaggio@windstream.net. Put "Query" in the subject line of your e-mail. For queries regarding children's and adult fiction, please send the first 20 pages in the body of your e-mail, along with a one-paragraph bio and a one-paragraph pitch. "I usually respond within three to six months. If you haven't received a response after six months, feel free to query me again."

Prior to becoming an agent, Ms. Dawson was an editor for 20 years, spending 11 years at William Morrow as vice president and 2 years at Putnam as executive editor. Ms. Blasdell was a senior editor at HarperCollins and Avon.

MEMBER AGENTS Liza Dawson, queryliza@LizaDawsonAssociates.com (plot-driven literary and popular fiction, historicals, thrillers, suspense, history,psychology [both popular and clinical], politics, narrative nonfiction and memoirs); **Caitlin Blasdell**, queryCaitlin@LizaDawsonAssociates.com (science fiction, fantasy [both adult and young adult], parenting, business, thrillers and women's fiction; **Hannah Bowman**, queryHannah@LizaDawsonAssociates.com, West coast office; (commercial fiction—especially science fiction and fantasy, women's

fiction, cozy mysteries, romance, young adult, also nonfiction in the areas of mathematics, science, and spirituality); **Caitie Flum**, querycaitie@LizaDawsonAssociates.com (commercial fiction, especially historical, women's fiction, mysteries, new adult and young adult, nonfiction in the areas of theater, memoir, current affairs and pop culture).

This agency specializes in readable literary fiction, thrillers, mainstream historicals, women's fiction, academics, historians, journalists, and psychology.

HOW TO CONTACT Query by e-mail only. No phone calls. Each of these agents has their own specific submission requirements, which you can find online at their website. queryHannah@LizaDawsonAssociates.com; query-havis@LizaDawsonAssociates.com; queryan na@LizaDawsonAssociates.com; queryCaitlin@Liza DawsonAssociates.com; queryliza@LizaDawsonAs sociates.com. Responds in 4 weeks to queries; 8 weeks to mss. Obtains most new clients through recommen dations from others, conferences.

TERMS Agent receives 15% commission on domestic sales. Agent receives 20% commission on foreign sales. Offers written contract.

Ⓓ DEFIORE & CO.

47 E. 19th St., 3rd Floor, New York NY 10003. (212)925-7744. **Fax:** (212)925-9803. **E-mail:** brian@ defliterary.com. **E-mail:** info@defliterary.com; sub missions@defliterary.com. **Website:** www.defiorean dco.com. Member of AAR.

Ⓞ Prior to becoming an agent, Mr. DeFiore was publisher of Villard Books (1997-1998), editor-in-chief of Hyperion (1992-1997), and editorial director of Delacorte Press (1988-1992).

MEMBER AGENTS Brian DeFiore (popular nonfic tion, business, pop culture, parenting, commercial fiction); **Laurie Abkemeier** (memoir, parenting, busi ness, how-to/self-help, popular science); **Kate Garrick** (literary fiction, memoir, popular nonfiction); **Mat thew Elblonk** (young adult, popular culture, narra tive nonfiction); **Caryn Karmatz-Rudy** (popular fic tion, self-help, narrative nonfiction); **Adam Schear** (commercial fiction, humor, YA, smart thrillers, his torical fiction, and quirky debut literary novels. For nonfiction: popular science, politics, popular culture, and current events); **Meredith Kaffel** (smart upmar ket women's fiction, literary fiction [especially debut] and literary thrillers, narrative nonfiction, nonfiction about science and tech, sophisticated pop culture/hu mor books); **Rebecca Strauss** (literary and commer cial fiction, women's fiction, urban fantasy, romance, mystery, YA, memoir, pop culture, and select nonfic tion); **Debra Goldstein** (nonfiction books on how to live better).

REPRESENTS nonfiction books, novels. **Considers these nonfiction areas:** autobiography, biography, business, child guidance, cooking, economics, foods, how-to, inspirational, money, multicultural, parent ing, popular culture, politics, psychology, religious, science, self-help, sports, young adult. **Considers these fiction areas:** ethnic, literary, mainstream, mid dle grade, mystery, paranormal, romance, short story collections, suspense, thriller, women's, young adult.

8➞🖈 "Please be advised that we are not considering poetry, adult science fiction and fantasy, or dramatic projects at this time."

HOW TO CONTACT Query with SASE or e-mail to submissions@defliterary.com. "Please include the word 'Query' in the subject line. All attachments will be deleted; please insert all text in the body of the e-mail. For more information about our agents, their in dividual interests, and their query guidelines, please visit our 'About Us' page on our website." There is more information (details, sales) for each agent on the agency website. Accepts simultaneous submissions. Obtains most new clients through recommendations from others.

TERMS Agent receives 15% commission on domes tic sales. Agent receives 20% commission on foreign sales. Offers written contract; 10-day notice must be given to terminate contract. Charges clients for pho tocopying and overnight delivery (deducted only after a sale is made).

Ⓓ SANDRA DIJKSTRA LITERARY AGENCY

1155 Camino del Mar, PMB 515, Del Mar CA 92014. (858)755-3115. **Fax:** (858)794-2822. **E-mail:** elise@ dijkstraagency.com. **Website:** www.dijkstraagency. com. Member of AAR. Other memberships include Authors Guild, PEN West, PEN USA, Organization of American Historians, Poets and Editors, MWA. Represents 100+ clients. 30% of clients are new/un published writers.

MEMBER AGENTS Sandra Dijkstra, president (adult only). Acquiring Sub-agents: **Elise Capron** (adult only), **Jill Marr** (adult only), **Thao Le** (adult and YA), **Roz Foster** (adult and YA), **Jessica Watter son** (subgenres of adult and new adult romance, and women's fiction).

REPRESENTS nonfiction books, novels. **Considers these nonfiction areas:** biography, business, creative nonfiction, design, history, memoirs, psychology, sci ence, self-help, narrative. **Considers these fiction ar eas:** commercial, horror, literary, middle grade, new adult, romance, science fiction, suspense, thriller, women's, young adult.

HOW TO CONTACT "Please see guidelines on our website, and note that we only accept e-mail submis sions. Due to the large number of unsolicited submis sions we receive, we are only able to respond those

NEW AGENT SPOTLIGHT

LYDIA SHAMAH
CAROL MANN AGENCY

Carolmannagency.com

@lydiablyf

ABOUT LYDIA: Lydia Shamah (nee Blyfield) is originally from London. After studying PR and Communications in the UK, she relocated to New York City where she gained a B.A. in English and American Literature at New York University.

SHE IS SEEKING: young adult and middle grade fiction. In YA and MG, she is looking for strong hooks and modern themes.

HOW TO SUBMIT: Please send a query letter (including a brief bio) and the first 25 pages of your manuscript to querylydia@carolmannagency.com. All material should be pasted into the body of the email message.

---

submissions in which we are interested." Accepts simultaneous submissions. Responds to queries of interest within 6 weeks.

TERMS Works in conjunction with foreign and film agents. Agent receives 15% commission on domestic sales and 20% commission on foreign sales. Offers written contract. No reading fee.

TIPS "Remember that publishing is a business. Do your research and present your project in as professional a way as possible. Only submit your work when you are confident that it is polished and ready for prime-time. Make yourself a part of the active writing community by getting stories and articles published, networking with other writers, and getting a good sense of where your work fits in the market.

⊕ DONAGHY LITERARY GROUP

(647)527-4353. **E-mail:** query@donaghyliterary.com. **Website:** www.donaghyliterary.com.

MEMBER AGENTS Stacey Donaghy (romantic suspense, LGBT stories standalone or series, mystery of all kinds, contemporary romance, erotica; Stacey also seeks nonfiction—authorized biographies, compelling stories written by celebrities, music industry professionals, pop culture, film/television, Canadian/international content; she is not seeking general nonfiction or memoirs unless you are a rock icon, or celebrity); **Valerie Noble** (science fiction and fantasy [think Kristin Cashore and Suzanne Collins] for young adults and adults).

REPRESENTS Considers these fiction areas: erotica, fantasy, mystery, romance, science fiction, young adult.

HOW TO CONTACT Check the website, because the agency can close to submissions at any time.

⦿ DUNHAM LITERARY, INC.

110 William St., Suite 2202, New York NY 10038. (212)929-0994. **E-mail:** query@dunhamlit.com. **Website:** www.dunhamlit.com. **Contact:** Jennie Dunham. Member of AAR. SCBWI Represents 50 clients. 15% of clients are new/unpublished writers. Currently handles: nonfiction books 25%, novels 25%, juvenile books 50%.

○ Prior to opening her agency, Ms. Dunham worked as a literary agent for Russell & Volkening. The Rhoda Weyr Agency is now a division of Dunham Literary, Inc.

REPRESENTS Considers these nonfiction areas: anthropology, archeology, biography, cultural interests, environment, ethnic, health, history, language, literature, medicine, popular culture, politics, psychology, science, technology, women's issues, women's studies. **Considers these fiction areas:** ethnic, juvenile, literary, mainstream, picture books, young adult.

HOW TO CONTACT Query with SASE. Responds in 3 weeks to queries; 2 months to mss. Obtains most new clients through recommendations from others, solicitations.

TERMS Agent receives 15% commission on domestic sales. Agent receives 20% commission on foreign sales.

RECENT SALES Sales include The Bad Kitty Series, by Nick Bruel (Macmillan); *The Little Mermaid*, by Robert Sabuda (Simon & Schuster); *The Gollywhopper Games* and Sequels, by Jody Feldman (HarperCollins); *Learning Not To Drown*, by Anna Shinoda (Simon & Schuster); *The Things You Kiss Goodbye*, by Leslie Connor (HarperCollins); *Gangsterland*, by Tod Goldberg (Counterpoint); *Ancestors and Others*, by Fred Chappell (Macmillan), *Forward From Here*, by Reeve Lindbergh (Simon & Schuster).

⭕ DUNOW, CARLSON, & LERNER AGENCY

27 W. 20th St., Suite 1107, New York NY 10011. (212)645-7606. **E-mail:** betsy@dclagency.com; jennifer@dclagency.com. **E-mail:** mail@dclagency.com. **Website:** www.dclagency.com. Member of AAR.

MEMBER AGENTS Jennifer Carlson (narrative nonfiction writers and journalists covering current events and ideas and cultural history, as well as literary and upmarket commercial novelists); **Henry Dunow** (quality fiction—literary, historical, strongly written commercial—and with voice-driven nonfiction across a range of areas – narrative history, biography, memoir, current affairs, cultural trends and criticism, science, sports); **Erin Hosier** (nonfiction: popular culture, music, sociology and memoir); **Betsy Lerner** (nonfiction writers in the areas of psychology, history, cultural studies, biography, current events, business; fiction: literary, dark, funny, voice driven); **Yishai Seidman** (broad range of fiction: literary, postmodern, and thrillers; nonfiction: sports, music, and pop culture); **Amy Hughes** (nonfiction in the areas of history, cultural studies, memoir, current events,

wellness, health, food, pop culture, and biography; also literary fiction); **Eleanor Jackson** (literary, commercial, memoir, art, food, science and history); **Julia Kenny** (fiction—adult, middle grade and YA—and is especially interested in dark, literary thrillers and suspense); **Edward Necarsulmer IV** (strong new voices in teen and middle grade, as well as picture books).

REPRESENTS nonfiction books, novels, juvenile. **Considers these nonfiction areas:** art, biography, creative nonfiction, cultural interests, current affairs, foods, health, history, memoirs, music, popular culture, psychology, science, sociology, sports. **Considers these fiction areas:** commercial, literary, mainstream, middle grade, mystery, picture books, thriller, young adult.

HOW TO CONTACT Query via snail mail with SASE, or by e-mail. No attachments. Responds if interested.

RECENT SALES A full list of agency clients is on the website.

◑ DYSTEL & GODERICH LITERARY MANAGEMENT

1 Union Square W., Suite 904, New York NY 10003. (212)627-9100. **Fax:** (212)627-9313. **Website:** www.dystel.com. Estab. 1994. Member of AAR. Other membership includes SCBWI. Represents 600+ clients.

MEMBER AGENTS Jane Dystel; Miriam Goderich, miriam@dystel.com (literary and commercial fiction as well as some genre fiction, narrative nonfiction, pop culture, psychology, history, science, art, business books, and biography/memoir); **Stacey Kendall Glick**, sglick@dystel.com (narrative nonfiction including memoir, parenting, cooking and food, psychology, science, health and wellness, lifestyle, current events, pop culture, YA, middle grade, and select adult contemporary fiction); **Michael Bourret**, mbourret@dystel.com (middle grade and young adult fiction, commercial adult fiction, and all sorts of nonfiction, from practical to narrative; he's especially interested in food and cocktail related books, memoir, popular history, politics, religion [though not spirituality], popular science, and current events); **Jim McCarthy**, jmccarthy@dystel.com (literary women's fiction, underrepresented voices, mysteries, romance, paranormal fiction, narrative nonfiction, memoir, and paranormal nonfiction); **Jessica Papin**, jpapin@dystel.com (literary and smart commercial fiction, narrative nonfiction, history with a thesis, medicine, science and

NEW AGENT SPOTLIGHT

LINDA CAMACHO
PROSPECT AGENCY

Prospectagency.com

@lindarandom

ABOUT LINDA: Linda joined Prospect Agency after nearly a decade in publishing. After graduating from Cornell University, Linda interned at Simon & Schuster and Writers House literary agency, and worked at Penguin before happily settling into children's marketing at Random House. She has an MFA in creative writing from the Vermont College of Fine Arts.

SHE IS SEEKING: She enjoys a variety of categories and genres, ranging from clean and lighthearted to edgy and dark. She is currently seeking: Adult, middle grade, and young adult fiction across many genres (romance, horror, fantasy, realistic, light sci-fi, and graphic novels); diversity of all types (ethnicity, disability, sexuality, etc.). Linda is not seeking early readers/chapter books, screenplays, poetry, and short stories.

HOW TO SUBMIT: Linda is currently accepting queries through Prospect Agency's Submissions page (see the website). Please include three chapters and a brief synopsis. Do not query by e-mail or postal mail, and do not submit unsolicited manuscripts or inquire about the status of submissions via e-mail.

religion, health, psychology, women's issues); **Lauren E. Abramo**, labramo@dystel.com (smart commercial fiction and well-paced literary fiction with a unique voice, including middle grade, YA, and adult and a wide variety of narrative nonfiction including science, interdisciplinary cultural studies, pop culture, psychology, reportage, media, contemporary culture, and history); **John Rudolph**, jrudolph@dystel.com (picture book author/illustrators, middle grade, YA, commercial fiction for men, nonfiction); **Rachel Stout**, rstout@dystel.com (literary fiction, narrative nonfiction, and believable and thought-provoking YA as well as magical realism); **Sharon Pelletier**, spelletier@dystel.com (witty literary fiction and smart commercial fiction featuring female characters, narrative nonfiction).

REPRESENTS nonfiction books, novels, cookbooks. **Considers these nonfiction areas:** animals, anthropology, archeology, autobiography, biography, business, child guidance, cultural interests, current affairs, economics, ethnic, gay/lesbian, health, history, humor, inspirational, investigative, medicine, metaphysics, military, New Age, parenting, popular culture, psychology, religious, science, technology, true crime, women's issues, women's studies. **Considers these fiction areas:** action, adventure, commercial, crime, detective, ethnic, family saga, gay, lesbian, literary, mainstream, middle grade, mystery, picture books, police, suspense, thriller, women's, young adult.

8—π "We are actively seeking fiction for all ages, in all genres." No plays, screenplays, or poetry.

HOW TO CONTACT Query via e-mail and put "Query" in the subject line. "Synopses, outlines, or sample chapters (say, one chapter or the first 25 pages of your ms) should either be included below the cover letter or attached as a separate document. We won't open attachments if they come with a blank e-mail." Accepts simultaneous submissions. Responds in 6 to 8 weeks to queries; within 8 weeks to mss. Obtains most new clients through recommendations from others, solicitations, conferences.

TERMS Agent receives 15% commission on domestic sales. Agent receives 19% commission on foreign sales. Offers written contract.

WRITERS CONFERENCES Backspace Writers' Conference; Pacific Northwest Writers' Association; Pike's Peak Writers' Conference; Writers League of Texas; Love Is Murder; Surrey International Writers Conference; Society of Children's Book Writers and Illustrators; International Thriller Writers; Willamette Writers Conference; The South Carolina Writers Workshop Conference; Las Vegas Writers Conference; Writer's Digest; Seton Hill Popular Fiction; Romance Writers of America; Geneva Writers Conference.

TIPS "DGLM prides itself on being a full-service agency. We're involved in every stage of the publishing process, from offering substantial editing on mss and proposals, to coming up with book ideas for authors looking for their next project, negotiating contracts and collecting monies for our clients. We follow a book from its inception through its sale to a publisher, its publication, and beyond. Our commitment to our writers does not, by any means, end when we have collected our commission. This is one of the many things that makes us unique in a very competitive business."

O EAST/WEST LITERARY AGENCY, LLC

1158 26th St., Suite 462, Santa Monica CA 90403. (310)573-9303. **Fax:** (310)453-9008. **E-mail:** dwarren@eastwestliteraryagency.com. **Contact:** Deborah Warren. Estab. 2000. Currently handles: juvenile books 90%, adult books 10%.

MEMBER AGENTS Deborah Warren, founder.

REPRESENTS Considers these fiction areas: middle grade, picture books, young adult.

HOW TO CONTACT By referral only. Submit proposal and first 3 sample chapters, table of contents (2 pages or fewer), synopsis (1 page). For picture books, submit entire ms. Requested submissions should be sent by mail as a Word document in Courier, 12-pt., double-spaced with 1.20-inch margin on left, ragged right text, 25 lines per page, continuously paginated, with all your contact info on the first page. Only responds if interested, no need for SASE. Responds in 60 days. Obtains new clients through recommendations from others.

TERMS Agent receives 15% commission on domestic sales. Agent receives 25% commission on foreign sales. Offers written contract; 30-day notice must be given to terminate contract. Charges for out-of-pocket expenses, such as postage and copying.

EDEN STREET LITERARY

P.O. Box 30, Billings NY 12510. **E-mail:** info@edenstreetlit.com. **E-mail:** submissions@edenstreetlit.com. **Website:** www.edenstreetlit.com. **Contact:** Liza Voges.

REPRESENTS Considers these fiction areas: juvenile, middle grade, picture books, young adult.

HOW TO CONTACT Send an e-mail (to submissions@edenstreetlit.com) with a picture book ms or dummy; a synopsis and 3 chapters of a middle grade or YA novel; or a proposal and 3 sample chapters for nonfiction. Responds only to submissions of interest.

RECENT SALES Recent Titles: *Dream Dog*, by Lou Berger; *Biscuit Loves the Library*, by Alyssa Capucilli; *The Scraps Book*, by Lois Ehlert; *Two Bunny Buddies*, by Kathryn O. Galbraith; *Between Two Worlds*, by Katherine Kirkpatrick.

EDUCATIONAL DESIGN SERVICES LLC

5750 Bou Ave, Suite 1508, N. Bethesda MD 20852. **E-mail:** blinder@educationaldesignservices.com. **Website:** www.educationaldesignservices.com. **Contact:** B. Linder. Estab. 1981. 80% of clients are new/unpublished writers.

8—π "We specialize in educational materials to be used in classrooms (in class sets), for staff development or in teacher education classes." Actively seeking educational, text materials. Not looking for picture books, story books, fiction; no illustrators.

HOW TO CONTACT Query by e-mail or with SASE or send outline and 1 sample chapter. Considers simultaneous queries and submissions if so indicated.

NEW AGENT SPOTLIGHT

ALEC SHANE
WRITERS HOUSE

Writershouse.com

@alecdshane

ABOUT ALEC: Alec majored in English at Brown University, a degree he put to immediate use by moving to Los Angeles after graduation to become a professional stunt man. Realizing that he prefers books to breakaway glass, he moved to New York City in 2008 to pursue a career in publishing. Alec quickly found a home at Writers House Literary Agency, where he worked under Jodi Reamer and Amy Berkower on a large number of YA and adult titles.

HE IS SEEKING: In the kidlit realm, he is looking for books geared toward young male readers (both YA and middle grade).

SUBMISSION GUIDELINES: Send the first 10 pages of your manuscript, along with your query letter, to ashane@writershouse.com with "Query for Alec Shane: TITLE" as your subject heading—no attachments.

Returns material only with SASE. Responds in 6-8 weeks to queries/mss. Obtains clients through recommendations from others, queries/solicitations, or through conferences.

TERMS Agent receives 15% commission on domestic sales; 25% on foreign sales. Offers written contract, binding until any party opts out. Terminate contract through certified letter.

RECENT SALES *How to Solve Word Problems in Mathematics*, by Wayne (McGraw-Hill*); Preparing for the* 8th *Grade Test in Social Studies*, by Farran-Paci (Amsco); *Minority Report*, by Gunn-Singh (Scarecrow Education); *No Parent Left Behind,* by Petrosino & Spiegel (Rowman & Littlefield*); Teaching Test-taking Skills* (R&L Education); *10 Languages You'll Need Most in the Classroom,* by Sundem, Krieger, Pickiewicz (Corwin Press*); Kids, Classrooms & Capital Hill,*

by Flynn (R&L Education); *Bully Nation*, by Susan Eva Porter (Paragon House).

ETHAN ELLENBERG LITERARY AGENCY

155 Suffolk St., No. 2R, New York NY 10002. (212)431-4554. **E-mail:** agent@ethanellenberg.com. **Website:** http://ethanellenberg.com. **Contact:** Ethan Ellenberg. Estab. 1984.

Prior to opening his agency, Mr. Ellenberg was contracts manager of Berkley/Jove and associate contracts manager for Bantam.

MEMBER AGENTS Evan Gregory, senior agent; **Bibi Lewis**, associate agent.

"We specialize in commercial fiction and children's books. In commercial fiction we want to see science fiction, fantasy, romance, mystery, thriller, women's fiction; all genres welcome. In children's books, we want to see everything:

picture books, early reader, middle grade and young adult.We do some nonfiction: history, biography, military, popular science, and cutting edge books about any subject. Does not want to receive poetry, short stories, or screenplays.

HOW TO CONTACT Query by e-mail. Paste the query, synopsis and first 50 pages (or 3 chapters) into the e-mail. For nonfiction, paste the proposal. For picture books, paste the entire text. Accepts simultaneous submissions. Responds in 2 weeks to queries (no attachments); 4-6 weeks to mss.

TERMS Agent receives 15% commission on domestic sales. Agent receives 10% commission on foreign sales. Offers written contract. Charges clients (with their consent) for direct expenses limited to photocopying and postage.

WRITERS CONFERENCES RWA National Conference; Novelists, Inc.; and other regional conferences.

⊘ THE ELAINE P. ENGLISH LITERARY AGENCY

4710 41st St. NW, Suite D, Washington DC 20016. (202)362-5190. **Fax:** (202)362-5192. **Website:** www.elaineenglish.com/. **Contact:** Elaine English. Member of AAR.

○　Ms. English has been working in publishing for more than 20 years. She is also an attorney specializing in media and publishing law.

MEMBER AGENTS Elaine English (novels).

REPRESENTS novels. **Considers these fiction areas:** historical, multicultural, mystery, suspense, thriller, women's, romance (single title, historical, contemporary, romantic, suspense, chick lit, erotic), general women's fiction. The agency is slowly but steadily acquiring in all mentioned areas.

⚷ Actively seeking women's fiction, including single-title romances. Does not want to receive any science fiction, time travel, or picture books.

HOW TO CONTACT Not accepting queries as of 2015. Keep checking the website for further information and updates. Responds in 4-8 weeks to queries; 3 months to requested submissions. Obtains most new clients through recommendations from others, conferences, submissions.

TERMS Agent receives 15% commission on domestic sales. Agent receives 20% commission on foreign sales. Offers written contract; 30-day notice must be given to terminate contract. Charges only for shipping expenses; generally taken from proceeds.

RECENT SALES Have been to Sourcebooks, Tor, Harlequin.

WRITERS CONFERENCES RWA National Conference; Novelists, Inc.; Malice Domestic; Washington Romance Writers Retreat, among others.

FINEPRINT LITERARY MANAGEMENT

115 W. 29th, 3rd Floor, New York NY 10001. (212)279-1282. **Website:** www.fineprintlit.com. Member of AAR.

MEMBER AGENTS Peter Rubie, CEO, peter@fineprintlit.com (nonfiction interests include narrative nonfiction, popular science, spirituality, history, biography, pop culture, business, technology, parenting, health, self help, music, and food; fiction interests include literate thrillers, crime fiction, science fiction and fantasy, military fiction and literary fiction, middle grade and YA fiction and nonfiction for boys); Stephany Evans, stephany@fineprintlit.com (nonfiction: health and wellness, especially women's health; spirituality, environment/sustainability, food and wine, memoir, and narrative nonfiction; fiction interests include stories with a strong and interesting female protagonist, both literary and upmarket commercial/book club fiction, romance [all subgenres], mysteries); Janet Reid (crime fiction and narrative nonfiction); Laura Wood, laura@fineprintlit.com (serious nonfiction, especially in the areas of science and nature, along with substantial titles in business, history, religion, and other areas by academics, experienced professionals, and journalists); June Clark (see juneclark.com).

REPRESENTS Considers these nonfiction areas: biography, business, creative nonfiction, foods, health, history, humor, law, memoirs, music, parenting, popular culture, science, self-help, spirituality, technology. **Considers these fiction areas:** commercial, crime, fantasy, middle grade, military, mystery, romance, science fiction, suspense, thriller, women's, young adult.

HOW TO CONTACT E-query. For fiction, send a query, synopsis, bio, and 30 pages pasted into the e-mail. No attachments. For nonfiction, send a query only; proposal requested later if the agent is interested. Obtains most new clients through recommendations from others, solicitations.

BRENT TAYLOR
TRIADA US

Triadaus.com

@naughtybrent

ABOUT BRENT: Prior to joining TriadaUS Literary Agency, Inc., he completed numerous internships in publishing, most recently at The Bent Agency. Find Brent on Twitter.

HE IS SEEKING: "My tastes are eclectic, but all of my favorite novels are similar in that they have big commercial hooks and fantastic writing. I am seeking smart, fun, and exciting books for readers of middle grade, young adult, new adult, and select mystery/crime and women's fiction. For middle grade: I am on the hunt for a humorous, intelligent fantasy; a scare-the-pants-off-me ghost or haunting story; fast-paced literary writing similar in style to Jerry Spinelli and Cynthia Lord. I have soft spots for larger-than-life characters and atmospheric setting (creepy and/or quirky). For young adult: I'm always looking for genre-bending books that can be an exciting puzzlement when thinking about how precisely to market; specifically mystery and crime for teens, the grittier the better; high-concept contemporary stories with addicting romantic tension. I'm a sucker for themes of finding your place in the world, new beginnings, and summer-before-college stories."

HOW TO SUBMIT: Send your query letter and first 10 pages pasted in the body of the message to brent@triadaus.com.

TERMS Agent receives 15% commission on domestic sales. Agent receives 20% commission on foreign sales.

FLANNERY LITERARY

1140 Wickfield Ct., Naperville IL 60563. (630)428-2682. **E-mail:** jennifer@flanneryliterary.com. **Contact:** Jennifer Flannery. Represents 40 clients. 50% of clients are new/unpublished writers. Currently handles: juvenile books 100%.
REPRESENTS Considers these fiction areas: juvenile, middle grade, young adult.

This agency specializes in children's and young adult fiction and nonfiction. It also accepts picture books. 100% juvenile books.

HOW TO CONTACT Query by mail with SASE. "Multiple queries are fine, but please inform us. Mail that requires a signature will be returned to sender, as we are not always available to sign for mail." Responds in 2 weeks to queries; 1 month to mss. Obtains new clients through referrals and queries.

TERMS Agent receives 15% commission on domestic sales. Agent receives 20% commission on foreign sales. Offers written contract, binding for life of book in print.

TIPS "Write an engrossing, succinct query describing your work. We are always looking for a fresh new voice."

FOLIO LITERARY MANAGEMENT, LLC

The Film Center Building, 630 Ninth Ave., Suite 1101, New York NY 10036. (212)400-1494. **Fax:** (212)967-0977. **Website:** www.foliolit.com. Member of AAR. Represents 100+ clients.

Prior to creating Folio Literary Management, Mr. Hoffman worked for several years at another agency; Mr. Kleinman was an agent at Graybill & English.

MEMBER AGENTS Claudia Cross, Scott Hoffman, Jeff Kleinman, Frank Weimann, Michelle Brower, Michael Harriot, Erin Harris, Molly Jaffa, Katherine Latshaw, Erin Niumata, Ruth Pomerance, Marcy Posner, Jeff Silberman, Michael Sterling, Steve Troha, Emily van Beek, Melissa Sarver White; John Cusick.

REPRESENTS nonfiction books, novels, short story collections. **Considers these nonfiction areas:** animals, art, biography, business, child guidance, cooking, creative nonfiction, economics, environment, foods, health, history, how-to, humor, inspirational, memoirs, military, parenting, popular culture, politics, psychology, religious, satire, science, self-help, technology, war, women's issues, women's studies. **Considers these fiction areas:** commercial, erotica, fantasy, horror, literary, middle grade, mystery, picture books, religious, romance, thriller, women's, young adult.

No poetry, stage plays, or screenplays.

HOW TO CONTACT Query via e-mail only (no attachments). Read agent bios online for specific submission guidelines and e-mail addresses.

TIPS "Please do not submit simultaneously to more than one agent at Folio. If you're not sure which of us is exactly right for your book, don't worry. We work closely as a team, and if one of our agents gets a query that might be more appropriate for someone else, we'll always pass it along. It's important that you check each agent's bio page for clear directions as to how to submit, as well as when to expect feedback."

FOUNDRY LITERARY + MEDIA

33 West 17th St., PH, New York NY 10011. (212)929-5064. **Fax:** (212)929-5471. **Website:** www.foundrymedia.com.

MEMBER AGENTS Peter McGuigan, pmsubmissions@foundrymedia.com; Yfat Reiss Gendell, yrgsubmissions@foundrymedia.com (practical nonfiction projects in the areas of health and wellness, diet, lifestyle, how-to, and parenting and a broad range of narrative nonfiction that includes humor, memoir, history, science, pop culture, psychology, and adventure/travel stories); Mollie Glick, mgsubmissions@foundrymedia.com (literary fiction, young adult fiction, narrative nonfiction, and a bit of practical nonfiction in the areas of popular science, medicine, psychology, cultural history, memoir, and current events); Chris Park, cpsubmissions@foundrymedia.com (memoirs, narrative nonfiction, sports books, Christian nonfiction and character-driven fiction); Hannah Brown Gordon, hbgsubmissions@foundrymedia.com (stories and narratives that blend genres, including thriller, suspense, historical, literary, speculative, memoir, pop-science, psychology, humor, and pop culture); Brandi Bowles, bbsubmissions@foundrymedia.com (literary and commercial fiction, especially high-concept novels that feature strong female bonds and psychological or scientific themes); Kirsten Neuhaus, knsubmissions@foundrymedia.com (platform-driven narrative nonfiction, in the areas of lifestyle (beauty/fashion/relationships), memoir, business, current events, history and stories with strong female voices, as well as smart, upmarket, and commercial fiction); Jessica Regel, jrsubmissions@foundrymedia.com (young adult and middle grade books, as well as a select list of adult general fiction, women's fiction, and adult nonfiction); Anthony Mattero, amsubmissions@foundrymedia.com (smart, platform-driven, nonfiction particularly in the genres of pop-culture, humor, music, sports, and pop-business); Matt Wise, mwsubmissions@foundrymedia.com (a wide array of projects, from controversial narrative nonfiction to literary fiction to art and design projects); Peter Steinberg, pssubmissions@foundrymedia.com (narrative nonfiction, commercial and literary fiction, memoir, health, history, lifestyle, humor, sports and young adult); Roger Freet, rfsubmis

NEW AGENT SPOTLIGHT

LANA POPOVIC
CHALBERG & SUSSMAN

Chalbergsussman.com

@LanaPopovicLit

ABOUT LANA: Lana holds a B.A. with honors from Yale University, a J.D. from the Boston University School of Law, where she focused on intellectual property, and an M.A. with highest honors from the Emerson College Publishing and Writing program. Prior to joining Chalberg & Sussman, Lana worked at Zachary Shuster Harmsworth, where she built a list of young adult and adult literary authors while managing foreign rights for the agency.

SHE IS SEEKING: In the kidlit realms of young adult and middle grade fiction: contemporary/realistic, mysteries, thrillers, fantasy, historical, horror, sci-fi.

HOW TO CONTACT: E-query lana@chalbergsussman.com with the first 10 pages of the ms included in the body of the e-mail.

sions@foundrymedia.com (narrative and idea-driven nonfiction clients in the areas of religion, spirituality, memoir, and cultural issues by leading scholars, pastors, historians, activists and musicians).
REPRESENTS Considers these nonfiction areas: creative nonfiction, current affairs, diet/nutrition, health, history, how-to, humor, medicine, memoirs, music, parenting, popular culture, psychology, science, sports, travel. **Considers these fiction areas:** commercial, historical, humor, literary, middle grade, suspense, thriller, women's, young adult.
HOW TO CONTACT Target one agent only. Send queries to the specific submission e-mail of the agent. For fiction: send query, synopsis, author bio, first three chapters—all pasted in the e-mail. For nonfiction, send query, sample chapters, table of contents, author bio (all pasted).
RECENT SALES *Tell the Wolves I'm Home*, by Carol Rifka Blunt; *The Rathbones*, by Janice Clark; *This is Your Captain Speaking*, by Jon Methven; *The War Against the Assholes* and *The November Criminals*, by Sam Munson; *Ready Player One*, by Ernest Cline.

TIPS "Consult website for each agent's submission instructions."

◐ FULL CIRCLE LITERARY, LLC

7676 Hazard Center Dr., Suite 500, San Diego CA 92108. **E-mail:** submissions@fullcircleliterary.com. **Website:** www.fullcircleliterary.com. **Contact:** Stefanie Von Borstel. Member of AAR. Represents 55 clients. 60% of clients are new/unpublished writers.
MEMBER AGENTS Lilly Ghahremani; Stefanie Von Borstel; Adriana Dominguez; Taylor Martindale (multicultural voices, young adult fiction).
REPRESENTS nonfiction books, juvenile. **Considers these nonfiction areas:** creative nonfiction, design, how-to, popular culture, women's issues. **Considers these fiction areas:** literary, middle grade, picture books, women's, young adult.
✎☛ "Our full-service boutique agency, representing a range of nonfiction and children's books (limited fiction), provides a one-stop resource for authors. Our extensive experience in the realms of law and marketing provide Full

Circle clients with a unique edge." Actively seeking nonfiction by authors with a unique and strong platform, projects that offer new and diverse viewpoints, and literature with a global or multicultural perspective. We are particularly interested in books with a Latino or Middle Eastern angle and books related to pop culture.

HOW TO CONTACT Agency accepts e-queries. Put "Query for [Agent]" in the subject line. Send a 1-page query letter (in the body of the e-mail) including a description of your book, writing credentials and author highlights. Following your query, please include the first 10 pages or complete picture book manuscript text within the body of the e-mail. For nonfiction, include a proposal with one sample chapter. Accepts simultaneous submissions. Obtains most new clients through recommendations from others, solicitations, conferences.

TERMS Agent receives 15% commission on domestic sales. Agent receives 20% commission on foreign sales. Offers written contract; up to 30-day notice must be given to terminate contract. Charges for copying and postage.

TIPS "Put your best foot forward. Contact us when you simply can't make your project any better on your own, and please be sure your work fits with what the agent you're approaching represents. Little things count, so copyedit your work. Join a writing group and attend conferences to get objective and constructive feedback before submitting. Be active about building your platform as an author before, during, and after publication. Remember this is a business and your agent is a business partner."

⊕ FUSE LITERARY

Website: www.fuseliterary.com.
MEMBER AGENTS Laurie McLean (only accepting referral inquiries and submissions from writers she meets at conferences); **Gordon Warnock**, query gordon@fuseliterary.com (high-concept commercial fiction, literary fiction, new adult, contemporary YA, graphic novels, memoir, cookbooks and food, politics, current events, pop science, pop culture, self-help, how-to, humor, pets, business, career); **Connor Goldsmith**, queryconnor@fuseliterary.com (in fiction: sci-fi/fantasy/horror, thrillers, upmarket commercial Fiction, and literary fiction with a unique and memorable hook; he is especially interested in

books by and about people from marginalized perspectives, such as LGBT people and/or racial minorities; in nonfiction: history [particularly of the ancient world], theater, cinema, music, television, mass media, popular culture, feminism and gender studies, LGBT issues, race relations, and the sex industry); **Sara Sciuto**, querysara@fuseliterary.com (middle grade, young adult, standout picture books); **Michelle Richter**, querymichelle@fuseliterary.com (primarily seeking fiction, specifically book club reads, literary fiction, and well-crafted women's commercial fiction, thrillers and mysteries [amateur sleuth, police procedurals and smart cozies]); **Jen Karsbeak** (women's fiction, upmarket commercial fiction, historical fiction, and literary fiction); **Emily S. Keyes**, queryemily@fuseliterary.com (young adult, middle grade, and also a select list of commercial fiction which includes fantasy & science fiction, women's fiction, new adult fiction, along with pop culture and humor titles); **Jennifer Chen Tran**, queryjennifer@fuseliterary.com (literary, commercial, women's, upmarket, contemporary romance, mature young adult, new adult, suspense/thriller and select graphic novels [adult, YA or MG]; "As a second-generation Taiwanese-American, I am particularly interested in voices from underrepresented and marginalized communities, strong and conflicted female characters, war and post-war fiction, and writers who are adept at creating a developed sense of place"; nonfiction areas of interest include memoir [but writers must have a sizable platform], narrative nonfiction in the areas of adventure, biography, business, current affairs, medical, history, how-to, pop-culture, psychology, social entrepreneurism, social justice, and travel).

HOW TO CONTACT E-query an individual agent. Check the website to see if any individual agent has closed themselves to submissions, as well as each agent's individual submission preferences.

WRITERS Conferences Agents from this agency attend many conferences. A full list of their appearances is available on the agency website.

◎ NANCY GALLT LITERARY AGENCY

273 Charlton Ave., South Orange NJ 07079. (973)761-6358. **Website:** www.nancygallt.com. **Contact:** Nancy Gallt, Marietta Zacker. Represents 40 clients. 30% of clients are new/unpublished writers.

NEW AGENT SPOTLIGHT

ALEXANDER SLATER
TRIDENT MEDIA GROUP

Tridentmediagroup.com

@abuckslater

ABOUT ALEXANDER: Alexander graduated from the University of Connecticut in 2007. He began his career in publishing that year with the Maria Carvainis Agency, first as an intern, and then as an assistant. He has been with Trident Media Group since 2010, where he started as the assistant to both agents Kimberly Whalen and Scott Miller. Moving on from there, he spent two years representing the entire agency's children's, middle grade, and young adult titles in the foreign market, attending books fairs in Bologna, London, and Frankfurt.

HE IS SEEKING: Alexander is interested in children's, middle grade, and young adult fiction and nonfiction, from new and established authors. He particularly loves authors like Frank Portman, Jim Shepard, Jenny Han, and Rainbow Rowell.

HOW TO SUBMIT: Send a query letter, pasted in the body of the email, to aslater@ TridentMediaGroup.com. Your query should include only a paragraph about yourself, a brief plot pitch, and your contact information. Please do not send a manuscript or proposal until you have been requested to do so.

Prior to opening her agency, Ms. Gallt was subsidiary rights director of the children's book division at Morrow, Harper and Viking.

MEMBER AGENTS Nancy Gallt; Marietta Zacker.

REPRESENTS juvenile. **Considers these fiction areas:** juvenile, middle grade, picture books, young adult.

"We only handle children's books." Actively seeking picture books, middle grade, and young adult novels.

HOW TO CONTACT Submit through online submission for on agency website. No e-mail queries, please. Accepts simultaneous submissions. Obtains new clients through recommendations from others.

TERMS Agent receives 15% commission on domestic sales. Agent receives 20% commission on foreign sales. Offers written contract; 30-day notice must be given to terminate contract.

RECENT SALES *Toya*, by Randi Revill; Rick Riordan's Books (Hyperion); *Something Extraordinary* by Ben Clanton (Simon & Schuster); *The Baby Tree* by Sophie Blackall (Nancy Paulsen Books/Penguin); *Fenway And Hattie* by Victoria J Coe (Putnam/Penguin); *The Meaning Of Maggie* by Megan Jean Sovern (Chronicle); *The Misadventures Of The Family Fletcher* by Dana Alison Levy (Random House); *Abrakapow!* by Isaiah Campbell (Simon & Schuster); *Subway Love* by Nora Raleigh Baskin (Candlewick).

TIPS "Writing and illustrations stand on their own, so submissions should tell the most compelling stories possible—whether visually, in words, or both."

GELFMAN SCHNEIDER/ICM PARTNERS

850 7th Ave., Suite 903, New York NY 10019. (212)245-1993. **Fax:** (212)245-8678. **E-mail:** mail@gelfman schneider.com. **Website:** www.gelfmanschneider.com. **Contact:** Jane Gelfman, Deborah Schneider. Member of AAR. Represents 300+ clients. 10% of clients are new/unpublished writers.

MEMBER AGENTS Deborah Schneider, Jane Gelfman, Victoria Marini, Heather Mitchell.

REPRESENTS fiction and nonfiction books. **Considers these nonfiction areas:** creative nonfiction, popular culture. **Considers these fiction areas:** historical, literary, mainstream, middle grade, mystery, science fiction, suspense, westerns, women's, young adult.

�—➤ Does not want to receive romance or illustrated children's books.

HOW TO CONTACT Query. Send queries via snail mail only. No unsolicited mss. Please send a query letter, a synopsis, and a sample chapter only. Consult website for each agent's submission requirements. Note that Ms. Marini is the only agent at this agency who accepts e-queries: victoria.gsliterary@gmail.com. If querying Marini, put "Query" in the subject line and paste all materials (query, 1-3 sample chapters) in the body of the e-mail. Responds in 1 month to queries. Responds in 2 months to mss.

TERMS Agent receives 15% commission on domestic sales. Agent receives 20% commission on foreign sales. Agent receives 15% commission on film sales. Offers written contract. Charges clients for photocopying and messengers/couriers.

BARRY GOLDBLATT LITERARY LLC

320 Seventh Ave. #266, Brooklyn NY 11215. (718)832-8787. **E-mail:** query@bgliterary.com. **Website:** www.bgliterary.com/. **Contact:** Barry Goldblatt. Estab. 2000.

MEMBER AGENTS Barry Goldblatt.

REPRESENTS Considers these fiction areas: middle grade, young adult.

�—➤ "Please see our website for specific submission guidelines and information on our particular tastes."

HOW TO CONTACT "E-mail queries can be sent to query@bgliterary.com and should include the word

'query' in the subject line. Please know that we will read and respond to every e-query that we receive, provided it is properly addressed and follows the submission guidelines below. We will not respond to e-queries that are addressed to no one, or to multiple recipients. While we do not require exclusivity, exclusive submissions will receive priority review. If your submission is exclusive to Barry Goldblatt Literary, please indicate so by including the word 'Exclusive' in the subject line of your e-mail. Your e-query should include the following within the body of the e-mail: your query letter, a synopsis of the book, and the first 5 pages of your ms. We will not open or respond to any e-mails that have attachments." Obtains clients through referrals, queries, and conferences.

TERMS Agent receives 15% commission on domestic sales; 20% on foreign and dramatic sales. Offers written contract. 60 days notice must be given to terminate contract.

RECENT SALES *Read Between the Lines*, by Jo Knowles; *Bright Before Sunrise*, by Tiffany Schmidt; *The Infamous Ratsos*, by Kara LaReau; *Wonders of the Invisible World*, by Christopher Barzak.

TIPS "We're a hands-on agency, focused on building an author's career, not just making an initial sale. We don't care about trends or what's hot; we just want to sign great writers."

IRENE GOODMAN LITERARY AGENCY

27 W. 24th St., Suite 700B, New York NY 10010. **Website:** www.irenegoodman.com. Member of AAR.

MEMBER AGENTS Irene Goodman (her fiction list includes upmarket women's fiction, middle grade, young adult, thrillers, historical fiction, and mysteries; her nonfiction list includes pop culture, science, Francophilia, and lifestyle); Beth Vesel (narrative nonfiction, cultural criticism, psychology, science and memoir; Miriam Kriss (commercial fiction and she represents everything from hardcover historical mysteries to all subgenres of romance, from young adult fiction to kick ass urban fantasies, and everything in between); Barbara Poelle (thrillers, literary suspense, young adult and upmarket fiction); Rachel Ekstrom (young adult, women's fiction, new adult, mysteries, thrillers, romance, and the occasional quirky work of nonfiction).

REPRESENTS nonfiction, novels. **Considers these nonfiction areas:** narrative nonfiction dealing with social, cultural and historical issues; an occasional

NEW AGENT SPOTLIGHT

LEON HUSOCK
L. PERKINS AGENCY

Lperkinsagency.com

@leonhusock

ABOUT LEON: Prior to joining the L. Perkins Agency, Leon was an associate agent at Anderson Literary Management. He has a BA in Literature from Bard College and attended the Columbia Publishing Course.

HE IS SEEKING: He has a particular interest in science fiction & fantasy, young adult and middle grade novels filled with strong characters and original premises, but keeps an open mind for anything that catches his eye.

HOW TO CONTACT: E-query leon@lperkinsagency.com.

memoir and current affairs book, parenting, social issues, francophilia, anglophilia, Judaica, lifestyles, cooking, memoir. **Considers these fiction areas:** crime, detective, historical, mystery, romance, thriller, women's, young adult.

"Specializes in the finest in commercial fiction and nonfiction. We have a strong background in women's voices, including mysteries, romance, women's fiction, thrillers, suspense. Historical fiction is one of Irene's particular passions and Miriam is fanatical about modern urban fantasies. In nonfiction, Irene is looking for topics on narrative history, social issues and trends, education, Judaica, Francophilia, Anglophilia, other cultures, animals, food, crafts, and memoir." Barbara is looking for commercial thrillers with strong female protagonists; Miriam is looking for urban fantasy and edgy sci-fi/young adult. No children's picture books, screenplays, poetry, or inspirational fiction.

HOW TO CONTACT Query. Submit synopsis, first 10 pages. E-mail queries only! See the website submission page. No e-mail attachments. Query one agent only. Responds in 2 months to queries. Consult website for each agent's submission guidelines.

RECENT SALES *The Ark*, by Boyd Morrison; *Isolation*, by C.J. Lyons; *The Sleepwalkers*, by Paul Grossman; *Dead Man's Moon*, by Devon Monk; *Becoming Marie Antoinette*, by Juliet Grey; *What's Up Down There*, by Lissa Rankin; *Beg for Mercy*, by Toni Andrews; *The Devil Inside*, by Jenna Black.

TIPS "We are receiving an unprecedented amount of e-mail queries. If you find that the mailbox is full, please try again in two weeks. E-mail queries to our personal addresses will not be answered. E-mails to our personal inboxes will be deleted."

Ⓘ DOUG GRAD LITERARY AGENCY, INC.
68 Jay Street, Suite N3, Brooklyn NY 11201. (718)788-6067. **E-mail:** doug.grad@dgliterary.com. **E-mail:** query@dgliterary.com. **Website:** www.dgliterary.com. **Contact:** Doug Grad. Estab. 2008.

Prior to being an agent, Doug Grad spent the last 22 years as an editor at 4 major publishing houses.

MEMBER AGENTS Doug Grad (narrative nonfiction, military, sports, celebrity memoir, thrillers, mysteries, historical fiction, music, style, business, home improvement, cookbooks, self-help, science and theater).

REPRESENTS Considers these nonfiction areas: business, cooking, creative nonfiction, military, music, popular culture, science, self-help, sports, theater, travel. **Considers these fiction areas:** historical, mystery, science fiction, thriller, young adult.

HOW TO CONTACT Query by e-mail first at query@ dgliterary.com. No sample material unless requested; no printed submissions by mail.

RECENT SALES *The Earthend Saga*, by Gillian Anderson and Jeff Rovin (Simon451); *Abandoned In Hell: The Fight for Vietnam's Fire Base Kate,* by William Albracht and Marvin Wolf (Berkley/Caliber); *Bounty* by Michael Byrnes (Bantam); *Sports Idioms and Words* by Josh Chetwynd (Ten Speed Press).

○ SANFORD J. GREENBURGER ASSOCIATES, INC.

55 Fifth Ave., New York NY 10003. (212)206-5600. **Fax:** (212)463-8718. **Website:** www.greenburger.com. Member of AAR. Represents 500 clients.

MEMBER AGENTS Matt Bialer, LRibar@sjga.com (fantasy, science fiction, thrillers, and mysteries as well as a select group of literary writers, and also loves smart narrative nonfiction including books about current events, popular culture, biography, history, music, race, and sports); **Brenda Bowen,** queryBB@ sjga.com (literary fiction, writers and illustrators of picture books, chapter books, and middle grade and teen fiction); **Lisa Gallagher,** lgsubmissions@sjga. com (accessible literary fiction, quality commercial women's fiction, crime fiction, lively narrative nonfiction); **Faith Hamlin,** fhamlin@sjga.com (receives submissions by referral); **Heide Lange,** queryHL@ sjga.com; **Daniel Mandel,** querydm@sjga.com (literary and commercial fiction, as well as memoirs and nonfiction about business, art, history, politics, sports, and popular culture); **Courtney Miller-Callihan,** cmiller@sjga.com (YA, middle grade, women's fiction, romance, and historical novels, as well as nonfiction projects on unusual topics, humor, pop culture, and lifestyle books); **Nicholas Ellison,** nellison@sjga. com; **Chelsea Lindman,** clindman@sjga.com (playful literary fiction, upmarket crime fiction, and forward thinking or boundary-pushing nonfiction); **Rachael Dillon Fried,** rfried@sjga.com (both fiction and nonfiction authors, with a keen interest in unique literary voices, women's fiction, narrative nonfiction, mem-

oir, and comedy); **Lindsay Ribar,** co-agents with Matt Bailer (young adult and middle grade fiction); **Thomas Miller** (primarily nonfiction projects in the areas of wellness and health, popular culture, psychology and self-help, business, diet, spirituality, cooking, and narrative nonfiction).

REPRESENTS nonfiction books and novels. **Considers these nonfiction areas:** art, biography, business, creative nonfiction, current affairs, ethnic, history, humor, memoirs, music, popular culture, politics, sports. **Considers these fiction areas:** crime, fantasy, historical, literary, middle grade, mystery, picture books, romance, science fiction, thriller, women's, young adult.

⚪ No Westerns. No screenplays.

HOW TO CONTACT E-query. "Please look at each agent's profile page for current information about what each agent is looking for and for the correct e-mail address to use for queries to that agent. Please be sure to use the correct query e-mail address for each agent." Accepts simultaneous submissions. Responds in 2 months to queries and mss. Obtains most new clients through recommendations from others.

TERMS Agent receives 15% commission on domestic sales. Agent receives 20% commission on foreign sales. Charges for photocopying and books for foreign and subsidiary rights submissions.

RECENT SALES *Inferno*, by Dan Brown; *Hidden Order*, by Brad Thor; *The Chalice*, by Nancy Bilveau; *Horns*, by Joe Hill.

⚪⚪ THE GREENHOUSE LITERARY AGENCY

4035 Ridge Top Road, Suite 550, Fairfax VA 22030. **E-mail:** submissions@greenhouseliterary.com. **Website:** www.greenhouseliterary.com. Member of AAR. Other memberships include SCBWI. Represents 20 clients. 100% of clients are new/unpublished writers. Currently handles: juvenile books 100%.

⚪ Sarah Davies has had an editorial and management career in children's publishing spanning 25 years; for 5 years prior to launching the Greenhouse she was Publishing Director of Macmillan Children's Books in London, and publishing leading authors from both sides of the Atlantic.

MEMBER AGENTS Sarah Davies, vice president (middle grade and young adult); **Polly Nolan,** agent (fiction by UK, Irish, Commonwealth—including

Australia, NZ and India—authors, from picture books to young fiction series, through middle grade and young adult).

REPRESENTS juvenile. **Considers these fiction areas:** juvenile, middle grade, picture books, young adult.

⏺—🖝 "We exclusively represent authors writing fiction for children and teens. The agency has offices in both the US and UK, and Sarah Davies (who is British) personally represents authors to both markets. The agency's commission structure reflects this—taking 15% for sales to both US and UK, thus treating both as 'domestic' market.'" All genres of children's and YA fiction—ages 5+. Does not want to receive nonfiction, poetry, picture books (text or illustration) or work aimed at adults; short stories, educational or religious/inspirational work, pre-school/novelty material, or screenplays.

HOW TO CONTACT Query one agent only. Put the target agent's name in the subject line. Paste the first 5 pages of your story (or your complete picture book) after the query. Obtains most new clients through recommendations from others, solicitations, conferences.

TERMS Agent receives 15% commission on domestic sales. Agent receives 25% commission on foreign sales. Offers written contract. This agency occasionally charges for submission copies to film agents or foreign publishers.

RECENT SALES *Vengeance*, by Megan Miranda (Bloomsbury); *Fiendish*, by Brenna Yovanoff (Razorbill); *The Very Nearly Honorable League Of Pirates*, by Caroline Carlson (Harpercollins); *We All Looked Up*, by Tommy Wallach (Simon & Schuster); *Shutter* by Courtney Alameda (Feiwel/Macmillan); *Can't Look Away*, by Donna Cooner (Scholastic); *Moonpenny Island*, by Tricia Springstubb (Harpercollins); *The Chapel Wars*, by Lindsey Leavitt (Bloomsbury); *The Third Twin*, by C.J.Omololu (Delacorte).

WRITERS CONFERENCES Bologna Children's Book Fair, ALA and SCBWI conferences, BookExpo America.

TIPS "Before submitting material, authors should read the Greenhouse's 'Top 10 Tips for Authors of Children's Fiction' and carefully follow our submission guidelines which can be found on the website."

🔵 KATHRYN GREEN LITERARY AGENCY, LLC

250 West 57th St., Suite 2302, New York NY 10107. (212)245-4225. **Fax:** (212)245-4042. **E-mail:** query@kgreenagency.com. **Contact:** Kathy Green. Other memberships include Women's Media Group. Represents approximately 20 clients. 50% of clients are new/unpublished writers.

🗩 Prior to becoming an agent, Ms. Green was a book and magazine editor.

REPRESENTS **Considers these nonfiction areas:** autobiography, biography, business, child guidance, cooking, current affairs, diet/nutrition, economics, education, foods, history, how-to, humor, interior design, investigative, juvenile nonfiction, memoirs, parenting, popular culture, psychology, satire, self-help, sports, true crime, women's issues, women's studies, juvenile. **Considers these fiction areas:** crime, detective, family saga, historical, humor, juvenile, literary, mainstream, middle grade, mystery, police, romance, satire, suspense, thriller, women's, young adult.

⏺—🖝 Keeping the client list small means that writers receive my full attention throughout the process of getting their project published. Does not want to receive science fiction or fantasy.

HOW TO CONTACT Query to query@kgreenagency.com. Send no samples unless requested. Accepts simultaneous submissions. Responds in 1-2 months to mss. Obtains most new clients through recommendations from others, solicitations, conferences.

TERMS Agent receives 15% commission on domestic sales. Agent receives 20% commission on foreign sales.

🔵 JILL GRINBERG LITERARY AGENCY

392 Vanderbilt Ave., Brooklyn NY 11238. (212)620-5883. **Fax:** (212)627-4725. **E-mail:** info@jillgrinbergliterary.com. **Website:** www.jillgrinbergliterary.com. Estab. 1999.

🗩 Prior to her current position, Ms. Grinberg was at Anderson Grinberg Literary Management.

MEMBER AGENTS Jill Grinberg, jill@jillgrinbergliterary.com; Cheryl Pientka, cheryl@jillgrinbergliterary.com; **Katelyn Detweiler**, katelyn@jillgrinbergliterary.com.

REPRESENTS nonfiction books, novels. **Considers these nonfiction areas:** biography, cooking, ethnic, history, science, travel. **Considers these fiction areas:**

fantasy, juvenile, literary, mainstream, romance, science fiction, young adult.

HOW TO CONTACT Please send your query letter to info@jillgrinbergliterary.com and attach the first 50 pages (fiction) or proposal (nonfiction) as a Word doc file. All submissions will be read, but electronic mail is preferred.

RECENT SALES *Cinder*, Marissa Meyer; *The Hero's Guide to Saving Your Kingdom*, Christopher Healy; *Kiss and Make Up*, Katie Anderson; i, T.J. Stiles; *Eon* and *Eona*, Alison Goodman; *American Nations*, Colin Woodard; HALO Trilogy, Alexandra Adornetto; *Babymouse*, Jennifer & Matthew Holm; Uglies/Leviathan Trilogy, Scott Westerfeld; *Liar*, Justine Larbalestier; *Turtle in Paradise*, Jennifer Holm; *Wisdom's Kiss* and *Dairy Queen*, Catherine Gilbert Murdock.

TIPS "We prefer submissions by mail."

○ HEACOCK HILL LITERARY AGENCY, INC.

West Coast Office, 1020 Hollywood Way, #439, Burbank CA 91505. (818)951-6788. **E-mail:** agent@heacockhill.com. **Website:** www.heacockhill.com. **Contact:** Catt LeBaigue or Tom Dark. Estab. 2009. Member of AAR. Other memberships include SCBWI.

○ Prior to becoming an agent, Ms. LeBaigue spent 18 years with Sony Pictures and Warner Bros.

MEMBER AGENTS Tom Dark (adult fiction, nonfiction); Catt LeBaigue (juvenile fiction, adult nonfiction including arts, crafts, anthropology, astronomy, nature studies, ecology, body/mind/spirit, humanities, self-help).

REPRESENTS nonfiction, fiction. **Considers these nonfiction areas:** art, business, gardening, politics. **Considers these fiction areas:** juvenile, middle grade, picture books, young adult.

⌐ Not presently accepting new clients for adult fiction. Please check the website for updates.

HOW TO CONTACT E-mail queries only. No unsolicited manuscripts. No e-mail attachments. Responds in 1 week to queries. Obtains most new clients through recommendations from others, solicitations.

TERMS Offers written contract.

TIPS "Write an informative original e-query expressing your book idea, your qualifications, and short excerpts of the work. No unfinished work, please."

① HERMAN AGENCY

350 Central Park West, New York NY 10025. (212)749-4907. **E-mail:** Ronnie@hermanagencyinc.com. **Website:** www.hermanagencyinc.com. Estab. 1999.

MEMBER AGENTS Ronnie Ann Herman.

REPRESENTS children's. **Considers these fiction areas:** picture books by author/artists only, not looking for manuscripts or artists and middle grade fiction and nonfiction.

HOW TO CONTACT Submit via e-mail

TIPS "Check our website to see if you belong with our agency."

① HSG AGENCY

287 Spring St., New York NY 10013. **E-mail:** channigan@hsgagency.com; jsalky@hsgagency.com; jgetzler@hsgagency.com; dburby@hsgagency.com. **Website:** http://hsgagency.com. **Contact:** Carrie Hannigan; Jesseca Salky; Josh Getzler; Danielle Burby. Estab. 2011.

○ Prior to opening HSG Agency, Ms. Hannigan, Ms. Salky. and Mr. Getzler were agents at Russell & Volkening.

MEMBER AGENTS Carrie Hannigan, Jesseca Salky (literary and mainstream fiction), Josh Getzler (foreign and historical fiction; both women's fiction, straight ahead historical fiction, and thrillers and mysteries); Danielle Burby (YA, women's fiction, mysteries).

REPRESENTS **Considers these nonfiction areas:** business, creative nonfiction, current affairs, education, foods, memoirs, photography, politics, psychology, science. **Considers these fiction areas:** commercial, crime, historical, literary, middle grade, mystery, picture books, thriller, women's, young adult.

⌐ Ms. Hannigan is actively seeking both fiction and nonfiction children's books in the picture book and middle grade age range, as well as adult women's fiction and select photography projects that would appeal to a large audience. Ms. Salky is actively seeking literary and commercial fiction that appeals to women and men; "all types of nonfiction, with a particular interest in memoir and narrative nonfiction in the areas of science, pop-psychology, politics, current affairs, business, education, food, and any other topic that is the vehicle for a great story." Mr. Getzler is actively seeking adult historical and crime-related fiction (mystery, thriller), select nonfiction and YA projects (particularly those that fit within historical or crime fiction). He is also interested in smart women's fiction.

HOW TO CONTACT Electronic submissions only. Send query letter, first 5 pages of ms within e-mail to appropriate agent. Avoid submitting to multiple agents within the agency. Picture books: include entire ms. Responds in 4-6 weeks.

RECENT SALES *The Beginner's Goodbye,* by Anne Tyler (Knopf); *Blue Sea Burning,* by Geoff Rodkey (Putnam); *The Partner Track,* by Helen Wan (St. Martin's Press); *The Thrill of the Haunt,* by E.J. Copperman (Berkley) *Aces Wild,* by Erica Perl (Knopf Books for Young Readers); *Steve & Wessley: The Sea Monster,* by Jennifer Morris (Scholastic); *Infinite Worlds,* by Michael Soluri (Simon & Schuster).

⊕ INKLINGS LITERARY AGENCY

8363 Highgate Drive, Jacksonville FL 32216. (904)527-1686. **Fax:** (904)758-5440. **Website:** www.inklingsliterary.com. Estab. 2013.

MEMBER AGENTS Michelle Johnson, michelle@inklingsliterary.com (in fiction, contemporary, suspense, thriller, mystery, horror, fantasy—including paranormal and supernatural elements within those genres), romance of every level, nonfiction in the areas of memoir and true crime); **Dr. Jamie Bodnar Drowley**, jamie@inklingsliterary.com (new adult fiction in the areas of romance [all subgenres], fantasy [urban fantasy, light sci-fi, steampunk], mystery and thrillers—as well as young adult [all subgenres] and middle grade stories); **Margaret Bail**, margaret@inklingsliterary.com (romance, science fiction, mystery, thrillers, action adventure, historical fiction, Western, some fantasy, memoir, cookbooks, true crime); **Naomi Davis**, naomi@inklingsliterary.com (romance of any variety—including paranormal, fresh urban fantasy, general fantasy, new adult and light sci-fi; young adult in any of those same genres; memoirs about living with disabilities, facing criticism, and mental illness); **Whitley Abell**, whitley@inklingsliterary.com (young adult, middle grade, and select upmarket women's fiction); **Alex Barba**, alex@inklingsliterary.com (YA fiction).

HOW TO CONTACT E-queries only. To query, type "Query (Agent Name)" plus the title of your novel in the subject line, then please send the following pasted into the body of the e-mail to query@inklingsliterary.com. Check the agency website to make sure that your targeted agent is currently open to submissions.

◐ INKWELL MANAGEMENT, LLC

521 Fifth Ave., 26th Floor, New York NY 10175. (212)922-3500. **Fax:** (212)922-0535. **E-mail:** submissions@inkwellmanagement.com. **Website:** www.inkwellmanagement.com. Represents 500 clients.

MEMBER AGENTS Stephen Barbara (select adult fiction and nonfiction); **Lizz Blaise** (literary fiction, women's and young adult fiction, suspense, and psychological thriller); **William Callahan** (nonfiction of all stripes, especially American history and memoir, pop culture and illustrated books, as well as voice-driven fiction that stands out from the crowd); **Michael V Carlisle**; **Catherine Drayton** (bestselling authors of books for children, young adults and women readers); **David Forrer** (literary, commercial, historical and crime fiction to suspense/thriller, humorous nonfiction and popular history); **Alexis Hurley** (literary and commercial fiction, memoir, narrative nonfiction and more); **Nathaniel Jacks** (memoir, narrative nonfiction, social sciences, health, current affairs, business, religion, and popular history, as well as fiction—literary and commercial, women's, young adult, historical, short story, among others); **Alyssa Mozdzen**; **Jacqueline Murphy**; (fiction, children's books, graphic novels and illustrated works, and compelling narrative nonfiction); **Richard Pine**; **Eliza Rothstein** (literary and commercial fiction, narrative nonfiction, memoir, popular science, and food writing); **Emma Schlee** (literary fiction, the occasional thriller, travel and adventure books, and popular culture and philosophy books); **Hannah Schwartz**; **David Hale Smith**; **Lauren Smythe** (smart narrative nonfiction [narrative journalism, modern history, biography, cultural criticism, personal essay, humor], personality-driven practical nonfiction [cookbooks, fashion and style], and contemporary literary fiction); **Kimberly Witherspoon**; **Monika Woods** (literary and commercial fiction, young adult, memoir, and compelling nonfiction in popular culture, science, and current affairs); **Lena Yarbrough** (literary fiction, upmarket commercial fiction, memoir, narrative nonfiction, history, investigative journalism, and cultural criticism).

REPRESENTS nonfiction books, novels. **Considers these nonfiction areas:** biography, business, cooking, creative nonfiction, current affairs, foods, health, history, humor, memoirs, popular culture, religious, science. **Considers these fiction areas:** commercial, crime, historical, literary, middle grade, picture books, romance, short story collections, suspense, thriller, women's, young adult.

HOW TO CONTACT In the body of your e-mail, please include a query letter and a short writing sample (1-2 chapters). We currently accept submissions in all genres except screenplays. Due to the volume of queries we receive, our response time may take up to two months. Feel free to put "Query for [Agent Name]: [Your Book Title]" in the e-mail subject line. Obtains most new clients through recommendations from others.

TERMS Agent receives 15% commission on domestic sales. Agent receives 20% commission on foreign sales. Offers written contract.

TIPS "We will not read mss before receiving a letter of inquiry."

⊘⊚ ICM PARTNERS

730 Fifth Ave., New York NY 10019. (212)556-5600. **Website:** www.icmtalent.com. **Contact:** Literary Department. Member of AAR. Signatory of WGA.

REPRESENTS nonfiction, fiction, novels, juvenile books.

� *"We do not accept unsolicited submissions."*

HOW TO CONTACT This agency is generally not open to unsolicited submissions. However, some agents do attend conferences and meet writers then. The agents take referrals, as well. Obtains most new clients through recommendations from others.

TERMS Agent receives 15% commission on domestic sales. Agent receives 20% commission on foreign sales.

ⓘ JABBERWOCKY LITERARY AGENCY

49 West 45th St., New York NY 10036. (718)392-5985. **Website:** www.awfulagent.com. **Contact:** Joshua Bilmes. Other memberships include SFWA. Represents 40 clients. 15% of clients are new/unpublished writers. Currently handles: nonfiction books 15%, novels 75%, scholarly books 5%, other 5% other.

MEMBER AGENTS Joshua Bilmes; Eddie Schneider; Lisa Rodgers; Sam Morgan.

REPRESENTS novels. **Considers these nonfiction areas:** autobiography, biography, business, cooking, current affairs, diet/nutrition, economics, film, foods, gay/lesbian, government, health, history, humor, language, law, literature, medicine, money, popular cul-

ture, politics, satire, science, sociology, sports, theater, war, women's issues, women's studies, young adult. **Considers these fiction areas:** action, adventure, contemporary issues, crime, detective, ethnic, family saga, fantasy, gay, glitz, historical, horror, humor, lesbian, literary, mainstream, middle grade, police, psychic, regional, satire, science fiction, sports, supernatural, thriller, young adult.

➤ This agency represents quite a lot of genre fiction and is actively seeking to increase the amount of nonfiction projects. It does not handle children's or picture books. Book-length material only—no poetry, articles, or short fiction.

HOW TO CONTACT "We are currently open to unsolicited queries. No e-mail, phone, or fax queries, please. Query with SASE. Please check our website, as there may be times during the year when we are not accepting queries. Query letter only; no ms material unless requested." Accepts simultaneous submissions. Responds in 3 weeks to queries. Obtains most new clients through solicitations, recommendation by current clients.

TERMS Agent receives 15% commission on domestic sales. Agent receives 20% commission on foreign sales. Offers written contract, binding for 1 year. Charges clients for book purchases, photocopying, international book/ms mailing.

RECENT SALES 188 individual deals done in 2014: 60 domestic and 128 foreign. *Alcatraz #5* by Brandon Sanderson; *Aurora Teagarden* by Charlaine Harris; *The Unnoticeables* by Robert Brockway; *Messenger's Legacy* by Peter V. Brett; *Slotter Key* by Elizabeth Moon. Other clients include Tanya Huff, Simon Green, Jack Campbell, Myke Cole, Marie Brennan, Daniel Jose Older, Jim Hines, Mark Hodder, Toni Kelner, Ari Marmell, Ellery Queen, Erin Tettensor, and Walter Jon Williams.

TIPS "In approaching with a query, the most important things to us are your credits and your biographical background to the extent it's relevant to your work. I (and most agents) will ignore the adjectives you may choose to describe your own work."

ⓞ JANKLOW & NESBIT ASSOCIATES

445 Park Ave., New York NY 10022. (212)421-1700. **Fax:** (212)980-3671. **E-mail:** submissions@janklow. com. **Website:** www.janklowandnesbit.com. Estab. 1989.

MEMBER AGENTS Morton L. Janklow; Anne Sibbald; Lynn Nesbit; Luke Janklow; Cullen Stanley; PJ Mark (interests are eclectic, including short stories and literary novels. His nonfiction interests include journalism, popular culture, memoir/narrative, essays and cultural criticism); **Richard Morris** (books that challenge our common assumptions, be it in the fields of cultural history, business, food, sports, science or faith); **Paul Lucas** (literary and commercial fiction, focusing on literary thrillers, science fiction and fantasy; also seeks narrative histories of ideas and objects, as well as biographies and popular science); **Emma Parry** (nonfiction by experts, but will consider outstanding literary fiction and upmarket commercial fiction. I'm not looking for children's books, middle grade, or fantasy); **Alexandra Machinist**; **Kirby Kim** (formerly of WME).

REPRESENTS nonfiction, fiction.

HOW TO CONTACT Query via snail mail or e-mail. Include a synopsis and the first 10 pages if sending fiction (no attachments). For nonfiction, send a query and full outline. Address your submission to an individual agent. Accepts simultaneous submissions. Responds in 8 weeks to queries/mss. Obtains most new clients through recommendations from others.

TIPS "Please send a short query with first 10 pages or artwork."

THE KNIGHT AGENCY

E-mail: submissions@knightagency.net. **Website:** http://knightagency.net/.

MEMBER AGENTS Deidre Knight (romance, women's fiction, commercial fiction, inspirational, memoir and nonfiction narrative, personal finance, business, popular culture, self-help, religion, health, and parenting); **Judson Knight**; **Pamela Harty** (contemporary and historical romance, romantic suspense, women's fiction, young adult, business, motivational, diet and health, memoir, parenting, pop culture, and true crime); **Elaine Spencer** (romance, women's fiction, young adult and middle grade material); **Lucienne Diver** (fantasy, science fiction, romance, romantica, suspense and young adult); **Nephele Tempest** (literary/commercial fiction, women's fiction, fantasy, science fiction, romantic suspense, paranormal romance, contemporary romance, historical fiction, young adult and middle grade fiction); **Melissa Jeglinski** (romance [contemporary, category, historical, inspirational], young adult, middle grade, women's

fiction and mystery); **Travis Pennington** (young adult, middle grade, mysteries, thrillers, commercial fiction, and romance [nothing paranormal/fantasy in any genre for now]).

REPRESENTS Considers these fiction areas: commercial, fantasy, middle grade, new adult, romance, science fiction, thriller, women's, young adult.

Does not want to receive screenplays, short stories, poetry, essays, or children's picture books.

HOW TO CONTACT E-queries only. "Your submission should include a 1-page query letter and the first 5 pages of your ms. All text must be contained in the body of your e-mail. Attachments will not be opened nor included in the consideration of your work. Queries must be addressed to a specific agent. Please do not query multiple agents."

BARBARA S. KOUTS, LITERARY AGENT

P.O. Box 560, Bellport NY 11713. (631)286-1278. **Fax:** (631) 286-1538. **Contact:** Barbara S. Kouts. Member of AAR. Represents 50 clients. 10% of clients are new/unpublished writers.

REPRESENTS juvenile.

This agency specializes in children's books.

HOW TO CONTACT Query with SASE. Accepts solicited queries by snail mail only. Accepts simultaneous submissions. Obtains most new clients through recommendations from others, solicitations, conferences.

TERMS Agent receives 10% commission on domestic sales. Agent receives 20% commission on foreign sales. This agency charges clients for photocopying.

RECENT SALES *Code Talker*, by Joseph Bruchac (Dial); *The Penderwicks*, by Jeanne Birdsall (Knopf); *Froggy's Baby Sister*, by Jonathan London (Viking).

TIPS "Write, do not call. Be professional in your writing."

KT LITERARY, LLC

9249 S. Broadway, #200-543, Highlands Ranch CO 80129. (720)344-4728. **Fax:** (720)344-4728. **E-mail:** queries@ktliterary.com. **Website:** http://ktliterary.com. **Contact:** Kate Schafer Testerman. Member of AAR. Other memberships include SCBWI. Represents 20 clients. 60% of clients are new/unpublished writers.

Prior to her current position, Ms. Schafer was an agent with Janklow & Nesbit.

MEMBER AGENTS Kate Schafer (middle grade and young adult); **Renee Nyen** (middle grade and young adult); **Sara Megibow**, saraquery@ktliterary.com (middle grade, young adult, new adult, romance, erotica, science fiction and fantasy; LGBTQ and diversity friendly).

REPRESENTS Considers these fiction areas: middle grade, young adult.

☞ "We're thrilled to be actively seeking new clients writing brilliant, funny, original middle grade and young adult fiction, both literary and commercial." Does not want picture books, serious nonfiction, and adult literary fiction.

HOW TO CONTACT "To submit to kt literary, please e-mail us a query letter with the first three pages of your ms in the body of the e-mail. The subject line of your e-mail should include the word 'Query' along with the title of your manuscript. Queries should not contain attachments. Attachments will not be read, and queries containing attachments will be deleted unread. We aim to reply to all queries within two weeks of receipt. No snail mail queries." Responds in 2 weeks to queries. Responds in 2 months to mss. Obtains most new clients through recommendations from others, solicitations, conferences.

TERMS Agent receives 15% commission on domestic sales. Agent receives 20% commission on foreign sales. Offers written contract; 30-day notice must be given to terminate contract.

RECENT SALES *Albatross*, by Julie Bloss; *The Last Good Place of Lily Odilon*, by Sara Beitia; *Texting the Underworld*, by Ellen Booraem. A full list of clients is available on the agency website.

WRITERS CONFERENCES Various SCBWI conferences, BookExpo.

TIPS "If we like your query, we'll ask for (more). Continuing advice is offered regularly on my blog 'Ask Daphne,' which can be accessed from my website."

◗ LIPPINCOTT MASSIE MCQUILKIN

27 West 20th Street, Suite 305, New York NY 10011. **Fax:** (212)352-2059. **E-mail:** info@lmqlit.com. **Website:** www.lmqlit.com.

MEMBER AGENTS Laney Katz Becker, laney@lmqlit.com (book club fiction, smart thrillers and suspense, memoir and nonfiction from platform-heavy authors); **Kent Wolf**, kent@lmqlit.com (literary and commercial fiction, including young adult and select middle grade, narrative nonfiction, memoir, essays, and pop culture); **Ethan Bassoff**, ethan@lmqlit.com (literary fiction, crime fiction, and narrative nonfiction in the areas of history, sports writing, journalism, science writing, pop culture, humor, and food writing); **Jason Anthony**, jason@lmqlit.com (commercial fiction of all types, including young adult, and nonfiction in the areas of memoir, pop culture, true crime, and general psychology and sociology); **Will Lippincott**, will@lmqlit.com (narrative nonfiction and nonfiction in the areas of politics, history, biography, foreign affairs, and health. He is not looking for fiction at this time); **Maria Massie**, maria@lmqlit.com (literary and upmarket commercial fiction [including select young adult and middle grade], memoir, and narrative nonfiction); **Rob McQuilkin**, rob@lmqlit.com (literary fiction as well as narrative nonfiction and nonfiction in the areas of memoir, history, biography, art history, cultural criticism, and popular sociology and psychology); **Amanda Panitch**, amanda@lmqlit.com (young adult and middle grade); **Rayhane Sanders**, rayhane@lmqlit.com (literary fiction, historical fiction, upmarket commercial fiction [including select YA], narrative nonfiction [including essays], and select memoir); **Stephanie Abou** (literary and upmarket novelists).

REPRESENTS nonfiction books, novels, short story collections, scholarly, graphic novels. **Considers these nonfiction areas:** animals, anthropology, archeology, architecture, art, autobiography, biography, business, child guidance, cultural interests, current affairs, design, economics, ethnic, film, gay/lesbian, government, health, history, inspirational, language, law, literature, medicine, memoirs, military, money, music, parenting, popular culture, politics, psychology, religious, science, self-help, sociology, technology, true crime, women's issues, women's studies, young adult. **Considers these fiction areas:** action, adventure, cartoon, comic books, confession, family saga, feminist, gay, historical, humor, lesbian, literary, mainstream, regional, satire.

☞ "LMQ focuses on bringing new voices in literary and commercial fiction to the market, as well as popularizing the ideas and arguments of scholars in the fields of history, psychology, sociology, political science, and current affairs. Actively seeking fiction writers who already have credits in magazines and quarterlies, as well as nonfiction writers who already have a media platform or some kind of a university affiliation." Does not want to receive romance, genre fiction, or children's material.

HOW TO CONTACT E-query. Include the word 'Query' in the subject line of your e-mail. Review the agency's online page of agent bios (lmqlit.com/contact.html), as some agents want sample pages with their submissions and some no not. If you have not heard back from the agency in 4 weeks, assume they are not interested in seeing more. Accepts simultaneous submissions. Obtains most new clients through recommendations from others, solicitations, conferences.

TERMS Agent receives 15% commission on domestic sales. Agent receives 20% commission on foreign sales. Offers written contract; 30-day notice must be given to terminate contract. Only charges for reasonable business expenses upon successful sale.

RECENT SALES Clients include: Peter Ho Davies, Kim Addonizio, Natasha Trethewey, Anne Carson, David Sirota, Katie Crouch, Uwen Akpan, Lydia Millet, Tom Perrotta, Jonathan Lopez, Chris Hayes, Caroline Weber.

○ LOWENSTEIN ASSOCIATES INC.

15 East 23rd St., Floor 4, New York NY 10010. (212)206-1630. **Fax:** (212)727-0280. **E-mail:** assistant@bookhaven.com. **Website:** www.lowensteinassociates.com. **Contact:** Barbara Lowenstein. Member of AAR.

MEMBER AGENTS Barbara Lowenstein, president (nonfiction interests include narrative nonfiction, health, money, finance, travel, multicultural, popular culture, and memoir; fiction interests include literary fiction and women's fiction).

REPRESENTS nonfiction books, novels. **Considers these nonfiction areas:** creative nonfiction, health, memoirs, money, multicultural, popular culture, travel. **Considers these fiction areas:** commercial, fantasy, literary, middle grade, science fiction, women's, young adult.

8—¬ Barbara Lowenstein is currently looking for writers who have a platform and are leading experts in their field, including business, women's issues, psychology, health, science and social issues, and is particularly interested in strong new voices in fiction and narrative nonfiction. Does not want Westerns, textbooks, children's picture books and books in need of translation.

HOW TO CONTACT "For fiction, please send us a 1-page query letter, along with the first 10 pages pasted in the body of the message by e-mail to assistant@bookhaven.com. If nonfiction, please send a 1-page query letter, a table of contents, and, if available, a proposal pasted into the body of the e-mail. Please put the word 'QUERY' and the title of your project in the subject field of your e-mail and address it to the agent of your choice. Please do not send an attachment as the message will be deleted without being read and no reply will be sent." Accepts simultaneous submissions. Responds in 6 weeks to queries. Obtains most new clients through recommendations from others, solicitations, conferences.

TERMS Agent receives 15% commission on domestic sales. Agent receives 20% commission on foreign sales. Offers written contract. Charges for large photocopy batches, messenger service, international postage.

TIPS "Know the genre you are working in and read!"

✛⊙ LR CHILDREN'S LITERARY

(224)848-4559. **E-mail:** submissions@LRchildrenslit erary.com. **Website:** www.lrchildrensliterary.com. **Contact:** Loretta Caravette.

REPRESENTS **Considers these fiction areas:** juvenile, middle grade, picture books, young adult.

8—¬ "I am very interested in the easy readers and early chapter books. I will take on an author/illustrator combination."

HOW TO CONTACT E-query only. Alert this agent if you are contacting other agencies at the same time. If submitting young adult or middle grade, submit the first 3 chapters and a synopsis. If submitting a picture book, send no more than 2 mss. Illustrations (no more than 5MB) can be sent as .JPG or .PDF formats. Responds in up to 6 weeks.

TIPS "No phone calls please."

SEAN MCCARTHY LITERARY AGENCY

E-mail: submissions@mccarthylit.com. **Website:** www.mccarthylit.com. **Contact:** Sean McCarthy.

○ Prior to his current position, Sean McCarthy began his publishing career as an editorial intern at Overlook Press and then moved over to the Sheldon Fogelman Agency.

REPRESENTS **Considers these fiction areas:** juvenile, middle grade, picture books, young adult.

8—¬ Sean is drawn to flawed, multifaceted characters with devastatingly concise writing in YA, and boy-friendly mysteries or adventures in MG.

In picture books, he looks more for unforgettable characters, off-beat humor, and especially clever endings. He is not currently interested in high fantasy, message-driven stories, or query letters that pose too many questions.

HOW TO CONTACT E-query. "Please include a brief description of your book, your biography, and any literary or relevant professional credits in your query letter. If you are a novelist: Please submit the first three chapters of your ms (or roughly 25 pages) and a one page synopsis in the body of the e-mail or as a Word or PDF attachment. If you are a picture book author: Please submit the complete text of your ms. We are not currently accepting picture book mss over 1,000 words. If you are an illustrator: Please attach up to 3 JPEGs or PDFs of your work, along with a link to your website."

⚪ GINA MACCOBY LITERARY AGENCY

P.O. Box 60, Chappaqua NY 10514. (914)238-5630. **E-mail:** query@maccobylit.com. **Website:** www. publishersmarketplace.com/members/GinaMaccoby/. **Contact:** Gina Maccoby. Member of AAR. AAR Board of Directors; Royalties and Ethics and Contracts subcommittees; Authors Guild. Represents 25 clients. Currently handles: nonfiction books 33%, novels 33%, juvenile books 33%.

MEMBER AGENTS Gina Maccoby.

REPRESENTS nonfiction books, novels, juvenile. **Considers these nonfiction areas:** autobiography, biography, cultural interests, current affairs, ethnic, history, juvenile nonfiction, popular culture, women's issues, women's studies. **Considers these fiction areas:** juvenile, literary, mainstream, mystery, thriller, young adult.

HOW TO CONTACT Query by e-mail only. Accepts simultaneous submissions. Owing to volume of submissions, may not respond to queries unless interested. Obtains most new clients through recommendations from clients and publishers.

TERMS Agent receives 15% commission on domestic sales. Agent receives 20-25% commission on foreign sales, which includes subagents commissions. May recover certain costs, such as legal fees or the cost of shipping books by air to Europe or Japan.

◑ MANSION STREET LITERARY MANAGEMENT

Website: http://mansionstreet.com. **Contact:** Jean Sagendorph; Michelle Witte.

MEMBER AGENTS Jean Sagendorph, querymansionstreet@gmail.com (pop culture, gift books, cookbooks, general nonfiction, lifestyle, design, brand extensions), **Michelle Witte**, querymichelle@mansionstreet.com (young adult, middle grade, juvenile nonfiction).

REPRESENTS Considers these nonfiction areas: cooking, design, popular culture. **Considers these fiction areas:** juvenile, middle grade, young adult.

HOW TO CONTACT Send a query letter and no more than the first 10 pages of your manuscript in the body of an e-mail. Query one specific agent at this agency. No attachments. You must list the genre in the subject line. If the genre is not in the subject line, your query will be deleted. Responds in up to 6 weeks.

RECENT SALES Authors: Paul Thurlby, Steve Ouch, Steve Seabury, Gina Hyams, Sam Pocker, Kim Siebold, Jean Sagendorph, Heidi Antman, Shannon O'Malley, Meg Bartholomy, Dawn Sokol, Hollister Hovey, Porter Hovey, Robb Pearlman.

⚪ HOWARD MORHAIM LITERARY AGENCY

30 Pierrepont St., Brooklyn NY 11201. (718)222-8400. **Fax:** (718)222-5056. **Website:** www.morhaimliterary. com. Member of AAR.

MEMBER AGENTS Howard Morhaim (no unsolicited submissions), **Kate McKean**, kmckean@morhaimliterary.com (adult fiction: contemporary romance, contemporary women's fiction, literary fiction, historical fiction set in the 20th Century, high fantasy, magical realism, science fiction, middle grade, young adult; in nonfiction, books by authors with demonstrable platforms in the areas of sports, food writing, humor, design, creativity, and craft [sewing, knitting, etc.], narrative nonfiction by authors with or without an established platform. Some memoir); **Paul Lamb**, paul@morhaimliterary.com (nonfiction in a wide variety of genres and subjects, notably business, political science, sociology, memoir, travel writing, sports, pop culture, and music; he is also interested in select literary fiction); **Maria Ribas**, maria@morhaimliterary. com (cookbooks, self-help, health, diet, home, parenting, and humor, all from authors with demonstrable platforms; she's also interested in narrative nonfiction and select memoir).

REPRESENTS Considers these nonfiction areas: business, cooking, crafts, creative nonfiction, design, health, humor, memoirs, parenting, self-help, sports.

Considers these fiction areas: fantasy, historical, literary, middle grade, new adult, romance, science fiction, women's, young adult, LGBTQ young adult, magical realism, fantasy should be high fantasy, historical fiction should be no earlier than the 20th century.

⚬━➤ Kate McKean is open to many subgenres and categories of YA and MG fiction. Check the website for the most details. Actively seeking fiction, nonfiction, and young adult novels.

HOW TO CONTACT Query via e-mail with cover letter and three sample chapters. See each agent's listing for specifics.

⊘⊚ ERIN MURPHY LITERARY AGENCY

2700 Woodlands Village, #300-458, Flagstaff AZ 86001. **Fax:** (928)525-2480. **Website:** http://emliterary.com. **Contact:** Erin Murphy, president; Ammi-Joan Paquette, senior agent; Tricia Lawrence, associate agent. 25% of clients are new/unpublished writers. Currently handles: juvenile books.

REPRESENTS Considers these fiction areas: middle grade, picture books, young adult.

⚬━➤ Specializes in children's books only.

TERMS Agent receives 15% commission on domestic sales; 20-30% on foreign sales. Offers written contract. 30 days notice must be given to terminate contract.

⚬ JEAN V. NAGGAR LITERARY AGENCY, INC.

216 E. 75th St., Suite 1E, New York NY 10021. (212)794-1082. **E-mail:** jweltz@jvnla.com; atasman@jvnla.com. **Website:** www.jvnla.com. **Contact:** Jean Naggar. Member of AAR. Other memberships include Women's Media Group, SCBWI, Pace University's Masters in Publishing Board Member. Represents 450 clients. 20% of clients are new/unpublished writers.

⚬ Ms. Naggar has served as president of AAR.

MEMBER AGENTS Jennifer Weltz (well researched and original historicals, thrillers with a unique voice, wry dark humor, and magical realism; enthralling narrative nonfiction; young adult, middle grade); **Jean Naggar** (taking no new clients); **Alice Tasman** (literary, commercial, YA, middle grade, and nonfiction in the categories of narrative, biography, music or pop culture); **Elizabeth Evans** (narrative nonfiction [travel/adventure], memoir, current affairs, pop science, journalism, health and wellness, psychology, history, pop culture, cookbooks and humor); **Laura**

Biagi (literary fiction, magical realism, psychological thrillers, young adult novels, middle grade novels, and picture books).

REPRESENTS nonfiction books, novels. **Considers these nonfiction areas:** biography, creative nonfiction, current affairs, health, history, humor, memoirs, music, popular culture, psychology, science. **Considers these fiction areas:** commercial, fantasy, literary, middle grade, picture books, thriller, young adult.

⚬━➤ This agency specializes in mainstream fiction and nonfiction and literary fiction with commercial potential. Does not want to receive screenplays.

HOW TO CONTACT "Visit our website, www.jvnla.com, for complete, up-to-date submission guidelines. Please be advised that Jean Naggar is no longer accepting new clients." Accepts simultaneous submissions.

TERMS Agent receives 15% commission on domestic sales. Agent receives 20% commission on foreign sales. Offers written contract. Charges for overseas mailing, messenger services, book purchases, long-distance telephone, photocopying—all deductible from royalties received.

RECENT SALES *Mort(e)* by Robert Repino; *The Paying Guests* by Sarah Waters; *Woman with a Gun* by Phillip Margolin; *An Unseemly Wife* by E.B. Moore; *The Man Who Walked Away* by Maud Casey; *A Lige in Men* by Gina Frangello; *The Tudor Vendetta* by C.W. Gortner; *Prototype* by M.D. Waters.

TIPS "We recommend courage, fortitude, and patience: the courage to be true to your own vision, the fortitude to finish a novel and polish it again and again before sending it out, and the patience to accept rejection gracefully and wait for the stars to align themselves appropriately for success."

⚬ NELSON LITERARY AGENCY

1732 Wazee St., Suite 207, Denver CO 80202. (303)292-2805. **Website:** www.nelsonagency.com. **Contact:** Kristin Nelson, president. Estab. 2002. Member of AAR. RWA, SCBWI, SFWA.

⚬ Prior to opening her own agency, Ms. Nelson worked as a literary scout and subrights agent for agent Jody Rein.

REPRESENTS Considers these fiction areas: commercial, fantasy, literary, mainstream, middle grade, romance, science fiction, women's, young adult.

⚬━➤ NLA specializes in representing commercial fiction and high-caliber literary fiction. They represent many pop genre categories, including things like historical romance, steampunk, and all subgenres of YA. Does not want short story collections, mysteries, thrillers, Christian, horror, children's picture books, or screenplays.

HOW TO CONTACT Query by e-mail. Put the word "Query" in the e-mail subject line. No attachments; querykristin@nelsonagency.com. Responds within 1 month.

RECENT SALES *Champion*, by Marie Lu (young adult); *Wool*, by Hugh Howey (science fiction); *The Whatnot*, by Stefan Bachmann (middle grade); *Catching Jordan*, by Miranda Kenneally (young adult); *Broken Like This*, by Monica Trasandes (debut literary fiction); *The Darwin Elevator*, by Jason Hough (debut science fiction). A full list of clients is available online.

⊕ ◑ NEW LEAF LITERARY & MEDIA, INC.

110 W. 40th St., Suite 410, New York NY 10018. (646)248-7989. **Fax:** (646)861-4654. **E-mail:** query@ newleafliterary.com. Member of AAR.

MEMBER AGENTS Joanna Volpe (women's fiction, thriller, horror, speculative fiction, literary fiction and historical fiction, young adult, middle grade, art-focused picture books); **Kathleen Ortiz**, Director of Subsidiary Rights and literary agent (new voices in YA nd animator/illustrator talent); **Suzie Townsend** (new adult, young adult, middle grade, romance [all subgenres], fantasy [urban fantasy, science fiction, steampunk, epic fantasy] and crime fiction [mysteries, thrillers]); **Pouya Shahbazian**, Director of Film and Television; **Mackenzie Brady** (her taste in nonfiction extends beyond science books to memoirs, lost histories, epic sports narratives, true crime and gift/lifestyle books; she represents select adult and YA fiction projects, as well).

REPRESENTS **Considers these fiction areas:** crime, fantasy, historical, horror, literary, mainstream, middle grade, mystery, new adult, paranormal, picture books, romance, thriller, women's, young adult.

HOW TO CONTACT "Only query us when your manuscript is complete. Do not query more than one agent at New Leaf Literary & Media, Inc. Put the word 'Query' in the subject line along with the target agent's name. No attachments. Responds if interested." Responds only if interested.

RECENT SALES *Four*, by Veronica Roth (Harper-Collins); *The Little World of Liz Climo*, by Liz Climo

(Running Press); *Ruin and Rising,g* by Leigh Bardugo (Henry Holt); *A Snicker of Magic*, by Natalie Lloyd (Scholastic).

◑ PARK LITERARY GROUP, LLC

270 Lafayette St., Suite 1504, New York NY 10012. (212)691-3500. **Fax:** (212)691-3540. **E-mail:** queries@parkliterary.com. **Website:** www.parkliterary.com. Estab. 2005.

MEMBER AGENTS Theresa Park (plot-driven fiction and serious nonfiction); **Abigail Koons** (popular science, history, politics, current affairs and art, and women's fiction); **Peter Knapp** (middle grade and young adult fiction).

REPRESENTS nonfiction books, novels. **Considers these nonfiction areas:** art, current affairs, history, politics, science. **Considers these fiction areas:** middle grade, suspense, thriller, women's, young adult.

⊶ The Park Literary Group represents fiction and nonfiction with a boutique approach: an emphasis on servicing a relatively small number of clients, with the highest professional standards and focused personal attention. Does not want to receive poetry or screenplays.

HOW TO CONTACT Please specify the first and last name of the agent to whom you are submitting in the subject line of the e-mail and send your query letter and accompanying material to queries@parkliterary.com. All materials must be in the body of the e-mail. Responds if interested. For fiction submissions to Abigail Koons or Theresa Park, please include a query letter with short synopsis and the first three chapters of your work. For middle grade and young adult submissions to Peter Knapp, please include a query letter and the first three chapters of your novel (no synopsis necessary). For nonfiction submissions, please send a query letter, proposal, and sample chapter(s).

RECENT SALES This agency's client list is on their website. It includes bestsellers Nicholas Sparks, Soman Chainani, Emily Giffin, and Debbie Macomber.

⊕ THE PURCELL AGENCY

E-mail: TPAqueries@gmail.com. **Website:** www.thepurcellagency.com. **Contact:** Tina P. Schwartz. Estab. 2012.

REPRESENTS **Considers these nonfiction areas:** juvenile nonfiction. **Considers these fiction areas:** juvenile, middle grade, young adult.

⊶ This agency also takes juvenile nonfiction for MG and YA markets. At this point, the agency is not considering fantasy, science fiction, or picture book submissions.

HOW TO CONTACT E-query. Mention if you are part of SCBWI. For fiction, send a query, the first 3 chapters, and synopsis. No attachments. For nonfiction, send table of contents + intro and sample chapter, author's credentials. Accepts simultaneous submissions. Responds in 1-3 months.

⊕ RUBIN PFEFFER CONTENT

648 Hammond St., Chestnut Hill MA 02467. **E-mail:** info@rpcontent.com. **Website:** www.rpcontent.com. **Contact:** Rubin Pfeffer. Estab. 2014.

○ Rubin has previously worked as the vice-president and publisher of Simon & Schuster Children's Books and as an independent agent at East West Literary Agency.

REPRESENTS Considers these fiction areas: juvenile, middle grade, picture books, young adult.

HOW TO CONTACT *Note: This agent accepts submissions by referral only. Specify the contact information of your reference when submitting.* Authors/illustrators should send a query and a 1-3 chapter ms via e-mail (no postal submissions). The query, placed in the body of the e-mail, should include a synopsis of the piece, as well as any relevant information regarding previous publications, referrals, websites, and biographies. The ms may be attached as a .doc or a .pdf file. Specifically for illustrators, attach a PDF of the dummy or artwork to the e-mail. Responds within 6-8 weeks.

RECENT SALES *Marti Feels Proud*, by Micha Archer; *Burning*, by Elana K. Arnold; *Junkyard*, by Mike Austin; *Little Dog, Lost*, by Marion Dane Bauer; *Not Your Typical Dragon*, by Tim Bowers; *Ghost Hawk*, by Susan Cooper.

◎ PIPPIN PROPERTIES, INC.

110 w. 40th Street, Suite 1704, New York NY 10018. (212)338-9310. **Fax:** (212)338-9579. **E-mail:** info@pippinproperties.com. **Website:** www.pippinproperties.com. **Contact:** Holly McGhee. Currently handles: juvenile books 100%.

○ Prior to becoming an agent, Ms. McGhee was an editor for 7 years and in book marketing for 4 years.

MEMBER AGENTS Holly McGhee; Elena Giovinazzo; Heather Alexander. Although each of the agents take children's books, you can find in-depth preferences for each agency on their website.

REPRESENTS Juvenile. **Considers these fiction areas:** middle grade, picture books, young adult.

✎ "We are strictly a children's literary agency devoted to the management of authors and artists in all media. We are small and discerning in choosing our clientele."

HOW TO CONTACT Query via e-mail. Include a synopsis of the work(s), your background and/or publishing history, and anything else you think is relevant. Accepts simultaneous submissions. Obtains most new clients through recommendations from others.

TERMS Agent receives 15% commission on domestic sales. Agent receives 25% commission on foreign sales. Offers written contract; 30-day notice must be given to terminate contract.

TIPS "Please do not start calling after sending a submission."

◑ PROSPECT AGENCY

551 Valley Road, PMB 377, Upper Montclair NJ 07043. (718)788-3217. **Fax:** (718)360-9582. **Website:** www.prospectagency.com. Estab. 2005. Member of AAR. Currently handles: 60% of material handled is books for young readers.

MEMBER AGENTS Emily Sylvan Kim, esk@prospectagency.com (romance, women's, commercial, young adult, new adult); **Rachel Orr**, rko@prospectagency.com (picture books, illustrators, middle grade, young adult); **Becca Stumpf**, becca@prospectagency.com (young adult, middle grade, fantasy, sci-fi, literary mysteries, literary thrillers, spicy romance); **Carrie Pestritto**, carrie@prospectagency.com (narrative nonfiction, general nonfiction, biography, and memoir; commercial fiction with a literary twist, women's fiction, romance, upmarket, historical fiction, new adult, YA, and upper middle grade); **Teresa Kietlinski,** tk@prospectagency.com (picture book artists and illustrators); **Linda Camacho** (adult, middle grade, and young adult fiction across all genres [romance, horror, fantasy, realistic, light sci-fi, and graphic novels]; select literary fiction [preferably with commercial bent] and picture books [both writers and illustrators welcome], select narrative nonfiction and memoir diversity of all types [ethnicity, disability, sexuality]).

REPRESENTS Considers these nonfiction areas: biography, memoirs. **Considers these fiction areas:** commercial, historical, juvenile, middle grade, mystery, new adult, picture books, romance, thriller, women's, young adult.

☞ "We're looking for strong, unique voices and unforgettable stories and characters."

HOW TO CONTACT Note that each agent at this agency has a different submission e-mail address and different submission policies. Check the agency website for the latest formal guideline per each agent. Obtains new clients through conferences, recommendations, queries, and some scouting.

TERMS Agent receives 15% on domestic sales, 20% on foreign sales sold directly and 25% on sales using a subagent. Offers written contract.

RECENT SALES Recent sales include: *Ollie and Claire* (Philomel), *Vicious* (Bloomsbury), *Temptest Rising* (Walker Books), *Where do Diggers Sleep at Night* (Random House Children's), *A DJ Called Tomorrow* (Little, Brown), The *Princesses of Iowa* (Candlewick).

☺ P.S LITERARY AGENCY

20033—520 Kerr St., Oakville ON L6K 3C7 Canada. **E-mail:** query@psliterary.com. **Website:** http://www. psliterary.com. **Contact:** Curtis Russell, principal agent; Carly Watters, agent; Maria Vicente, associate agent. Estab. 2005. Currently handles: nonfiction books 50%, novels 50%.

MEMBER AGENTS Curtis Russell (young adult and middle grade books); **Carly Watters** (young adult, book club fiction, commercial fiction, women's fiction, contemporary romance, cookbooks, unique memoirs, pop science and psychology, literary thrillers and mysteries, platform-heavy nonfiction); **Maria Vicente** (young adult, middle grade and illustrated picture books); **Kurestin Armada** (particular affection for science fiction and fantasy, especially books that recognize and subvert typical tropes of genre fiction).

REPRESENTS nonfiction, novels, juvenile books. **Considers these nonfiction areas:** autobiography, biography, business, child guidance, cooking, current affairs, diet/nutrition, economics, environment, foods, government, health, history, how-to, humor, law, memoirs, military, money, parenting, popular culture, politics, science, self-help, sports, technology, true crime, war, women's issues, women's studies. **Considers these fiction areas:** action, adventure, detective, erotica, ethnic, family saga, historical, horror, humor, juvenile, literary, mainstream, middle grade,

mystery, new adult, picture books, romance, sports, thriller, women's, young adult, biography/autobiography, business, child guidance/parenting, cooking/food/nutrition, current affairs, government/politics/law, health/medicine, history, how-to, humor, memoirs, military/war, money/finance/economics, nature/environment, popular culture, science/technology, self-help/personal improvement, sports, true crime/investigative, women's issues/women's studies.

☞ "What makes our agency distinct: We take on a small number of clients per year in order to provide focused, hands-on representation. We pride ourselves in providing industry-leading client service." Actively seeking both fiction and nonfiction. Seeking both new and established writers. Does not want to receive poetry or screenplays.

HOW TO CONTACT Queries by e-mail only. Submit query letter and bio. "Please limit your query to one page." Accepts simultaneous submissions. Responds in 4-6 weeks to queries/proposals; mss 4-8 weeks. Obtains most new clients through solicitations.

TERMS Agent receives 15% commission on domestic sales. Agent receives 25% commission on foreign sales. We offer a written contract, with 30-days notice terminate. Fees for postage/messenger services only if project is sold. "This agency charges for postage/messenger services only if a project is sold."

TIPS "Please review our website for the most up-to-date submission guidelines. We do not charge reading fees. We do not offer a critique service."

◑ RED SOFA LITERARY

2163 Grand Ave., #2, St. Paul MN 55105. (651)224-6670. **E-mail:** dawn@redsofaliterary.com; jennie@redsofaliterary.com; laura@redsofaliterary.com; amanda@redsofaliterary.com. **Website:** www.redsofaliterary.com. **Contact:** Dawn Frederick, literary agent and owner; Jennie Goloboy, agent; Laura Zats, associate agent; Amanda Rutter, associate agent. Red Sofa is a member of the Authors Guild and the MN Publishers Round Table Represents 20 clients. 80% of clients are new/unpublished writers.

◑ Prior to her current position, Ms. Frederick spent 5 years at Sebastian Literary Agency. In addition, Ms. Frederick worked more than 10 years in indie and chain book stores, and at an independent children's book publisher. Ms. Frederick has a master's degree in library and information sciences from an ALA-accredited institution. In Fall 2011, Jennie Goloboy joined Red Sofa Literary as an associate agent. Jennie Goloboy has a PhD in the History of American Civilization from Harvard. She is also a published author of both history and fiction, and a member of SFWA, RWA, SHEAR, OAH, the AHA, and Codex Writer's Group. Her funny, spec-fic short stories appear under her pen name, Nora Fleischer. Laura Zats became an associate agent in December 2013; she graduated from Grinnell College with degrees in English and anthropology.

REPRESENTS nonfiction, fiction, juvenile books. **Considers these nonfiction areas:** animals, anthropology, archeology, crafts, cultural interests, current affairs, gay/lesbian, government, health, history, hobbies, humor, investigative, popular culture, politics, satire, sociology, true crime, women's issues, women's studies, extreme sports. **Considers these fiction areas:** erotica, fantasy, middle grade, romance, science fiction, young adult.

⚮ Does not want to receive any personal memoirs.

HOW TO CONTACT Query by e-mail or mail with SASE. No attachments, please. Submit full proposal plus 3 sample chapters and any other pertinent writing samples. Accepts simultaneous submissions. Obtains most new clients through recommendations from others, solicitations.

TERMS Agent receives 15% commission on domestic sales. Agent receives 20% commission on foreign sales. Offers written contract.

TIPS "Always remember the benefits of building an author platform, and the accessibility of accomplishing this task in today's industry. Most importantly, research the agents queried. Avoid contacting every literary agent about a book idea. Due to the large volume of queries received, the process of reading queries for unrepresented categories (by the agency) becomes quite the arduous task. Investigate online directories, printed guides (like *Writer's Market)*, individual agent websites, and more, before beginning the query process. It's good to remember that each agent has a vision of what s/he wants to represent and will communicate this information

accordingly. We're simply waiting for those specific book ideas to come in our direction."

RED TREE LITERARY AGENCY

403 12th St., #4, Brooklyn, NY 11215. **Website:** www.redtreeliterary.com. **Contact:** Elana Roth.

◯ Elana is a graduate of Barnard College and the Jewish Theological Seminary, where she earned degrees in English literature and Bible.

REPRESENTS Considers these fiction areas: juvenile, middle grade, young adult.

HOW TO CONTACT E-query elana@redtreeliterary.com "Include 'QUERY: [title]' in the e-mail subject field. Please also include publisher submission history and previous publishing credits, if applicable. If you are a debut author, do not worry. After your query letter, paste the first 5-10 pages of your novel into the body of the email. If you are an author/illustrator and have not yet realized it's a necessity, I highly recommend creating an online portfolio, which you can link to in your query instead of attaching sample artwork to an email."

RECENT SALES *Doug-Dennis and the Flyaway Fib*, by Darren Farrel; *Juniper Berry*, by M.P. Kozlowsky; *The Selection*, by Kiera Cass; *Unison Spark*, by Andy Marino.

◑ REGAL LITERARY AGENCY

236 W. 26th St., #801, New York NY 10001. (212)684-7900. **Fax:** (212)684-7906. **E-mail:** submissions@regal-literary.com. **Website:** www.regal-literary.com. London Office: 36 Gloucester Ave., Primrose Hill, London NW1 7BB, United Kingdom, uk@regal-literary.com Estab. 2002. Member of AAR. Represents 70 clients. 20% of clients are new/unpublished writers.

MEMBER AGENTS Michelle Andelman (all categories of children's books); **Claire Anderson-Wheeler**; **Markus Hoffmann** (international and literary fiction, crime, [pop] cultural studies, current affairs, economics, history, music, popular science, and travel literature); **Joseph Regal** (literary fiction, international thrillers, history, science, photography, music, culture, and whimsy).

REPRESENTS Considers these nonfiction areas: creative nonfiction, memoirs, psychology, science. **Considers these fiction areas:** literary, middle grade, picture books, thriller, women's, young adult.

⚮ Actively seeking literary fiction and narrative nonfiction. "We do not consider romance, science fiction, poetry, or screenplays."

HOW TO CONTACT "Query with SASE or via e-mail. No phone calls. Submissions should consist of a 1-page query letter detailing the book in question, as well as the qualifications of the author. For fiction, submissions may also include the first 10 pages of the novel or one short story from a collection." Responds if interested. Accepts simultaneous submissions. Responds in 4-8 weeks.

TERMS Agent receives 15% commission on domestic sales. Agent receives 20% commission on foreign sales. "We charge no reading fees."

RECENT SALES Audrey Niffenegger's *The Time Traveler's Wife* (Mariner) and *Her Fearful Symmetry* (Scribner), Gregory David Roberts' *Shantaram* (St. Martin's), Josh Bazell's *Beat the Reaper* (Little, Brown), John Twelve Hawks' *The Fourth Realm Trilogy* (Doubleday), James Reston, Jr.'s *The Conviction of Richard Nixon* (Three Rivers) and *Defenders of the Faith* (Penguin), Michael Psilakis' *How to Roast a Lamb: New Greek Classic Cooking* (Little, Brown), Colman Andrews' *Country Cooking of Ireland* (Chronicle) and *Reinventing Food: Ferran Adria and How He Changed the Way We Eat* (Phaidon).

TIPS "WE ARE deeply committed to every aspect of our clients' careers, and are engaged in everything from the editorial work of developing a great book proposal or line editing a fiction ms to negotiating state-of-the-art book deals and working to promote and publicize the book when it's published. We are at the forefront of the effort to increase authors' rights in publishing contracts in a rapidly changing commercial environment. We deal directly with co-agents and publishers in every foreign territory and also work directly and with co-agents for feature film and television rights, with extraordinary success in both arenas. Many of our clients' works have sold in dozens of translation markets, and a high proportion of our books have been sold in Hollywood. We have strong relationships with speaking agents, who can assist in arranging author tours and other corporate and college speaking opportunities when appropriate. We also have a staff publicist and marketer to help promote our clients' and their work."

🄳 RODEEN LITERARY MANAGEMENT

3501 N. Southport #497, Chicago IL 60657. **E-mail:** submissions@rodeenliterary.com. **Website:** www.rodeenliterary.com. **Contact:** Paul Rodeen. Estab. 2009.

Paul Rodeen established Rodeen Literary Management in 2009 after 7 years of experience with the literary agency Sterling Lord Literistic, Inc.

REPRESENTS nonfiction books, novels, juvenile books, illustrations, graphic novels. **Considers these fiction areas:** juvenile, middle grade, picture books, young adult, graphic novels, comics.

Actively seeking "writers and illustrators of all genres of children's literature including picture books, early readers, middle grade fiction and nonfiction, graphic novels and comic books, as well as young adult fiction and nonfiction." This is primarily an agency devoted to children's books.

HOW TO CONTACT Unsolicited submissions are accepted by e-mail only to submissions@rodeenliterary.com. Cover letters with synopsis and contact information should be included in the body of your e-mail. An initial submission of 50 pages from a novel or a longer work of nonfiction will suffice and should be pasted into the body of your e-mail. Electronic portfolios from illustrators are accepted but please keep the images at 72 dpi—a link to your website or blog is also helpful. Electronic picture book dummies and picture book texts are accepted. Graphic novels and comic books are accepted. Accepts simultaneous submissions. Response time varies.

⊕ SADLER CHILDREN'S LITERARY

(815)209-6252. **E-mail:** jodell.sadlerliterary@gmail.com. **E-mail:** submissions.sadlerliterary@gmail.com. **Website:** www.sadlercreativeliterary.com. **Contact:** Jodell Sadler.

REPRESENTS Considers these fiction areas: juvenile, middle grade, picture books, young adult.

HOW TO CONTACT E-query only. Your subject line should read "QUERY—Name or Title—Genre." Alert this agency if submitting to other agencies at the same time. Along with your query, include an attached Word doc with your complete picture book text or the first 10 pages or your book. If you are an illustrator, send a link to online portfolio, or send PDF with pictures.

🄳 VICTORIA SANDERS & ASSOCIATES

40 Buck Rd., Stone Ridge NY 12484. (212)633-8811. **Fax:** (212)633-0525. **E-mail:** queriesvsa@gmail.com. **Website:** www.victoriasanders.com. **Contact:** Victo-

ria Sanders. Estab. 1992. Member of AAR. Signatory of WGA. Represents 135 clients. 25% of clients are new/unpublished writers.

MEMBER AGENTS Victoria Sanders, Chris Kepner, Bernadette Baker-Baughman.

REPRESENTS nonfiction books, novels. **Considers these nonfiction areas:** autobiography, biography, cultural interests, current affairs, ethnic, film, gay/lesbian, government, history, humor, law, literature, music, popular culture, politics, psychology, satire, theater, translation, women's issues, women's studies. **Considers these fiction areas:** action, adventure, contemporary issues, crime, ethnic, family saga, feminist, lesbian, literary, mainstream, mystery, new adult, picture books, thriller, young adult.

HOW TO CONTACT Query by e-mail only. "We will not respond to e-mails with attachments or attached files."

TERMS Agent receives 15% commission on domestic sales. Agent receives 20% commission on foreign/film sales. Offers written contract. Charges for photocopying, messenger, express mail. If in excess of $100, client approval is required.

RECENT SALES Sold 20+ titles in the last year.

TIPS "LIMIT QUERY to letter (no calls) and give it your best shot. A good query is going to get a good response."

WENDY SCHMALZ AGENCY

402 Union St., #831, Hudson NY 12534. (518)672-7697. **E-mail:** wendy@schmalzagency.com. **Website:** www.schmalzagency.com. **Contact:** Wendy Schmalz. Estab. 2002. Member of AAR.

REPRESENTS Considers these nonfiction areas: , Many nonfiction subjects are of interest to this agency. **Considers these fiction areas:** literary, mainstream, middle grade, young adult.

⌐Not looking for picture books, science fiction, or fantasy.

HOW TO CONTACT Accepts only e-mail queries. Paste all text into the e-mail. Do not attach the ms or sample chapters or synopsis. Replies to queries only if they want to read the ms. (2015: Not currently accepting submissions of genre fiction or children's picture books.) If you do not hear from this agency within 6 weeks, consider that a no. Obtains clients through recommendations from others.

TERMS AGENT RECEIVES 15% commission on domestic sales; 20% on foreign sales; 25% for Asian sales.

SUSAN SCHULMAN LITERARY AGENCY

454 W. 44th St., New York NY 10036. (212)713-1633. **Fax:** (212)581-8830. **E-mail:** Susan@Schulmanagency.com. **Website:** www.publishersmarketplace.com/members/Schulman/. **Contact:** Susan Schulman. Estab. 1980. Member of AAR. Signatory of WGA. Other memberships include Dramatists Guild. 10% of clients are new/unpublished writers. Currently handles: nonfiction books 50%, novels 25%, juvenile books 15%, stage plays 10%.

REPRESENTS Considers these nonfiction areas: biography, business, cooking, ethnic, health, history, money, religious, science, travel, women's issues, women's studies. **Considers these fiction areas:** juvenile, literary, mainstream, women's.

⌐"We specialize in books for, by and about women and women's issues including nonfiction self-help books, fiction and theater projects. We also handle the film, television and allied rights for several agencies as well as foreign rights for several publishing houses." Actively seeking new nonfiction. Considers plays. Does not want to receive poetry, television scripts or concepts for television.

HOW TO CONTACT "For fiction: query letter with outline and three sample chapters, résumé and SASE. For nonfiction: query letter with complete description of subject, at least one chapter, résumé and SASE. Queries may be sent via regular mail or e-mail. Please do not submit queries via UPS or Federal Express. Please do not send attachments with e-mail queries." Accepts simultaneous submissions. Responds in 6 weeks to queries/mss. Obtains most new clients through recommendations from others, solicitations, conferences.

TERMS Agent receives 15% commission on domestic sales. Agent receives 20% commission on foreign sales. Offers written contract; 30-day notice must be given to terminate contract.

RECENT SALES Sold 50 titles in the last year; hundred of subsidiary rights deals.

WRITERS CONFERENCES Geneva Writers' Conference (Switzerland); Columbus Writers' Conference; Skidmore Conference of the Independent Women's Writers Group.

TIPS "KEEP WRITING!" Schulman describes her agency as "professional boutique, long-standing, eclectic."

SERENDIPITY LITERARY AGENCY, LLC

305 Gates Ave., Brooklyn NY 11216. (718)230-7689. **Fax:** (718)230-7829. **E-mail:** rbrooks@serendipitylit.com; info@serendipitylit.com. **Website:** www.serendipitylit.com; facebook.com/serendipitylit. **Contact:** Regina Brooks. Represents 50 clients. 50% of clients are new/unpublished writers. Currently handles: nonfiction books 50%, other 50% fiction.

- Prior to becoming an agent, Ms. Brooks was an acquisitions editor for John Wiley & Sons, Inc. and McGraw-Hill Companies.

MEMBER AGENTS Regina Brooks; **Dawn Michelle Hardy** (sports, pop culture, blog and trend, music, lifestyle and social science), **Karen Thomas** (narrative nonfiction, celebrity, pop culture, memoir, general fiction, women's fiction, romance, mystery, self-help, inspirational, Christian based fiction and nonfiction including Evangelical), **John Weber** (unique YA and middle grade); **Folade Bell** (literary and commercial women's fiction, YA, literary mysteries & thrillers, historical fiction, African-American issues, gay/lesbian, Christian fiction, humor and books that deeply explore other cultures); **Nadeen Gayle** (romance, memoir, pop culture, inspirational/ religious, women's fiction, parenting young adult, mystery and political thrillers, and all forms of nonfiction).

REPRESENTS Considers these nonfiction areas: creative nonfiction, current affairs, humor, inspirational, investigative, memoirs, music, parenting, popular culture, religious, self-help, spirituality, sports. **Considers these fiction areas:** commercial, gay, historical, humor, lesbian, literary, middle grade, mystery, romance, thriller, women's, young adult.

- African-American nonfiction, commercial fiction, young adult novels, and juvenile books. No stage plays, screenplays or poetry.

HOW TO CONTACT Check the website, as there are online submission forms for fiction, nonfiction and juvenile. Accepts simultaneous submissions. Obtains most new clients through conferences, referrals.

TERMS Agent receives 15% commission on domestic sales. Agent receives 20% commission on foreign sales. Offers written contract; 2-month notice must be given to terminate contract. Charges clients for office fees, which are taken from any advance.

RECENT SALES *How I Discovered Poetry* by Marilyn Nelson; *Cooking Allergy Free* by Jenna Short; *Cleo Edison Oliver* by Sundee Frazier; *Flight Of The Seahawks* by Jerry Brewer; *It's Not A Game* by Kent Babb; *Drop The Act: It's Exhausting* by Beth Thomas Cohen; *College, Quicker: The Fast-Track To a More Affordable College Degree* by Katherine Stephens; *Every Closed Eye Ain't Sleep* by Marita Teague Tips "

TIPS "See The books *Writing Great Books For Young Adults* and *You Should Really Write A Book: How To Write Sell And Market Your Memoir*. We are looking for high concept ideas with big hooks. If you get writer's block try possibiliteas.co, it's a muse in a cup."

THE SEYMOUR AGENCY

475 Miner St., Canton NY 13617. (315)386-1831. **E-mail:** marysue@twcny.rr.com; nicole@theseymouragency.com; julie@theseymouragency.com; lane@theseymouragency.com. **Website:** www.theseymouragency.com. Member of AAR. Signatory of WGA. Other memberships include RWA, Authors Guild.

- Ms. Seymour is a retired New York State certified teacher. Ms. Resciniti was recently named "Agent of the Year" by the ACFW.

MEMBER AGENTS Mary Sue Seymour (accepts queries in Christian, inspirational, romance, and nonfiction); **Nicole Resciniti** (accepts all genres of romance, young adult, middle grade, new adult, suspense, thriller, mystery, sci-fi, fantasy); **Julie Gwinn** (Christian and inspirational fiction and nonfiction, women's fiction [contemporary and historical], new adult, Southern fiction, literary fiction and young adult); Lane Heymont (science fiction, fantasy, nonfiction).

REPRESENTS nonfiction books, novels. **Considers these nonfiction areas:** business, health, how-to, self help, Christian books; cookbooks; any well-written nonfiction that includes a proposal in standard format and 1 sample chapter. **Considers these fiction areas:** action, fantasy, inspirational, middle grade, mystery, new adult, religious, romance, science fiction, suspense, thriller, young adult.

HOW TO CONTACT For Mary Sue: E-query with synopsis, first 50 pages for romance. Accepts e-mail queries. For Nicole and Julie: E-mail the query plus first 5 pages of the manuscript pasted into the e-mail. Accepts simultaneous submissions. Responds in 1 month to queries. Responds in 3 months to mss.

TERMS Agent receives 12-15% commission on domestic sales.

○ THE SPIELER AGENCY

27 W. 20 St., Suite 305, New York NY 10011. **E-mail:** thespieleragency@gmail.com. **Contact:** Joe Spieler. Represents 160 clients. 2% of clients are new/unpublished writers.

○ Prior to opening his agency, Mr. Spieler was a magazine editor.

MEMBER AGENTS Eric Myers, eric@TheSpielerAgency.com (pop culture, memoir, history, thrillers, young adult, middle grade, new adult, and picture books [text only]); **Victoria Shoemaker**, victoria@TheSpielerAgency.com (environment and natural history, popular culture, memoir, photography and film, literary fiction and poetry, and books on food and cooking); **John Thornton**, john@TheSpielerAgency.com (nonfiction); **Joe Spieler**, joe@TheSpielerAgency.com (nonfiction and fiction and books for children and young adults).

REPRESENTS novels, juvenile books. **Considers these nonfiction areas:** cooking, environment, film, foods, history, memoirs, photography, popular culture. **Considers these fiction areas:** literary, middle grade, New Age, picture books, thriller, young adult.

HOW TO CONTACT "Before submitting projects to the Spieler Agency, check the listings of our individual agents and see if any particular agent shows a general interest in your subject (e.g. history, memoir, YA, etc.). Please send all queries either by e-mail or regular mail. If you query us by regular mail, we can only reply to you if you include a self-addressed, stamped envelope." Accepts simultaneous submissions. Cannot guarantee a personal response to all queries. Obtains most new clients through recommendations, listing in *Guide to Literary Agents*.

TERMS Agent receives 15% commission on domestic sales. Charges clients for messenger bills, photocopying, postage.

WRITERS CONFERENCES London Book Fair.

TIPS "Check http://www.publishersmarketplace.com/members/spielerlit/."

STIMOLA LITERARY STUDIO

308 Livingston Ct., Edgewater NJ 07020. **E-mail:** info@stimolaliterarystudio.com. **Website:** www.stimolaliterarystudio.com. **Contact:** Rosemary B. Stimola. Estab. 1997. Member of AAR. Represents 45

clients. 15% of clients are new/unpublished writers. Currently handles: 10% novels, 90% juvenile books.

○ Agency is owned and operated by a former educator and children's bookseller with a Ph.D in Linguistics.

MEMBER AGENTS Rosemary B. Stimola.

➤ Actively seeking remarkable young adult fiction and debut picture book author/illustrators. No institutional books.

HOW TO CONTACT Query via e-mail. Author/illustrators of picture books may attach text and sample art. A PDF dummy is preferred. Accepts simultaneous submissions. Responds in 3 weeks to queries "we wish to pursue further." Responds in 2 months to requested mss. While unsolicited queries are welcome, most clients come through editor, agent, client referrals.

TERMS Agent receives 15% commission on domestic sales. Agent receives 20% (if subagents are employed) commission on foreign sales. Offers written contract, binding for all children's projects. 60 days notice must be given to terminate contract.

TIPS Agent is hands-on, no-nonsense. May request revisions. Does not line edit but may offer suggestions for improvement before submission. Well-respected by clients and editors. "A firm but reasonable deal negotiator."

THE STRINGER LITERARY AGENCY, LLC

E-mail: mstringer@stringerlit.com. **Website:** www.stringerlit.com. **Contact:** Marlene Stringer.

REPRESENTS Considers these fiction areas: fantasy, middle grade, mystery, romance, thriller, women's, young adult.

➤ This agency specializes in fiction. This agency is seeking all kinds of romance, except inspirational or erotic. Does not want to receive picture books, plays, short stories, or poetry. The agency is also seeking nonfiction as of this time.

HOW TO CONTACT Electronic submissions through website submission form only. Accepts simultaneous submissions.

RECENT SALES *The Secret History*, by Stephanie Thornton (NAL); *The Bone Song*, by Alex Bledsoe (Tor); *Red*, by Alyxandra Harvey (Entangled); *Mer*, by Katie Schickel (Forge); The Paper Magician series, by Charlie Holmberg (47 North); *Fly by Night*, by Andrea Thalasinos (Forge); *Duty of Evil*, by April Taylor (Carina); The Joe Gale mysteries, by Brenda Buchanan

(Carina); *Wreckage,* by Emily Bleeker (Lake Union); *A Wicked Way to Win an Earl,* by Anna Bradley (Berkley); *The Stilt House,* by Charlie Donlea (Kensington).

TIPS "If your ms falls between categories, or you are not sure of the category, query and we'll let you know if we'd like to take a look. We strive to respond as quickly as possible. If you have not received a response in the time period indicated on website, please re-query."

◯ THE STROTHMAN AGENCY, LLC

63 East 9th St., 10X, New York NY 10003. **E-mail:** info@strothmanagency.com. **Website:** www.strothmanagency.com. **Contact:** Wendy Strothman, Lauren MacLeod. Member of AAR. Other memberships include Authors' Guild. Represents 50 clients.

◗ Prior to becoming an agent, Ms. Strothman was head of Beacon Press (1983-1995) and executive vice president of Houghton Mifflin's Trade & Reference Division (1996-2002).

MEMBER AGENTS Wendy Strothman; Lauren MacLeod.

REPRESENTS nonfiction, juvenile books. **Considers these nonfiction areas:** business, current affairs, environment, government, history, language, law, literature, politics, travel. **Considers these fiction areas:** literary, middle grade, young adult.

⊶ "Because we are highly selective in the clients we represent, we increase the value publishers place on our properties. We specialize in narrative nonfiction, memoir, history, science and nature, arts and culture, literary travel, current affairs, young adult, middle grade, and some business." The Strothman Agency seeks out scholars, journalists, and other acknowledged and emerging experts in their fields. We are now actively looking for authors of well-written young adult fiction and nonfiction. Browse the Latest News to get an idea of the types of books that we represent. For more about what we're looking for, read Pitching an Agent: The Strothman Agency on the publishing website www.strothmanagency.com." Does not want to receive adult fiction or self-help.

HOW TO CONTACT Accepts queries only via e-mail at strothmanagency@gmail.com. See submission guidelines online. Accepts simultaneous submissions. Responds in 4 weeks to queries. Responds in 8 weeks to mss. Obtains most new clients through recommendations from others.

TERMS Agent receives 15% commission on domestic sales. Agent receives 20% commission on foreign sales. Offers written contract; 30-day notice must be given to terminate contract.

◐ TALCOTT NOTCH LITERARY

2 Broad St., Second Floor, Suite 10, Milford CT 06460. (203)876-4959. **Fax:** (203)876-9517. **E-mail:** editorial@talcottnotch.net. **Website:** www.talcottnotch.net. **Contact:** Gina Panettieri, President. Represents 35 clients. 25% of clients are new/unpublished writers.

◗ Prior to becoming an agent, Ms. Panettieri was a freelance writer and editor.

MEMBER AGENTS Gina Panettieri, gpanettieri@talcottnotch.net (history, business, self-help, science, gardening, cookbooks, crafts, parenting, memoir, true crime and travel, women's fiction, paranormal, urban fantasy, horror, science fiction, historical, mystery, thrillers and suspense); **Paula Munier**, pmunier@talcottnotch.net (mystery/thriller, SF/fantasy, romance, YA, memoir, humor, pop culture, health & wellness, cooking, self-help, pop psych, New Age, inspirational, technology, science, and writing); **Rachael Dugas**, rdugas@talcottnotch.net (young adult, middle grade, romance, and women's fiction); **Jessica Negron**, jnegron@talcottnotch.net (commercial fiction, sci fi and fantasy (and all the little sub genres), psychological thrillers, cozy mysteries, romance, erotic romance, YA); **Suba Sulaiman**, ssulaiman@talcottnotch.net (upmarket literary and commercial fiction, romance [all subgenres except paranormal], character-driven psychological thrillers, cozy mysteries, memoir, young adult [except paranormal and sci-fi), middle grade, and nonfiction humor).

REPRESENTS Considers these nonfiction areas: business, cooking, crafts, gardening, health, history, humor, inspirational, memoirs, parenting, popular culture, psychology, science, self-help, technology, travel, true crime. **Considers these fiction areas:** commercial, fantasy, historical, horror, literary, mainstream, middle grade, mystery, New Age, paranormal, romance, science fiction, suspense, thriller, urban fantasy, women's, young adult.

HOW TO CONTACT Query via e-mail (preferred) with first 10 pages of the ms pasted within the body of the e-mail, not as an attachment. Accepts simultaneous submissions. Responds in 1 week to queries. Responds in 4-6 weeks to mss.

TERMS Agent receives 15% commission on domestic sales. Agent receives 20% commission on foreign sales. Offers written contract, binding for 1 year.

RECENT SALES Sold 36 titles in the last year. *Delivered From Evil*, by Ron Franscell (Fairwinds) and *Sourtoe* (Globe Pequot Press); *Hellforged*, by Nancy Holzner (Berkley Ace Science Fiction); *Welcoming Kitchen*; *200 Allergen- and Gluten-Free Vegan Recipes*, by Kim Lutz and Megan Hart (Sterling); *Dr. Seteh's Love Prescription*, by Dr. Seth Meyers (Adams Media); *The Book of Ancient Bastards*, by Brian Thornton (Adams Media); *Hope in Courage*, by Beth Fehlbaum (Westside Books) and more.

TIPS "Know your market and how to reach them. A strong platform is essential in your book proposal. Can you effectively use social media/Are you a strong networker: Are you familiar with the book bloggers in your genre? Are you involved with the interest-specific groups that can help you? What can you do to break through the 'noise' and help present your book to your readers? Check our website for more tips and information on this topic."

○○ TRANSATLANTIC LITERARY AGENCY

2 Bloor St., Suite 3500, Toronto ON M4W 1A8 Canada. (416)488-9214. **E-mail:** info@transatlanticagency. com. **Website:** http://transatlanticagency.com.

MEMBER AGENTS Trena White (nonfiction); **Amy Tompkins** (fiction, nonfiction, juvenile); **Stephanie Sinclair** (fiction, nonfiction); **Fiona Kenshole** (juvenile, illustrators); **Samantha Haywood** (fiction, nonfiction, graphic novels); **Jesse Finkelstein** (nonfiction); **Marie Campbell** (middle grade fiction); **Shaun Bradley** (referrals only); **Sandra Bishop** (fiction, nonfiction, serious narratives to inspirational romance); **Barb Miller**; **Lynn Bennett**; **David Bennett**.

REPRESENTS nonfiction books, novels, juvenile.

ℰ➞ "In both children's and adult literature, we market directly into the US, the United Kingdom and Canada." Actively seeking literary children's and adult fiction, nonfiction. Does not want to receive picture books, poetry, screenplays or stage plays.

HOW TO CONTACT Always refer to the website, as guidelines will change, and only various agents are open to new clients at any given time. Obtains most new clients through recommendations from others.

TERMS Agent receives 15% commission on domestic sales. Agent receives 20% commission on foreign sales. Offers written contract; 45-day notice must be given to terminate contract. This agency charges for photocopying and postage when it exceeds $100.

RECENT SALES Sold 250 titles in the last year.

⊘◉ SCOTT TREIMEL NY

434 Lafayette St., New York NY 10003. (212)505-8353. **E-mail:** general@scotttreimelny.com. **Website:** ScottTreimelNY.blogspot.com; www.ScottTreimelNY.com. Estab. 1995. Member of AAR. Other memberships include Authors Guild, SCBWI. 10% of clients are new/unpublished writers. Currently handles: other 100% junvenile/teen books.

◯ Prior to becoming an agent, Mr. Treimel was an assistant to Marilyn E. Marlow at Curtis Brown, a rights agent for Scholastic, a book packager and rights agent for United Feature Syndicate, a freelance editor, a rights consultant for HarperCollins Children's Books, and the founding director of Warner Bros. Worldwide Publishing.

MEMBER AGENTS Scott Treimel.

REPRESENTS nonfiction books, novels, juvenile, children's, picture books, young adult.

ℰ➞ This agency specializes in tightly focused segments of the trade and institutional markets.

HOW TO CONTACT No longer accepts simultaneous submissions. Wants queries only from writers he has met at conferences.

TERMS Agent receives 15% commission on domestic sales. Agent receives 20% commission on foreign sales. Offers verbal or written contract. Charges clients for photocopying, express postage, messengers, and books needed to sell foreign, film and other rights.

RECENT SALES *The Hunchback Assignments*, by Arthur Slade (Random House, HarperCollins Canada; HarperCollins Australia); *Shotgun Serenade*, by Gail Giles (Little, Brown); *Laundry Day*, by Maurie Manning (Clarion); *The P.S. Brothers*, by Maribeth Boelts (Harcourt); *The First Five Fourths*, by Pat Hughes (Viking); *Old Robert and the Troubadour Cats*, by Barbara Joosse (Philomel); *Ends*, by David Ward (Abrams); *Dear Canada*, by Barbara Haworth-Attard (Scholastic); *Soccer Dreams*, by Maribeth Boelts (Candlewick);

Lucky Me, by Richard Scrimger (Tundra); *Play, Louie, Play*, by Muriel Harris Weinstein (Bloomsbury).

WRITERS CONFERENCES SCBWI NY, NJ, PA, Bologna; The New School; Southwest Writers' Conference; Pikes Peak Writers' Conference.

TIPS "We look for dedicated authors and illustrators able to sustain longtime careers in our increasingly competitive field. I want fresh, not derivative story concepts with overly familiar characters. We look for gripping stories, characters, pacing, and themes. We remain mindful of an authentic (to the age) point-of-view, and look for original voices. We spend significant time hunting for the best new work, and do launch debut talent each year. It is best *not* to send mss with lengthy submission histories already."

ⓓ TRIDENT MEDIA GROUP

41 Madison Ave., 36th Floor, New York NY 10010. (212)333-1511. **Website:** www.tridentmediagroup. com. **Contact:** Ellen Levine. Member of AAR.

MEMBER AGENTS Kimberly Whalen, ws.assistant@tridentmediagroup (commercial fiction and nonfiction, women's fiction, suspense, paranormal, and pop culture); **Scott Miller**, smiller@tridentmediagroup.com (thrillers, crime fiction, women's and book club fiction, and a wide variety of nonfiction, such as military, celebrity and pop culture, narrative, sports, prescriptive, and current events); **Melissa Flashman**, mflashman@tridentmediagroup. com (pop culture, memoir, wellness, popular science, business and economics, and technology—also fiction in the genres of mystery, suspense or YA); **Alyssa Eisner Henkin**, ahenkin@tridentmediagroup.com (juvenile, children's, young adult); **Don Fehr**, dfehr@tridentmediagroup.com (literary and commercial fiction, narrative nonfiction, memoirs, travel, science, and health); **John Silbersack**, silbersack.assistant@tridentmediagroup.com (commercial and literary fiction, science fiction and fantasy, narrative nonfiction, young adult, thrillers); **Erica Spellman-Silverman**; **Ellen Levine**, levine.assistant@tridentmediagroup.com (popular commercial fiction and compelling nonfiction—memoir, popular culture, narrative nonfiction, history, politics, biography, science, and the odd quirky book); **MacKenzie Fraser-Bub**, MFraserBub@tridentmediagroup.com (many genres of fiction—specializing in women's fiction); **Mark Gottlieb** (in fiction, he seeks science fiction, fantasy, young adult, comics, graphic novels, historical, history, horror, literary, middle grade, mystery, thrillers and new adult; in nonfiction, he seeks arts, cinema, photography, biography, memoir, self-help, sports, travel, world cultures, true crime, mind/body/spirit, narrative nonfiction, politics, current affairs, pop culture, entertainment, relationships, family, science, technology); **Alexander Slater**, aslater@tridentmediagroup. com (children's, middle grade, and young adult fiction and nonfiction, from new and established authors).

REPRESENTS Considers these nonfiction areas: biography, business, creative nonfiction, current affairs, economics, health, history, memoirs, military, popular culture, politics, science, sports, technology, travel. **Considers these fiction areas:** commercial, crime, fantasy, juvenile, literary, middle grade, mystery, paranormal, science fiction, suspense, thriller, women's, young adult.

➑➔Actively seeking new or established authors in a variety of fiction and nonfiction genres.

HOW TO CONTACT While some agents are open to e-queries, all seem open to submissions through the agency's online submission form on the agency website. Query only one agent at a time. If you e-query, include no attachments.

RECENT SALES *Sacred River*, by Syl Cheney-Coker; *Saving Quinton*, by Jessica Sorensen; *The Secret History of Las Vegas*, by Chris Abani; *The Summer Wind*, by Mary Alice Munroe.

TIPS "If you have any questions, please check FAQ page before e-mailing us."

ⓓ THE UNTER AGENCY

23 W. 73rd St., Suite 100, New York NY 10023. (212)401-4068. **E-mail:** Jennifer@theunteragency. com. **Website:** www.theunteragency.com. **Contact:** Jennifer Unter. Estab. 2008.

Ⓠ　Ms. Unter began her book publishing career in the editorial department at Henry Holt & Co. She later worked at the Karpfinger Agency while she attended law school. She then became an associate at the entertainment firm of Cowan, DeBaets, Abrahams & Sheppard LLP where she practiced primarily in the areas of publishing and copyright law.

REPRESENTS Considers these nonfiction areas: biography, environment, foods, health, memoirs, popular culture, politics, travel, true crime, nature subjects. **Considers these fiction areas:** commercial, mainstream, middle grade, picture books, young adult.

This agency specializes in children's and nonfiction, but does take quality fiction.

HOW TO CONTACT Send an e-query. There is also an online submission form. If you do not hear back from this agency within 3 months, consider that a no.

RECENT SALES A full list of recent sales/titles is available on the agency website.

◑ UPSTART CROW LITERARY

244 Fifth Avenue, 11th Floor, New York NY 10001. **E-mail:** danielle.submission@gmail.com. **Website:** www.upstartcrowliterary.com. **Contact:** Danielle Chiotti, Alexandra Penfold. Estab. 2009.

MEMBER AGENTS Michael Stearns (not accepting submissions); **Danielle Chiotti** (young adult, middle grade, adult upmarket commercial that explores deep emotional relationships in an interesting or unusual way, and nonfiction in the areas of narrative/memoir, lifestyle, relationships, humor, current events, food, wine, and cooking); **Ted Malawer** (accepting queries only through conference submissions and client referrals); **Alexandra Penfold** (not accepting submissions).

REPRESENTS Considers these **nonfiction areas:** cooking, creative nonfiction, foods, humor, memoirs. **Considers these fiction areas:** middle grade, picture books, women's, young adult.

HOW TO CONTACT Submit a query and 20 pages pasted into an e-mail.

◎ WELLS ARMS LITERARY

E-mail: info@wellsarms.com. **Website:** www.wellsarms.com. **Contact:** Victoria Wells Arms. Estab. 2013.

Prior to opening her agency, Victoria was a children's book editor for Dial Books.

REPRESENTS Considers these **fiction areas:** juvenile, middle grade, picture books, young adult.

We focus on books for readers of all ages, and we particularly love board books, picture books, readers, chapter books, middle grade, and young adult fiction—both authors and illustrators. We do not represent to the textbook, magazine, adult romance or fine art markets.

HOW TO CONTACT E-query. Put "Query" in your e-mail subject line. No attachments.

WOLF LITERARY SERVICES, LLC

Website: http://wolflit.com. Estab. 2008.

MEMBER AGENTS Kirsten Wolf (no queries); **Adriann Ranta** (all genres for all age groups with a penchant for edgy, dark, quirky voices, unique settings, and everyman stories told with a new spin; she loves gritty, realistic, true-to-life stories with conflicts based in the real world; women's fiction and nonfiction; accessible, pop nonfiction in science, history, and craft; and smart, fresh, genre-bending works for children); **Kate Johnson** (literary fiction, particularly character-driven stories, psychological investigations, modern-day fables, and the occasional high-concept plot; she also represents memoir, cultural history and narrative nonfiction, and loves working with journalists); **Allison Devereux** (literary and upmarket commercial fiction, everyman characters in unlikely situations, debut voices, and psychologically adept narratives with a surreal bent; she loves narrative nonfiction, examinations of contemporary culture, pop science, cultural history, illustrated/graphic memoir, humor, and blog-to-book).

REPRESENTS Considers these **nonfiction areas:** art, crafts, creative nonfiction, history, memoirs, science, women's issues. **Considers these fiction areas:** literary, women's, young adult, magical realism.

HOW TO CONTACT To submit a project, please send a query letter along with a 50-page writing sample (for fiction) or a detailed proposal (for nonfiction) to queries@wolflit.com. Samples may be submitted as an attachment or embedded in the body of the e-mail.

RECENT SALES *Hoodoo*, by Ronald Smith (Clarion); *Binary Star*, by Sarah Gerard (Two Dollar Radio); *Conviction*, by Kelly Loy Gilbert (Hyperion); *The Empire Striketh Back*, by Ian Doescher (Quirk Books).

◑ WRITERS HOUSE

21 W. 26th St., New York NY 10010. (212)685-2400. **Fax:** (212)685-1781. **Website:** www.writershouse.com. Estab. 1973. Member of AAR.

MEMBER AGENTS Amy Berkower; Stephen Barr, sbarr@writershouse.com; Susan Cohen; Dan Conaway; Lisa DiMona; Susan Ginsburg; Merrilee Heifetz; Brianne Johnson; Daniel Lazar; Simon Lipskar; Steven Malk; Jodi Reamer, Esq.; Robin Rue; Rebecca Sherman; Geri Thoma; Albert Zuckerman; Alec Shane; **Sarah Nagel**, sarahsubmissions@writershouse.com (psychological thrillers, horror, mystery, suspense, literary fiction, young adult, middle grade; nonfiction in the areas of medical ethics, true crime, humor books and memoir); **Stacy Testa**, stesta@writershouse.com (literary fiction, commercial fiction, young adult, some nonfiction); **Lisa DiMona**. **REPRESENTS** nonfiction books, novels, juvenile. **Considers these nonfiction areas:** animals, art, autobiography, biography, business, child guidance, cooking, decorating, diet/nutrition, economics, film, foods, health, history, humor, interior design, juvenile nonfiction, medicine, military, money, music, parenting, psychology, satire, science, self-help, technology, theater, true crime, women's issues, women's studies. **Considers these fiction areas:** adventure, cartoon, contemporary issues, crime, detective, erotica, ethnic, family saga, fantasy, feminist, frontier, gay, hi-lo, historical, horror, humor, juvenile, literary, mainstream, middle grade, military, multicultural, mystery, New Age, occult, picture books, police, psychic, regional, romance, spiritual, sports, thriller, translation, war, women's, young adult.

☛ This agency specializes in all types of popular fiction and nonfiction. Does not want to receive scholarly, professional, poetry, plays, or screenplays.

HOW TO CONTACT Query with SASE. Do not contact two agents here at the same time. While snail mail is OK for all agents, some agents do accept e-queries (see below). Check the website for individual agent bios. "Please send us a query letter of no more than 2 pages, which includes your credentials, an explanation of what makes your book unique and special, and a synopsis. (If submitting to Steven Malk: Writers House, 7660 Fay Ave., #338H, La Jolla, CA 92037. Note that Malk only accepts queries on an exclusive basis.)" Accepts simultaneous submissions. Obtains most new clients through recommendations from authors and editors.

TERMS Agent receives 15% commission on domestic sales. Agent receives 20% commission on foreign sales. Offers written contract, binding for 1 year. Agency charges fees for copying mss/proposals and overseas airmail of books.

TIPS "Do not send mss. Write a compelling letter. If you do, we'll ask to see your work. Follow submission guidelines and please do not simultaneously submit your work to more than 1 Writers House agent."

ART REPS

CAROL BANCROFT & FRIENDS

P.O. Box 2030, Danbury CT 06813. (203)730-8270 or (800)720-7020. **Fax:** (203)730-8275. **E-mail:** cb_friends8270@sbcglobal.net; cbfriends@sbcglobal.net. **Website:** www.carolbancroft.com. **Contact:** Joy Elton Tricarico, owner; Carol Bancroft, founder. "Internationally known for representing artists who specialize in illustrating art for all aspects of the children's market. We also represent many artists who are well known in other aspects of the field of illustration." Clients include, but not limited to, Scholastic, Houghton Mifflin Harcourt, HarperCollins, Marshall Cavendish, McGraw Hill, Hay House. **REPRESENTS** Specializes in illustration for children's publishing-text and trade; any children's-related material.

TERMS Rep receives 25% commission. Advertising costs are split: 75% paid by talent; 25% paid by representative.

HOW TO CONTACT Either e-mail 2-3 samples with your address or mail 6-10 samples, along with a SASE to the P.O. Box address. For promotional purposes, artists must provide "laser copies (not slides), tearsheets, promo pieces, good color photocopies, etc.; 6 pieces or more is best; narrative scenes and children interacting."

TIPS "We look for artists who can draw animals and people with imagination and energy, depicting engaging characters with action in situational settings."

CRAVEN DESIGN, INC.

1202 Lexington Ave., Box 242, New York, NY 10028. (212)288-1022. **Fax:** (212)249-9910 **E-mail:** cravendesign@mac.com. **Website:** www.cravendesignstudios.com. **Contact:** Meryl Jones.

REPRESENTS "We represent more than 20 professional illustrators with experience in a full range of genres, from humorous to realistic, decorative and technical, electronic and traditional, including maps, charts and graphs."

RECENT Sales Specializes in textbook illustration for all ages, juvenile through adult, elementary through secondary school.

HOW TO CONTACT E-mail with any inquiries.

FAMOUS FRAMES

5839 Green Valley Circle, Suite 104, Culver City, CA 90230. (855)530-3375. Additional phone numbers: (212)980-7979 (NY); (310)642-2721 (LA). **Fax:** 310.642.2728. **Website:** www.famousframes.com.

REPRESENTS A "roster of 100+ of the world's top illustrators."

RECENT SALES Sells to a wide client base made up of many commercial organizations and some publishers.

HOW TO CONTACT E-mail portfolio@famousframes.com and include samples/links along with contact information within the body of the e-mail.

FRIEND + JOHNSON

Contact information varies based upon location. East: 244 Fifth Ave, Suite D-146, New York, NY 10001. (212)337-0055. West/Southwest 388 Market St. Suite 1300, San Francisco, CA 94111. (415)927-4500. **E-mail:** bjohnson@friendandjohnson.com. **Contact:** Beth Johnson. Midwest: 901 W Madison St Suite 918., Chicago, IL 60607. (312)435-0055. **E-mail:** sfriend@friendandjohnson.com. **Contact:** Simone Friend. **Website:** www.friendandjohnson.com

REPRESENTS A diverse and original group of artists, photographers, designers, illustrators and typographists.

HOW TO CONTACT Please send your inquiry and a link to your website in an e-mail to agent@friendandjohnson.com. Don't contact the agents directly. Will reply only if interested.

HEART ARTIST'S AGENCY

Heart USA Inc., 611 Broadway Suite 734, New York, NY 10012 . (212)995-9386 **Fax:** (212)995-9386. **E-mail:** nyc@heartagency.com. London: Heart Top Floor 100 De Beauvoir Road, London N1 4EN, Tel 020 7254 5558 email: info@heartagency.com **Website:** www.heartagency.com

REPRESENTS Currently open to illustrators seeking representation. Is highly selective.

HOW TO CONTACT Accepts submissions in the form of website links via e-mail to mail@heartagency.com. If no website exists please provide printed samples by post. If you would like your samples returned, please supply a stamped self-addressed-envelope in your package.

SCOTT HULL ASSOCIATES

3875 Ferry Road, Bellbrook, Ohio 45305. (937)433-8383. **Fax:** (937)433-0434 **E-mail:** scott@scotthull.com. **Website:** www.scotthull.com.

REPRESENTS A very large group of illustrators who specialize in a vairety of fields, including publishing.

RECENT SALES Has done business with Scholastic, Harper Collins, Chronicle Books, Crown Publishing, Bantam Books, and many other publishers

HOW TO CONTACT E-mail with inquiries or fill out the form on the website.

ILLUSTRATORSREP.COM

5 W. Fifth Street, Suite 300, Covington, KY 41011. (513)861-1400. **Fax:** (859)980-0820. **E-mail:** bob@illustratorsrep.com. **Website:** www.illustratorsrep.com.

REPRESENTS Small group of illustrators and photographers.

RECENT SALES "We have serviced such accounts as Disney, Rolling Stone Magazine and Procter & Gamble, just to name a few."

HOW TO CONTACT For information about representation, e-mail samples to info@illustratorsrep.com.

THE JULY GROUP

(212) 932-8583. Website: www.thejulygroup.com.

REPRESENTS Currently open to illustrators seeking representation. Their current group of illustrators' and animators' professional skills include: licensed images, children's book illustration, science fiction and fantasy art, graphic novels, CD art, educational illustration, and multimedia animation."

RECENT SALES Works with a variety of clients, including publishers and commercial.

HOW TO CONTACT Work can be submitted via a form on the website.

KID SHANNON

Shannon Associates, 333 West 57th Street, Suite 809, New York, New York 10019. (212)333-2551. **E-mail:** Use e-mail form online. **Website:** www.shannonassociates.com/kidshannon.

REPRESENTS Very large group of illustrators, some photographers and some authors.

RECENT SALES Sells to many major publishing companies, including Penguin and Random House,

HOW TO CONTACT Fill out the form on the website.

LEMONADE ILLUSTRATION AGENCY

347 Fifth Ave. Suite 1402, New York, NY 10016. E-mail: info@lemonadeillustration.com. **Website:** www.lemonadeillustration.com.

REPRESENTS A wide variety of illustrators, including those for children's books.

RECENT SALES Sells to many major book publishers, including Penguin Books, Pearson, McGraw-Hill, Scholastic, and Random House.

HOW TO CONTACT Only replies to inquiries if interested. "We only accept links to your own website or sample copies via snail mail, addressed to either our NYC office or: Submissions Dept., Lemonade Illustration Agency, Hill House, Suite 231, 210 Upper Richmond Road, London, SW15 6NP." Email your website link to : studio@lemonadeillustration.com. Please address Lemonade in your email inquiry, we will not accept generalised emails or emails addressed to other Agents/Reps in the same subject line.

TIPS "Please try and write a little about yourself and your work in your e-mail. A professional presentation of your illustrations is key."

MARTHA PRODUCTIONS, INC.

7550 West 82nd Street, Playa Del Rey, CA 90293. (310)670-5300. Fax: (310) 670-3644. E-mail: contact@marthaproductions.com. Website: www.marthaproductions.com.

REPRESENTS Wide range of illustration styles, all categorized on website.

HOW TO CONTACT "We always welcome submissions from illustrators considering representation. Please e-mail us a few small digital files of your work or mail us non-returnable samples. We will contact you if we think we would be able to sell your work or if we'd like to see more."

MB ARTISTS

775 Sixth Ave., #6, New York NY 10001. (212)689-7830. **E-mail:** mela@mbartists.com. **Website:** www.mbartists.com. **Contact:** Mela Bolinao.

REPRESENTS Specializes in illustration for juvenile markets. Markets include: advertising agencies; editorial/magazines; publishing/books, board games, stationary, etc. We are not actively seeking more artists at this time. But we are always interested in seeing work by talented artists, particularly if their work is appropriate for children's books.

TERMS Rep receives 25% commission. No geographic restrictions. Advertising costs are split: 75% paid by talent; 25% paid by representative.

HOW TO CONTACT For first contact, send query letter, direct mail flier/brochure, website address, tearsheets, slides, photographs or color copies and SASE or send website link to mela@mbartists.com. Portfolio should include at least 12 images appropriate for the juvenile market.

MGI KIDS (MORGAN GAYNIN INC.)

149 Madison Avenue, Suite 1140, New York, NY 10016. (212)475-0440. **E-mail:** info@morgangaynin.com. **Website:** www.morgangaynin.com.

REPRESENTS "Select international illustrators." Features many of Morgan Gaynin's illustrators who also specialize in children's illustration.

RECENT SALES Has a wide client base. Artists have won several awards from organizations like American Illustration and Society of Illustrators New York and Los Angles.

HOW TO CONTACT Not accepting submissions at this time.

RILEY ILLUSTRATION

PO Box 92, New Paltz, NY 12561. (845)255-3309. 212.989.8770 **E-mail:** info@rileyillustration.com. **Website:** www.rileyillustration.com.

REPRESENTS Several award winning illustrators.

RECENT SALES Works with "art directors and designers, publishers, corporations, organizations, architects, and product developers."

HOW TO CONTACT E-mail any inquiries to info@rileyillustration.com.

LIZ SANDERS AGENCY

2415 E. Hangman Creek Ln., Spokane WA 99224-8514. (509)993-6400. **E-mail:** liz@lizsanders.com; artsubmissions@lizsanders.com. **Website:** www.lizsanders.com. **Contact:** Liz Sanders, owner. Commercial illustration representative. Represents Kyle Poling, Amy Ning, , Sudi McCollum, Suzanne Beaky, Maria Paula Dufour, Lois Rosio Sprague, Thodoris Tibilis and more.

REPRESENTS Markets include publishing, licensed properties, entertainment and advertising. Currently open to illustrators seeking representation. Open to both new and established illustrators.

TERMS Receives 30% commission against pro bono mailing program. Offers written contract.

HOW TO CONTACT For first contact, send If you would like to be considered by LSA for possible representation, please submit a link to your portfolio's website addressed to artsubmissions@lizsanders. com. If interested, Liz Sanders Agency looks forward to contacting you or e-mail to artsubmissions@lizsanders.com. Obtains new talent through recommendations from industry contacts, conferences and queries/solicitations, Literary Market Place.

RICHARD SOLOMON ARTISTS REPRESENTATIVE, LLC

110E 30th St., Suite 501, New York, NY, 10016. (212)223-9545. **Fax:** (212)223-9633 **E-mail:** richard@ richardsolomon.com. **Website:** www.richardsolomon.com.

REPRESENTS "We represent an ever-expanding 'big tent' of award-winning illustrators and fine artists, who work collaboratively with the best art directors and designers throughout the world. Looking for a signature style that shows consistency and a breadth of applications. Contact form on website."

RECENT SALES Has done work with Harper Collins, Random House, Scholastic, and many others

HOW TO CONTACT Send inquiries via e-mail or fill out the submission form on the website.

STORE 44 REPS

PO Box 251, Flagstaff, AZ 86002 . (323)230-0044. **E-mail:** art@store44.com. **Website:** www.store44.com.

REPRESENTS Photopgraphers, fine artists, and illustrators on an international level.

RECENT SALES WORKS with a wide client base, including Macmillan Publishing Group

HOW TO CONTACT "We consider new artists for representation during our internal quarterly portfolio reviews. We also hold an open annual portfolio review during September. Attach up to 16 JPG images, or a PDF Portfolio. Include your contact info, résumé, client or gallery list, along with links to examples of your work. Use the body of your e-mail to briefly describe why you are seeking representation, and be sure to reference 'Artist Submission' in the subject line. You should also include keywords in your email like 'fashion' and 'photographer.' Please do not attach ZIP files or Word documents."

T2 CHILDREN'S ILLUSTRATORS

Tugeau2 2231 Grandview Avenue, Cleveland Heights, OH 44106. (216)707-0854. **E-mail:** nicole@tugeau2. com. **Website:** www.tugeau2.com **Contact:** Nicole Tugeau.

REPRESENTS Currently open to children's illustrators seeking representation.

RECENT SALES Works with a variety of publishers, such as Tricycle (division of Random House), Raven Tree Press, and Harper Collins.

HOW TO CONTACT "To submit your work for consideration, please send Nicole a short e-mail with a link to your personal website and/or five pictures of your best and most recent artwork."

THOROGOOD KIDS/GOOD ILLUSTRATION

11-15 Betterton St., Covent Garden, London WC2H 9BPUnited Kingdom UK: +44 (0)208 123 0243 USA:. (347)627-0243. **E-mail:** draw@goodillustration.com. **Website:** www.goodillustration.com. Represents 30 illustrators including: Bill Dare, Kanako and Yuzuru, Nicola Slater, Dan Hambe, David Bromley, , Anja Boretzki, Olivier Latyk, Al Sacui, John Woodcock, Carol Morley, Leo Timmers, Christiane Engel, Anne Yvonne Gilbert, Philip Nicholson, Adria Fruitos, Ester Garcia Cortes, Lisa Zibamanzar, Alessandra Cimatoribus, Marta and Leonor, Iryna Bodnaruk. Open to illustrators seeking representation. Accepting both new and established illustrators.

HOW TO CONTACT "We would love to view your work. Please email submissions@goodillustration. com with no more than 10 examples of your work (maximum of 3mb total size). Please include a link to your website and/or blog. We prefer images that are sent as RGB JPGs. Printed material can be sent to the above address. Please note: We will not return work unless a stamped addressed envelope is included.

TIPS "Be unique and research your market. Talent will win out!"

GWEN WALTERS ARTIST REPRESENTATIVE

20 Windsor Lane, Palm Beach Gardens FL 33418. (561)805-7739. **E-mail:** artincgw@gmail.com. **Website:** www.gwenwaltersartrep.com. **Contact:** Gwen Walters.

REPRESENTS Currently open to illustrators seeking representation. Looking for established illustrators only.

RECENT SALES Sells to "All major book publishers."

TERMS Receives 30% commission. Artist needs to supply all promo material. Offers written contract.

HOW TO CONTACt For first contact, send e-mail including samples. Finds illustrators through recommendations from others.

TIPS "You need to pound the pavement for a couple of years to get some experience under your belt. Don't forget to sign all artwork. So many artists forget to stamp their samples."

WILKINSON STUDIOS, INC.

1121 E. Main St., Suite 310, St. Charles, IL 06174. (630)549-0504. **Website:** www.wilkinsonstudios.com.

REPRESENTS Represents several professional illustrators, including those specializing in children's illustration. "What sets us apart from the other rep firms is that we also offer art management services for large volume blackline and color illustration programs."

RECENT SALES Works with a wide variety of clients, nationally and internationally.

HOW TO CONTACT Has a contact form online. Accepts appropriate hard copy samples, tear sheets, color copies, or digital print-outs only via mail. Accepts digital submissions from non-US artists only.

CLUBS & ORGANIZATIONS

Contacts made through organizations such as the ones listed in this section can be quite beneficial for children's writers and illustrators. Professional organizations provide numerous educational, business, and legal services in the form of newsletters, workshops, or seminars. Organizations can provide tips about how to be a more successful writer or artist, as well as what types of business cards to keep, health and life insurance coverage to carry, and competitions to consider.

An added benefit of belonging to an organization is the opportunity to network with those who have similar interests, creating a support system. As in any business, knowing the right people can often help your career, and important contacts can be made through your peers. Membership in a writer's or artist's organization also shows publishers you're serious about your craft. This provides no guarantee your work will be published, but it gives you an added dimension of credibility and professionalism.

Some of the organizations listed here welcome anyone with an interest, while others are only open to published writers and professional artists. Organizations such as the Society of Children's Book Writers and Illustrators (SCBWI, www.scbwi.org) have varying levels of membership. SCBWI offers associate membership to those with no publishing credits, and full membership to those who have had work for children published. International organizations such as SCBWI also have regional chapters throughout the US and the world. Write or call for more information regarding any group that interests you, or check the websites of the many organizations that list them. Be sure to get information about local chapters, membership qualifications, and services offered.

ARIZONA AUTHORS ASSOCIATION

6145 West Echo Ln., Glendale AZ 85302. (623)847-9343. **E-mail:** info@azauthors.com. **Website:** www.azauthors.com. Purpose of organization: to offer professional, educational and social opportunities to writers and authors, and serve as a network. Members must be authors, writers working toward publication, agents, publishers, publicists, printers, illustrators, etc. Publishes bimonthly newsletter and *Arizona Literary Magazine.* Sponsors Annual Literary Contest in poetry, essays, short stories, novels, and published books with cash prizes and awards bestowed at a public banquet. Winning entries are also published or advertised in the *Arizona Literary Magazine.* First and second place winners in poetry, essay and short story categories are entered in the Pushcart Prize. Learn more online. **Contact:** Toby Heathcotte, president.

THE AUTHORS GUILD, INC.

31 E. 32nd St., 7th Floor, New York NY 10016. (212)564-5904. **Fax:** (212)564-5363. **E-mail:** staff@authorsguild.org. **Website:** www.authorsguild.org. Purpose of organization: to offer services and materials intended to help authors with the business and legal aspects of their work, including contract problems, copyright matters, freedom of expression and taxation. Guild has 8,000 members. Qualifications for membership: Must be book author published by an established American publisher within 7 years or any author who has had 3 works (fiction or nonfiction) published by a magazine or magazines of general circulation in the last 18 months. Associate membership also available. Different levels of membership include: associate membership with all rights except voting available to an author who has a firm contract offer or is currently negotiating a royalty contract from an established American publisher. "The Guild offers free contract reviews to its members. The Guild conducts several symposia each year at which experts provide information, offer advice and answer questions on subjects of interest and concern to authors. Typical subjects have been the rights of privacy and publicity, libel, wills and estates, taxation, copyright, editors and editing, the art of interviewing, standards of criticism, and book reviewing. Transcripts of these symposia are published and circulated to members. The *Authors Guild Bulletin,* a quarterly journal, contains articles on matters of interest to writers, reports of Guild activities, contract surveys, advice on problem

clauses in contracts, transcripts of Guild and League symposia and information on a variety of professional topics. Subscription included in the cost of the annual dues." **Contact:** Mary Rasenberger, executive director.

○ CANADIAN SOCIETY OF CHILDREN'S AUTHORS, ILLUSTRATORS AND PERFORMERS

104-40 Orchard View Blvd., Lower Level, Toronto ON M4R 1B9Canada . (416)515-1559. **E-mail:** office@canscaip.org. **Website:** www.canscaip.org. Purpose of organization: development of Canadian children's culture and support for authors, illustrators and performers working in this field. Qualifications for membership: Members—professionals who have been published (not self-published) or have paid public performances/records/tapes to their credit. Friends—share interest in field of children's culture. Sponsors workshops/conferences. Manuscript evaluation services; publishes newsletter: includes profiles of members; news round-up of members' activities countrywide; market news; news on awards, grants, etc; columns related to professional concerns. **Contact:** Lena Coakley, administrative director.

INTERNATIONAL READING ASSOCIATION

P.O. Box 8139, Newark DE 19714. (302)731-1600 ext. 293. **Fax:** (302)731-1057. **E-mail:** councils@reading.org. **Website:** www.reading.org. "The International Reading Association seeks to promote high levels of literacy for all by improving the quality of reading instruction through studying the reading process and teaching techniques; serving as a clearinghouse for the dissemination of reading research through conferences, journals, and other publications; and actively encouraging the lifetime reading habit. Its goals include professional development, advocacy, partnerships, research, and global literacy development." Sponsors annual convention. Publishes a newsletter called "Reading Today." Sponsors a number of awards and fellowships. More information online.

INTERNATIONAL WOMEN'S WRITING GUILD

274 Madison Ave., Suite 1202, New York NY 10016. (917)720-6959. **E-mail:** iwwgquestions@gmail.com. **Website:** www.iwwg.org. IWWG is "a network for the personal and professional empowerment of women through writing." Open to any woman connected to the written word regardless of professional portfolio. "IWWG sponsors several annual conferences a year

in all areas of the US. The major conference is held in June of each year at Yale University in New Haven, Connecticut. It is a week-long conference attracting 350 women internationally." Also publishes a 32-page newsletter, *Network*, 4 times/year; offers dental and vision insurance at group rates, referrals to literary agents. **Contact:** Kristin Rath, director of operations.

NATIONAL WRITERS ASSOCIATION

10940 S. Parker Rd., #508, Parker CO 80138. (303)841-0246. **Fax:** (303)841-2607. **E-mail:** natlwritersassn@hotmail.com. **Website:** www.nationalwriters.com. Association for freelance writers. Qualifications for membership: associate membership—must be serious about writing; professional membership—must be published and paid writer (cite credentials). Sponsors workshops/conferences: TV/screenwriting workshops, NWAF Annual Conferences, Literary Clearinghouse, editing and critiquing services, local chapters, National Writer's School. Open to non-members. Publishes industry news of interest to freelance writers; how-to articles; market information; member news and networking opportunities. Sponsors poetry contest; short story contest; article contest; novel contest. Awards cash for top 3 winners; books and/or certificates for other winners; honorable mention certificate places 5-10. Contests open to nonmembers.

NATIONAL WRITERS UNION

256 W. 38th St., Suite 703, New York NY 10018. (212)254-0279. **Fax:** (212)254-0673. **E-mail:** nwu@nwu.org. **Website:** www.nwu.org. Advocacy for freelance writers. Qualifications for membership: "Membership in the NWU is open to all qualified writers, and no one shall be barred or in any manner prejudiced within the Union on account of race, age, sex, sexual orientation, disability, national origin, religion or ideology. You are eligible for membership if you have published a book, a play, three articles, five poems, one short story or an equivalent amount of newsletter, publicity, technical, commercial, government, or institutional copy. You are also eligible for membership if you have written an equal amount of unpublished material and you are actively writing and attempting to publish your work." Holds workshops throughout the country. Members only section on website offers rich resources for freelance writers. Skilled contract advice and grievance help for members.

PEN AMERICAN CENTER

588 Broadway, Suite 303, New York NY 10012. (212)334-1660. **Fax:** (212)334-2181. **E-mail:** info@pen.org. **Website:** www.pen.org. "An association of writers working to advance literature, to defend free expression, and to foster international literary fellowship. The standard qualification for a writer to become a member of PEN is publication of two or more books of a literary character, or one book generally acclaimed to be of exceptional distinction. Also eligible for membership: editors who have demonstrated commitment to excellence in their profession (usually construed as five years' service in book editing); translators who have published at least two book-length literary translations; playwrights whose works have been produced professionally; and literary essayists whose publications are extensive even if they have not yet been issued as a book. Candidates for membership may be nominated by a PEN member or they may nominate themselves with the support of two references from the literary community or from a current PEN member. PEN members receive a subscription to the PEN journal, the PEN Annual Report, and have access to medical insurance at group rates. Members living in the New York metropolitan and tri-state area, or near the Branches, are invited to PEN events throughout the year. Membership in PEN American Center includes reciprocal privileges in PEN American Center branches and in foreign PEN Centers for those traveling abroad. Application forms are available online. PEN American Center is the largest of the 141 centers of PEN International, the world's oldest human rights organization and the oldest international literary organization. PEN International was founded in 1921 to dispel national, ethnic, and racial hatreds and to promote understanding among all countries. PEN American Center, founded a year later, works to advance literature, to defend free expression, and to foster international literary fellowship. The Center has a membership of 3,400 distinguished writers, editors, and translators. In addition to defending writers in prison or in danger of imprisonment for their work, PEN American Center sponsors public literary programs and forums on current issues, sends prominent authors to inner-city schools to encourage reading and writing, administers literary prizes, promotes international literature that might otherwise go unread in the US, and offers

grants and loans to writers facing financial or medical emergencies."

PUPPETEERS OF AMERICA, INC.

Sabathani Community Center, 310 East 38th St., Suite 127, Minneapolis MN 55409. (888)568-6235. **E-mail:** membership@puppeteers.org; execdir@puppeteers.org. **Website:** www.puppeteers.org. Purpose of organization: to promote the art and appreciation of puppetry as a means of communications and as a performing art. The Puppeteers of America boasts an international membership. There are 9 different levels of membership, from family to youth to library to senior and more. See the website for all details. Costs are $35-90 per year.

SCIENCE-FICTION AND FANTASY WRITERS OF AMERICA, INC.

P.O. Box 3238, Enfield CT 06083. **Website:** www.sfwa.org. Purpose of organization: to encourage public interest in science fiction literature and provide organization format for writers/editors/artists within the genre. Qualifications for membership: at least 1 professional sale or other professional involvement within the field. Different levels of membership include: active—requires 3 professional short stories or 1 novel published; associate—requires 1 professional sale; or affiliate—which requires some other professional involvement such as artist, editor, librarian, bookseller, teacher, etc. Workshops/conferences: annual awards banquet, usually in April or May. Open to nonmembers. Publishes quarterly journal, the *SFWA Bulletin*. Nonmember subscription: $18/year in U.S. Sponsors Nebula Awards for best published science fiction or fantasy in the categories of novel, novella, novelette and short story. Awards trophy. Also presents the Damon Knight Memorial Grand Master Award for Lifetime Achievement, and, beginning in 2006, the Andre Norton Award for Outstanding Young Adult Science Fiction or Fantasy Book of the Year.

SOCIETY OF CHILDREN'S BOOK WRITERS AND ILLUSTRATORS

8271 Beverly Blvd., Los Angeles CA 90048. (323)782-1010. **Fax:** (323)782-1892. **E-mail:** scbwi@scbwi.org; membership@scbwi.org. **Website:** www.scbwi.org. Purpose of organization: to assist writers and illustrators working or interested in the field. Qualifications for membership: an interest in children's literature and illustration. Membership cost: $80/year. Plus one time $90 initiation fee. Different levels of membership

include: P.A.L. membership—published by publisher listed in SCBWI Market Surveys; full membership—published authors/illustrators (includes self-published); associate membership—unpublished writers/illustrators. Holds 100 events (workshops/conferences) worldwide each year. National Conference open to nonmembers. Publishes bi-monthly magazine on writing and illustrating children's books. Sponsors annual awards and grants for writers and illustrators who are members. **Contact:** Stephen Mooser, president; Lin Oliver, executive director.

SOCIETY OF ILLUSTRATORS

128 E. 63rd St., New York NY 10065. (212)838-2560. **Fax:** (212)838-2561. **E-mail:** info@societyillustrators.org. **Website:** www.societyillustrators.org. "Our mission is to promote the art and appreciation of illustration, its history and evolving nature through exhibitions, lectures and education. Annual dues for nonresident illustrator members (those living more than 125 air miles from SI's headquarters): $300. Dues for resident illustrator members: $500 per year; resident associate members: $500. Artist members shall include those who make illustration their profession and earn at least 60% of their income from their illustration. Associate members are those who earn their living in the arts or who have made a substantial contribution to the art of illustration. This includes art directors, art buyers, creative supervisors, instructors, publishers and like categories. The candidate must complete and sign the application form, which requires a brief biography, a listing of schools attended, other training and a résumé of his or her professional career. Candidates for illustrators membership, in addition to the above requirements, must submit examples of their work." **Contact:** Anelle Miller, executive director.

SOCIETY OF SOUTHWESTERN AUTHORS

Fax: (520)751-7877. **E-mail:** azwritten@gmail.com. **Website:** www.ssa-az.org. Purpose of organization: to promote fellowship among professional and associate members of the writing profession, to recognize members' achievements, to stimulate further achievement, and to assist persons seeking to become professional writers. Qualifications for membership: Professional Membership—proof of publication of a book, articles, TV screenplay, etc; Associate Membership—proof of desire to write, and/or become a professional. Self-published authors may receive status of Professional

Membership at the discretion of the board of directors. Membership cost: see website. Sometimes this organization hosts writing events, such as its cosponsorship of the Arizona Writing Workshops in Phoenix and Tucson in November 2014. **Contact:** Chris Stern.

THEATRE FOR YOUNG AUDIENCES/USA

c/o The Theatre School, 2135 N. Kenmore Ave., Chicago IL 60657. (773)325-7981. **Fax:** (773)325-7920. **E-mail:** info@tyausa.org. **Website:** www.assitej-usa. org. Purpose of organization: to promote theater for children and young people by linking professional theaters and artists together; sponsoring national, international and regional conferences and providing publications and information. Also serves as U.S. Center for International Association of the Theatre for Children and Young People. Different levels of memberships include: organizations, individuals, students, retirees, libraries. TYA Today includes original articles, reviews and works of criticism and theory, all of interest to theater practitioners (included with membership). Publishes *Marquee*, a directory that focuses on information on members in US.

○ WRITERS' FEDERATION OF NOVA SCOTIA

1113 Marginal Rd., Halifax NS B3H 4P7Canada . (902)423-8116. **Fax:** (902)422-0881. **E-mail:** director@writers.ns.ca. **Website:** www.writers.ns.ca. Purpose of organization: "to foster creative writing and the profession of writing in Nova Scotia; to provide advice and assistance to writers at all stages of their careers; and to encourage greater public recognition of Nova Scotian writers and their achievements." Regional organization open to anybody who writes. Currently has 800+ members. Offerings include resource library with over 2,500 titles, promotional services, workshop series, annual festivals, mentorship program. Publishes *Eastword*, a bimonthly newsletter containing "a plethora of information on who's doing what; markets and contests; and current writing events and issues." Members and nationally known writers give readings that are open to the public. Additional information online.

○ WRITERS GUILD OF ALBERTA

11759 Groat Rd., Edmonton AB T5M 3K6Canada . (780)422-8174. **E-mail:** mail@writersguild.ab.ca. **Website:** www.writersguild.ab.ca. Purpose of organization: to support, encourage and promote writers and writing, to safeguard the freedom to write and to read, and to advocate for the well-being of writers in Alberta. Currently has over 1,000 members. Offerings include retreats/conferences; monthly events; bimonthly magazine that includes articles on writing and a market section; weekly electronic bulletin with markets and event listings; and the Stephan G. Stephansson Award for Poetry (Alberta residents only). Holds workshops/conferences. Publishes a newsletter focusing on markets, competitions, contemporary issues related to the literary arts (writing, publishing, censorship, royalties etc.). Sponsors annual literary awards in 5 categories (novel, nonfiction, children's literature, poetry, drama). Awards include $1,500, leather-bound book, promotion and publicity. Open to nonmembers.

CONFERENCES
& WORKSHOPS

///

Writers and illustrators eager to expand their knowledge of the children's publishing industry should consider attending one of the many conferences and workshops held each year. Whether you're a novice or seasoned professional, conferences and workshops are great places to pick up information on a variety of topics and network with experts in the publishing industry, as well as with your peers.

Listings in this section provide details about what conference and workshop courses are offered, where and when they are held, and the costs. Some of the national writing and art organizations also offer regional workshops throughout the year. Write, call, or visit websites for information.

Members of the Society of Children's Book Writers and Illustrators (SCBWI) can find information on conferences in national and local SCBWI newsletters. Nonmembers may attend SCBWI events as well. (Some SCBWI regional events are listed in this section.) For information on SCBWI's annual national conferences and all of their regional events, check their website (scbwi.org) for a complete calendar of conferences and happenings.

ALABAMA WRITING WORKSHOP

Website: www.alabamawritingworkshop.com. Estab. 2015. The 2016 event is set for Friday, February 19, 2016. Organized by Writing Day Workshops. The workshop is a one-day, all-day "How to Get Published" conference with instructional sessions and panels. Multiple literary agents are in attendance at the workshop to meet with writers and hear pitches.

COSTS Early-bird tuition is $129; later tuition is $149; agent meetings are $29 per appointment.

ACCOMMODATIONS Rooms available at the event hotels.

ADDITIONAL INFORMATION Query critique options available. Check the website for contact and registration information.

ALASKA WRITERS CONFERENCE

Alaska Writers Guild, PO Box 670014, Chugiak AK 99567. **E-mail:** alaskawritersguild.awg@gmail.com. **Website:** alaskawritersguild.com. Annual event held in the fall—usually September. Duration: 2 days. There are many workshops and instructional tracks of courses. This event sometimes teams up with SCBWI and Alaska Pacific University to offer courses at the event. Literary agents are in attendance each year to hear pitches and meet writers.

ANAM CARA WRITER'S AND ARTIST'S RETREAT

Eyeries, Beara, Co. Cork Ireland. (353)(027)74441. **Fax:** (353)(027)74448. **E-mail:** anamcararetreat@gmail.com. **Website:** www.anamcararetreat.com. **Contact:** Sue Booth-Forbes, director.

ACCOMMODATIONS 2015 cost: residency fee ranges from 600-700 Euro/week for individual retreats (full room and board). The event also features editorial consulting, laundry, sauna, hot tub overlooking Coulagh Bay, 5 acres of gardens, meadows, riverbank and cascades, river island, swimming hole, and several unique working spots, such as the ruin of a stone mill and a sod-roofed beehive hut. Overflow from workshops stay in nearby B&Bs, a 10-minute walk or 2-minute drive away. Transportation provided if needed. Details regarding workshops scheduled for 2015 and their fees as well as transportation to Anam Cara are available on the website.

ADDITIONAL INFORMATION Requests for specific information about rates and availability can be made through the website.

ANNUAL SPRING POETRY FESTIVAL

City College, 160 Convent Ave., New York NY 10031. (212)650-6356. **Website:** www.ccny.cuny.edu/prospective/humanities/poetry. Writer workshops geared to all levels. **Open to students.** Annual poetry festival. 2015 dates: May 8, 2015. Registration limited to 325. Cost of workshops and festival: free. Write for more information. Site: Theater B of Aaron Davis Hall.

ANTIOCH WRITERS' WORKSHOP

c/o Antioch University Midwest, 900 Dayton St., Yellow Springs OH 45387. (937)769-1803. **E-mail:** info@antiochwritersworkshop.com. **Website:** www.antiochwritersworkshop.com. **Contact:** Sharon Short, director. Estab. 1986. Average attendance: 80. Programs are offered year-round; see the website for details. The dates of the 2015 conference are July 11-17. Workshop concentration: fiction, poetry, personal essay, memoir. Workshop located at Antioch University Midwest in the Village of Yellow Springs. Literary agents attend. Writers of all levels (beginner to advanced) of fiction, memoir, personal essay, and poetry are warmly welcomed to discover their next steps on their writing paths--whether that's developing craft or preparing to submit for publication. An agent and an editor will be speaking and available for meetings with attendees.

ACCOMMODATIONS Accommodations are available at local hotels and bed & breakfasts.

ADDITIONAL INFORMATION The easiest way to contact this event is through the online website contact form.

ARKANSAS WRITERS' CONFERENCE

(501)833-2756. **E-mail:** breannacone1@yahoo.com. **Website:** www.arkansaswritersconference.org. 2015 dates: June 5-6. Held at Pulaski Technical College NLR Campus in Little Rock. There is a keynote speaker, events, contests, and more.

ASJA ANNUAL WRITERS CONFERENCE

American Society of Journalists and Authors, 355 Lexington Ave., 15th Floor, New York NY 10017. (212)997-0947. **E-mail:** asjaoffice@asja.org; director@asja.org. **Website:** www.asjaconferences.org. **Contact:** Alexandra Owens, executive director. Estab. 1971. Annual conference held in April. Conference duration: 3 days. Average attendance: 600. Covers nonfiction. Held at the Roosevelt in New York. Speakers have included Arianna Huffington, Kitty Kelley, Barbara Ehrenreich, and Stefan Fatsis.

COSTS $200 minimum, depending on when you sign up (includes lunch). Check website for updates.

ACCOMMODATIONS The hotel holding our conference always blocks out discounted rooms for attendees.

ADDITIONAL INFORMATION Conference program online by mid-January. Registration is online only. Sign up for e-mail updates online.

ASPEN SUMMER WORDS LITERARY FESTIVAL & WRITING RETREAT

Aspen Words, 110 E. Hallam St., #116, Aspen CO 81611. (970)925-3122. **Fax:** (970)925-5700. **E-mail:** aspenwords@aspeninstitute.org. **Website:** www.aspenwords.org. **Contact:** Caroline Tory, programs coordinator. Estab. 1976. 2015 dates: June 21-26. The 39th annual Aspen Summer Words Writing Retreat and Literary Festival offers workshops in fiction, memoir, novel editing, and playwriting. The faculty includes fiction writers Ann Hood, Richard Russo, Akhil Sharma, and Hannah Tinti; memoir writers Andre Dubus III and Dani Shapiro; and playwright Sharr White. Aspen Summer Words features lectures, readings, panel discussions, and the opportunity to meet with agents and editors. Tuition for the writing workshops ranges from $1,100 to $1,375, which includes some meals. Financial aid is available on a limited basis. To apply for a juried workshop, submit up to 10 pages of prose with a $30 application fee by February 27. Registration to non-juried workshops (Beginning Fiction and Playwriting) is first-come, first-served. A pass to all the public panels is $150, tickets to individual events are $20. Call, e-mail, or visit the website for an application and complete guidelines.

ASSOCIATION OF WRITERS & WRITING PROGRAMS ANNUAL CONFERENCE

Association of Writers & Writing Programs, George Mason University, 4400 University Drive, MSN 1E3, Fairfax VA 22030-4444. (703)993-4317. **Fax:** (703)993-4302. **E-mail:** conference@awpwriter.org; events@awpwriter.org. **Website:** www.awpwriter.org/awp_conference. Estab. 1992. Each year, AWP holds its Annual Conference & Bookfair in a different city to celebrate the authors, teachers, writing programs, literary centers, and independent publishers of that region. The conference typically features hundreds of readings, lectures, panel discussions, and forums, as well as hundreds of book signings, receptions, dances, and informal gatherings. AWP's is now the largest literary conference in North America.

ADDITIONAL INFORMATION Upcoming conference locations include Minneapolis (2015), Los Angeles (March 30-April 2, 2016), and Washington, D.C. (February 8-11, 2017).

ATLANTA WRITERS CONFERENCE

E-mail: awconference@gmail.com. **E-mail:** gjweinstein@yahoo.com. **Website:** www.atlantawritersconference.com. **Contact:** George Weinstein. The Atlanta Writers Conference happens twice a year (May and October/November) with 10 agents and publishing editors who critique ms samples and query letters, and also respond to pitches. There also are sessions with authors and industry professionals.

ACCOMMODATIONS Westin Airport Atlanta Hotel

ADDITIONAL INFORMATION There is a free shuttle that runs between the airport and the hotel.

ATLANTA WRITING WORKSHOP

Website: www.atlantawritingworkshop.com. Estab. 2015. The 2016 event is set for Saturday, February 20, 2016. Organized by Writing Day Workshops. The workshop is a one-day, all-day "How to Get Published" conference with instructional sessions and panels. Multiple literary agents are in attendance at the workshop to meet with writers and hear pitches.

COSTS Early-bird tuition is $129; later tuition is $149; agent meetings are $29 per appointment.

ACCOMMODATIONS Rooms available at the event hotel: Hyatt Place Cobb Galleria (NW of Atlanta).

ADDITIONAL INFORMATION Query critique options available. Check the website for contact and registration information.

BALTIMORE WRITERS' CONFERENCE

English Department, Liberal Arts Bldg., Towson University, 8000 York Rd., Towson MD 21252. (410)704-3695. **E-mail:** prwr@towson.edu. **Website:** baltimorewritersconference.org. Estab. 1994. "Annual conference held in November at Towson University. Conference duration: 1 day. Average attendance: 150-200. Covers all areas of writing and getting published. Held at Towson University. Session topics include fiction, nonfiction, poetry, magazine and journals, agents and publishers. Sign up the day of the conference for quick critiques to improve your stories, essays, and poems."

ACCOMMODATIONS Hotels are close by, if required.

ADDITIONAL INFORMATION Writers may register through the BWA website. Send inquiries via e-mail.

BAY TO OCEAN WRITERS CONFERENCE

P.O. Box 1773, Easton MD 21601. (443)786-4536. E-mail: info@baytoocean.com. **Website:** www.baytoocean.com. Estab. 1998. Annual conference held the last Saturday in February. Average attendance: 200. Approximately 30 speakers conduct workshops on publishing, agents, editing, marketing, craft, the Internet, poetry, fiction, nonfiction, and freelance writing. Site: Chesapeake College, Rt. 213 and Rt. 50, Wye Mills, on Maryland's historic Eastern Shore. Accessible to individuals with disabilities.

COSTS Adults $115, students $55. A paid ms review is also available—details on website. Includes continental breakfast and networking lunch.

ADDITIONAL INFORMATION Registration is on website. Pre-registration is required; no registration at door. Conference usually sells out one month in advance. Conference is for all levels of writers.

BIG SUR WRITING WORKSHOP

Henry Miller Library, Highway One, Big Sur CA 93920. (831)667-2574. **E-mail:** writing@henrymiller.org. **Website:** bigsurwriting.wordpress.com. Annual workshops focusing on children's and young adult writing (picture books, middle grade, and young adult). (2015 dates: March 6-8.) Workshop held in Big Sur Lodge in Pfeiffer State Park. Cost of workshop includes meals, lodging, workshop, Saturday evening reception. This event is helmed by the literary agents of the Andrea Brown Literary Agency, which is the most successful agency nationwide in selling kids books. All attendees meet with at least 2 faculty members, so work is critiqued.

Full editorial schedule and much more available online. The Lodge is located 25 miles south of Carmel in Big Sur's Pfeiffer State Park, 47225 Highway One Big Sur, CA 93920.

BOOMING GROUND ONLINE WRITERS STUDIO

Buch E-462, 1866 Main Mall, UBC, Vancouver BC V6T 1Z1Canada . **Fax:** (604)648-8848. **E-mail:** contact@boomingground.com. **Website:** www.boomingground.com. Writer mentorships geared toward beginner, intermediate, and advanced levels in novel, short fiction, poetry, nonfiction, and children's writing, and more. **Open to students.** Online mentorship program—students work for 6 months with a mentor by e-mail, allowing up to 120-240 pages of material to be created. Based in British Columbia. Check the website for more specifics.

BOSTON WRITING WORKSHOP

Website: www.bostonwritingworkshop.com. The 2015 event is set for Saturday, November 14, 2015. Organized by Writing Day Workshops. The workshop is a one-day, all-day "How to Get Published" conference with instructional sessions and panels. At least 8 literary agents are in attendance at the workshop to meet with writers and hear pitches.

COSTS Early-bird tuition is $149; later tuition is $179; agent meetings are $29 per appointment.

ACCOMMODATIONS Rooms available at the event hotel: The Sheraton Boston in Back Bay.

ADDITIONAL INFORMATION Query critique options available. Check the website for contact and registration information.

BREAD LOAF WRITERS' CONFERENCE

Middlebury College, Middlebury College, Middlebury VT 05753. (802)443-5286. **Fax:** (802)443-2087. **E-mail:** blwc@middlebury.edu. **Website:** www.middlebury.edu/bread-loaf-conferences/bl_writers. Estab. 1926. Annual conference held in late August. Conference duration: 10 days. Offers workshops for fiction, nonfiction, and poetry. Agents and editors will be in attendance.

ACCOMMODATIONS Bread Loaf Campus in Ripton, Vermont.

ADDITIONAL INFORMATION 2015 Conference Dates: August 12-22. Location: mountain campus of Middlebury College in Vermont. Average attendance: 230. The application deadline for the 2015 event is March 1, 2015; there is $15 application fee.

CAPE COD WRITERS CENTER ANNUAL CONFERENCE

P.O. Box 408, Osterville MA 02655. **E-mail:** writers@capecodwriterscenter.org. **Website:** www.capecodwriterscenter.org. **Contact:** Nancy Rubin Stuart, executive director. Duration: 3 days; held during first week in August. Offers workshops in fiction, commercial fiction, nonfiction, poetry, writing for children, memoir, pitching your book, screenwriting, digital communications, and getting published. There are ms evaluation and mentoring sessions with faculty.

COSTS Vary, depending on the number of courses selected.

ACCOMMODATIONS Held at Resort and Conference Center of Hyannis, Hyannis, MA.

CAPON SPRINGS WRITERS' WORKSHOP

2836 Westbrook Dr., Cincinnati OH 45211-7617. (513)481-9884. **E-mail:** whbeckman@gmail.com. **Website:** wendyonwriting.com. Estab. 2000. Event will be in October 2015. Conference duration: 2.5 days. Covers fiction, creative nonfiction, and publishing basics. Conference is held at Capon Springs and Farms Resort, a secluded 5,000-acre mountain resort in West Virginia.

COSTS Check website.

ACCOMMODATIONS Facility has swimming, hiking, fishing, tennis, badminton, volleyball, basketball, ping pong, etc. A 9-hole golf course is available for an additional fee.

ADDITIONAL INFORMATION Brochures available for SASE. Inquire via e-mail.

CAT WRITERS' ASSOCIATION ANNUAL WRITERS CONFERENCE

E-mail: loriehuston@pet-health-care-gazette.com. **Website:** www.catwriters.org. **Contact:** President Lorie Huston, DVM. Conference in the fall. The Cat Writers' Association holds an annual conference at varying locations around the US. The agenda for the conference is filled with seminars, editor appointments, an autograph party, networking breakfast, reception and annual awards banquet, as well as the annual meeting of the association. As of 2014, the event merged with BarkWorld Pet Expo to present BarkWorld/MeowWorld. See website for details.

CELEBRATION OF SOUTHERN LITERATURE

Southern Lit Alliance, 3069 S. Broad St., Suite 2, Chattanooga TN 37408-3056. (423)267-1218. **Fax:** (866)483-6831. **E-mail:** srobinson@southernlitalliance.org. **Website:** www.southernlitalliance.org. **Contact:** Susan Robinson. "The Celebration of Southern Literature stands out because of its unique collaboration with the Fellowship of Southern Writers, an organization founded by towering literary figures like Eudora Welty, Cleanth Brooks, Walker Percy, and Robert Penn Warren to recognize and encourage literature in the South. The 2015 celebration marked 26 years since the Fellowship selected Chattanooga for its headquarters and chose to collaborate with the Celebration of Southern Literature. The Fellowship awards 11 literary prizes and induct new members, making this event the place to discover up-and-coming voices in Southern literature. The Southern Lit Alliance's Celebration of Southern Literature attracts more than 1,000 readers and writers from all over the US. It strives to maintain an informal atmosphere where conversations will thrive, inspired by a common passion for the written word. The Southern Lit Alliance (formerly The Arts & Education Council) started as 1 of 12 pilot agencies founded by a Ford Foundation grant in 1952. The Alliance is the only organization of the 12 still in existence. The Southern Lit Alliance celebrates southern writers and readers through community education and innovative literary arts experiences."

This event happens every other year in odd-numbered years.

CHICAGO WRITERS CONFERENCE

E-mail: ines@chicagowritersconference.org; mare@chicagowritersconference.org. **Website:** chicagowritersconference.org. **Contact:** Mare Swallow. Estab. 2011. This conference happens every year in October. Find them on Twitter at @ChiWritersConf. The conference brings together a variety of publishing professionals (agents, editors, authors) and brings together several Chicago literary, writing, and bookselling groups. The conference often sells out. Past speakers have included *New York Times* bestselling author Sara Paretsky, children's author Allan Woodrow, YA author Erica O'Rourke, novelist Eric Charles May, and novelist Loretta Nyhan.

CHRISTOPHER NEWPORT UNIVERSITY WRITERS' CONFERENCE & WRITING CONTEST

(757)269-4368. **E-mail:** eleanor.taylor@cnu.edu. **Website:** www.facebook.com/cnuwriters. Estab. 1981. Conference held in the first few months of each year. This is a working conference. Presentations made by editors, agents, fiction writers, poets, and more. Breakout sessions in fiction, nonfiction, poetry, juvenile fiction, and publishing. Previous panels included "Publishing," "Proposal Writing," "Internet Research."

ACCOMMODATIONS Provides list of area hotels.

ADDITIONAL INFORMATION 2016 conference dates are set for May 6-7.

CLARKSVILLE WRITERS CONFERENCE

1123 Madison St., Clarksville TN 37040. (931)551-8870. **E-mail:** artsandheritage@cdelightband.net; burawac@apsu.edu. **E-mail:** artsandheritage@cde lightband.net; burawac@apsu.edu. **Website:** www.artsandheritage.us/writers. **Contact:** Ellen Kanervo. Annual conference held in the summer at Austin Peay State University. The conference features a variety of presentations on fiction, nonfiction, and more. Past presenting authors include Tom Franklin, Frye Gaillard, William Gay, Susan Gregg Gilmore, Will Campbell, John Seigenthaler Sr., Alice Randall, George Singleton, Alanna Nash, and Robert Hicks. Our presentations and workshops are valuable to writers and interesting to readers.

COSTS Costs available online; prices vary depending on how long attendees stay and if they attend the banquet dinner.

ADDITIONAL INFORMATION Multiple literary agents are flown in to the event every year to meet with writers and take pitches.

CONFERENCE FOR WRITERS & ILLUSTRATORS OF CHILDREN'S BOOKS

Book Passage, 51 Tamal Vista Blvd., Corte Madera CA 94925. (415)927-0960, ext. 234. **E-mail:** lberkler@bookpassage.com. **Website:** www.bookpassage.com. Conference for writers and illustrators geared toward beginner and intermediate levels. Sessions cover such topics as the nuts and bolts of writing and illustrating, publisher's spotlight, market trends, developing characters, finding voice in your writing, and the author/agent relationship. Held each summer with a conference length of 4 days. Includes opening night dinner, 3 lunches and a closing reception. 2015 dates: June 18-21.

CONNECTICUT WRITING WORKSHOP

Website: www.connecticutwritingworkshop.com. The 2015 event is set for Friday, November 13, 2015. Organized by Writing Day Workshops. The workshop is a one-day, all-day "How to Get Published" conference with instructional sessions and panels. Multiple literary agents are in attendance at the workshop to meet with writers and hear pitches.

COSTS Early-bird tuition is $129; later tuition is $149; agent meetings are $29 per appointment.

ACCOMMODATIONS Rooms available at the event hotel.

ADDITIONAL INFORMATION Query critique options available. Check the website for contact and registration information.

CRESTED BUTTE WRITERS CONFERENCE

P.O. Box 1361, Crested Butte CO 81224. **E-mail:** coordinator@conf.crestedbuttewriters.org. **Website:** www.crestedbuttewriters.org/conf.php. **Contact:** Barbara Crawford or Theresa Rizzo, co-coordinators. Estab. 2006. Annual conference held in June.

COSTS $330 nonmembers; $300 members; $297 Early Bird; The Sandy Writing Contest Finalist $280; and groups of 5 or more $280.

ACCOMMODATIONS The conference is held at The Elevation Hotel, located at the Crested Butte Mountain Resort at the base of the ski mountain. The quaint historic town lies nestled in a stunning mountain valley 3 short miles from the resort area of Mt. Crested Butte. A free bus runs frequently between the 2 towns. The closest airport is 30 miles away, in Gunnison. The conference website lists 3 lodging options besides rooms at the event facility. All condos, motels, and hotel options offer special conference rates. No special travel arrangements are made through the conference; however, information for car rental from Gunnison airport or the Alpine Express shuttle is listed on the online conference FAQ page.

ADDITIONAL INFORMATION "Our conference workshops address a wide variety of writing craft and business. Our most popular workshop is Our First Pages Readings—with a twist. Agents and editors read opening pages volunteered by attendees-with a few best selling authors' openings mixed in. Think the A/E can identify the bestsellers? Not so much. Each year one of our attendees has been mistaken for a bestseller and obviously garnered requests from some on the panel. Writers may request additional information by e-mail."

WRITERS IN PARADISE

Eckerd College, 4200 54th Ave. South, St. Petersburg FL 33711. (727) 864-7994. **Fax:** (727) 864-7575. **E-mail:** wip@eckerd.edu. **Website:** writersinparadise.eckerd.edu/. Estab. 2005. Annual. January. 2015 dates: Jan 16-23. Conference duration: 8 days. Average attendance: 84 maximum. Workshop. Offers college credit. "Writers in Paradise Conference offers workshop classes in fiction (novel and short story), poetry, and nonfiction. Working closely with our award-winning faculty, students will have stimulating opportunities to ask questions and learn valuable skills from fellow students and authors at the top of their form. Most importantly, the intimate size and secluded location of the Writers in Paradise experience allows you the time and opportunity to share your mss, critique one another's work, and discuss the craft of writing with experts and peers who can help guide you to the next level." Previous faculty includes Andre Dubus III (*House of Sand and Fog*), Michael Koryta (*So Cold the River*), Dennis Lehane (*The Given Day*), Laura Lippman (*I'd Know You Anywhere*), Seth Fishman (literary agent), Johnny Temple (Akashic Books), and more." Editors and agents attend the conference.

ADDITIONAL INFORMATION Application (December deadline) materials are required of all attendees.

ERMA BOMBECK WRITERS' WORKSHOP

University of Dayton, 300 College Park, Dayton OH 45469. **E-mail:** erma@udayton.edu. **Website:** humorwriters.org. **Contact:** Teri Rizvi. This is a specialized writing conference for writers of humor (books, articles, essays, blogs, film/TV). It happens every 2 years. The 2016 conference dates are March 31-April 2. The Bombeck Workshop is the only one in the country devoted to both humor and human interest writing. Through the workshop, the University of Dayton and the Bombeck family honor one of America's most celebrated storytellers and humorists. Over the past decade, the workshop has attracted such household names as Dave Barry, Art Buchwald, Phil Donahue, Nancy Cartwright, Don Novello, Garrison Keillor, Gail Collins, Connie Schultz, Adriana Trigiani and Alan Zweibel. The workshop draws approximately 350 writers from around the country and typically sells out very quickly, so don't wait once registration opens.

ADDITIONAL INFORMATION Connect with the event on social media: facebook.com/ermabombeck, and @ebww.

FLATHEAD RIVER WRITERS CONFERENCE

P.O. Box 7711, Kalispell MT 59904-7711. (406)881-4066. **E-mail:** answers@authorsoftheflathead.org. **Website:** www.authorsoftheflathead.org/conference.asp. Estab. 1990. Two-day conference packed with energizing speakers. Highlights include 2 literary agents who will review 12 ms one-on-one with the first 24 paid attendees requesting this opportunity, a synopsis writing workshop, a screenwriting workshop, and more.

COSTS Check the website for updated cost information and more.

ACCOMMODATIONS Rooms are available at a discounted rate.

ADDITIONAL INFORMATION Watch website for additional speakers and other details. Register early as seating is limited.

FLORIDA WRITING WORKSHOPS

Website: www.floridawritingworkshops.com. Estab. 2015. The 2016 calendar year includes events in the Tampa area (Friday, Match 25, 2016) and the Fort Lauderdale area (Saturday, March 26, 2016) at hotel locations. Organized by Writing Day Workshops. The workshops are separate yet identical "How to Get Published" one-day conferences with instructional sessions all day. Multiple literary agents are in attendance at both events to meet with writers and hear pitches.

COSTS Early-bird tuition is $129; later tuition is $149; agent meetings are $29 per appointment.

ACCOMMODATIONS Rooms available at the event hotels.

ADDITIONAL INFORMATION Query critique options available. Check the website for contact and registration information.

GENEVA WRITERS CONFERENCE

Geneva Writers Group, Switzerland. **E-mail:** info@GenevaWritersGroup.org. **Website:** www.genevawritersgroup.org. Estab. 1993. Biennial conference (even years) held at Webster University in Bellevue/Geneva, Switzerland. (The 2014 dates were January 31-February 2.) Conference duration: 2.5 days, welcoming more than 200 writers from around the world. Speakers and presenters have included Peter Ho Davies, Jane Alison, Russell Celyn Jones, Patricia Hampl, Robert Root, Brett Lott, Dinty W. Moore, Naomi Shihab Nye, Jo Shapcott, Wallis Wilde Menozzi, Susan Tiberghien, Jane Dystel, Laura Longrigg, and Colin Harrison.

GULF COAST WRITERS CONFERENCE

P.O. Box 35038, Panama City FL 32412. (800)628-6028. **E-mail:** PulpwoodPress@gmail.com. **Website:** www.gulfcoastwritersconference.com. Estab. 1999. Annual conference held in September in Panama City, Fla. Conference duration: 1 day. Average attendance: 100+. This conference is deliberately small and writer-centric with an affordable attendance price. (As of this listing being updated, the conference is completely free.) Speakers include writers, editors and agents. Cricket Freeman of the August Agency is often in attendance. A former keynote speaker was mystery writer Michael Connelly.

HAMPTON ROADS WRITERS CONFERENCE

P.O. Box 56228, Virginia Beach VA 23456. **E-mail:** hrwriters@cox.net. **Website:** hamptonroadswriters.org. 2015 dates: Sept. 17-20, 2015. Workshops cover fiction, nonfiction, memoir, poetry, and the business of getting published. A bookshop, 3 free contests with cash prizes, free evening networking social, and many networking opportunities will be available. Multiple literary agents are in attendance each year to meet with writers and hear 10-minute pitches. Much more information available on the website.

COSTS Maximum of $255. Costs vary. There are discounts for members, for early bird registration, for students and more

HIGHLAND SUMMER CONFERENCE

Box 7014, Radford University, Radford VA 24142-7014. **E-mail:** tburriss@radford.edu; rbderrick@radford.edu. **Website:** tinyurl.com/q8z8ej9. **Contact:** Dr. Theresa Burriss, Ruth Derrick. Estab. 1978. 2015 dates: June 15-19. The Highland Summer Writers' Conference is a 4-day lecture-seminar workshop combination conducted by well-known guest writers. It offers the opportunity to study and practice creative and expository writing within the context of regional culture. The course is graded on Pass/Fail basis for undergraduates and letter grades for graduate students. It may be taken twice for credit. The evening readings are free and open to the public. Services at a reduced rate for continuing education credits or to simply participate.

HIGHLIGHTS FOUNDATION FOUNDERS WORKSHOPS

814 Court St., Honesdale PA 18431. (570)253-1122. **Fax:** (570)253-0179. **E-mail:** klbrown@highlights foundation.org. **E-mail:** jo.lloy@highlightsfounda tion.org. **Website:** highlightsfoundation.org. **Contact:** Kent L. Brown, Jr. Estab. 2000. Offers more than three dozen workshops per year. Conference duration: 3-7 days. Average attendance: limited to 10-14. Genre specific workshops and retreats on children's writing: fiction, nonfiction, poetry, promotions. "Our goal is to improve, over time, the quality of literature for children by educating future generations of children's authors." Highlights Founders' home in Boyds Mills, Pa.

COSTS Prices vary based on workshop. Check website for details.

ACCOMMODATIONS Coordinates pickup at local airport. Offers overnight accommodations. Participants stay in guest cabins on the wooded grounds surrounding Highlights Founders' home adjacent to the house/conference center.

ADDITIONAL INFORMATION Some workshops require pre-workshop assignment. Brochure available for SASE, by e-mail, on website, by phone, by fax. Accepts inquiries by phone, fax, e-mail, SASE. Editors attend conference. "Applications will be reviewed and accepted on a first-come, first-served basis, applicants must demonstrate specific experience in writing area of workshop they are applying for—writing samples are required for many of the workshops."

HOUSTON WRITERS GUILD CONFERENCE

P.O. Box 42255, Houston TX 77242. (281)736-7168. **E-mail:** HoustonWritersGuild@Hotmail.com. **Website:** houstonwritersguild.org/annual-conference. 2015 dates: Saturday, April 24-26. This annual conference, organized by the Houston Writers Guild, happens in the spring, and has concurrent sessions and tracks on the craft and business of writing. Each year, multiple agents are in attendance taking pitches from writers. The 2015 keynote speaker was Jane Friedman.

COSTS Costs are different for members and non-members. Costs depend on how many days and events you sign up for.

ADDITIONAL INFORMATION There is a writing contest at the event. There is also a for-pay pre-conference workshop the day before the conference.

IDAHO WRITERS LEAGUE WRITERS' CONFERENCE

601 W. 75 S., Blackfoot ID 83221-6153. (208)684-4200. **Website:** www.idahowritersleague.com. Estab. 1940. Annual floating conference, usually held in September. This conference has at least one agent in attendance every year, along with other writers and presenters.

COSTS A minimum of $145, depending on early bird pricing and membership. Check the website for updates on cost.

INDIANA UNIVERSITY WRITERS' CONFERENCE

464 Ballantine Hall, 1020 E. Kirkwood Ave., Bloomington IN 47405-7103. (812)855-1877. **Fax:** (812)855-9535. **E-mail:** writecon@indiana.edu. **Website:** www.

indiana.edu/~writecon. Estab. 1940. Annual. Conference/workshops held in May. 2015 dates: May 30-June 3. Average attendance: 115. "The Indiana University Writers' Conference believes in a craft-based teaching of fiction writing. We emphasize an exploration of creativity through a variety of approaches, offering workshop-based craft discussions, classes focusing on technique, and talks about the careers and concerns of a writing life."

ACCOMMODATIONS Information on accommodations available on website.

ADDITIONAL INFORMATION Connect on Twitter at @iuwritecon.

IOWA SUMMER WRITING FESTIVAL

The University of Iowa, C215 Seashore Hall, University of Iowa, Iowa City IA 52242. (319)335-4160. **Fax:** (319)335-4743. **E-mail:** iswfestival@uiowa.edu. **Website:** uiowa.edu/~iswfest. Estab. 1987. Annual festival held in June and July. 2015 event will have 138 workshops with 72 instructors. Conference duration: Workshops are 1 week or a weekend. Average attendance: Limited to 12 people/class, with over 1,500 participants throughout the summer. "We offer courses across the genres: novel, short story, poetry, essay, memoir, humor, travel, playwriting, screenwriting, writing for children, and women's writing. Held at the University of Iowa campus." Speakers have included Marvin Bell, Lan Samantha Chang, John Dalton, Hope Edelman, Katie Ford, Patricia Foster, Bret Anthony Johnston, Barbara Robinette Moss, among others.

ACCOMMODATIONS Accommodations available at area hotels. Information on overnight accommodations available by phone or on website.

ADDITIONAL INFORMATION Brochures are available in February. Inquire via e-mail or on website.

IWWG ANNUAL CONFERENCE

International Women's Writing Guild, (212)737-7536. **Fax:** (212)737-9469. **E-mail:** iwwgquestions@gmail.com. **Website:** www.iwwg.org. Writer and illustrator workshops geared toward all levels. Offers over 50 different workshops—some are for children's book writers and illustrators. Also sponsors other events throughout the US. Annual workshops. Workshops held every summer for a week. Length of each session: 90 minutes; sessions take place for an entire week. Registration limited to 500. Write for more in-

formation. The 2015 spring conference was March 15 in Los Angeles.

JACKSON HOLE WRITERS CONFERENCE

PO Box 1974, Jackson WY 83001. (307)413-3332. **E-mail:** nicole@jacksonholewritersconference.com. **Website:** jacksonholewritersconference.com. Estab. 1991. Annual conference held in late June. Conference duration: 4 days. Average attendance: 110. Covers fiction, creative nonfiction, and young adult and offers ms critiques from authors, agents, and editors. Agents in attendance will take pitches from writers. Paid manuscript critique programs are available.

COSTS $365 if registered by May 12. Accompanying teen writer: $175. Pre-Conference Writing Workshop: $150.

ADDITIONAL INFORMATION Held at the Center for the Arts in Jackson, Wyoming and online.

JAMES RIVER WRITERS CONFERENCE

2319 East Broad St., Richmond VA 23223. (804)433-3790. **Fax:** (804)291-1466. **E-mail:** info@jamesriverwriters.com; fallconference@jamesriverwriters.com. **Website:** www.jamesriverwriters.com. Estab. 2003. Annual conference held in October. The event has master classes, agent pitching, editor pitching, critiques, sessions, panels, and more. Previous attending agents have included Kimiko Nakamura, Kaylee Davis, Peter Knapp, and more.

COSTS $240-290.

ACCOMMODATIONS Hilton Garden Inn, 501 E. Broad St.

KACHEMAK BAY WRITERS' CONFERENCE

Kenai Peninsula College - Kachemak Bay Campus, 533 East Pioneer Ave., Homer AK 99603. (907)235-7743. **E-mail:** iyconf@uaa.alaska.edu. **Website:** writersconference.uaa.alaska.edu. Annual writers conference held in June. 2015 dates: June 12-16. 2015 keynote speaker was Andre Dubus III. Sponsored by Kachemak Bay Campus-Kenai Peninsula College / UAA. This nationally recognized writing conference features workshops, readings and panel presentations in fiction, poetry, nonfiction, and the business of writing. There are "open mic" sessions for conference registrants; evening readings open to the public; agent/editor consultations, and more.

COSTS See the website. Some scholarships available.

ACCOMMODATIONS Homer is 225 miles south of Anchorage, Alaska on the southern tip of the Kenai

Peninsula and the shores of Kachemak Bay. There are multiple hotels in the area.

KENTUCKY WRITERS CONFERENCE

Southern Kentucky Book Fest, Knicely Conference Center, 2355 Nashville Road, Bowling Green KY 42101. (270)745-4502. **E-mail:** kristie.lowry@wku.edu. **Website:** www.sokybookfest.org/KYWritersConf. **Contact:** Kristie Lowry. This event is entirely free to the public. 2015 date: April 17. Duration: 1 day. Precedes the Southern Kentucky Book Fest the next day. Authors who will be participating in the Book Fest on Saturday will give attendees at the writers' conference the benefit of their wisdom on Friday. Free workshops on a variety of writing topics will be presented during this day-long event. Sessions run for 75 minutes and the day begins at 9 a.m. and ends at 3:30 p.m. The conference is open to anyone who would like to attend, including high school students, college students, teachers, and the general public.

KENYON REVIEW WRITERS WORKSHOP

Kenyon College, Gambier OH 43022. (740)427-5207. **Fax:** (740)427-5417. **E-mail:** kenyonreview@kenyon.edu; writers@kenyonreview.org. **Website:** www.kenyonreview.org. **Contact:** Anna Duke Reach, director. Estab. 1990. Annual 8-day workshop held in June. Participants apply in poetry, fiction, creative nonfiction, literary hybrid/book arts or writing online, and then participate in intensive daily workshops which focus on the generation and revision of significant new work. Held on the campus of Kenyon College in the rural village of Gambier, Ohio. Workshop leaders have included David Baker, Carl Phillips, Mary Szybist, Rebecca McClanahan, Dinty Moore, Caitlin Horrocks, Lee K. Abbott, and Nancy Zafris.

COSTS $1,995; includes tuition, room and board.

ACCOMMODATIONS The workshop operates a shuttle to and from Gambier and the airport in Columbus, Ohio. Offers overnight accommodations. Participants are housed in Kenyon College student housing. The cost is covered in the tuition.

ADDITIONAL INFORMATION Application includes a writing sample. Admission decisions are made on a rolling basis. Workshop information is available online at www.kenyonreview.org/workshops in November. For brochure send e-mail, visit website, call, or fax. Accepts inquiries by SASE, e-mail, phone, fax.

KINDLING WORDS EAST

Website: www.kindlingwords.org. Annual retreat held early in the year near Burlington, Vermont. 2015 dates: February 5-8. A retreat with three strands: writer, illustrator and editor; professional level. Intensive workshops for each strand, and an open schedule for conversations and networking. Registration limited to approximately 70. Hosted by the 4-star Inn at Essex (room and board extra). Participants must be published by a CCBC listed publisher, or if in publishing, occupy a professional position. Registration opens August 1 or as posted on the website, and fills quickly. Check website to see if spaces are available, to sign up to be notified when registration opens each year, or for more information. No contact email is available for this organization, but there is a contact form on the website.

KINDLING WORDS WEST

Website: www.KindlingWords.org. Annual retreat specifically for children's book writers held in late April/early May out west. 2015 location is in Marble Falls, TX. 2015 dates are April 7-14. KWW is an artist's colony-style week with workshops by gifted teachers followed by a working retreat. Participants gather just before dinner to have white-space discussions; evenings include fireside readings, star gazing and songs. Participants must be published by CBC-recognized publisher.

LA JOLLA WRITERS CONFERENCE

P.O. Box 178122, San Diego CA 92177. **E-mail:** akuritz@san.rr.com. **Website:** www.lajollawritersconference.com. **Contact:** Jared Kuritz, director. Annual conference held in November. 2015 dates: November 6-8. Conference duration: 3 days. Average attendance: 200. The LJWC covers all genres and both fiction and nonfiction as well as the business of writing. "We take particular pride in educating our attendees on the business aspect of the book industry and have agents, editors, publishers, publicists, and distributors teach classes. There is unprecedented access to faculty at the LJWC. Our conference offers lecture sessions that run for 50 minutes, and workshops that run for 110 minutes. Each block period is dedicated to either workshop or lecture-style classes, with 6-8 classes on various topics available each block. For most workshop classes, you are encouraged to bring written work for review. Literary agents from prestigious agencies such as The Andrea Brown Literary

Agency, The Dijkstra Agency, The McBride Agency and Full Circle Literary Group, the Zimmerman Literary Agency, the Van Haitsma Literary Agency, the Farris Literary Agency, and more have participated in the past, teaching workshops in which they are familiarized with attendee work. Late night and early bird sessions are also available. The conference creates a strong sense of community, and it has seen many of its attendees successfully published."

COSTS $295 early bird registration for 2015. Conference limited to 200 attendees.

LAS VEGAS WRITERS CONFERENCE

Henderson Writers' Group, PO Box 92032, Henderson NV 89009. (702)564-2488; or, toll-free, (866)869-7842. **E-mail:** lasvegaswritersconference@gmail.com. **Website:** www.lasvegaswritersconference.com. Annual. Held April 28-30. Conference duration: 3 days. Average attendance: 150 maximum. "Join writing professionals, agents, industry experts, and your colleagues for 3 days in Las Vegas as they share their knowledge on all aspects of the writer's craft. While there are formal pitch sessions, panels, workshops, and seminars, the faculty is also available throughout the conference for informal discussions and advice. Workshops, seminars, and expert panels cover topics in both fiction and nonfiction, screenwriting, marketing, indie-publishing and the craft of writing itself. There will be many Q&A panels for you to ask the experts all your questions." Site: Sam's Town Hotel and Gambling Hall in Las Vegas (Henderson, Nevada).

COSTS 2015 prices: $375 until October 31, 2015; $450 starting February 1, 2015; $500 at door; $300 for one day.

ADDITIONAL INFORMATION Sponsors contest. Agents and editors participate in conference.

LEAGUE OF UTAH WRITERS' ANNUAL WRITER'S CONFERENCE

E-mail: Luwriters@gmail.com. **Website:** www.luwriters.org/index.html. **Contact:** Tim Keller. Annual spring and fall conferences. Faculty includes novelists, screenwriters, agents, and editors. Writer workshops geared toward beginner, intermediate or advanced. Annual conference.

MENDOCINO COAST WRITERS CONFERENCE

1211 Del Mar Dr., second address is P.O. Box 2087, Fort Bragg CA 95437. (707)485-4032. **E-mail:** info@mcwc.org. **Website:** www.mcwc.org. Estab. 1988.

Annual summer conference. 2015 dates: August 6-8, 2015. Average attendance: 90. Offers intensive workshops in fiction, creative nonfiction, poetry, YA, and seminars/panels about writing and publishing. Located at a community college on the Northern California Coast. Workshop leaders at the 2015 event: Ellen Bass, David Corbett, Catherine Ryan Hyde, Albert DeSilver, Lisa Locascio. Opportunities to meet informally or in private manuscript consultations with agents and editors.

COSTS $525 (minimum) includes morning intensives, afternoon panels and seminars, social events, and most meals. Scholarships available. Early application advised.

ADDITIONAL INFORMATION Emphasis is on encouragement, expertise and inspiration in a literary community where authors are also fantastic teachers. Registration opens March 15.

MIDWEST WRITERS WORKSHOP

Ball State University, Department of Journalism, Muncie IN 47306. (765)282-1055. **E-mail:** midwestwriters@yahoo.com. **Website:** www.midwestwriters.org. **Contact:** Jama Kehoe Bigger, director. Annual workshop held in late July in eastern Indiana. Writer workshops geared toward writers of all levels. Topics include most genres. Faculty/speakers have included Joyce Carol Oates, George Plimpton, Clive Cussler, Haven Kimmel, William Kent Krueger, Wiliam Zinsser, John Gilstrap, Lee Martin, Jane Friedman, Chuck Sambuchino, and numerous bestselling mystery, literary fiction, young adult, and children's authors. Workshop also includes agent pitch sessions ms evaluation and a writing contest. Registration tentatively limited to 200.

COSTS $185-395. Most meals included.

ADDITIONAL INFORMATION Offers scholarships. See website for more information. Keep in touch with the MWW at facebook.com/MidwestWriters and twitter.com/MidwestWriters.

MISSOURI WRITERS' GUILD CONFERENCE

St. Louis MO **E-mail:** mwgconferenceinfo@gmail.com. **Website:** www.missouriwritersguild.org. **Contact:** Tricia Sanders, vice president/conference chairman. Writer and illustrator workshops geared to all levels. **Open to students.** Conference "gives writers the opportunity to hear outstanding speakers and to receive information on marketing, research, and writing techniques." Agents, editors, and published authors in attendance. There was no 2015 event, but keep checking the guild website for future events because a return is planned. The keynote speaker in 2014 was Writer's Digest Books editor Chuck Sambuchino.

ADDITIONAL INFORMATION The primary contact individual changes every year, because the conference chair changes every year. See the website for contact info.

OHIO KENTUCKY INDIANA CHILDREN'S LITERATURE CONFERENCE

Northern Kentucky University, 405 Steely Library, Highland Heights KY 41099. (859)572-6620. **Fax:** (859)572-5390. **E-mail:** smithjen@nku.edu. **Website:** http://oki.nku.edu. **Contact:** Jennifer Smith. Annual conference for writers and illustrators geared toward all levels. **Open to all.** Emphasizes multicultural literature for children and young adults. Conference held annually in November. Contact Jennifer Smith for more information.

COSTS $75; includes registration/attendance at all workshop sessions, *Tri-state Authors and Illustrators of Childrens Books Directory*, continental breakfast, lunch, author/illustrator signings. Manuscript critiques are available for an additional cost. E-mail or call for more information.

MONTEVALLO LITERARY FESTIVAL

Sta. 6420, University of Montevallo, Montevallo AL 35115. (205)665-6420. **Fax:** (205)665-6422. **E-mail:** murphyj@montevallo.edu. **Website:** http://www.montevallo.edu/arts-sciences/college-of-arts-sciences/departments/english-foreign-languages/student-organizations/montevallo-literary-festival/. **Contact:** Dr. Jim Murphy, director. Estab. 2003. 2015 dates: March 20. "Each April, the University of Montevallo's Department of English and Foreign Languages hosts the annual Montevallo Literary Festival, a celebration of creative writing dedicated to bringing literary writers and readers together on a personal scale. Our friendly, relaxed festival runs all day into the evening featuring readings by all invited writers, book signings, a Q&A panel, social gatherings and dinner with live music."

JENNY MCKEAN MOORE COMMUNITY WORKSHOPS

English Department, George Washington University, 801 22nd St. NW, Rome Hall, Suite 760, Washington DC 20052. (202)994-6180. **Fax:** (202)994-7915. **E-mail:** lpageinc@gwu.edu. **Website:** www.gwu.edu/~english/creative_jennymckeanmoore.html. **Contact:** Lisa Page, acting director of creative writing. Estab. 1976. Workshop held each semester at the university. Average attendance: 15. Concentration varies depending on professor—usually fiction or poetry. The Creative Writing department brings an established poet or novelist to campus each year to teach a writing workshop for GW students and a free community workshop for adults in the larger Washington community. Details posted on website in June, with an application deadline at the end of August or in early September.

ADDITIONAL INFORMATION Admission is competitive and by decided by the quality of a submitted ms.

MUSE AND THE MARKETPLACE

Grub Street, 162 Boylston St., 5th Floor, Boston MA 02116. (617)695-0075. **E-mail:** info@grubstreet.org. **Website:** www.grubstreet.org/muse. The conferences are held in the late spring, such as early May. (2015 dates were May 1-3.) Conference duration: 3 days. Average attendance: 400. Dozens of agents are in attendance to meet writers and take pitches. The conference has workshops on all aspects of writing.

ACCOMMODATIONS Boston Park Plaza Hotel.

NAPA VALLEY WRITERS' CONFERENCE

Napa Valley College, 1088 College Ave., St. Helena CA 94574. (707)967-2900. **E-mail:** writecon@napavalley.edu. **Website:** www.napawritersconference.org. **Contact:** Andrea Bewick, managing director. Estab. 1981. Established 1981. Annual weeklong event. 2015 dates: July 26 - July 31. Location: Upper Valley Campus in the historic town of St. Helena, 25 miles north of Napa in the heart of the valley's wine growing community. Average attendance: 48 in poetry and 48 in fiction. "Serious writers of all backgrounds and experience are welcome to apply." Offers poets and fiction writers workshops, lectures, faculty readings at Napa Valley wineries, and one-on-one faculty counseling. "Poetry session provides the opportunity to work both on generating new poems and on revising previously written ones."

COSTS $975; $25 application fee.

NIMROD ANNUAL WRITERS' WORKSHOP

800 S. Tucker Dr., Tulsa OK 74104. (918)631-3080. **E-mail:** nimrod@utulsa.edu. **Website:** www.utulsa.edu/nimrod. **Contact:** Eilis O'Neal, editor-in-chief. Estab. 1978. Annual conference held in October. Conference duration: 1 day. Offers one-on-one editing sessions,

readings, panel discussions, and master classes in fiction, poetry, nonfiction, memoir, and fantasy writing. Speakers have included Ted Kooser, Colum McCann, Molly Peacock, Peter S. Beagle, Aimee Nezhukumatathil, Philip Levine, and Linda Pastan. Full conference details are online in August.

COSTS Approximately $50. Lunch provided. Scholarships available for students.

ADDITIONAL INFORMATION *Nimrod International Journal* sponsors literary awards: The Katherine Anne Porter Prize for fiction and The Pablo Neruda Prize for poetry. Poetry and fiction prizes: $2,000 each and publication (top prize); $1,000 each and publication (other winners). Deadline: must be postmarked no later than April 30.

NORTH CAROLINA WRITERS' NETWORK FALL CONFERENCE

P.O. Box 21591, Winston-Salem NC 27120. (336)293-8844. **E-mail:** mail@ncwriters.org. **Website:** www.ncwriters.org. Estab. 1985. Annual conference held in November in different NC venues. Average attendance: 250. This organization hosts 2 conferences: 1 in the spring and 1 in the fall. Each conference is a weekend full of workshops, panels, book signings, and readings (including open mic). There will be a keynote speaker, a variety of sessions on the craft and business of writing, and opportunities to meet with agents and editors.

COSTS Approximately $250 (includes 4 meals).

ACCOMMODATIONS Special rates are usually available at the conference hotel, but conferees must make their own reservations.

ADDITIONAL INFORMATION Available at www.ncwriters.org.

NORTHERN COLORADO WRITERS CONFERENCE

2107 Thunderstone Court, Fort Collins CO 80525. (970)556-0908. **E-mail:** kerrie@northerncoloradowriters.com. **Website:** www.northerncoloradowriters.com. Estab. 2006. Annual conference held in March in Fort Collins. 2015 dates: March 27-28. Conference duration: 2-3 days. The conference features a variety of speakers, agents and editors. There are workshops and presentations on fiction, nonfiction, screenwriting, children's books, marketing, magazine writing, staying inspired, and more. Previous agents who have attended and taken pitches from writers include Jessica Regel, Kristen Nelson, Rachelle Gardner, Andrea

Brown, Ken Sherman, Jessica Faust, Gordon Warnock, and Taylor Martindale. Each conference features more than 30 workshops from which to choose from. Previous keynotes include Chuck Sambuchino, Andrew McCarthy, and Stephen J. Cannell.

COSTS $255-541, depending on what package the attendee selects, whether you're a member or nonmember, and whether you're renewing your NCW membership.

ACCOMMODATIONS The conference is hosted at the Fort Collins Hilton, where rooms are available at a special rate.

OHIO KENTUCKY INDIANA CHILDREN'S LITERATURE CONFERENCE

Northern Kentucky University, 405 Steely Library, Highland Heights KY 41099. (859)572-6620. **Fax:** (859)572-5390. **E-mail:** smithjen@nku.edu. **Website:** http://oki.nku.edu. **Contact:** Jennifer Smith. Annual conference for writers and illustrators geared toward all levels. **Open to all.** Emphasizes multicultural literature for children and young adults. Conference held annually in November. Contact Jennifer Smith for more information.

COSTS $75; includes registration/attendance at all workshop sessions, *Tri-state Authors and Illustrators of Childrens Books Directory*, continental breakfast, lunch, author/illustrator signings. Manuscript critiques are available for an additional cost. E-mail or call for more information.

OKLAHOMA WRITERS' FEDERATION, INC. ANNUAL CONFERENCE

9800 South Hwy. 137, Miami OK 74354. **Website:** www.owfi.org. Annual conference held just outside Oklahoma City. Held first weekend in May each year. Writer workshops geared toward all levels. The goal of theconference is to create good stories with strong bones. We will be exploring cultural writing and cultural sensitivity in writing. Several literary agents are in attendance each year to meet with writers and hear pitches.

COSTS Costs vary depending on when registrants sign up. Cost includes awards banquet and famous author banquet. Three extra sessions are available for an extra fee. Visit the eventwebsite for a complete faculty list and conference information

OUTDOOR WRITERS ASSOCIATION OF AMERICA ANNUAL CONFERENCE

615 Oak St., Suite 201, Missoula MT 59801. (406)728-7434. **E-mail:** info@owaa.org. **Website:** http://owaa.org. **Contact:** Jessica Seitz, conference and membership coordinator. Outdoor communicator workshops geared toward all levels. Annual three-day conference. Craft improvement seminars; newsmaker sessions. 2016 conference to be held in Billings, MT. Cost includes attendance at all workshops and most meals. Visit owaa.org/2016conference for additional information on the 2016 event.

COSTS $425-449.

OZARK CREATIVE WRITERS, INC. CONFERENCE

P.O. Box 9076, Fayetteville AR 72703. **E-mail:** ozarkcreativewriters1@gmail.com. **Website:** www.ozarkcreativewriters.org. The annual event is held in October at the Inn of the Ozarks, in the resort town of Eureka Springs, Arkansas. Approximately 200 attend each year; many also enter the creative writing competitions. Open to professional and amateur writers, workshops are geared to all levels and all forms of the creative process and literary arts. Sessions sometimes include songwriting, with presentations by best-selling authors, editors, and agents. The OCW Conference promotes writing by offering writing competitions in all genres.

A full list of sessions and speakers is online. The conference usually has agents and/or editors in attendance to meet with writers.

PACIFIC COAST CHILDREN'S WRITERS WHOLE-NOVEL WORKSHOP: FOR ADULTS AND TEENS

P.O. Box 244, Aptos CA 95001. **Website:** www.childrenswritersworkshop.com. 2015 dates: Oct. 2-4. "Our seminar offers semi-advanced through published adult writers an editor and/or agent critique on their full novel or 15-30 page partial. (Mid-book and synopsis critique may be included with the partial.) A concurrent workshop is open to students age 13 and up, who give adults target-reader feedback. There is a focus on craft as a marketing tool. Team-taught master classes (open clinics for ms critiques) explore such topics as "Story Architecture and Arcs." Continuous close contact with faculty, who have included Andrea Brown, agent, and Simon Boughton, VP/executive editor at 3 Macmillan imprints. **Past seminars**:

Annually, the first weekend of October. Registration limited to 16 adults and 10 teens. For the most critique options, submit sample chapters and synopsis with e-application by mid May; open until filled. **Content:** Character-driven novels with protagonists ages 11 and older. Collegial format; 90 percent hands-on. Our pre-workshop anthology of peer manuscripts maximizes learning and networking. Several past attendees have landed contracts as a direct result of our seminar. **Details:** visit our website and e-mail Director Nancy Sondel via the contact form."

PENNWRITERS CONFERENCE

5706 Sonoma Ridge, Missouri City TX 77459. **E-mail:** conferenceco@pennwriters.org. **Website:** www.pennwriters.org/prod. **Contact:** Carol A. Silvis, conference coordinator. Estab. 1987. The Mission of Pennwriters Inc. is to help writers of all levels, from the novice to the award-winning and multi-published, improve and succeed in their craft. The annual Pennwriters conference is held every year in May in Pennsylvania, switching between locations—Lancaster in even years and Pittsburgh in odd years. 2015 event dates: May 15-17 in Pittsburgh.

ACCOMMODATIONS $289 for members, $324 for nonmembers.

ADDITIONAL INFORMATION Sponsors contest. Published authors judge fiction in various categories. Agent/editor appointments are available on a first-come, first serve basis.

PHILADELPHIA WRITERS' CONFERENCE

P.O. Box 7171, Elkins Park PA 19027-0171. (215) 619-7422. **E-mail:** info@pwcwriters.org. **E-mail:** info@pwcwriters.org. **Website:** pwcwriters.org. Estab. 1949. Annual. Conference held in June. Average attendance: 160-200. Conference covers many forms of writing: novel, short story, genre fiction, nonfiction book, magazine writing, blogging, juvenile, poetry.

ACCOMMODATIONS Wyndham Hotel (formerly the Holiday Inn), Independence Mall, Fourth and Arch Streets, Philadelphia, PA 19106-2170. Hotel offers discount for early registration.

ADDITIONAL INFORMATION Accepts inquiries by e-mail. Agents and editors attend the conference. Many questions are answered online.

PIKES PEAK WRITERS CONFERENCE

Pikes Peak Writers, PO Box 64273, Colorado Springs CO 80962. (719)244-6220. **Website:** www.pikespeakwriters.com/ppwc/. Estab. 1993. Annual conference held in April. 2016 dates: April 15-17. Conference duration: 3 days. Average attendance: 300. Workshops, presentations, and panels focus on writing and publishing mainstream and genre fiction (romance, science fiction/fantasy, suspense/thrillers, action/adventure, mysteries, children's, young adult). Agents and editors are available for meetings with attendees on Saturday. 2015 speakers included R.L. Stine and Mary Kay Andrews.

COSTS $300-500 (includes all meals).

ACCOMMODATIONS Marriott Colorado Springs holds a block of rooms at a special rate for attendees until late March.

ADDITIONAL INFORMATION Readings with critiques are available on Friday afternoon. Also offers a contest for unpublished manuscripts; entrants need not attend the conference. Deadline: November 1. Registration and contest entry forms are online; brochures are available in January. Send inquiries via e-mail.

PIMA WRITERS' WORKSHOP

Pima College, 2202 W. Anklam Rd., Tucson AZ 85709. (520)206-6084. **Fax:** (520)206-6020. **E-mail:** mfiles@pima.edu. **Contact:** Meg Files, director. Annual conference geared toward beginner, intermediate and advanced levels. **Open to students.** The conference features presentations and writing exercises on writing and publishing stories for children and young adults, among other genres. Participants may attend for college credit. Meals and accommodations not included. Features a dozen authors, editors, and agents talking about writing and publishing fiction, nonfiction, poetry, and stories for children. E-mail us for more info, or check the website.

RT BOOKLOVERS CONVENTION

55 Bergen St., Brooklyn NY 11201. **Website:** rtconvention.com. Annual conference with a varying location. 2016 details: April 12-16 in Las Vegas. Features 125 workshops, agent and editor appointments, a book fair, and more. More than 800 authors were at the 2015 event.

COSTS $489 normal registration; $425 for industry professionals (agents, editors). Many other pricing options available. See website.

ACCOMMODATIONS Rooms available nearby.

SALT CAY WRITERS RETREAT

Salt Cay Bahamas. (732)267-6449. **E-mail:** admin@saltcaywritersretreat.com. **Website:** www.saltcaywritersretreat.com. **Contact:** Karen Dionne and Christopher Graham. 5-day retreat held in the Bahamas in October. "The Salt Cay Writers Retreat is particularly suited for novelists (especially those writing literary, upmarket commercial fiction, or genre novelists wanting to write a break-out book), memoirists and narrative nonfiction writers. However, any author (published or not-yet-published) who wishes to take their writing to the next level is welcome to apply." Speakers have included or will include editors Chuck Adams (Algonquin Books) and Amy Einhorn (Amy Einhorn Books); agents Jeff Kleinman, Michelle Brower, Erin Niumata, and Erin Harris (all of Folio Literary Management); authors Robert Goolrick and Jacquelyn Mitchard.

COSTS $2,450 through May 1; $2,950 after.

ACCOMMODATIONS Comfort Suites, Paradise Island, Nassau, Bahamas.

SAN DIEGO STATE UNIVERSITY WRITERS' CONFERENCE

SDSU College of Extended Studies, 5250 Campanile Dr., San Diego State University, San Diego CA 92182-1920. (619)594-3946. **Fax:** (619)594-8566. **E-mail:** sdsuwritersconference@mail.sdsu.edu. **Website:** ces.sdsu.edu/writers. Estab. 1984. Annual conference held in January. Conference duration: 2.5 days. Average attendance: 350. Covers fiction, nonfiction, scriptwriting and e-books. Held at the San Diego Marriott Mission Valley Hotel. Each year the conference offers a variety of workshops for the beginner and advanced writers. This conference allows the individual writer to choose which workshop best suits his/her needs. In addition to the workshops, editor reading appointments and agent/editor consultation appointments are provided so attendees may meet with editors and agents one-on-one to discuss specific questions. A reception is offered Saturday immediately following the workshops, offering attendees the opportunity to socialize with the faculty in a relaxed atmosphere. Last year, approximately 60 faculty members attended.

COSTS Approximately $399-435. Parking is available for $8/day.

ACCOMMODATIONS Attendees must make their own travel arrangements. A conference rate for attendees is available at the event hotel (Marriott Mission Valley Hotel).

SAN DIEGO WRITING WORKSHOP

Website: www.sandiegowritingworkshop.com. The 2016 event is set for Friday, October 9, 2015. Organized by Writing Day Workshops. The workshop is a one-day, all-day "How to Get Published" conference with instructional sessions and panels. Multiple literary agents are in attendance at the workshop to meet with writers and hear pitches.

COSTS Early-bird tuition is $149; later tuition is $179; agent meetings are $29 per appointment.

ACCOMMODATIONS Rooms available at the event hotel: The Crowne Plaza in Mission Valley.

ADDITIONAL INFORMATION Query critique options available. Check the website for contact and registration information.

SAN FRANCISCO WRITERS CONFERENCE

1029 Jones St., San Francisco CA 94109. (415)673-0939. **E-mail:** Barbara@sfwriters.org. **Website:** sfwriters. org. **Contact:** Barbara Santos, marketing director. Estab. 2003. "Annual conference held President's Day weekend in February. Average attendance: 500 minimum. More than 100 top authors, respected literary agents, and major publishing houses are at the event so attendees can make face-to-face contact with all the right people. Writers of nonfiction, fiction, poetry, and specialty writing (children's books, cookbooks, travel, etc.) will all benefit from the event. There are important sessions on marketing, self-publishing, technology, and trends in the publishing industry. Plus, there's an optional 4-hour session called Speed Dating for Agents where attendees can meet with 20+ agents. Speakers have included Jennifer Crusie, R.L. Stine, Richard Paul Evans, Jamie Raab, Mary Roach, Jane Smiley, Debbie Macomber, Clive Cussler, Guy Kawasaki, Lisa See, Steve Berry, and Jacquelyn Mitchard. More than 20 agents and editors participate each year, many of whom will be available for meetings with attendees."

COSTS Check the website for pricing on later dates. 2015 pricing was $650-795 depending on when you signed up and early bird registration, etc.

ACCOMMODATIONS The Intercontinental Mark Hopkins Hotel is a historic landmark at the top of Nob Hill in San Francisco. The hotel is located so that everyone arriving at the Oakland or San Francisco airport can take BART to either the Embarcadero or Powell Street exits, then walk or take a cable car or taxi directly to the hotel.

ADDITIONAL INFORMATION "Present yourself in a professional manner and the contacts you will make will be invaluable to your writing career. Fliers, details and registration information are online."

SAN MIGUEL WRITERS' CONFERENCE AND LITERARY FESTIVAL

220 N. Zapata Hwy. #11, Laredo TX 78043. (510)295-4097. **E-mail:** susan@susanpage.com. **Website:** www. sanmiguelwritersconference.org. Estab. 2005. Annual conference held in February. 3 days with 2-day intensive retreats on either end of the conference. 2016 dates: Feb. 10-14. Average attendance: 150. Covers poetry, fiction, nonfiction, memoir, screenwriting. "San Miguel de Allende is a magical town, a UNESCO World Heritage Site filled with charm and history. It is completely safe and very far from any of the border violence." 2015 keynote speakers were: Alice Walker, Scott Turow, and more.

COSTS $325 before January 20th; $375 after Jan. 20th for 2011, includes meals sessions, workshops, open mic and readings, planned excursions. Optional fee consultations and two-day Intensives not included.

ACCOMMODATIONS Consultants work with attendees to arrange accommodations. Cost in the conference hotel is $75/night, double occupancy. "We assist with making airline reservations and transportation arrangements from airport."

ADDITIONAL INFORMATION "The entire conference is simultaneously translated into Spanish. We offer workshops in a broad range of writing topics. We offer seven general session speakers or panels, 90-minute workshops from a choice of 36, 2 optional 2-day intensive workshops, open mic sessions, author readings, individual consultations, and a spectacular Mexican fiesta." Guidelines available as of November 1.

SANTA BARBARA WRITERS CONFERENCE

27 W. Anapamu St., Suite 305, Santa Barbara CA 93101. (805)568-1516. **E-mail:** info@sbwriters.com. **Website:** www.sbwriters.com. Estab. 1972. Annual conference held in June. 2015 dates: June 7-12. Average attendance: 200. Covers fiction, nonfiction, journalism, memoir, poetry, playwriting, screenwriting, travel writing, young adult, children's literature, humor, and marketing. Speakers have included Ray Bradbury, William Styron, Eudora Welty, James Mi-

chener, Sue Grafton, Charles M. Schulz, Clive Cussler, Fannie Flagg, Elmore Leonard, and T.C. Boyle. Agents will appear on a panel; in addition, there will be an agents and editors day that allows writers to pitch their projects in one-on-one meetings.

COSTS Early conference registration is $575, and regular registration is $650.

ACCOMMODATIONS Hyatt Santa Barbara.

ADDITIONAL INFORMATION Register online or contact for brochure and registration forms.

☾ SASKATCHEWAN FESTIVAL OF WORDS

217 Main St. N., Moose Jaw SK S6J 0W1 Canada. **Website:** www.festivalofwords.com. Estab. 1997. Annual 4-day event, third week of July (2015 dates: July 16-19). Location: Moose Jaw Library/Art Museum complex in Crescent Park. Average attendance: about 4,000 admissions. "Canadian authors up close and personal for readers and writers of all ages in mystery, poetry, memoir, fantasy, graphic novels, history, and novel. Each summer festival includes more than 60 events within 2 blocks of historic Main Street. Audience favorite activities include workshops for writers, audience readings, drama,performance poetry, concerts, panels, and music."

ACCOMMODATIONS Information available at www.templegardens.sk.ca, campgrounds, and bed and breakfast establishments. Complete information about festival presenters, events, costs, and schedule also available on website.

SCBWI; ANNUAL CONFERENCES ON WRITING AND ILLUSTRATING FOR CHILDREN

E-mail: scbwi@scbwi.org. **Website:** www.scbwi.org. **Contact:** Lin Oliver, conference director. Writer and illustrator workshops geared toward all levels. **Open to students.** Covers all aspects of children's book and magazine publishing—the novel, illustration techniques, marketing, etc. Annual conferences held in August in Los Angeles and in New York in February. Cost of conference includes all 4 days and one banquet meal. Write for more information or visit website.

☾ These are very large events—SCBWI's biggest, and both events draw 50+ publishing professionals (agents and editors) as well as many authors.

SCBWI—ARIZONA; EVENTS

P.O. Box 26384, Scottsdale AZ 85255-0123. **E-mail:** RegionalAdvisor@scbwi-az.org. **Website:** www.scbwi-az.org. **Contact:** Michelle Parker-Rock, regional advisor. SCBWI Arizona will offer a variety of workshops, retreats, intensives, conferences, meetings and other craft and industry-related events throughout the year. Open to members and nonmembers, published and nonpublished. Registration to major events is usually limited. Pre-registration always required. Visit website, write, or e-mail for more information.

☋ SCBWI BOLOGNA BIENNIAL CONFERENCE

E-mail: kathleenahrens@gmail.com. **Website:** http://bologna.scbwi.org. The SCBWI Showcase Booth at the Bologna Book Fair: The next SCBWI Showcase Booth will take place during the February 2016 fair.

SCBWI—CALIFORNIA (SAN FRANCISCO/ SOUTH); GOLDEN GATE CONFERENCE AT ASILOMAR

Website: http://sfsouth.scbwi.org. **Contact:** Naomi Kinsman, regional advisor. Annual conference. 2015 dates: March 16-18. Welcomes published and not-yet-published writers and illustrators. Lectures and workshops are geared toward professionals and those striving to become professional. Program topics cover aspects of writing or illustrating, and marketing, from picture books to young adult novels. Past speakers include editors, agents, art directors, Newbery Award-winning authors, and Caldecott Award-winning illustrators. For more information, including exact costs and dates, visit website.

☾ SCBWI—CANADA EAST

E-mail: canadaeast@scbwi.org; almafullerton@almafullerton.com. **Website:** www.canadaeast.scbwi.org. **Contact:** Alma Fullerton, regional advisor. Writer and illustrator events geared toward all levels. Usually offers one event in spring and another in the fall. Check website Events pages for updated information.

SCBWI COLORADO/WYOMING (ROCKY MOUNTAIN); EVENTS

E-mail: lindsayeland@me.com; todd.tuell@rmcscbwi.org. **Website:** www.rmc.scbwi.org. **Contact:** Todd Tuell and Lindsay Eland, co-regional advisors. SCBWI Rocky Mountain chapter (CO/WY) offers special events, schmoozes, meetings, and conferences throughout the year. Major events: Fall Con-

ference (annually, September); Summer Retreat, "Big Sur in the Rockies" (bi- and tri-annually). More info on website.

SCBWI–EASTERN PENNSYLVANIA

E-mail: donnaboock@hotmail.com; easternpas cbwi@yahoo.com. **Website:** http://epa.scbwi.org; https://easternpennpoints.wordpress.com/. The Eastern Pennsylvania chapter of SCBWI plans conferences and local events that feature lessons on the craft of writing and illustrating books for children. Active members will have the opportunity to make connections to editors, agents, art directors and authors, and have the pleasure of meeting others who also love writing and/or illustrating for children. 2015 events include a Pocono Retreat May 1-3.

SCBWI–FLORIDA; MID-YEAR WRITING WORKSHOP

12973 SW 112 Ct., Miami FL 33186. (305)382-2677. **E-mail:** lindabernfeld@gmail.com; gabytriana@gmail. com. **Website:** florida.scbwi.org. **Contact:** Linda Bernfeld, co-regional advisor. Annual workshop held in June in Orlando. 2015 dates: June 5-6. Workshop is geared toward helping everyone hone their writing skills. Attendees choose one track and spend the day with industry leaders who share valuable information about that area of children's book writing. There are a minimum of 3 tracks, picture book, middle grade and young adult. The 4th and 5th tracks are variable, covering subjects such as poetry, non-iction, humor or writing for magazines. E-mail for more information.

SCBWI–FLORIDA; REGIONAL CONFERENCE

12973 SW 112 Ct., Miami FL 33186. (305)382-2677. **E-mail:** lindabernfeld@gmail.com; gabytriana@ gmail.com. **Website:** florida.scbwi.org. **Contact:** Linda Bernfeld, regional advisor. Annual conference held in January in Miami. (2015 dates: January 16-18. The Midyear Workshops at Walt Disney World are June 5-6, 2015.) Past keynote speakers have included Linda Sue Park, Richard Peck, Bruce Coville, Bruce Hale, Arthur A. Levine, Judy Blume, Kate Dicamillo. The 3-day conference will have workshops Friday afternoon and a field trip to Books and Books Friday evening.

SCBWI–ILLINOIS; PRAIRIE WRITERS DAY

E-mail: alicebmcginty@gmail.com. **Website:** http:// illinois.scbwi.org. **Contact:** Alice McGinty, co-regional advisor. Full day of guest speakers, editors/

agents TBD. Ms critiques available as well as breakout sessions on career and craft. See website for complete description. This event is usually held in the early fall.

SCBWI–IOWA CONFERENCES

E-mail: hecklit@aol.com. **Website:** http://iowa.scb wi.org/. **Contact:** Connie Heckert, regional advisor. Writer and illustrator workshops in all genres of children writing. The Iowa Region offers conferences of high quality events usually over a three-day period with registration options. Holds spring and fall events on a regional level, and network events across that state. Individual critiques and portfolio review offerings vary with the program and presenters. For more information e-mail or visit website. (The most recent event was in October 2015.) Literary agents and editors are present at the events.

SCBWI–MICHIGAN; CONFERENCES

Website: http://michigan.scbwi.org. Three-day fall conference held in September. Workshops periodically. Speakers TBA. See website for details on all upcoming events.

SCBWI--MIDATLANTIC; ANNUAL FALL CONFERENCE

P.O. Box 3215, Reston VA 20195. **E-mail:** scbwimidat lantic@gmail.com. **Website:** midatlantic.scbwi.org/. For updates and details visit website. Registration limited to 275. Conference fills quickly.Includes continental breakfast and boxed lunch. Optional craft-focused workshops and individual consultations with conference faculty are available for additional fees.

🎧   This conference takes place in the fall—usually October. Previous conferences have been held in Virginia.

SCBWI–MIDSOUTH FALL CONFERENCE

P.O. Box 396, Cordova TN 38088. **E-mail:** ktubb@ comcast.net. **Website:** http://midsouth.scbwi.org. **Contact:** Kristin Tubb, regional advisor. Annual conference for writers and illustrators of all experience. Usually held in the fall (September). In the past, workshops were offered on Plotting Your Novel, Understanding the Language of Editors, Landing an Agent, How to Prepare a Portfolio, Negotiating a Contract, The Basics for Beginners, and many others. Attendees are invited to bring a ms and/or art portfolio to share in the optional, no-charge critique group session. Illustrators are invited to bring color copies of their art (not originals) to be displayed in the illustrators' showcase. For an additional fee, attendees may schedule a 15-minute ms critique or portfolio critique by the editor, art director or other expert consultant.

○ Some agents and editors attend to meet with writers.

SCBWI—MISSOURI; CHILDREN'S WRITER'S CONFERENCE

Website: http://missouri.scbwi.org/. **Contact:** Kimberly Piddington, regional advisor. Open to students. Speakers include editors, writers, agents, and other professionals. Topics vary from year to year, but each conference offers sessions for both writers and illustrators as well as for newcomers and published writers. Previous topics included: "What Happens When Your Manuscript is Accepted" by Dawn Weinstock, editor; "Writing—Hobby or Vocation?" by Chris Kelleher; "Mother Time Gives Advice: Perspectives from a 25 Year Veteran" by Judith Mathews, editor; "Don't Be a Starving Writer" by Vicki Berger Erwin, author; and "Words & Pictures: History in the Making," by author-illustrator Cheryl Harness. Annual conference held in early November. For exact date(s), see the website.

SCBWI—NEW ENGLAND; ANNUAL CONFERENCE

Nashua NH 03063. **E-mail:** nescbwi2015@gmail.com. **Website:** http://newengland.scbwi.org. 2015 dates: April 24-26. Conference is for all levels of writers and illustrators. Open to students. Offers many workshops at each conference, and often there is a multi-day format. Examples of subjects addressed: manuscript development, revision, marketing your work, productive school visits, picture book dummy formatting, adding texture to your illustrations, etc. Annual conference held in Spring. Registration limited to 450. Cost: TBD; includes pre-conference social, great keynote speaker, many workshop options, lunch, snacks, etc. Details (additional speakers, theme, number of workshop choices, etc.) will be posted to website as they become available. Registration doesn't start until March. Opportunities for one-on-one ms critiques and portfolio reviews will be available at the conference.

○ Agents and editors in attendance to meet with writers.

SCBWI—NEW JERSEY; ANNUAL SUMMER CONFERENCE

SCBWI-New Jersey: Society of Children's Book Writers & Illustrators, **Website:** http://njscbwi.com. **Contact:** Leeza Hernandez, regional advisor. This weekend conference is held in thesummer. Multiple one-on-one critiques; "how to" workshops for every level, first page sessions, agent pitches and interaction with the faculty of editors, agents, art director and authors are some of the highlights of the weekend. On Friday attendees can sign up for writing intensives or register for illustrators' day with the art directors. Published authors attending the conference can sign up to participate in the bookfair to sell and autograph their books; illustrators have the opportunity to display their artwork. Attendees have the option to participate in group critiques after dinner on Saturday evening and attend a mix and mingle with the faculty on Friday night. Meals are included with the cost of admission. Conference is known for its high ratio of faculty to attendees and interaction opportunities.

SCBWI—NEW MEXICO; HANDSPRINGS: A CONFERENCE FOR CHILDREN'S WRITERS AND ILLUSTRATORS

PO Box 1084, Socorro NM **E-mail:** carolinestarr@yahoo.com. **Website:** http://newmexico.scbwi.org. **Contact:** Linda Tripp, regional advisor; Caroline Starr, assistant advisor. Annual conference held in October for beginner and intermediate writers and illustrators. Conference features editors, agents, art directors and/or illustrators and authors. Offers intensive craft-based workshops and large-group presentations. See website for details. Monthly offerings include Schmoozes, Critique Groups, and Illustrator Meetings.

SCBWI—NORTHERN OHIO; ANNUAL CONFERENCE

E-mail: vselvaggio@windstream.net. **Website:** nohscbwi.org/conference.html. **Contact:** Victoria A. Selvaggio, regional advisor. Northern Ohio's conference is crafted for all levels of writers and illustrators of children's literature. 2015 dates: September 18-19. "Our annual event will be held at the Sheraton Cleveland Airport Hotel. Conference costs will be posted on our website with registration information. SCBWI members receive a discount. Additional fees apply for late registration, critiques, or portfolio reviews. Cost includes an optional Friday evening Opening Banquet from 6-10 p.m. with a keynote speaker; Saturday event from 8:30 a.m. to 5 p.m. which includes breakfast snack, full-day conference with headliner presentations, general sessions, breakout workshops, lunch, panel discussion, bookstore, and autograph session. The Illustrator Showcase is open to all attendees at no additional cost. Grand door prize drawn at the end of the day Saturday, is free admission to the following year's conference. Further information, including Headliner Speakers will be posted on our website." Literary agents and acquiring editors are brought in every year.

SCBWI—OREGON CONFERENCES

E-mail: suhligford@gmail.com; oregon@scbwi.org. **Website:** http://oregon.scbwi.org. **Contact:** Sue Ford, co-regional advisor; Judith Gardiner, co-regional advisor. Writer and illustrator workshops and presentations geared toward all levels. Invites editors, art directors, agents, attorneys, authors, illustrators and others in the business of writing and illustrating for children. Faculty members offer craft presentations, workshops, first-page sessions and individual critiques as well as informal networking opportunities. Critique group network opportunities for local group meetings and regional retreats; see website for details. Two main events per year: Writers and Illustrators Retreat: held near Portland Thurs-Sun in October; Spring Conference: Held in the Portland area (2 day event in May (one-day attendance is permitted). SCBWI Oregon is a regional chapter of the Society of Children's Book Writers and Illustrators. SCBWI Members receive a discount for all events. Oregon and South Washington members get preference.

SCBWI—POCONO MOUNTAINS RETREAT

E-mail: easternpascbwi@yahoo.com. **Website:** http://easternpennpoints.wordpress.com; http://epa.scbwi.org. Annual retreat held in early May. (2015 dates: May 1-3.) Faculty addresses craft, web design, school visits, writing, illustration and publishing. Registration limited to 150. For information, online registration and brochure, visit website.

SCBWI—SOUTHERN BREEZE; SPRINGMINGLE

P.O. Box 26282, Birmingham AL 35260. **Website:** http://southern-breeze.scbwi.org. **Contact:** Kathleen Bradshaw, co-regional advisor. Writer and illustrator conference geared toward intermediate, advanced and professional levels. Speakers typically include

agents, editors, authors, art directors, illustrators. Open to SCBWI members, non-members, and college students. Annual conference held in Atlanta, Georgia. Usually held in late March. Registration limited. Manuscript critiques and portfolio reviews available for additional fee. Pre-registration is necessary. Visit website for more information.

SCBWI—SOUTHERN BREEZE; WRITING AND ILLUSTRATING FOR KIDS

P.O. Box 26282, Birmingham AL 35260. **E-mail:** klbradshaw@kathleenbradshaw.com. **Website:** http://southern-breeze.scbwi.org. **Contact:** Kathleen Bradshaw, co-regional advisor; Claudia Pearson, co-regional advisor. Fall event. Writer and illustrator workshops geared toward all levels. Open to SCBWI members, non-members and college students. All sessions pertain specifically to the production and support of quality children's literature. This one-day conference offers about 30 workshops on craft and the business of writing. Picture books, chapter books, novels covered. Entry and professional level topics addressed by published writers and illustrators, editors and agents. Annual fall conference is held the third weekend in October in the Birmingham, AL, metropolitan area. All workshops are limited to 30 or fewer people. Pre-registration is necessary. Some workshops fill quickly. Mss critiques and portfolio reviews are available for an additional fee; mss must be sent early. Registration is by mail ahead of time. Ms and portfolio reviews must be pre-paid and scheduled.

SCBWI—VENTURA/SANTA BARBARA; FALL CONFERENCE

Simi Valley CA 93094-1389. **E-mail:** maryafraser@gmail.com. **Website:** http://cencal.scbwi.org. **Contact:** Mary Ann Fraser, regional advisor. Writers' & illustrators' events geared toward all levels. Annual. 2015 "Writers' Day" is October 17. Speakers include editors, authors, illustrators and agents. Fiction and nonfiction picture books, middle grade and YA novels, and magazine submissions addressed. Annual writing contest in all genres plus illustration display. Conference held in October. For fees and other information, e-mail or visit website.

SCBWI—WESTERN WASHINGTON STATE; CONFERENCE & RETREAT

Western Region of SCBWI, **E-mail:** info@scbwiwashington.org; danajsullivan@comcast.net. **Website:** http://chinookupdate.blogspot.com; http://wwa.

scbwi.org. **Contact:** Dana Arnim, co-regional advisor; Dana Sullivan, co-regional advisor. The Western Washington region of SCBWI hosts an annual conference in April, a retreat in November, and monthly meetings and events throughout the year. Visit the website for complete details.

SCBWI–WISCONSIN; FALL RETREAT FOR WORKING WRITERS

E-mail: scbwijamieswenson@gmail.com;. **Website:** http://wisconsin.scbwi.org. Writer and illustrator conference geared toward all levels. All sessions pertain to children's writing/illustration. Faculty addresses writing/illustrating/publishing. Annual conference held in the fall (usually October). Visit website for information.

☺ THE SCHOOL FOR WRITERS FALL WORKSHOP

The Humber School for Writers, Humber Institute of Technology & Advanced Learning, 3199 Lake Shore Blvd. W., Toronto ON M8V 1K8 Canada. (416)675-6622. **E-mail:** antanas.sileika@humber.ca; hilary. higgins@humber.ca. **Website:** www.humber.ca/scapa/programs/school-writers. The School for Writers Workshop has moved to the fall with the International Festival of Authors. The workshop runs during the last week in October. Conference duration: 1 week. Average attendance: 60. New writers from around the world gather to study with faculty members to work on their novels, short stories, poetry, or creative nonfiction. Agents and editors participate in the conference. Include a work-in-progress with your registration. Faculty has included Martin Amis, David Mitchell, Kevin Barry, Rachel Kuschner, Peter Carey, Roddy Doyle, Tim O'Brien, Andrea Levy, Barry Unsworth, Edward Albee, Ha Jin, Julia Glass, Mavis Gallant, Bruce Jay Friedman, Isabel Huggan, Alistair MacLeod, Lisa Moore, Kim Moritsugu, Francine Prose, Paul Quarrington, Olive Senior, D.M. Thomas, Annabel Lyon, Mary Gaitskill, and M.G. Vassanji.

COSTS around $850 (in 2014). Some limited scholarships are available.

ADDITIONAL INFORMATION Accepts inquiries by e-mail, phone, and fax.

SEWANEE WRITERS' CONFERENCE

735 University Ave., 119 Gailor Hall, Stamler Center, Sewanee TN 37383-1000. (931)598-1654. **E-mail:** allatham@sewanee.edu. **Website:** www.sewaneewriters.org. **Contact:** Adam Latham. Estab. 1990. Annual conference. 2015 dates: July 21-Aug. 2. Average attendance: 150. "The University of the South will host the 26th session of the Sewanee Writers' Conference. Thanks to the generosity of the Walter E. Dakin Memorial Fund, supported by the estate of the late Tennessee Williams, the Conference will gather a distinguished faculty to provide instruction and criticism through workshops and craft lectures in poetry, fiction, and playwriting. During an intense 12-day period, participants will read and critique each other's mss under the leadership of some of our country's finest fiction writers, poets, and playwrights. All faculty members and fellows give scheduled readings; senior faculty members offer craft lectures; open-mic readings accommodate many others. Additional writers, along with a host of writing professionals, visit to give readings, participate in panel discussions, and entertain questions from the audience. Receptions and mealtimes offer opportunities for informal exchange. This year's faculty includes fiction writers Richard Bausch, Tony Earley, Adrianne Harun, Randall Kenan, Jill McCorkle, Alice McDermott, Tim O'Brien, Christine Schutt, Allen Wier, and Steve Yarbrough; and poets Daniel Anderson, Claudia Emerson, B.H. Fairchild, Andrew Hudgins, Maurice Manning, Charles Martin, Mary Jo Salter, and A.E. Stallings. Dan O'Brien and Paula Vogel will lead the playwriting workshop. Erin McGraw and Wyatt Prunty will read from their work. The conference fee reflects but two-thirds of the actual cost to attend. Additional funding is awarded to fellows and scholars."

COSTS $1,000 for tuition and $800 for room, board, and activity costs.

ACCOMMODATIONS Participants are housed in single rooms in university dormitories. Bathrooms are shared by small groups.

THE SOUTHAMPTON WRITERS CONFERENCE

239 Montauk Highway, Southampton NY 11968. (631)632-5030. **E-mail:** southamptonarts@stonybrook.edu. **Website:** www.stonybrook.edu/southampton/mfa/summer/cwl_home.html. Estab. 1975. 2015 dates: July 8-19. "Since 1976, the Southampton Writers Conference has brought together writers at all stages of their careers with world-class novelists, essayists, editors, poets and children's book authors for lectures, readings, panels and workshops. All writers are welcome to attend the Conference, including those who seek a 12-day writers residency in the

Hamptons. This year's offerings include a 5-part craft lecture series with Roger Rosenblatt. Admission to a 5-day writing workshop is competitive and requires additional application materials."

SOUTH CAROLINA WRITERS WORKSHOP

4840 Forest Drive, Suite 6B: PMB 189, Columbia SC 29206. **E-mail:** scwwliaison@gmail.com; scww2013@gmail.com. **Website:** www.myscww.org. Estab. 1991. Conference in October held at the Hilton Myrtle Beach Resort in Myrtle Beach, SC. Held almost every year. Conference duration: 3 days. The conference features critique sessions, open mic readings, presentations from agents and editors and more. The conference features more than 50 different workshops for writers to choose from, dealing with all subjects of writing craft, writing business, getting an agent and more. Agents will be in attendance.

SOUTH COAST WRITERS CONFERENCE

Southwestern Oregon Community College, P.O. Box 590, 29392 Ellensburg Ave., Gold Beach OR 97444. (541)247-2741. **Fax:** (541)247-6247. **E-mail:** scwc@socc.edu. **Website:** www.socc.edu/scwriters. Estab. 1996. Annual conference held Presidents Day weekend in February. Conference duration: 2 days. Covers fiction, poetry, children's, nature, songwriting, and marketing. Melissa Hart was the keynote speaker in 2014, and presenters include Stevan Allred, Mark Bennion, Dan Berne, Mark Graham, Nina Kiriki Hoffman, Elena Passarello, Liz Prato, Jeffrey Shultz, Tess Thompson.

ADDITIONAL INFORMATION See website for cost and additional details.

SOUTHEASTERN WRITERS ASSOCIATION—ANNUAL WRITERS WORKSHOP

161 Woodstone, Athens GA 30605. **E-mail:** purple@southeasternwriters.org. **Website:** www.southeasternwriters.com. **Open to all writers**. (2015 dates: June 19-23.) Contests with cash prizes. Instruction offered for novel and short fiction, nonfiction, writing for children, humor, inspirational writing, and poetry. Manuscript deadline April 1; includes free evaluation conference(s) with instructor(s). Agent in residence. Annual 4-day workshop held in June. Cost of workshop: $445 for 4 days or lower prices for daily tuition. (See online.) Accommodations: Offers overnight accommodations on workshop site. Visit website for more information and cost of overnight

accommodations. Tuition pricing online. Multiple hotels available in St. Simon's Island, GA.

SQUAW VALLEY COMMUNITY OF WRITERS

P.O. Box 1416, Nevada City CA 95959-1416. (530)470-8440. **E-mail:** info@squawvalleywriters.org. **Website:** www.squawvalleywriters.org. **Contact:** Brett Hall Jones, executive director. Estab. 1969.

COSTS Tuition is $1,075, which includes 6 dinners. Limited financial aid is available.

ACCOMMODATIONS The Community of Writers rents houses and condominiums in the Valley for participants to live in during the week of the conference. Single room (1 participant): $700/week. Double room (twin beds, room shared by conference participant of the same sex): $465/week. Multiple room (bunk beds, room shared with 2 or more participants of the same sex): $295/week. All rooms subject to availability; early requests are recommended. Can arrange airport shuttle pick-ups for a fee.

ADDITIONAL INFORMATION Online submittal process, see squawvalleywriters.org/writers_ws.htm#APPLY for instructions and application form. Send inquiries via e-mail to info@squawvalleywriters.org.

STEAMBOAT SPRINGS WRITERS CONFERENCE

Steamboat Springs Arts Council, Eleanor Bliss Center for the Arts at the Depot, 1001 13th St., Steamboat Springs CO 80487. (970)879-9008. **Fax:** (970)879-8138. **E-mail:** info@steamboatwriters.com. **Website:** www.steamboatwriters.com. **Contact:** Susan de Wardt. Estab. 1982. Writers' workshops geared toward intermediate levels. Open to professionals and amateurs alike.

COSTS Tuition: $60 early registration, $75 after May 16.

ADDITIONAL INFORMATION For additional information, please consult the website.

SUMMER WRITING PROGRAM

Naropa University, 2130 Arapahoe Ave., Boulder CO 80302. (303)245-4862. **Fax:** (303)546-5287. **E-mail:** swpr@naropa.edu. **Website:** www.naropa.edu/swp. **Contact:** Kyle Pivarnik, special projects manager. Estab. 1974. Annual event in summer. Workshop duration: 4 weeks. Average attendance: 250. Offers college credit. Accepts inquiries by e-mail, phone. With 13 workshops to choose from each of the 4 weeks of the program, students may study poetry, prose, hybrid/

cross-genre writing, small press printing, or book arts. Site: All workshops, panels, lectures and readings are hosted on the Naropa University main campus. Located in downtown Boulder, the campus is within easy walking distance of restaurants, shopping, and the scenic Pearl Street Mall.

ADDITIONAL INFORMATION Writers can elect to take the Summer Writing Program for noncredit, graduate, or undergraduate credit. The registration procedure varies, so consider whether or not you'll be taking the SWP for academic credit. All participants can elect to take any combination of the first, second, third, and/or fourth weeks. To request a catalog of upcoming program or to find additional information, visit naropa.edu/swp. Naropa University also welcomes participants with disabilities.

☼ SURREY INTERNATIONAL WRITERS' CONFERENCE

151-10090 152 St., Suite 544, Surrey BC V3R 8X8Canada . **E-mail:** kathychung@siwc.ca. **Website:** www.siwc.ca. **Contact:** Kathy Chung, proposals contact and conference coordinator. Annual writing conference outside Vancouver, Canada, held every October. Writing workshops geared toward beginner, intermediate, and advanced levels. More than 70 workshops and panels, on all topics and genres, plus pre-conference master classes. Blue Pencil and agent/editor pitch sessions included. Different conference price packages available. Check the conference website for more information. This event has many literary agents in attendance taking pitches.

TAOS SUMMER WRITERS' CONFERENCE

Department of English Language and Literature, MSC 03 2170, 1 University of New Mexico, Albuquerque NM 87131-0001. **E-mail:** swarner@unm.edu. **Website:** taosconf.unm.edu. **Contact:** Sharon Oard Warner. Estab. 1999. Annual conference held in July. 2015 dates: July 12-19. Offers workshops and master classes in the novel, short story, poetry, creative nonfiction, memoir, prose style, screenwriting, humor writing, yoga and writing, literary translation, book proposal, the query letter and revision.Participants may also schedule a consultation with a visiting agent/editor.

COSTS Week-long workshop registration $700, weekend workshop registration $400, master classes between $1,350 and $1,625, publishing consultations are $175.

TIN HOUSE SUMMER WRITERS WORKSHOP

P.O. Box 10500, Portland OR 97296. (503)219-0622. **Website:** http://www.tinhouse.com/blog/workshop. Estab. 2003. Annual workshops held in Oregon. 2015 dates: fiction workshop is Jan. 30 - Feb. 2; nonfiction workshop is Feb. 6-9. Full list of faculty members is available online.

COSTS $40 application fee; $1,200 for program + room and board (breakfast and one dinner).

ACCOMMODATIONS Sylvia Beach Hotel.

ADDITIONAL INFORMATION Attendees must apply; all information available online. "A board composed of Tin House editorial staff members decides upon applications. Acceptance is based on the strength and promise of the submitted writing sample, as well as how much the board feels an applicant might benefit from the Winter Workshop. We will notify applicants of acceptance or rejection within 4 weeks of the application's receipt. Once accepted, enrollment into the program is granted on a first-come, first-serve basis (meaning you need to register in-order to guarantee your spot). We encourage you to apply early, as workshops can fill quickly."

TONY HILLERMAN WRITERS CONFERENCE

1063 Willow Way, Santa FE NM 87505. (505)471-1565. **E-mail:** wordharvest@wordharvest.com. **Website:** www.wordharvest.com. **Contact:** Anne Hillerman and Jean Schaumberg, co-founders. Estab. 2004. Annual event held in November. Conference duration: 3 days. Average attendance: 100. Site: Hilton Santa Fe Historic Plaza. Full days of presentations on the craft of writing. We honor the winner of the $10,000 Tony Hillerman Prize for best first mystery at the Hillerman luncheon. A flash critique session-"Writing With the Stars"-is open to any interested attendee and adds to the fun and information. A book signing/reception is followed by the keynote dinner.

COSTS A full registration is $695, but there are many options in terms of lower prices if the attendee only comes 1-2 days. All information available on website.

ACCOMMODATIONS Hilton Santa Fe Historic Plaza.

UNICORN WRITERS CONFERENCE

P.O. Box 176, Redding CT 06876. (203)938-7405. **E-mail:** unicornwritersconference@gmail.com. **Website:** www.unicornwritersconference.com. This writers conference draws upon its close proximity to New York City and pulls in many literary agents and editors to pitch each year. There are ms review sessions (40 pages equals 30 minutes with an agent/editor), query/ms review sessions, and five different workshops every hour. $300 cost includes all workshops and 3 meals.

ACCOMMODATIONS Held at Reid Castle, Purchase, N.Y. Directions available on event website.

UNIVERSITY OF NORTH DAKOTA WRITERS CONFERENCE

Department of English, 110 Merrifield Hall, 276 Centennial Dr., Stop 7209, Grand Forks ND 58202. (701)777-2393. **Fax:** (701)777-2373. **E-mail:** crystal. alberts@e-mail.und.edu. **Website:** http://und.edu/orgs/writers-conference. **Contact:** Crystal Alberts, director. Estab. 1970. Annual event of 3-5 days. 2016 dates: April 6-8. Offers panels, readings, and films focused around a specific theme. Almost all events take place in the UND Memorial Union, which has a variety of small rooms and a 1,000-seat main hall. Past speakers include Art Spiegelman, Truman Capote, Sir Salman Rushdie, Allen Ginsberg, Alice Walker, and Louise Erdrich.

COSTS All events are free and open to the public. Donations accepted.

ACCOMMODATIONS Accommodations available at area hotels. Information on overnight accommodations available on website.

ADDITIONAL INFORMATION Schedule and other information available on website.

UNIVERSITY OF WISCONSIN AT MADISON WRITERS INSTITUTE

21 N. Park St., Madison WI 53715-1218. (608)262-3447. **Website:** https://uwwritersinstitute.wisc.edu/. Estab. 1990. Annual conference. 2016 dates: April 15-17. Conference on fiction and nonfiction held at the University of Wisconsin at Madison. Guest speakers are published authors, editors, and agents.

COSTS $125-260, depending on discounts and if you attend one day or multiple days.

ACCOMMODATIONS The 2016 location is at the Madison Concourse Hotel.

UW-MADISON WRITERS' INSTITUTE

21 North Park St., Room 7331, Madison WI 53715. (608)265-3972. **Fax:** (608)265-2475. **E-mail:** lscheer@dcs.wisc.edu. **Website:** www.uwwritersinstitute.org. **Contact:** Laurie Scheer. Estab. 1989. Annual. Conference usually held in the spring. Site: Madison Concourse Hotel, downtown Madison. Average attendance: 600. Conference speakers provide workshops and consultations. For information, send e-mail, visit website, call, fax. Accepts inquiries by SASE, e-mail, phone, fax. Agents and editors participate in conference.

COSTS $260-310; includes materials, breaks.

ACCOMMODATIONS Provides a list of area hotels or lodging options.

ADDITIONAL INFORMATION Sponsors contest.

WESLEYAN WRITERS CONFERENCE

Wesleyan University, 294 High St., Room 207, Middletown CT 06459. (860)685-3604. **Fax:** (860)685-2441. **E-mail:** agreene@wesleyan.edu. **Website:** www.wesleyan.edu/writing/conference. Estab. 1956. Annual conference. 2015 dates: June 10-14. Average attendance: 100. Focuses on the novel, fiction techniques, short stories, poetry, screenwriting, nonfiction, literary journalism, memoir, mixed media work and publishing. The conference is held on the campus of Wesleyan University, in the hills overlooking the Connecticut River. Features a faculty of award-winning writers, seminars and readings of new fiction, poetry, nonfiction and mixed media forms - as well as guest lectures on a range of topics including publishing. Both new and experienced writers are welcome. Participants may attend seminars in all genres. Speakers have included Esmond Harmsworth (Zachary Schuster Agency), Daniel Mandel (Sanford J. Greenburger Associates), Amy Williams (ICM and Collins McCormick), and many others. Agents will be speaking and available for meetings with attendees. Participants are often successful in finding agents and publishers for their mss. Wesleyan participants are also frequently featured in the anthology *Best New American Voices*.

ACCOMMODATIONS Meals are provided on campus. Lodging is available on campus or in town.

ADDITIONAL INFORMATION Ms critiques are available, but not required.

WESTERN RESERVE WRITERS & FREELANCE CONFERENCE

7700 Clocktower Dr., Kirtland OH 44094. (440)525-7812. **E-mail:** deencr@aol.com. **Website:** www.deannaadams.com. **Contact:** Deanna Adams, director/conference coordinator. Estab. 1983. Biannual. Last conference held September 26, 2015. Conference duration: 1 day or half-day. Average attendance: 120. "The Western Reserve Writers Conferences are designed for all writers, aspiring and professional, and offer presentations in all genres—nonfiction, fiction, poetry, essays, creative nonfiction, and the business of writing, including Web writing and successful freelance writing." Site: "Located in the main building of Lakeland Community College, the conference is easy to find and just off the I-90 freeway. The Fall 2013 conference featured top-notch presenters from newspapers and magazines, along with published authors, freelance writers, and professional editors. Presentations included 'Writing Believable Dialogue,' 'Creating a Sense of Place,' 'Writing Your Life Story,' 'First Fiction,' 'Writing and Researching Crime Stories,' as well as tips on submissions, getting books into stores, and storytelling for both fiction and nonfiction writers. Included throughout the day are one-on-one editing consults, Q&A panel, and book sale/author signings."

COSTS Fall all-day conference includes lunch: $105. Spring half-day conference, no lunch: $69.

ADDITIONAL INFORMATION Brochures for the conferences are available by January (for spring conference) and July (for fall). Also accepts inquiries by e-mail and phone. Check Deanna Adams' website for all updates. Editors always attend the conferences. Private editing consultations are available, as well.

WHIDBEY ISLAND WRITERS' CONFERENCE

(360)331-0307. **E-mail:** http://writeonwhidbey.org. **Website:** http://writeonwhidbey.org. P.O. Box 1289, Langley, WA 98260. (360)331-6714. **E-mail:** writers@whidbey.com. **Website:** www.writeonwhidbey. org. **Writers Contact:** Conference Director. Three days focused on the tools you need to become a great writer. Learn from a variety of award-winning children's book authors and very experienced literary agents. Variety of preconference workshops and conference topics. Conference held in early spring. Registration limited to 290. Cost: $395; early bird and member discounts available. Registration includes workshops, fireside chats, book-signing reception, various activities, and daily luncheons. The conference offers consultation appointments with editors and agents. Registrants may reduce the cost of their conference by volunteering. See the website for more information. "The uniquely personal and

friendly weekend is designed to be highly interactive." Annual conference held in early spring. Registration limited to 290. Registration includes workshops, fireside chats, book-signing reception, various activities, and daily luncheons. The conference offers consultation appointments with editors and agents. Registrants may reduce the cost of their conference by volunteering. See the website for more information. "The uniquely personal and friendly weekend is designed to be highly interactive." There are a variety of sessions on topics such as fiction, craft, poetry, platform, agents, screenwriting, and much more. Topics are varied, and there is something for all writers. Multiple agents and editors are in attendance. The schedule and faculty change every year, and those changes are reflected online

COSTS Cost: $395; early bird and member discounts available

WILDACRES WRITERS WORKSHOP

233 S. Elm St., Greensboro NC 27401. (336)255-8210. **E-mail:** judihill@aol.com. **Website:** www.wildacreswriters.com. **Contact:** Judi Hill, Director. Estab. 1985. 2015 summer workshop dates: July 4-11. Conference duration: 1 week. Average attendance: 100. Workshop focuses on novel, short story, flash fiction, poetry, and nonfiction. 10 on faculty include Ron Rash, Carrie Brown, Dr. Janice Fuller, Phillip Gerard, Luke Whisnant, Dr. Joe Clark, John Gregory Brown, Dr. Phebe Davidson, Lee Zacharias, and Vicki Lane. This group also has a week-long writing retreat that is different from the workshop.

COSTS The current price is $790. Check the website for more info.

ADDITIONAL INFORMATION Include a 1-page writing sample with your registration. See the website for information.

WILLAMETTE WRITERS CONFERENCE

2108 Buck St., West Linn OR 97068. (503)305-6729. **Fax:** (503)344-6174. **Website:** willamettewriters. com/wwcon/. Estab. 1981. Annual conference held in August. 2015 dates: Aug. 7-9. Conference duration: 3 days. Average attendance: 600. "Willamette Writers is open to all writers, and we plan our conference accordingly. We offer workshops on all aspects of fiction, nonfiction, marketing, the creative process, screenwriting, etc. Also, we invite top-notch inspirational speakers for keynote addresses. We always include at least 1 agent or editor panel and offer a variety of topics of interest to both fiction and nonfiction writers and screenwriters." Agents will be speaking and available for meetings with attendees.

COSTS Pricing schedule available online.

ACCOMMODATIONS If necessary, arrangements can be made on an individual basis through the conference hotel. Special rates may be available. 2015 location was the Lloyd Center DoubleTree Hotel.

ADDITIONAL INFORMATION Brochure/guidelines are available for a catalog-sized SASE.

🔵 THE UNIVERSITY OF WINCHESTER WRITERS' FESTIVAL

University of Winchester, Winchester Hampshire WA S022 4NR United Kingdom. 44(0)1962-827238. **E-mail:** judith.heneghan@winchester.ac.uk. **Website:** www.writersfestival.co.uk. The dates for the 35th Winchester Writers' Festival (2015) are June 19-21, held at the University of Winchester. Sebastian Faulks, internationally acclaimed author of *Birdsong, A Possible Life* and *Human Traces* will give the keynote address and will lead an outstanding team of 60 best-selling authors, commissioning editors and literary agents offering day-long workshops, 32 talks and 700 one-to-one appointments to help writers harness their creative ideas, turn them into marketable work and pitch to publishing professionals. Participate by entering some of the 11 writing competitions, even if you can't attend. More than 130 writers have now reported major publishing successes as a direct result of their attendance at past festivals. This leading international literary event offers a magnificent source of support, advice, inspiration and networking opportunities for new and published writers working in all genres. Enjoy a creative writing weekend in Winchester, the oldest city in England and only one hour from London.To view Festival details, including all the competition details please go to the official event website.

WRITE-BY-THE-LAKE WRITER'S WORKSHOP & RETREAT

21 N. Park St., 7th Floor, Madison WI 53715. (608)262-3447. **E-mail:** cdesmet@dcs.wisc.edu. **Website:** www.dcs.wisc.edu/lsa/writing. **Contact:** Christine DeSmet, director. Open to all writers and students; 12 workshops for all levels. Includes classes for full-novel critique and one Master Class for 50 pages. Held the third week of June on UW-Madison campus. Registration limited to 15 each section; fewer in Master Classes. Writing facilities available; computer labs, wi-fi in all buildings and on the outdoor lakeside terrace. E-mail for more information. "Registration opens every January for following June."

COSTS Costs $365 before May 18; $415 after May 18. Additional cost for Master Classes and college credits. Cost includes instruction, welcome luncheon, and pastry/coffee each day.

WRITING WORKSHOPS AT CASTLE HILL

10 Meetinghouse Rd., P.O. Box 756, Truro MA 02666. (508)349-7511. **Fax:** (508)349-7513. **E-mail:** info@castlehill.org. **Website:** www.castlehill.org/workshopwriting.html. Workshops about poetry, fiction, narrative nonfiction, memoir, and more; these writing workshops are geared toward intermediate and advanced levels. **Open to students.** The dates, courses, and instructors change each year, so check the website for individual details of upcoming events. Held at the Truro Center for the Arts at Castle Hill in Massachusetts.

THE WRITING CONFERENCE OF LOS ANGELES

Website: www.writingconferenceoflosangeles.com. The 2015 event is set for Saturday, October 10, 2015. Organized by Writing Day Workshops. The workshop is a one-day, all-day "How to Get Published" conference with instructional sessions and panels. Multiple literary agents are in attendance at the workshop to meet with writers and hear pitches.

COSTS Early-bird tuition is $149; later tuition is $179; agent meetings are $29 per appointment.

ACCOMMODATIONS Rooms available at the event hotel: The Four Points Sheraton in Culver City.

ADDITIONAL INFORMATION Query critique options available. Check the website for contact and registration information.

WYOMING WRITERS CONFERENCE

Cheyenne WY **E-mail:** president@wyowriters.org. **Website:** wyowriters.org. **Contact:** Chris Williams. This is a statewide writing conference for writers of Wyoming and neighboring states. 2015 conference dates: June 5-7, 2015 in Cheyenne, WY. Each year, multiple published authors, editors, and literary agents are in attendance to meet with writers and take pitches.

CONTESTS, AWARDS & GRANTS

//

Publication is not the only way to get your work recognized. Contests and awards can also be great ways to gain recognition in the industry. Grants, offered by organizations like the Society of Children's Book Writers and Illustrators (SCBWI), offer monetary recognition to writers, giving them more financial freedom as they work on projects.

When considering contests or applying for grants, be sure to study guidelines and requirements. Regard entry deadlines as gospel and follow the rules to the letter.

Note that some contests require nominations. For published authors and illustrators, competitions provide an excellent way to promote your work. Your publisher may not be aware of local competitions such as state-sponsored awards—if your book is eligible, have the appropriate person at your publishing company nominate or enter your work for consideration.

To select potential contests and grants, read through the listings that interest you, then send for more information about the types of written or illustrated material considered and other important details. A number of contests offer information through websites given in their listings.

If you are interested in knowing who has received certain awards in the past, check your local library or bookstores or consult *Children's Books: Awards & Honors*, compiled and edited by the Children's Book Council (www.cbcbooks.org). Many bookstores have special sections for books that are Caldecott and Newbery Medal winners. Visit the American Library Association website, www.ala.org, for information on the Caldecott, Newbery, Coretta Scott King and Printz Awards. Visit www.hbook.com for information on The Boston Globe-Horn Book Award. Visit www.scbwi.org/awards.htm for information on The Golden Kite Award.

JANE ADDAMS CHILDREN'S BOOK AWARDS

777 United Nations Plaza, 6th Floor, New York NY 10017. (212)682-8830. **E-mail:** japa@igc.org. **Website:** www.janeaddamspeace.org. **Contact:** Ann Carpenter, chair. The Jane Addams Children's Book Awards are given annually to the children's books published the preceding year that effectively promote the cause of peace, social justice, world community, and the equality of the sexes and all races as well as meeting conventional standards for excellence. Books eligible for this award may be fiction, poetry, or nonfiction. Books may be any length. Entries should be suitable for ages 2-12. See website for specific details on guidelines and required book themes. Deadline: December 31. Judged by a national committee of WILPF members concerned with children's books and their social values is responsible for making the changes each year.

☮ ALCUIN SOCIETY BOOK DESIGN AWARDS

P.O. Box 3216, Vancouver BC V6B 3X8. Canada. (604)732-5403. **Fax:** (604)985-1091. **E-mail:** awards@alcuinsociety.com; info@alcuinsociety.com. **Website:** www.alcuinsociety.com. **Contact:** Leah Gordon. The Alcuin Society Awards for Excellence in Book Design in Canada is the only national competition for book design in Canada. Winners are selected from books designed and published in Canada. Awards are presented annually at appropriate ceremonies held in each year. Winning books are exhibited nationally and internationally at the Tokyo, Frankfurt, and Leipzig Book Fairs, and are Canada's entries in the international competition in Leipzig, "Book Design from all over the World" in the following spring. Submit previously published material from the year before the award's call for entries. Submissions made by the publisher, author or designer. Deadline: March 15. Prizes: 1st, 2nd, and 3rd in each category (at the discretion of the judges). Judging by professionals and those experienced in the field of book design.

AMERICA & ME ESSAY CONTEST

P.O. Box 30400, Lansing MI 48909. **E-mail:** lfedewa@fbinsmi.com. **Website:** www.farmbureauinsurance-mi.com. Focuses on encouraging students to write about their personal Michigan heroes: someone they know personally who has encouraged them and inspired them to want to live better and achieve more. Open to Michigan eighth graders. Contest rules and entry form available on website. Encourages Michigan youth to explore their roles in America's future. Deadline: November 18. Prizes: $1,000, plaque, and medallion for top 10 winners.

AMERICAN ASSOCIATION OF UNIVERSITY WOMEN AWARD IN JUVENILE LITERATURE

4610 Mail Service Center, Raleigh NC 27699-4610. (919)807-7290. **E-mail:** michael.hill@ncdcr.gov. **Website:** www.ncdcr.gov. **Contact:** Michael Hill, awards coordinator. Annual award. Book must be published during the year ending June 30. Submissions made by author, author's agent or publisher. SASE for contest rules. Author must have maintained either legal residence or actual physical residence, or a combination of both, in the state of North Carolina for 3 years immediately preceding the close of the contest period. Only published work (books) eligible. Recognizes the year's best work of juvenile literature by a North Carolina resident. Deadline: July 15. Prize: Awards a cup to the winner and winner's name inscribed on a plaque displayed within the North Carolina Office of Archives and History. Judged by three-judge panel. Competition receives 10-15 submissions per category.

AMERICAS AWARD

Website: http://claspprograms.org/americasaward. **Contact:** Claire Gonzalez. The Américas Award encourages and commends authors, illustrators, and publishers who produce quality children's and young adult books that portray Latin America, the Caribbean, or Latinos in the US. Up to 2 awards (for primary and secondary reading levels) are given in recognition of US published works of fiction, poetry, folklore, or selected nonfiction (from picture books to works for young adults). The award winners and commended titles are selected for their (1) distinctive literary quality; (2) cultural contextualization; (3) exceptional integration of text, illustration and design; and (4) potential for classroom use. To nominate a copyright title from the previous year, publishers are invited to submit review copies to the committee members listed on the website. Publishers should send 8 copies of the nominated book. Deadline: January 18. Prize: $500, plaque and a formal presentation at the Library of Congress, Washington DC.

🌑 HANS CHRISTIAN ANDERSEN AWARD

Nonnenweg 12, Postfach Basel CH-4003Switzerland
. **E-mail:** liz.page@ibby.org. **E-mail:** ibby@ibby.org.
Website: www.ibby.org. **Contact:** Liz Page, director.
The Hans Christian Andersen Award, awarded every
two years by the International Board on Books for
Young People (IBBY), is the highest international
recognition given to an author and an illustrator of
children's books. The Author's Award has been given
since 1956, the Illustrator's Award since 1966. Her
Majesty Queen Margrethe II of Denmark is the Pa-
tron of the Hans Christian Andersen Awards. The
awards are presented at the biennial congresses of
IBBY. Awarded to an author and to an illustrator,
living at the time of the nomination, who by the outstanding value of their work are judged to have made
a lasting contribution to literature for children and
young people. The complete works of the author and
of the illustrator will be taken into consideration in
awarding the medal, which will be accompanied by a
diploma. Candidates are nominated by National Sections of IBBY in good standing. Prizes: Awards medals according to literary and artistic criteria. Judged
by the Hans Christian Andersen Jury.

🌑 ATLANTIC WRITING COMPETITION FOR UNPUBLISHED MANUSCRIPTS

1113 Marginal Rd., Halifax NS B3H 4P7. (902)423-
8116. **Fax:** (902)422-0881. **E-mail:** programs@writ
ers.ns.ca. **Website:** www.writers.ns.ca. **Contact:**
Robin Spittal, communications and development
officer. Annual program designed to honor work by
unpublished writers in all 4 Atlantic Provinces. Entry is open to writers unpublished in the category
of writing they wish to enter. Prizes are presented
in the fall of each year. Categories include: novel,
writing for children, poetry, short story, juvenile/
young adult novel, creative nonfiction, and play.
Judges return written comments when competition
is concluded. Page lengths and rules vary based on
categories. See website for details. Anyone resident
in the Atlantic Provinces since September 1st immediately prior to the deadline date is eligible to
enter. Only one entry per category is allowed. Each
entry requires its own entry form and registration
fee. Deadline: February 2. Prizes vary based on categories. See website for details.

🌑 MARILYN BAILLIE PICTURE BOOK AWARD

40 Orchard View Blvd., Suite 217, Toronto ON M4R
1B9 Canada. (416)975-0010, ext. 222. **Fax:** (416)975-
8970. **E-mail:** meghan@bookcentre.ca. **Website:**
www.bookcentre.ca. **Contact:** Meghan Howe. The
Marilyn Baillie Picture Book Award honors excellence in the illustrated picture book format. To be eligible, the book must be an original work in English,
aimed at children ages 3-8, written and illustrated
by Canadians and first published in Canada. Eligible
genres include fiction, non-fiction and poetry. Books
must be published between Jan. 1 and Dec. 31 of the
previous calendar year. New editions or re-issues of
previously published books are not eligible for submission. Send 5 copies of title along with a completed submission form. Deadline: December 17. Prize:
$20,000.

MILDRED L. BATCHELDER AWARD

Website: http://www.ala.org/alsc/awardsgrants/
bookmedia/batchelderaward. The Batchelder Award
is given to the most outstanding children's book originally published in a language other than English in a
country other than the US, and subsequently translated into English for publication in the US. Visit website for terms and criteria of award. The purpose of the
award, a citation to an American publisher, is to encourage international exchange of quality children's
books by recognizing US publishers of such books in
translation. Deadline: December 31.

JOHN AND PATRICIA BEATTY AWARD

2471 Flores St., San Mateo CA 94403. (650)376-0886.
Fax: (650)539-2341. **E-mail:** bartlett@scfl.lib.ca.us.
Website: www.cla-net.org. **Contact:** Diane Bartlett,
award chair. The California Library Association's
John and Patricia Beatty Award, sponsored by Baker
& Taylor, honors the author of a distinguished book
for children or young adults that best promotes an
awareness of California and its people. Must be a children's or young adult books published in the previous year, set in California, and highlight California's
cultural heritage or future. Send title suggestiosn to
the committee members. Deadline: January 31. Prize:
$500 and an engraved plaque. Judged by a committee
of CLA members, who select the winning title from
books published in the US during the preceding year.

THE GEOFFREY BILSON AWARD FOR HISTORICAL FICTION FOR YOUNG PEOPLE

40 Orchard View Blvd., Suite 217, Toronto ON M4R 1B9Canada. (416)975-0010, ext. 222. **Fax:** (416)975-8970. **Website:** www.bookcentre.ca. **Contact:** Meghan Howe. Awarded annually to reward excellence in the writing of an outstanding work of historical fiction for young readers, by a Canadian author, published in the previous calendar year. Open to Canadian citizens and residents of Canada for at least 2 years. Books must be published between January 1 and December 31 of the previous year. Books must be first foreign or first Canadian editions. Autobiographies are not eligible. Jury members will consider the following: historical setting and accuracy, strong character and plot development, well-told, original story, and stability of book for its intended age group. Send 5 copies of the title along with a completed submission form. Deadline: December 17. Prize: $5,000.

THE IRMA S. AND JAMES H. BLACK AWARD

Bank Street College of Education, 610 W. 112th St., New York NY 10025-1898. (212)875-4458. **Fax:** (212)875-4558. **E-mail:** kfreda@bankstreet.edu. **Website:** http://bankstreet.edu/center-childrens-literature/irma-black-award/. **Contact:** Kristin Freda. Award give to an outstanding book for young children—a book in which text and illustrations are inseparable, each enhancing and enlarging on the other to produce a singular whole. Entries must have been published during the previous calendar year. Publishers submit books. Submit only one copy of each book. Does not accept unpublished mss. Deadline: mid-December. Prize: A scroll with the recipient's name and a gold seal designed by Maurice Sendak. Judged by a committee of older children and children's literature professionals. Final judges are first-, second-, and third-grade classes at a number of cooperating schools.

BOSTON GLOBE-HORN BOOK AWARDS

300 The Fenway, Palace Road Building, Suite P-311, Boston MA 02115. (617)628-0225. **Fax:** (617)628-0882. **E-mail:** info@hbook.com; khedeen@hbook.com. **Website:** hbook.com/bghb/. **Contact:** Katrina Hedeen. Offered annually for excellence in literature for children and young adults (published June 1-May 31). Categories: picture book, fiction and poetry, nonfiction. Judges may also name up to 2 honor books in each category. Books must be published in the US, but may be written or illustrated by citizens of any country. The Horn Book Magazine publishes speeches given at awards ceremonies. Guidelines for SASE or online. Submit a book directly to each of the judges. See website for details on submitting, as well as contest guidelines. Deadline: May 15. Prize: $500 and an engraved silver bowl; honor book recipients receive an engraved silver plate. Judged by a panel of 3 judges selected each year.

ANN CONNOR BRIMER BOOK AWARD

(902)490-2742. **Website:** www.atlanticbookawards.ca/. **Contact:** Laura Carter, Atlantic Book Awards Festival Coordinator. In 1990, the Nova Scotia Library Association established the Ann Connor Brimer Award for writers residing in Atlantic Canada who have made an outstanding contribution to writing for Atlantic Candian young people. Author must be alive and residing in Atlantic Canada at time of nomination. Book intended for youth up to the age of 15. Book in print and readily available. Fiction or nonfiction (except textbooks). Book must have been published within the previous year. Prize: $2,000.

BUCKEYE CHILDREN'S BOOK AWARD

Website: www.bcbookaward.info. **Contact:** Christine Watters, president. The Buckeye Childeren's Book Award Program is designed to encourage children to read literature critically, to promote teacher and librarian involvement in children's literature programs, and to commend authors of such literature, as well as to promote the use of libraries. Open to Ohio students. Award offered every year. Students may only nominate books published in the previous 2 years (for paperbacks, check the original hardcover publication date), and the book must be originally published in the US. A book in a series that has previously won the award are not eligible for nonfiction. Deadline: March 10. Nominations for the following year's contest begins on March 15 and continues year-round.

RANDOLPH CALDECOTT MEDAL

50 E. Huron, Chicago IL 60611-2795. (312)944-7680. **Fax:** (312)440-9374. **E-mail:** alsc@ala.org; lschulte@ala.org. **Website:** www.ala.org. **Contact:** Laura Schulte-Cooper, program officer. The Caldecott Medal was named in honor of nineteenth-century English illustrator Randolph Caldecott. It is awarded annually by the Association for Library Service to Children, a division of the American Library Association, to the art-

ist of the most distinguished American picture book for children. Illustrator must be US citizen or resident. Must be published year preceding award. SASE for award rules. Entries are not returned. Honors the artist of the most outstanding picture book for children published in the US. Deadline: December 31.

CALIFORNIA YOUNG PLAYWRIGHTS CONTEST

3675 Ruffin Rd., Suite 330, San Diego CA 92123-1870. (858)384-2970. **Fax:** (858)384-2974. **E-mail:** write@ playwrightsproject.org. **Website:** www.playwright sproject.org. **Contact:** Cecelia Kouma, executive director. Annual contest open to Californians under age 19. Annual contest. "Our organization and the contest is designed to nurture promising young writers. We hope to develop playwrights and audiences for live theater. We also teach playwriting." Submissions are required to be unpublished and not produced professionally. Submissions made by the author. SASE for contest rules and entry form. Scripts must be a minimum of 10 standard typewritten pages; send 2 copies. Scripts will *not* be returned. If requested, entrants receive detailed evaluation letter. Guidelines available online. Deadline: June 1. Prize: Scripts will be produced in spring at a professional theatre in San Diego. Writers submitting scripts of 10 or more pages receive a detailed script evaluation letter upon request.. Judged by professionals in the theater community, a committee of 5-7; changes somewhat each year.

✪ CANADIAN SHORT STORY COMPETITION

Unit #6, 477 Martin St., Penticton BC V2A 5L2 Canada. (778)476-5750. **Fax:** (778)476-5750. **E-mail:** dave@redtuquebooks.ca. **Website:** www.redtuque books.ca. **Contact:** David Korinetz, contest director. Offered annually for unpublished works. Purpose of award is to promote Canada and Canadian publishing. Stories require a Canadian element. There are three ways to qualify. They can be written by a Canadian, written about Canadians, or take place somewhere in Canada. Deadline: December 31. Prizes: 1st Place: $500; 2nd Place: $150; 3rd Place: $100; and 10 prizes of $25 will be given to honorable mentions. All 13 winners will be published in an anthology. They will each receive a complimentary copy. Judged by Canadian authors in the fantasy/sci-fi/horror field. Acquires first print rights. Contest open to anyone.

CASCADE WRITING CONTEST & AWARDS

1075 Willow Lake Road N., Keizer Oregon 97303. **E-mail:** cascade@oregonchristianwriters.org. **Website:** http://oregonchristianwriters.org/. **Contact:** Marilyn Rhoads and Julie McDonald Zander. The Cascade Awards are presented at the annual Oregon Christian Writers Summer Conference (held at the Red Lion on the River in Portland, Oregon each August) attended by national editors, agents, and professional authors. The contest is open for both published and unpublished works in the following categories: contemporary fiction book, historical fiction book, speculative fiction book, nonfiction book, memoir book, young adult/middle grade fiction book, young adult/middle grade nonfiction book, children's chapter book and picture book (fiction and nonfiction), poetry, devotional, article, column, story, or blog post. Two additional special Cascade Awards are presented each year, the Trailblazer Award to a writer who has distinguished him/herself in the field of Christian writing and a Writer of Promise Award for a writer who demonstrates unusual promise in the field of Christian writing. For a full list of categories, entry rules, and scoring elements, visit website. Guidelines and rules available on the website. Entry forms will be available on the first day for entry. Annual multi-genre competition to encourage both published and emerging writers in the field of Christian writing. Deadline: March 31. Submissions period begins February 14. Prize: Award certificate presented at the Cascade Awards ceremony during the Oregon Christian Writers Annual Summer Conference. Finalists are listed in the conference notebook and winners are listed online. Cascade Trophies are awarded to the recipients of the Trailblazer and Writer of Promise Awards. Judged by published authors, editors, librarians, and retail book store owners and employees. Final judging by editors, agents, and published authors from the Christian publishing industry.

CHILDREN'S AFRICANA BOOK AWARD

c/o Rutgers University, 132 George St., New Brunswick NJ 08901. (732)932-8173; (301)585-9136. **Fax:** (732)932-3394. **E-mail:** africaaccess@aol.com. **E-mail:** harrietmcguire@earthlink.net. **Website:** www. africaaccessreview.org. **Contact:** Brenda Randolph, chairperson. The Children's Africana Book Awards are presented annually to the authors and illustrators of the best books on Africa for children and young people published or republished in the US. The awards were created by the Outreach Council of the African Studies Association (ASA) to dispel stereotypes and encourage the publication and use of accurate, balanced children's materials about Africa. The awards are presented in 2 categories: Young Children and Older Readers. Entries must have been published in the calendar year previous to the award. Work submitted for awards must be suitable for children ages 4-18; a significant portion of books' content must be about Africa; must by copyrighted in the calendar year prior to award year; must be published or republished in the US. Books should be suitable for children and young adults, ages 4-18. A significant portion of the book's content should be about Africa. Books must be copyrighted the previous year to be eligible for the awards. Judged by African Studies and Children's Literature scholars. Nominated titles are read by committee members and reviewed by external African Studies scholars with specialized academic training.

CHILDREN'S BOOK GUILD AWARD FOR NONFICTION

E-mail: theguild@childrensbookguild.org. **Website:** www.childrensbookguild.org. Annual award. "One doesn't enter. One is selected. Our jury annually selects one author for the award." Honors an author or illustrator whose total work has contributed significantly to the quality of nonfiction for children. Prize: Cash and an engraved crystal paperweight. Judged by a jury of Children's Book Guild specialists, authors, and illustrators.

CHILDREN'S WRITER WRITING CONTESTS

95 Long Ridge Rd., West Redding CT 06896-0811. (203)792-8600. **Fax:** (203)792-8406. **Website:** www.childrenswriter.com. Contest offered twice a year by *Children's Writer*, the monthly newsletter of writing and publishing trends. Each contest has its own theme. Any original unpublished piece, not accepted by any publisher at the time of submission, is eligible. Submissions made by the author. To obtain the rules and theme for the current contest go to the website and click on "Writing Contests," or send a SASE to *Children's Writer* at the above address. Put "Contest Request" in the lower left of your envelope. Open to any writer. Entries are judged on age targeting, originality, quality of writing and, for nonfiction, how well the information is conveyed and accuracy. Promotes higher quality children's literature. Deadline: Middle of February and October. Prizes: 1st place: $250 or $500, a certificate and publication in *Children's Writer*; 2nd place: $100 or $250, and certificate; 3rd-5th places: $50 or $100 and certificates. Judged by a panel of 4 selected from the staff of the Institute of Children's Literature.

CHRISTIAN BOOK AWARDS

9633 S. 48th St., Suite 140, Phoenix AZ 85044. (480)966-3998. **Fax:** (480)966-1944. **E-mail:** info@ecpa.org; mkuyper@ecpa.org. **Website:** www.ecpa.org. **Contact:** Mark W. Kuyper, president and CEO. The Evangelical Christian Publishers Association recognizes quality and encourages excellence by presenting the ECPA Christian Book Awards (formerly known as Gold Medallion) each year. Categories include children, fiction, nonfiction, Bibles, Bible reference, inspiration, and new author. All entries must be evangelical in nature and submitted through an ECPA member publisher. Books must have been published in the calendar year prior to the award. Publishing companies submitting entries must be ECPA members in good standing. See website for details. The Christian Book Awards recognize the highest quality in Christian books and is among the oldest and most prestigious awards program in Christian publishing. Deadline: September 30. Submission period begins September 1.

☉ THE CITY OF VANCOUVER BOOK AWARD

Woodward's Heritage Building, 111 W. Hastings St., Suite 501, Vancouver BC V6B 1H4 Canada . (604) 829-2007. **Fax:** (604)871-6005. **E-mail:** marnie.rice@vancouver.ca; culture@vancouver.ca. **Website:** https://vancouver.ca/people-programs/city-of-vancouver-book-award.aspx. The annual City of Vancouver Book Award recognizes authors of excellence of any genre who contribute to the appreciation and understanding of Vancouver's history, unique character, or the achievements of its residents. The book must exhibit excellence in one or more of the following areas: content, illustration, design, format. The book must not be copyrighted prior to the previous year. Submit four copies of book. See website for details and guidelines. Deadline: May 14. Prize: $3,000. Judged by an independent jury.

◑ CLA YOUNG ADULT BOOK AWARD

1150 Morrison Dr.,, Suite 400, Ottawa ON K2H 8S9 Canada. (613)232-9625. **Fax:** (613)563-9895. **E-mail:** svollick@shaw.ca. **Website:** www.cla.ca. **Contact:** Stephanie Vollick, chair. This award recognizes an author of an outstanding English language Canadian book which appeals to young adults between the ages of 13 and 18. To be eligible for consideration, the following must apply: it must be a work of fiction (novel, collection of short stories, or graphic novel), the title must be a Canadian publication in either hardcover or paperback, and the author must be a Canadian citizen or landed immigrant. The award is given annually, when merited, at the Canadian Library Association's annual conference. Deadline: December 31. Prize: $1,000.

COLORADO BOOK AWARDS

(303)894-7951, ext. 19. **Fax:** (303)864-9361. **E-mail:** stephanie@coloradohumanities.org. **Website:** www. coloradohumanities.org. **Contact:** Stephanie March. An annual program that celebrates the accomplishments of Colorado's outstanding authors, editors, illustrators, and photographers. Awards are presented in at least ten categories including anthology/collection, biography, children's, creative nonfiction, fiction, history, nonfiction, pictorial, poetry, and young adult. To be eligible for a Colorado Book Award, a primary contributor to the book must be a Colorado writer, editor, illustrator, or photographer. Current Colorado residents are eligible, as are individuals engaged in ongoing literary work in the state and authors whose personal history, identity, or literary work reflect a strong Colorado influence. Authors not currently Colorado residents who feel their work is inspired by or connected to Colorado should submit a letter with his/her entry describing the connection. Submissions should have been published in the previous year. Deadline: January 2.

CRICKET LEAGUE

P.O. Box 300, Peru IL 61354. **E-mail:** cricket@carus pub.com. **E-mail:** mail@cricketmagkids.com. **Website:** www.cricketmagkids.com. Cricket League contests encourage creativity and give young people an opportunity to express themselves in writing, drawing, painting or photography. There is a contest in each issue. Possible categories include story, poetry, art, or photography. Each contest relates to a specific theme described on each *Cricket* issue's Cricket League page and on the website. Signature verifying originality, age and address of entrant and permission to publish required. Entries which do not relate to the current month's theme cannot be considered. Unpublished submissions only. Cricket League rules, contest theme, and submission deadline information can be found in the current issue of *Cricket* and via website. Deadline: The 25th of each month. Prizes: Certificates. Judged by *Cricket* editors.

CWW ANNUAL WISCONSIN WRITERS AWARDS

6973 Heron Way, De Forest WI 53532. **E-mail:** kar lahuston@gmail.com. **Website:** www.wiswriters.org. **Contact:** Geoff Gilpin, president and annual awards co-chair; Karla Huston, secretary and annual awards co-chair; Marilyn L. Taylor, annual awards chair; Alice D'Allesio, annual awards co-chair. Offered annually for work published by Wisconsin writers during the previous calendar year. Nine awards: Major Achievement (presented in alternate years); short fiction; short nonfiction; nonfiction book; poetry book; fiction book; children's literature; Lorine Niedecker Poetry Award; Christopher Latham Sholes Award for Outstanding Service to Wisconsin Writers (presented in alternate years); Essay Award for Young Writers. Open to Wisconsin residents. Entries may be submitted via postal mail or e-mail, based on category. See website for guidelines and entry forms. Deadline: January 31. Submissions open on November 1. Prizes: First place prizes: $500. Honorable mentions: $50.

MARGARET A. EDWARDS AWARD

50 East Huron St., Chicago IL 60611-2795. (312)280-4390 or (800)545-2433. **Fax:** (312)280-5276. **E-mail:** yalsa@ala.org. **Website:** www.ala.org/yalsa/edwards. **Contact:** Nichole O'Connor. Annual award administered by the Young Adult Library Services Association (YALSA) of the American Library Association (ALA) and sponsored by *School Library Journal* magazine. Awarded to an author whose book or books, over a period of time, have been accepted by young adults as an authentic voice that continues to illuminate their experiences and emotions, giving insight into their lives. The book or books should enable them to understand themselves, the world in which they live, and their relationship with others and with society. The book or books must be in print at the time of the nomination. Submissions must be previously published no less than 5years prior to the first meeting of

the current Margaret A. Edwards Award Committee at Midwinter Meeting. Nomination form is available on the YALSA website. Deadline: December 1. Prize: $2,000. Judged by members of the Young Adult Library Services Association.

SHUBERT FENDRICH MEMORIAL PLAYWRITING CONTEST

P.O. Box 4267, Englewood CO 80155. (303)779-4035. **Fax:** (303)779-4315. **E-mail:** editors@pioneerdrama. com. **E-mail:** submissions@pioneerdrama.com. **Website:** www.pioneerdrama.com. **Contact:** Lori Conary, submissions editor. Annual competition that encourages the development of quality theatrical material for educational, community and children's theatre markets. Previously unpublished submissions only. Only considers mss with a running time between 20-90 minutes. Open to all writers not currently published by Pioneer Drama Service. Guidelines available online. No entry fee. Cover letter, SASE for return of ms, and proof of production or staged reading must accompany all submissions. Deadline: Ongoing contest; a winner is selected by June 1 each year from all submissions received the previous year. Prize: $1,000 royalty advance in addition to publication. Judged by editors.

DOROTHY CANFIELD FISHER CHILDREN'S BOOK AWARD

578 Paine Tpke. N., Berlin VT 05602. (802)828-6954. **E-mail:** grace.greene@state.vt.us. **Website:** www. dcfaward.org. **Contact:** Mary Linney, chair. Annual award to encourage Vermont children to become enthusiastic and discriminating readers by providing them with books of good quality by living American or Canadian authors published in the current year. E-mail for entry rules. Titles must be original work, published in the US, and be appropriate to children in grades 4-8. The book must be copyrighted in the current year. It must be written by an American author living in the US or Canada, or a Canadian author living in Canada or the US Deadline: December of year book was published. Prize: Awards a scroll presented to the winning author at an award ceremony. Judged by children, grades 4-8, who vote for their favorite book.

✪ THE NORMA FLECK AWARD FOR CANADIAN CHILDREN'S NONFICTION

40 Orchard View Blvd., Suite 217, Toronto ON M4R 1B9 Canada. (416)975-0010 ext. 222. **Fax:** (416)975-

8970. **E-mail:** meghan@bookcentre.ca. **Website:** www.bookcentre.ca. **Contact:** Meghan Howe. The Norma Fleck Award was established by the Fleck Family Foundation to recognize and raise the profile of exceptional nonfiction books for children. Offered annually for books published between January 1 and December 31 of the previous calendar year. Open to Canadian citizens or landed immigrants. Books must be first foreign or first Canadian editions. Nonfiction books in the following categories are eligible: culture and the arts, science, biography, history, geography, reference, sports, activities, and pastimes. Deadline: December 17. Prize: $10,000. The award will go to the author unless 40% or more of the text area is composed of original illustrations, in which case the award will be divided equally between author and illustrator. Judged by at least 3 of the following: a teacher, a librarian, a bookseller, and a reviewer. A judge will have a deep understanding of, and some involvement with, Canadian children's books.

FLICKER TALE CHILDREN'S BOOK AWARD

Morton Mandan Public Library, 609 W. Main St., Mandan ND 58554. **E-mail:** laustin@cdln.info. **Website:** www.ndla.info/ftaward.htm. **Contact:** Linda Austin. Award gives children across the state of North Dakota a chance to vote for their book of choice from a nominated list of 20: 4 in the picture book category; 4 in the intermediate category; 4 in the juvenile category (for more advanced readers); 4 in the upper grade level nonfiction category. Also promotes awareness of quality literature for children. Previously published submissions only. Submissions nominated by librarians and teachers across the state of North Dakota. Deadline: April 1. Prize: A plaque from North Dakota Library Association and banquet dinner. Judged by children in North Dakota.

DON FREEMAN ILLUSTRATOR GRANTS

8271 Beverly Blvd., Los Angeles CA 90048. (323)782-1010. **Fax:** (323)782-1892. **E-mail:** grants@scbwi.org; sarahbaker@scbwi.org. **Website:** www.scbwi.org. **Contact:** Sarah Baker. The grant-in-aid is available to both full and associate members of the SCBWI who, as artists, seriously intend to make picture books their chief contribution to the field of children's literature. Applications and prepared materials are available in October. Grant awarded and announced in August. SASE for award rules and entry forms. SASE for return of entries. Enables picture book artists to further their understanding, training, and work in the picture book genre. Deadline: March 31. Submission period begins March 1. Prizes: Two grants of $1,000 each awarded annually. One grant to a published illustrator and one to a pre-published illustrator.

THEODOR SEUSS GEISEL AWARD

50 E. Huron, Chicago IL 60611. (800)545-2433. **E-mail:** alscawards@ala.org. **Website:** www.ala.org. The Theodor Seuss Geisel Award is given annually to the author(s) and illustrator(s) of the most distinguished American book for beginning readers published in English in the US during the preceding year. The award is to recognize the author(s) and illustrator(s) who demonstrate great creativity and imagination in his/her/their literary and artistic achievements to engage children in reading. Terms and criteria for the award are listed on the website. Entry will not be returned. Deadline: December 31. Prize: Medal, given at awards ceremony during the ALA Annual Conference.

☼ AMELIA FRANCES HOWARD GIBBON ILLUSTRATOR'S AWARD

1150 Morrison Drie, Suite 400, Ottawa ON K 2H859 Canada. (613)232-9625. **Fax:** (613)563-9895. **Website:** www.cla.ca. **Contact:** Stirling Prentice, chair. Annually awarded to an outstanding illustrator of a children's book published in Canada during the previous calendar year. The award is bestowed upon books that are suitable for children up to and including age 12. To be eligible for the award, an illustrator must be a Canadian citizen or a permanent resident of Canada, and the text of the book must be worthy of the book's illustrations. Deadline: December 31. Prize: A plaque and a check for $1,000 (CAD).

GOLDEN KITE AWARDS

SCBWI Golden Kite Awards, 8271 Beverly Blvd., Los Angeles CA 90048-4515. (323)782-1010. **Fax:** (323)782-1892. **E-mail:** sararutenberg@scbwi.org. **Website:** www.scbwi.org. Given annually to recognize excellence in children's literature in 4 categories: fiction, nonfiction, picture book text, and picture book illustration. Books submitted must be published in the previous calendar year. Both individuals and publishers may submit. Submit 4 copies of book. Submit to one category only, except in the case of picture books. Must be a current member of the SCBWI. Deadline: December 1. Submission period begins July 1. Prizes: One Golden Kite Award Winner and one

Honor Book will be chosen per category. Winners and Honorees will receive a commemorative poster also sent to publishers, bookstores, libraries, and schools; a press release; an announcement on the SCBWI website; and on SCBWI Social Networks..

☼ GOVERNOR GENERAL'S LITERARY AWARDS

150 Elgin St., P.O. Box 1047, Ottawa ON K1P 5V8 Canada. (613)566-4414, ext. 5573. **Website:** www.canadacouncil.ca. Established by Parliament, the Canada Council for the Arts provides a wide range of grants and services to professional Canadian artists and art organizations in dance, media arts, music, theater, writing, publishing, and the visual arts. Books must be first edition trade books written, translated, or illustrated by Canadian citizens or permanent residents of Canada and published in Canada or abroad in the previous year. Collections of poetry must be at least 48 pages long, and at least half the book must contain work not published previously in book form. In the case of translation, the original work must also be a Canadian-authored title. Books must be submitted by publishers with a Publisher's Registration Form, which is available by request from the Writing and Publishing Section of the Canada Council for the Arts. Guidelines and current deadlines are available on our website, by mail, telephone, fax, or e-mail. The Governor General's Literary Awards are given annually for the best English-language and French-language work in each of 7 categories, including fiction, nonfiction, poetry, drama, children's literature (text), children's literature (illustration), and translation. Deadline: Depends on the book's publication date. See website for details. Prizes: Each GG winner receives $25,000. Non-winning finalists receive $1,000. Judged by fellow authors, translators, and illustrators. For each category, a jury makes the final selection.

HACKNEY LITERARY AWARDS

1305 2nd Ave. N, #103, Birmingham AL 35203. (205)226-4921. **E-mail:** info@hackneyliteraryawards.org. **Website:** www.hackneyliteraryawards.org. **Contact:** Myra Crawford, PhD, executive director. Offered annually for unpublished novels, short stories (maximum 5,000 words), and poetry (50 line limit). Guidelines on website. Deadline: September 30 (novels), November 30 (short stories and poetry). Prizes: $5,000 in annual prizes for poetry and short fiction ($2,500 national and $2,500 state level). 1st Place: $600; 2nd

Place: $400; 3rd Place: $250); plus $5,000 for an unpublished novel. Competition winners will be announced on the website each March.

THE MARILYN HALL AWARDS FOR YOUTH THEATRE

P.O. Box 148, Beverly Hills CA 90213. **Website:** www.beverlyhillstheatreguild.com. **Contact:** Candace Coster, competition coordinator. The Marilyn Hall Awards consist of 2 monetary prizes for plays suitable for grades 6-8 (middle school) or for plays suitable for grades 9-12 (high school). The 2 prizes will be awarded on the merits of the play scripts, which includes its suitability for the intended audience. The plays should be approximately 45-75 minutes in length. There is no production connected to any of the prizes, though a staged reading is optional at the discretion of the BHTG. Unpublished submissions only. Authors must be US citizens or legal residents and must sign entry form personally. Deadline: The last day of February. Submission period begins January 15. Prizes: 1st Prize: $700; 2nd Prize: $300..

HIGHLIGHTS FOR CHILDREN FICTION CONTEST

803 Church St., Honesdale PA 18431-1824. (570)253-1080. **Fax:** (570)251-7847. **E-mail:** eds@highlights-corp.com. **Website:** www.highlights.com. **Contact:** Christine French Cully, editor-in-chief. Unpublished submissions only. Open to any writer 16 years of age or older. Winners announced in May. Length up to 800 words. Stories for beginning readers should not exceed 500 words. Stories should be consistent with Highlights' editorial requirements. No violence, crime or derogatory humor. Send SASE or visit website for guidelines and current theme. Stimulates interest in writing for children and rewards and recognizes excellence. Deadline: January 31. Submission period begins January 1. Prizes: Three prizes of $1,000 or tuition for any Highlights Foundation Founders Workshop.

MARILYN HOLINSHEAD VISITING SCHOLARS FELLOWSHIP

113 Anderson Library, 222 21st Ave. South, Minneapolis MN 55455. **Website:** http://www.lib.umn.edu/clrc/awards-grants-and-fellowships. Marilyn Hollinshead Visiting Scholars Fund for Travel to the Kerlan Collection is available for research study. Applicants may request up to $1,500. Send a letter with the proposed purpose and plan to use specific research materials (manuscripts and art), dates, and budget (including airfare and per diem). Travel and a written report on the project must be completed and submitted in the previous year. Deadline: January 30.

HRC SHOWCASE THEATRE PLAYWRITING CONTEST

P.O. Box 940, Hudson NY 12534. (518)851-7244. **E-mail:** hrcshowcaseplaycontest@gmail.com. **Website:** www.hrc-showcasetheatre.com. **Contact:** Jesse Waldinger, chair. HRC Showcase Theatre invites submissions of full-length plays to its annual contest from new, aspiring, or established playwrights. Each submitted play should be previously unpublished, run no more than 90 minutes, require no more than 6 actors, and be suitable for presentated as a staged reading by Equity actors. Deadline: March 1. Prizes: $500. Four runner-ups will receive $100 each.

CAROL OTIS HURST CHILDREN'S BOOK PRIZE

Westfield Athenaeum, 6 Elm St., Westfield MA 01085. (413)568-7833. **Website:** www.westath.org. The Carol Otis Hurst Children's Book Prize honors outstanding works of fiction and nonfiction, including biography and memoir, written for children and young adults through the age of eighteen that exemplify the highest standards of research, analysis, and authorship in their portrayal of the New England Experience. The prize will be presented annually to an author whose book treats the region's history as broadly conceived to encompass one or more of the following elements: political experience, social development, fine and performing artistic expression, domestic life and arts, transportation and communication, changing technology, military experience at home and abroad, schooling, business and manufacturing, workers and the labor movement, agriculture and its transformation, racial and ethnic diversity, religious life and institutions, immigration and adjustment, sports at all levels, and the evolution of popular entertainment. The public presentation of the prize will be accompanied by a reading and/or talk by the recipient at a mutually agreed upon time during the spring immediately following the publication year. Books must have been copyrighted in their original format during the calendar year, January 1 to December 31, of the year preceding the year in which the prize is awarded. Any individual, publisher, or organization may nominate a book. See website for details and guidelines. Prize: $500.

INSIGHT WRITING CONTEST

Fax: (301)393-4055. **E-mail:** insight@rhpa.org. **Website:** www.insightmagazine.org. **Contact:** Omar Miranda, editor. Annual contest for writers in the categories of student short story, general short story, and student poetry. Unpublished submissions only. General category is open to all writers; student categories must be age 22 and younger. Deadline: July 31. Prizes: Student Short and General Short Story: 1st Prize: $250; 2nd Prize: $200; 3rd Prize: $150. Student Poetry: 1st Prize: $100; 2nd Prize: $75; 3rd Prize: $50.

INTERNATIONAL READING ASSOCIATION CHILDREN'S AND YOUNG ADULTS BOOK AWARDS

P.O. Box 8139, 800 Barksdale Rd., Newark DE 19714-8139. (302)731-1600, ext. 221. **E-mail:** kbaughman@reading.org. **E-mail:** committees@reading.org. **Website:** www.reading.org. **Contact:** Kathy Baughman. The IRA Children's and Young Adults Book Awards are intended for newly published authors who show unusual promise in the children's and young adults' book field. Awards are given for fiction and nonfiction in each of three categories: primary, intermediate, and young adult. Books from all countries and published in English for the first time during the previous calendar year will be considered. See website for eligibility and criteria information. Entry should be the author's first or second book. Deadline: October 31. Prize: $1,000.

☼ THE IODE JEAN THROOP BOOK AWARD

The Lillian H. Smith Children's Library, 239 College St., Toronto ON M5T 1R5 Canada. (905)522-9537. **E-mail:** mcscott@torontopubliclibrary.ca; iodeontario@bellnet.ca. **Website:** www.iodeontario.ca. **Contact:** Martha Scott. Each year, the Municipal Chapter of Toronto IODE presents an award intended to encourage the publication of books for children between the ages of 6-12 years. The award-winner must be a Canadian citizen, resident in Toronto or the surrounding area, and the book must be published in Canada. Deadline: January 31. Prize: Award and cash prize of $2,000. Judged by a selected committee.

IRA SHORT STORY AWARD

International Reading Association, 800 Barksdale Rd., PO Box 8139, Newark DE 19714-8139. (302)731-1600. **Fax:** (302)731-1057. **E-mail:** committees@reading.org. **Website:** www.reading.org. Offered to reward author of an original short story published for the first time in a periodical for children. (Periodicals should generally be aimed at readers around age 12.) Write for guidelines or download from website. Award is non-monetary. Both fiction and nonfiction stories are eligible; each will be rated according to the characteristics that are appropriate for the genre. The story should: create a believable world for the readers, be truthful and authentic in its presentation of information, serve as a reading and literary standard by which readers can measure other writing, and encourage young readers by providing them with an enjoyable reading experience. Deadline: November 15.

JEFFERSON CUP AWARD

P.O. Box 56312, Virginia Beach VA 23456. (757)689=0594. **E-mail:** catlettsm@gmail.com. **Website:** www.vla.org. **Contact:** Susan M. Catlett, current chairperson. The Jefferson Cup honors a distinguished biography, historical fiction, or American history book for young people. The Jefferson Cup Committee's goal is to promote reading about America's past; to encourage the quality writing of US history, biography, and historical fiction for young people; and to recognize authors in these disciplines. Deadline: January 31.

EZRA JACK KEATS/KERLAN MEMORIAL FELLOWSHIP

University of Minnesota Libraries, 499 Wilson Library, 309 19th Ave. S, Minneapolis MN 55455. **E-mail:** asc-clrc@umn.edu. **Website:** https://www.lib.umn.edu/clrc/awards-grants-and-fellowships. This fellowship from the Ezra Jack Keats Foundation will provide $1,500 to a talented writer and/or illustrator of children's books who wishes to use the Kerlan Collection for the furtherance of his or her artistic development. Special consideration will be given to someone who would find it difficult to finance a visit to the Kerlan Collection. The Ezra Jack Keats Fellowship recipient will receive transportation costs and a per diem allotment. See website for application deadline and for digital application materials. Winner will be notified in February. Study and written report must be completed within the calendar year. Deadline: January 30.

THE EZRA JACK KEATS NEW WRITER AND NEW ILLUSTRATOR AWARDS

450 14th St., Brooklyn NY 11215-5702. **E-mail:** foundation@ezra-jack-keats.org. **Website:** www.ezra-jack-keats.org. Annual award to recognize and encourage new authors and illustrators starting out in the field of children's books. Many past winners of the Ezra Jack Keats Book Award have gone on to distinguished careers, creating books beloved by parents, children, librarians, and teachers around the world. Writers and illustrators must have had no more than 3 books previously published. Prize: $1,000 honorarium for each winner. Judged by a distinguished selection committee of early childhood education specialists, librarians, illustrators and experts in children's literature.

KENTUCKY BLUEGRASS AWARD

Northern Kentucky University, 405 Steely Library, Nunn Drive, Highland Heights KY 41099. (859)572-6620. **E-mail:** smithjen@nku.edu. **Website:** kba.nku.edu. The Kentucky Bluegrass Award is a student choice program. The KBA promotes and encourages Kentucky students in kindergarten through grade 12 to read a variety of quality literature. Each year, a KBA committee for each grade category chooses the books for the four Master Lists (K-2, 3-5, 6-8 and 9-12). All Kentucky public and private schools, as well as public libraries, are welcome to participate in the program. To nominate a book, see the website for form and details. Deadline: March 1.. Judged by students who read books and choose their favorite.

CORETTA SCOTT KING BOOK AWARDS

50 E. Huron St., Chicago IL 60611-2795. (800)545-2433. **Website:** www.ala.org/emiert/cskbookawards. The Coretta Scott King Book Awards are given annually to outstanding African American authors and illustrators of books for children and young adults that demonstrate an appreciation of African American culture and universal human values. This award commemorates the life and work of Dr. Martin Luther King, Jr., and honors his wife, Mrs. Coretta Scott King, for her courage and determination to continue the work for peace and world brotherhood. Must be written for a youth audience in one of three categories: preschool-4th grade; 5th-8th grade; or 9th-12th grade. Book must be published in the year preceding the year the award is given, evidenced by the copyright date in the book. See website for full details, criteria, and eligibility concerns. Deadline: December 1..

LEAGUE OF UTAH WRITERS CONTEST

The League of Utah Writers, P.O. Box 64, Lewiston UT 84320. (435)755-7609. **E-mail:** luwcontest@gmail.com. **Website:** www.luwriters.org. Open to any writer, the LUW Contest provides authors an opportunity to get their work read and critiqued. Multiple categories are offered; see website for details. Entries must be the original and unpublished work of the author. Winners are announced at the Annual Writers Round-Up in September. Those not present will be notified by e-mail. Deadline: June 15. Submissions period begins March 15. Prizes: Cash prizes are awarded. Judged by professional authors and editors from outside the League.

◐ MARSH AWARD FOR CHILDREN'S LITERATURE IN TRANSLATION

The English-Speaking Union, Dartmouth House, 37 Charles St., London En W1J 5EDUnited Kingdom . 020 7529 1591. **E-mail:** melanie.aplin@esu.org. **Website:** www.marshchristiantrust.org; www.esu.org. **Contact:** Melanie Aplin, senior education officer. The Marsh Award for Children's Literature in Translation, awarded biennially, was founded to celebrate the best translation of a children's book from a foreign language into English and published in the UK. It aims to spotlight the high quality and diversity of translated fiction for young readers. The Award is administered by the ESU on behalf of the Marsh Christian Trust. Submissions will be accepted from publishers for books produced for readers from 5 to 16 years of age. Guidelines and eligibility criteria available online.

MCLAREN MEMORIAL COMEDY PLAY WRITING COMPETITION

2000 W. Wadley, Midland TX 79705. (432)682-2544. **Fax:** (432)682-6136. **Website:** www.mctmidland.org. The McLaren Memorial Comedy Play Writing Competition was established to honor long-time MCT volunteer Mike McLaren who loved a good comedy, whether he was on stage or in the front row. Open to students. Annual contest. Unpublished submissions only. Submissions made by author. Rights to winning material acquired or purchased. First right of production or refusal is acquired by MCT. The contest is open to any playwright, but the play submitted must be unpublished and never produced in a for-profit setting. One previous production in a nonprofit theatre is acceptable. "Readings" do not count as productions. Deadline: February 28. Prize: $400. Judged by the audience present at the McLaren festival when the staged readings are performed.

THE VICKY METCALF AWARD FOR LITERATURE FOR YOUNG PEOPLE

460 Richmond St. W., Suite 600, Toronto ON M5V 1Y1 Canada. (416)504-8222. **E-mail:** info@writer strust.com. **Website:** www.writerstrust.com. **Contact:** Amanda Hopkins. The Vicky Metcalf Award is presented to a Canadian writer for a body of work in children's literature at The Writers' Trust Awards event held in Toronto each Fall. Open to Canadian citizens and permanent residents only.

MILKWEED PRIZE FOR CHILDREN'S LITERATURE

1011 Washington Ave. S., Suite 300, Minneapolis MN 55415. (612)332-3192. **Fax:** (612)215-2550. **E-mail:** editor@milkweed.org. **Website:** www.milkweed.org. Milkweed Editions will award the Milkweed Prize for Children's Literature to the best mss for young readers that Milkweed accepts for publication during the calendar year by a writer not previously published by Milkweed. All mss for young readers submitted for publication by Milkweed are automatically entered into the competition. Seeking full-length fiction between 90-200 pages. Does not consider picture books or poetry collections for young readers. Recognizes an outstanding literary novel for readers ages 8-13 and encourage writers to turn their attention to readers in this age group. Prize: $10,000 cash prize in addition to a publishing contract negotiated at the time of acceptance. Judged by the editors of Milkweed Editions.

MINNESOTA BOOK AWARDS

325 Cedar Street, Suite 555, St. Paul MN 55101. **E-mail:** mnbookawards@thefriends.org; friends@the friends.org; info@thefriends.org. **Website:** www.the friends.org. A year-round program celebrating and honoring Minnesota's best books, culminating in an annual awards gala. Recognizes and honors achievement by members of Minnesota's book community. All books must be the work of a Minnesota author or primary artistic creator (current Minnesota resident who maintains a year-round residence in Minnesota). All books must be published within the calendar year of the competition.

NATIONAL BOOK AWARDS

The National Book Foundation, 90 Broad St., Suite 604, New York NY 10004. (212)685-0261. **E-mail:** na tionalbook@nationalbook.org; agall@nationalbook. org. **Website:** www.nationalbook.org. **Contact:** Amy Gall. The National Book Foundation and the National Book Awards celebrate the best of American literature, expand its audience, and enhance the cultural value of great writing in America. The contest offers prizes in 4 categories: fiction, nonfiction, poetry, and young people's literature. Books should be published between December 1 and November 30 of the past year. Submissions must be previously published and must be entered by the publisher. General guidelines available on website. Interested publishes should phone or e-mail the Foundation. Deadline: Entry form and payment by May 15; a copy of the book by July 1. Prize: $10,000 in each category. Finalists will each receive a prize of $1,000. Judged by a category specific panel of 5 judges for each category.

NATIONAL OUTDOOR BOOK AWARDS

921 S. 8th Ave., Stop 8128, Pocatello ID 83209. (208)282-3912. **E-mail:** wattron@isu.edu. **Website:** www.noba-web.org. **Contact:** Ron Watters. Nine categories: History/biography, outdoor literature, instructional texts, outdoor adventure guides, nature guides, children's books, design/artistic merit, natural history literature, and nature and the environment. Additionally, a special award, the Outdoor Classic Award, is given annually to books which, over a period of time, have proven to be exceptionally valuable works in the outdoor field. Application forms and eligibilty requirements are available online. Applications for the Awards program become available in early June. Deadline: September 1. Prize: Winning books are promoted nationally and are entitled to display the National Outdoor Book Award (NOBA) medallion.

NATIONAL WRITERS ASSOCIATION NONFICTION CONTEST

10940 S. Parker Rd., #508, Parker CO 80134. (303)841-0246. **E-mail:** natlwritersassn@hotmail.com. **Website:** www.nationalwriters.com. Only unpublished works may be submitted. Judging of entries will not begin until the contest ends. Nonfiction in the following areas will be accepted: articles—submission should include query letter, 1st page of ms, separate sheet citing 5 possible markets; essay—the complete essay and 5 possible markets on separate sheet; nonfiction book proposal including query letter, chapter by chapter outline, first chapter, bio and market analysis. Those unsure of proper ms format should request Research Report #35. The purpose of the National Writers Association Nonfiction Contest is to encourage the writing of nonfiction and recognize those who excel in this field. Deadline: December 31. Prizes: 1st-5th place awards. Other winners will be notified by March 31st. 1st Prize: $200 and Clearinghouse representation if winner is book proposal; 2nd Prize: $100; 3rd Prize: $50; 4th-10th places will receive a book. Honorable Mentions receive a certificate. Judging will be based on originality, marketability, research, and reader interest. Copies of the judges evaluation sheets will be sent to entrants furnishing an SASE with their entry.

NATIONAL WRITERS ASSOCIATION SHORT STORY CONTEST

10940 S. Parker Rd., #508, Parker CO 80134. (303)841-0246. **E-mail:** natlwritersassn@hotmail.com. **Website:** www.nationalwriters.com. Opens April 1. Any genre of short story ms may be entered. All entries must be postmarked by July 1. Only unpublished works may be submitted. All manuscripts must be typed, double-spaced, in the English language. Maximum length is 5,000 words. Those unsure of proper ms format should request Research Report #35. The entry must be accompanied by an entry form (photocopies are acceptable) and return SASE if you wish the material and rating sheets returned. Submissions will be destroyed, otherwise. Receipt of entry will not be acknowledged without a return postcard. Author's name and address must appear on the first page. Entries remain the property of the author and may be submitted during the contest as long as they are not published before the final notification of winners. Final prizes will be awarded in June. The purpose of the National Writers Assn. Short Story Contest is to encourage the development of creative skills, recognize and reward outstanding ability in the area of short story writing. Prizes: 1st Prize: $250; 2nd Prize: $100; 3rd Prize: $50; 4th-10th places will receive a book. 1st-3rd place winners may be asked to grant one-time rights for publication in *Authorship* magazine. Honorable Mentions receive a certificate. Judging will be based on originality, marketability, research, and reader interest. Copies of the judges evaluation sheets will be sent to entrants furnishing an SASE with their entry.

NATIONAL YOUNGARTS FOUNDATION

2100 Biscayne Blvd., Miami FL 33137. (305)377-1140. **Fax:** (305)377-1149. **E-mail:** info@nfaa.org. **Website:** www.youngarts.org. The National YoungArts Foundation (formerly known as the National Foundation for Advancement in the Arts) was established in 1981 by Lin and Ted Arison to identify and support the next generation of artists and to contribute to the cultural vitality of the nation by investing in the artistic development of talented young artists in the visual, literary, design and performing arts. Each year, there are approximately 11,000 applications submitted to YoungArts from 15-18 year old (or grades 10-12) artists, and from these, approximately 700 winners are selected who are eligible to participate in programs in Miami, New York, Los Angeles, and Washington D.C. (with Chicago and other regions in the works). YoungArts provides these emerging artists with life-changing experiences and validation by renowned mentors, access to significant scholarships, national recognition and other opportunities throughout their careers to help ensure that the nation's most outstanding emerging artists are encouraged to pursue careers in the arts. See website for details about applying.

JOHN NEWBERY MEDAL

50 E. Huron, Chicago IL 60611. (800)545-2433, ext. 2153. **Fax:** (312)280-5271. **E-mail:** alscawards@ala.org. **Website:** www.ala.org. The Newbery Medal is awarded annually by the American Library Association for the most distinguished contribution to American literature for children. Previously published submissions only; must be published prior to year award is given. SASE for award rules. Entries not returned. Medal awarded at Caldecott/Newbery banquet during ALA annual conference. Deadline: December 31. Judged by Newbery Award Selection Committee.

NEW ENGLAND BOOK AWARDS

1955 Massachusetts Ave., #2, Cambridge MA 02140. (617)547-3642. **Fax:** (617)547-3759. **E-mail:** nan@neba.org. **Website:** http://www.newenglandbooks.org/BookAwards. **Contact:** Nan Sorenson, administrative coordinator. Annual award. Previously published submissions only. Submissions made by New England booksellers; publishers. Submit written nominations only; actual books should not be sent. Member bookstores receive materials to display winners' books. Award is given to a specific title, fiction, nonfiction, children's. The titles must be either about New England, set in New England or by an author residing in the New England. The titles must be hardcover, paperback orginal or reissue that was published between

September 1 and August 31. Entries must be still in print and available. Deadline: June 13. Prizes: Winners will receive $250 for literacy to a charity of their choice. Judged by NEIBA membership.

NEW VOICES AWARD

Website: www.leeandlow.com. Open to students. Annual award. Lee & Low Books is one of the few minority-owned publishing companies in the country and has published more than 100 first-time writers and illustrators. Winning titles include *The Blue Roses*, winner of a Patterson Prize for Books for Young People; *Janna and the Kings*, an IRA Children's Book Award Notable; and *Sixteen Years in Sixteen Seconds*, selected for the Texas Bluebonnet Award Masterlist. Submissions made by author. SASE for contest rules or visit website. Restrictions of media for illustrators: The author must be a writer of color who is a resident of the US and who has not previously published a children's picture book. For additional information, send SASE or visit Lee & Low's website. Encourages writers of color to enter the world of children's books. Deadline: September 30. Prize: New Voices Award: $1,000 prize and standard publication contract (regardless of whether or not writer has an agent) along with an advance against royalties; New Voices Honor Award: $500 prize. Judged by Lee & Low editors.

NORTH AMERICAN INTERNATIONAL AUTO SHOW HIGH SCHOOL POSTER CONTEST

1900 W. Big Beaver Rd., Troy MI 48084-3531. (248)643-0250. **Fax:** (248)283-5148. **E-mail:** sherp@ dada.org. **Website:** www.naias.com. Open to students. Annual contest. Submissions made by the author and illustrator. Entrants must be Michigan high school students enrolled in grades 10-12. Winning posters may be displayed at the NAIAS and reproduced in the official NAIAS program, which is available to the public, international media, corporate executives and automotive suppliers. Winning posters may also be displayed on the official NAIAS website at the sole discretion of the NAIAS. Contact Detroit Auto Dealers Association (DADA) for contest rules and entry forms or retrieve rules from website. Deadline: November 25. Prize: Chairman's Award: $1,000; State Farm Insurance Award: $1,000; Designer's Best of Show (Digital and Traditional): $500; Best Theme: $250; Best Use of Color: $250; Most Creative: $250. A winner will be chosen in each category from grades 10, 11, and 12.

Prizes: 1st place in 10, 11, 12: $500; 2nd place: $250; 3rd place: $100. Judged by an independent panel of recognized representatives of the art community.

NORTHERN CALIFORNIA BOOK AWARDS

c/o Poetry Flash, 1450 Fourth St. #4, Berkeley CA 94710. (510)525-5476. **E-mail:** ncbr@poetryflash.org; editor@poetryflash.org. **Website:** www.poetryflash. org. **Contact:** Joyce Jenkins, executive director. Annual Northern California Book Award for outstanding book in literature, open to books published in the current calendar year by Northern California authors. NCBR presents annual awards to Bay Area (northern California) authors annually in fiction, nonfiction, poetry and children's literature. Previously published books only. Must be published the calendar year prior to spring awards ceremony. Submissions nominated by publishers; author or agent could also nominate published work. Send 3 copies of the book to attention: NCBR. Encourages writers and stimulates interest in books and reading. Deadline: December 28. Prize: $100 honorarium and award certificate. Judging by voting members of the Northern California Book Reviewers.

OHIOANA BOOK AWARDS

274 E. First Ave., Suite 300, Columbus OH 43201-3673. (614)466-3831. **Fax:** (614)728-6974. **E-mail:** ohioana@ ohioana.org. **Website:** www.ohioana.org. **Contact:** David Weaver, executive director. Writers must have been born in Ohio or lived in Ohio for at least 5 years, but books about Ohio or an Ohioan need not be written by an Ohioan. Finalists announced in May and winners in July. Winners notified by mail in early summer. Offered annually to bring national attention to Ohio authors and their books, published in the last year. (Books can only be considered once.) Categories: Fiction, nonfiction, juvenile, poetry, and books about Ohio or an Ohioan. Deadline: December 31. Prize: $1,000 cash prize, certificate, and glass sculpture. Judged by a jury selected by librarians, book reviewers, writers and other knowledgeable people.

OKLAHOMA BOOK AWARDS

200 NE 18th St., Oklahoma City OK 73105. (405)521-2502. **Fax:** (405)525-7804. **E-mail:** connie.arm strong@libraries.ok.gov. **Website:** www.odl.state. ok.us/ocb. **Contact:** Connie Armstrong, executive director. This award honors Oklahoma writers and books about Oklahoma. Awards are presented to best books in fiction, nonfiction, children's, design

and illustration, and poetry books about Oklahoma or books written by an author who was born, is living or has lived in Oklahoma. SASE for award rules and entry forms. Winner will be announced at banquet in Oklahoma City. The Arrell Gibson Lifetime Achievement Award is also presented each year for a body of work. Previously published submissions only. Submissions made by the author, author's agent, or entered by a person or group of people, including the publisher. Must be published during the calendar year preceding the award. Deadline: January 10. Prize: Awards a medal. Judging by a panel of 5 people for each category, generally a librarian, a working writer in the genre, booksellers, editors, etc.

ONCE UPON A WORLD CHILDREN'S BOOK AWARD

1399 S. Roxbury Dr., Los Angeles CA 90035-4709. (310)772-7605. **Fax:** (310)772-7628. **E-mail:** boo kaward@wiesenthal.com. **Website:** www.museu moftolerance.com. **Contact:** Adaire J. Klein, award director. The Simon Wiesenthal Center/Museum of Tolerance welcomes submissions for the Once Upon a World Children's Book Award. Book publishers and members of the public are invited to nominate children's books that meet the following criteria: young readers' books for ages 6-8 that promote the themes of tolerance, diversity, and social justice; older readers' books for ages 9-12 that promote the themes of tolerance, diversity, respect, and social justice. Books may be a picture book, fiction, nonfiction, or poetry. Deadline: February 28. Prize: $1,000 award in each category.

ORBIS PICTUS AWARD FOR OUTSTANDING NONFICTION FOR CHILDREN

1111 W. Kenyon Rd., Urbana IL 61801-1096. (217)328-3870. **Fax:** (217)328-0977. **E-mail:** elementary@ncte. org. **Website:** www.ncte.org/awards/orbispictus. The NCTE Orbis Pictus Award promotes and recognizes excellence in the writing of nonfiction for children. Orbis Pictus commemorates the work of Johannes Amos Comenius, *Orbis Pictus—The World in Pictures* (1657), considered to be the first book actually planned for children. Submissions should be made by an author, the author's agent, or by a person or group of people. Must be published in the calendar year of the competition. Deadline: December 31. Prize: A plaque given at the NCTE Elementary Section Lun-

cheon at the NCTE Annual Convention in November. Up to 5 honor books awarded. Judged by members of the Orbis Pictus Committee.

OREGON BOOK AWARDS

925 SW Washington St., Portland OR 97205. (503)227-2583. **Fax:** (503)241-4256. **E-mail:** la@literary-arts. org. **Website:** www.literary-arts.org. **Contact:** Susan Denning, director of programs and events. The annual Oregon Book Awards celebrate Oregon authors in the areas of poetry, fiction, nonfiction, drama and young readers' literature published between August 1 and July 31 of the previous calendar year. Awards are available for every category. See website for details. Entry fee determined by initial print run; see website for details. Entries must be previously published. Oregon residents only. Accepts inquiries by phone and e-mail. Finalists announced in January. Winners announced at an awards ceremony in November. List of winners available in April. Deadline: August 29. Prize: Grant of $2,500. (Grant money could vary.). Judged by writers who are selected from outside Oregon for their expertise in a genre. Past judges include Mark Doty, Colson Whitehead, and Kim Barnes.

OREGON LITERARY FELLOWSHIPS

925 S.W. Washington, Portland OR 97205. (503)227-2583. **E-mail:** susan@literary-arts.org. **Website:** www. literary-arts.org. **Contact:** Susan Denning, director of programs and events. Oregon Literary Fellowships are intended to help Oregon writers initiate, develop or complete literary projects in poetry, fiction, literary nonfiction, drama and young readers literature. Writers in the early stages of their career are encouraged to apply. The awards are merit-based. Guidelines available in February for SASE. Accepts inquiries by e-mail, phone. Oregon residents only. Recipients announced in January. Deadline: Last Friday in June. Prize: $2,500 minimum award, for approximately 10 writers and 2 publishers. Judged by out-of-state writers

THE ORIGINAL ART

128 E. 63rd St., New York NY 10065. (212)838-2560. **Fax:** (212)838-2561. **E-mail:** kim@societyillustrators. org; info@societyillustrators.org. **Website:** www.so cietyillustrators.org. **Contact:** Kate Feirtag, exhibition director. The Original Art is an annual exhibit created to showcase illustrations from the year's best children's books published in the US. For editors and art directors, it's an inspiration and a treasure trove

of talent to draw upon. Previously published submissions only. Request "call for entries" to receive contest rules and entry forms. Works will be displayed at the Society of Illustrators Museum of American Illustration in New York City October-November annually. Deadline: July 18. Judged by 7 professional artists and editors.

HELEN KEATING OTT AWARD FOR OUTSTANDING CONTRIBUTION TO CHILDREN'S LITERATURE

10157 SW Barbur Blvd. #102C, Portland OR 97219. (503)244-6919. **Fax:** (503)977-3734. **E-mail:** sharperl@kent.edu. **Website:** www.cslainfo.org. **Contact:** S. Meghan Harper, awards chair. Annual award given to a person or organization that has made a significant contribution to promoting high moral and ethical values through children's literature. Recipient is honored in July during the conference. Awards certificate of recognition, the awards banquet, and one-night's stay in the hotel. A nomination for an award may be made by anyone. An application form is available online. Elements of creativity and innovation will be given high priority by the judges.

PATERSON PRIZE FOR BOOKS FOR YOUNG PEOPLE

One College Blvd., Paterson NJ 07505. (973)684-6555. **Fax:** (973)523-6085. **E-mail:** mgillan@pccc.edu. **Website:** www.pccc.edu/poetry. **Contact:** Maria Mazziotti Gillan, executive director. Award for a book published in the previous year in each age category (Pre-K-Grade 3, Grades 4-6, Grades 7-12). Deadline: March 15. Prize: $500.

THE KATHERINE PATERSON PRIZE FOR YOUNG ADULT AND CHILDREN'S WRITING

Vermont College of Fine Arts, 36 College St., Montpelier VT 05602. (802)828-8517. **E-mail:** hungermtn@vcfa.edu. **Website:** www.hungermtn.org. **Contact:** Miciah Bay Gault, editor. The annual Katherine Paterson Prize for Young Adult and Children's Writing honors the best in young adult and children's literature. Submit young adult or middle grade mss, and writing for younger children, short stories, picture books, or novel excerpts, under 10,000 words. Guidelines available on website. Deadline: June 30. Prize: $1,000 and publication for the first place winner; $100 each and publication for the three category winners.. Judged by a guest judge every year. The 2015 judge

was Ammi-Joan Paquette, a Senior Agent with Erin Murphy Literary Agency and published author of numerous children's books.

PENNSYLVANIA YOUNG READERS' CHOICE AWARDS PROGRAM

Website: www.psla.org. **Contact:** Alice L. Cyphers, coordinator. Submissions nominated by a person or group. Must be published within 5 years of the award—for example, books published in 2011 to present are eligible for the 2015-2016 award. Check the Program wiki at pyrca.wikispaces.com for submission information. View information at the Pennsylvania School Librarians' website or the Program wiki. Must be currently living in North America. The purpose of the Pennsylvania Young Reader's Choice Awards Program is to promote the reading of quality books by young people in the Commonwealth of Pennsylvania, to encourage teacher and librarian collaboration and involvement in children's literature, and to honor authors whose works have been recognized by the students of Pennsylvania. Deadline: October 15. Prizes: Framed certificate to winning authors. Four awards are given, one for each of the following grade level divisions: K-3, 3-6, 6-8, YA. Judged by children of Pennsylvania (they vote).

PEN/PHYLLIS NAYLOR WORKING WRITER FELLOWSHIP

PEN American Center, 588 Broadway, Suite 303, New York NY 10012. **E-mail:** awards@pen.org. **Website:** www.pen.org. **Contact:** Arielle Anema, literary awards coordinator. Offered annually to an author of children's or young-adult fiction. The Fellowship has been developed to help writers whose work is of high literary caliber but who have not yet attracted a broad readership. The Fellowship is designed to assist a writer at a crucial moment in his or her career to complete a book-length work-in-progress. Candidates have published at least two novels for children or young adults which have been received warmly by literary critics, but have not generated suficient income to support the author. Writers must be nominated by an editor or fellow author. See website for eligibility and nomination guidelines. Deadline: December 19. Submission period begins September 1. Prize: $5,000.

PLEASE TOUCH MUSEUM BOOK AWARD

Memorial Hall in Fairmount Park, 4231 Avenue of the Republic, Philadelphia PA 19131. (215)578-5153. **Fax:** (215)578-5171. **E-mail:** hboyd@pleasetouchmu seum.org. **Website:** www.pleasetouchmuseum.org. **Contact:** Heather Boyd. This prestigious award has recognized and encouraged the publication of high quality books. The award was exclusively created to recognize and encourage the writing of publications that help young children enjoy the process of learning through books, while reflecting PTM's philosophy of learning through play. The awards to to books that are imaginative, exceptionally illustrated, and help foster a child's life-long love of reading. To be eligible for consideration, a book must be distinguished in text, illustration, and ability to explore and clarify an idea for young children (ages 7 and under). **Deadline:** October 1. Books for each cycle must be published within previous calendar year (September-August). Judged by a panel of volunteer educators, artists, booksellers, children's authors, and librarians in conjunction with museum staff.

PNWA LITERARY CONTEST

(452)673-2665. **Fax:** (452)961-0768. **E-mail:** pnwa@pnwa.org. **Website:** www.pnwa.org. Annual literary contest with 12 different categories. See website for details and specific guidelines. Each entry receives 2 critiques. Winners announced at the PNWA Summer Conference, held annually in mid-July. **Deadline:** February 20. **Prize:** 1st Place: $700; 2nd Place: $300. Judged by an agent or editor attending the conference.

POCKETS FICTION-WRITING CONTEST

P.O. Box 340004, Nashville TN 37203-0004. (615)340-7333. **Fax:** (615)340-7267. **E-mail:** pockets@upperroom.org. **Website:** www.pockets.upperroom.org. **Contact:** Lynn W. Gilliam, senior editor. Designed for 6- to 12-year-olds, *Pockets* magazine offers wholesome devotional readings that teach about God's love and presence in life. The content includes fiction, scripture stories, puzzles and games, poems, recipes, colorful pictures, activities, and scripture readings. Freelance submissions of stories, poems, recipes, puzzles and games, and activities are welcome. Stories should be 750-1,000 words. Multiple submissions are permitted. Past winners are ineligible. The primary purpose of *Pockets* is to help children grow in their relationship with God and to claim the good news of the gospel of Jesus Christ by applying it to their daily lives. *Pockets* espouses respect for all human beings and for God's creation. It regards a child's faith journey as an integral part of all of life and sees prayer as undergirding that journey. **Deadline:** August 15.

Submission period begins March 15. **Prize:** $500 and publication in magazine.

EDGAR ALLAN POE AWARD

1140 Broadway, Suite 1507, New York NY 10001. (212)888-8171. **Fax:** (212)888-8107. **E-mail:** mwa@mysterywriters.org. **Website:** www.mysterywriters.org. Mystery Writers of America is the leading association for professional crime writers in the US. Members of MWA include most major writers of crime fiction and nonfiction, as well as screenwriters, dramatists, editors, publishers, and other professionals in the field. Categories include: Best Novel, Best Frist Novel by an American Author, Best Paperback/E-Book Original, Best Fact Crime, Best Critical/Biographical, Best Short Story, Best Juvenile Mystery, Best Young Adult Myster, Best Television Series Episode Teleplay, and Mary Higgins Clark Award. Purpose of the award: Honor authors of distinguished works in the mystery field. Previously published submissions only. Submissions made by the author, author's agent; "normally by the publisher." Work must be published/produced the year of the contest. **Deadline:** November 30. **Prize:** Awards ceramic bust of "Edgar" for winner; scrolls for all nominees. Judged by professional members of Mystery Writers of America (writers).

MICHAEL L. PRINTZ AWARD

50 E. Huron, Chicago IL 60611. (800)545-2433. **Fax:** (312)280-5276. **E-mail:** yalsa@ala.org; ala@ala.org. **Website:** www.ala.org/yalsa/printz. **Contact:** Nichole O'Connor, program officer for events and conferences. The Michael L. Printz Award annually honors the best book written for teens, based entirely on its literary merit, each year. In addition, the Printz Committee names up to 4 honor books, which also represent the best writing in young adult literature. The award-winning book can be fiction, nonfiction, poetry or an anthology, and can be a work of joint authorship or editorship. The books must be published between January 1 and December 31 of the preceding year and be designated by its publisher as being either a young adult book or one published for the age range that YALSA defines as young adult, e.g. ages 12 through 18. **Deadline:** December 1. Judged by an award committee.

PURPLE DRAGONFLY BOOK AWARDS

4696 W. Tyson St., Chandler AZ 85226-2903. (480)940-8182. **Fax:** (480)940-8787. **E-mail:** cristy@

fivestarpublications.com; fivestarpublications@gmail.com. **Website:** www.purpledragonflybookawards.com; www.fivestarpublications.com; www.fivestar bookawards.com. **Contact:** Cristy Bertini, contest coordinator. Five Star Publications presents the Purple Dragonfly Book Awards, which were conceived and designed with children in mind. "Not only do we want to recognize and honor accomplished authors in the field of children's literature, but we also want to highlight and reward up-and-coming, newly published authors and younger published writers." The Purple Dragonfly Book Awards are divided into 3 distinct subject categories, ranging from books on the environment and cooking to sports and family issues. (Click on the "Categories" tab on the website for a complete list.) The Purple Dragonfly Book Awards are geared toward stories that appeal to children of all ages. Looking for stories that inspire, inform, teach or entertain. "A Purple Dragonfly seal on your book's cover tells parents, grandparents, educators and care-givers they are giving children the very best in reading excellence." Being honored with a Purple Dragonfly Award confers credibility upon the winner, as well as provides positive publicity to further their success. The goal of these awards is to give published authors the recognition they deserve and provide a helping hand to further their careers. The awards are open to books published in any calendar year and in any country that are available for purchase. Books entered must be printed in English. Traditionally published, partnership published and self-published books are permitted, as long as they fit the above criteria. Submit materials to: Cristy Bertini, Attn: Five Star Book Awards, 1271 Turkey St., Ware, MA 01082. **Deadline:** May 1 (postmarked). Submissions postmarked March 1 or earlier that meet all submission requirements are eligible for the Early Bird reward: A free copy of *The Economical Guide to Self-Publishing* or *Promote Like a Pro: Small Budget, Big Show*. **Prizes:** Grand Prize winner will receive a $300 cash prize, 100 foil award seals (more can be ordered for an extra charge), 1 hour of marketing consultation from Five Star Publications, and $100 worth of Five Star Publications' titles, as well as publicity on Five Star Publications' websites and inclusion in a winners' news release sent to a comprehensive list of media outlets. The Grand Prize winner will also be placed in the Five Star Dragonfly Book Awards virtual bookstore with a thumbnail of the book's cover, price, 1-sentence description and link to Amazon.com for purchasing purposes, if applicable. 1st Place: All first-place winners of categories will be put into a drawing for a $100 prize. In addition, each first-place winner in each category receives a certificate commemorating their accomplishment, 25 foil award seals (more can be ordered for an extra charge) and mention on Five Star Publications' websites. Judged by industry experts with specific knowledge about the categories over which they preside.

QUILL AND SCROLL INTERNATIONAL WRITING AND PHOTO CONTEST, AND BLOGGING COMPETITION

School of Journalism, Univ. of Iowa, 100 Adler Journalism Bldg., Iowa City IA 52242-2004. (319)335-3457. **Fax:** (319)335-3989. **E-mail:** quill-scroll@uiowa.edu. **E-mail:** vanessa-shelton@uiowa.edu. **Website:** quillandscroll.org. **Contact:** Vanessa Shelton, contest director. Entries must have been published in a high school or profesional newspaper or website during the previous year, and must be the work of a currently enrolled high school student, when published. Open to students. Annual contest. Previously published submissions only. Submissions made by the author or school media adviser. **Deadline:** February 5.. **Prize:** Prize: Winners will receive *Quill and Scroll*'s National Award Gold Key and, if seniors, are eligible to apply for one of the scholarships offered by *Quill and Scroll*. All winning entries are automatically eligible for the International Writing and Photo Sweepstakes Awards. Engraved plaque awarded to sweepstakes winners.

THE RED HOUSE CHILDREN'S BOOK AWARD

Red House Children's Book Award, 123 Frederick Road, Cheam, Sutton, Surrey SM1 2HT United Kingdom. **E-mail:** info@rhcba.co.uk. **Website:** www.red housechildrensbookaward.co.uk. **Contact:** Sinead Kromer, national coordinator. The Red House Children's Book Award is the only national book award that is entirely voted for by children. A shortlist is drawn up from children's nominations and any child can then vote for the winner of the three categories: Books for Younger Children, Books for Younger Readers and Books for Older Readers. The book with the most votes is then crowned the winner of the Red House Children's Book Award. Deadline: December 31.

REGINA BOOK AWARD

315-1102 8th Ave., Regina SK S4R 1C9 Canada. (306)569-1585. **E-mail:** director@bookawards.sk.ca. **Website:** www.bookawards.sk.ca. **Contact:** Courtney Bates-Hardy, administrative director. Offered annually. In recognition of the vitality of the literary community in Regina, this award is presented to a Regina author for the best book, judged on the quality of writing. Books from the following categories will be considered: Children's; drama; fiction (short fiction by a single author, novellas, novels); nonfiction (all categories of nonfiction writing except cookbooks, directories, how-to books, or bibliographies of minimal critical content); poetry. Part of a larger group of awards, the Saskatchewan Book Awards. Deadline: November 3. Prize: $2,000 (CAD).

TOMÁS RIVERA MEXICAN AMERICAN CHILDREN'S BOOK AWARD

Dr. Jesse Gainer, Texas State University, 601 University Drive, San Marcos TX 78666-4613. (512)245-2357. **E-mail:** riverabookaward@txstate.edu. **Website:** www.riverabookaward.org. **Contact:** Dr. Jesse Gainer, award director. Texas State University College of Education developed the Tomas Rivera Mexican American Children's Book Award to honor authors and illustrators who create literature that depicts the Mexican American experience. The award was established in 1995 and was named in honor of Dr. Tomas Rivera, a distinguished alumnus of Texas State University. The book will be written for younger children, ages pre-K to 5th grade (awarded in even years), or older children, ages 6th grade to 12 grade (awarded in odd years). The text and illustrations will be of highest quality. The portrayal/representations of Mexican Americans will be accurate and engaging, avoid stereotypes, and reflect rich characterization. The book may be fiction or nonfiction. See website for more details and directions. Deadline: November 1.

ROCKY MOUNTAIN BOOK AWARD: ALBERTA CHILDREN'S CHOICE BOOK AWARD

Box 42, Lethbridge AB T1J 3Y3 Canada. (403)381-0855. **Website:** http://www.rmba.info. **Contact:** Michelle Dimnik, contest director. Annual contest open to Alberta students. No entry fee. Awards: Gold medal and author tour of selected Alberta schools. Judging by students. Canadian authors and/or illustrators only. Submit entries to Richard Chase. Previously unpublished submissions only. Submissions made by author's agent or nominated by a person or group. Must be published within the 3 years prior to that year's award. Register before January 20th to take part in the Rocky Mountain Book Award. SASE for contest rules and entry forms. Purpose of contest: "Reading motivation for students, promotion of Canadian authors, illustrators, and publishers."

ROYAL DRAGONFLY BOOK AWARDS

4696 W. Tyson St., Chandler AZ 85226. (480)940-8182. **Fax:** (480)940-8787. **E-mail:** cristy@fivestarpublications.com; fivestarpublications@gmail.com. **Website:** www.fivestarpublications.com; www.fivestarbookawards.com; www.royaldragonflybookawards.com. **Contact:** Cristy Bertini. Offered annually for any previously published work to honor authors for writing excellence of all types of literature—fiction and nonfiction—in 52 categories, appealing to a wide range of ages and comprehensive list of genres. Open to any title published in English. Entry forms are downloadable at www.royaldragonflybookawards.com. Guidelines available online. Send materials to Cristy Bertini, Attn.: Five Star Book Awards, 1271 Turkey St., Ware, MA 01082. Deadline: October 1. Prizes: Grand Prize winner receives $300, while another entrant will be the lucky winner of a $100 drawing. All first-place winners receive foil award seals and are included in a publicity campaign announcing winners. All first- and second-place winners and honorable mentions receive certificates.

SASKATCHEWAN FIRST BOOK AWARD

315-1102 8th Ave., Regina SK S4R 1C9 Canada. (306)569-1585. **E-mail:** director@bookawards.sk.ca. **Website:** www.bookawards.sk.ca. **Contact:** Courtney Bates-Hardy, administrative director. Offered annually. This award is presented to a Saskatchewan author for the best first book, judged on the quality of writing. Books from the following categories will be considered: Children's; drama; fiction (short fiction by a single author, novellas, novels); nonfiction (all categories of nonfiction writing except cookbooks, directories, how-to books, or bibliographies of minimal critical content); and poetry. Deadline: November 3. Prize: $2,000 (CAD).

SCBWI MAGAZINE MERIT AWARDS

8271 Beverly Blvd., Los Angeles CA 90048. (323)782-1010. **Fax:** (323)782-1892. **E-mail:** grants@scbwi.org. **Website:** www.scbwi.org. **Contact:** Stephanie Gordon, award coordinator. The SCBWI is a professional organization of writers and illustrators and others interested in children's literature. Membership is open to the general public at large. All magazine work for young people by an SCBWI member—writer, artist or photographer—is eligible during the year of original publication. In the case of co-authored work, both authors must be SCBWI members. Members must submit their own work. Requirements for entrants: 4 copies each of the published work and proof of publication (may be contents page) showing the name of the magazine and the date of issue. Previously published submissions only. For rules and procedures see website. Must be a SCBWI member. Recognizes outstanding original magazine work for young people published during that year, and having been written or illustrated by members of SCBWI. Deadline: December 15 of the year of publication. Submission period begins January 1. Prizes: Awards plaques and honor certificates for each of 4 categories (fiction, nonfiction, illustration and poetry). Judged by a magazine editor and two "full" SCBWI members.

SCBWI WORK-IN-PROGRESS GRANTS

8271 Beverly Blvd., Los Angeles CA 90048. (323)782-1010. **Fax:** (323)782-1892. **E-mail:** grants@scbwi.org. **E-mail:** wipgrant@scbwi.org. **Website:** www.scbwi.org. The SCBWI Work-in-Progress Grants have been established to assist children's book writers in the completion of a specific project. Five categories: Picture Book Text, Chapter Books/Early Readers, Middle Grade, Young Adult Fiction, Nonfiction, and Multi-Cultural Fiction or Nonfiction. SASE for applications for grants. The grants are available to both full and associate members of the SCBWI. They are not available for projects on which there are already contracts. Previous recipients not eligible to apply. Deadline: March 31. Submission period begins March 1..

SHEEHAN YA BOOK PRIZE

P.O. Box 172873, Tampa FL 33672. **E-mail:** elephantrockbooksya@gmail.com. **Website:** elephantrockbooks.com/ya.html. **Contact:** Jotham Burrello and Amanda Hurley. Guidelines are available on the website: http://www.elephantrockbooks.com/about.html#submissions. "Elephant Rock Books' teen imprint is looking for a great story to follow our critically acclaimed novel, *The Carnival at Bray*. We're after quality stories with heart, guts, and a clear voice. We're especially interested in the quirky, the hopeful, and the real. We are not particularly interested in genre fiction and prefer standalone novels, unless you've got the next *Hunger Games*. We seek writers who believe in the transformative power of a great story, so show us what you've got." Deadline: July 1. Prize: $1,000 as an advance.

SKIPPING STONES BOOK AWARDS

Website: www.skippingstones.org. Open to published books, publications/magazines, educational videos, and DVDs. Annual awards. Submissions made by the author or publishers and/or producers. Send request for contest rules and entry forms or visit website. Many educational publications announce the winners of our book awards. The winning books and educational videos/DVDs are announced in the July-September issue of *Skipping Stones* and also on the website. In addition to announcements on social media pages, the reviews of winning titles are posted on website. *Skipping Stones* multicultural magazine has been published for over 25 years. Recognizes exceptional, literary and artistic contributions to juvenile/children's literature, as well as teaching resources and educational audio/video resources in the areas of multicultural awareness, nature and ecology, social issues, peace, and nonviolence. Deadline: February 1. Prize: Winners receive gold honor award seals, attractive honor certificates and publicity via multiple outlets. Judged by a multicultural selection committee of editors, students, parents, teachers, and librarians.

SKIPPING STONES YOUTH HONOR AWARDS

P.O. Box 3939, Eugene OR 97403-0939. (541)342-4956. **E-mail:** editor@SkippingStones.org. **Website:** www.SkippingStones.org. Now celebrating its 26th year, *Skipping Stones* is a winner of N.A.M.E.EDPRESS, Newsstand Resources and Parent's Choice Awards. Open to students. Annual awards. Submissions made by the author. The winners are published in the September-October issue of *Skipping Stones*. Everyone who enters the contest receives the September-October issue featuring Youth Awards. SASE for contest rules or download from website. Entries must include certificate of originality by a parent and/or teacher and a cover letter that included cultural background information on the author. Submissions can either be mailed or e-mailed. Up to 10 awards are given in three categories: (1) Compositions (essays, poems, short stories, songs, travelogues, etc.): Entries should be typed (double-spaced) or neatly handwritten. Fiction or nonfiction should be limited to 1,000 words; poems to 30 lines. Non-English writings are also welcome. (2) Artwork (drawings, cartoons, paintings or photo essays with captions): Entries should have the artist's name, age and address on the back of each page. Send the originals with SASE. Black & white photos are especially welcome. Limit: 8 pieces. (3) Youth Organizations: Describe how your club or group works to: (a) preserve the nature and ecology in your area, (b) enhance the quality of life for low-income, minority or disabled or (c) improve racial or cultural harmony in your school or community. Use the same format as for compositions. Recognizes youth, 7 to 17, for their contributions to multicultural awareness, nature and ecology, social issues, peace, and nonviolence. Also promotes creativity, self-esteem and writing skills and to recognize important work being done by youth organizations. Deadline: June 25. Judged by *Skipping Stones* staff.

KAY SNOW WRITING CONTEST

Willamette Writers, 2108 Buck St., West Linn OR 97068. (503)305-6729. **Fax:** (503)344-6174. **E-mail:** reg@willamettewriters.com. **Website:** www.willamettewriters.com. Willamette Writers is the largest writers' organization in Oregon and one of the largest writers' organizations in the United States. It is a nonprofit, tax-exempt Oregon corporation led by volunteers. Elected officials and directors administer an active program of monthly meetings, special seminars, workshops and annual writing conference. Continuing with established programs and starting new ones is only made possible by strong volunteer support. See website for specific details and rules. There are fivedifferent categories writers can enter: Adult Fiction, Adult Non-Fiction, Poetry, Juvenile Short Story, and Student Writer. The purpose of this annual writing contest, named in honor of Willamette Writer's founder, Kay Snow, is to help writers reach professional goals in writing in a broad array of categories and to encourage student writers. Deadline: April 23. Submission deadline begins January 15. Prizes: One first prize of $300, one second place prize of $150, and

a third place prize of $50 per winning entry in each of the six categories.

SOCIETY OF MIDLAND AUTHORS AWARD

Society of Midland Authors, P.O. Box 10419, Chicago IL 60610-0419. **E-mail:** marlenetbrill@comcast.net. **Website:** www.midlandauthors.com. **Contact:** Marlene Targ Brill, awards chair. Since 1957, the Society has presented annual awards for the best books written by Midwestern authors. The contest is open to any title published within the year prior to the contest year. Open to authors or poets who reside in, were born in, or have strong ties to a Midland state, which includes Illinois, Indiana, Iowa, Kansas, Michigan, Minnesota, Missouri, Nebraska, North Dakota, South Dakota, Ohio and Wisconsin. The Society of Midland Authors (SMA) Award is presented to one title in each of six categories: adult nonfiction, adult fiction, adult biography and memoir, children's nonfiction, children's fiction, and poetry. Books and entry forms must be mailed to the 3 judges in each category; for a list of judges and the entry form, visit the website. Do not mail books to the society's P.O. box. Deadline: January 3.. Prize: Prize: cash prize of $500 and a plaque that is awarded at the SMA banquet in May in Chicago..

SOUTHWEST WRITERS ANNUAL WRITING CONTEST

3200 Carlisle Blvd., NE Suite #114, Albuquerque NM 87110. (505)830-6034. **E-mail:** swwriters@juno.com. **Website:** www.southwestwriters.com. The SouthWest Writers Writing Contest encourages and honors excellence in writing. In addition to competing for cash prizes, contest entrants may receive an optional written critique of their entry from a qualified contest critiquer. Non-profit organization dedicated to helping members of all levels in their writing. Members enjoy perks such as networking with professional and aspiring writers; substantial discounts on mini-conferences, workshops, writing classes, and annual and quarterly SWW writing contest; monthly newsletter; two writing programs per month; critique groups, critique service (also for nonmembers); discounts at bookstores and other businesses; and website linking. Deadline: May 1 (up to May 15 with a late fee). Submissions begin February 1. Prize: A 1st, 2nd, and 3rd place winner will be judged in each of the categories. 1st place: $300; 2nd place: $200; 3rd place: $150. Judged by a panel; the top 10 in each category will be sent to appropriate editors or literary agents to determine the final top 3 places.

SYDNEY TAYLOR BOOK AWARD

P.O. Box 1118, Teaneck NJ 07666. (212)725-5359. **E-mail:** chair@sydneytaylorbookaward.org; mls-4bug@sbcglobal.net. **Website:** www.sydneytaylorbookaward.org. **Contact:** Diane Rauchwerger, chair. The Sydney Taylor Book Award is presented annually to outstanding books for children and teens that authentically portray the Jewish experience. Deadline: December 31, "but we cannot guarantee that books received after November 30 will be considered." Prizes: Gold medals are presented in 3 categories: younger readers, older readers, and teen readers. Honor books are awarded in silver medals, and notable books are named in each category.

SYDNEY TAYLOR MANUSCRIPT COMPETITION

Sydney Taylor Manuscript Award Competition, 204 Park St., Montclair NJ 07042-2903. **E-mail:** stmacajl@aol.com. **Website:** www.jewishlibraries.org/main/Awards/SydneyTaylorManuscriptAward.aspx. **Contact:** Aileen Grossberg. This competition is for unpublished writers of fiction. Material should be for readers ages 8-13, with universal appeal that will serve to deepen the understanding of Judaism for all children, revealing positive aspects of Jewish life. Download rules and forms from website. Must be an unpublished fiction writer or a student; also, books must range from 64-200 pages in length. "AJL assumes no responsibility for publication, but hopes this cash incentive will serve to encourage new writers of children's stories with Jewish themes for all children." Deadline: September 30. Prize: $1,000. Judging by qualified judges from within the Association of Jewish Libraries.

☺ TD CANADIAN CHILDREN'S LITERATURE AWARD

40 Orchard View Blvd., Suite 217, Toronto ON M4R 1B9 Canada. (416)975-0010, ext. 222. **Fax:** (416)975-8970. **Website:** www.bookcentre.ca. **Contact:** Meghan Howe. The TD Canadian Children's Literature Award is for the most distinguished book of the year. All books, in any genre, written and illustrated by Canadians and for children ages 1-12 are eligible. Only books first published in Canada are eligible for submission. Books must be published between January 1 and December 31 of the previous calendar year.

Open to Canadian citizens and/or permanent residents of Canada. Submission deadline: December 17. Prizes: Two prizes of $30,000, 1 for English, 1 for French. $20,000 will be divided among the Honour Book English titles and Honour Book French titles, to a maximum of 4; $2,500 shall go to each of the publishers of the English and French grand-prize winning books for promotion and publicity.

☺ TORONTO BOOK AWARDS

Cultural Partnerships, City Hall, 9E, 100 Queen St. W., Toronto ON M5H 2N2 Canada. **E-mail:** cjones2@toronto.ca. **Website:** www.toronto.ca/book_awards. The Toronto Book Awards honor authors of books of literary or artistic merit that are evocative of Toronto. There are no separate categories; all books are judged together. Any fiction or nonfiction book published in English for adults and/or children that are evocative of Toronto are eligible. To be eligible, books must be published between January 1 and December 31 of previous year. Deadline: April 30. Prizes: Each finalist receives $1,000 and the winning author receives the remaining prize money ($15,000 total in prize money available).

VEGETARIAN ESSAY CONTEST

P.O. Box 1463, Baltimore MD 21203. (410)366-VEGE. **Fax:** (410)366-8804. **E-mail:** vrg@vrg.org. **Website:** www.vrg.org. Write a 2-3 page essay on any aspect of vegetarianism. Entrants should base their paper on interviewing, research, and/or personal opinon. You need not be a vegetarian to enter. Three different entry categories: age 14-18; age 9-13; and age 8 and under. Prize: $50.

VFW VOICE OF DEMOCRACY

406 W. 34th St., Kansas City MO 64111. (816)968-1117. **E-mail:** kharmer@vfw.org. **Website:** http://www.vfw.org/Community/Voice-of-Democracy/. The Voice of Democracy Program is open to students in grades 9-12 (on the Nov. 1 deadline), who are enrolled in a public, private or parochial high school or home study program in the United States and its territories. Contact your local VFW Post to enter (entry must not be mailed to the VFW National Headquarters, only to a local, participating VFW Post. Purpose is to give high school students the opportunity to voice their opinions about their responsibility to our country and to convey those opinions via the broadcast media to all of America. Deadline: November 1. Prize: Winners receive awards ranging from $1,000-30,000.

⚫ WESTERN AUSTRALIAN PREMIER'S BOOK AWARDS

State Library of Western Australia, Perth Cultural Centre, 25 Francis St., Perth WA 6000Australia . (61) (8)9427-3151. **E-mail:** premiersbookawards@slwa. wa.gov.au. **Website:** pba.slwa.wa.gov.au. **Contact:** Karen de San Miguel. Annual competition for Australian citizens or permanent residents of Australia, or writers whose work has Australia as its primary focus. Categories: children's books, digital narrative, fiction, nonfiction, poetry, scripts, writing for young adults, West Australian history, and Western Australian emerging writers. Submit 5 original copies of the work to be considered for the awards. All works must have been published between January 1 and December 31 of the prior year. See website for details and rules of entry. Deadline: January 31. Prize: Awards $25,000 for Premier's Prize; awards $15,000 each for the Children's Books, Digital Narrative, Fiction, and Nonfiction categories; awards $10,000 each for the Poetry, Scripts, Western Australian History, Western Australian Emerging Writers, and Writing for Young Adults; awards $5,000 for People's Choice Award.

WESTERN HERITAGE AWARDS

1700 NE 63rd St., Oklahoma City OK 73111-7997. (405)478-2250. **Fax:** (405)478-4714. **Website:** www. nationalcowboymuseum.org. **Contact:** Jessica Limestall. The National Cowboy & Western Heritage Museum Western Heritage Awards were established to honor and encourage the legacy of those whose works in literature, music, film, and television reflect the significant stories of the American West. Accepted categories for literary entries: western novel, nonfiction book, art book, photography book, juvenile book, magazine article, or poetry book. Previously published submissions only; must be published the calendar year before the awards are presented. Requirements for entrants: The material must pertain to the development or preservation of the West, either from a historical or contemporary viewpoint. Literary entries must have been published between December 1 and November 30 of calendar year. Five copies of each published work must be furnished for judging with each entry, along with the completed entry form. Works recognized during special awards ceremonies held annually at the museum. There is an autograph party preceding the awards. Awards ceremonies are sometimes broadcast. The WHA are pre-sented annually to encourage the accurate and artistic telling of great stories of the West through 16 categories of western literature, television, film and music; including fiction, nonfiction, children's books and poetry. See website for details and category definitions. Deadline: November 30. Prize: Awards a Wrangler bronze sculpture designed by famed western artist, John Free. Judged by a panel of judges selected each year with distinction in various fields of western art and heritage.

WESTERN WRITERS OF AMERICA

271CR 219, Encampment WY 82325. (307)329-8942. **Fax:** (307)327-5465 (call first). **E-mail:** wwa. moulton@gmail.com. **Website:** www.westernwriters. org. **Contact:** Candy Moulton, executive director. 17 Spur Award categories in various aspects of the American West. Send entry form with your published work. Accepts multiple submissions, each with its own entry form. The nonprofit Western Writers of America has promoted and honored the best in Western literature with the annual Spur Awards, selected by panels of judges. Awards, for material published last year, are given for works whose inspirations, image and literary excellence best represent the reality and spirit of the American West.

JACKIE WHITE MEMORIAL NATIONAL CHILDREN'S PLAY WRITING CONTEST

1800 Nelwood, Columbia MO 65202-1447. (573)874-5628. **E-mail:** bybetsy@yahoo.com. **Website:** www. cectheatre.org. **Contact:** Betsy Phillips, contest director. Annual contest that encourages playwrights to write quality plays for family audiences Previously unpublished submissions only. Submissions made by author. Play may be performed during the following season. All submissions will be read by at least 3 readers. Author will receive a written evaluation of the script. Guidelines available online. Send materials to: Betsy Phillips, Jackie White Memorial National Children's Playwriting Contest, 309 Parkade Blvd., Columbia, MO 65202-1447. Deadline: June 1.. Prize: $500 with production possible. Judging by current and past board members of CEC and by non-board members who direct plays at CEC.

LAURA INGALLS WILDER MEDAL

50 E. Huron, Chicago IL 60611. (800)545-2433. **E-mail:** alscawards@ala.org;. **Website:** www.ala.org/ alsc/awardsgrants/bookmedia/wildermedal. Award offered every 2 years. The Wilder Award honors an

author or illustrator whose books, published in the US, have made, over a period of years, a substantial and lasting contribution to literature for children. The candidates must be nominated by ALSC members. Medal presented at Newbery/Caldecott banquet during annual conference. Judging by Wilder Award Selection Committee.

WILLA LITERARY AWARD

E-mail: cynipid@comcast.net. **Website:** www.wom enwritingthewest.org. **Contact:** Cynthia Becker. The WILLA Literary Award honors the year's best in published literature featuring women's or girls' stories set in the West. Women Writing the West (WWW), a nonprofit association of writers and other professionals writing and promoting the Women's West, underwrites and presents the nationally recognized award annually (for work published between January 1 and December 31). The award is named in honor of Pulitzer Prize winner Willa Cather, one of the country's foremost novelists. The award is given in 7 categories: historical fiction, contemporary fiction, original softcover fiction, creative nonfiction, scholarly nonfiction, poetry, and children's/young adult fiction/nonfiction. Entry forms available on the website. Deadline: November 1-February 1. Prize: $100 and a trophy. Finalist receives a plaque. Both receive digital and sticker award emblems for book covers. Notice of Winning and Finalist titles mailed to more than 4,000 booksellers, libraries, and others. Award announcement is in early August, and awards are presented to the winners and finalists at the annual WWW Fall Conference.. Judged by professional librarians not affiliated with WWW.

RITA WILLIAMS YOUNG ADULT PROSE PRIZE CATEGORY

E-mail: SoulKeats@mail.com. **Website:** www.soul makingcontest.us. **Contact:** Eileen Malone. For writers in grades 9-12 or equivalent age. Up to 3,000 words in prose form of choice. Complete rules and guidelines available online. Deadline: November 30 (postmarked). Prizes: $100 for first place; $50 for second place; $25 for third place. Judged (and sponsored) by Rita Wiliams, an Emmy-award winning investigative reporter with KTVU-TV in Oakland, California.

PAUL A. WITTY OUTSTANDING LITERATURE AWARD

P.O. Box 8139, Newark DE 19714-8139. (800)336-7323. **Fax:** (302)731-1057. **Website:** www.reading.org. **Con-**tact:** Marcie Craig Post, executive director. This award recognizes excellence in original poetry or prose written by students. Elementary and secondary students whose work is selected will receive an award. Deadline: February 2. Prize: Not less than $25 and a citation of merit.

WRITE NOW

Indiana Repertory Theatre, 140 W. Washington St., Indianapolis IN 46204. 480-921-5770. **E-mail:** info@ writenow.co. **Website:** www.writenow.co. The purpose of this biennial workshop is to encourage writers to create strikingly original scripts for young audiences. It provides a forum through which each playwright receives constructive criticism and the support of a development team consisting of a professional director and dramaturg. Finalists will spend approximately one week in workshop with their development team. At the end of the week, each play will be read as a part of the Write Now convening. Guidelines available online. Deadline: July 31.

WRITER'S DIGEST SELF-PUBLISHED BOOK AWARDS

10151 Carver Road, Suite #200, Blue Ash OH 45242. (715)445-4612, ext. 13430. **E-mail:** WritersDigest SelfPublishingCompetition@fwmedia.com. **Website:** www.writersdigest.com. **Contact:** Nicole Howard. Contest open to all English-language, self-published books for which the authors have paid the full cost of publication, or the cost of printing has been paid for by a grant or as part of a prize. Categories include: Mainstream/Literary Fiction, Genre Fiction, Nonfiction, Inspirational (spiritual/new age), Life Stories (biographies/autobiographies/family histories/memoirs), Children's Books, Reference Books (directories/encyclopedias/guide books), Poetry, and Middle-Grade/Young Adult Books. Judges reserve the right to re-categorize entries. Judges reserve the right to withhold prizes in any category. All winners will be notifed by October 12. Entrants must send a printed and bound book. Entries will be evaluated on content, writing quality, and overall quality of production and appearance. No handwritten books are accepted. Books must have been published within the past 5 years from the competition deadline. Books which have previously won awards from *Writer's Digest* are not eligible. Early bird deadline: April 1; Deadline: May 1. Prizes: Grand Prize: $8,000, a trip to the Writer's Digest Conference, promotion in *Writer's Digest*, 10 copies of the book will be sent to major review houses, and a guaranteed review in *Midwest Book Review*; 1st Place (9 winners): $1,000 and promotion in *Writer's Digest*; Honorable Mentions: $50 worth of Writer's Digest Books and promotion on writersdigest.com. All entrants will receive a brief commentary from one of the judges.

WRITER'S DIGEST SELF-PUBLISHED E-BOOK AWARDS

10151 Carver Road, Suite #200, Blue Ash OH 45242. (715)445-4612, ext. 13430. **E-mail:** WritersDigest-SelfPublishingCompetition@fwmedia.com. **Website:** www.writersdigest.com. **Contact:** Nicole Howard. Contest open to all English-language, self-published e-books for which the authors have paid the full cost of publication, or the cost of publication has been paid for by a grant or as part of a prize. Categories include: Mainstream/Literary Fiction, Genre Fiction, Nonfiction (includes reference books), Inspirational (spiritual/new age), Life Stories (biographies/autobiographies/family histories/memoirs), Children's Books, Poetry, and Middle-Grade/Young Adult Books. Judges reserve the right to re-categorize entries. Judges reserve the right to withhold prizes in any category. All winners will be notifed by December 31. Entrants must enter online. Entrants may provide a file of the book or submit entry by the Amazon gifting process. Acceptable file types include: .epub, .mobi, .ipa. Word processing documents will not be accepted. Entries will be evaluated on content, writing quality, and overall quality of production and appearance. Books must have been published within the past 5 years from the competition deadline. Books which have previously won awards from *Writer's Digest* are not eligible. Early bird deadline: August 1; Deadline: September 19. Prizes: Grand Prize: $3,000, promotion in *Writer's Digest*, a full 250-word (minimum) editorial review, $200 worth of Writer's Digest Books, and more; 1st Place (9 winners): $1,000 and promotion in *Writer's Digest*; Honorable Mentions: $50 worth of Writer's Digest Books and promotion on writersdigest.com. All entrants will receive a brief commentary from one of the judges.

WRITERS-EDITORS NETWORK INTERNATIONAL WRITING COMPETITION

E-mail: contestentry@writers-editors.com. **E-mail:** info@writers-editors.com. **Website:** www.writers-editors.com. **Contact:** Dana K. Cassell, executive

director. Annual award to recognize publishable talent. Categories: Nonfiction (previously published article/essay/column/nonfiction book chapter; unpublished or self-published article/essay/column/nonfiction book chapter); fiction (unpublished or self-published short story or novel chapter); children's literature (unpublished or self-published short story/nonfiction article/book chapter/poem); poetry (unpublished or self-published free verse/traditional). Guidelines available online. Open to any writer. Maximum length: 5,000 words. Accepts inquiries by e-mail, phone and mail. Entry form online. Results announced May 31. Winners notified by mail and posted on website. Results available for SASE or visit website. Deadline: March 15. Prizes: 1st Place: $100; 2nd Place: $75; 3rd Place: $50. All winners and Honorable Mentions will receive certificates as warranted. Judged by editors, librarians, and writers.

○ WRITERS GUILD OF ALBERTA AWARDS

Percy Page Centre, 11759 Groat Rd., Edmonton AB T5M 3K6 Canada. (780)422-8174. **Fax:** (780)422-2663. **E-mail:** mail@writersguild.ab.ca. **Website:** www.writersguild.ab.ca. **Contact:** Executive Director. Offers the following awards: Wilfrid Eggleston Award for Nonfiction; Georges Bugnet Award for Fiction; Howard O'Hagan Award for Short Story; Stephan G. Stephansson Award for Poetry; R. Ross Annett Award for Children's Literature; Gwen Pharis Ringwood Award for Drama; Jon Whyte Memorial Essay Prize; James H. Gray Award for Short Nonfiction. Eligible entries will have been published anywhere in the world between January 1 and December 31 of the current year. The authors must have been residents of Alberta for at least 12 of the 18 months prior to December 31. Unpublished mss, except in the drama and essay categories, are not eligible. Anthologies are not eligible. Works may be submitted by authors, publishers, or any interested parties. Deadline: December 31. Prizes: Winning authors receive $1,500; essay prize winners receive $700.

WRITERS' LEAGUE OF TEXAS BOOK AWARDS

611 S. Congress Ave., Suite 200A-3, Austin TX 78704. (512)499-8914. **Fax:** (512)499-0441. **E-mail:** wlt@writersleague.org. **E-mail:** sara@writersleague.org. **Website:** www.writersleague.org. Open to Texas authors of books published the previous year. Authors

are required to show proof of Texas residency, but are not required to be members of the Writers' League of Texas. Deadline: Open to submissions from October 1 to January 15. Prize: $750, a commemorative award, and an appearance at a WLT Third Thursday panel at BookPeople in Austin, TX.

WRITING CONFERENCE WRITING CONTESTS

P.O. Box 664, Ottawa KS 66067-0664. (785)242-2947. **Fax:** (785)242-2473. **E-mail:** jbushman@writingconference.com. **E-mail:** support@studentq.com. **Website:** www.writingconference.com. **Contact:** John H. Bushman, contest director. Unpublished submissions only. Submissions made by the author or teacher. Purpose of contest: To further writing by students with awards for narration, exposition and poetry at the elementary, middle school, and high school levels. Deadline: January 8. Prize: Awards plaque and publication of winning entry in The Writers' Slate online, April issue. Judged by a panel of teachers.

YEARBOOK EXCELLENCE CONTEST

100 Adler Journalism Building, Iowa City IA 52242-2004. (319)335-3457. **Fax:** (319)335-3989. **E-mail:** quill-scroll@uiowa.edu. **Website:** www.quilland scroll.org. **Contact:** Vanessa Shelton, executive director. High school students who are contributors to or staff members of a student yearbook at any public or private high school are invited to enter the competition. Awards will be made in each of the 18 divisions. There are two enrollment categories: Class A: more than 750 students; Class B: 749 or less. Winners will receive Quill and Scroll's National Award Gold Key and, if seniors, are eligible to apply for one of the Edward J. Nell Memorial or George and Ophelia Gallup scholarships. Open to students whose schools have Quill and Scroll charters. Previously published submissions only. Submissions made by the author or school yearbook adviser. Must be published in the 12-month span prior to contest deadline. Visit website for list of current and previous winners. Purpose is to recognize and reward student journalists for their work in yearbooks and to provide student winners an opportunity to apply for a scholarship to be used freshman year in col-lege for students planning to major in journalism. Deadline: November 1..

YOUNG READER'S CHOICE AWARD

E-mail: hbray@missoula.lib.mt.us. **Website:** www.pnla.org. **Contact:** Honore Bray, president. The Pacific Northwest Library Association's Young Reader's Choice Award is the oldest children's choice award in the US and Canada. Nominations are taken only from children, teachers, parents and librarians in the Pacific Northwest: Alaska, Alberta, British Columbia, Idaho, Montana, and Washington. Nominations will not be accepted from publishers. Nominations may include fiction, nonfiction, graphic novels, animae, and manga. Nominated titles are those published 3 years prior to the award year. Deadline: February 1. Books will be judged on popularity with readers. Age appropriateness will be considered when choosing which of the three divisions a book is placed. Other considerations may include reading enjoyment; reading level; interest level; genre representation; gender representation; racial diversity; diversity of social, political, economic, or religions viewpoints; regional consideration; effectiveness of expression; and imagination. The Pacific Northwest Library Association is committed to intellectual freedom and diversity of ideas. No title will be excluded because of race, nationality, religion, gender, sexual orientation, political or social view of either the author or the material.

THE YOUTH HONOR AWARD PROGRAM

Skipping Stones Magazine, P.O. Box 3939, Eugene OR 97403. (541)342-4956. **E-mail:** info@skippingstones.org. **E-mail:** editor@skippingstones.org. **Website:** www.skippingstones.org. **Contact:** Arun N. Toke, Editor and Publisher. Original writing and art from youth, ages 7 to 17, should be typed or neatly handwritten. The entries should be appropriate for ages 7 to 17. Prose under 1,000 words; poems under 30 lines. Non-English and bilingual writings are welcome. To promote multicultural, international, and nature awareness. Deadline: June 25. Prize: An Honor Award Certificate, a subscription to Skipping Stones and five nature and/or multicultural books. They are also invited to join the Student

Review Board. Everyone who enters the contest receives the autumn issue featuring the 10 winners.

ANNA ZORNIO MEMORIAL CHILDREN'S THEATRE PLAYWRITING COMPETITION

Department of Theatre and Dance, PCAC, 30 Academic Way, Durham NH 03824. (603)862-3038. **Fax:** (603)862-0298. **E-mail:** mike.wood@unh.edu. **Website:** http://cola.unh.edu/theatre-dance/resource/zornio. **Contact:** Michael Wood. Offered every 4 years for unpublished well-written plays or musicals appropriate for young audiences with a maximum length of 60 minutes. May submit more than 1 play, but not more than 3. Honors the late Anna Zornio, an alumna of The University of New Hampshire, for dedication to and inspiration of playwriting for young people, K-12th grade. Deadline: March of 2017. Prize: $500.

SUBJECT INDEX

SUSPENSE/MYSTERY

TEXTBOOKS

TRAVEL

EDITOR AND AGENT
NAMES INDEX

AGE-LEVEL INDEX

YOUNG READERS

PHOTOGRAPHY INDEX

ILLUSTRATION INDEX

MAGAZINES:

GENERAL INDEX